THE
WORLD'S
MOST
EVIL MONSTERS

THE WORLD'S
MOST
EVIL MONSTERS

BB Bounty
Books

This collection first published in 2014 by Bounty Books,
a division of Octopus Publishing Group Ltd,
Endeavour House, 189 Shaftesbury Avenue,
London WC2H 8JY
www.octopusbooks.co.uk

An Hachette UK company
www.hachette.co.uk

The material in this book originally appeared in three separate titles:
The World's Most Evil Men by Neil Blandford & Bruce Jones
The World's Greatest Crooks & Conmen by Nigel Blundell
The World's Greatest Serial Killers by Nigel Cawthorne

ISBN: 978-0-753727-76-8

Printed and bound by CPI Group (UK) Ltd, Croydon, CR0 4YY

THE WORLD'S

MOST

EVIL MONSTERS

THE
WORLD'S MOST
EVIL MEN

Contents

ACKNOWLEDGEMENTS

In a factual book such as this, the authors must draw on many reference works in the course of their research. Some of these are specifically mentioned in the text. But two invaluable books deserve particular acknowledgement and are highly recommended for further reading. They are: *The Directory Of Infamy* by Jonathon Green (Mills & Boon 1980), and *A Criminal History Of Mankind* by Colin Wilson (Granada, 1984). Other authors to whom acknowledgements are due are: Gordon Honeycombe (*The Murders Of The Black Museum* Hutchinson, 1982), David Mitchell (*Pirates* Thames & Hudson, 1976), Dennis Elsenburg, Uri Dan and Ell Landau (*Meyer Lansky: Mogul Of The Mob* Paddington Press, 1979), John Beattie (*Klaus Barbie – His Life And Career* Methuen/Daily Star, 1984) and Herbert Walther (editor of *Hitler* Bison Books, 1978).

The publishers would like to thank the following for their kind permission to reproduce the pictures used in this book:
Keystone Press Agency 13, 24, 37, 103, 111, 112, 124, 144, 149; Topham Picture Library 21, 141, 144, 156, 157, 162; Mary Evans Picture Library 43, 54, 59, 65, 72, 81, 86, 191; Popperfoto 93, 99; Fox Photos 106; Central Press Photos 117.

'I never wonder to see men wicked but I often wonder to see them not ashamed.'

Jonathan Swift (1711)

Chapter
One

TWENTIETH-CENTURY TYRANTS

Regimes whose rule is terror . . . led by men to whom power has meant a licence to corrupt, maim and murder.

'Some men delight in things for no other reason but because they are ugly and infamous.'
Samuel Butler (1680)

Idi Amin

The dimming of the street lights on the warm, tropical nights in Kampala was always an accurate barometer of the morale of the people of Uganda.

Privileged visitors, arms salesmen and foreign diplomats in the two showpiece hotels would grumble loudly when the cocktail bars were plunged into darkness and the elevators jammed between floors.

But the uncomplaining residents of Kampala would leave the unlit cinemas and cheap little coffee shops in fearful silence to go home and spend a sleepless night behind barricaded doors.

Fitful blackouts in the power supply were a sign that Uganda's President Idi Amin had just completed another busy day of butchery. The drop in the voltage usually meant only one thing . . .

That the hydro-electric generators at Owen Falls Dam, 40 miles west of Kampala, were once again clogged with rotting corpses.

Despite the constant boat patrols on Lake Victoria, the source of the waters of the Nile, the maintenance engineers couldn't hope to spot every dead body swept by the currents towards their filter grids. They had allies helping them to scavenge the lake clear of the harvest of murder victims: the teeming colonies of crocodiles. But even these voracious reptiles became bloated and lazy. The pickings were too rich for them.

Time after time the generators had to be shut down and the water inlets cleared of that day's toll of death, usually 40 or 50 bodies in a 24-hour period.

In eight years of ruling his country in a torrent of blood and terror, Idi Amin had 500,000 of his fellow Ugandans ruthlessly and systematically butchered. He ordered the grisly mutilation of one of his own wives. He killed crusading clergymen, nosy journalists, his own diplomats and a helpless, frail elderly hijack hostage. He even tasted the flesh of some of his victims in cannibal ritual.

He killed political opponents, real and imagined, to stay in power. And he killed countless ordinary men and women for profit, sometimes for the sake of a few hundred pounds.

He personally supervised the actions of Uganda's 'State Research Bureau', an organisation which was a cross between the Gestapo and Murder Incorporated, dealing in state-sponsored torture, contract killing, drug running and currency smuggling.

For almost a hundred years, the fertile land of Uganda had been part of the

British Empire, 'The Pearl of Africa' according to its colonial administrators. Spread over the hills and valleys of a high plateau, its gentle climate makes it a pleasant garden nudging the Equator. It had enormous strategic value but when the 'wind of change' blew through Africa, the pressure for independence for Uganda became irresistible.

An astute lawyer and professional politician, Milton Obote became the first Prime minister when he triumphed in the hastily organized elections in 1962. His first priority was to forge some sort of unity among the 14 million Ugandans who owed more allegiance to their tribal chiefs than to any government in Kampala.

The ruling edicts of some of the chiefs of the 40 different tribes of Uganda often seemed to carry more authority than the decisions of any ballot-box Government. Mindful of this, Obote, a member of the minority Langi tribe, appointed the powerful ruler of the Buganda tribe, King Freddy, as President of Uganda. The Buganda tribe, largely Anglicized by colonial commissioners and missionaries, were the largest single tribal group. They considered themselves an elite.

But in placating them, Milton Obote earned himself the growing distrust of all the other tribes. Shortly after independence, however, he began slowly to reduce the powers of King Freddy.

By 1966 Buganda tribesmen were agitating more and more violently for Obote's overthrow. He needed to pit some military muscle against them and chose the deputy commander of the army, Idi Amin.

Amin had all the qualifications. He was an outsider, a Kakwa tribesman from the furthest flung province of Uganda, bordering Sudan. He was a Moslem who spoke virtually no English and was only semi-literate. He wouldn't be loath to dish out some rough justice to the Bugandans.

A former sergeant in the King's African Rifles, Amin was the ex-heavyweight-boxing champion of Uganda, a hulk of a man who, at six feet four inches tall and weighing more than twenty stone, easily dominated his fellow Ugandan Army staff officers.

His British commanding officer before independence had enthusiastically earmarked Amin as 'a tremendous chap to have around.' And though he was tough and swaggering, he was slow-witted and had never shown even the slightest tendency to try to grasp the complexities of politics.

Amin responded swiftly and energetically to the task the Prime Minister had given him. Using a 122mm gun mounted on his personal Jeep, he blew gaping holes in King Freddie's Palace. The Bugandan leader, warned of the danger just before the attack, fled into hiding and eventually made his way to Britain where he died in lonely exile.

For the next four years, Idi Amin was the Prime Minister's trusted strong arm man. Milton Obote was calm and relaxed when he flew off to Singapore in January 1971 to attend a Commonwealth Conference. He was about to fly home to Uganda when he heard the news on the radio . . . Idi Amin had just mobilized the Army and declared himself the country's new ruler.

The overgrown village bully turned military chief had decided that if he was to do the dirty work in Uganda he might just as well install himself as its supreme authority.

Milton Obote went into exile having learned an embarrassing political lesson. For the people of Uganda, cautiously celebrating his overthrow, the experience was to be painful to the point of torture and death.

Amin's first move was to pacify tribal enemies and buy valuable breathing space. He persuaded Buganda leaders that he himself had actually tipped off King Freddy and given him time to flee to safety. He arranged for the release of many political prisoners detained by Obote and had the body of the dead tribal King flown back from Britain for a ceremonial burial.

Amin was deeply affected by the ritual outpouring and lavish expense of the Buganda tribesmen at the burial ceremony. The experience was to be put to hideous use later.

Amin then moved against the most potent potential threat to his new power – the officers of the Ugandan Army.

He announced a new programme of army re-structuring and began by ordering 36 senior officers, Langi and Acholi tribesmen, to report to Makindye Prison for training in internal security. Disgruntled, but seduced by the thought of forming part of a government of military men instead of politicians, the officers arrived at Makindye. They were locked in cells and bayonetted to death.

The former army chief-of-staff, Brigadier Suleiman Hussein, was arrested and taken to yet another prison where he was beaten to death with rifle butts. His head was severed and taken to Amin's new palatial home in Kampala where the president preserved it in the freezer compartment of his refrigerator.

In two widely separated army barracks, at Mbarara and Jinja, the elite of the officer corps were lined up on the parade ground to take a salute from an armoured column. The tanks swept across the square, swung into line abreast formation and crushed most of the officers to death. Those left alive were used for target practice by riflemen. At another barracks, the remaining staff officers were herded into a briefing room for a lecture by Amin. As they saw his gleaming black Mercedes sweep into the square, the doors were locked from outside and grenades were lobbed through the windows.

Within five months Amin had killed most of the trained professional officers in his army. Yet the news was kept secret from the Ugandan people, who were simply told that a few disloyal officers had been court-martialled and executed. To make up the gaps in the ranks, Amin promoted fellow Kakwa tribesmen. Cooks and drivers, mess orderlies and wireless operators became majors and colonels overnight.

Idi Amin, one-time Life President of Uganda

But the word of the massacres had filtered out to two inquiring Americans, Nicholas Stroh, son of a wealthy Detroit brewer and a former writer for the *Philadelphia Bulletin* newspaper, was working as a freelance journalist in Africa. He joined forces with another American, Robert Siedle, a sociologist at Makere University in Kampala, to start asking questions about the army massacres.

At Mbarara barracks they were granted an interview with the new commander, Major Juma Aiga, a former taxi driver who had won an instant army commission. When their persistent questioning became too much, Major Aiga telephoned President Amin. His reply was terse: 'Kill them'.

Both men were gunned down on the spot and a few days later Aiga was openly driving around Kampala in Stroh's Volkswagen car. When the American Embassy demanded an investigation into the disappearance of the two men, they got nowhere.

As Amin went off on his first foreign trip as a head of government, he had already broken the backbone of the Ugandan Army. He was all-powerful, but he returned from his journeys to Israel and Britain empty-handed. His outright demands to both countries for millions of pounds in cash donations were refused. And the word went round the tight community of international diplomacy that the new president was not just a stupid, arrogant man. He was mad and dangerous.

Within a year Uganda was bankrupt. Amin's reaction was to order the Bank of Uganda to print millions of worthless banknotes to pump into the economy. All that remained of the reserves of U.S. dollars and sterling were made available for his personal use.

In Kampala the price of a bar of soap rose to £6, two weeks' wages for the average worker on the coffee plantations which were among the country's few sources of income.

Temporary salvation was offered by one other extravagant dictator, Libya's Colonel Ghadaffi. The price was one Amin was only too happy to pay for their newly formed alliance. As Libyan money poured into Kampala to keep the country barely afloat, Amin kept his side of the bargain. He ranted and raved against the State of Israel and kicked out the small group of skilled Israeli engineers employed on the construction projects which formed Israel's limited aid to Uganda.

Angered and hurt, the Israelis pulled out with their bulldozers and a meticulous mass of paperwork and blueprints. The documents included one slim volume which was later to help make history – the plans of Israel's last gift to Uganda, the new passenger terminal, control tower and runway layout of Entebbe Airport.

Amin, anxious to prove to Ghadaffi that he was a worthy protégé, opened an office in Kampala for the Palestine Liberation Organization with full diplomatic status. He capped it by pronouncing his admiration for his political hero, Adolf Hitler. As Amin drew up plans for a memorial to Hitler in the centre of Kampala, the world began to realize that some awful disaster was beginning to unfold.

They didn't have long to wait.

The Libyan money was barely propping up Uganda, and now Amin had hundreds of his chosen henchmen on the payroll of his new police force, The State Research Bureau. He bought their loyalty with lavish gifts of money and expensive cars, luxuries like video tape recorders and whisky and clothes imported from London and Paris.

One hot August night in 1972, dinner guests at Amin's palace, State House in Entebbe, were shocked and revolted when he left the table and returned from the kitchen with the frost-encrusted head of Brigadier Hussein from the freezer. In a ranting fit of rage Amin screamed abuse at the severed head, heaving cutlery at it, then ordered his guests to leave.

Two nights later he turned up unexpectedly in eastern Uganda and announced that God had appeared to him and told him that Uganda's population of 50,000 Asians, mainly tradesmen and merchants, doctors and nurses, were causing all Uganda's economic problems. He ordered them to leave the country within 90 days.

For the next three months Amin's voice could be heard on Uganda radio, making a daily count down to his deadline. Although most of the Asians had lived in Uganda for generations, forming the backbone of the nation's commerce, they fled in terror leaving behind their homes, offices, shops and plantations.

In November that year, Amin gave away the choice businesses to his friends and cronies. Pharmacies and surgeries were handed over to motor mechanics from the State Research Bureau, textile warehouses were given to Research Bureau telephone operators and army corporals. Within weeks the shops were deserted, their stocks sold and the shelves never filled again . . . and the men of the State Research Bureau wanted to be paid again.

With no money or property left to meet their demands, Amin gave them the only asset he had left, the lives of his fellow Ugandans.

It was the most bestial mass murder contract in history. Amin gave his bureau torturers the licence to kill for profit.

He knew the tradition of Ugandans, their deep reverence for the last remains of dead relatives and how they will spend every last Ugandan shilling of their money and part with anything of value to recover the body of a loved one for burial. In many of the tribes 'body finders' will earn their rewards by tracking through the bush to find the body of some father or son who has died in some

remote cattle grazing area or drowned in the fast flowing waters of the Nile.
The State Research Bureau became the killers – and the body finders.

Cruising through the street of Kampala in their imported cars, wearing their 'uniform' of gaudy silk shirts and bell bottom trousers, they openly arrested ordinary townspeople. And at their headquarters, only a few hundred yards from Amin's palatial home, they ruthlessly butchered their victims.

As the corpses piled up in the basement cells of the three storey building, other Research Bureau jailers were despatched to tell grieving families that their loved ones had disappeared after being arrested and were feared dead. For a body finding fee of £150, or every last possession the family owned, the State Research murderers drove the widows and weeping sons and daughters to a lush forest on the outskirts of Kampala.

Almost every gulley and bush concealed a dead body. Many nights as many as a hundred families made the grisly trip. The bodies not reclaimed were thrown into Lake Victoria, useless assets written off as a 'business' loss until they floated through the sluced gates of the Owens Falls Dam and the hydro-electric generators.

But the executions by firing squads at the Research Bureau became a problem. The neighbouring French Embassy staff complained directly to Amin about the constant gunfire throughout the night. Amin, sinking deeper and deeper into depravity, discussed a solution with the head of the Bureau, Lieutenant Isaac Malyamungu.

Malyamungu, a gatekeeper at a textile factory before Amin made him a government official, was a notoriously sadistic killer. Before executing the mayor of the provincial town of Masaka, he had paraded the badly mutilated man through the streets carrying his own amputated genitals in his hands. Now he and Amin calmly came up with the answer to the problem of maintaining the horrendous flow of lucrative killings without the disturbing, continuous rattle of gunfire. The murder victim would be kept alone in the basement, while another prisoner was offered the promise of reprieve if he would batter the solitary man to death with a 16lb sledgehammer.

Terrified and pleading for their lives, few prisoners were brave enough to refuse the offer. But once they had carried out their sickening task, the roles were changed. The unwilling executioner, usually sobbing and demented, would be left alone. He would become the solitary man, while in the cell next door another Ugandan was being given the sledgehammer and the heartless promise of life if he would repeat the procedure.

Even as the death toll rose, Amin still found time to indulge in personal episodes of unbelievable horror.

In March 1974 he went through a simple Moslem ritual to divorce three of his four wives. He accused them of meddling in his affairs and ordered them out of his home. Three months later one of the young ex-wives, Kay Amin, died in an apartment in Kampala as the result of a clumsy abortion attempt. She had been four months pregnant. Amin, in a state of fury, rushed to the mortuary to see her body. A few minutes later, quiet and unemotional, he gave a series of orders to the hospital surgeons and then left.

Two hours later he returned and satisfied himself that his orders had been carried out. Then he strode into the hospital morgue with his most junior wife, Sarah, and six-year-old Aliga Amin, the young son of Kay.

'Pay close attention to what you see,' he roared at them. 'Kay was a wicked woman, now look at what has become of her.'

Kay Amin's mutilated torso lay on the operating table. Her head and all her limbs had been amputated. Now her head had been reversed and sewn back on face down on her torso. Her legs had been neatly sutured on to her shoulders and her arms attached firmly to her bloodstained pelvis.

The swaggering arrogance of Idi Amin came to an end on 4 July 1976 although his brutality was to continue for almost another three years.

On 28 June an Air France airliner hijacked by a team of Palestinians arrived at Entebbe Airport. The plane had been en route from Tel Aviv to Paris when it had been commandeered shortly after a stop-over in Athens. It carried some 300 passengers.

In the heart of an African country governed by a Hitler-worshipper, far from any hope of rescue, the Palestinians confidently drew up their demands while Amin looked on, gloating and basking in the world limelight.

Amin helped to draft the blackmail demand that all the passengers would be killed in 48 hours if 53 Palestinian prisoners in jail in Israel and Europe were not released. As international tension mounted, the deadline was extended until the early hours of July 4, and passengers who were not Jewish were allowed to go.

Two days before the deadline, as the terrified hostages were huddled in the passenger terminal, one elderly Londoner, Dora Bloch, who held dual British-Israeli nationality, choked on a piece of food and was driven 20 miles from the airport to hospital in Kampala.

But as Idi Amin was being seen world-wide on television, badgering the hostages in the passenger lounge, the Israeli engineers in Tel Aviv unlocked a filing cabinet and began to pore over the vital blueprints of the airport they had helped to build.

Up and down the east coast of Africa an incredible international humanitarian conspiracy began to take shape. Shortly after midnight on 3 July, a task force of Israeli Air Force planes filled with commandoes came swooping over Lake Victoria. In silent co-operation they had been allowed to refuel and fly through the radar screens of Kenya, Uganda's neighbour.

The Israeli planes, guided by their own blueprints, landed swiftly and taxied to the precise spot in the terminal buildings where the hostages were being held. In less than an hour they took off again with the rescued hostages, leaving behind 20 of Idi Amin's troops dead and the seven hijackers killed on the spot. They also took with them the bodies of two of their own men caught in the crossfire.

But elderly Dora Bloch remained behind in hospital in Kampala, frail and barely able to breathe. Amin decided to vent his fury on her.

Sixteen hours after the Entebbe rescue mission, British High Commissioner Peter Chandley was allowed to visit Mrs Bloch. He tried to reassure the frightened woman and left the hospital briefly to prepare some food for her.

Shortly after he left, two State Research Bureau officials crashed through the doors of the hospital ward. They pistol-whipped the frail widow and dragged her down three flights of steps. Half an hour later they dumped her bullet-riddled body in a field on the outskirts of Kampala.

When the High Commissioner returned to the hospital, Amin simply announced that Mrs Bloch had gone the day before, returned to the airport under escort before the Entebbe Raid.

Idi Amin's last desperate mad gamble to hold the reins of power collapsed in April 1979. To scare the Ugandan people into submission, he claimed that the country was threatened by bloody invasion from its southern neighbour, Tanzania.

To give substance to his fantasies, he ordered small contingents of his troops across the Tanzanian border on raids against the 'invaders'. Such provocation was too much for Tanzanian President Julius Nyrere. His soldiers repelled the attacks and then drove deep into Uganda. They were welcomed with open arms by the long-suffering Ugandans as they advanced swiftly towards Kampala.

In one final broadcast, Idi Amin urged his troops to join him in a last stand at the town of Jinja, near the Owens Falls Dam. The soldiers didn't turn up. But then neither did Idi Amin. He had fled in his personal aircraft to the safety of Libya to seek sanctuary with his ally, Colonel Ghadaffi.

Five years after his overthrow, Idi Amin was still safely living in luxury in a private suite of an hotel in Saudi Arabia, the guest of the Moslem royal rulers of that country.

He would still rant about his return to Uganda and his self-appointed role in international politics. But this time no one was listening.

Prime Minister Milton Obote was back in power in Kampala. The country still suffered the ravages of the long years of Amin's tyranny. But the power supply flowed smoothly from the Owens Falls Dam hydro-electric generators, and the crocodiles in Lake Victoria had only the birds' nests in the swamps to prey on for a decent meal.

Pol Pot

He has a broad, chubby face with sparkling, grandfatherly eyes and thick lips which split into a toothy, genial grin. He looks slightly comical, an impression not dispelled by his peculiar name, Pol Pot. But there is nothing funny about Pol Pot . . . he is a tyrannical fanatic responsible for the coldly calculated extermination of three million people.

Pol Pot spent just four years on the world stage, as the shadowy leader of Kampuchea (formerly Cambodia) after the overthrow of President Lon Nol in 1975. Yet in that short period he virtually destroyed a nation – all for the sake of an unworkable creed that he imposed unyieldingly on a starving and terrorized population. Under his rule, a once-beautiful country became known as 'The Land of the Walking Dead'.

Little is known of Pol Pot's background, and what is known could easily have been the invention of his propaganda machine. It is said that he was brought up in a peasant community in Cambodia's Kampong Thom province and was educated at a Buddhist temple where, for two years, he was a monk. In the 1950s he won a scholarship to study electronics in Paris where, like so many other students at the time, he found it fashionable to espouse left-wing causes.

Also in Paris in the 1950s was another left-wing Cambodian student, Khieu Samphan, who used his political science courses to formulate an extraordinary philosophy of rural revolution. His theory was that to rid itself of the vestiges of colonial rule and to avoid capitalist exploitation, Cambodia must regress to a peasant economy – without towns, without industry, without currency, without education.

It is unlikely that Pol Pot and Khieu Samphan ever met in Paris. But back among the Khmer people of Cambodia, they teamed up and set about making Khieu's crackpot creed come true, using as their instrument the newly-formed and Chinese-backed Communist Party of Kampuchea.

After a decade of political intrigue and rural guerrilla warfare, in 1975 the communists finally overthrew President Lon Nol and became masters of the capital, Phnom Penh. By now the party was known as the Khmer Rouge. Khieu Samphan became its figurehead. But the real power lay in the hands of the former peasant from the provinces, Prime Minister Pol Pot. And he immediately put political daydreams into horrific, brutal, uncompromising reality.

The capital was emptied. As many as three million of its citizens were stripped of all they possessed and were ordered out of their homes. Irrespective of whether they were old, sick, pregnant, crippled, newly born or dying, they were marched into the countryside and herded into vast communes of as many as 10,000. No town was left inhabited. Even villages were emptied of their people. Everybody had to work in the fields.

Of course, not everyone could. The aged and the ill died of exhaustion. The young died of starvation. And the crippled and the lame were clubbed to death.

Living in malaria-ridden swamps, with no proper shelter or sanitation, the new 'peasants' were frogmarched into the paddy fields to work a minimum of eleven hours a day. They were fed a daily bowl of gruel and a morsel of dried fish. They worked nine days on and one day off . . . but that tenth day of rest was taken up with political indoctrination. Children began their working lives at the age of seven.

Not only did the Khmer Rouge abolish towns and communities, they abolished families, husbands and wives being split up and placed in different co-operatives. They also abolished personal property, apart from the one sleeping mat and one pair of black overalls handed out no more than once a year. Since there was no property and no trade, there was no need for money, so they abolished that too.

Because there was no education apart from political indoctrination, Pol Pot abolished the schools and colleges. All books were burned. With education thereby shown to be non-essential, he abolished the educated classes – and had them murdered by the tens of thousands. Also eliminated, by bayonet or pickaxe, were priests, political reactionaries, prison inmates and the defeated soldiers of ex-president Lon Nol.

Anyone who complained, or even questioned the system, would be instantly executed by clubbing. Special offenders, like those starving peasants found cannibalizing dead bodies, would be buried up to their heads in the ground and left to die. Their heads would then be cut off and stuck on stakes as a warning to others.

The extermination continued for four years, with no hope of help from the outside world. Refugees reaching neighbouring countries told stories of horrors that were unbelievable. Yet, with no diplomatic ties, no travel, not even a postal service, the renamed nation of Kampuchea was an impenetrable armed camp seemingly set on the genocide of its own people.

The world's repugnance was unheeded; protest appeared futile. In March 1978, Britain reported Kampuchea to the United Nations Commission On Human Rights. The Khmer Rouge's embassy in Peking issued an hysterical response, saying: 'The British imperialists have no right to speak of the rights of man. The world knows well their barbarous and abject nature. Britain's leaders are living in opulence on top of a pile of rotting corpses while the proletariat have only the right to be unemployed, to steal and to become prostitutes.' There was

A grim scene in the Museum of Genocidal Crime outside Phnom Penh

little chance of a reasoned debate . . . and indeed Pol Pot's ministers sent their regrets that they could find no one with the time to spare to attend the United Nations human rights hearings.

Predictably, it was military might, not moral right, that brought the overthrow of Pol Pot and his murderous henchmen. Vietnam signed a pact with Kampuchea's only ally, China, and in 1978 Vietnamese forces which had been skirmishing with the Khmer Rouge for years launched a full-scale invasion. The Chinese did not step in to aid Pol Pot, and in January 1979 his regime fell to the invading Vietnamese. So swift was his overthrow that the chubby little despot had to flee from Phnom Penh in a white Mercedes limousine only two hours before the first of Hanoi's troops arrived.

Pol Pot fought on from his power base among his dedicated followers in the countryside. He formed the Khmer People's National Liberation Front and announced a hypocritical manifesto promising political and religious freedom. Khieu Samphan remained titular head of the Khmer Rouge. In a rare interview with foreign journalists in 1980, he said the mistakes made by his regime were mainly in implementation of policy. For instance, he said, over-zealous commune leaders had often forgotten to give workers their one day off in ten. And as for the massacres, he said: 'To talk about systematic murder is odious. If we had really killed at that rate, we would have no one to fight the Vietnamese.'

No one will ever know the truth about how many Khmers died of disease, starvation, neglect, brutalization, murder or massacre. But in June 1979, Foreign Minister Ieng Sary admitted to three million deaths since the Khmer Rouge came to power. As there were only eight million Khmers in the pre-revolutionary census, it was pointed out by journalists that this did not seem a good record for a four-year-old government. The Minister was apologetic. He had an explanation, he said. The orders from Pol Pot had been 'misunderstood.' The massacres had, he said, been 'a mistake'.

'Emperor' Bokassa

For a brief period just before the 'coronation' of self-styled Emperor Jean Bedel Bokassa it seemed as if some glimmer of humanity might be creeping into his tyrannical madness. Important diplomats and influential international businessmen from many parts of the world were preparing to attend his spectacular enthronement ceremony in Bangui, capital of the land-locked Central African Republic, the sprawling former French colony in the heart of the continent.

At the beginning of December 1977, as rehearsals began for the great event, Bokassa had locked himself away in his palace 50 miles outside the capital watching endless re-runs of a film which had been specially flown to him from London. The film showed the majesty and splendour of the Coronation of Britain's Queen Elizabeth. Bokassa, a violent, squat, ugly little man, seemed to be genuinely moved by the scenes of the splendid pageantry and the spontaneous, heart-felt joy and devotion of the Queen's loyal subjects.

His own coronation, he decided, would be a similarly historic occasion. Even if he couldn't hope to win the hearts of the people he ruled, at least his guests couldn't fail to be impressed. Apparently on a whim, he ordered the governor of Bangui Prison to select a dozen prisoners for more humane treatment. They were to be moved to less cramped cells, given better food than the other inmates and allowed some fresh air in the prison yard. Some prison guards even talked excitedly of a partial amnesty to celebrate the coronation. The prisoners, Bokassa promised, wouldn't be in jail much longer.

Then Bokassa busied himself again supervising the last-minute preparations for the ceremony. The Government of France, headed by his frequent holiday guest, President Valéry Giscard D'Estaing, had generously provided him with credit of £1 million to buy a fleet of Mercedes limousines for his guests and to equip their ceremonial escort with 200 new BMW motorcycles.

It mattered little to the 58-year-old dictator that his country ranked as one of the poorest in the world, with barely ten per cent of the two million population able to read and write and more than a quarter of their children dying of disease and malnutrition before they reached their first birthday.

He planned to spend £10 million in a 48-hour spectacular binge, a regal extravaganza to rival the coronation of his 'hero', the Emperor Napoleon. President Bokassa himself would assume the title Emperor Bokassa and his bankrupt country would be grandly re-named The Central African Empire.

Many political leaders had no stomach for his lunacy and returned their gold-lettered invitation cards with scant apologies for their absence. Even the formally polite British Foreign Office were blunt and rude when they refused to attend. American President Jimmy Carter, outraged by Bokassa's insane claim to Napoleonic grandeur, promptly responded by cutting off all aid to the country.

Bokassa was unrepentant. His rag-tag army formed most of the unenthusiastic onlookers at the triumphal parade through Bangui where the new Emperor would ride in a gilded carriage drawn by eight white horses along the city's only two miles of paved road.

The coronation went ahead with all the panoply of crowns and ermine robes in the sweltering African heat, and the guests were treated to a mouth-watering imperial banquet in Bokassa's palace at Berengo.

Protected by screens of bullet-proof glass in a landscaped garden amid fountains and ornate ivory carvings, they were pampered by uniformed servants who brought them elaborately cooked delicacies served on gold and white porcelain dishes specially imported from the workshops of the master designer, Berardaud of Limoges.

Some of the French and African diplomats, and the Italian and German businessmen, seemed ill at ease in the absurd splendour of their bizarre surroundings. They would have felt distinctly more queasy if they had realized the origins of some of the tastiest morsels served up to them on the Limoges porcelain.

Bokassa had kept his promise to the prison governor. The inmates who had been given food, fresh air and exercise had found their new privileges short-lived. As soon as they had been restored to near normal health, they had been killed, expertly butchered and served up to the unsuspecting guests at Bokassa's celebration feast.

His obsession with the trappings of the power and grace of the age of Napoleon were flattering to many of his French VIP visitors. At least most of them found his mania for all things French to be understandable. His character had been moulded by his long years as a soldier in the French colonial army, where all new

The Coronation of Emperor Bokassa, 28 December, 1977

recruits were thoroughly indoctrinated in the glories of French history and the awesome achievements of its finest soldier, Napoleon Bonaparte.

In 1960, when the French gave independence to the republic, an area almost as large as France itself, most of them were glad to be rid of the task of governing its vast, arid waste. There was some embarassed amusement in 1966 when Colonel Bokassa seized power in a coup from the Republic's civilian government and began to boast of his devotion to France. He swore undying loyalty to French President Charles De Gaulle, whom he lovingly called 'Papa'. The French Government responded with generous aid in return for some minor business concessions and a military foothold in a strategic part of Africa.

In 1975, the new French President Valéry Giscard D'Estaing took advantage of Bokassa's welcome to make several big-game hunting trips to his private game reserve, an area covering most of the eastern half of the country.

There were reports that Bokassa was never slow to shower his visitors with lavish gifts, including fistfuls of diamonds, one of his country's few precious resources, which should have gone to help alleviate the crushing poverty of its people.

By the time Bokassa was in the full grip of his 'imperial' mania, the soaring price of oil had made the country's only other asset, uranium deposits, look like a promising commercial prospect for French developers. Wary of growing evidence of Bokassa's brutality, the French uneasily indulged his regal fantasies while keeping a discreet eye on his appetite for power and showmanship. Within two years of the ludicrous coronation, he had become more than a posturing embarrassment to Paris. He was a bloodthirsty, dangerous liability.

Apparently determined to transform his dusty capital city into a model of French 'provincial' fashion, Bokassa ordered the barefoot schoolchildren of Bangui's only high school to buy expensively tailored school uniforms to be worn at all lessons. Their parents could hardly afford to buy the text books their children needed if they were to have even a basic education. And it hadn't passed unnoticed that the Emperor owned the only clothing factory which produced the school uniforms. It was yet another impossible order from the Emperor which they couldn't obey even if they wanted to. No one foresaw the consequences.

President Bokassa, who had seen his demands for national opera, ballet and art societies dismissed by his weary people, had at one time seemingly grown accustomed to being ignored. But *Emperor* Bokassa, the Napoleon-worshipper, expected every order to be carried out without question.

Two hundred ragged schoolchildren were rounded up by the 'Imperial Guard'. Bokassa gathered them in the yard of Bangui Prison, swaggering among them with his gold-topped cane, bullying the overawed, frightened pupils. 'You will not need school uniforms as long as you stay in prison,' the Empe or screamed at them. Under the threatening guns of the guards, the children were herded into the already overcrowded cells.

Over the next few weeks the killings began. One by one the children were led from the cells for 'school uniform inspection' . . . and mercilessly beaten to death.

News of the mass murders finally reached the disbelieving ears of officials of the French Embassy in Bangui. At first they couldn't bring themselves to accept the evidence. But witness after witness from the prison repeated the same story. And Paris finally woke up to the fact that Jean Bedel Bokassa was more than a comic opera Emperor with his crown and robes and sceptre. He was a monster.

For the honour of France, for the sake of common decency, the Emperor had to go.

The opportunity came a month later when the demented Emperor left Bangui for a visit to another dictator, Colonel Ghadaffi of Libya. As Bokassa stepped off his plane in Tripoli, he learned a lesson in the true French art of power politics and military muscle which would have delighted his long dead hero Napoleon.

At his home in Paris where he had lived since being ousted by Bokassa, African politician David Dacko was roughly shaken awake by French Secret Service agents and given a prepared speech to rehearse and memorize before being bundled into a waiting car. Ten hours later he stumbled from a French military jet at Bangui and asked the French Foreign Legion troops who landed immediately after him to help him to a 'spontaneous' humanitarian overthrow of the evil Bokassa.

Within 24 hours the 'Empire' was effectively back under French control. The deposed Emperor went into exile from Libya to the Ivory Coast in West Africa and then to a run-down château in an unfashionable Paris suburb.

The hardened Legionnaires who searched the grounds of the prison had the grim task of uncovering the mass grave which held the bodies of the dead schoolchildren.

Later, when they stormed the Emperor's Napoleonic palace, they found the bones of another 37 children lying on the tiled floor of the Olympic standard swimming pool. Lounging by the poolside were the predators who had enjoyed the grisly feast, Bokassa's four pet crocodiles. And in the cold storage rooms of the palace kitchens, they found the half-eaten remains of another dozen unnamed victims who had been served up at the Emperor's dining table only the week before.

As the uniform-obsessed Emperor began a new career in exile as a supplier of khaki safari suits to African tourist boutiques, President Giscard D'Estaing announced in Paris that he had sent a personal cheque for £10,000, the value of the diamonds given to him as gifts, to a charity school for children in Bangui.

Papa Doc

Many tyrants have held power over nations by preying on simple human emotions, like fear of invasion by hostile neighbours or by nationalistic pride in conquest over weaker countries. Others have kept themselves in government by rigged elections or by armed suppression of their own downtrodden populations.

But only one modern dictator has ever managed to keep his people enslaved by a grisly combination of machine-gun and mysticism, by the force of a vicious police state and an unholy alliance with the Devil himself and his legions of demons and ghosts, vampires and zombies.

In the era that saw astronauts land on the moon and orbiting laboratories in space, President 'Papa Doc' Duvalier still ruled the republic of Haiti by bullets and black magic, by real live bogeymen who carried very real automatic pistols and by a supernatural 'police force' of living skeletons raised from the dead. Millions of Haitians who suffered the terrors of his 15 years of brutal dictatorship are convinced that he still reigns from beyond the grave, controlling his country's destiny from within the gates of Hell.

The bitter irony of the plight of the 5 million inhabitants of Haiti is that their struggling nation was once hailed as the most progressive in the Caribbean, a proud democracy which showed the way for other countries to free themselves from exploiters and foreign rule.

Haiti shares the island of Hispaniola with the Dominican Republic, and its lush and rolling sub-tropical forests were one of the wondrous sights of the New World for explorer Christopher Columbus when his ship foundered and was wrecked there in December 1492. It was an inauspicious start for a new nation. And over the centuries the people of that island have paid a terrible price for its accidental introduction to the adventurers from the Old World.

By the end of the 16th century most of the original population of Arawak Indians had been wiped out. Many fell victim to newly introduced European diseases. The survivors were literally worked to death on the plantations of their new Spanish masters. When the Spaniards moved on, there was little left to plunder for the next occupants, the rapacious pirates who used Hispaniola as their base for marauding, murder and looting. The buccaneers who controlled the whole western part of the island renamed their territory by its original Indian name – Haiti.

They were soon ousted by a new set of colonial rulers, the French, who revived the plantation system and peopled Haiti with black slaves captured on the west coast of Africa and packed into stinking hulks for the voyage to their new 'home'. The wretched slaves brought with them only two possessions – hatred of their new oppressors and their age-old belief in African witchcraft and demons. The first of these two emotions was to lead to uprisings so passionate and violent that even the all-conquering Emperor Napoleon eventually had to concede defeat in 1804 and Haiti, with its short history of bloodshed and superstition, became the first independent black-governed republic in the world.

Over the years this unhappy land lurched from one incompetent or greedy regime to another. From 1915 to 1934 it was occupied by US Marines. There followed a string of provincial presidents, mostly mulatto descendants of mixed French-negro marriages, each being toppled in the midst of scandal and crisis which only made the already poverty-stricken population more miserable.

But in 1957 a popular new president emerged: François Duvalier, known to his friends and foes alike as 'Papa Doc'. Duvalier was a trained doctor, working on a US medical aid scheme before he turned to politics. Since they provided almost the only source of income for Haiti, the Americans were pleased to see a modern man of medicine as the new ruler. But the black peasants who formed 95 per cent of the population welcomed him for a totally different reason.

To them Duvalier was not so much a doctor, more a medicine man and a pure descendant of African slaves. They were enthralled by his open boast that he was a skilled witch doctor with experience in the dark practices of their voodoo religion, a mixture of French-inspired Christianity and ancient African superstitions. Papa Doc promised that by witchcraft and black magic ritual he would summon the Devil himself to share his power with all the voodoo worshippers of Haiti. On a more practical note, to placate the more educated political opposition, he vowed that the millions of dollars in American aid would be used to raise living standards. At that time, only 10 per cent of the population were literate, the national income averaged £1 a week, and most Haitians died of malnutrition and disease by the age of 35.

Within a few years of gaining control, Papa Doc made it plain he would share his power with no-one. Most of the finance from the United States was funnelled into his own private bank accounts while he lived in seclusion in his palatial presidential mansion. In 1961 he declared himself president for life and ordered the ill-disciplined Haitian Army to murder scores of political opponents. Their bodies were strung up on lamp posts around the capital, Port-au-Prince, with bloody voodoo symbols engraved on their corpses.

They had been killed, Papa Doc warned, by the forces of 'Baron Samedi', the avenging zombie of witchcraft. Baron Samedi, a hellish figure dressed in a black hat and a suit of mourning, was a voodoo demon, a soul raised from the dead to prowl the earth and carry out the wishes of the Devil.

To ensure that his own Army was in fear of him, Duvalier raised a secret police force, the Ton Ton Macoute – voodoo bogeymen who swore allegiance to him as the supreme witch doctor. The 10,000 members of the Ton Ton were given the task of killing hundreds of Army officers who were threatening rebellion against the bloodthirsty tyrant. In return they were given free rein to terrorise the countryside, looting and stealing from the starving peasants, carrying out murders which were always staged to bear the hallmarks of terrifying religious ritual.

The savagery of Papa Doc and his declaration of the grotesque cult of voodoo as Haiti's official national religion looked certain to prove his downfall. In the United States, recently elected President John F. Kennedy reacted with fury and indignation. Reflecting the civilised world's revulsion with Pap Doc's depravity, Kennedy announced that American aid to Haiti would cease as long as the Devil-worshipper was in power. It was thought to be only a matter of time before the pangs of hunger of the Haitians overcame their fear of demons and zombies. As the rumblings of discontent grew, even the gunmen of the Ton Ton Macoute were hard pressed to silence the increasing number of voices raised in anger against Duvalier.

For Papa Doc there was only one source of help to which he could turn. With power slowly beginning to slip from his grasp, he announced that he had performed a nightmarish voodoo ceremony to raise the Devil from Hell to put a curse on the American President. Six weeks later, John F. Kennedy died of an assassin's bullets in Dallas.

In Haiti the news was greeted with stunned despair. Nothing could shake the belief of terrified Haitians that the trigger of the assassin's gun had been pulled by the bony finger of the grinning zombie, Baron Samedi. Now Duvalier found new ways to bleed his people dry – literally. Still grasping for American dollars, he used the Ton Ton Macoute to round up thousands of Haitians daily and march them to medical centres in the capital, Port-au-Prince. There, each was given a week's wages of £1 in exchange for a litre of blood. The blood was flown to America and sold for transfusion at £12 a litre.

Papa Doc continued to rule supreme in Haiti. Any challenge to his power was met swiftly by the murder squads of the Ton Ton Macoute. In 1971, dying of diabetes and heart disease, he altered the constitution of Haiti to allow his podgy playboy son Jean-Claude, known as Baby Doc, to assume the mantle of power . . . Papa Doc had been president for life. Now he was trying to ensure that his devilish dynasty survived even in death.

Josef Stalin

Bolshevik bullets finally ended 400 years of repressive rule by Russia's Tsars. Nicholas II, gunned down with his haemophilic son Alexei in the cellar of a house in Ekaterinburg in July 1918, had fought to the last against what he called the 'senseless dream' of the people having a say in how their lives were governed. Bolstered in his belief in absolute autocracy by the sinister 'mad monk' Rasputin, he allowed ruthless henchmen to try to silence with savagery the growing clamour for basic human rights.

Chief of police Vyacheslav von Plehve mounted pogroms in Kishiniov and Gomel to 'drown the revolution in Jewish blood.' Minister of the Interior Peter Stolypin executed so many people for political offences – 5,000 in less than two years – that the gallows were nicknamed Stolypin's Necktie. And on Bloody Sunday, 22 January 1905, when riflemen and Cossack horsemen killed 150 defenceless men, women and children and injured a thousand more by brutally attacking a peaceful protest march to the St Petersburg Winter Palace, the Tsar's only question was: 'Have they killed enough?'

But there was by then no way that the revolution could be prevented. All it needed was a catalyst . . . and that came with the carnage of World War One, in which Russia lost vast tracts of land and 4 million men.

By 1916 abysmal leadership and terrible suffering had sapped the army's strength. And a year later, when soldiers and sailors garrisoned near St Petersburg sided with the strikers protesting at food shortages, inflation and corruption, the Tsar was forced to abdicate. The dreaded Ochrana, the secret police who maintained his reign of terror, were disbanded. Land confiscated from the rich was given to the peasants. Workers were promised an eight-hour day. Genuinely free elections were called. To the suddenly unsuppressed masses, Utopia seemed theirs.

But the revolutionaries had inherited a bitter legacy. In maintaining power at all costs, the Tsars had neglected the nation's interests. Revolutionaries like Lenin, returning from exile, knew from first-hand experience in Europe how backward the country was. 'Our task,' Lenin told his Politburo colleagues, 'is to take the lead of the exhausted masses who are wearily seeking a way out and lead them along the true path, along the path of labour discipline . . .'

But Lenin died in 1924, having taken only a few steps along that path. And his successor was to turn the democratic dream into a blood-soaked nightmare of tyranny on a scale that even the most sadistic Tsars never contemplated. In just

30 years of power, Josef Stalin killed more people than the Tsars had accounted for in four centuries. He turned a popular revolution based on ideals of freedom and equality into a totalitarian dictatorship maintained solely by terror. Although in the process he turned the Soviet Union into one of the world's two great super-powers, and extended its empire far beyond the boundaries established by the Tsars, even the communists who succeeded him denounced his monstrous excesses.

The dying Lenin had warned the communist Central Committee against Stalin, the shoemaker's son who had robbed banks in his native Georgia to raise funds for the Bolshevik cause, and rose to become party General Secretary in 1922. Lenin urged his colleagues to find someone 'more tolerant, more loyal, more polite, more considerate, less capricious,' and added: 'Comrade Stalin has concentrated boundless authority in his hands and I am not sure whether he will always be capable of using that authority with sufficient caution . . .' The party hierarchy did what they could, appointing Comrades Zinoviev and Kamenev to share leadership with Stalin. But already he was too powerful to be shackled. Adroit manoeuvring of the Politburo power blocs enabled him to demote, expel, even exile all potential rivals. By 1928 he was undisputed master of Moscow. Nikolai Bukhanin, one of Lenin's closest aides, confided to a friend when he was ousted: 'Stalin is a Genghis Khan who will kill us all.' It was a chillingly accurate prediction.

Stalin decided to accelerate Russian development. Huge new coal, iron and steel complexes were built all over Russia at a tremendous cost in human life. One of the American engineers called in as a consultant said: 'I would wager that Russia's battle of ferrous metallurgy alone involved more casualties than the Battle of the Marne.'

The programme was partly financed by swingeing taxes on richer peasants, the kulaks, who had been allowed by Lenin to sell surplus food to ease shortages. Dogmatic Stalin allowed no such 'deviations.' Soon the kulaks lost not only the

---

Walter Krivitsky was Stalin's military intelligence chief in Western Europe until he defected to escape a purge in 1936. He told a British interrogator: 'If you ever hear I have committed suicide, don't believe it. I will have been murdered.' In February 1941 his body was found in a hotel room in Washington DC. An inquest studied farewell notes before deciding that bullet wounds to his head were self-inflicted. But Krivitsky's widow Tania said of the notes: 'The writing is Walter's but the words are not.'

right to sell but their land and livestock. Stalin announced the elimination of the kulaks as a class. Millions were ordered to join vast state-run collective farms. Millions more were herded to towns to become forced labour in the new state-owned factories. Others disappeared into the growing network of 'corrective labour camps', the harsh 'Gulags' much later exposed by writer Alexander Solzhenitsyn. More than 25 million were forcibly evicted. More than three million were killed.

Stalin – the revolutionary name meant 'Man of Steel' – imposed his Marxist will on all walks of life. The party and government bureaucracies were purged of 'unreliable' workers – 164,000 Moscow civil servants were kicked out in 18 months. Church publications were suppressed, church buildings confiscated and the leaders exiled or jailed. Local nationalism in satellite states was dismissed as another 'deviation' and ruthlessly eradicated. Writers were subjected to intense censorship to ensure they wrote only work to inspire the proletariat. 'Where else do they kill people for writing poetry?' one artist asked plaintively. The grip of the secret police, the OGPU, tightened over everyone. Internal passports were re-introduced to make keeping track of people easier. Often alleged enemies of the state were quietly liquidated without troubling the courts. After all, the OGPU were working for a man who said: 'The death of a man is a tragedy; the death of a thousand is a statistic.'

Statistically the first five-year plan was a success. By 1935 industrial production was four times greater than in 1913. But progress had been bought at staggering cost. Results of a census in 1937 were so appalling they were suppressed. Two years later experts estimated that Russia's population was an astounding 20 million short of what it should have been. Emigration and famine

---

Stalin set up a special overseas sabotage and murder squad within his secret service in January 1946. Its first chief, war hero Pavl Anatolevich Sudoplatov, gave one officer – who later defected – this advice on recruiting killers: 'Go search for people who are hurt by fate or nature – the ugly, those suffering from an inferiority complex, craving power and influence but defeated by unfavourable circumstances. The sense of belonging to an influential, powerful organization will give them a feeling of superiority over the handsome and prosperous people around them and for the first time in their lives they will experience a sense of importance. It is sad and humanly shallow but we are obliged to profit from it.'

were factors. But Stalin's purges and the breakneck pace of industrialization accounted for many millions more. Historian E.H. Carr wrote: 'Seldom perhaps in history has so monstrous a price been paid for so monumental an achievement.'

In November 1932 Stalin's wife Nadezhda Alliluevna committed suicide with a revolver. At one time she had helped Stalin, telling him secrets learned from her job as a confidential code clerk in Lenin's private office. Now she was appalled at his increasingly brutal nature. He had become a foul-mouthed drunkard prone to violent rages, abusing underlings and indulging in debauched delights to test their loyalty. On one occasion he rolled five slim tubes of paper and stuck them on his secretary's fingers. Then he lit each like a candle and grinned as the man writhed in agony, not daring to remove them. Nadezhda's death removed one of the few remaining checks on Stalin's absolute authority. Their daughter Svêtlana said later: 'It deprived his soul of the last vestiges of human warmth.'

Then, in December 1934, a young communist shot dead party secretary Sergei Kirov in St Petersburg – which had been renamed Leningrad. Stalin instantly ordered the security services to speed up cases against people accused of executing or preparing to execute acts of terror. And he told courts to carry out death sentences immediately, since the government would no longer consider petitions for possible pardons. The ruling, as Nikita Khruschev later said, was 'the basis for mass acts of abuse against socialist legality.'

Stalin now began moving against old revolutionary colleagues. Zinoviev, Kamenev, Bukhanin and OGPU chief Yahoda were just four of the prominent communists accused of conspiring against the state in a series of show trials which lasted from 1936 to 1938. Astonishingly, they all pleaded guilty, perhaps through loyalty to the revolution, but more probably because they had been broken by torture and warned that their families would suffer if they caused a stir. By 1939, of the 139-strong Central Committee, 98 had been shot, and every member of Lenin's Politburo except Stalin himself and Trotsky, exiled in 1929, had been condemned by the courts.

New massive purges began throughout society. The Red Army leadership was more than halved. Naval top brass was devastated. The Communist Party rank and file was cleansed of intellectual idealists who put principles before the new politics of power, privilege and practicalities. Ruthless sycophants took their places, men with whom Stalin felt more secure. The secret police were shaken up and renamed the NKVD, under the notorious Beria. Even secret agents abroad, including spies who recruited and controlled English traitors Philby, Blunt and Burgess, were summoned back to Moscow and eliminated. Stalin, who knew more than most about conspiracy, saw plots everywhere. Others had to die because they knew too much about his previous misdeeds.

THE WORLD'S MOST EVIL MEN

More than 500,000 people were summarily shot. Millions more were tortured and incarcerated. Even President Kalinin's wife spent seven years in a prison camp to guarantee her husband's behaviour.

The purges suddenly ceased in 1939. With the promise of a new, liberal constitution, people began to breathe more easily. But their relief was short-lived, for World War Two was about to begin . . .

To the war-weary nations allied against the Nazis, Soviet Marshal Stalin was avuncular Uncle Joe, a hero helping America and Britain end the evil of Hitler. Winston Churchill posed for photographs with him at the Yalta summit, and told journalists Stalin's life was 'precious to the hopes and hearts of us all.' He added: 'I walk through this world with greater courage when I find myself in a relation of friendship and intimacy with this great man.' It was not a sentiment shared by many of the millions who entered the war under Stalin, or the peoples he subjected during the hostilities. For Stalin's smiles at Yalta concealed a cruel and calculating nature prepared to condone and commit war crimes at least as evil as those of the enemy, and an ambition which was already bent on betraying the leaders who sang his praises.

Stalin had already betrayed the Allies once when, in August 1939, he had signed a non-aggression pact with Hitler. It was a cynical deal between a man who secretly planned to murder 30 million Slavs and a man who was already well on his way to doing so. Under its terms, the NKVD and the Gestapo compared notes on dissident refugees. Jewish prisoners in Soviet Gulags were swapped for concentration camp inmates Stalin wanted to get his hands on. Germany was allowed to use Murmansk as a submarine base and Russia supplied the Nazis with vital war materials. Most importantly for Stalin, he was given a free hand in certain areas to extend his reign of terror.

The Red Army marched into the Balkan states, ostensibly to preserve their neutrality. When Finland refused to hand over strategically useful land and islands, Stalin invaded to force the transfer at gunpoint. But it was Poland, a traditional enemy of Russia for centuries, which was most callously abused. The two dictators had drawn a line down the middle of the independent state. When Hitler invaded from the west, forcing Britain and France to declare war, Stalin's troops went in from the east, taking cruel advantage of Polish preoccupation with the Nazi attack. More than a quarter of a million Polish officers and men were captured – and 14,000 were never seen alive again.

In all the captured countries, the sinister NKVD arrived soon after the army had established control. They eliminated political and cultural leaders who might stand in the way of Stalin's planned Russification of the different nationalities. Millions were transported to the remote wastelands of Russia. Others were simply shot. As were Russians returned from captivity by the Finns. Stalin had no time for Soviet soldiers who failed him.

The fate of some of the missing Poles was revealed in 1943. The bodies of 4,000 officers were unearthed in shallow graves beneath a grove of young conifers at Katyn, near Smolensk. Most had their hands tied behind their backs and bullet wounds in the back of their necks. A few had smashed skulls. Some had straw or sawdust stuffed in their mouths, to kill them while saving ammunition. What happened to the remaining 10,000 who vanished has never been conclusively established, but some experts suspect they were loaded on barges and drowned in the White Sea by the NKVD. The missing included 800 doctors and 12 university professors.

Stalin was able to indulge himself in such blood-letting against his own and other peoples because he trusted Hitler. But by late 1940, the Führer was the master of mainland Europe, and able to prepare for the move he had planned all along: Operation Barbarossa, the invasion of Russia.

When Hitler's troops crossed the border at dawn on 22 June, 1941, Stalin was stunned. For 11 days he did nothing as the Red Army, weakened by purges and assured by their leader that invasion was impossible, fell back in disarray. But Stalin was eventually stung into action, when it became clear that many of his subjects were not resisting the Nazis, but welcoming them as liberators.

Long-silent church bells rang out in occupied towns as a religious people, denied the right to worship for years, joyously assembled for services. Civilians began hoping for the freedoms promised in 1917. Even the Jews, victims of Stalin's anti-semitism, responded willingly to Nazi posters asking them to register with the invaders. Nobody dreamed that Hitler could be as murderous a master as Stalin. Disillusioned Russian troops surrendered in droves. In less than six months, the invading army of just over 3 million captured nearly 4 million of the Red Army.

But Hitler and his army threw away their chances of capitalizing on Russian misery. Freed towns were soon appalled by the cruelty of the occupying forces. Hitler himself refused to allow nearly 800,000 Russian volunteers to fight for him

---

Stalin was a sadist. He liked to watch interrogations of political suspects by his secret police, and is quoted as ordering them to 'beat, beat and beat again until they come crawling to you on their bellies with confessions in their teeth.' Some historians attribute such brutality to the savage beatings he took from his father, a Georgian shoemaker who drank heavily. A childhood attack of smallpox, which left Stalin pockmarked for life, also contributed to his bitter inferiority complex.

against Stalin under rebel general Alexander Vlasov. And when Stalin appealed over the radio to 'his friends' the Russian people, they rose heroically to throw off the Nazi yoke.

Yet while his troops were battling back with courage, and Stalin was appealing to the Allies to send him battalions of reinforcements or to invade Europe to open a second front, the NKVD were waging war on the Russian people. Fearful of anyone who might try to topple him for his earlier savagery or for his military mistakes, Stalin launched yet another great purge. Army officers were killed by the hundred. Gulag inmates were slaughtered by the thousand. Potential 'enemies of the people' were massacred in every area that might fall into German hands. In his book *Stalin's Secret War*, Count Nikolai Tolstoy wrote: 'At Lvov, as the Soviet 4th Army battled against odds to save the city, the NKVD was working for a week with machine guns, grenades and high explosives in its frantic effort to liquidate thousands of Ukrainian prisoners. Thousands more were being transferred east under heavy armed guard.'

The Germans knew how Stalin dealt with Ukrainians. They had uncovered a mass grave of 9,000 bodies, clinically laid head to toe to save space, in the Ukrainian town of Vinnitsa, population 70,000. Again, most had their hands bound and bullet wounds in the back of the neck. Nazi propaganda chief Joseph Goebbels was making a rare excursion into truth when he said: 'If the Germans lay down their arms, the whole of eastern and south-eastern Europe, together with the Reich, would come under Russian occupation. Behind an iron screen, mass butcheries of people would begin, and all that would remain would be a crude automaton, a dull fermenting mass of millions of proletarians and despairing slave animals knowing nothing of the outside world.'

Slowly the Red Army pushed back the Germans and began pursuing them beyond Russia's borders. At their Yalta summit, the Allied leaders had agreed how to divide the spoils, once Hitler was forced into unconditional surrender. American forces held back to allow Stalin's troops to take Prague. In Poland, the Russians roused the Warsaw resistance via radio to attack their German oppressors and help the liberating army. Then the advance was halted for several days, giving Nazis time to kill as many Poles as possible.

By the end of the war, Stalin had added parts of Finland, Romania and Czechoslovakia, half of Poland and East Prussia, and most of the Baltic States to the Soviet Union. He had also established sympathetic buffer states in the rest of Czechoslovakia, Hungary, Bulgaria and Romania. And by entering the fighting against Japan after America dropped its A-bombs, he legitimized his annexation of the Kurile Islands, Sakhalin Island and parts of Mongolia. His sinister rule now stretched from the South China Sea to the River Elbe in Germany. And, just as Goebbels predicted, mass butchery began behind heavily policed borders.

Stalin in 1949

Beria's NKVD took savage revenge on anyone suspected of collaborating with the Nazis. Whole peoples from outlying areas – the Crimean Tatars, Kalmyks, Karachi-Balkars, Chechens – were transported to starvation in Siberia and Central Asia. Russian soldiers, returning either from captivity or victorious invasion, were thoroughly vetted. Those impressed by what they had seen in the West were shot or incarcerated. Stalin could not allow anyone to spread the word that the capitalist masses actually enjoyed a better standard of living than his Soviet proletariat. Even heroes suffered. Author Alexander Solzhenitsyn, twice decorated for bravery as an artillery officer, vanished into a Gulag for 8 years for 'insulting Stalin.' In the new satellite countries, loyal

Marxist-Leninists were executed or jailed after show trials and the communist parties purged of anyone not proved to be a committed Stalinist.

But the most terrible retribution leaked out only years later. At Yalta, Western leaders agreed to return to Stalin not just prisoners of war, but all refugees from his iron rule. The list ranged from Soviet citizens and soldiers who had tried to fight for Hitler to White Russians who had fled after the civil war ended in 1921. More than three million desperate escapees were in Western hands in 1945. By 1948 almost all had been forcibly repatriated. Britain alone sent 30,000. At Scarisbrook camp on Merseyside, one man hanged himself rather than fall into Stalin's clutches. Another cut his throat as he was led towards a ship on Liverpool dockside. In Rimini, Italy, British soldiers forced reluctant returnees to board trains at gunpoint. One man beat his brains out with a stone. Another was shot by troops as he tried to break free.

Back in the USSR, thousands of the helpless hostages were marched straight off boats and trains into makeshift execution yards. At ports on the north coast and in the Crimea, Soviet air force planes flew low to try to drown the sound of shooting. Those who escaped the quayside massacres were bundled into closed trains for a lingering death in the Gulags.

If Western governments hoped such sacrifices would satisfy Stalin, they were in for a shock. Instead of planning for peace, he ordered exhausted Russia into massive rearmament. Iron and steel production was trebled. Coal and oil targets were doubled. Hundreds of captured German scientists and technicians were forced to try to bridge the technology gap between the USSR and the West. The growing army of Moscow moles abroad was ordered to steal the secrets of the A-bomb. And the Soviet communist party was purged of anyone who refused to toe the hard-line Stalinist policy of cold war.

But the man hell-bent on imposing his brand of Soviet slavery on free nations was now a prisoner of his own terror. Otto Kuusinen, a Finn who knew Stalin better than most, said: 'The more ruthless and cold-blooded he became, the more he lived in an almost insane fear of his life.' Stalin's daughter Svetlana described her father as being 'as bitter as he could be against the whole world. He saw enemies everywhere. It had reached the point of being pathological, of persecution mania.'

Even in the Kremlin, Stalin wore a special bullet-proof vest. Tunnels were dug to link his office with other government buildings. Moscow's underground railway was secretly extended to his villa at Kuntsevo. When forced to appear above ground, Stalin used only an armour-plated car with bullet-proof windows 3 inches thick. NKVD squads checked out every route, and lined the roads when their leader drove past. All Stalin's food came from farms run by the NKVD. It was analyzed by a special team of doctors, served by bodyguards posing as waiters, and always tested for poison by companions before Stalin took a mouthful. His tea had to come from specially sealed packs which were used just once, the rest being thrown away. When the woman who always prepared his tea was spotted taking leaves from a pack with a broken seal, she was thrown into Lubianka prison.

But even a man as powerful as Stalin could not cheat death for ever. On 5 March, 1953, he collapsed with a cerebral haemorrhage, aged 73, apparently in a fury because some of the Politburo opposed his plans to transport thousands of Soviet Jews to wasteland near the Chinese border. According to Czech defector Karel Kaplan, he had even more sinister plans in mind. Kaplan, who fled to the West in 1976, reported that in 1951 Stalin told leaders of the East European satellite states to prepare for all-out war to occupy Western Europe 'in three or four years at the most.'

Stalin had taken Russia from the wooden plough to the nuclear age in 30 years. He had caught up with the advanced countries who had spent centuries making the transition. But in the process, the lives of more than 20 million Soviet citizens had been sacrificed. Another 14 million were still in Gulag camps when he died. Count Nikolai Tolstoy wrote that, in a nation of 200 million people, 'scarcely a family had been untouched by tragedy.' It was too much even for the stomachs of those who succeeded Stalin as Soviet leaders.

The NKVD apparatus of fear, which had mushroomed to $1\frac{1}{2}$ million men and women, was slimmed down and renamed the KGB. Beria and other powerful aides were shot within months of their patron's death. In 1956 Nikita Khruschev accused the man for whom he had once worked of unjustified harshness against 'punished peoples' and Russians captured by the Nazis. He also attacked Stalin for killing 'many thousands of honest and innocent communists.' And he added: 'Arbitrary behaviour by one person encouraged and permitted arbitrariness in others. Mass arrests and deportations of many thousands of people, execution without trial and without normal investigation created conditions of insecurity, fear and even desperation.'

Slowly Stalin slipped from public adulation in Russia as revelations about the means he used overshadowed the ends he achieved. In 1961 his remains were removed from the Red Square mausoleum and buried outside the Kremlin walls. His entry in Soviet encyclopaedias shrank. In 1977 his name vanished from the national anthem, though Lenin's stayed. But the most telling blow was a name change which symbolized the passing of two of the world's most repressive regimes. The Volga town of Tsaritsyn was retitled Stalingrad in honour of Stalin's gallant defence of it during the Russian civil war. Within a few years of his death, it became known as Volgograd.

Chapter Two

MERCILESS DESPOTS

The scourge of the sword . . . throughout history it
has been the violent recourse of rulers who
tortured and ravaged in their greed for conquest
and power.

'Power takes as ingratitude the writings of its
victims.'

Rabindranath Tagore (1916)

Attila the Hun

Mass slaughter, rape and pillage were an integral part of life for most of northern Europe for centuries. Though the Greeks and Romans established the Mediterranean as the cradle of civilization, it was constantly rocked by murderous incursions from barbarian hordes to the north. Greek historian Herodotus, born in 484 BC, described savage Scythians north of the Black Sea who skinned opponents to make coats, sawed off the top of their skulls to make drinking cups and drank the blood of their victims. Wild Goths swept south from Sweden, and in AD 410 sacked Rome in a six-day orgy of rape and killing. Vicious Vandals reached the city less than 50 years later after storming through Germany, Gaul, Spain and North Africa, leaving death and destruction in their wake. Saxons, Franks and Vikings were other warlike and unmerciful raiders. But of all the brutal barbarians who terrorized Europe, none struck greater fear in men's hearts than a tribe whose roots were in the harsh steppes of Mongolia.

The Huns were wild horsemen driven out of their homeland by the Chinese in the second century AD. They rode west, conquering and cold-bloodedly massacring any tribe that stood in their way. Eventually they settled north of the river Danube, between the Volga and the Don, and established uneasy detente with neighbouring Romans, even helping the legions subdue troublesome tribes. Rome paid the Huns' King Ruas an annual tribute of 350 pounds of gold, but in return took hostages as a guarantee of good behaviour. The king's nephew, Attila, born in AD 406, spent part of his youth as a hostage in Italy. It was invaluable experience for a leader whose bloodthirsty campaigns were to earn him the title 'Scourge Of God'. Attila the Hun was 27 when King Ruas died. At first he ruled jointly with his brother Bleda, strengthening the kingdom by defeating Teutonic tribes like the Ostrogoths and Gepidae. By AD 444 he had complete control of the territory known today as Hungary and Romania. And he was absolute ruler after having his brother murdered. Now his ruthless ambition was ready to take on the Romans. The plaintive plea of a damsel in distress gave him the pretext for war.

Honoria, sister of Roman emperor Valentinian III, caused a scandal by having an affair with a court chamberlain and getting pregnant. Valentinian had her sent off to Constantinople, where she lived with religious relatives virtually a prisoner. Frustrated and bored, she smuggled her ring together with a message for help to Attila at his camp near Budapest, offering herself as his

Attila, King of the Huns

bride if he rescued her. The Hun chieftain already had as many wives as he needed, but he made the most of the request. He asked Valentinian for Honoria's hand – and half the Roman Empire as dowry. Rejected, he unleashed a furious onslaught.

His hordes swept south, through Macedonia – now mostly part of Greece – to the gates of Constantinople in AD 447. The Romans bought him off, increasing their yearly tribute to 2,100 pounds of gold, and paying a heavy indemnity for withdrawal. Attila went home with his booty, but four years later he led a vast army of Huns, Franks and Vandals across the Rhine into Gaul.

Town after town was ravaged and razed, but as the unscrupulous barbarians were about to storm the city of Orléans, the city was saved by the arrival of Roman legions allied to an army of Visigoths. Attila withdrew to the plains near Châlons-sur-Marne and prepared for battle. It lasted all day, with appalling carnage on both sides. One eye-witness later described the hand-to-hand fighting as 'ruthless, immense, obstinate.' The Visigoth king was just one of the thousands slaughtered. But Attila was forced to retreat back beyond the Rhine. Historians describe the battle as one of the most crucial ever. Had the Romans not won, they say, Europeans might today have slant-eyed, Mongol-like features.

Attila was bloodied but unbowed. A year later his men again swarmed south into Italy. Aquileia, the major city in the province of Venetia, was completely destroyed after appalling atrocities against its inhabitants. The Hun hordes swept on to the Adriatic sea, slaughtering the civilians of Concordia, Altinum and Padua before burning their properties. Frightened refugees fled to the islands and lagoons where horsemen could not follow. There they established the city we know as Venice.

The power-crazed heathen turned his army towards the Lombardy plain and Milan, plundering and pillaging until northern Italy was devastated. As Rome itself was threatened, Pope Leo I courageously left the Vatican for a personal interview with the irresistible invader. Attila, his fury subdued by such a bold move, agreed to lead his men home, though he talked menacingly of returning if Honoria's wrongs were not righted.

But there were to be no more atrocities from the most ruthless despot the world had then known. On 15 March, AD 453, he hosted a gigantic banquet to celebrate the taking of yet another wife, the beautiful virgin Ildico. That night, as he tried to consummate the marriage, an artery burst, and bloodthirsty Attila bled to death.

History has hailed Peter the Great as the Tsar who civilized Russia by introducing European customs and by fostering trade. In fact, he could be just as barbarous as Ivan the Terrible. When troops mutinied in Moscow in 1698, Peter personally supervised bloody reprisals which left 1,200 of them dead. For two months, men were flogged, broken on the rack or roasted slowly over flames. Peter was seen wielding an executioner's axe with relish. And he insisted that mutilated bodies be left on display for months as a warning to others.

Genghis Khan

Nearly 800 years after Attila's demise, Europe was reeling from the onslaught of another Mongol conqueror whose callous cunning and cruelty have never been matched. He was born in 1162 and named Temuchin after a tribal chief his father Yesukai had just defeated. At the age of 13 Yesukai's death in an ambush plunged the boy into the terror and treachery of tribal infighting. But he proved equal to every challenge. He cold-bloodedly killed one of his brothers in a dispute over a fish. He slaughtered every man, woman and child in a tribe of nomads who dared to kidnap his wife. And though rivals battled bitterly – one boiled 70 of his followers alive in cooking pots – by the spring of 1206 Temuchin was powerful enough to impose his power on all the Mongol tribes. He summoned leaders of dozens of warring factions to a conference on the banks of the river Onon and proclaimed himself their chief. He also took a new name – Genghis Khan, which meant perfect warrior.

China was first to feel his wrath. The Kin Tartars ruled the northern half of the country, and had been glad to accept when Genghis offered them some of his troops to suppress troublemakers. In 1211 that move rebounded on them. The troops had gained a comprehensive knowledge of the land inside the Great Wall, and even subverted sentries at some of the gates. The Mongol armies poured south, besieging and sacking cities, trampling and burning crops. By 1214 Genghis Khan controlled almost all the country north of the Yellow River. He offered the Kin emperor peace, adding: 'It will be necessary that you distribute largess to my officers and men to appease their fierce hostility.' Two royal princesses, 500 young men and girls, 3,000 horses and a herd of rare white camels were among the prizes the Mongol armies carried home. But within a year they were back, ruthlessly besieging the few cities that had survived the previous invasion.

Genghis Khan's empire was soon secure, ruled by a regime of fear which meant instant death to any rebel. The savage warlord now looked to the west and his neighbours the Khwarizms. Their vast territories stretched from the Ganges to the Tigris, and included present-day Turkistan, Iran and northern India. Genghis sent envoys to Shah Mohammed, promising peace and proposing trade. The reply seemed favourable. But when the first caravan of 100 Mongol traders arrived in the border town of Otrar, governor Inaljuk had them all massacred as spies. Furious Genghis sent more envoys, demanding the governor's extradition. Mohammed beheaded their leader and sent the rest home minus their beards. The insult was to cost the Shah his kingdom – and bring unprecedented horror to Europe's door.

More than 400,000 Khwarizm troops were strung along the Syr Daria river to repel the invasion, but they were like lambs to the slaughter when the Mongol armies struck in a three-pronged attack. One army attacked in the south, threatening the strategic cities of Bukhara and Samarkand. Two others crossed the mountains to the north and besieged Otrar. A bitter battle ended with the errant governor being executed as painfully as possible – molten metal was poured into his eyes and ears. Then, while one army turned south to link with the first near Bukhara, 40,000 men led by Genghis Khan vanished into the vast Kizylkum desert. They re-emerged behind Bukhara and behind the enemies' lines. The Shah fled as the city suffered the Mongol victory rites. Its mercenary defenders were slaughtered, and the civilians ordered outside what was left of the walls to allow uninterrupted looting. Then the women were raped in front of their families, craftsmen were taken as slaves and the remaining residents put to the sword.

The terror-struck Khwarizms had no answer to the Mongols' devastating military efficiency. Their infantry was helpless against hordes of horsemen who unleashed waves of arrows which decimated defenders, then moved in to finish them off ruthlessly with their curved sabres and lances. If a city or a pass seemed too secure, the Mongols would appear to retreat, then turn and scatter their pursuers with savage ferocity. As they moved further into Khwarizm territory, they herded crowds of captives in front of them as a human shield. Giant catapults, manned by up to 100 Mongol warriors, hurled rocks at city walls. Other defences were breached by means of a weapon unknown to the West, gunpowder.

Towns which opened their gates to the invaders were spared. Those that fought, like Samarkand, were not. The Mongols arrived in May 1220 to find a garrison of 50,000 men well dug in. When the attackers pretended to flee, the defenders poured after them and were cut to ribbons. When half the mercenaries deserted to Genghis Khan, the civilians surrendered, leaving soldiers besieged in the citadel. They were starved out and killed – then the turncoat mercenaries were massacred for treachery. Nearly 30,000 civilians were herded away to form a living shield at the next siege.

At Urgenj, the Mongols slaughtered every man and took the women and children as slaves before breaching dykes to flood the burning ruins. In Termez every body was cut open after Genghis discovered that one old woman had swallowed some pearls. At Nisa, Genghis's son Tulé had all the inhabitants' hands tied behind their backs, then watched them die in a hail of arrows. At Merv the poor were beheaded while the rich were savagely tortured to reveal the whereabouts of their treasures. When Nishapur surrendered, the severed heads of the residents were arranged in three gruesome pyramids of men, women and children.

Shah Mohammed had been broken by the speed and savagery with which his empire had been destroyed. He fled to a village on the Caspian Sea, and died of pleurisy. Genghis pursued his son and successor, Jelaleddin, south through Afghanistan, slaughtering hundreds of thousands of innocent civilians as he went. When his quarry took refuge with the Sultan of Delhi, the Mongols ravaged Lahore, Peshawar and Melikpur before turning north west again. News had reached Genghis that the people of Herat, spared after surrendering without a fight, had deposed the governor he installed. A six-month siege by 80,000 men ended the rebellion. Then a week of unbridled murder meted out the punishment. Thousands of corpses lay in the rubble of the city when Genghis at last headed for home. He had unfinished business with the Tangut tribe, who had declined to send troops to aid his Khwarizm campaign. He vowed to exterminate them all.

But age and weakness following a hunting accident were finally to achieve what no foe could manage. Genghis Khan was besieging the Tangut capital of Ninghsia in August 1227, when he fell ill and died, aged 65. His will named his son Ogotai as successor, but the warlord's aides decided that the death must remain secret until Ogotai was safely in command. The final victims of the man described by one historian as the 'mightiest and most bloodthirsty conqueror of all time' were the innocent souls who accidentally spotted the funeral procession as it headed for the burial ground in the valley of Kilien. Without exception, they were put to the sword.

Genghis Khan left an empire stretching from the China Sea to the Persian Gulf. But trembling neighbours who hoped his death would spare them further conquest were sadly mistaken. For the mighty Mongol had fathered a dynasty of ruthless rulers almost as callous and cruel. And they had their own territorial ambitions to extend their legacy.

Genghis's successor, Ogotai, spent his first years in power consolidating his grip on China and extending his empire in Korea. Then his avaricious eyes strayed westward again. The Mongol warriors surged through central Asia, laying waste to the cities of Tiflis and Ryazan, in Georgia, and massacring the

---

Not all deaths ordered by Genghis Khan were gory. Once he defeated another tribe led by a childhood friend. He offered to spare his life, but the rival insisted on execution. So Genghis decided to kill him without spilling blood. He was wrapped in a carpet and kicked to death.

inhabitants. Moscow, then an insignificant wooden township, was quickly taken. At Koselsk, revenge for an earlier reversal resulted in such a carnival of death that the laughing invaders renamed the town Mobalig, 'city of woe'. Finally Kiev, known as 'the mother of cities', was battered into submission. The residents were slaughtered and the buildings razed.

Now the Mongol army split. One of Genghis Khan's old lieutenants, Subatai, led a three-pronged assault on Hungary, aiming to rendezvous with the rest of the army at the Danube. But first the armies of Poland, Germany and Bohemia had to be prevented from coming to the aid of Hungary's fearsome Magyars. The rest of the invasion force swarmed into Poland, moving at a pace which staggered generals accustomed to slow-moving traditional battle strategy. The Poles were routed at Szydlow and the Germans at Liegnitz. The Bohemians beat a hasty retreat. In less than a month the Mongols had covered 400 miles, won two decisive battles, captured four major cities and cleared the way to the main objective – Hungary.

Hungarian King Bela IV had massed his men to meet Subatai at the Danube. But the Mongol commander declined to fight on ground which did not suit his horsemen. He began a calculated retreat to the Sajo river, and for six days the Hungarians followed, being lured further from their stronghold and reinforcements. Then Subatai turned for a savage dawn attack. Most of Bela's army was still asleep. By mid-day, more than 70,000 Magyars had been massacred. 'They fell to the left and right like leaves in winter,' wrote one chronicler. 'The roads for two days' journey from the field of battle were strewn with corpses as the rest tried to flee.'

Subatai stormed Budapest while part of his force chased King Bela to the Adriatic coast, burning and destroying everything in their path. On Christmas Day 1241 he led his forces across the iced-up Danube and took the city of Esztergom. But as Europe waited in trepidation for the next move, the Mongols again turned back. News had reached them that Ogotai was dead, and a bitter battle for succession was likely. No one wanted to miss it.

It was ten years before Genghis Khan's grandson Mangu, son of the tyrant Tulé, emerged as undisputed Mongol leader. Unrest in Persia, fostered by the Ismailites, prompted him to send his brother Halagu to the Middle East to storm the strongholds of a sinister sect known as the Assassins. Halagu rode on to Baghdad, then the major city in the region. After resisting for a month, the city

---

Genghis Khan gave the Mongols their first written laws, the Great Jasagh. Refusing to work, urinating in running water and gluttony all received the same sentence – death.

surrendered in February 1258. Halagu's marauders massacred everybody inside, trampling the sultan to death under horses. They set fire to the city, then turned towards Syria. Aleppo was sacked, Damascus surrendered, and Halagu was about to attack Jerusalem when, once again, a single death prevented thousands. The news was received that Mangu had died, and the hordes rode home.

Mangu's brother was Kubla Khan, celebrated in Coleridge's verse. Alone amongst the family, he treated captives humanely and banned indiscriminate massacres. For 34 years he concentrated on conquests in the East, in southern China, Tibet and Vietnam. He even tried to invade Japan without success. And after his death, the empire fell apart as his heirs squabbled. Even the Chinese cast off the Mongol yoke as the Ming Dynasty forced the wild warriors back to their Mongolian homeland.

Tamerlane the Great

The world had not heard the last of the merciless Mongols. In 1336 a boy called Timur was born at Kesh, near Samarkand. He was the great-great-grandson of Genghis Khan and conceived the desperate dream of rebuilding his forefather's empire, by then divided into a multitude of smaller principalities. Locals nicknamed him Timur i Leng, or Timur the Lame, because of a disability which made him limp. But the world remembers him as Tamerlane the Great, a wicked warmonger with a savage sadistic streak.

At 33 he usurped the Transoxian throne at Samarkand and gained the power base he needed for his conquests. Superb military management earned him mastery of Persia, Turkistan, the Ukraine, the Crimea, Georgia, Mesopotamia and Armenia. Governors who appealed to him for help frequently found themselves betrayed once he had restored their realms. He dethroned a rival khan to occupy Russia, then over-ran India, leaving a trail of carnage all the way to Delhi, where he reduced the city to rubble and massacred 100,000 inhabitants.

Like his ancestors, Tamerlane, tall with a huge head and white-haired from childhood, found that fear was no way to establish allegiance among the peoples he conquered. Revolts in the growing empire were frequent, but repressed ruthlessly. Whole cities were destroyed out of spite and their populations slaughtered. Massive towers or pyramids of skulls were constructed for the emperor's enjoyment. Twice he had thousands of opponents bricked up alive for agonising slow suffocation and starvation. Another time he hurled all his prisoners to their deaths over a cliff.

After his Indian campaign, Tamerlane stormed into Syria to settle old scores with leaders who refused to help in his earlier wars. Aleppo was seized and sacked and Damascus occupied in 1400. Baghdad, still smarting from Halagu's atrocities a century earlier, was devastated again by fire, and 20,000 people put to the sword. In 1402 Tamerlane unleashed his wrath on Anatolia – now Turkey – and beheaded 5,000 Ottoman fighters after one siege. Their sultan was killed in captivity in a barbarous iron cage.

The nightmare return to the depravity of an earlier age ended only with Tamerlane's death. His hordes were on their way to attack China when, in January, 1405, he fell ill while camping on the Syr Daria river and died. By a bizarre twist of fate, it happened at Otrar – the town whose governor had unwittingly sparked off the fury of the Mongols under Genghis Khan nearly 200 years earlier when he executed 100 traders. Millions had since paid the Mongols' bloody price for that rash act.

Ivan the Terrible

In July 1662, a mob of 5,000 angry Russians marched to the palace of Tsar Alexis in the suburbs of Moscow. Poor harvests and a long war with Poland had exhausted their patience over harsh taxation, currency devaluation and corrupt officialdom, and they extracted a promise from the Tsar that he would act on their grievances. But his solution to the problems was not what they had in mind. According to historian V.O. Klyuchevsky, 'Tsar Alexis called on the streltsy (musketeers who formed the Tsar's bodyguard) and his courtiers for assistance, and an indiscriminate slaughter ensued, followed by tortures and executions. Hundreds were drowned in the River Moskva and whole families were exiled permanently to Siberia.'

Alexis was pious and artistically-minded. He tried to leave government to ministers. But he had been born into a succession of Tsars who inherited absolute rule from the Mongols – and were equally merciless about maintaining it. Any challenge to their authority was met by torture, exile and execution. The loyalty of a few select aristocrats was bought with land and honours. The peasants – 90 per cent of the population – were shackled in medieval-style serfdom; denied education, the right to change jobs, even the right to choose their own marital partners. And if they grew restless about their lot, soldiers and a secret army of informers soon brought them back into line with bloodshed. For four centuries, the Tsars ruled Russia by fear. And few rulers inspired more fear than Ivan the Terrible.

Ivan, born in August 1530, was an orphan by the age of eight. His father Vasily, Grand Duke of Moscow, died when he was three. Five years later his mother Elena, who acted as Regent, was poisoned. After that, Ivan was to claim that he received 'no human care from any quarter.' Vicious power battles between leading families marked his early years. Ivan was used as a pawn by rival factions wrestling for control, only to lose it, in a succession of bloodbaths. He watched one of his uncles carried off to death by a Moscow mob in one uprising. But he quickly learned how to fight back. He was just 13 when he ordered his first assassination. Then he threw the body of his victim, a troublesome Shuisky prince, to his dogs.

In 1547, Ivan had himself crowned Tsar and, at a parade of the nation's most beautiful and eligible virgins, he selected himself a bride – 15-year-old Anastasia. She produced six children for him, but only two were still alive when she died in 1560. Their deaths, plus the loss of his wife's calming influence and the trauma of his childhood, may all have played a part in the horrors that followed.

First Ivan banished his closest advisers, his personal priest Father Silvestr, and nobleman Alexei Adashev, accusing them of plotting to kill Anastasia. Then he left Moscow for virtual monastic seclusion in the provinces. All sections of the community begged him to return, fearing a power vacuum. Ivan agreed – but only if he was allowed to govern without any interference. When his terms were accepted, he split the nation into two vast sections. In one, he was absolute master. The rest of the country was to be governed for him by bureaucrats.

Now Ivan unleashed unprecedented terror on his people, using the sinister oprichniki. They were black-cloaked riders on black horses, whose saddles carried the symbols of a broom and a dog's head. With unbridled fury, they slaughtered anyone suspected of opposition to Ivan, and settled many of his old scores from the turmoil of his teenage days. More than 4,000 aristocrats were purged. The Staritsky family, relatives of Ivan but potential rivals for power, were wiped out. When Metropolitan Philip, leader of the Orthodox Church in Moscow, condemned the oprichnikis' attacks and refused to bless the Tsar, the ruthless riders tracked him down and savagely executed him.

Ivan himself often took part in their orgies of rape, torture and death. And his rage really ran wild when an informant told him civic leaders of Novgorod, then Russia's second city, were planning rebellion. Without bothering to check the allegation, which was almost certainly untrue, Ivan led his oprichniki north, pillaging and plundering aristocratic homes, monasteries and churches within 50 miles of the city. Having laid waste to the fields that fed Novgorod, he then built a wooden wall around the metropolis to prevent anyone fleeing. And for five weeks, he watched, or took part in, wholesale slaughter.

Husbands and wives were forced to watch as their partners – and sometimes their children – were tortured. Many women were roasted alive on revolving spears. Other killings were treated almost as sport. One German mercenary wrote: 'Mounting a horse and brandishing a spear, he (Ivan) charged in and ran people through while his son watched the entertainment . . .'

Though Soviet scholars have claimed recently that no more than 2,000 people died, Western historians put the total toll in the annihilation of Novgorod at over 60,000. And Ivan's sadistic savagery there, and at Pskov, also suspected of plotting, certainly had an effect on later opponents. When he invaded neighbouring Livonia, one beseiged garrison blew themselves up rather than fall into his cruel clutches.

In 1572 Ivan suddenly disbanded the oprichniki and banned all mention of them. Throughout his life, his sadism alternated with periods of manic religious depression, when he would publicly confess his sins and don sackcloth. So perhaps genuine shame ended the six-year reign of terror. Perhaps an attack on Russia from the south by Turks forced him to call off internal vendettas. Or perhaps his assassins had eliminated almost everyone Ivan wanted out of the way.

Ivan got away with his ruthless rule because he had the support of the Orthodox Church. Western Europe was undergoing the religious crisis of the Reformation, and Orthodox leaders were terrified of free-thinking Protestantism which would weaken their hold on the unthinking masses. In exchange for a hard line on all religious dissent, including burning for 'heresy', the Church backed the Tsar and became an effective propaganda machine on his behalf. When peasant revolts were crushed with total brutality, the causes and the consequences were never attributed to Ivan. They were blamed on the corruption or excessive zeal of those who worked for him.

For a few Russians, Ivan was not so terrible. They were the people granted lands and power in the territories the Tsar added to his empire, north of the Black Sea and in Siberia. But the wars that won them, and campaigns which won nothing, forced an ever-increasing tax burden on Russian landowners and their peasants. And by the end of Ivan's reign, English ambassador Giles Fletcher was reporting to London: 'The desperate state of things at home maketh the people for the most part to wish for some foreign invasion, which they suppose to be the only means to rid them of the heavy yoke of his tyrannous government.'

In fact there was another way – Ivan's death. It came in March 1584, three years after he killed his son and heir Ivan with a spear during a quarrel. A life of licentiousness – six more wives and innumerable mistresses – had left the Tsar riddled with disease. As British trader Sir Jerome Horsey put it: 'The emperor began grievously to swell in his cods, with which he had most horribly offended above 50 years, boasting of a thousand virgins he had deflowered and thousands of children of his begetting destroyed.' Ivan collapsed and died as he prepared to play a game of chess.

Yet even his departure did not spare Russia agony. His heir's death left Ivan's imbecilic son Theodore as successor and he soon proved hopelessly unable to govern. The country was plunged into 30 years of chaos, which included occupation by the armies of both Poland and Sweden, before the Romanovs – relatives of Ivan's wife Anastasia – were able to reimpose the authority of the Tsars.

Historians still dispute whether Tsarist Russia's most bloodthirsty tyrant was consciously bad or completely mad. Some seek excuses in his traumatic childhood. Others blame a painful spinal defect for his excesses. It was nearly 350 years before Ivan the Terrible found sympathetic consideration from someone who believed his oprichniki had played a 'progressive role', someone who claimed his only mistake was not taking his purges further. That sympathiser was Josef Stalin. And as the earlier chapter on Stalin shows, he did not make the same 'mistake'.

The Ottoman Sultans

Turkey was known as the sick man of Europe throughout the 19th Century. Crisis followed crisis – one culminated in the bloody Crimea War – as the continent's super-powers bolstered the weak and crumbling regime of the once-great Ottoman Sultans to prevent rivals like Russia from seizing Constantinople and threatening trade routes. Then the outraged western world learned that Turkey was even sicker than they feared – but in a very different sense.

Like the Mongols before them, early Ottoman armies conquered mercilessly. Massacres of captives were commonplace, an accepted aspect of warfare. And by 1588 – the year Spain's Armada was routed by England – the Sultans ruled an empire which circled most of the Mediterranean. It stretched from the Red

Mahomet III

Sea port of Aden to Budapest and Belgrade, from the Crimea north of the Black Sea to Algeria. Huge chunks of present-day Hungary, Poland and Russia shared the same masters as the people of Greece, Egypt, Tunisia, Libya, Lebanon, Syria, Israel, Yugoslavia, Romania and Bulgaria. Any revolts among the 30 million subjects were ruthlessly suppressed.

But the absolute power of the Sultans not only corrupted them, it blinded them to the changing world outside their realms. In 1876 a rebellion in Bulgaria was repressed with traditional carnage. Ottoman troops ran amok in an orgy of killing, and more than 12,000 men, women and children were slaughtered. But by then the western world had newspapers, and millions were appalled to realise that medieval-style tyranny still went on in the 'modern' age. Historians were to discover that such tyranny had run virtually unchecked for 350 years – and would carry on well into the 20th Century.

The sinister Sultans had more reason than most absolute rulers to be paranoid about plots. A strong tradition of strangulation by deaf mutes, using silk bowstrings, existed inside the walls of their Grand Seraglio palace. Mahomet the Conqueror (1431–81) formulated a law by which his successors as Sultan had 'the right to execute their brothers to ensure the peace of the world.' It was designed to stop disputes over succession. But when Mahomet III took the throne in 1595, his father Murad III's prowess in the harem meant he had to murder 19 brothers, all aged under 11, and throw seven pregnant concubines into the Bosporus tied up in sacks.

Thereafter, close male relatives of the incoming Sultan were locked up in a windowless building within the Grand Seraglio complex until the Sultan's death called them to the throne. Cut off from the outside world, with only deaf mutes and sterilized concubines for company, many were completely deranged when they came to power, sometimes after more than 30 years incarceration. It was 1789 before the practice was abolished - and by then, madness was in the blood of the Ottoman dictators.

Suleiman the Magnificent, who ruled from 1520 to 1566, is regarded by most historians as the last great Sultan. In 1526 he seized more of Hungary, massacring 200,000 -- 2,000 were killed for his enjoyment as he watched from a throne – and taking 100,000 slaves back to Constantinople. Three years later, when Vienna stubbornly refused to surrender, he scoured the surrounding countryside and selected the most nubile girls for Turkey's harems. Then he threw hundreds of unwanted peasants on a gigantic fire in view of the city walls. Such 'sanity' in the name of military strength was succeeded by a dynasty of Sultans who were weak, debauched, indecisive or insane – or sometimes all four.

Suleiman's son Selim II was a drunkard, despite the proscription of alcohol by the Koran, and decided to wrest Cyprus, source of his favourite wine, from its Venetian rulers. His soldiers sacked Nicosia, slaughtering 30,000. When the key fortress of Famagusta fell after a two-year siege, the Turks promised to spare the heroic garrison – then killed them all. Their commander was flayed alive, then paraded in front of the Turkish troops, his body stuffed with straw. Venice, Spain and Austria retaliated with the humiliating naval triumph of Lepanto, at which 50,000 Turks died. But the Ottomans still held Cyprus when, in 1574, Selim lost his footing climbing into his bath after a drinking session, and died from a fractured skull.

His son, Mahomet III, the man who killed his 19 young brothers, was a man with a fiery temper who enjoyed the sight of women's breasts being scorched off with hot irons. Osman II, who ruled for less than a year before his 1618 murder, enjoyed archery – but only if his targets were live prisoners-of-war or page boys. And while these two, and a string of insignificant Sultans, indulged themselves, the empire began to fall to pieces. Neglect and oppression ravaged the countryside, with tax income tumbling as famine laid waste to whole areas. The rigid disciplines which had made the Ottoman empire strong were also disintegrating.

Murad IV, a savage, dark-eyed giant, tried to reimpose them when he took over in 1623. After the Janissaries, the Sultan's special army, forced him to sack the chief minister and 16 other officials, he later revenged himself for their impudence by having more than 500 of their leaders strangled in their barracks. Then he set about the rest of the nation, as author Noel Barber records in his excellent book, *Lords Of The Golden Horn.*

'Murad quickly found a simple panacea for the ills of the country,' writes Barber. 'He cut off the head of any man who came under the slightest suspicion. In 1637 he executed 25,000 subjects in the name of justice, many by his own hand. He executed the Grand Mufti because he was dissatisfied with the state of the roads. He beheaded his chief musician for playing a Persian air. He liked to patrol the taverns at night and if he caught anyone smoking he declared himself and executed the offender on the spot. When he caught one of his gardeners and his wife smoking, he had their legs amputated and exhibited them in public while they bled to death.'

A Venetian who added a room to the top of his house was hanged because Murad thought he had done it to spy on the Sultan's harem. A Frenchman who arranged a date with a Turkish girl was impaled. And, according to Barber, Murad 'spent hours . . . exercising the royal prerogative of taking ten innocent lives a day as he practised his powers with the arquebus on passers-by who were too near the palace walls. On one occasion he drowned a party of women when he chanced to come across them in a meadow and took exception to the noise they were making. He ordered the batteries to open fire and sink a boatload of women on the Bosporous when their craft came too near the Seraglio walls . . .'

Murad's atrocities were not confined to home. In 1638 he led his troops to the Persian capital, Baghdad. After a six-week siege, during which he sliced in half the head of a Persian champion in single-handed combat, he ordered the massacre of the defending garrison of 30,000. When an accidental ammunition explosion killed some Turkish troops, Murad slaughtered 30,000 men, women and children.

But Murad was the last of the all-conquering Ottoman despots. His son Ibrahim's most notable conquest was deflowering the virgin daughter of the Grand Mufti, Turkey's highest religious leader. Then, when one concubine from his harem was seduced by an outsider, he had all 280 girls tied in weighted sacks and thrown into the Bosporus. Even Constantinople, which could forgive its Sultans almost anything, could not condone that. The Grand Mufti took revenge by organising a coup which toppled Ibrahim, then had him, his mother and his favourite lover strangled.

The Ottoman armies had long lost their invincible reputation. In 1683 an alliance of European forces crushed another attempt to take Vienna. In 1790 the Russian forces of Catherine the Great took Ismail, 40 miles north of the Black Sea, and dropped the corpses of 34,000 fallen Turks into the Danube through holes in the ice. In 1827, a six-year war, with massacres on both sides, ended with the Greeks winning independence. Egypt achieved a large measure of self-government.

The Ottoman empire was in steady decline. Elsewhere in the world, such events as the French Revolution, the American Constitution, with its declaration of rights, the Industrial Revolution, a more general right to vote and the introduction of newspapers had all helped foster an awareness of human rights which forced governments to act more humanely. But in 1876, the Ottoman Sultan showed just how far behind the tide of civilization his country had fallen.

In that year, the Bulgarians, who had been part of the Ottoman empire for nearly 500 years, revolted – and Sultan Abdul Aziz unleashed the bloodlust of unpaid troops who were rewarded only by what they could loot. Within days 12,000 men, women and children were dead and 60 villages burned to the ground. The Sultan gave the commander of the troops a medal.

The carnage in the town of Batak was witnessed by American journalist J. A. MacGahan and, when his report appeared in the *Daily News*, the stunned world had its first eye-witness account of an Ottoman atrocity. 'On every side as we entered the town were the skulls and skeletons of women and children,' he wrote. 'We entered the churchyard. The sight was more dreadful. The whole churchyard for three feet deep was festering with dead bodies partly covered. Hands, legs, arms and heads projected in ghastly confusion . . . I never imagined anything so fearful. There were three thousand bodies in the churchyard and the church. In the school 200 women and children had been burnt alive . . . no crime invented by Turkish ferocity was left uncommitted.'

Western governments at first refused to accept the reports, labelling them 'picturesque journalism.' But when Britain sent an investigator from the Constantinople embassy, he told Whitehall the troops had perpetrated 'perhaps the most heinous crime that has stained the history of the present century.' Ex-Prime Minister William Gladstone issued a pamphlet describing the Turks as 'the great anti-human specimen of humanity.' The storm of worldwide protest caused a coup which installed Abdul Aziz's drunken nephew Murad as Sultan. His reign lasted three months, until he was declared insane, and his brother Abdul Hamid II took over.

Abdul was so paranoid about possible plots that he built an entire village, designed only for his safety. Behind the barricades he kept loaded pistols in every room – two hung beside his bath – and constructed glass cupboards which, when opened, blasted the room with bullets from remote-controlled guns. He personally shot dead a gardener and a slave girl whose sudden movements alarmed him. He countered the growing revolt of the Young Turks with a network of spies and a torture chamber under a cruel executioner who delighted in slowly drowning broken men.

But his most astonishing act was to order the monstrous slaughter of the Armenians, a minority race whose homeland was in the north-east of the dwindling empire, close to the Russian border. He regarded the business-minded Armenians much as Hitler later regarded the Jews. First he banned the word 'Armenian' from newspapers and school books. Then he told Moslems they could seize Armenian goods – and kill the owners if they resisted.

Clearly, Abdul had learned nothing from the 1876 atrocities. And his massacres were far worse. It was cold-blooded, premeditated genocide. For days a bugle at dawn and dusk called the faithful to murder. Nearly 100,000 Armenians were killed. And Westerners witnessed the terror in Trebizond, where every Christian house was plundered before the owners were ritually slaughtered, their throats cut as if they were sheep. Those who jumped into the river to flee were caught and drowned by Moslem boatmen. At Urfa 3,000 men, women and children were roasted alive in the cathedral after seeking sanctuary. Sultan Abdul noted every detail as his spies sent detailed reports.

If the Sultan hoped to curry favour with his people, using racial prejudice to blind them to the economic ruin of his empire, he was sadly mistaken. Many Moslems felt only shame, labelling him Abdul the Damned. And this time, it was not only Europe that was outraged. Two Armenian professors at an American missionary school were arrested, taken in chains for trial for printing seditious leaflets, and sentenced to die. America was scandalized. Finally, when 7,000 Armenians were slaughtered in Constantinople in reprisal for a band raid carried out by 20, every European power signed an open telegram to the Sultan. If the massacres did not end at once, it read, the Sultan's throne and his dynasty would be imperilled.

Sultan Abdul Hamid survived to celebrate his Silver Jubilee as the new century dawned. But he was now an obsolete leftover from another age. And in 1908, the Young Turks – whose numbers and influence had been growing, first in exile, then in Turkey – seized power. The Sultan was exiled to Salonika and his brother, a stooge figurehead, installed as constitutional monarch. Sacks of gold and precious gems, a fortune in foreign bank accounts and shares in international companies were discovered at Abdul's palace, all obtained with money milked from the Turkish treasury.

The repressive rule of the Ottomans had finally ended. But if Turks and the West thought they had seen the end of evil and tyranny, they were in for a shock. For in 1915, Enver Bey, one of the three Young Turk leaders, ordered a new massacre of Armenians, even more ruthless than that of the Sultan. Using the

Abdul Hamid II, overthrown by the Young Turks in 1908

excuse that some Armenians had collaborated with the Russians during World War I battles – Turkey fought on the Kaiser's side – he made his brother-in-law Djevet Bey governor of the region, with orders to exterminate the Christians.

The inhabitants of more than 80 villages were rounded up and shot. Thousands of women were raped. Men were tortured, often by having horseshoes nailed to their feet. One official admitted he 'delved into the records of the Spanish Inquisition and adopted all the suggestions found there.' More than 18,000 Armenians were sent on a forced march of exile across the Syrian desert to Aleppo. Then Kurdish rebels were encouraged to attack them. Only 150 women and children reached Aleppo, 70 days after setting out.

The official British report on the atrocities, presented to Parliament, estimated that, of two million Armenians in Turkey in 1915, a third died and another third fled to Russia. The American Ambassador in Constantinople asked Enver Bey to condemn his underlings for the outrages. To his astonishment, the callous leader accepted responsibility for everything that had taken place. His co-leader, Talaat Bey, said it was unwise to punish only those Armenians who had actually helped the Russians 'since those who are innocent today might be guilty tomorrow.' And he had the audacity to ask the American Ambassador for a full list of Armenians covered by U.S. insurance companies. As their relatives were probably dead, he said, life assurance payments should go to the government.

Enver, Talaat and Djevet fled in November 1918, denounced for choosing the wrong side in a war which cost Turkey half a million battle casualties and for profiteering in food at a time of famine. The victorious allies took control in Constantinople. The empire was now smashed, and Turkey pushed back almost to its present borders. But to head off feared Italian territorial ambitions, the allies allowed the Greeks to occupy the port of Smyrna. Revenge for centuries of repression resulted in massacres of Turks – and fuelled the fury that, in atoning for wrongdoing, would make Turkey once again an international outcast.

Patriot Mustafa Kemal was the focus for Turkish anger at the allied occupation, and the loss of Smyrna. Though he was courtmartialled and sentenced to death in his absence, his support grew, and the allies were unable to control his rebel forces. Finally the Greeks offered their army to restore order. In 1920 their campaign pressed the Turks back. But in August 1921, Mustafa's men won a three-week battle along a 60-mile front at Sakkaria river. The Greeks fled towards the coast. The following year, reinforced by arms from France, Italy and Russia, the Turks again routed their most bitter foes, forcing them back to Smyrna. In September, Mustafa arrived in triumph at the port, and decreed that any Turkish soldier who molested civilians would be killed.

Peter the Great set up the first efficient secret police force in Russia and ruled by fear through a network of spies. He financed his almost constant wars by seizing Church assets and introducing bizarre taxes on beards, bee-keeping, coffins, clothes and foodstuffs. By the end of his reign, the peasants who made up 90 per cent of Russia's population were far worse off than when he came to power.

But within hours, the Greek Patriarch had been torn to pieces by a Turkish mob, under the eyes of the town's new commander. Mass looting, raping and killing began, Turkish troops methodically moving from house to house in the Greek and Armenian areas in the north of the town. 'By evening dead bodies were lying all over the streets,' said one American witness. Worse was to come. On Wednesday 13 September, Westerners saw squads of Turkish soldiers setting fire to houses in the Armenian quarter using petroleum. The wind spread the flames northwards, and thousands of flimsy homes were engulfed. Five hundred people perished in a church set ablaze deliberately. The reek of burning flesh filled the air. Tens of thousands fled to the waterfront, pursued by a rapidly growing wall of fire. In the bay lay warships from Britain, America, Italy and France. They were there to protect their nationals – but they had strict orders to maintain neutrality in the war between Greek and Turk. The sailors watched in horror as the inferno changed the colour of the sea and silhouetted the throng of helpless refugees on the wharfs. Then, at midnight, they heard what one described as 'the most awful scream one could ever imagine.'

Humanity over-rode orders next morning, when a massive rescue attempt began. Mustafa Kemal had said as he watched the fire: 'It is a sign that Turkey is purged of the traitors, the Christians, and of the foreigners, and that Turkey is for the Turks.' Three days after the blaze began, he announced that all Greek and Armenian men aged between 15 and 50 were to be deported inland in labour gangs. Women and children had to be out of Smyrna by 30 September or they too would be rounded up. He was later persuaded to extend the deadline by six days. Military and merchant ships performed a miracle, ferrying nearly 250,000 people to safety. No-one has ever been able to say how many corpses were left behind, though most estimates start at 100,000.

Mustafa Kemal always maintained that the Greeks and Armenians started the great fire of Smyrna. But a report for the American State Department said all the evidence pointed to an attempt by the Turks to hide evidence of 'sack, massacre and raping that had been going on for four days.'

Mustafa, oddly, later changed his name to Kamal Atatürk and instigated massive reforms throughout the government and society which finally dragged Turkey into the 20th Century. The last vestiges of the scourge of the Ottomans were buried forever.

Chapter
Three

FOR GOD, KING AND COUNTRY

Twisted minds . . . of evil men who used the mask of religion or patriotism as an excuse for some of the most horrifying crimes in history.

'The belief in a supernatural source of evil is not necessary. Men alone are capable of every wickedness.'

Joseph Conrad (1911)

The Borgias

It was a city where the brazenly licentious indulged in perverse orgies and incestuous relationships. Where ambitious and greedy men grabbed power and personal fortune by bribery and extortion. And where anyone who stood in their way was ruthlessly eliminated. Yet the city where all this happened was not the hub of a barbarian empire. This citadel of sin was the Vatican City in Rome. And the evil masterminds putting vice before virtue, riches before religion and power before piety were the Pope, Alexander VI, alias Rodrigo Borgia, and his illegitimate son Cesare.

For centuries, the Catholic Church was the only Christian faith in Europe. But its monopoly on salvation brought corruption. It sanctioned merciless killing in crusades against so-called heathen-races who worshipped other gods. It exterminated as heretics all who dared question its edicts about the world and life. And it amassed immense wealth by charging a high price for forgiveness of sins. By the 15th Century, the Pope was not only a religious leader, but a powerful political force. Secular rulers in the confusing cluster of small states that made up the Italian peninsula competed for his favours and support – and his requests, backed by the threat of excommunication if they were refused, were compelling even for the strongest kings and princes.

Rodrigo Borgia was well grounded in the intrigues and intricacies of the Holy See long before he assumed its highest office. In April 1455, his mother's brother became Pope Calixtus III. Rodrigo, born 24 years earlier at Xativa, near Valencia in Spain, was immediately made a bishop, and quickly progressed up the Catholic hierarchy, to cardinal and vice-chancellor. He served in the Curia under five Popes.

But behind the facade of faith, hope and chastity, Rodrigo was busy seducing as many young virgins as he could lay his hands on. A highly sexed, handsome charmer, he could not resist the temptations of the flesh and one of his brazen open-air orgies earned him a reprimand from the Pope. In 1470 he began a torrid romance with a 28-year-old beauty, Vanozza dei Catanei. She bore him three sons, Giovanni (1474), Cesare (1476) and Goffredo (1481) and a daughter, Lucrezia (1480) before he tired of her and fell for the charms of the 16-year-old Giulia Farnese. For appearance's sake, he had Giulia betrothed to his young nephew – but he forbade the boy to consummate the marriage.

When Pope Innocent VIII died in 1492, Rodrigo was one of three contenders to become Pontiff. On the first poll, the electoral college of cardinals voted for

Cesare Borgia, Renaissance tyrant

Giuliano della Rovere, the successor nominated by Innocent. But Borgia began handing out huge bribes and promised delegates luxurious palaces and lucrative posts if he was chosen. On 10 August he duly became Pope, taking the name Alexander VI.

Instantly he showered his illegitimate children with riches. Cesare, aged just 16, was appointed Archbishop of Valencia. A year later he became a cardinal. But the titles meant little to the ambitious teenager. He was furious that his older brother had been given command of the Papal army. Cesare rode disdainfully round Rome, fully armed, with a succession of shapely mistresses at his side. He canoodled outrageously in public with his sister Lucrezia. And he rivalled his father's scandalous sexual exploits. When Sanchia, promiscuous teenage daughter of the King of Naples, arrived at the Vatican as a prospective bride for Goffredo Borgia, both the Pope and Cesare made a rigorous check on her credentials between the sheets of their own beds.

One of Cesare Borgia's few admirers was a man whose name later became synonymous with evil cunning: Niccolo Machiavelli. When the Papal army threatened Florence, Machiavelli, a city official, was sent to gauge Cesare's intentions. Borgia demanded gold in return for not attacking Florence. Machiavelli stalled while accompanying the army on conquests of other cities. He studied Cesare's ruthless methods, and used them as the basis for his book *The Prince*.

Its cynical dictates made survival of the state an end which justified any means. 'A prudent ruler ought not to keep faith when doing so would be against his interests,' Machiavelli wrote. Using force was justified if the rule of law proved insufficient, and governors were urged to give 'no consideration to either justice or injustice, to kindness or cruelty or to actions being praiseworthy or ignominious.' But Machiavelli was not an innovator advocating calculated corruption. He was a patriot who despaired because the squabbling states of Italy were too fragmented to stop France and Spain dominating the Italian peninsula. In Cesare Borgia he saw a man strong and unscrupulous enough to forge those states into a united nation. When Cesare lost power, Machiavelli passed on his hard-hearted philosophy in the hope that a later warrior would achieve the dream. And as a contemporary noted, Machiavelli's work contained little that was new. Though pious people thought him heretical and good people branded him wicked, the chronicler wrote: 'To the evil ones, he was merely too knowledgable in their ways.'

Rodrigo's reign began in embarrassing fashion. When King Ferrante of Naples died, the new Pope recognized the king's son Alphonso, father of saucy Sanchia, as successor. But the French King, Charles VIII, thought he had a better claim – and invaded Rome to prove it. Rodrigo grovelled and agreed to let Charles take Cesare along as a hostage on his journey south to the Naples coronation. But Cesare slipped away during the trip, returned to Rome and helped his father form an anti-French alliance with the rulers of Spain, Milan and Venice. Charles, afraid of being cut off from his homeland, scurried back to France and Alphonso was reinstated.

The Borgias then set about punishing those who had helped Charles to humiliate them. Cesare seized some Swiss mercenaries who had broken into his mother's home during the French occupation of Rome, and tortured them unmercifully. Rodrigo ordered the people of Florence to arrest and torture Girolamo Savonarola, a puritan monk who had denounced corruption in the Church and had welcomed Charles as a redeemer arrived to restore Catholicism's old values. The Florentines responded with enthusiasm, because the kill-joy cleric had forced them to abandon their carefree carnivals. He was stretched on the rack 14 times in one day during weeks of persecution before being publicly hanged. His body was then burned.

The Pope sent his son Giovanni off with the army to attack the fortresses of the Orsini family, who had also collaborated with the French. But he proved a hopeless general and returned to Rome in disgrace early in 1497 after losing a battle against the foes he was supposed to punish. Months later, on 14 June, he dined with his mother and brother Cesare. The two men left separately on horseback. Next morning Giovanni's body was dragged from the river Tiber. He had been stabbed nine times.

Giovanni's assassin was never caught, and officially the murder remained a mystery. But wagging tongues noted that one man gained more from the death than most – younger brother Cesare. It meant he could give up the religious positions he held so reluctantly and become the Pope's political and military strong man. That was good news for the Pope, too. Rodrigo could send Cesare away from Rome on business and quell the growing clamour of scandalized gossip. The cardinal's sexual proclivities – he found young boys as alluring as girls, and was far from discreet about his flings with either sex – were the talk of the town. Most embarrassing was his continuing affair with his own sister, Lucrezia. She was placed in a convent when her first husband fled for fear of Cesare's jealous rages. But six months later, after visits from Cesare and his father, she became pregnant. The baby boy was later taken to the Vatican and made heir to the Borgia fortune.

Cesare's new duties took him first to Naples, then to France. The new French king, Louis XII, wanted to annul his marriage and wed his mistress. Rodrigo agreed. In return, Cesare was made Duke of Valentinois and given a bride, the 16-year-old sister of the King of Navarre. More importantly, he was offered French armed help to subdue rebellious nobles in northern Italy and carve out a kingdom for himself in Romagna, south of Venice. The joint invasion began in 1499.

Cesare proved as cunning and unscrupulous in war as he had proved in love. When he crushed the forces of Caterina Sforza and captured her castle at Forli, he insisted that she also surrender her body to him. He wrote a gloating description of their love-making to his father in Rome before confining her in a convent. He took the town of Faenza after stubborn resistance by a population devoted to their 18-year-old master, Astorre Manfredi. The teenager agreed to surrender only after he was promised that his life would be spared. But Cesare sent him to Rome and had him horribly tortured, then killed.

Friends and allies of Cesare had as much to fear from him as from their foes. He betrayed the trust of the Duke of Urbino, marching his men past the city, then doubling back to launch a surprise attack. He appointed a ruthless governor to rule his new lands in Romagna – but when protests about the man's cruelty became impossible to ignore, he had him hacked in two and left on display in Sesena town square. Soon even some of Cesare's lieutenants were alienated by the reign of terror imposed by their morose, unsympathetic leader. Afraid that he might reclaim estates he had given them, they began plotting against him with princes he had deposed. Cesare learned of the conspiracy and lured some of the unsuspecting plotters to a banquet at the town of Senigallia. When they arrived, unarmed, they were seized. Two were instantly strangled.

Cesare's costly campaigns were funded by the Pope. Rodrigo sold cardinal's hats to wealthy aspirants, some of whom died mysteriously only months later leaving their estates to the Vatican. He declared the year 1500 a Jubilee, which meant pilgrims prepared to pay would receive total absolution for their trespasses. As an added inducement, he announced the unveiling of a 'secret holy door' in St Peter's which was only ever revealed once every 100 years. Grateful and gullible sinners paid handsomely for the rare privilege of viewing the door, which had been cut in the wall shortly before their arrival.

Rome's death rate rose every time Cesare returned from his territorial conquests. He answered insults, real or imagined, with murder. Many of his homosexual partners were also found poisoned, or dragged from the Tiber with fatal knife wounds. The Venetian ambassador wrote: 'Every night four or five murdered men are discovered – bishops, prelates and others – so that all Rome is trembling for fear of being destroyed by the Duke Cesare.' Then, in 1500, Cesare's fiery passion for sister Lucrezia led to a sensational killing.

Rodrigo had quietly annulled his daughter's first marriage after her husband fled Cesare's jealousy. And in the wake of the scandal over Lucrezia's baby, the Pope had rushed her to the altar with Alphonse, Duke of Bisceglie and the brother of Sanchia. Sadly, Lucrezia had genuinely fallen in love with him. That infuriated Cesare, who still prefered his sister's embraces to those of his wife.

In July 1500, Alphonse was walking across St Peter's Square after sharing supper with the Pope when a gang of thugs disguised as pilgrims attacked him with knives. He survived, though seriously wounded, and was given a room near the Pope's quarters to ensure his future safety. Lucrezia nursed him devotedly. But one night, having left his bedside briefly, she returned to find him dead. Amazingly, Cesare confessed to strangling him, saying the Duke had earlier tried to murder him with a crossbow. But no action was taken. And in less than two weeks Cesare was again forcing his attentions on his grief-stricken sister. Their incestuous liaison continued until Rodrigo arranged another match for Lucrezia, with the Duke of Ferraro's son. On their last night together before she left for the nuptials, Cesare arranged a special treat in his Vatican rooms – 50 local socialites rolled naked on the floor, scrambling for hot roasted chestnuts tossed to them by the illicit lovers.

But the debauched days of the unholy Borgia alliance were numbered. In August 1503, Rodrigo and Cesare both fell ill with malaria after attending a party thrown by a cardinal in a vineyard just outside Rome. Within a week the 72-year-old Pope was dead. And Cesare, who knew that all his power derived from his father's protection, was too weak to look after his own interests.

For a while he had reason to hope that he could still maintain power. Rodrigo's successor as Pope was an ineffectual old man who bore no grudge against Cesare. But he died just one month after taking office. Unluckily for Cesare, the old man's successor was Giuliano della Rovere, who still resented his defeat by Rodrigo in the election of 1492.

Cesare was arrested and forced to relinquish his Romagna kingdom. He left Rome for Naples, then under Spanish rule, hoping to be allowed to build a new power base. Instead he was again arrested, for disturbing the peace of Italy, and taken to Spain where he spent two years in jail. In 1506 he escaped and sought sanctuary with his brother-in-law, the King of Navarre. But, on 12 March, 1507, he was wounded leading a siege of the town of Viana during a territorial dispute with Spain. His captors showed him as much mercy as he had shown his own victims – they stripped him naked and left him to die of thirst.

The Conquistadores

Christian fervour reigned in Catholic Spain in the 16th Century. The dreaded Inquisition spread its bloody tyranny, the entire Dutch people were excommunicated and an invasion armada was sent to convert Protestant England. But missionary mania was not confined to Europe. When explorers sailed home with news of distant lands across the Atlantic full of strange peoples and untold riches, armed expeditions set out to claim them for

King and Pope. Natives of the Caribbean, Mexico and Central America were conquered and tamed in the name of Christ. Then the discovery of the Pacific Ocean opened up fresh horizons.

In 1527 a Spanish galleon investigating the new sea captured a balsa raft crammed with beautiful gold and silver objects studded with precious gems. The natives crewing the raft were the first clue to an unexpected and extraordinary civilization which had prospered in total isolation from the known world – the Incas. And the cargo they carried was enough to condemn their well-ordered empire to destruction. For although Spanish conquistadores, led by Francisco Pizarro, justified their invasion as a crusade for God and the Bible, they committed every sin in the book in pursuit of their real aim – treasure.

Pizarro, illegitimate son of a soldier from Trujillo, had spent 30 years in the new world subjugating 'savages'. Though an important member of Panama's Spanish community, he had not yet found the crock of gold that would make his fortune. With seizure of the Inca raft, he saw his chance. He obtained royal permission to explore and conquer Peru. Dominican monk Friar Vicente de Valverde was to go with him as 'protector' of the Indians.

The expedition left Panama in December 1530. Pizarro established a coastal base, killing the local chief to intimidate nearby natives, then moved inland with 168 soldiers, 62 on horses. He could not have arrived at a better time for Spain. Disease had ravaged the Inca court, killing the Inca himself, Huayna-Capac, and his heir. Two more of his sons, Huascar and Atahualpa, had begun a civil war for control of the empire, which stretched 3,000 miles through Chile, Bolivia, Ecuador and south Colombia as well as Peru. The conquistadores found towns in ruins and Indian corpses dangling from trees as they pressed up into the mountains.

Atahualpa, who commanded the area of Peru where the Spanish had landed, was none too pleased when his scouts reported that the strangers were pillaging the countryside as they advanced. But he sent the conquistadores gifts and invited them to meet him at Cajamarca. His army was camped beyond the town, and Atahualpa told Pizarro's envoys he would visit their leader in the town's central square next day. But when he arrived, carried on a litter by 80 men and surrounded by thousands of unarmed natives, the conquistadores stayed hidden in the buildings around the square. Friar Valverde emerged with an interpreter, carrying a cross and a Bible, and began explaining his religion to the baffled chief. Then he handed Atahualpa the book. But the Incas did not understand writing. They worshipped the sun, and claimed their images of it spoke to them. When the pages of the Bible did not speak, Atahualpa threw the book to the ground. The furious priest screamed for the insult to be avenged – and Pizarro unleashed a brutal and carefully planned ambush.

'The Spaniards began to fire their muskets and charged upon the Indians with horses, killing them like ants,' Inca nobleman Huaman Poma told chroniclers. 'At the sound of the explosions and the jingle of bells on the horses' harnesses, the shock of arms and the whole amazing novelty of the attackers' appearance, the Indians were terror-stricken. The pressure of their numbers caused the walls of the square to crumble and fall. They were desperate to escape from being trampled by horses and in their headlong flight a lot of them were crushed to death. So many Indians were killed that it was impractical to count them.' After two hours of horrific slaughter, nearly 7,000 natives were dead and thousands more maimed by sword slashes. All 80 carriers of Atahualpa were massacred, but he himself was spared. Pizarro needed him alive as insurance for the invaders' safety until reinforcements arrived.

The captive Inca noted the conquistadores' glee as they ravaged his camp for treasure, and made a shrewd offer. He would buy his freedom by filling a room 22 feet (6.7m) long by 17 feet (5.1m) wide with treasure, to a depth of 8ft (2.4m). He would fill it once with gold and twice with silver. Pizarro accepted, promising to restore Atahualpa to his stronghold at Quito as long as he instigated no plots against the Spanish. The Inca told the invaders where to find his temples and directed a scouting party to his capital, Cuzco. It returned with 285 llamas loaded with gold and silver stripped from palaces, tombs and holy places. Other treasure trains poured in from all over the empire. Pizarro crushed jars, jugs and sculptures so the room would hold more. Then he set up furnaces to melt all the precious metals into bars. There were six tons (6,096kg) of 22 carat gold and 12 tons (12,192kg) of silver, a total then worth nearly £3 million.

Atahualpa, confident of release, had secretly continued his civil war, having his troops kill Huascar and two of his half-brothers. But all he was doing was playing into Pizarro's hands by weakening the empire's chances of ever repelling the invaders. Pizarro had no intention of letting the Inca go. Now he had Atahualpa's treasure, he planned to march on to Cuzco with recently arrived reinforcements, and could not afford to take the native leader along as a magnet for possible attacks. Rumours of an approaching Inca army, out to rescue their chief, were the excuse Pizarro needed. He sent out search parties to check the reports. But before they returned, Atahualpa was dead. Condemned without trial for treason, he was tied to a stake on 26 July, 1533, and told he would be burned alive unless he became a Christian. He agreed to be converted, taking the name Francisco in honour of Pizarro. Then he was garrotted.

The death caused a furore in Spain and its other colonies. In Madrid the King was angry that a fellow royal had been illegally executed. The governor of Panama said Atahualpa had 'done no harm to any Spaniard'. But Pizarro survived the storm. He reasoned, rightly, that the crown's one-fifth share of all booty would calm humanitarian qualms.

The march to Cuzco started uneventfully. The invaders were going through

Francisco Pizarro

Huascar country, and locals welcomed the death of Atahualpa. They were trusting, gentle people – their homes did not have doors, let alone locks – and were in awe of the magnificent appearance of the newcomers. Having never seen horses before, some thought mount and rider were one being. Others believed the armour-plated conquistadores, white-faced and wearing strange beards, heralded the return of their sun god Viracocha. They were to pay for their naïveté by losing their wealth, their land, their women, their religion – and, for thousands, their lives.

The first armed opposition to Pizarro's men came 17 months after he landed in Peru. Troops loyal to Atahualpa attacked at Jauja, 250 miles north of Cuzco. But they were trying to fight cavalry armed with pistols, lances and steel swords using only clubs, bronze axes and stone slingshots. The native forces were routed by charging horses and mercilessly pursued and cut down as they fled. When the futile ambushes continued, Pizarro burned captive commander Chulcuchima alive, accusing him of inspiring the raids. The Inca general defiantly refused to spare himself agony by becoming a Christian.

The town of Cuzco welcomed the Spanish as liberators. And Huascar's son Manco welcomed them most. He was ready to collaborate if they made him Inca. Pizarro willingly installed him, then organized systematic looting of the empire's richest city. Temple walls, priceless statues, jewels and vases buried with the dead, even a unique artificial garden of intricate golden plants, were melted down. A young priest who watched with horror wrote: 'Their only concern was to collect gold and silver to make themselves rich . . . What was being destroyed was more perfect than anything they enjoyed or possessed.' But clerical concern at the abuse of a peaceful people in the Church's name could not stop it. As the governor of Panama reported to the King: 'The greed of Spaniards of all classes is so great as to be insatiable. The more the native chiefs give, the more the Spaniards kill or torture them to give more.'

Reports of the riches available in the Inca land sparked off a gold rush in other colonies. In Puerto Rico, the governor banned anyone leaving. When he caught a boatload of would-be treasure-hunters, he flogged them and cut off their feet. But still new adventurers reached Peru, committing atrocities in the race to get rich quickly.

Pedro de Alvarado marched into northern Peru, chaining up hundreds of native porters from the tropical coastal areas and watching them die cruelly in the icy Andes. Men, women and children were killed as towns were sacked, and local chieftains were hanged, burned or thrown to dogs when, under torture, they refused to divulge the whereabouts of treasure. Sebastian de Benalcazar burned the feet of chiefs to force them to reveal treasure troves. In one village, where all the men had fled to join Inca armies, he massacred the remaining women and children because there were not enough riches to satisfy his cravings. It was 'cruelty unworthy of a Castillian', according to the official chronicler of the Peruvian conquest. Other Spaniards buried native chiefs up to their waists in pits to try to force them to give away the hiding places of gold. When they would not – or could not – they were flogged, then buried up to their necks before being killed.

Reports of cruelty flooded into Cuzco, angering the Inca Manco. He also had personal reasons to regret collaborating with the Spanish. The town was in the control of Pizzaros's brothers, Juan, Hernando and Gonzalo, after Francisco left for the coast to found the new city of Lima. The Inca was continually pestered to reveal more treasure caches. His mother and sisters were raped. Then Gonzalo stole his wife. Such humiliation of himself and his people was more than the proud prince could stand. He and his elders decided to rebel. In 1535 he slipped out of the town at night, but was recaptured by horsemen and returned in chains. Spaniards urinated on him and tortured him, burning his eyelashes with a candle. But a year later he successfully escaped, determined to make the invaders pay for treating him so disgustingly.

Manco had secretly mobilized a vast native army, and began deploying it with devastating effect. He lured Cuzco's cavalry to nearby Calca, allowing them to seize a treasure train. While they counted their plunder, thousands of natives surrounded Cuzco, diverting irrigation canals to flood fields, making them impossible for horses to operate on. It was the start of a four-month siege. Three squads of Spaniards marching to the rescue were wiped out by native ambushers, who hurled giant boulders down deep gorges to knock them off tortuous mountain paths. Spaniards in Jauja were all killed in a dawn raid. But the conquistadores hit back with subterfuge and savagery to quell the rebellion.

Four shaved off their beards and blacked their faces to appear like Indians. Then, with the help of a native traitor, they got into an inaccessible fortress and opened the gates for colleagues to run amok. Hundreds of Indians leapt to their deaths off cliffs to escape Spanish swords. Morgovejo de Quinones, riding to relieve Cuzco, decided to avenge the death of 5 Spanish travellers by herding 24 chiefs and elders of a nearby town into a thatched building, then setting light to it and burning them alive. When the encircled horsemen in Cuzco broke out to attack a native fortress – Juan Pizarro was killed by a sling stone in the raid – so many Indians leapt from the battlements that the last to jump were cheated of death because the bodies piled beneath them broke their fall. More than 1,500 natives still in the fort were put to the sword. Conquistadores led by Gonzalo Pizarro surprised an indian army and massacred the men. Those who plunged into a lake to try to escape were pursued by horsemen and 'speared like fish.'

Horror and mutilation were deliberately used by the Spanish to demoralize their foes. Hernando Pizarro ordered that all women caught near battlefields were to be killed. They were the Inca soldiers' wives and mistresses. When brother Gonzalo captured 200 Indian fighters, he paraded them in the square at Cuzco and sliced off all their right hands. Then he sent them back to their comrades as 'a dreadful warning.' Later male captives had their noses cut off. Women who escaped death had their breasts chopped. In the Huaylas area, Francisco de Chaves instituted a three-month reign of terror. Homes and fields were destroyed, men and women burned or impaled, and 600 children aged under three were slaughtered.

The final blow to Manco's hopes came when an army led by his commander Quizo tried to take Francisco Pizarro's capital, Lima. Cavalry devastated the foot soldiers as they advanced across the coastal plain, and the horsemen massacred survivors of the charge as they fled towards safety in the mountains. Quizo and 40 fellow generals were among the dead.

Manco now realized he could not save Peru from the Spanish. More than 20,000 of his people had died trying. He retreated to Vilcabamba, a desolate valley screened by misty crags, and escaped his pursuers by hiding with forest Indians. But the Spaniards caught his wife, Cura Ocllo. And Francisco Pizarro took out his anger on her. Pizarro had proved during the siege of Lima that he had no qualms about killing women. Atahualpa's sister Azarpay was his prisoner there. He suspected her of encouraging the native attackers and had her garrotted. He had an even worse fate in mind for Cura Ocllo.

The poor woman only escaped rape at the hands of her escort soldiers by smearing herself with excrement. When she reached Cuzco, where Pizarro was waiting for news of the pursuit of the Inca, she was stripped naked, tied to a stake and savagely beaten. Finally she was killed by arrow shots. Her battered body was loaded into a basket and floated on a river which flowed into Vilcabamba, so the Inca could see the fate of his spouse. It was yet another horror to appal decent-minded Spaniards. One called it 'an act totally unworthy of a sane Christian gentleman.' Sadly, such acts were becoming all too common in the conquest of Peru.

But Pizarro's days were numbered. The lure of gold had led Spaniards to fight each other. Hernando Pizarro was recalled to Spain and jailed for garrotting without trial Diego de Almagro, one of the first conquistadores, who had rebelled for a bigger share of the booty. On 26 June, 1541, Almagro's followers took revenge. Twenty of them stormed Francisco Pizarro's Lima palace and stabbed him to death. Another victim of the raid was the cruel child-killer Francisco de Chaves. Friar Vicente de Valverde, the man who had helped dupe Atahualpa, panicked at the death of his patron Pizarro and took ship for Panama. On an island off Peru, he was captured by cannibals and eaten.

Pizarro had succeeded in his quest. Contemporaries praised him for acquiring more gold and silver than any other commander the world had seen. But the religious cause which justified his exploits played little part in his epitaph. His achievements were best summed up in the coat of arms awarded him by the King of Spain when he made him a marquis. It showed seven native chiefs with chains round their necks, and a shackled Atahualpa, his hands delving into two treasure chests.

Pizarro's passing did not end the suffering his invasion inflicted on Peru. And deaths resisting his takeover accounted for just a fraction of the estimated five million drop in the empire's native population between 1530 and the end of the century. The other reasons were spelled out damningly in John Hemming's authoritative book, *The Conquest Of The Incas*. They were:

Disease: Peruvians had no immunity to European ailments such as smallpox, measles, the plague. Epidemics raged uncontrollably. The town of Quito lost 30,000 in just one.

Neglect: Preoccupied by gold and silver, the Spaniards failed to maintain precious irrigation canals, agricultural terraces, roads and bridges. Where the Incas filled communal storehouses for times of hardship, the Spanish merely looted them.

Hunger: Apart from taking the natives' precious metals, the conquistadores and their successors seized, slaughtered and sold at ridiculously cheap prices their herds of llama. Harvests were also grabbed for cheap sale.

Exploitation: Francisco Pizarro had divided the nation into vast estates. Natives living on them had to provide annual tribute – gold, silver, livestock, grain, potatoes, eggs, salt, timber, utensils, clothing – whether the land provided them or not. Get-rich-quick landlords increased their demands until many natives worked all year just to provide the tribute, with no time or energy to look after their families. Many became wandering vagabonds to escape impossible obligations.

Plantations: Indians from the snowbound Andes were herded down to humid forests to harvest lucrative crops of coca, the plant that provides cocaine. They died in their thousands from heat and coca-related diseases.

Expeditions: Greedy Spaniards followed up every rumour of another rich El Dorado, however remote the gold was said to be. Hundreds of natives were chained to act as porters. They died like flies from exhaustion, exposure or abuse.

Forced labour: Giant silver and mercury mines were set up by the Spanish, and natives from catchment areas up to 600 miles wide were forced to work them. Conscripts chipped at narrow, unsafe faces for six days at a stretch, sleeping in the fetid air of the galleries, full of acrid smoke from tallow candles which were the only lighting. Toxic gases containing arsenic added to the toll of exhaustion, heat and bad diet in the mercury mines. A monk, Domingo de Santo Tomas, called the mines 'the mouth of hell, into which a great mass of people enter every year, and are sacrificed by the greed of the Spaniards to their god.' But the carnage was too profitable to stop. The royal fifth of the annual output at the Potosi silver mine alone came to $4\frac{1}{2}$ tons (4,550kg).

Yet according to John Hemming, none of these evils was the biggest killer. The main cause of death, he says, was 'profound culture shock.' The Inca people had lived without money in a benevolent welfare state which cared for them. Now, after decades of fighting, they were expected to work for cash wages by a government which cared nothing for them. Hemming quotes an Inca elder as saying: 'The Indians, seeing themselves dispossessed and robbed, allow themselves to die and do not apply themselves to anything as they did in Inca times.' They lost the will to live – and recreate. The birth rate fell as dramatically as the death toll rose.

The Madrid government tried to impose liberal laws, but the settlers rebelled – once led by Gonzalo Pizarro – insisting it was their right to exploit the land they had won as they thought fit. Rather than risk losing the flow of New World riches, the King made concessions. The exploitation went on.

The final nails in the coffin of the Inca empire were driven in by Francisco de

Toledo, who arrived as Viceroy in 1569. In two years, $1\frac{1}{2}$ million natives from isolated farms and villages were forcibly uprooted and settled in towns where they were easier to convert and control. Then the Church began a drive against native religions, seizing leaders, smashing relics and rooting out rites. And the last Inca king was captured and killed.

The murder of a Spanish messenger, trying to deliver letters to the new Inca, Tupac Amaru, was the excuse Toledo needed to invade Vilcabamba, the mysterious last refuge of the Peruvian royal family. Native sticks and stones were no match for the cannons and muskets of the 250-strong Spanish force. The Inca and his generals were caught as they tried to flee through the forests, and dragged to Cuzco in chains. Tupac Amaru was accused of ruling a heathen state which allowed heathen practices and raided Spanish Peru. He was also charged with specific murders, including that of the messenger. Despite pleas for mercy from all over Peru, and despite an astonishing public admission that the Inca religion of sun worship was a sham, Tupac Amaru was beheaded in front of vast, emotional crowds. It was almost 40 years to the day since the death of his great-uncle Atahualpa.

Toledo wanted to rid Peru of all Inca influence. He married princesses to Spaniards against the girls' wills, and sentenced several relatives of Tupac Amaru to Mexican exile – a decision over-ruled by Madrid. But all his efforts were in vain. Over 200 years later, when Peruvians successfully fought for independence from Spain, one of their heroes was Jose Gabriel Condorcanqui Tupac Amaru – great-great-great-grandson of the last Inca.

Pirates: evil on the high seas

The Venetian ambassador to London, Giovanni Scaramelli, wrote to his city's Doge and senate in 1603: 'How just is the hatred which all peoples bear to the English, for they are the disturbers of the whole world. The whole strength and repute of the nation rests on its vast number of corsairs. To such a state has this unhappy kingdom come, that from a lofty religion has fallen into the abyss of infidelity.'

Scaramelli was writing home in dismay at the realization that a mighty nation had granted a licence to criminals to guard its furthest colonial frontiers and boost its revenues. Those criminals called themselves corsairs, privateers, buccaneers or, grandly, 'the brethren of the coast.' In reality, they were no more than pirates. In the service of the English Crown, carrying no-questions-asked commissions, they were seaborne merchants of death and destruction.

Since the early sixteenth century, deserters, felons and shipwrecked smugglers had been abandoned to their fate on the coasts of the Caribbean islands, mainly Cuba, Jamaica and Hispaniola. They lived off wild pigs, the meat of which they cured by smoking in long strips over wood-and-dung fires. The dried meat was known as *boucan* and the wild men of the islands were termed *boucaniers*.

Through trade with passing ships, they acquired an arsenal of weapons, which they used to good effect in raids on the ill-defended colonial outposts – mainly Spanish – then being established throughout the islands. They drank a fearsome mixture of rum and gunpowder, wore trousers of uncured rawhide and shirts stained with pigs' blood. They must have smelt revolting and looked like savages. They certainly struck fear into the hearts of the Spaniards . . . with good reason.

In the first half of the seventeenth century, these buccaneers took to the sea. They stole small boats or fashioned canoes from hollowed tree trunks and sailed out of coves to attack Spanish shipping. The buccaneers would manoeuvre outside the line of fire of the Spanish guns, then race in close under constant covering fire and clamber aboard the sterns of the great galleons. Captured ships would be looted and occasionally impounded into the service of the attackers. The age of the pirate was born.

With names like Roche Braziliano, Red Legs Greaves, Pierre le Grand and Montbars the Exterminator, they harried Spain's treasure fleets and repeatedly sacked her outposts in the Central American isthmus, torturing the inhabitants without mercy until they revealed their hidden hoards. Most feared among them was a Breton captain, François Lolonois.

At the head of an army of 700 men, Lolonois razed Maracaibo to the ground and rampaged through what is now Nicaragua, lining Spanish prisoners before him and slaughtering them a dozen at a time for the sheer fun of it. According to one chronicler, Lolonois once 'grew outrageously passionate in so much that he drew his cutlass, slashed open the heart of a poor Spaniard and, pulling it out, began to gnaw it, saying to the rest that he would serve them all alike if they did not talk.' Among his other delights, Lolonois would 'cut a man to pieces, first some flesh, then a hand, an arm, a leg, sometimes tying a cord about his head and with a stick twisting it till his eyes shoot out, which is called woolding.' Lolonois met a fittingly unpleasant fate himself, being torn limb from limb by Indians.

The ease with which the buccaneers were able to relieve the Spanish of the gold they had themselves stolen from the natives of central and south America ushered in a new and, if anything, even bloodier age of piracy. For, under the guise of a crusade against Popery, Britain entered the arena and effectively gave its citizens a free hand in ravaging, robbing and persecuting neighbouring colonies with whom they were not even at war. These sea-going criminals were issued with commissions which were no more than licences to kill.

Foremost amongst them was Henry Morgan, a farmer's son born in Llanrhymney, Glamorgan. How he got to the West Indies is not known. He may have been transported, he may have been an indentured servant or he may have arrived in 1655 with Oliver Cromwell's army. In 1663 his uncle, Sir Edward Morgan, was appointed Deputy Governor-General of Jamaica and, although there is no evidence, it is likely that this valuable family connection helped the young Welshman launch his piratical career. For Jamaica's Government House was the principal source of buccaneers' commissions, handed out freely under the guise of guarding the colony against Spanish 'invasion'. In return for the commissions, the governor, the notoriously corrupt planter Sir Thomas Modyford, and his deputy received their own 'commission' – a share in the pirate plunder.

First records of Morgan's activities date from 1665 when he was involved in skirmishes with the Spanish in Costa Rica. Two years later, despite a British peace treaty with Spain, Modyford authorized Henry Morgan to assemble a fleet of 12 ships and to sweep the Spanish colonies for booty.

Morgan fast gained a reputation for barbarity. In Puerto del Principe, Cuba, he systematically tortured the townspeople until he was satisfied no hidden treasures remained. Then he sailed south to the Panama isthmus where he launched an ambitious attack on the impressively fortified town of Portobello. His men scaled the walls of the town by forcing captured priests and nuns up the scaling ladders as a human shield.

Morgan's savage rampage almost came to an early end in 1669 when, about to raid Maracaibo, he called all his captains and senior officers to a council of war aboard his flagship, the *Oxford*, in Port Royal harbour. Midway through the discussions, the *Oxford* was torn apart by an explosion in the powder magazine. Two hundred men, including five captains, died. Among the council of war, only Morgan and 25 others survived – watching horrified as everyone on the opposite side of a chart table was blown to bits. Morgan was unharmed but his reputation was dented.

The following year Morgan determined to restore his prestige and to ensure riches that would last him a lifetime by carrying out a single, dramatic raid on the richest city of the west. He planned to attack 'the Cup of Gold' – Panama City itself.

In 1670, ignoring yet another newly signed treaty between Spain and Britain,

THE WORLD'S MOST EVIL MEN

Henry Morgan assembled more than 2,000 men and 36 ships, victualled his fleet by sacking a dozen or more townships and set sail for Panama. En route he stopped at Providence Island where the governor agreed to surrender if Morgan staged a mock attack using gunpowder but no ammunition. This charade over and the garrison town sacked, the fleet sailed to the mouth of the River Chagre, which breaches the Darien isthmus, and took the sentinel Fort San Lorenzo with the loss of 100 buccaneers.

The city of Panama was only 50 miles away but they were 50 miles of disease-ridden swamp and dense jungle inhabited by unfriendly natives. After five days his men, starving and shot at by Indians, urged him to turn back and relaunch the attack with greater supplies. Morgan refused. The Spanish withdrew before them, burning villages and leaving the pirates without food or fresh water. The invaders ate cats, dogs and their own leather bags before, on the tenth day, they reached Panama, routed the defenders on the plains outside the city and burned it to the ground.

The looting of Panama and the murder, rape and torture of its inhabitants produced an unrecorded fortune. But the men who had gone through hell for Henry Morgan got little reward. Morgan claimed that the booty had been far less than expected – and accordingly gave his men pathetically small hand-outs for their sacrifices. Even the widows of those who had died in his service were cheated of their agreed recompense by Morgan. The only people satisfied with the share-out were the expedition's principal backers, some of the captains . . . and Morgan himself.

Rich and famous, he was ordered to England by King Charles II to serve a period of so-called 'detention' for what was known as 'the crime of Panama'. It was no more than a feint to appease the angry Spanish. Morgan spent two years in London, a hero feted by society, before returning in 1674 to Jamaica as Sir Henry Morgan, Lieutenant-Governor, plantation owner and justice of the peace. As such, he sat in judgement on many pirates and sentenced them to prison, and to death, without mercy – this, despite his own continuing financial links with the pirate trade. He died a rich man in 1688.

The lessons in terror and barbarity of François Lolonois and Henry Morgan were well learned by pirates who followed them in the early years of the eighteenth century. Monstrous Edward Teach (better known as Blackbeard) was a sadistic psychotic who ravaged the West Indies and America's eastern seaboard under the protection of North Carolina's corrupt governor. Dashing, dandified Bartholomew 'Black Bart' Roberts was reported to have treated prisoners with 'barbarous abuse . . . some almost whipped to death, others had their ears cut off, others fixed to yardarms and fired at as a mark'.

But the pirates' crimes often seem in restrospect to have been overshadowed by a more insidious evil – on the part of the corrupt, greedy authorities who not

Henry Morgan,
pirate king

Captain Kidd,
before the House of Commons

only tolerated but encouraged pirate activities.

The example of royal duplicity and hypocrisy displayed by Charles II and his loyal servant Henry Morgan was exceeded by their immediate successors: King William III and a New York-based privateer called Captain Kidd. In 1695 the king granted 'to our trusty and well-beloved William Kidd' two commissions, one to seize French shipping and the other to subdue piracy (a euphemism for the confiscation of booty from other privateers). For this the king expected a 'commission' of his own of 10 per cent of the haul. After Kidd's share, the remainder would go to the expedition's backers – a syndicate of bankers, peers and Whig politicians including the Lord Chancellor and the First Lord of the Admiralty.

Kidd little needed the adventure or the money. Born in Greenock, Scotland in 1645, the son of a Presbyterian minister, he had already made his mark and his fortune as a privateer against the French in the West Indies. He had then settled in New York, married a wealthy widow and retired to a mansion in Wall Street. It was only his wish to give evidence to a British Board of Trade inquiry about the corrupt practices of an arch enemy, New York's Governor Benjamin Fletcher, that brought Kidd to London and to the attention of the king.

In 1696 Kidd, duly commissioned, sailed from England to New York, where he recruited a crew from among pirates who had once worked for Governor Fletcher. He then sailed south, around the Cape of Good Hope to the Indian Ocean, on a buccaneering rampage that brought protests from almost every major maritime nation. The British government were forced to tear up his royal commissions and order his capture. Dismayed when he heard the news, Kidd fled to the West Indies, lost most of his plunder to mutinous crews and ended up in Boston, throwing himself upon the mercy of the authorities.

The man who had the power of life or death over Kidd at that stage was the new Governor of New York, the Earl of Bellomont. The noble Earl had got the job with the help of Kidd's evidence against his predecessor. He had also been one of the secret backers of Kidd's expedition. Yet Bellomont had the captain clapped in irons and thrown into a dungeon for six months before sending him back to Britain to stand trial. Bellomont meanwhile appropriated the £14,000 which was all that Kidd had left of his haul from the South Seas.

On 23 May 1701, drunk and insensible, William Kidd was hanged at Wapping and his body suspended in chains 'to serve as a greater terror to all persons from committing the like crimes'.

François Lolonois and Henry Morgan were among the most pitiless, brutal, bloodthirsty pirates who ever put to sea – but the unfortunate Captain Kidd was very different. Though his actions were certainly criminal, the real evil was displayed by those who, to line their own pockets, secretly and hypocritically authorized piracy and murder . . . and who, when their plot began to rebound on them, covered their traces by sending the instrument of their greed to the gallows. They were men like the duplicitous New York governor and Irish peer, the Earl of Bellomont; the Lord Chancellor, Sir John Somers; the First Lord of the Admiralty, Edward Russell, later Earl of Orford; the Master of Ordnance, the Earl of Romney; Secretary of State, the Duke of Shrewsbury – and the king himself, William III.

As Kidd told the judge at his trial: 'It is a very hard sentence. I am the innocentest person of them all, only I have been sworn against by perjured persons'. It was his last appeal to those evil men in high office – and it went unheeded.

Marat and Robespierre: evil in the name of Liberty

Hailing the almost-bloodless start of the French Revolution, Honoré Gabriel Riqueti, Comte de Mirabeau, said in May 1789: 'History has too often recounted the actions of nothing more than wild animals . . . Now we are given hope that we are beginning the history of man.' But, within five years, that hope had been wiped out by one of the world's worst outbreaks of mass murder. Frenchmen freed by negotiation from almost-feudal tyranny turned into brutal, barbaric beasts on the pretext of achieving liberty, equality and fraternity. And the most poignant epitaph for Mirabeau's dream was the anguished cry of a fallen revolutionary as she was led to the guillotine: 'Oh liberty, what crimes are committed in your name.'

The Revolution erupted when public patience with the King's absolute power to impose taxes and laws ran out. Louis XVI and the privileged nobility were forced to make concessions to democracy and individual freedom. But each concession merely made the increasingly strong citizens greedy for more. 'The difficulty is not to make a revolution go, it is to hold it in check,' said Mirabeau shortly before his death in 1791. For as the people realized they had the power of life or death, negotiation was abandoned for naked force. After the storming of the Bastille, symbol of the old regime's authority, revolutionaries advocating cautious progress were drowned by the clamour of radical factions urging war on France's neighbours and dissidents at home. Then a more sinister voice demanded massacres.

Jean-Paul Marat was not even French – his father came from Sardinia, his mother was Swiss. But when the Revolution began, he abandoned his career as a scientist and doctor to become one of Paris's most vitriolic pamphleteers. His early extremism was unpopular, and several times he was forced into hiding. Once, when he took refuge in the city sewers, he contracted a painful and unpleasant skin disease, which added to his bitter persecution complex. But as the mob became increasingly impatient with a Revolution which seemed to be doing nothing to reduce raging inflation and food shortages, and with leaders who were prevaricating over the fate of Louis and his hated Austrian wife Marie Antoinette, Marat's messages began to find a receptive audience. And he spoke with chilling clarity. 'In order to ensure public tranquility,' he wrote, '200,000 heads must be cut off.'

On 10 August, 1791, an armed procession of 20,000 Parisians marched towards the royal residence, the Tuileries. The King and Queen, and their two children, were smuggled out by elected representatives and taken to the National Assembly building for protection. The Palace's Swiss Guards held the mob at bay until their ammunition ran out. They surrendered – but the mob was in no mood for mercy. More than 500 soldiers were slaughtered with pikes, bayonets, swords and clubs. Another 60 were massacred as they were marched away as captives. Palace staff, even cooks, maids and the royal children's tutor, were slashed to pieces as the Parisians ran riot. Bodies were strewn in rooms and on staircases. The grounds were littered with corpses. And onlookers were sickened to see children playing with decapitated heads. Women, 'lost to all sense of shame, were committing the most indecent mutilations on the dead bodies, from which they tore pieces of flesh and carried them off in triumph.'

The hideous orgy of blood lust instantly brought fears of a backlash from royalists or counter-revolutionaries. Marat had the answer. Many opponents of the Revolution were already packed in the jails of Paris, and might break out to seek revenge. 'Let the blood of the traitors flow,' wrote Marat. 'That is the only way to save the country.' Hysteria was whipped up by pamphlets warning of a plot to assassinate all good citizens in their beds. In September, the good citizens took steps to make that impossible.

A party of priests who had refused to take a new vow severing their allegiance to Rome were being escorted to prison in six carriages. A mob ambushed them, plunging swords through the carriage windows to wound and mutilate indiscriminately. Then, at the gates of the jail, another mob was waiting. When the convoy arrived, and the priests tried to dash inside for safety, they were slaughtered. Soon afterwards, a bunch of thugs burst into a convent where 150 more priests were being held, along with an archbishop. He was stabbed first. Then the others were killed in pairs, their bodies thrown down a well.

Over the next week, gangs broke into jails, prison hospitals and mental asylums all over Paris, massacring inmates with swords, axes and iron bars. Only prisons for prostitutes and debtors were spared. Women were on hand with food and drink for the executioners. Drunken killers held mock trials for some of the victims. One woman awaiting trial for mutilating her lover had her breasts cut off and her feet nailed to the floor before being burned alive. Marie Thérèse de Savoie-Carignan, Princesse de Lamballe, a friend of Marie Antoinette, was stripped and raped. Then her body was ripped to pieces. A leg was stuffed into a cannon, her head was stuck on a pole, and her heart cut out, roasted and eaten.

Ghastly scenes of grisly glee were reported as the piles of corpses built up. Drunken women sat watching the debauched death-dealers, laughing and applauding at each new depravity. Some pinned cut-off ears to their skirts as gruesome souvenirs. Others drank aristocratic blood handed round by the killers, or dipped bread in it. Men sat on bloodied bodies, smoking and joking while they rested from their labours. In six days, during which the gutters ran red, half the prison population, nearly 1,200 people, were murdered. And those who took a day off work to join the extermination squads were paid compensation for lost wages by delighted leaders of the Paris Commune.

The excesses appalled many of the most radical revolutionaries. But Marat was unrepentant. He signed a letter sent by the Commune to its counterparts in provincial towns, explaining that the 'act of justice' was 'indispensable in order to restrain by intimidation the thousands of traitors hidden within our walls.' And the letter went on: 'We do not doubt that the whole nation will be anxious to adopt this most necessary method of public security; and that all Frenchmen will exclaim, with the people of Paris, "We are marching against the foe, but we will not leave these brigands behind us to cut the throats of our children and wives."' Republicans in many towns took that as their cue to match the capital's atrocities by massacring the inmates of their own jails.

In January 1793, the Revolution reached the point of no return. The elected national assembly, now called the Convention, unanimously condemned Louis XVI to death for trying to 're-establish tyranny on the ruins of liberty.' He was executed in the Place de la Révolution, formerly the Place de Louis XV. Within weeks, every major country in Europe had declared war on France, and civil war raged as peasants resisted compulsory call-up to the armed forces.

Minister of Justice Charles Danton set up a Revolutionary Tribunal to try to maintain order and avoid atrocities like the September massacres. 'Let us be terrible to prevent the people from being terrible,' he thundered. But Convention moderates believed the people would stay terrible as long as Marat was free to incite them. They ordered he be tried by the Tribunal. To their consternation, he was cleared. Carried back to the parliament in triumph by the mob, he forced through a decree ordering the arrest of 22 of his accusers.

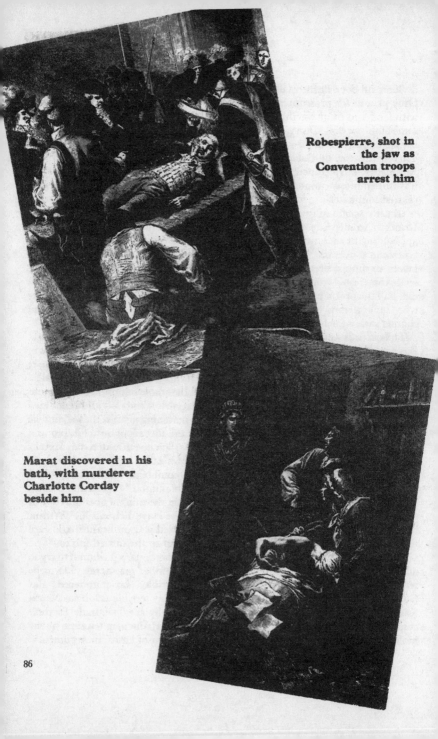

Robespierre, shot in the jaw as Convention troops arrest him

Marat discovered in his bath, with murderer Charlotte Corday beside him

Marat did not savour his victory for long. On 13 July, 1793, he was at home, wrapped in towels in a copper bath to ease the pain of his skin affliction, when a young girl arrived, claiming to know of moderates who were plotting an anti-leftist coup against Marat's party. 'They will all soon be guillotined,' Marat assured her as he jotted down the names. But the girl, Charlotte Corday, was not what she seemed. She suddenly drew a knife from her cleavage and stabbed Marat. He fell dying as aides manhandled Charlotte to the ground. She seemed oblivious to their blows. 'The deed is done,' she shouted. 'The monster is dead.'

But once again the moderates had miscalculated. Marat the monster became the mob's martyr. All over France, streets and squares were named after him. More than 30 towns changed their name to his. And his death did not divert the Revolution from the path of blood. For an even more evil man had taken over leadership of the lethal extremists, a man prepared to sacrifice even the parents of his godson at the altar of his ambitions.

Maximilien Robespierre, a cold, humourless barrister from Arras, was despised by many of his fellow revolutionaries for his fastidious appearance and his squeamishness at the sight of bloodshed. Yet by 1793 the dapper lawyer who shunned public executions because they corrupted the human soul was the most feared man in France. And he used his power, as chief of the ironically named Committee of Public Safety, to institute one of the most cruel reigns of terror in history.

Robespierre's committee directed the Revolutionary Tribunal in eradicating enemies of the republic. France was still in danger of invasion by its European neighbours, and Robespierre could justify early severity on those grounds. He ruled that all foreign nationals not living in France on 14 July, 1789 – the day the Bastille was stormed – should be arrested. And he executed the most famous foreigner on French soil – Austrian-born Queen Marie Antoinette. Charges against her included conspiracy with her brother, the Austrian Emperor, and incest with her son. Though she denied them all, she followed her husband to the guillotine on 16 October, 1793.

Soon the dreaded tumbrils were speeding almost daily to the scaffold in the Place de la Révolution bringing new victims. Pierre Vergniand, former president of the Revolutionary parliament, had warned: 'It is to be feared that the Revolution, like Saturn, will end up by devouring its own children.' Now his prophecy was coming true. He was among 20 moderates accused and condemned to death at a show trial. One stabbed himself to death in the courtroom with a concealed dagger – but his lifeless body accompanied his luckless colleagues for ritual decapitation next day.

More than 3,000 Parisians followed them to the blade. They included former royal mistress Madame Du Barry, accused of mourning the executed king while she was in London; a general who 'surrounded himself with aristocratic officers and never had good republicans at his table'; an innkeeper who 'furnished to the defenders of the country sour wine injurious to health'; a gambler who insulted patriots during a card game dispute; and a man who rashly shouted 'Vive le Roi' after a court jailed him for 12 years for another offence. Author Christopher Hibbert, in his authoritative book *The French Revolution*, says alleged speculators and hoarders died for 'starving the people' and one man paid the penalty 'for not giving his testimony properly.'

Vast crowds watched the executions, eating, drinking and laying bets on the order in which each batch of victims would lose their heads. English writer William Hazlitt reported: 'The shrieks of death were blended with the yell of the assassin and the laughter of buffoons. Whole families were led to the scaffold for no other crime than their relationship; sisters for shedding tears over the death of their brothers; wives for lamenting the fate of their husbands; innocent peasant girls for dancing with Prussian soldiers; and a woman giving suck . . . for merely saying, as a group were being conducted to slaughter, "Here is much blood shed for a trifling cause."'

The Place de la Révolution guillotine was so busy that, according to author Hibbert, people living in nearby Rue Saint-Honoré – ironically the street where Robespierre had lodgings – complained that the smell of stale blood from the stones was a health hazard and lowered the value of their houses.

Outside Paris, the vicious purges were even worse. 'The whole country seemed one vast conflagration of revolt and vengeance,' wrote Hazlitt. More than 14,000 people died as sadists and butchers in positions of office in the provinces made the most of Robespierre's instructions. Others killed to keep up with them, afraid they might be labelled weak or counter-revolutionaries. At Lyons, the Committee of Public Safety mowed down 300 convicted prisoners with a cannon. At Bordeaux a woman who wept when her husband was guillotined was forced to sit beneath the blade while his blood dripped on to her. Then she too was beheaded.

At Nantes, Jean-Baptiste Carrier was busy earning himself immortality as one of the worst brutes in the annals of infamy. Mass-killer Carrier, a lawyer like Robespierre, found the guillotine too slow for his taste. He packed victims into barges, towed them to the middle of the river Loire, then drowned them. Some couples were stripped naked and strapped together, face to face. Men waited with hatchets on the shore, to make sure no one got away. More than 2,000 people died in the river. Ships setting sail brought corpses up with their anchors, and the water became so polluted that catching fish in it was banned.

Carrier was also a child-killer. The guillotine was unsatisfactory – tiny heads were chopped in half because the necks made too small a target for the blade. And one executioner collapsed and died from the trauma of beheading four little sisters. So Carrier had 500 children taken to fields outside the town, where they were shot and cudgelled to death. But disease cheated the butcher of some of his prey. An epidemic swept through his overcrowded prisons, killing 3,000 inmates.

Millions of Frenchmen lived in terror of the midnight knock on the door that spelt arrest. Robespierre's spies were everywhere, and his assistants ensured that the pace of persecution never slackened. 'Liberty must prevail at any price,' declared Louis de Saint-Just, nicknamed Robespierre's Angel of Death. 'We must rule by iron those who cannot be ruled by justice,' he ordered. 'You must punish not merely traitors, but the indifferent as well.'

Early in 1794 Robespierre arrested more than 20 Convention members suspected of being critical of the way their Revolution was going. One of them was Camille Desmoulins. Robespierre was godfather to his son, but that made no difference. Desmoulins had said: 'Love of country cannot exist when there is neither pity nor love for one's fellow countrymen, but only a soul dried up and withered by self-adulation.' He named no names, but everyone knew who his target was. Saint-Just hit back: 'A man is guilty of a crime against the republic when he takes pity on prisoners. He is guilty because he has no desire for virtue.' Desmoulins died – and so did his 23-year-old widow, because she appealed to Robespierre for mercy.

Danton, too, was among this consignment of children of the Revolution to be devoured. Robespierre had decided that the notorious womanizer could never be a fit champion of freedom. Danton confided to friends that he would not fight his accuser, because 'far too much blood has been shed already.' He added: 'I had the Revolutionary Tribunal set up. I pray to God and men to forgive me for it.'

With his main potential rivals purged, Robespierre again stepped up the slaughter. The Committee of Public Safety decreed that death was henceforth the only sentence it would impose. Defence lawyers, witnesses and preliminary investigations were all banned, and an official said: 'For a citizen to become suspect, it is now sufficient that rumour accuses him.' Hundreds more aristocrats were executed – 1,300 in Paris in one month alone. 'At the point we are now, if we stop too soon we will die,' Robespierre told the Convention. 'Freedom will be extinguished tomorrow.'

But in the Convention, more and more delegates shared Danton's belated repugnance at the killings – and, at last, summoned the courage to resist Robespierre. For 24 hours the Convention was split, with both sides drawing up indictments to arrest their opponents. Finally, the vote went against Robespierre, Saint-Just and 18 of their closest associates. But in the confusion, troops detailed to escort Robespierre to jail proved loyal to him, and installed him in a safe house. The Convention summoned more soldiers to recapture him. When they burst in, a shot smashed Robespierre's jaw. Next day, 28 July, 1794, he was in agony as the Revolutionary Tribunal he had used so lethally sentenced him and his aides to death. Hours later, the tumbrils took all the arrested men to the guillotine, pausing momentarily outside Robespierre's lodgings while a boy smeared blood from a butcher's shop on the door. Robespierre was the last to die. When his turn came, a woman screamed at him: 'You monster spewed out of hell, go down to your grave burdened with the curses of the wives and mothers of France.'

The new Revolutionary regime revenged itself on Robespierre's followers. Many were executed after trials – Carrier was guillotined on 16 November – and hundreds more were lynched in jails all over the country. The people's revolution was at last over.

The French had paid a bloody price for allowing the likes of Marat and Robespierre to lead them towards their dream of liberty, equality and fraternity.

Rev. Jim Jones

I t is just possible that the Reverend Jim Jones set out to be a loving religious leader who would champion the cause of the poor and the oppressed.

Certainly, thousands of sincere worshippers, inspired by his message of brotherhood and justice, flocked to join his faithful congregation. Politicians and civic leaders hailed Jones as a selfless, tireless worker whose personal sacrifices pointed the way towards building a better society for millions in the United States.

But somewhere along the line, it all went grotesquely wrong.

Jones changed from Good Shepherd to tyrant, from benign pastor to brutal torturer. In the end he led nearly 1,000 of his followers into a nightmare in a tropical jungle in South America with the promise of building them a paradise on earth. And when concerned relatives began to plead for an investigation into the plight of the faithful in the jungle settlement of Jonestown, he had the inquiring visitors assassinated to stop them telling the outside world the truth about the living hell he had created in the name of social progress and humanity.

As his religious empire came crashing down under the weight of the terrible suffering he had inflicted on his own followers, he ordered them to commit mass suicide.

FOR GOD, KING AND COUNTRY

Chanting and singing his praises, elderly women and young couples cheerfully drank the deadly arsenic potion of 'holy water' he offered them. Loving parents fed their children a sweet mixture of poison and lemonade. And for those whose nerve failed them, the elders of Jones's church were ready to slit their throats or put a .38 bullet in their heads. The whole congregation died.

Jim Warren Jones was born on 13 May, 1931 in the small farming town of Lynn, Indiana, and he was doomed to grow up a lonely child. His father was a World War One veteran who suffered a disabling lung disease and who could only contribute a meagre Government pension towards the support of his family. Embittered and partly crippled, he reserved most of his strength for the fiery rallies of his favourite political cause, the racist Klu Klux Klan.

Jones's mother, Lynetta, was forced to take a factory job to make ends meet. As an adult, Jones was to claim that she was a full-blooded Cherokee Indian. Certainly he took his dark complexion and handsome features from her. And it was obvious from an early age he felt compelled to spread a different message from that of his father's racial hatred. Only an average student at school, he showed an unusual zeal for Bible studies. While his schoolmates demonstrated their energy on the football field, the Jones boy would stand on the porch of the family's run-down home and preach sermons at passers-by.

In 1949, at the age of 18, he took a part-time job as a hospital porter in nearby Richmond to support himself through religious studies at Indiana University. He also married hospital nurse Marceline Baldwin, four years his senior. The following year, although not yet an ordained minister, he became a pastor at a church in Indianapolis and helped to run its racially integrated youth centre.

For the next ten years, Jones suffered abuse at the hands of Indiana's racial bigots. Even the more conservative members of the church where he served protested about his plans to welcome black worshippers into their midst. Eventually Jones quit, but not before he had learned a valuable lesson about human behaviour. Members of the congregation who had only been lukewarm about their young pastor had closed ranks and rallied round him when Jones was attacked by outsiders. The message was clear: even people who don't enthusiastically share each other's beliefs can become loyally bound together if they feel threatened by a common enemy.

With money from his followers he eventually bought his own church, grandly named The People's Temple, in a run-down part of Indianapolis which had changed from a poor white area to a black ghetto. He preached racial integration and equality, not because it was fashionable, but because he honestly believed in it.

He and his wife adopted seven children, black, white and Asian. Boasting of his mother's Cherokee blood, he called himself 'biracial'.

Now that his new parish was to consist mainly of black churchgoers, he set out to study the style and technique of black preachers who commanded rapturous devotion from their flocks. And in Philadelphia he watched one black preacher who held his congregation absolutely spellbound. Father Divine was a hellfire-and-damnation orator, faith healer and showman who lived a life of luxury on the offerings of totally trusting followers who even believed his claims to be able to raise the dead. Jones was enthralled – and decided to test the level of allegiance of his own churchgoers.

Overnight the campaign of racist abuse against him mysteriously reached a sinister climax. He claimed he had been concussed when a Klan member smashed a bottle in his face on his doorstep. A stick of dynamite thrown into his garden caused a tremendous explosion but no damage or injuries. Newspaper reports, based mainly on information supplied by Jones himself, told of how he bravely stood up to the threats against himself and his family.

In recognition of his courageous stand, the mayor of Indianapolis appointed Jones to a £3,000-a-year job on the city's Human Rights Commission. And his congregation, feeling their young pastor to be beleaguered, gave him their unswerving devotion. Jones decided the time had come to weld the congregation even more tightly together with a common fear that was more terrifying than the threat of racism.

In 1960, when the country was going through 'nuclear war fever', millions of worried Americans built backyard nuclear fallout shelters. A popular magazine ran a tongue-in-cheek article, claiming to be a scientific survey of the 'ten safest places to live in the event of nuclear war'. Jones seized on the idea as a perfect trial of how thoroughly he could rule the lives of his followers. Two of the safest 'bolt-holes' from nuclear destruction were reported by the magazine to be Belo Horizonte in Brazil and the rural backwoods of Ukiah in California, 120 miles north of San Francisco.

The Rev. Jones suddenly announced to his church members that he had experienced 'a personal vision of the nuclear holocaust' and he told them they should be prepared to follow him to distant pastures to escape. Leaving abruptly with his family, at church expense, for a visit to Brazil, he ordered them to be ready to sell up their homes and withdraw their savings from their banks.

Jones returned from his South American trip unimpressed by Brazil but curiously interested in the prospects of the tiny, newly independent country of Guyana where he had stopped over for a few days. The former British colony, now a left-wing socialist republic, fulfilled many of his dreams of social justice, he told his congregation. As an afterthought he added that his terrible premonition of the nuclear holocaust had receded for the time being.

Emboldened and flattered by the number of devotees who had already put their homes up for sale just because of his 'premonition', Jones decided the option of fleeing from civilization should be held for a future emergency. If they

The Rev. Jim Jones

believed in him enough to let his fantasies rule their lives, he reckoned, they would believe in just about anything he told them. Now was the ideal time to launch himself into the lucrative faith-healing market.

The healing services were spectacular, profitable and fraudulent. In a religious frenzy, Jones would pass among the 'sick' and 'crippled' newcomers to his church, laying his hands on them. Selected patients would then leap joyously to their feet saying their injuries and diseases had been totally cured.

But when Jones's inner circle of church officials began to claim that he had raised forty followers from the dead, newspapers and the State Board of Psychology began to take a close interest.

The time had come to make a quick move before the press and local authorities began to pry too deeply. The ideal bolt-hole proved to be in California's Redwood Valley, near Ukiah, one of the so-called 'nuclear safe zones'.

California of the mid-sixties provided the perfect camouflage for the People's Temple. The arrival of three hundred religious enthusiasts preaching love and peace blended in neatly with a culture which had more than its fair share of 'flower children', 'peaceniks' and hippy communes.

For his so-called People's Temple to grow and flourish it only remained for Jones to convert the two potential troublemakers, civic busybodies and the press, into allies. He succeeded almost overnight. Temple members who became hard-working shop assistants and farm labourers were always the first to volunteer to work long unpaid hours organizing local charities. The church-goers acted as foster parents to take in scores of problem children from orphanages. Jones himself wooed local politicians until he was elected as foreman of the county grand jury and a director of free legal aid services.

Jones now had hundreds of supporters whose regard for him had been cleverly nurtured from respect to allegiance, from devotion to mindless blind loyalty. One shortcut for him to bring about social justice, he explained to them, was to work tirelessly in elections and canvassing to get him more political power – and to hand over most of their earnings to him.

With the dollars pouring in and the People's Temple a respectable state-registered, tax-exempt, religious organization with the worthiest ideals, he was ready for the big-time.

Jones and his flock left the backwoods for the bright lights of San Francisco. Their reputation as an industrious band of do-gooders quickly followed them as Jones set up a new Temple in downtown San Francisco. The membership swelled to 7,500.

City officials, impressed by Jones's boundless energy and his flair for organization, soon turned over to him part of their welfare programme and his Temple took over the task of dispensing thousands of free hot meals in their dining hall every day. No one realized that among the grateful recipients of the meals were many of Jones's own followers who had handed over to him their wages, their savings and even their social security payments.

In 1976 a naïve local political worker who feared an embarrassingly small turnout at a meeting for Rosalynn Carter, wife of presidential candidate Jimmy, asked Jones for help to swell the numbers at the election rally. Jones packed the hall with his supporters and received a standing ovation from the crowd. The next day the papers ran his photograph with Rosalynn Carter and when Jimmy was duly elected, Jones received an invitation to the presidential inauguration in Washington.

In the eyes of the local community he was a pillar of respectability. He openly boasted about funnelling hundreds of thousands of dollars from his Temple funds to South America to aid starving children in Guyana.

But the first defectors from his Temple began to tell a different story. They spoke of Jones's long tirades about sex during his sermons and how he demanded that happily married couples should be forced to divorce each other and remarry partners he had chosen for them among his inner circle of church elders.

They revealed how Jones insisted that, as their spiritual leader, he had the right to have sex with any woman or girl in the congregation and how he forced them to submit to his sexual demands.

They gave details of how browbeaten Temple members were made to confess publicly to imagined sins of homosexuality. And they revealed how young children were cruelly beaten on a platform in the Temple by Jones to 'make them show respect'. Young girls were made to take part in 'boxing matches', outnumbered by teams of bigger, stronger opponents who knocked them senseless. Other children vanished into a private room to meet 'the blue-eyed monster'. No sounds of beatings came from the room, only the screams of the young victims and the crackling noise of an electric cattle prod which sent surges of high voltage electricity through their bodies.

And all the time, hundreds of thousands of dollars poured into the Temple funds.

Many San Francisco newspapers had been the proud winners of hefty cash bonuses from Jones through his Temple awards for 'outstanding journalistic contributions to peace and public enlightenment'. Even the local police department had benefitted from his generous donations to the widows and orphans of officers killed in the line of duty.

There was a deep sense of disappointment in the highest circles, even up to the level of President Carter in the White House, that Jones the civic hero might just be a vicious crackpot.

As the bubble began to burst, Jones put into action his escape plan. The millions of dollars he had salted away in Guyana had already been put to use buying a lease on 20,000 acres of jungle and swamp near Port Kaituma on the country's Caribbean coast. A pavilion had been built as headquarters of 'Jonestown' and dormitories were ready for a thousand followers to join Jones in setting up a 'new, just, socialist society'.

Amazingly, a thousand loyal volunteers did go with him to Jonestown in November 1977 and San Francisco's politicians breathed a sigh of relief that a growing scandal had removed itself 2,000 miles from their doorstep. But they reckoned without the tenacity of one tough, independently-minded Congressman who wasn't prepared to leave the scandal uncovered.

Fifty-three-year-old Leo Ryan was a politician who believed in confronting problems first-hand. He had left the comfort and safety of his plush Congress office to spend time in the solitary confinement cell of Folsom Prison, California's toughest maximum security jail, to see for himself the treatment of prisoners. And he had worked undercover as a teacher in ghetto schools to expose failures in the education system.

When worried constituents told him they feared many of their loved ones – husbands and wives, sons and daughters – had discovered the truth about Jones in Guyana but were held there against their will, Ryan pressured the U.S. State Department to force a reluctant Guyanese government to allow him to fly to Jonestown to speak to Temple members himself.

Accompanied by a group of newspaper and television reporters, he arrived by chartered plane at the settlement on 17 November 1978 and walked straight into the lion's den. Jones himself was holding court in Jonestown's central pavilion. Locked away in a strongroom at the rear were 1,000 American passports which he had taken from his followers. Armed guards patrolled the outskirts of the remote settlement – 'to keep away bandits', Jones explained to the Congressman. Settlement pioneers were gaunt and hungry but most of them appeared to be still fanatically devoted to Jones.

Ryan was characteristically blunt. Addressing a meeting of the worshippers, under the gaze of the Jonestown armed guards, he explained: 'I am sure there are some of you who think this is the best thing that has ever happened to you in your lives.' He was drowned in a crescendo of shouting and cheering. 'But I promise if any of you want to leave you can come with me under my personal guarantee of protection.'

There was sullen silence.

Jones was seething. Any defectors who left with the Congressman would tell the truth about Jonestown as soon as they were away from the power of his evil spell. The façade cracked a little when one volunteer stepped forward.

That night Ryan was allowed to stay in Jonestown to talk to the settlers. The party of journalists was sent packing, to stay in Port Kaituma, six miles away. When they got there, TV reporter Don Harris reached into his pocket for a note which had been secretly thrust into his hand in Jonestown. It bore four names and the plaintive cry for help: 'Please, please get us out of here before Jones kills us'.

The following day when the journalists returned, Ryan was waiting for them with 20 terrified worshippers who wanted to leave. One by one Jones hugged them as they lined up to ride in an earth-moving truck through the jungle to the airstrip. But there were too many of them for the small plane to carry in one trip and Ryan bravely volunteered to stay behind until the plane could make a second journey.

Then there was a scuffle and a spurt of blood, followed by a grisly cheer. One of Jones's elders had pulled a knife and accidentally slashed himself as he tried to stab Ryan. The journalists pulled the blood-stained Congressman aboard the truck and roared away towards the airfield. They were still trembling beside the runway, briefing the pilot, when a tractor drove through the undergrowth on to the concrete. A volley of shots rang out from the men on the tractor. Ryan was killed instantly, his face blown off. Don Harris, the TV reporter, died as he took the full force of a blast from an automatic rifle. His cameraman was killed as he filmed the scene. A young photographer from the *San Francisco Examiner* was slain in a hail of bullets.

To add to the horror, one of the Jonestown 'defectors' suddenly pulled a gun from his shirt and began pumping bullets at the pilot. It was carnage.

At the settlement, the Reverend Jim Warren Jones called his loving

---

For centuries, European knights launched crusades in the name of God against the 'heathen' Turks occuping the Holy Land. But the murderous missionaries were out to kill rather than convert. The most bloodthirsty expedition was led by Godfrey of Bouillon, in response to pleas from Pope Urban II, who alleged Christians in the Middle East were being persecuted by the Turks. Godfrey's forces besieged the Syrian city of Antioch for seven months in 1097. When the inhabitants finally surrendered, every Turk within the walls was slaughtered. The evangelical army then marched on Jerusalem. Huge siege towers enabled the soldiers to swarm over the battlements and begin another orgy of death. Jews who sought sanctuary in their synagogue were burned alive. Historian Salomon Reinach wrote: 'It is said that 70,000 persons were put to death in less than a week to attest the superior morality of the Christian faith!'

The dead of Jonestown lie strewn around a vat of the poisoned drink

congregation around him for the last time. 'I warned you this would happen,' he told them sobbing. 'We were too good for this world. Now come with me and I will take you to a better place.'

There was some crying and praying as the elders of the People's Temple struggled from the pavilion carrying huge vats of poison laced with Kool-Aid soft drink. Gospel singing began as the mesmerized followers queued up to drink the cups of death.

The babes in arms died first, the poison squirted into their helpless mouths with syringes. Then the children, then their parents.

When Guyanese troops arrived the next day, they found the corpses of entire families with their arms locked around each other in a last loving embrace.

Jones himself lay sprawled with a bullet in his brain. The People's Temple had held its last prayer meeting.

One devotee had left behind a suicide note addressed to Jim Jones. It said: 'Dad, I can see no way out, I agree with your decision. Without you the world may not make it to Communism. I am more than tired of this wretched, merciless planet and the hell it holds for so many masses of beautiful people. Thank you for the only life I've known.'

Congressman Leo Ryan had a more fitting epitaph for Jones. Just before he died in the airstrip massacre, he was interviewed by the television crew. His last words faithfully preserved on their tape recorder, found under the pile of bodies, were: 'Jim Jones talks a lot about love, brotherhood and humanity and his faith and the power of religion. But never once did I hear him mention God.'

Chapter
Four

THE NAZIS

Chronicling the rise of Adolf Hitler . . . and the eager disciples of the Fascist demagogue who graduated over two decades from thuggery to genocide.

'Kill a man and you are a murderer. Kill millions of men and you are a conqueror. Kill everyone and you are a god.'

Jean Rostard (1955)

Hitler:
the Making Of A Monster

There was nothing to set the young Adolf Hitler apart from his schoolmates. He was a studious lad, his report cards showing regular columns of A grades. He was seldom absent, his stern father saw to that. If his teachers had any criticism of his work, it was that his mind tended easily to wander. He could not concentrate for long on a single subject. He was a bit of a dreamer.

In later years, a glorious legend would be carefully fabricated about young Adolf's schooldays in Austria. That he was a born leader whom his classmates followed instinctively. That, as well as extraordinary artistic gifts, he was also possessed of a formidable political understanding. And that at the age of 11, he gained an 'insight into the meaning of history'. All bunkum, of course. The true character of Adolf Hitler was subordinated to the Nazis' needs to make a myth, a superman and a master race. And buried so well that today psychiatrists can only guess at the boy's mental and emotional state.

Yet, at the turn of the century, *someone* should have had an inkling that there was something a little different about the blue-eyed, dark-haired, impish youngster with the intense gaze who sat scribbling at a desk in a drab secondary school in the Austrian town of Linz. Someone should have seen into the dark depths of his young mind when the pattern of his future – and therefore the future of the entire world – was being settled.

That very someone could have prevented the making of a monster, and he failed. That man was his father.

Alois Hitler was a customs official in the Austrian town of Braunau-am-Inn, close to the border with Bavaria. He was a stern man and the young Adolf had little affection for him. Alois had risen from the most modest background to a position of lower-middle-class respectability, adopting along the way a severe conservatism, a self-conscious caution and a strict, pedantic, pompous attitude towards his job and his family. He felt that he had a great deal to be proud of and even his long suffering colleagues had to admit that he had achieved much in life.

Alois Hitler's father had been a poor country miller who had apprenticed his son to a cobbler while still a child. Alois married young but details of his first wife are scant. His second wife, Franziska Matzelberger, bore two children before dying of consumption. He married for a third time but tragedy still dogged him.

Hitler in one of a series of photographs he had taken in 1925 to perfect his oratorical manner

Klara Hitler produced two children who died in infancy. A third child, a son, was born at Braunau at 18.30 pm on 20 April, 1889, and survived. He was given the name Adolf.

There were to be two further children. Another son, Edmund, died at the age of six, causing an early trauma in the elder brother Adolf's life. Then came a sister, Paula, who survived.

Apart from the death of his brother, there was a further detail of family history that was to plague Adolf Hitler throughout his life. It was that his father had been born out of wedlock. This resulted in the wholly erroneous claim, loudly proclaimed by political opponents in the 1930s and by the Allies during World War Two, that Adolf himself was illegitimate and that his real name was Schicklgruber. The stigma stuck despite the fact that Hitler's father's birth had subsequently been legitimized by the marriage of Hitler's grandfather to the unmarried mother, Maria Schicklgruber.

THE WORLD'S MOST EVIL MEN

There is believed to have been conflict between Adolf Hitler and his father Alois throughout the boy's schooldays. Faithfully protective of his mother, Adolf found his father a boorish brute. There were stories of young Adolf having to support his drunken father home from late-night drinking houses and of having to watch his mother being verbally abused by her husband. There is some doubt about these tales but there is every indication that, while adopting many of his father's middle-class prejudices, Adolf nevertheless detested the man. And in return, Alois Hitler, the one man whose behaviour could have changed the boy's character, showed no interest in his dreaming son's high-flown aspirations.

Adolf was 14 when his father died and the family moved to Linz where Klara managed to keep herself and the two children on a government pension. It was here that Hitler decided that his future lay as an artist. The fact that his talent was slight did not dissuade him and in 1907, at the age of 18, he travelled to Vienna to pursue his calling.

It is here again that fact and fiction diverge. According to the Nazis' rewriting of the history books and Hitler's own romanticized version of events, Adolf struggled in poverty, living the life of a typical garret-dwelling artist while, in pavement cafés, he pursued a soul-deep search for a political philosophy that would lead him to his destiny.

What Hitler was doing in Vienna was somewhat less romantic. Having quarrelled fiercely with his mother, who wanted him to pursue his studies, the pampered Hitler persuaded her to give him a generous allowance. He then approached the Vienna Academy of Art which, after viewing his test drawings, firmly rejected his application to become a student. At his second attempt a year later, he was not even offered a test for entry. He had no greater luck at the Academy of Architecture, where he was told that he had not completed to an adequate level his studies back at Linz.

The vision of himself at this time of his life later presented by Hitler soon became even more ludicrously divorced from reality when just before Christmas 1908 his mother died. Adolf was genuinely distraught but her demise did mean that he could pursue his sojourn in the cloud-cuckoo-land he had created for himself with even greater ease. He was provided with a healthy inheritance, including the proceeds of the sale of Klara's house in Linz. On top of this, he claimed part of his mother's continued pension on the basis that he was still a full-time student – an act which was no less than fraud.

Hitler now spent his time lounging around cafés and joining in any and every discussion on politics and philosophy. There would also be visits to the opera, an occasional water-colour, the writing of a never-to-be-performed play. But most of the time his life was idle and unproductive as he used up the money that his late father had spent all his life amassing.

At this stage in his life, he still did not have a single close friend. And despite stories of an assault on an artist's model and of his contracting syphilis from a prostitute, there is no indication of an interest in women. The well-known syndrome of bullying father and cossetting mother may have produced an oedipus complex making it difficult for him to form such relationships.

What he was acquiring, however, was a fierce, fiery unremitting hatred of the Jewish people. In classic style, the self-blame that should have been brought to bear on his own failures was transferred to another 'guilty' party. The Jews were an easy target in the early years of the twentieth century as more and more of their peasant communities in Russia and eastern Europe were driven west by the pogroms being conducted against them. Hitler encountered these dispossessed people in his early, jobless days and, like others before and since, blamed the immigrant minority for taking work away from the 'more deserving' majority. Other traits that characterized his later life revealed themselves at this time . . . his inability to establish ordinary human relationships, his hatred of the establishment and his sudden, passionate, ranting outbursts. He was beginning to live in a fantasy world to evade the reality of his own failure.

In 1912 Hitler's inheritance ran out and he took a job on a building site, returning at night to a malodorous doss-house. For a few months his lifestyle really did match the accounts later given to an adoring nation. But not for long.

Adolf Hitler was later to relate how he made up his mind to live in the Fatherland, the heart of the German peoples, of whom the Austrians were no more than a provincial part. True, in 1913 he moved to Munich – but not for the reason he gave. The cross-border flit was to avoid his conscription into the

---

Only one member of Hitler's family survived to see his rise to power: his younger sister Paula. But there were those among his less immediate relatives with whom he remained close.

One of these was his half-sister Angela, the daughter of Adolf's father, Alois, by his second wife. In 1939 Hitler rented a country home at Berchtesgaden in the majestic Bavarian Alps and asked Angela to run it for him as housekeeper.

She agreed and moved in with her own daughter, Angelika, who was addressed by her Uncle Adolf as 'Geli'. He became deeply infatuated with her and clumsily pursued her, although – it is assumed – without his feelings being fully reciprocated. It will never be known to what degree and with what success Hitler pressed his suit . . . but Geli was to commit suicide under the pressure.

Adolf Hitler and Rudolph Hoess, outside Hitler's Bavarian retreat

Austrian Imperial Army. When the Munich police caught up with him and handed him over to the Austrian authorities, he sent a letter to Vienna pleading that he be excused military service. It was an unnecessary humiliation as he was shortly afterwards rejected on medical grounds.

In 1914, the events that led to World War One set off the slow time-bomb that exploded into World War Two. Through those first hostilities, Hitler, the 25-year-old failed artist, realized that he really could become a German hero. He decided that action, not words, would be his way.

Though still an Austrian citizen, he succeeded, through a personal petition to the Kaiser, in joining a Bavarian infantry regiment. Sent to the front, he was employed in what was considered the most dangerous job in the trenches – as a company runner, forever exposed to the machine-guns, shrapnel and sniper-fire from across no-man's-land. His valour was redoubtable and he soon gained a Mercury-like reputation as a man immune to enemy bullets. He was decorated twice, the second time with the Iron Cross, first class.

Corporal Hitler avoided bullets but he was unable to escape the greatest horror of that war, mustard gas. It was while he was recovering, half-blinded, in hospital that news of Germany's capitulation came through. Like most of the rank and file of the German army, Hitler believed the armistice to be an act of treason on the part of the politicians and blamed it on a communist and Jewish conspiracy. Still in the army, though certified disabled through gas poisoning, he returned to Munich and became card-carrying member number five of the newly formed German Workers Party. He attended meetings, became elected to its executive, quit the army and threw himself into the task of recruiting members. He changed the party's title to the National Socialist German Workers' Party – Nazis for short. He adopted the swastika armband and discovered his gift for oratory. He found he could manipulate the minds of the masses.

The machinations that led Hitler to final and supreme power are well documented. There was no steady rise to his eventual position as Führer; his political and brutal struggle was one of Machiavellian successes and sudden disappointments. During one reversal, when he was languishing in Landsberg Prison for his part in the bungled 1923 putsch to overthrow the Bavarian government, he wrote the major part of his book *Mein Kampf* (My Struggle) outlining his vision of the future of Germany. This and his other pronouncements gave a clear warning to the races that were to suffer most to avenge the insults, real or imagined, visited on the Fatherland at their hands.

It was a ranting, sometimes unreadable, diatribe against Jews, Slavs, communists, pacifists, gipsies, the mentally ill, the 'subversive' and the 'inferior'. Because of this doctrine of hate, not one life in Europe or throughout most of the world would remain unchanged. The dreaming artist who had no friends, whom no one loved, whose work was derided, who was shunned even by his own father, wrote:

'What we must fight for is to safeguard the existence and reproduction of our race and our people, the sustenance of our children and the purity of our blood, the freedom and independence of the Fatherland, so that our people may mature for the fulfilment of the mission allotted it by the Creator of the universe.'

It was a creed that was to destroy Germany, sentence eastern Europe to the Russian yoke, cause civilian suffering on a scale never before known, and leave many millions dead.

SS Bloodbath In The Ghettoes

When Hitler's evil genius dreamed up the genocide of the Jews as his 'Final Solution' for the Jewish 'problem', he could have wished for no more willing, obedient and ruthless lieutenants than Heinrich Himmler and Reinhard Heydrich. With cold-blooded relish, they became the most methodical mass murderers of all time, forever seeking 'improvements' in their machinery for massacring an entire race. And they logged their lethal efficiency with the pride of obsequious civil servants.

Himmler's big regret was having been too young to fight in World War One. The Munich schoolteacher's son, born in October 1900, idolized the veterans returning from the front and shared their conviction that their efforts had been foiled by traitors at home. Jews, Freemasons, Bolsheviks, Slavs and Poles were all scapegoats for the right-wing radicals whose para-military retribution squads flourished under the weak Weimar administration. The young Himmler was carried along with the anti-semitic tide, and saw nothing wrong in the motto that it was better to kill a few innocent people than let one guilty party escape.

He was far from the Nazi ideal of a strong blond Aryan superman. A weak stomach barred him from the traditional Bavarian drinking duels and an attack of paratyphoid in his teens had ruled out strenuous physical work. But his orderly mind and diligent clerical skills made him useful to the organizations springing up in the effort to build a new Germany. He became an invaluable administrator and an effective propagandist.

Himmler was also Hitler's most slavishly sycophantic follower. As the future Führer emerged from political infighting as the strongman of the right, Himmler praised him as the German Messiah, 'the greatest genius of all time.' But it was 1927 before Hitler rewarded 'Loyal Heinrich' with more than a mundane task. Worried that many men in his para-military *Sturmabteilung* (SA) were more loyal to their brigade leaders than to him, he set up the rival *Schutzstaffel* (SS) and made Himmler its deputy leader, with orders that his instructions were to be obeyed without question.

At first Himmler had only 280 men to command. But he was shrewd and patient. Slowly he compiled dossiers on enemies of Hitler, real or imagined, and built up his leader's trust by regularly telling him of assassination plots, actual or invented. After two years he became SS chief. But he was still bogged down in Bavaria while the action was switching to Berlin and the North. Then luck presented him the accomplice he needed to achieve his ambitions.

Reinhard Heydrich was also a teacher's son, born at Halle in the Teutoburg Forest in 1904. At the age of 18 he joined the navy. Tall, blond and handsome, he was an expert on the ski slopes and a fine fencer, and a delicate violinist who shared weekends of croquet and chamber music at the home of cultured Admiral Canaris. But at 26 he impregnated the daughter of an influential industrialist and refused to marry her, declaring that any woman who made love before wedlock was not a worthy wife. The navy gave him a dishonourable discharge for 'impropriety', but he was not jobless for long. In October 1931 Himmler appointed him to his personal staff. Heydrich's quick brain and imaginative cruelty, allied to Himmler's plodding thoroughness, produced a deadly double act that would become the most feared combination in Germany.

Hitler's election as Chancellor in January 1933 opened the door to unprecedented power for the SS. Within three months, Himmler set up the first concentration camp, at Dachau, and crammed it with Bavarian communists and other anti-Nazis. Heydrich formed the *Sicherheitsdienst* (SD), a counter-espionage corps, to tighten the net around potential opponents. Its targets included Admiral Canaris, rightly suspected by Heydrich of clandestine contact with the British as war approached. By 1934 Himmler controlled the police of almost every German state. That April he also took over the Gestapo, the secret police network founded by Göring. Heydrich was second-in-command. Two months later, the two organized their first massacre.

Hitler's distrust of the SA had been carefully nurtured by the SS chiefs. Now Himmler and Heydrich stepped up their warnings that an SA coup was imminent. As the damning revelations piled up, angry Hitler summoned SA leaders to a meeting at Bad Wiesse, Bavaria. They were marched off to jail and shot. SA supremo Ernst Röhm had been Himmler's patron 12 years earlier, arranging for him to join a para-military unit. Himmler had been his flag-bearer in the abortive Munich *putsch* of 1923. But now he had no qualms about ordering the death of his former leader. The Bad Wiesse killings were the signal for the SS to run amok throughout Germany, liquidating prominent politicians on lists meticulously prepared by Himmler and Heydrich. Hitler told the Reichstag that 79 died on the so-called 'Night of the Long Knives'. Most historians put the total of victims at over 500.

Hitler now declared the SS his executive arm, completely independent within the Nazi Party. And in May 1935, in an astonishing ruling, the Prussian High Court decreed that actions of the Gestapo could not be contested in court if the secret police were carrying out the will of the leadership. Himmler and Heydrich were now beyond all criticism except that of the Führer. The SS was the spearhead of Himmler's drive for racial purity. Applicants had to prove there had been no Jewish blood in their family since 1800. For officers the date was 1750. The SS leadership had to approve marriage between true Aryan types, who were rewarded with gifts for every child. SS men who preferred to remain single took advantage of the *Lebensborn* – a system which enabled them to father children by attractive, racially pure German girls. Most SS personnel were country peasants, for Himmler had a maniacal belief that towns were evil and controlled by Jews. 'Cowards are born in towns,' he once said. 'Heroes are born in the country.' But the job Himmler had in mind for his troops was hardly one for heroes.

In October 1938, 17,000 Polish Jews living in Germany were stripped of their citizenship by the Polish government. Days later, the SS told them that Germany did not want them either. Heydrich organised a massive round-up, and the Jews were taken by truck and train to the Polish border, and dumped in no-man's-land between the two frontiers. The 17-year-old son of one of the victims was in Paris when he heard of the savage treatment. He went to the German embassy, intent on shooting the ambassador. Instead he killed a minor envoy, and was instantly arrested.

Here was a chance Heydrich could not miss. He wrote to every German police chief warning that anti-Jewish demonstrators 'are to be expected' on the night of 9 November, and instructed the officers to inform local political organizers of the rules of the game. No German life or property was to be endangered. And 'synagogues may only be set on fire if there is no danger of fire spreading to adjoining properties.' He added: 'Houses of Jews may only be destroyed, not plundered.'

The 'spontaneous' demonstrations that followed left 35 people dead, nearly 180 synagogues destroyed and 7,500 businesses wrecked. Insurers estimated the damage at more than £3 million. *Kristallnacht* – so called for the amount of glass

Heinrich Himmler, head of the SS and the Gestapo

smashed – was a clear warning to the Jews of Europe. Those who were able to fled to more friendly countries. Those who could not faced far worse atrocities in the near future.

Before the Nazi invasion of Poland on 1 September, 1939, Hitler warned his army generals: 'Things will happen which will not be to your taste. But you should not interfere. Restrict yourself to your military duties.' It was an order Wehrmacht officers, ingrained with a traditional sense of fair play in war, were to find hard to obey. For it was in Poland, the Baltic states and Russia that the full horror of Hitler's policies, ruthlessly implemented by Himmler and Heydrich, was to be revealed.

The SS had paved the way for war by helping Hitler purge his High Command of waverers. Many generals felt the Führer's timetable of invasions too demanding and too dangerous. Some were unwise enough to ask for postponements. Himmler and Heydrich gave Hitler rigged evidence that

Reinhard Heydrich, the 'brains' behind the concentration camps

enabled him to dismiss and replace the 'faint hearts' with men more ready to follow orders blindly. Heydrich then devised a cunning way to check on the loyalty of all Nazi leaders. He set up an exclusive Berlin brothel, Madame Kitty's, and staffed it with the most attractive call-girls in the country. But each bedroom was wired with microphones, and all careless pillow talk was taped.

Heydrich was also the brains behind one of the SS's most lucrative money-spinning schemes. After the 1938 union with Austria – the SS prepared for it by assassinating Austrian Chancellor Engelbert Dollfuss – an Office of Jewish Emigration opened in Vienna. For extortionate sums, Jews could buy exit visas rather than risk death or incarceration in concentration camps. By the end of 1939, 60 per cent of Austrian Jews had sold everything to the SS and fled. A second Office in Prague after the occupation of Czechoslovakia proved equally profitable.

And it was Heydrich who came up with the propaganda ploy to 'justify' invasion of Poland. On the evening of 31 August, a German radio station in the border town of Gleiwitz was attacked by Polish soldiers. They soon withdrew, leaving the area strewn with Polish and German bodies. Next day, as Nazi tanks rolled into Poland, German newspapers justified the move as retaliation for provocation. But the Polish soldiers had been SS men in disguise. And the corpses were inmates from concentration camps, dumped from trucks during the charade.

Within days of the invasion, the Wehrmacht knew that Hitler's warnings had been no joke. SS men were discovered shooting 50 Jews in a synagogue and arrested. Himmler instantly ordered their release. The generals had been told men, women and children would be killed without mercy. At the time it seemed impossible. Now it appeared all too probable. They pleaded for the slaughter to be delayed until the army withdrew once conquest was complete. They feared the world would blame them for any atrocities. But Himmler and Heydrich refused to compromise on the Führer's orders. They began herding Jews behind the high walls and barbed wire of 55 city ghettoes. And Himmler started his duties as head of the Reich's Commissariat for the Strengthening of German Nationhood.

The people of the conquered North were to be evicted to provide land for Germans to farm. In Nazi parlance, this was 'population exchange'. But the euphemism hid a multitude of sins. Himmler spoke of killing 30 million Slavs during the Russian invasion. And of the first year in Poland he said: 'We had to drag away hundreds of thousands of people. We had to have the toughness to shoot thousands of leading Poles, otherwise revenge would have been taken on us later.'

Mass murder was soon second nature to the SS. Nearly 45,000 Jews died in the Polish ghettoes in 1941 alone after Himmler reduced rations to starvation level. On the Russian front, appalled Wehrmacht officers watched units of the military Waffen-SS send hundreds of bullet-riddled bodies tumbling into blood-soaked mass graves. At the war trials in Nuremburg, one SS leader estimated that his squads liquidated 90,000 men, women and children in that way in 12 months. Ironically, the practice decreased after Himmler witnessed the machine-gunning of 100 helpless captives at Minsk. The man who condemned millions with each stroke of his pen retched at the sight. In future, he ordered, victims were to be eliminated in mobile gas coaches.

Meanwhile, Heydrich had been appointed Reich Protector for Bohemia and Moravia. Within weeks he was known as the Butcher of Prague, as the Gestapo ruthlessly destroyed Czech resistance movements. The Czech premier was condemned to death after a bogus trial. But Czechoslovakian agents were the link between London and a vital spy in the Nazi hierarchy, code-named Franta. Heydrich was getting too close to unmasking him. British intelligence chiefs and the Czech government in exile agreed that Heydrich was too dangerous to live, and parachuted two assassins into the country.

Jan Kubis and Josef Gabcik set their ambush for a hairpin bend on the road that took Heydrich from his country villa to his office in Prague's Hradcany Palace. As the SS chief's Mercedes slowed to negotiate it on 27 May, 1942, Gabcik stepped into the road and raised his sten-gun. The trigger jammed. As the car halted, Kubis threw a grenade. Heydrich leapt from the car wielding his revolver. Then he staggered and fell. After a nine-day battle for life, he died in hospital. The SS and Gestapo made 10,000 arrests. But the most brutal reprisal was on the village of Lidice. It was burned to the ground, and all 1,300 male inhabitants were shot.

Himmler was left alone to carry through Hitler's ghastly plans for German supremacy.

'Final Solution' Of The Exterminators

S treet shootings, starvation in the ghettoes, gassing in rail coaches . . . this was how Jews, communists and other 'undesirables' died by the hundreds of thousands in the 1930s. But still this unprecedented genocide was not fast enough for the coldly efficient masters of the SS. So the concentration camps, established years before to house political prisoners, were turned into extermination camps. Gas chambers and cremation ovens were added. And, to meet demand, new 'purpose-built' camps were erected.

There were 16 extermination camps throughout the Reich but the busiest were in Poland, at Auschwitz and Treblinka. And their sinister efficiency was a tribute to the untiring efforts of Adolf Eichmann.

Born in the Rhineland in 1906 and brought up in Austria, Eichmann was an unemployed travelling salesman before joining the SS as a 'researcher', studying the 'evils' of Freemasonry. When Reinhard Heydrich opened the Offices Of Jewish Emigration, Eichmann found his niche. By streamlining the bureaucracy, he dealt with more applications than ever before – and thereby raked even more money into the SS coffers. He was so successful in Vienna and Prague that, when Poland was invaded, Eichmann was called to Berlin and appointed chief of the Reich Centre for Jewish Emigration.

But in August 1941 Heydrich told him that the days of milking escaping Jews was over. From now on, the policy was their total extermination.

Eichmann was put in charge of transporting Jews from all over Europe to the death camps. It was his responsibility to round them up and provide the special trains to take them to eternity. Nobody minded much if some died on the way in the over-crowded cattle trucks. Once a train returning to France from Auschwitz was found to contain the bodies of 25 children aged from two to four. Guards at the camp had not bothered to unload the tiny corpses.

Eichmann's hideous success became horrifyingly clear at the Nuremburg trials. Rudolf Hoess was commandant at Auschwitz from August 1941 to December 1943. Under cross-examination, he estimated that 2,500,000 men, women and children died in the gas chambers at that time, and a further 500,000 from starvation or disease. Jews were sent to him from Germany, Holland, France, Belgium, Hungary, Czechoslovakia and Greece as well as Poland. More than 400,000 Hungarian Jews were liquidated in the summer of 1944 alone, he said.

Then Hoess clinically drew macabre comparisons between his camp and Treblinka, which dealt mostly with inmates of the Warsaw Ghetto. 'They used monoxide gas, which I considered not particularly effective,' he said. 'I decided to use Zyklon-B, a crystallized prussic acid . . . A further improvement we introduced was that we built gas chambers which could take 2,000 people at once, while the ten chambers at Treblinka only had a capacity of 200 each.' The Zyklon-B chambers were Eichmann's brainchild, after a painstaking study of the alternatives. They speeded up the business of extermination, enabling 24,000 Jews a day to be eliminated and cremated. The air at Auschwitz was constantly full of the nauseating stench of burning bodies.

The SS exploited every aspect of genocide. Gold rings were ripped from the fingers of corpses, and gold teeth torn out. Bones were ground down for fertiliser. In 1942 all camp commandants received a stunning directive from SS economics chief Oswald Pohl: 'Human hair must be collected. Women's hair can be used in the manufacture of socks for U-boat personnel and for employees of the State railways . . . As to men's hair, it is only of use to us if it has a length of at least 20 millimetres.'

Crude medical experiments were carried out on captive 'guinea pigs' before execution. Sterilizations without anaesthetic, injections to test new drugs and bizarre tests of human resistance to pain, heat and cold were all encouraged. Some patients did not survive for the gas chambers. Yet in the midst of death, Himmler was concerned about life. He took particular interest in a herb garden just yards from the Auschwitz slaughter houses. He was anxious to help Germans revert to natural foods and remedies.

Utter disregard for human life coupled with concern for seeming trivialities seem the hallmarks of madmen. Yet the most guilty Nazis knew full well that what they were doing was evil and wrong. Eichmann, in particular, always took great care to cover his tracks. And as the Allied armies closed in on Germany, SS leaders destroyed their carefully compiled dossiers on who had died where. The world might not understand . . .

After July 1944, when Hitler survived a bomb attack by army chief Count Claus von Stauffenberg, Himmler's power was further boosted. In addition to his SS, police and Gestapo responsibilities, he was given command of the vast Reserve Army. Paranoid Hitler could no longer trust a military man with the job.

Himmler knew it was already too late to save Germany. The Allies were consolidating after their D-Day landings, and he was soon trying to save his skin by offering secret peace initiatives to them behind the Führer's back. But that did not stop his brutality. Field marshals and generals convicted of complicity in Stauffenberg's plot were hanged in agony on piano wire strung from butcher's hooks. Would-be deserters from the Reserve Army were warned to remember their families' well-being. They could see the corpses of deserters hanging from trees, with placards pinned to their chests which read: 'I left my unit without permission.'

Even after Hitler's suicide, as the Allies closed in on Berlin, Himmler believed he had a future as a German leader. Only after the Führer's successor, Grand Admiral Dönitz, dismissed him from all his posts as 'politically questionable' did he go to ground. With false papers in the name of Heinrich Hitzinger, and without his glasses and moustache, he tried to lose himself in the huge crowds of refugees and soldiers heading for home in the chaos of beaten Germany. But his civil service mentality gave him away. He joined a long queue shuffling across a narrow bridge at Meinstedt under the casual scrutiny of British soldiers – and was the only man in the line to volunteer his papers. He was instantly suspected and arrested, though not then recognized.

In prison he confessed his real identity and demanded to be taken to Field Marshal Montgomery. The request was declined. His captors had found one cyanide suicide pill in his clothing, but another was hidden in a dental cavity. As British intelligence men arrived to interrogate him, he chewed on it. On 26 May, 1945, his body was taken to the woods near Lüneburg and buried without ceremony in an unmarked grave. Only the burial detail of five knew where the second most sinister man in the Reich ended his days.

Adolf Eichmann was also arrested in May 1945 – but he was not recognised. When American soldiers stopped him, he was disguised as a Luftwaffe pilot, and the Allies were not too interested in ordinary airmen. Eichmann took advantage of the confusion to slip away and vanish.

It was 1957 before Israeli agents hunting the monster who supervised the murder of six million Jews received their first real lead to his whereabouts. The German secret service passed on a report from a former inmate of Dachau who had emigrated to Argentina after the war. A schoolmate of his daughter had been making violently anti-semitic statements. His name was Nikolaus Klement. And from the girl's description of the schoolboy's father, the man was convinced he was Eichmann.

The name Klement rang bells in Tel Aviv. Israeli agents had traced the escape routes of 30 high-ranking Nazis via Spain and Italy. One had headed for Latin America on refugee papers issued by Vatican authorities. His name was Ricardo Clementi. Now the Germans had passed on an address for the Klement family – 4261 Chacabuco Street, Olivos, Buenos Aires.

After delicate negotiations with the Argentinian government, Israeli agents were given permission to put Klement under surveillance. Long-range photographs were sent back to Tel Aviv and shown to death camp survivors, but none could positively identify the man as Eichmann, and the Israelis dared not make a move without irrefutable proof. Seizing the wrong man would make them an international laughing stock.

Adolf Eichmann at his trial in Jerusalem, 1961

Then a bunch of flowers gave the game away. Klement bought them on 21 March, 1960, as he left work at the Mercedes Benz factory in the Suarez suburb of Buenos Aires. He was still carrying them when he got off the bus outside his Olivos home. It was enough to finally convince the watchers. They knew 21 March was the Eichmanns' wedding anniversary.

Israeli intelligence chiefs gave the go-ahead for what was later described as one of the world's best-organized kidnappings. Simply killing Eichmann would not have been enough. Ace Nazi hunter Simon Wiesenthal had said, 'If you kill him, the world will never learn what he did. There must be an accounting, a record for history.' On 11 May, Klement was bundled into a car as he got off the bus and driven to a safe house. He was stripped and examined for distinguishing marks. The appendicitis scar, the scar above the left eyebrow, and the SS blood group tattooed under the left armpit all proved he was Eichmann.

He was drugged and driven to Buenos Aires airport, his captors posing as nurses and relatives. Forged papers declared him to be an Israeli car crash victim, fit enough to travel but not to be disturbed. He was waved through to an El-Al jet which had brought Israeli politicians to help celebrate the 150th anniversary of Argentina's independence. Within 24 hours the man the Jews hated most was in Tel Aviv.

His trial began on 12 December, 1961. The 15 charges included deporting and causing the deaths of millions of Jews, being party to the murder of thousands of gipsies, and being party to the murder of 91 children. Eichmann claimed that, by streamlining Jewish emigration in the early years of his SS career, he was only doing what Zionists proposed – sending Jews out of Europe to find a new homeland. He said he tried to organize Jewish settlements in Poland and even Madagascar, but was thwarted by others in the Nazi hierarchy. When told in 1941 that the Führer had ordered extermination of the Jews, 'I lost all joy in my work, all initiative, all interest.' Thereafter he simply did his duty and carried out orders.

The Israelis were scrupulous in ensuring a fair trial, and the full procedure of appeals. But at 11.53 pm on 31 May, 1962, Adolf Eichmann was hanged at Ramleh Prison, outside Tel Aviv. His defence cut no ice with a people who knew that, when Himmler tried to stop the activity of extermination camps as the end of the war loomed, Eichmann protested violently. They preferred to believe the words of Dieter Wisliceny, executed in Czechoslovakia for war crimes as one of Eichmann's lieutenants. 'He told me in 1944 that he did not care what happened if Germany lost the war,' Wisliceny said. 'He said he would leap into his grave laughing because the feeling that he had five million Jews on his conscience only filled his heart with gladness.'

Klaus Barbie, The Butcher of Lyons

Wartime occupied France was a place without sanctuary for those in fear of the Nazis. The German armies occupied the north. In the south the puppet government of Marshal Philippe Pétain did the Nazis' dirty work for them with an unseemly willingness. And everywhere the SS and the Gestapo ruled by terror.

In greatest fear were the Jews, who knew that unless their identities could be disguised they would end up in transports heading eastward to the terrible death camps like Auschwitz, Mauthausen and Ravensbruck. In the southern part of France, where arrest seemed less imminent, many persecuted families sent their children off to homes in the country, surreptitiously set up as refuges for Jewish infants.

France was dotted with such homes, and generally the local German commanders turned a blind eye to this slight lapse in the otherwise rigid pursuance of the Final Solution to eradicate the Jewish race. But one SS leader thought differently. He was Klaus Barbie, the 'Butcher of Lyons'.

Barbie discovered that a refuge for Jewish children had been established in a large drab, grey house in the centre of the village of Izieu, high in the hills close to France's border with Switzerland. Early in the morning of 6 April 1944 Barbie sent a number of trucks up the steep winding road to the village. Soldiers ordered the children and staff out of the home and into the trucks and they were driven away.

On the night of the raid on the children's home, Klaus Barbie sent a telex message to the Gestapo headquarters in Paris detailing his latest achievement. It read:

'In the early hours of this morning the Jewish children's home, Colonie Enfant, at Izieu was raided. In total 41 children aged from three to 13 were taken. Furthermore, the entire Jewish staff of 10, five of them females, were arrested. Cash and other assets were not taken. Transportation to Drancy follows tomorrow. – Barbie.'

Drancy was the 'holding camp' in a Paris suburb, from where two months later the children were transported by cattle train to the most notorious death camp of all, Auschwitz.

Not one of the children survived the gas chambers.

Today on the wall of the grey old house in Izieu there is a plaque bearing the names of all 41 children. It was put there after the war, to remind the people of the region of the blackest period in their history . . . Of the valour of the resistance fighters, of the shame of the collaborators who made the Nazis' task so easy, of the terror reign of the SS and Gestapo, and above all of the horrors perpetrated in the name of Hitler by one of his most ardent henchmen, Klaus Barbie.

Thirty-nine years after the capture of the innocents, memories of Barbie's infamy came flooding back. In February 1983 he was expelled from Bolivia and flown to France to stand trial for crimes against humanity. He was placed in a special wing of St Joseph's prison, Lyons, while prosecutors sifted through a mountain of evidence to build a damning case against him.

The files reveal a youthful fanaticism that helped build the 'perfect' Nazi. Klaus Barbie was born on 25 October 1913 at Bad Godesberg, near Bonn. He was illegitimate, though his parents later married. He joined the Hitler Youth and at 22 volunteered for the SS (*Schutzstaffell*, or Protection Squads) and he was posted to Dortmund to work in the SS's own elite security branch. There he met Regina Willms and they became engaged. Their marriage was conducted with full SS guard of honour in Berlin in 1940. Two years later, promoted to Oberstürmführer, he was sent to Lyons as head of the Gestapo in the city.

He quickly discovered that his task of 'cleansing' the region of Jews and subversives was far simpler than he had imagined. Collaborators and informers abounded, ready to turn on their own countrymen to win favour, reward and acclaim from their new masters.

Marshal Pétain's puppet government ensured that no more German troops than absolutely necessary were occupied controlling the country. Indeed, the French often enforced law and order more harshly than the Germans. They rounded up Jews for deportation even before being ordered to by the Nazis. Still more thorough in their new duties were French paramilitary units called the

---

Death's Head Units of the Waffen-SS fought alongside the regular German army in France – and sickened battle-hardened soldiers by their butchery. Near Bailleul in May 1940, British forces defending La Bassée canal ran up the white flag after fighting bravely though outnumbered. As they walked towards the enemy, arms above their heads, SS company commander Lieutenant Fritz Knoechlein ordered his men to mow them down. Dead and wounded were then dumped in a nearby farmyard. But one man survived, and testified when Knoechlein was brought to trial after the war.

Architect Albert Speer was Hitler's Minister for War Production from 1942 to 1944, and historians believe his success in stepping up the supply of tanks, planes and armaments delayed peace by two years. But Speer realized the folly of his slavish devotion to the Führer when he became aware of the atrocities Hitler condoned. He complained that Himmler's brutal SS killers were robbing him of 40,000 foreign workers a month in 1944, and even considered a nerve gas attack on Hitler's bunker to end the evil of the Third Reich. He was the only defendant to plead guilty at the Nuremburg war crimes trials, and served 20 years in Spandau Prison, Berlin, before release in 1966.

Milice who carried out many executions at their masters' behest.

Barbie's headquarters were in Lyons' Ecole Santé Militaire where he installed torture chambers equipped with whips, chains, spiked coshes, electric-shock boxes and welders' torches.

In an astonishing book about the Butcher of Lyons (entitled *Klaus Barbie – His Life And Career*), author John Beattie uncovered some of his horrifying practices.

Barbie installed twin baths at his headquarters, one filled with near-boiling water, the other with ice-cold water. Prisoners would be ducked in them alternately until they submitted.

Women were stripped, tied down and covered in raw meat. Then Barbie's German shepherd dogs would be set loose on them. Other tortures involved acid injections, burning by blow torch or being wired up for electric shock treatment.

Author John Beattie traced Barbie's old interpreter, Gottlieb Fuchs, who spoke of the interrogation of a young Jewish boy and girl who adamantly refused to divulge the whereabouts of the rest of their family. In a rage, Barbie picked them up one at a time and smashed their heads against the cell wall.

Fuchs revealed that on another occasion Barbie's over-abundance of zeal lost the Nazis a valuable prisoner. General de Gaulle's top resistance organizer in France, Jean Moulin, was betrayed and captured with eight comrades at a secret meeting in Lyons in June 1942. He was tortured until he passed out and was then dragged by his feet down several flights of stone stairs until his head was battered beyond recognition. He was sent to Germany for further interrogation but died of his injuries.

Barbie's greatest mistake, however, was employing Fuchs as his interpreter. He was a double agent, working for the allies and feeding information gleaned from Barbie to the Swiss secret service across the border.

Within three months of D-Day, the allies were on the outskirts of Lyons. By then, Barbie's sadistic excesses had reached extraordinary proportions. He would conduct torture sessions seated with a naked woman on his knee, getting a perverted pleasure out of his victims' agonies.

After a café popular with German officers was damaged he took revenge. Barbie ordered a Gestapo raid; five innocent young men were hauled out of the café and shot dead in the street.

He once called local gendarmes to his headquarters to clear out a cellar. They found it piled with the corpses of young men, all machine-gunned, their blood lying deep on the floor.

He took 110 men and women from Montluc prison and had them driven to the village of St Genis-Laval. There, in an upstairs room of an old fort, they were machine-gunned to death until their blood literally ran through the ceiling.

Allied troops entered Lyons on 3 September 1944, but by then Barbie had fled. The Butcher had ruled the city by fear for just 657 days. In that time he had organized the executions of more than 4,000 people, including many collaborators who could have borne witness to his crimes.

Barbie laid low at the end of the war, earning a living in Frankfurt from the black-market. He kept in close touch with other ex-SS men, whose tip-offs saved him from capture on at least one occasion. He thought his luck had run out in August 1946, however, when he was arrested by Americans and driven towards their base in the back of a Jeep. He leaped out of the vehicle which, in the ensuing confusion, crashed into a tree. Barbie was once again a free man.

> **Sadistic doctor Marcel Petiot cashed in on desperation in the chaos of Nazi-occupied Paris. He told rich Jews and others wishing to flee Gestapo persecution that he could smuggle them out to Spain and Cuba for a price. But when they arrived at his mansion in Rue Lesueur laden with money, jewellery, furs, gold and silver, he gave them a lethal injection, then watched through specially drilled peepholes as they died in a windowless triangular room. Once he was pulled in by the Gestapo, puzzled by the disappearance of Jews destined for the death camps. But he was freed, presumably because he convinced the Nazis he was saving them time and effort. Only after the Allies freed France was Petiot arrested. His meticulous records showed that 63 people perished in the triangular room – and that their payments made Petiot a millionaire. He died on the guillotine on 26 May 1946.**

John Beattie asserts that Barbie spent a period after the war working first for British Intelligence and then the Americans, feeding them information about undercover Communist groups. He lived under the name Klaus Altmann in the Bavarian town of Augsburg until 1951 when he, his wife Regina and their two children set sail for South America from the Italian port of Genoa.

They settled in the Bolivian capital, La Paz, where Barbie became a respected businessman, owner of a saw mill and friend of politicians. He was even able to travel abroad on business trips with impunity.

The good life for Klaus Barbie ended in the 'eighties. His son died in a hang-gliding accident and his wife died of cancer. Shortly afterwards a new, more liberal president, Siles Zuazo, came to power, vowing to rid his country of Nazis.

France's constant pressure on the Bolivians to extradite the Butcher bore fruit on 4 February 1983, when Barbie was arrested and told he was to be sent abroad. He was driven to La Paz airport and put on an unmarked transport plane. Barbie was unruffled – until the crew of the plane revealed themselves as French officers. The Butcher of Lyons was on his way to jail in the city where he had imprisoned, maimed and murdered so many innocent people.

The Ones That Got Away With Murder

On 15 May, 1984, a cryptic agency dispatch was sent to newspapers. It read: 'Nazi killer Walter Rauff, blamed for the deaths of thousands of Jews in the SS gas chambers during World War Two, has died of lung cancer in South America, aged 77'.

An Israeli official who had been fighting for Rauff's extradition said: 'God has closed the case'. But there was one man who wished that he, and not God, had been given a chance of concluding the case against Walter Rauff for crimes against humanity. That man was Nazi hunter Dr Simon Wiesenthal, who believed that Rauff was responsible for the deaths of 250,000 people.

Dr Wiesenthal had long found that his unflagging crusade to bring to justice the surviving Nazi murderers was being hampered by diplomatic stalling and a protective conspiracy on the part of the fast-decreasing band of Hitler's henchmen still on the run.

Josef
Mengele

Rauff, for instance, led a charmed life after the downfall of the Nazis. Like so many of his compatriots, he escaped to South America, ending up in Chile where he ran a meat-freezing plant – quite openly under his own name. On occasions, he even answered letters sent to him by inquisitive journalists.

It was rumoured that Rauff was involved in drug-smuggling in the Punta Arenas area and that at one time he was employed by the right-wing Chilean government as an anti-communist agent.

His hatred of communists is well documented. As commander of the units which provided gas trucks for concentration camps, Rauff was known as Hitler's 'ambulance man'. He had tens of thousands of left-wingers, intellectuals, mental defectives, Jews and others regarded as 'racially undesirable' herded into what looked like Red Cross ambulances. Gas was then released into the airtight trucks until all inside were dead.

Rauff was one of ten names on a list that Dr Wiesenthal produced at the time of the extradition of Klaus Barbie in 1983. The ten names were, he said in a statement from his Jewish Documentation Centre in Vienna, those of Nazis whom he most wished to be brought to justice to fulfill his 'compact with the dead'. The 76-year-old doctor said: 'If I could get all ten, it would be an achievement. But if I could get only Josef Mengele, I think my soul would be at peace'.

Mengele was the Auschwitz concentration camp doctor who carried out horrifying experiments on humans and was given the title 'Angel of Death' by the inmates. At one time, Wiesenthal believed he had traced Dr Mengele to a remote Mennonite religious community on the border of Bolivia and Paraguay. But as a registered refugee and a Paraguayan citizen, he was thought to be immune from extradition.

Dr Mengele's qualifications for his infamous work were impeccable. He was a medical graduate of both Munich and Frankfurt universities, and it was this expertise that won him the post of chief medical officer at Auschwitz where, according to Wiesenthal, he was directly responsible for the deaths of 400,000 people.

Mengele's main preoccupation at Auschwitz was his attempt to prove Hitler's theory of the Teutonic master race. He would alter the hair and eye colouring of human 'guinea pigs' by genetic manipulation. Most of his patients died, were crippled or were blinded.

After the war, Mengele fled to Italy and then Argentina. He eventually settled in Paraguay where he became a naturalized citizen in 1973. Despite the efforts of the Nazi hunters, he continued to enjoy the effective protection of the Paraguayan government, although staying constantly on the move to avoid kidnap or assassination attempts.

In 1979 his Nazi friends in the country put about a story that the evil doctor was dead. They even released a photograph of a man on a mortuary slab, showing a scar on the right arm where his SS tattoo had been removed. However, Wiesenthal discovered that the body was not Mengele's but that of SS Captain Eduardo Roschmann who sent 80,000 Jews to their deaths in Riga concentration camp.

But neither Rauff nor Mengele were at the top of Dr Wiesenthal's list of most-wanted Nazis. That dishonour went to a man who probably never pulled the trigger on any of his victims, who seldom visited a concentration camp and who may never have witnessed an execution. Heinrich Müller, head of the Gestapo, just gave the orders.

Müller was responsible for the deaths of millions of Jews, according to Wiesenthal. Yet the inveterate Nazi hunter never came close to catching him and often had to admit that he had lost the scent of his hated adversary.

The Gestapo chief was at first thought to have died in the ruins of Berlin. But when his grave was later opened it was found to contain three skulls – none of them Müller's. He is since reported to have been in the Soviet Union, Albania, Spain and Egypt.

Four of Adolf Eichmann's closest aides were on the list. Rolf Guenther was Eichmann's deputy, Anton Burger was his field officer and Josef Schwamberger and Alois Brunner his assistants.

At his trial Eichmann accused Guenther of taking a special initiative in the death camps. Willingly accepting the task of organizing the 'Final Solution', he was sent to Denmark to rid the country of all Jews. So successful was he that he later asked to advise on similar operations in Hungary and Greece, carrying with him confidential instructions to arrange sterilization, medical experiments and the gassing of concentration camp inmates.

Guenther disappeared after the war.

Anton Burger was deputy commander of Theresienstadt concentration camp on the German-Czech border. This 'model' camp was open to neutral visitors as a propaganda exercise to dispel stories of mass extermination. But, behind the scenes, horrific experiments including poisonings, sterilization and abortions were being carried out on inmates.

Burger was arrested after the war. In 1948 he escaped from prison and was never seen again.

Eichmann's third principal aide to escape justice was Alois Brunner, responsible for the deaths of thousands of Jews in Czechoslovakia, Greece and France, where he organized the transportation of Jews to the concentration camps.

After the war Brunner fled to Syria and settled in Damascus under the name of Dr Fisher.

Eichmann's other assistant, Josef Schwamberger, was commander of the Jewish ghetto at Przemysl, Poland, where he is reckoned to have organized the extermination of 15,000 people.

The SS took terrible revenge on a French village when one of its officers was shot by the Resistance in June 1944. All 642 inhabitants of Oradour-sur-Glane, near Limoges, were rounded up. The men were herded into the village square, while the women and more than 200 children were crammed into the village church. At a signal from the SS commander, the men were mown down by machine guns. Then the church was set alight. Children who stumbled out of the inferno were thrown back. Everyone burned alive.

At the war's end, Schwamberger was hidden by the Odessa escape group, then sent to Italy and finally Argentina. In 1973 West Germany requested his extradition and he was arrested – only to be released when extradition was refused due to pressure from local Nazis.

Three other concentration camp chiefs were on Dr Wiesenthal's list . . .

Friedrich Wartzog was commander of the Polish Lemberg-Janowska camp where he ordered the deaths of 40,000 people. Some of the most damning evidence against him was given by Eichmann at his trial when he spoke of a 'spring of blood gushing from the earth' where executed Jews had been buried.

Prisoners were starved for days then, if found unfit for work, shot. Camp guards were encouraged to use prisoners for target practice, aiming only for their extremities. Only after they had suffered appalling agonies did an executioner finish them off.

Wartzog, who presided over these horrors, escaped at the war's end and has never been heard of since.

Dr Aribert Heim was director of Mauthausen concentration camp in Austria where prisoners would end up after 'death marches' from other camps like Auschwitz. Survivors said that on these marches people were so hungry that they resorted to cannibalism.

In 1941 the Germans made their first mass arrests in Holland by rounding up 400 Amsterdam Jews and sending them to Mauthausen. According to the Red Cross, only one survived. When Allied troops reached Mauthausen, they discovered the camp's log book which revealed that 35,318 prisoners had died there.

After the war Heim vanished without trace.

Perhaps the most gruesomely intriguing name on Dr Wiesenthal's list is that of Richard Gluecks, Inspector-General of all concentration camps. Less is known about him than almost any other Nazi war criminal, except that he was a Gruppenführer and was head of administration at the Reich Security Head Office which was in overall control of the death camps. Dachau, Buchenwald and Ravensbruck were under his command, as was Auschwitz where more than a million people died.

Like the others, Gluecks vanished at the end of the war.

Despite Dr Wiesenthal's efforts, chances of tracing these missing monsters became slimmer with the years. As was the case with Walter Rauff, death rather than justice is most likely to catch up with the Nazis who got away with mass murder.

Chapter
Five

EVIL IS BIG BUSINESS

The cold, calculating villains of organized crime who kill and corrupt for cash.

'Love of money is the root of all evil.'
First Epistle of Paul to Timothy

The Mafia:
Network of Evil

The newspapers of the time reported it in typically racy, lurid terms, as befitted the occasion . . . 'Mafia Godfather Carmine Galante was shot dead over a plate of spaghetti in New York's Knickerbocker Avenue last night. The cigar-chewing 'boss of all bosses' was sipping chianti as two black limousines drew up outside Joe and Mary's Italian restaurant. Four neatly dressed men strolled calmly from the cars into the eating house and opened fire.

'Galante, who rubbed out all gangland opposition to become America's most powerful mobster since Lucky Luciano, tried to rise from his chair but was cut down in a hail of bullets. His bodyguard Nino Copolla also died instantly. The restaurant owner and his 17-year-old son were also wounded, and the boy died later in hospital.'

A typical gangland killing of the 1930s? A regular act of savagery from the days of prohibition, bootlegging, tommy guns and Al Capone? No, that report appeared in the London *Daily Express* of 13 July, 1979 – a full 50 years after the infamous St Valentine's Day Massacre which first brought the full horrors of mobster rule to the shocked attention of the world.

In those 50 years and more, organized crime has become bigger and bigger business. But, as evidenced by the shooting of Carmine Galante, its face is just as ugly. And, as ever, this sordid sub-culture and black economy is run by the same, sinister, all-encompassing organization . . .

They may call it 'The Mob', 'The Syndicate', or 'The National Network of Organized Crime'. Older and more sentimental members call it 'Cosa Nostra' – literally, 'Our Thing'. Most people, however, know it simply as The Mafia.

Its roots are as shadowy as its present-day operations. Even the derivation of the word Mafia is unknown. It may come from a Sicilian dialect term for bravado or possibly from an Arabic word, mehia, which means boastful. All that is certain about the Mafia's origins is that it was formed in the thirteenth century as a patriotic underground movement to resist Sicily's unwelcome rulers, the French. And on Easter Monday, 1282, these freedom fighters led a bloody massacre of the foreign invaders as the bells of the capital, Palermo, rang for vespers.

A similar society, the Camorra, was founded later in Naples. Over the centuries both flourished as secret brotherhoods vowed to protect the local populace from the despotic rulers of their regions. But, almost inevitably, both abused their autocratic powers to exploit and subjugate their people rather than protect them.

America's Italian immigrants took both societies across the Atlantic with them in the last century – and it was in the city slums of the U.S. that the two groups merged. An early boost to the fledgling 'families' in exile came in 1890 when 11 immigrant Mafiosi were lynched in New Orleans. The government paid $30,000 compensation to the widows and families of the hanged men. But the money was expropriated by the criminal brotherhood.

With further massive influxes of southern Italians around the turn of the century, the Mafia took its hold on immigrant ghettoes of the major cities. At first, they were a protection agency – at a price. Then their activities spread to illegal gambling, loan sharking, prostitution and finally drugs.

The introduction of Prohibition in 1920 was probably the biggest single factor in the success story of the Mafia. The market in bootleg liquor to help America

La Cosa Nostra	**literally translates as 'This Thing of Ours'**
Capo di Tutti Capi	**boss of bosses, the Godfather**
consigliore	**counsellor, a family leader's chief of staff**
caporegima	**leader of a family's bodyguard, muscle squad or hit men**
soldier	**rank-and-file strongarm man or hit man**
regime	**a group of such soldiers**
going to the matresses	**going to war with another group**
Moustache Pete	**derisive term for old-style, trigger-happy Mafia gangster**
making his bones	**murder carried out to prove loyalty**
omersa	**Mafia vow of silence**
bootleg	**illicit, as in bootleg booze – a boot being the ideal place to hide it**
hijack	**'Hi, Jack' was the greeting when a bootleg liquor truck was being held up**
speakeasy	**bar selling bootleg liquor – so-named because customers didn't speak of it too loudly**

drown its sorrows through the Depression was seemingly limitless. Every one of the several, fragmented, ill-organized Mafia families spread across the nation worked together to fulfil that demand . . . at enormous profits.

When Prohibition was repealed in 1933, the profits dried up and new forms of investment had to be found. Loan sharking, the numbers games, 'protection' rackets and prostitution kept the money rolling in. But new areas of exploitation were needed.

The growing drugs market was one of the most potentially lucrative and the Mafia built up French and Far Eastern Connections. Another was legal gambling, with the golden boom in casino cities like Las Vegas, Reno and more recently Atlantic City. The third was the labour movement.

Trade unions were cynically milked for the funds that could be misappropriated and, more importantly, for the 'muscle' they could lend to any extortion situation where a strike could prove costly.

Early this century, the trades unions were manipulated by New York Mafia boss Jacob 'Little Augie' Orgen, whose labour rackets earned him a huge fortune until his death at the hands of gunmen in 1927. Such Mafia notables as Albert Anastasia, Vito Genovese, Meyer Lansky and Lucky Luciano all worked for and learned from Orgen in those early days.

If Orgen's operation was the training ground for union corruption, Jimmy Hoffa's was the finishing school. No trade union has been infiltrated to a more infamous degree than the Teamsters Union. And Hoffa, the Teamsters boss, was its notorious leader.

Hoffa appointed a number of aides who had criminal records. Many were chosen for their expertise in terror and extortion. He also poured millions of dollars into his own pockets and then bought a Miami bank to look after the money. When the crusading Robert Kennedy became chairman of the Senate Rackets Committee, Hoffa became his prime and very personal target. He described Hoffa's leadership of the Teamsters as a 'conspiracy of evil.'

Because of the shady deals revealed by the committee, Hoffa was jailed in 1967, sentenced to serve 13 years for jury tampering and defrauding the union's pension fund of almost two million dollars. Four years later President Nixon issued a pardon and freed Hoffa on condition that he held no union office until 1980. That was not good enough for the still-ambitious Hoffa, who fought in the appeal court for the lifting of the ban.

Nixon's orders were not Hoffa's only problem. While in jail, he had appointed his long-time ally Frank Fitzsimmons as president of the union in his stead, on the firm understanding that he was no more than a 'caretaker' until the former boss was freed. But Fitzsimmons came to enjoy his taste of supreme power and had no intention of giving up the job. The union's Detroit headquarters became the battleground for the feud between Fitzsimmons and Hoffa.

James – 'Jimmy' – Hoffa

THE WORLD'S MOST EVIL MEN

Although Hoffa had many allies within the union ranks, observers believed that his outlandish style no longer suited the 'respectable' image required by the shadowy figures who wanted to get their hands on the union's purse strings. Jimmy Hoffa was an embarrassment.

Shortly after midday on 30 July, 1975, Hoffa got into his bullet-proof car to drive to a mysterious luncheon meeting. An anonymous telephone caller later told the police where they could find the car. It was empty. Jimmy Hoffa was never seen again.

Hoffa's crime in Mafia eyes was that he had broken the rule of silence. The low-profile approach ordered by the families since the last war was being endangered by the loud-mouthed union boss.

The Mafia always had a vow of silence. A new recruit would hold a scrap of burning paper in his hand while he recited the oath: 'This is the way I will burn if I betray the secrets of the family'. But beyond this natural secrecy lay a more productive lesson for the Mafia chiefs – that they could operate more effectively, more profitably and with less interference from law enforcement agencies if they did not advertise their shadowy organization's existence with public killings and scandals.

Salvatore Maranzano was first to see this. The first man to claim the title Il Capo di Tutti Capi – The Boss of All Bosses – Maranzano called a conference of the major families in 1931 and proposed a constitution that would end the bitter rivalries within their ranks. But he was ahead of his time. Within five months, he and 40 of his men were murdered.

Gang warfare on such an overt scale alerted Americans to the magnitude of the crime problem in their midst. It also alerted the Mafiosi themselves to the dangers of advertising their power in blood.

The man who ordered Maranzano's killing, Meyer Lansky, learned the lesson best of all. He took up his assassinated rival's theme of cooperation. Lansky and his contemporaries, 'Lucky' Luciano and Vito Genovese, made themselves millions by adopting the low-profile approach to organized crime.

If Maranzano first voiced the new Mafia philosophy and Lansky espoused it, then Carlo Gambino perfected it. Gambino was the inspiration for the character featured as Il Capo di Tutti Capi in the novel and film *The Godfather*. Under the iron rule of this frail old man, the Mafia flourished. By 1976, when Carlo Gambino died peacefully in his bed at the age of 73, the Mafia had apparently vanished into the woodwork.

But there was just one more act necessary to make the transformation complete. And that was the removal of ambitious, brutal, old-time mafioso Carmen Galante, who saw himself as the new Godfather following Carlo Gambino's death.

Galante's life story is almost the story of the American Mafia itself. His parents

> A tough, fresh 'super-cop' was called in by New York's
> police commissioner in 1911 and given a brief to close down
> the city's illegal gambling joints. The man entrusted with
> this task was Lieutenant Charles Becker – the most corrupt
> policeman on the force. Within months, Becker was running
> his own gambling club and taking a rake-off for 'protection'
> from several others.
>
> Becker's eventual downfall was his greed. He fell out with
> a partner over his share in a casino and had the man
> gunned down outside a restaurant. The gunmen were
> hauled in by a police team untainted by Becker's
> corruption. They all implicated the lieutenant in the crime.
> Becker went to the electric chair in 1915.

were Sicilian immigrants who settled in the tough East Harlem district of New York. He never weighed more than 10 stone 10 lbs but his usefulness with a gun quickly won him respect among mobsters as a 'good soldier'.

On Christmas Eve 1930 he was involved in a shoot-out in which a detective and a six-year-old girl were wounded. He was jailed for 15 years but was released after 12 and returned to the Mafia brotherhood.

Galante was a man of contradictions and surprises. He made a subordinate marry his mistress of 22 years so that her children by him would be legitimate. He was responsible for destroying thousands of lives with the drugs he made available. He ordered countless killings. Yet he loved kittens and was a keen gardener. He controlled prostitutes and a pornography empire but was furious if he heard a man use bad language in the presence of a woman.

Galante's specialized business interests were drug peddling to teenagers, organized prostitution, loan sharking and crooked gambling. He was instrumental in setting up the 'French Connection' to flood the East Coast of the USA with hard drugs from Marseilles.

He had always lived by the gun and it was this loud, loutish and overtly brutal approach that brought about his premature demise at the age of 69.

Believing that no one would dare stand in his way after the death of Carlo Gambino in 1976, Galante began to encroach on the territories of other Mafia families. He was thought to be trying to amass a $50 million personal fortune to pass on to his relatives. To this end, he risked warfare with other families and put his own gang at risk from the police and the FBI.

In January 1979 he was told to give up his leadership but he refused. The decision meant that he had signed his own death warrant.

That was why Galante's assassins, carrying scatter-guns and wearing ski masks, visited Joe and Mary's restaurant on 'unlucky' 13 July 1979 and killed him so quickly that his trademark cigar was still clenched at a jaunty angle in his mouth as he hit the floor. Then a .45 bullet was calmly fired into his left eye – a traditional Mafia calling card.

Less than a mile away from the bloody scene, when the news was brought that Galante was dead, 20 ruthless Mafia bosses raised their glasses in a macabre toast. They had gathered at another New York restaurant to discuss underworld strategy following the removal of their former associate.

A senior detective on the case said: 'It shows you how cold-blooded and businesslike these people are'.

The FBI first got wind of the underworld summit meeting when a Mafia chief from California flew into New York. They saw him rent a car and tailed him to a restaurant in a seedy Brooklyn side-street. To their astonishment, it was lined with gleaming black Cadillacs and Lincoln Continentals.

Among those at the meeting was Frank 'Funzi' Tieri, boss of New York's Genovese family. Galante had been pushing hard to take over the Genovese mob and police believed that Tieri, 74, had a part in the assassination. He certainly reaped the benefits . . . for he was shortly afterwards voted the new Godfather.

Tieri had done similar 'business' in the past. He had taken control of the Genovese family seven years earlier after the shooting of the former boss Tommy Eboli – a killing that police also put down to Tieri.

The style of Frank 'Funzi' Teiri was much more suited to the new image of Mafia business-men. Unlike Galante, he could keep his nose clean, his mouth shut and maintain a low profile. He had learned his trade as a lieutenant of the infamous Vito Genovese in the bloody 1950's gangster battles for control of the lucrative empire of Lucky Luciano after he was deported to Italy. But since then he had turned to the more orthodox range of Mafia rackets – with the exception of drugs, which he declined to touch.

The Mafia was called in by the CIA spy agency to assassinate Cuban leader Fidel Castro, according to a self-confessed Cosa Nostra gangster. Jimmy Fratianno claimed in 1981 that the plots suggested included poisoned cigars and a Capone-style machine-gun ambush. There was even a suggestion that he could be publicly humiliated by exposing him to powder that would make his beard fall out.

His legitimate businesses included a sportswear firm, a sales corporation and companies operating school bus services.

Shortly after coming to power, Tieri was described by New York Police Department as the biggest loan shark in the country. They said: 'He controls most of the gambling and loan sharking in the Bronx, East Harlem, Brooklyn and Queens. And he controls gambling in New Jersey, Florida, Puerto Rico, California and Las Vegas'.

Tieri's lifestyle suited the mob. He lived in a neat, three-storey house on a tree-lined street in a middle-class suburb. Every morning he would kiss his wife (her first name was, strangely, America) and leave for work wearing a conservative business suit. He would then be driven by his chauffeur one mile to the home of his mistress, Rita Perelli, from where he ran his operation.

He was said never to use the telephone and never to commit any note of his activities to paper. And he kept the loyalty of his criminal family not by threats but by a profit-sharing scheme. The Mafia's transformation from a gang of gunfighters to a band of multi-million-dollar businessmen was complete.

By the 1980s the Mafia had infiltrated almost every area of American business life. The U.S. Justice Department named the following industries as having the biggest Mafia involvement: music, video recording, haulage, garbage collection, clothes manufacturing, commercial banking, insurance, meat supply and processing, hotel and casino operation, funeral parlours, tobacco distribution, building construction, baking, cheese making, cooking oil wholesaling and pizza retailing.

Today an American may start his life wrapped in a Mafia nappy, listen to rock music from a Mafia record company, dine out on a Mafia steak, drive a car bought on a Mafia bank loan, holiday at a Mafia hotel, buy a house in a Mafia development and finally be buried by a Mafia funeral service.

Ralph Salerno, a leading US authority on organized crime, has said: 'If New York's five Mafia families conspired to paralyse the city, they could halt every car, taxi, bus, truck, train, ship and plane. They could also shut down literally thousands of wholesale and retail businesses. And they could close down services like laundering, dry cleaning, catering, garbage collection and dozens more.

It is no exaggeration to say that in New York every morsel of food you eat at home or in a restaurant, every item of clothing you wear and every journey you make is tainted by The Mob'.

The influence of the Mafia is now so all-pervasive that more than 2,000 past and potential witnesses to Mafia crimes are being guarded by the Witness Protection Program of the US government. The bill for keeping these 'squealers' safe from Mafia hit-men is currently $20 million a year.

At one time, the Mafia was estimated to have between 3,000 and 5,000 criminals working for it across the country. Nowadays this is a small proportion of the payroll, compared with the thousands of 'front men' and perfectly honest employees who look after The Mob's business interests. A *Time* magazine survey put profits from the Mafia's 10,000-plus legitimate firms at $12 billion a year – five times as high as the profits of America's largest industrial corporation, Exxon. Add to that the Mafia's profits from crime: an estimated $48 billion.

Such fabulous rewards come mainly from extortion. Companies are forced to buy Mafia products or shut down.

The US Justice Department believes that the cost of bribing a government meat inspector in New York is as low as $25 a day. For that, he will say that kangaroo- or horse-meat is '100 per cent beef'. It is then sold, not to pet food manufacturers for whom it was intended, but to market traders and restaurants. Similarly, Mafia vegetables often seem crisper – but only because they have been treated with a chemical that can cause cancer.

The Mob controls the supply of goods to companies by its union power. Mafia men stand for election as union officials – rival candidates being discouraged with baseball bats, knives or guns. A company which resists Mafia extortion can easily have its supplies cut off by a strike or union blacking. Few can afford to resist. Most, whether they know it or not, are contributing generously to the Mafia's billion-dollar profits.

Jacob Orgen and Jimmy Hoffa may be dead. But their methods are reaping fortunes of which even they never dared to dream.

The reach of the Mafia can sometimes be longer than the arm of the law. In 1984 a Mafia gang leader was incarcerated in a Spanish jail in Barcelona. Every evening, the prisoner, 34-year-old Raymond Vaccarizi, was visited by his wife, who stood in the street below his cell and called up to him. Vaccarizi would lean out of the window for a half-hour's chat.

The prison authorities knew of this innocent arrangement and allowed it to continue. Unfortunately, the Mafia also knew about it . . . and they were concerned that their colleague might begin to talk more than sweet nothings after his expected extradition to France to face murder, robbery and arms charges.

One sultry evening in July, the wife made her usual visit. Vaccarizi leaned out of the cell window – and two shots rang out from a high-powered rifle. The prisoner was hit in the heart and the face. He was dead before he hit the cell floor.

Meyer Lansky, 'Lucky' Luciano and Victor Genovese: The First Mob Magnates and Founders of Murder Incorporated

Meyer Lansky, born Maier Suchowjansky, was a respectable 16-year-old Polish immigrant who had settled with his family in New York and taken a job as an engineering apprentice. One day he passed a doorway on the city's lower East Side and saw a girl being assaulted. Lansky rushed to her rescue, fists flying.

In the ensuing fight, police were called and all three men were arrested and kept in prison 48 hours for brawling. They were 48 hours that changed Meyer Lansky's life.

The girl's two attackers were young thugs named Salvatore Lucania and Benjamin Siegel . . . who later preferred to be known as 'Lucky' Luciano and 'Bugsy' Siegel. Despite his attack on them, they took Lansky under their wings and Luciano, in particular, tutored him in a life of crime.

Luciano was five years older than Lansky. A Sicilian immigrant, he had been in and out of trouble ever since his arrival in New York at the age of ten. He was first arrested within hours of disembarking from his migrant ship – for stealing fruit from a handcart. His life of petty crime led him to jail for the first time in 1915 for drug peddling, and shortly after his release he met and teamed up with Meyer Lansky.

Luciano was at first Lansky's mentor and later his associate. They controlled a number of New York gangs, mainly Italian and Irish, involved in robbing homes, shops and warehouses.

But there was an area of crime in which Luciano specialized and which Lansky abhorred – prostitution. The Jew would have no part in the vice trade because, when a teenager, he had fallen desperately in love with a young prostitute – then found her one night in an alley with her throat cut, probably by her pimp.

Between 1918 and 1932 Lansky was arrested seven times on charges ranging from disorderly conduct to murder. But he had to be released on every one because of lack of witnesses.

Luciano was more successful in keeping out of police custody. He and Lansky had both become members of the gang of Jacob 'Little Augie' Orgen, who made a fortune from union and organized labour rackets. While Lansky concentrated on less violent crimes, Luciano became New York's most feared hit-man, whose favoured weapon was an ice pick. His reward was a string of Manhattan brothels which, by the mid-Twenties, were estimated to be earning him more than $1 million a year.

In 1920 came the ill-judged turn of events that was to turn Luciano, Lansky and others into multi-millionaires . . . Prohibition.

The soft-spoken Lansky paved the way for a new breed of tommy-gun wielding thugs to take over the illegal liquor business in the north and ensure the supply of whiskey to New York. Principal among these was Alfonso 'Al' Capone, who was fiercely loyal to Lanksy and Luciano.

In 1927, Luciano and Lansky were joined by a third ruthless killer and future crime czar, Vito Genovese. Born in Naples in 1897, Genovese had been a friend and neighbour of Luciano since the former's arrival in New York at the age of 16. A petty thief with only one arrest, for carrying a revolver, he too had graduated to organized crime while working 'under contract' to Jacob Orgen.

Despite the combined reputations of Lansky, Luciano and Genovese, the gang of three were still not the most powerful mobsters in New York. That accolade was being fought for between two old-style Mafia leaders, Salvatore Maranzano and Giuseppe Masseria, bitter rivals whose territorial battles had left as many as 60 of their 'soldiers' shot dead in a single year.

Both gang bosses tried to woo Luciano, Lansky and Genovese to their side, probably fearful of the trio's growing power. They refused. By way of persuasion, Maranzano lured Luciano to an empty garage where a dozen masked men lay in wait. Maranzano had him strung up by his thumbs from the rafters and punched and kicked until he lost consciousness. Luciano was repeatedly revived so that the torture could continue anew. Finally, Maranzano slashed him across the face with a knife. The wound required 55 stitches.

Not surprisingly, Luciano told his tormentor that he had changed his mind and was now happy to join the Maranzano mob. He was offered the Number Two job if he would first wipe out the Mafia rival, Masseria.

Luciano invited Masseria for a meal, pretending that he was now keen to join forces with him. They sealed the deal and toasted one another across the table at Scarpato's Restaurant, Coney Island. But when Luciano retired to the lavatory,

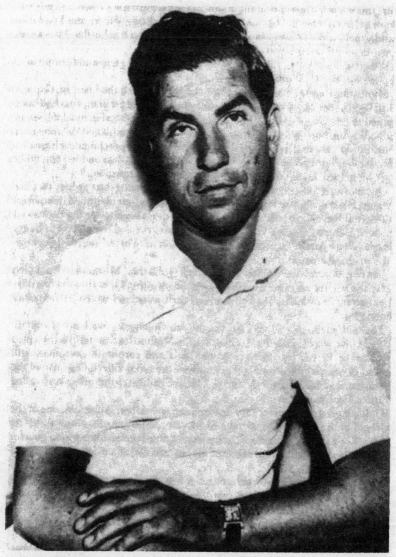

'Lucky' Luciano

four gunmen burst into the dining-room. Masseria must have known his fate the moment he saw them. They were Vito Genovese, Bugsy Siegel and two other Lansky men, Albert Anastasia and Joe Adonis. Masseria tried to flee but was cut down in a hail of 20 bullets.

Which now left only Maranzano between the Lansky gang and the pinnacle of power in the U.S. underworld.

Maranzano, aged 63, could have claimed to have been the first true Capo di Tutti Capi. After Masseria's death, this elegantly dressed Sicilian, who had once trained to be a priest, called a meeting of the New York families in a hall where the walls were hung with crucifixes and other religious emblems. He drew up a constitution of what he termed La Cosa Nostra and proclaimed himself its effective Godfather. Lansky and his associates had other ideas and in September 1931 he helped Luciano settle his old score with Maranzano.

One morning four 'taxmen' called at Maranzano's real estate agency on Park Avenue. His bodyguards kept their guns hidden as the four identified themselves as Internal Revenue Service investigators and demanded to see the books and the boss. Ushered in to his private office, the four revealed themselves as Bugsy Siegel, Albert Anastasia, Red Levine and Thomas 'Three Fingers' Lucchese. All four drew knives.

Just five months after pronouncing himself Godfather, Maranzano was killed – stabbed several times and then shot for good measure. Over the next few days about 40 more of Maranzano's team and their associates were systematically eliminated.

The mob magnates – Lansky, Luciano and Genovese – were now firmly in power. Gone were the old-style trigger-happy Mafioso leaders derisively termed 'Moustache Petes'. In came the accountants and corporate executives, still backed of course by the ultimate persuaders, the hired killers. One arm of the operation was labelled the National Crime Syndicate, the other was called Murder Incorporated.

Helping set up this mercenary death squad was Albert Anastasia, one of the killers of both Giuseppe Masseria and Salvatore Maranzano. Known as New York's 'Lord High Executioner', he meted out murder on contract for a quarter of a century, becoming head of one of the city's five Mafia clans, the Mangano family.

His growing power finally became too much of a threat to his principal New York rivals, including Genovese, two of whose henchmen followed Anastasia to his barber's shop one morning in 1957. As a warm towel was draped over his face, he did not see the two gunmen position themselves behind the barber's chair. Then they calmly blew his head off.

It was a scene of which Meyer Lansky probably disapproved. He was the man who, more than any other, welded previously fiery-tempered Mafia families scattered around the nation into a 'federal' unit. Autonomous in their own area, they nevertheless came together to seek agreement on major policy issues. Above all, they maintained a low profile; the days of street warfare were over for good.

In their book *Meyer Lansky: Mogul of The Mob*, authors Dennis Elsenburg, Uri Dan and Ell Landau quote their subject as saying: 'Crime moved out of the small ghettoes and became nationwide.'

An associate, Joseph Doc Stacher, says of Lansky and Luciano: 'They were an unbeatable team. If they had become President and Vice-President of the United States, they would have run the place far better than the idiot politicians'.

Lansky was certainly a wily politician within the crime syndicate. Despite being a Jew in a predominantly Italian society, he became trusted as an 'independent' Mafia mogul, more concerned with money-making than internal power struggles. His value to his associates was his ability secretly to invest the mob's ill-gotten gains in respectable industries and in the gambling casinos of Las Vegas, Cuba and the Bahamas.

Lansky made millions for the Mafia and an estimated personal fortune of $300 million. Seemingly safe from criminal charges, his main concern in his old age was the taxman. He even left the United States on one occasion – to live in an hotel he owned in Israel, much to the displeasure of the Israeli government. But he returned to America to spend his last years in the land that had made his organization fabulously rich. As he himself described it: 'We're bigger than U.S. Steel.'

Like Lansky, his old friend Vito Genovese also seemed to lead a charmed life. Before World War Two he salted an estimated $2 million into secret Swiss bank accounts and fled to Naples. A vociferous supporter of Mussolini (he contributed generously to fascist funds), he switched sides hurriedly when the tide of war changed and offered his services to the occupying American forces.

Genovese pinpointed black-market operations in post-war Italy and helped close them down. He then resurrected them with one of his own 'front men' in charge. His Italian Connection came to an end when he was extradited back to the U.S. to face an old murder charge. It failed to stick after the principal witness was shot dead, and Genovese returned to his New York stamping ground.

His former lieutenant, Albert Anastasia, having been eliminated along with other rivals, Genovese savoured the fruits of power for only a year before being jailed in 1959 for drug smuggling. He had served ten years of a 15-year sentence when he was found dead from a heart attack.

The third of the triumvirate, 'Lucky' Luciano, did not always live up to his name. He must have thought his luck had finally run out when he was sent to jail to serve a 30- to 50-year sentence for 90 vice offences. Then, in November 1942, he got a visit from his old friend Lansky.

'Lucky' Luciano – dead of
a heart attack

All the pomp of an
Italian funeral for
Luciano

Lansky told him that he had just done a deal with U.S. naval intelligence who were concerned that information about Allied convoys was being leaked by pro-Mussolini Italian immigrants working on the New York waterfront. The fears seemed to have been confirmed by the burning of the French liner *Normandie* at its moorings in New York. So many fires had broken out at the same time that the U.S. Navy, which was due to use the ship to carry troops and supplies to Europe, was certain Italian saboteurs were to blame.

The deal Lansky had struck was that the Mafia, under Luciano's direction from his prison cell, would work in conjunction with a special unit of naval intelligence to flush out Italian spies and saboteurs. In return, Luciano would win his freedom after the war. He readily agreed.

At least one other Mafia man was immediately freed from jail at Luciano's request. He was Johnny 'Cockeye' Dunn who was responsible for the no-questions-asked removal of two suspected German spies. Apart from keeping peace on the waterfront, the team was also credited with pinpointing an enemy submarine off Long Island. Four German spies were captured as they came ashore from it and, under interrogation, revealed a North American network of Nazi agents.

Before the Allies invaded Sicily, Luciano sent word to local Mafia leaders that all help should be given to the Americans. Four Italian-speaking U.S. naval intelligence officers joined up with the Sicilian Mafia and successfully raided German and Italian bases for secret defence blueprints. Later, in Rome, the Mafia foiled an assassination attempt against Britain's General Sir Harold Alexander and, as a footnote to history, seized Mussolini's entire personal archives.

The American authorities kept their part of the bargain and, in 1945, within a few months of the war in Europe ending, Luciano was freed from jail but was told he was to be deported to Italy.

His comrade in crime, Lansky, was there to bid him farewell – after first giving him $500,000 to help him start his new life. He lived in Rome for a while but grew restless for the 'big time' and shortly afterwards turned up in Cuba. Luciano issued an invitation to leaders of U.S. organized crime to meet him in Havana. But before his empire-building in exile could begin, U.S. pressure on Cuba's President Batista forced his dispatch back to Italy.

On 26 January 1962, Luciano went to Naples airport to await the arrival of an American producer who was considering filming the Mafia chief's life. But Luciano's luck had at last run out. He dropped dead of a heart-attack in the airport lounge.

Extraordinarily, after a lifetime of corruption, torture and violent death, America's three moguls of organized crime – Meyer Lansky, Vito Genovese and 'Lucky' Luciano – all died of natural causes.

Al Capone and the Chicago Mob

A l Capone, 'Legs' Diamond, 'Machine Gun' McGurn, 'Bugs' Morgan, 'Dutch' Schultz . . . they are names that have gone down in America's violent folklore. In books, films and TV series, they have been dramatized, often glamorized and sometimes turned into heroes.

But the stark truth about these gangsters of the Twenties is far from glamorous. They lived tawdry lives and, in the main, died violently. A principal exception to that rule was the most infamous gangster of the age, Al Capone himself. He died peacefully but deranged, from syphilis.

Alphonse Capone, born in New York in 1899, was one of nine children of Italian immigrants. A street-fighting thug, he gained his lifelong nickname, Scarface, while working as a bouncer for a Brooklyn brothel.

This small-time hoodlum could have faded into criminal obscurity but for a strange quirk of fate. Capone urgently needed to get out of New York where he was wanted for questioning over the death of a policeman. He contacted Chicago gangster Johnny Torrio, who remembered the young thug from his own street-fighting days in New York and immediately invited him to join his team.

Capone arrived in Chicago in 1919 to find Torrio working for old-time mafioso tycoon 'Diamond' Jim Colosimo. This strange character, so called because of his penchant for jewellery, ran just about every brothel in the city, as well as various labour rackets. Torrio, a cousin of Colosimo's wife, was his principal lieutenant, sworn to guard his boss with his life. It was no informal oath of allegiance: Torrio, like the rest of Colosimo's hired army, had to swear fidelity to their leader on his family Bible.

Colosimo, with his second wife, singer Dale Winter, held court nightly at his retaurant on South Wabash Avenue, surrounded by unsavoury 'heavies' as well as by politicians and entertainers. With the introduction of Prohibition, Torrio tried to persuade Colosimo to expand his business to take advantage of the new market in illicit liquor. The older man refused.

On 11 May 1920 Torrio asked Colosimo if he would be at his restaurant at a particular time to sign for a delivery of whiskey. As Colosimo waited in the empty restaurant, Al Capone stepped out of a phone booth and, acting on Torrio's orders, shot Colosimo dead then took his wallet to make the killing look like a robbery. An hour later he was back at Torrio's side ready to shed tears and swear vengeance upon receiving the news of their boss's death. Torrio and Capone took over the Colosimo crime empire, added bootleg liquor to it and began to amass a fortune.

In the early Twenties, Chicago's underworld was split between the Torrio-Capone mafia axis and the mainly Irish gang of Charles Dion 'Deanie' O'Bannion.

O'Bannion was perhaps the most remarkable of all the hoodlums of his day. Angelically baby-faced, an ex-choirboy once destined for the priesthood, O'Bannion fell into crime almost by accident. He worked for William Randolph Hearst's newspaper the *Herald Examiner* while moonlighting at night as a singing waiter in a club which was the haunt of criminals. It was these villains who introduced O'Bannion to the richer pickings on the wrong side of the law.

'Deanie' O'Bannion was a criminal with a great sense of humour and a considerable style. Unlike his Italian rivals in neighbouring parts of Chicago, the Irishman would not allow brothels in his area, refused to sell any but the finest liquor from his chain of breweries and distilleries and ran his business from the grandest flower shop in Chicago, catering for the city's high society weddings and funerals.

O'Bannion laughed at the crudities of the Italian overlords. But in 1924 he cracked his most costly joke at their expense – he sold Johnny Torrio a half-share in a brewery for half a million dollars. He did not tell Torrio that he had received a tip-off that the brewery was about to be raided. The police swoop left O'Bannion in the clear. But Torrio, who had been meticulous in his efforts to avoid any police record, was booked. Furious, he sought instant revenge.

On 10 November 1924 three men called at O'Bannion's flower shop to buy a wreath. The baby-faced proprietor did not realize who the wreath was for. The men, Alberto Anselmi, John Scalise and Frank Yale, were killers hired by Torrio and Capone. Yale held O'Bannion down while the others shot him dead.

O'Bannion's funeral was the grandest Chicago had seen. The rich and the famous mingled with murderers, thieves and bootleggers to pay their respects to the supplier of the best booze in town. 'Deanie' would have been proud of the floral tributes. The wreaths alone were worth $50,000.

O'Bannion's funeral was the first of many over the next few years. Torrio and Capone had started a gangland war that they could not finish. Before the Twenties were out, more than 1,000 bodies were to end up on the streets of Chicago in a string of bloody reprisal raids. And the first raid was against Torrio himself.

O'Bannion's loyal henchmen, Hymie Weiss and George 'Bugs' Moran, ambushed Torrio as he left home. They gunned him down and left him for dead. But he survived, was himself arrested over the illicit brewery raid and was jailed for nine months.

The following year, shaken by events in Chicago and doubtless concerned that Capone's own ambitions may not have included him in future plans, Torrio 'retired' at the age of 43. Pursued first out of Chicago and then Florida with Weiss and Moran on his tail, he settled in Naples until he felt safe enough to return to New York in 1928. He worked behind the scenes for Meyer Lansky until 1939 when he was jailed for two years for non-payment of taxes. He died of a heart attack in 1967.

Torrio's flight from Chicago in 1925 meant that Capone was now lord of the richest territory in the underworld. Torrio had taken with him a 'golden handshake' estimated at more than $50 million but that still left a thriving empire in prostitution, bootlegging, gambling and extortion which Capone ran in a grandiose manner.

But Capone's showmanship almost cost him his life. He controlled his $5 million-a-year business from the Hawthorn Hotel in the wholly corrupt Chicago suburb of Cicero. In September 1926, 'Bugs' Moran and Hymie Weiss, having failed to settle their score with Johnny Torrio, attempted to wipe out his successor. They drove in a motorcade past the Hawthorn Hotel and sprayed it with hundreds of rounds of submachine-gun fire.

Astonishingly, Capone was unhurt. But his pride was ruffled. He had Weiss gunned down in the street at the first opportunity. Moran, however, proved more elusive. Capone had to wait another two years to attempt revenge on him in the infamous St Valentine's Day Massacre.

But first there were other items of business Al Capone had to clear up. The Genna family, a gang led by four Sicilian brothers, were Capone's main suppliers of rot-gut whiskey and gin. The liquor was cheap, foul and dangerous. Produced at 40 cents a gallon, it was sold to Capone at two dollars and passed on to drinking dens at six dollars. Many of the customers who drank it were blinded and some even died.

Capone fell out with the influential Gennas, not over the quality of their whiskey but because they were vying with him for power and influence among the Italian criminal fraternity. One by one, the Gennas and their gang were gunned down until the remaining members of the family fled, some to Sicily, some to other parts of the United States.

Another victim of this war was a crook-turned-politician called Joseph Esposito. Nicknamed 'Diamond Joe' because of the $50,000 worth of gems studded into his belt, Esposito was Committeeman for Chicago's notorious 19th Ward where he controlled police, politicians and union leaders – as well as running a string of distilleries for Capone. Caught up in the Capone-Genna war, he was gunned down in the street by unknown assailants in 1928.

Another supplier of bootleg liquor to Capone was policeman's son Roger Touhy. Capone wanted him out of the way so that he could take over his

Al Capone, the head of the Chicago mob

business. First he kidnapped Touhy's partner Matt Kilb, held him to ransom and, when Touhy paid the $50,000 asked, shot him anyway. When Touhy still held out against Capone's demands, he was framed for a kidnapping and sentenced to 199 years imprisonment. He served nine years before escaping and proving his innocence. Within days of finally winning his freedom, he was shot dead in a Chicago street.

Capone's blood-letting stretched to New York where Frank Yale, one of the men who had been hired to assassinate Dion O'Bannion, was thought by Capone to have cheated him on liquor deals. In 1927 Yale was lured to a fake appointment in Brooklyn where he was machine-gunned to death from a passing car.

But Capone's most longed-for victim was still 'Bugs' Moran, the O'Bannion aide who had tried to kill Johnny Torrio in that first round of revenge shootings back in 1924. For the task, Capone employed the most deadly hit-man of them all, 'Machine Gun' Jack McGurn.

McGurn's real name was James Vincenzo de Mora, born in Chicago's Little Italy in 1904. A professional boxer, his connection with Capone was through his father who worked in one of the Genna family's distilleries. When his father was killed by Genna lieutenants, McGurn joined Capone as a hired gunman. His reputation was fearsome. His trademark was a nickel coin pressed into the palm of the victim's hand. By 1929 at least 15 bodies had been found with McGurn's 'calling card'. His fees for such contract killings were high and allowed him to buy shares in a number of Chicago clubs. He married one of his club's showgirls. In 1927 when a comedian, Joe E. Lewis, refused to work at one of the clubs, he was beaten up by McGurn and had his vocal cords cut.

On 14 February, St Valentine's Day, 1929, Jack McGurn was ordered by Capone to rid him finally of his arch enemy Moran, who had recently been publicly bad-mouthing 'Alphonse The Beast'.

Moran's gang were expecting a liquor delivery that day at a garage at 2122 North Clark Street. Seven of Moran's men were inside the garage when three 'policemen' burst in carrying machine guns. They ordered the bootleggers to line up with their faces against a wall and mowed them down in a hail of bullets. The 'policemen' were Capone's men – one of them McGurn.

'Bugs' Moran was not among the victims, however. He turned up late for the liquor delivery and fled when he witnessed the supposed police raid.

The St Valentine's Day Massacre, as the newspapers labelled it, at last brought the measure of public outrage that forced politicians and police – even the crooked ones – to act to put to curb the violence on Chicago's streets. 'Machine Gun' McGurn, whose role in the slaughter was well known, was no longer wanted as a hired gun by Capone. He was simply not good news to have around.

McGurn believed he could hang up his gun and make a good enough living out of his clubs. But the Depression put paid to that. Hard-up but still flashily dressed in three-piece suit, white spats and highly polished shoes, McGurn was walking down a quiet street on 14 February 1936, seven years to the day after the St Valentine's Day massacre, when two gunmen approached and blasted him. When police arrived at the scene they found a nickel pressed into his palm and a cut-out valentine heart by his side.

McGurn's killers were never traced but it is believed that one of them was

'Bugs' Moran. O'Bannion's loyal Irish lieutenant had disappeared from public view after his men were massacred in the garage on North Clark Street. After the war he turned up again in Ohio where he was arrested for bank robbery. He died in Leavenworth Jail in 1957.

'Bugs' Moran had survived almost every other member of the Chicago gangs of the bloody Twenties. And he had outlived by ten years the most notorious of them all, Al Capone.

After forcing Moran to flee for his life following the 1929 massacre, Capone had taken over control of the entire criminal network of the city of Chicago. But his victory was short-lived . . .

In 1931, what the police failed to achieve in a decade the taxman achieved in a few weeks. On 24 October after a speedy trial, Al Capone was found guilty of tax evasion. He was fined $50,000 and ordered to pay $30,000 costs – chickenfeed to him. But he was also sentenced to a jail term of 11 years. It broke him.

When he was released in 1939, he was already sliding into insanity from sylphilis. He hid himself away on his Florida estate, shunned by his neighbours and by the new breed of Mafia leaders who wanted nothing to do with the loud-mouthed, brutish scar-faced relic of a bloody past best forgotten. Al Capone died alone in 1947.

'Bugsy' Siegel:
the Hollywood Gangster

It wasn't a pretty sight when they found the bullet-riddled body of 'Bugsy' Siegel. And that wouldn't have pleased the man who had the reputation of being the Casanova of the Mafia.

Siegel was gunned down as he sat on a sofa in his girlfriend's house. A final bullet was fired into his left eye – the coup de grâce that was the Mafia's 'calling card'. Tall, good-looking, well-groomed and smartly dressed, 'Bugsy' would have abhorred such messy methods. He would have preferred a more dignified death.

Benjamin Siegel, born in Brooklyn in 1906, had always been convinced that he was headed for the big-time. But he started small – stealing cars, driving trucks of illicit liquor and guarding illegal gambling houses.

It was when, in his teens, he teamed up with the much lighter, more calculating Meyer Lansky that his fortunes changed. He called his group of small-time criminals the Bug And Meyer Gang and, by the mid-thirties, through his loyalty to Lansky, became a trusted associate of the top racketeers on America's east coast.

In 1935 Siegel was indicted in New York for shooting a rival gang member, one of 'Dutch' Schultz's men. Lansky decided his friend must leave town, so he set him up with a £500,000 investment and sent him to California to team up with local mobster Jack Dragna.

Life in the Californian sunshine was paradise to the impetuous Siegel. Soon after his arrival, he was seducing one starlet after another. A millionairess divorcée, Countess Dorothy Di Frasso, took him under her wing. She travelled with him to Italy, where they met Mussolini. Siegel and the countess launched an expedition to seek Spanish treasure on the Cocos Islands – but after blasting an island with dynamite they returned empty-handed.

In Hollywood, Siegel was on first-names terms with stars like Jean Harlow, Gary Cooper and Clark Gable. But his greatest friend was actor George Raft, famous for his film gangster roles. He and Raft went on a gambling spree on the French Riviera – until Siegel got a cable from Lansky ordering him to 'stop acting like a movie star' and get back to work.

But it was not all play for Siegel. He and Dragna operated a string of illegal Los Angeles gambling houses and offshore casino ships, as well as drug smuggling operations and even a wire service. The money rolled in throughout World War Two, and in 1945 Lansky helped organize for him a $3 million loan to build a casino hotel in Las Vegas – forerunner of the many monolithic emporia that were to make the desert town into a mobsters' Mecca.

Siegel matched $3 million of his own money with the crime syndicate's stake and started building The Flamingo, a name chosen by his girlfriend of the moment, Virginia Hill. But, during construction, large sums of money were salted away into Swiss bank accounts, some of them said to be in the name of Miss Hill.

In late 1946 many of America's leading gangsters, including Siegel's east-coast associates Lansky, 'Lucky' Luciano and Vito Genovese, met at a hotel in Havana to spend a holiday, to attend a Frank Sinatra concert and to discuss the problem of the errant 'Bugsy'. Lansky, who considered Siegel a blood-brother, argued the case for his friend. But he was over-ruled. It was decided that Siegel be asked to repay with interest all of the syndicate investment as soon as the hotel was open. If he failed, then . . .

'Bugsy' Siegel's luck was out. He opened the Flamingo Hotel on 26 December 1946 with Virginia Hill at his side. The event was a disaster. Bad weather grounded planes in Los Angeles and few of the invited famous faces turned up. The razmatazz of the grand opening fell flat, publicity was scant, interest dimmed and the punters stayed away. For two weeks Siegel struggled on. The casino alone lost more than $100,000 before he ordered it closed.

The demands for repayment of the Mob's loan became more and more insistent. But Siegel's money was largely tied up in the hotel, and the sums siphoned off to Switzerland did not add up to what the syndicate demanded. Siegel thought he could bluff his way out of the crisis, under the protection of his old friend Lansky.

Lansky, however, had reluctantly washed his hands of him. 'Lucky' Luciano, who had known 'Bugsy' even longer than Lansky, accepted the task of arranging his execution. He asked for the money one last time. Siegel refused.

On the night of 20 June 1947 Siegel was sitting on the sofa in the living room of Virginia Hill's rented house in North Linden Drive, Los Angeles, when an unknown killer or killers fired five bullets at him.

His rich and famous friends steered well clear of Benjamin 'Bugsy' Siegel once his fame had turned to notoriety. There were only five mourners at his funeral.

'Legs' Diamond and 'Dutch' Schultz: the New York Bootleggers

Jack 'Legs' Diamond and 'Dutch' Schultz were two hoodlums who brought an unwelcome taste of Chicago-style gang warfare to the heart of New York. Both thought themselves smart, stylish, wise guys. Both changed their names to glamorize their image. Both died by the gun – cold-bloodedly executed by their own kind.

Jack 'Legs' Diamond was born John Noland in 1896 in Philadelphia. Moving to New York in his teens, he followed the classic criminal pattern of street-fighting, theft and 'protection'. In the early Twenties he worked for racketeer Jacob 'Little Augie' Orgen, carrying out inter-gang killings at his behest.

The money he earned from Orgen was spent on a lavish lifestyle. Although married, he supported a string of mistresses and earned the nickname 'Legs' from a brief spell as a professional dancer. He bought shares in a number of nightclubs and eventually purchased a top nightspot of his own.

Everything had come easily to Diamond. But in 1927 'Little Augie' Orgen was assassinated and Diamond wounded. He backed out of the impending inter-gang warfare and instead set himself up in the bootlegging business. He went into partnership with an already established bootlegger calling himself 'Dutch' Schultz.

Schultz's real name was Arthur Fliegenheimer, born in New York in 1902 and following the same criminal path as 'Legs' Diamond. Perhaps they were too much alike – for as partners, Diamond and Schultz made great adversaries. They seemed incapable of keeping their bargains with one another.

When Diamond fled the scene after killing a drunk at his club, Schultz took over much of his business. Diamond retaliated by hijacking Schultz's liquor trucks.

Diamond had felt safe in his activities as long as he had the patronage of his new gangland protector, New York gaming club and brothel owner Arnold Rothstein. But just as he had lost a friend in the assassinated Orgen, so he did again in 1928 when Rothstein was found dying in a gambling club after refusing to pay a $320,000 debt due from a single poker game.

Schultz deemed it a safe time to get rid of Diamond. A hit squad dispatched to kill him found Diamond in bed with his mistress and sprayed the room with gunfire. Five bullets entered his body but he survived. Two further attempts on his life failed. But on 17 December 1931 Schultz's gangsters finally got their man.

Diamond had been celebrating his acquittal from charges that he had beaten up two rival bootleggers, and in the early hours visited a girlfriend's apartment. From there, he went home. As he lay in bed, the door was shattered from its hinges and 'Legs' Diamond was finally shot dead.

'Dutch' Schultz now had a free hand to run his liquor, gambling and protection rackets which together brought in an estimated $20 million a year. But his gun-slinging style of business was inimical to the new, rising breed of Mafia leader such as 'Lucky' Luciano, Vito Genovese and Meyer Lansky.

After a sensational tax evasion case, in which Schultz was acquitted after having the trial moved to a small and 'manageable' upstate courthouse, Luciano and his associates decided to spare the Mafia further embarrassment. On 23 October 1935 'Dutch' Schultz was dining with three friends at a Newark, New Jersey, restaurant when a man with a machine-gun entered and shot them all.

The last of New York's old-style gun-slinging gangsters was out of action for good.

Death of a President

The Mafia organization is America's 'Public Enemy Number One'. But for a long time the Mafia itself also had its own very public enemy . . . The Kennedy Clan.

The feud went back half a century to the days when, according to mobsters' stories, the Kennedy patriarch, Joseph, made a fortune from the profits of Prohibition whiskey illegally imported from Ireland to Boston.

In 1927 one of the Irish cargoes was hijacked by The Mob and 11 smugglers were killed in the shoot-out. It was, believe the Mafia, the start of a long campaign, instigated by Joseph Kennedy and continued by his children – principally John, who became President of the United States, and Robert, who became Attorney General.

Robert Kennedy was responsible for pursuing Teamsters union boss Jimmy Hoffa to jail in the U.S. Justice Department's relentless drive to crush Mafia influence within the organized labour movement. It was elder brother John who, as President, failed to give full backing to the disastrous Bay of Pigs invasion attempt of Cuba, planned by the CIA with Mafia assistance.

Many years later, after the assassination of both men, the question was being asked: was the Mafia linked with the killing of the U.S. President in 1963? At one time, such a question would have been unthinkable. But when dealing with organized crime in the USA, the unthinkable often becomes the perfectly feasible.

That was what happened in 1979 when a committee set up by the U.S. House of Representatives suggested it was likely that a contract killer was involved in the assassination that shocked the world, in Dallas, Texas, on 22 November 1963. After a $3 million investigation lasting two years, the committee's experts reported: 'An individual crime leader or a small combination of leaders might have participated in a conspiracy to assassinate President Kennedy.'

The report went on to name the 'most likely family bosses of organized crime to have participated in such a unilateral assassination plan' – Carlos Marcello of New Orleans and Santos Trafficante of Miami. Both men immediately issued the strongest denials of any involvement with Kennedy's death.

The circumstantial evidence to back a conspiracy theory was that Lee Harvey Oswald, who is presumed to have fired the shots that killed the President, had some links with underworld figures. So had Jack Ruby, the man who gunned down Oswald before the latter could be brought to court.

Oswald's connection was through his uncle, Charles Murret, and an acquaintance, David Ferrie – both of whom worked for Carlos Marcello.

Murret took Oswald under his wing when his favourite nephew moved from Dallas to New Orleans in 1963. He gave Oswald a home, a job in his book-making business and treated him like a son. The investigative committee described Murret as 'a top deputy for a top man in Carlos Marcello's gambling apparatus.' Murret died in 1964.

David Ferrie also worked for Marcello, as a pilot. He had flown him back to the U.S. after he was deported to Guatemala in 1961 by Robert Kennedy. Ferrie had also had secret connections with the CIA and had trained pilots who later took part in the Bay of Pigs invasion. Oswald's New Orleans work address in 1963 was the same as Ferrie's, and Oswald was in the same air club in which Ferrie was a pilot.

Such evidence, quoted in the House of Representatives committee's report, is circumstantial in the extreme. But judged alongside the evidence linking Oswald's executioner, Jack Ruby, to the Mafia, the conspiracy theory becomes stronger.

Club-owner Ruby's connections with underworld figures were well-established. His telephone records showed that he had been in contact with Mob

Moments before the fatal shot on 22 November, 1963 . . .

personalities in Miami, New Orleans and Chicago. He had visited Santos Trafficante. And on 21 November, the day before Kennedy's death, Ruby was seen drinking with a friend of pilot David Ferrie.

Whoever may have been pulling the strings, the evidence points to Ruby's public execution of Oswald being a certain way of keeping him quiet and preventing him naming accomplices during his trial. Ruby's own life would not have been of high account . . . he died in prison shortly afterwards of cancer.

Ruby's connection with Santos Trafficante brings the amazing web full circle.

When Meyer Lansky, 'Lucky' Luciano and their associates ran the Havana hotel and casino business under corrupt Cuban dictator Fulgencio Batista, Trafficante was a small cog in the business. Fidel Castro overthrew the Batista regime in 1959 and threw the Mob's men either into jail or out of the country. Among them was Trafficante.

The fact that Trafficante's pilot, David Ferrie, worked for the CIA may not have been known to his boss. If he did know, he might not have been concerned. He may even have approved of the connection. For the CIA, the Mafia and big business interests had all been involved in various plots to overthrow Castro and return Cuba to 'democratic' – and capitalist – rule. The CIA, with the unpublicized but tacit agreement of the U.S. government, wanted to remove the

and moments after

communist threat from the Caribbean. The Mafia and big business wanted to restore Cuba's profitable tourist industry, complete with acquiescent officials, politicians susceptible to bribes plus gambling and vice interests.

The CIA and the Mafia had previously worked together successfully, even launching joint military operations before and during the allied invasion of Sicily. A similar link-up made sound sense in the organizing of the Bay of Pigs invasion.

Even the world's richest businessman was involved. The eccentric Howard Hughes was said to have volunteered to fund one particular part of the Cuban invasion – the assassination of Fidel Castro. The plan was discussed by the CIA. Through their connections in Las Vegas, where Hughes had interests in 17 casinos, his aides recruited two Mafia hoodlums. But the invasion was a debacle, the assassination never took place – and the hoodlums died under mysterious circumstances in the 1970s.

Another sensational case in which politics and crime are sinisterly intertwined is the death of Marilyn Monroe. Again, the central characters are John and Robert Kennedy, both of whom were rumoured to have had affairs with the world's leading sex symbol. But this time the government agency suspected of being involved was not the CIA but the FBI.

J. Edgar Hoover, chief of the FBI, had long been hampered by the Kennedys in his autocratic handling of the agency's affairs. Attorney-General Robert, with his brother's White House backing, clipped the wings of the all-powerful Hoover – and earned himself an unforgiving enemy.

Hoover's agents collected every scrap of information about the private lives of every leading politician in the country. It was one of the reasons that Hoover's eccentric handling of the FBI had previously gone unchallenged. In the Kennedys' case, the FBI's personal files bulged with scandal.

Neither John nor his younger brother had been suitably secretive in their extra-marital activities. They had both known Marilyn Monroe and, in her developing state of depression and nervous disorder, it was thought that she might make public some of their indiscretions.

Such stories, which were no more than rumours at the time of Monroe's death, have since become common currency. And in 1981 a reformed criminal, Ronald 'Sonny' Gibson, wrote a book adding some startling new allegations.

In the book, *Mafia Kingpin*, Gibson said that while working for the Mob, he had been told that Marilyn had been murdered by a Mafia hit-man. J. Edgar Hoover, he said, had been furious about the actress's affairs with top politicians. So the Mafia had taken upon themselves the task of silencing her as a means of repaying favours done for them by the FBI.

Gibson is not alone in his assertion that Marilyn died not because she had swallowed an overdose of barbiturates, but because drugs had been injected into her. Even top pathologists who investigated the case have since gone into print to say the same.

Was Marilyn Monroe murdered by the Mafia? Was John F. Kennedy assassinated with the help of the Mob? The theories sound preposterous . . . Almost as preposterous an idea as that the U.S. government and the Mafia would collaboate in a Caribbean invasion. But it happened . . .

There are rich pickings for crooks along France's glittering south coast, sun-soaked playground of millionaires and 'beautiful people'. In the early 1980s police estimated that more than £70 million a year was being raked in from drugs, casino rackets, prostitution and extortion.

Chicago-style gang warfare arrived on the Riviera in 1970 when more than 100 people died in a wave of shootings which began with the jailing of crime czar 'Mimi' Guerini, 70, for his part in a gangland murder.

The spate of killings was stepped up in February 1977 after the shooting of ex-jockey Jacques 'Tomcat' Imbert. Imbert, who owed his nickname to his reputation for having nine lives, ran a nightclub in the small Riviera resort of Cassis. He was believed to have clashed with a gang who had taken over the Marseilles end of the 'French Connection' drug ring after the former boss had been jailed. Living up to his nickname, Imbert survived the shooting – though he lost an eye – spent six months in hospital and was permanently crippled.

A month after Imbert's shooting, one of his three attackers was shot dead while leaving a cemetery after visiting his son's grave. Next day the second man was killed in the street. The third man was murdered a few weeks later, shot as his car stopped at traffic lights.

The battle for power on the Riviera erupted into bloody violence again in October 1978 when nine people were gunned down in a Marseilles bar. They were riddled with 91 bullets. Five of the victims had police records, but the other four were thought to be innocent customers, shot to keep them quiet. Police, who were working closely with the FBI, said they believed the killings were 'Mafia-linked'.

The Kray Twins: the 'Mafia' of London's East End

When London gangsters, the Kray twins, were sentenced in 1969, the judge Mr Justice Melford Stevenson told them with scornful understatement: 'In my view society has earned a rest from your activities'. These activities included theft, extortion and finally murder, in a reign of terror that marred the memory of Britain's 'swinging sixties'.

The Krays held London's underworld in a mafia-like grip. In their heyday, they were feted by showbusiness personalities. They were photographed with the famous. They were generous in their support of charities. And they were feared like no other criminals. In every way, they were a British version of America's thirties gangsters, whose exploits they studied avidly and emulated slavishly.

Even after the full extent of their crimes was revealed in court and the pair were jailed for life, many people in the East End of London still spoke affectionately of the Krays. Some regarded them as 'Robin Hood' characters. Others, more realistically, saw them as people who maintained gangland peace and kept the seedy streets safe. Few at the time asked any questions as to how such a peace was being maintained and by what sort of men.

The Kray twins were born on 17 October 1933 at Hoxton in the East End. Ronnie was the elder. Reggie arrived 45 minutes later. They also had an older brother, Charles.

The boys had Jewish, Irish and Romany blood in their veins. Their father Charles, who was 25 at the time of the twins' birth, was a dealer in old clothes, silver and gold. Their mother Violet was just 21.

Just before the war, the family moved to one of the toughest, most run-down areas of Bethnal Green, shortly to become even more decrepit thanks to visits from the Luftwaffe. Ronnie and Reggie became known as the Terrible Twins because of their love of fighting – at first with fists and later with bicycle chains and flick-knives.

By the age of 16, they were carrying guns. A year later, they made their first appearance in court. They were accused of seriously beating up a 16-year-old rival but the case was dismissed for lack of evidence.

The twins were fighters in every sense. At 17, they became professional boxers. A year later they were called up for their National Service and punched the recruiting corporal on the nose. Much of their subsequent military service was spent in jails.

After their dishonourable discharge in 1954, they went into the protection business. If a bookmaker, store or club owner wanted to ensure 'no trouble', a weekly payment to Ronnie and Reggie would do the trick. As the easy money rolled in, so their gang of collectors grew. Their territory covered the East End and much of North London.

They founded their own clubs – at first in the East End, where a sports hall provided a front for their rackets, and later in fashionable Knightsbridge where the West End found the pair a rough and ready attraction.

By now, Ronnie was known as 'the Colonel', Reggie was 'the Quiet One' and their home in Vallance Road termed 'Fort Vallance.'

The Krays could be magnanimous, loyal and charming. They could also be frighteningly, unpredictably brutal. But mainly it was Ronnie who took the lead, egging his brother on to prove himself by being tough enough to follow his lead.

In 1956 Ronnie shot a man in the leg. When picked out at an identity parade, he avoided being charged by claiming he was Reggie – thus making nonsense of the evidence. Later that year Ronnie was caught and convicted. He received a three-year sentence for stabbing a man with a bayonet in a raid on a rival gang's territory.

It was at this time that Ronnie Kray's dangerous instability became apparent. He went berserk in jail. He became obsessively fearful that someone was trying to have him 'put away'. He even had to be shown his reflection in a mirror to prove he was still in one piece. Finally, he was sent from prison to a mental hospital where he was certified insane.

In true flamboyant Kray style, the family moved in to help – and Ronnie moved out. Reggie paid a visit to the mental hospital and swapped clothes with his brother. When Ronnie was safely away, Reggie owned up to his little trick.

Ronnie remained free for some weeks, during which time his sense of bravado induced him to make surprise calls on East End pubs to taunt the police. But his strange state of mind worried his family and, after a suicide attempt, they allowed the police to recapture him. After further treatment, he was deemed fit to be released, in 1958.

But Ronnie Kray was far from cured – and no one knew it better than his brother. Reggie had a good business brain, and the family's commercial enterprises had flourished during Ronnie's spell in jail. There was the original 'Double R Club' in Bow, a new club in Stratford, a car sales business and even an illegal gambling club a stone's throw away from Bow police station. But

The Kray twins, Reggie (left) and Ronnie (right), with brother Charles

Ronnie's return from prison also meant a return of the heavy-handed gangsterism that put such businesses in peril.

The brothers argued about their 'firm'. But when in 1960 Reggie was jailed for 18 months for demanding money with menaces, it was his brother's turn to have a free hand at running the business.

Ronnie took a contract from the notorious slum landlord, Peter Rachman. The Krays' hoodlums would guard Rachman's rent collectors in return for a healthy commission. The result was not only added riches for Ronnie but his introduction to a more sophisticated society. His new Knightsbridge club, 'Esmerelda's Barn', became a favourite rendezvous for entertainers and sports people. It also became a haven for penniless young men on the make . . . for Ronnie was by now openly homosexual.

Reggie was otherwise inclined. When released from prison in 1961, he fell hopelessly in love with a 16-year-old East End girl. For the first time in their lives, the brother's lifestyles were now widely different – Ronnie veered towards his swinging friends 'up West' while Reggie returned to his roots on the east side of town. Largely thanks to Reggie's business acumen, the Krays added a restaurant and several other clubs to their empire. And Reggie got married – tragically for his teenage bride who could not cope with the gangster's crazy world and eventually committed suicide in 1967.

It may have been due to the strain of Reggie's failing marriage or it may have been due to the Al Capone fantasy world of brother Ronnie, but the regime of the Krays took an even more violent turn in the second half of the Sixties.

There were beatings, brandings and knifings. One former friend who drunkenly insulted Ronnie needed 70 stitches to face wounds. There were also at least three unsuccessful attempts on the Krays' lives, and Ronnie took to sleeping with a gun under his pillow.

Warfare flared between the Krays and Charles Richardson's gang, based in south London but intent on muscling in on West End protection rackets.

In March 1966, a small-time 'heavy' working for Richardson strayed into Kray territory. The brothers were told that George Cornell had been announcing to East Enders that 'Ronnie Kray is a big, fat poof and don't take any notice of him . . . He can't protect you from anything.'

Ronnie was tipped off that Cornell was in a well-known Whitechapel pub called the Blind Beggar. Ronnie walked calmly into the bar and, as he later described in his own words, 'put a gun at his head, looked him in the eyes and pulled the trigger. Then I put the gun in my pocket. His body fell off the stool and I walked out.'

Later he justified the murder by saying: 'Cornell was vermin. He was a drunkard and a bully. He was simply nothing. I done the Earth a favour ridding it of him.'

The following year, Reggie made his own violent contribution to the murder statistics.

By now, the brothers' business had expanded to drugs and pornography, areas that did not endear them to their traditional East End friends. Ronnie's homosexual proclivities were the talk of their 'manor' – quite apart from his by-now obvious paranoia. And Reggie 'the Quiet One', following his wife's suicide, had taken to drink and to shooting at the legs of people who gave him offence.

The Krays were becoming bad news. They were being shunned by the rich and famous as well as by the poor and infamous. They were trouble. The twins became concerned about their 'image' and decided to hold a test of their 150-strong gang's loyalty – a meaningless murder.

The victim was to be Jack 'The Hat' McVitie, so called because of the hat he wore to hide his baldness. McVitie's crime was to owe the brothers £500 and to have insulted them in their absence during a drunken binge.

Four of the Krays' men lured McVitie to a 'party' in a borrowed house in Stoke Newington where Ronnie, Reggie and two henchmen lay in wait. As their victim entered he realized his impending fate and turned to flee. Ronnie pinned him against a wall and told him: 'Come on, Jack, be a man.' McVitie said: 'I will be a man but I don't want to die like one.'

Ronnie led him into a basement room where the killing became near-farcical. As McVitie walked through the door, Reggie pointed a gun at his head and pulled the trigger . . . nothing happened. Ronnie then picked up a carving knife and thrust it at McVitie's back. But it failed to pierce his thick coat.

McVitie made a dash for the window. He dived through, only to be grabbed by his feet and hauled back in. Ronnie pinioned his arms from behind and screamed at his brother: 'Kill him, Reg. Do it. Don't stop now.' Reggie picked up the knife and stabbed his pleading victim in the face and then through the throat. The knife passed through his gullet and pinned him to the floor.

McVitie's body was never found.

Flushed with their success, the twins decided to form a Murder Incorporated organization along the lines of the American model. But, by now, every move they made was being monitored by a Scotland Yard team led by Detective Superintendent Leonard 'Nipper' Read.

Plans were laid to kill a minor crook who was appearing as a witness at an Old Bailey trial. The murder weapons were a crossbow and a briefcase with a hidden hypodermic syringe filled with cyanide. Another plan was for the contract killing of a gambler who owed an unspecified debt to the Krays' prospective paymasters in Las Vegas. A third plot was to be the murder of a Maltese club owner by blowing up his car with dynamite.

Detective Superintendent 'Nipper' Read's case against the Krays was now strong. But he knew that, unless the twins were safely behind bars, prospective witnesses would suffer 'memory loss' or simply vanish.

Then the police got lucky. A Kray associate was stopped while about to board a plane from Glasgow to London. He was carrying four sticks of dynamite, presumably destined for the Maltese club-owner's car. Detectives raided his home and found the crossbow and briefcase complete with poisonous syringe.

On the night of 8 May 1968 Ronnie and Reggie went drinking at the Old Horn pub in Bethnal Green. They went on to the Astor Club in fashionable Berkeley Square, returning to their mother's new council flat in Shoreditch at four in the morning. Reggie went to bed with a girlfriend, Ronnie with a boyfriend. At dawn 'Nipper' Read's men swooped on the flat and arrested them.

The Kray twins were charged with the murders of George Cornell and Jack McVitie. Eight other members of their 'firm', including their brother Charles, were charged with various lesser crimes.

The twins pleaded not guilty but after a sensational 39-day trial at the Old Bailey, they were jailed for life with a recommendation that they should serve no less than 30 years. They were 35 years of age when the trial ended on 8 March 1969, which meant that they would be pensioners before they were released.

Ronnie and Reggie were sent to separate top-security prisons. In 1972 they were briefly reunited at Parkhurst jail on the Isle of Wight. But in 1979 Ronnie was again certified and sent to Broadmoor hospital for the criminally insane.

Reggie found his sentence harder to take than his brother. He was classified as a Category A prisoner – highly dangerous and liable to escape. Shadowed at all times by two prison officers, his movements were logged and monitored while his visits were screened and limited. While of Category A status, no parole board could consider his case. All his appeals fell on deaf ears. In 1982, he unsuccessfully attempted suicide by cutting his wrists.

Ronnie was luckier in his time behind bars. Being an inmate of Broadmoor, he was allowed more privileges than his brother. He received visits from old East End associates and from showbusiness and sporting friends. They brought him parcels of food from Harrods – smoked salmon and game pie – and classical records for the hi-fi in his cell. He also had a colour television set.

Ronnie Kray would regale visitors with details of his exploits in the days when he and his brother wrote headlines in blood. In 1983 he told a visiting journalist, long-time friend Brian Hitchen: 'We never hurt ordinary members of the public. We only took money off other villains and gave a bundle of that away to decent people who were on hard times.

'I look back on those days and naturally remember the good times. Then, people could take ladies into pubs with them without the risk of their being insulted. Old people didn't get mugged, either. It couldn't have happened when we were looking after the East End.'

About life in Broadmoor he said: 'There are some really bad ones in here,

Brian, some really bad ones. But they are all some mother's sons – and that's where the heartbreak is. Because no matter what they've done or how bad they've been, the mothers don't stop coming and don't stop loving them. When I see these mums, I feel really sorry for them having to come here.'

In 1982 the twins' strongest link with the outside world ended. Their most constant visitor, their mother Violet, died one week before her seventy-third birthday. Violet Kray had become an East End legend in her own right and was said to have been the only person on earth who had any control over the twins.

Ronnie and Reggie were allowed out for a day to attend her funeral, which was turned into a star-studded East End occasion.

Reggie said after his return to Parkhurst jail: 'It's so lonely without visits from our mum. They were always the best ones. I shall miss her so much. Throughout the funeral, Ronnie and I were handcuffed to police officers who must have been 6ft. 3ins. (1.9 metres) tall. But they needn't have worried. Violence is not part of my life anymore.

'I get angry when I read about the way things are in the East End nowadays – like those attacks on old ladies. Years ago, if we saw an old lady we would help her across the road and wish her goodnight. Now they rape 80-year-old women and kill them for their pensions. It makes me sick.'

And of the hopelessness of life in jail, he said: 'You can so easily give up after all these years. They have passed quickly. But it is only when I see the youngsters come in here that I realize what a terrible waste of life it is.'

The Richardson Gang: Scourge of South London

If the Krays were infamous for meting out instant vengeance, the rival Richardson gang, based on the south side of the Thames, were the masters of the slower punishment. They vied with the Krays for the reputation of being the most monstrous merchants of terror in London. Known as the 'torture gang', their speciality was pinning their enemies to the floor with six-inch (15 cm) nails and removing their toes with bolt cutters.

The gang's leader was Charles Richardson, born in Camberwell in 1934. He and his younger brother Eddie turned to crime after their father left home –

leaving the family without any source of income – while the children were still schoolboys.

From petty theft, the brothers slowly built up a thriving string of businesses – some legitimate, others not – throughout south London. Charles specialized in scrap metal but he also ran furniture and fancy goods firms. Eddie operated fruit machines and a wholesale chemists' supplier.

On their own, these companies would have made the brothers comfortably well off, although not rich. But largely they were no more than fronts for the other and more profitable sides of their business – fraud, theft and receiving stolen goods.

Eddie's fruit machine business, for instance, was more successful than most in the same line. The reason was simple – if a pub or club owner was offered one of Eddie's machines, he would be wise to accept. If not, he knew his premises would be broken into, and vandalized, or quite openly smashed up, by 'heavies' in broad daylight.

The Richardsons' most masterful money-making strokes, however, involved what were known as 'long firms'. A company would be set up under a Richardson nominee and begin trading perfectly legitimately. Goods would be ordered from suppliers and paid for promptly, so creating good credit ratings. After a few months' operation, massive orders would be placed on credit with all the suppliers. The goods would be quickly sold, the Richardsons would pocket the money, and the company would seemingly evaporate into thin air.

Charles was once arrested for receiving stolen goods, but police had to drop the charge for lack of evidence. They kept a careful watch on the gang's activities, however, and in 1965 they got an insight into the full horrors of the Richardsons' methods for keeping order and repaying old scores.

In July of that year one of the gang's victims walked into a South London police station and related a horrific story of how he had been tortured by the gang after a kangaroo court had found him guilty of disloyalty. Finally, he had been forced to mop up his own blood from the floor.

The trials and torture sessions were, police discovered, the sadistic speciality of Eddie. Sick with fear, the victims would be hauled in by gang members and tried before Eddie and the others in a mock court. Then the punishments were meted out – anything from beatings to more fearsome forms of torture. Men were whipped, burned with cigarettes, had their teeth pulled out with pliers, were nailed to the floor, had their toes removed by bolt cutters or leaped in agony from the effects of an electric shock machine. Afterwards if the victims were too badly injured they would be taken to a struck-off doctor for emergency treatment.

In 1966 the police decided they had enough evidence to act. The clincher was the murder trial of a man accused of killing a South African mining speculator to whom Charles Richardson was said to have entrusted a considerable sum of money which had never been returned. There were also stories about Charles being involved with the South African secret service, BOSS – and even talk of an attempt to bug the telephone of Prime Minister Harold Wilson.

Eddie was by now already inside jail, serving five years for affray. In July 1966 police mopped up the rest of the gang in a series of raids throughout south-east London.

It was not until April 1967 that the Old Bailey trial began, with charges of fraud, extortion, assaults and grievous bodily harm. Despite an attempt to bribe a juror, the Richardsons were found guilty after 46 days of evidence. Eddie had another ten years added to his existing sentence. Charles was jailed for 25 years for grievous bodily harm, demanding money with menaces and robbery with violence.

The judge, Mr Justice Lawton, told him: 'You terrorized those who crossed your path in a way that was vicious, sadistic and a disgrace to society . . . One is ashamed to think one lives in a society that contains men like you. You must be prevented from committing further crime. It must be made clear that all those who set themselves up as gang leaders will be struck down, as you have been struck down.'

Like the Kray brothers, Charles Richardson was later to issue an apologia for his crimes. He said: 'The men I was involved with were professional swindlers. I was only trying to get my own money back. I feel sick about the way I have been portrayed. I'm a scapegoat. I got 25 years for grievous bodily harm and not one of them need an aspirin.'

He told the London *Sunday Times* in 1983 that his links with South Africa and the shadowy BOSS organization had been an embarrassment to the British

---

Pride swelled in Jimmy Eppolito's chest as he posed for a photograph beside U.S. President Jimmy Carter's wife Rosalynn. But when Eppolito later flaunted the picture, his underworld bosses were far from amused. They sentenced him to death for 'showboating' – attracting unwanted publicity to the Mafia.

Eppolito, 34, who worked for Carlo Gambino's New York crime family as well as helping out the Carters' favourite children's charity in his spare time, was lured to a non-existent business appointment in March 1980. As he and his 64-year-old father waited in their car, they were machine-gunned to death by unknown assailants.

government. 'I was a pawn,' he said. 'The bigger a criminal the British made me out to be, the more leverage they could apply on the South Africans for having used me. Most business is pressure and blackmail, isn't it?

'I never tapped Harold Wilson's phone – it could have been done but it wasn't. But people here got very upset about that. They wanted to get rid of me for as long as possible.'

A vociferous campaign for his early release was launched by Charles Richardson's loyal family and friends, backed by parole board reports stating that he was no longer a danger to society. They fell on deaf ears.

In 1980 he walked out of an open prison and went on the run for nearly a year, supposedly to publicize his claims for freedom. He even dressed up as Father Christmas and handed out presents at a children's party. On his return to prison, he was allowed a day release to work with the handicapped. In 1983, anticipating his early release within a year or two, he was allowed home for a long, quiet weekend to prepare himself for life again on the outside.

A preview of the lifestyle befitting one of the biggest ex-crooks in London was revealed when he was collected at the gates of Coldingley Open Prison, Berkshire, by Rolls-Royce. He was driven home for a family reunion, then took his relatives – including his freed brother Eddie – to a champagne lunch.

In the following days the festivities continued at a nightclub and a public house. At the Sidmouth Arms, off the Old Kent Road in the Richardsons' old stamping ground, 350 people thronged the bars and lounges to pay their respects to Charles.

'Look around you,' he told reporters. 'I love these people and they love me. I get 200 Christmas cards a year in jail. That's what a bad man I am.'

Charles Richardson was finally freed from prison in July 1984.

Chapter
Six

BLOOD LUST

More savage than any animal, these men
committed the most horrifying crimes of all. Mass
murderers, sex monsters, cannibals or vampires,
they all enjoyed letting blood. From the insane
Roman Emperor who butchered his countrymen
and turned his sisters into prostitutes to the
insidious writer who polluted the minds of the
weak with his creed of cruelty – and gave the
world the word Sadism.

'Man is the only animal who causes pain to others
with no other object than wanting to do so.'

Arthur Schopenhauer (1851)

Caligula

There was relief and rejoicing in Rome in AD 37 when 25-year-old Gaius Caesar succeeded to the title of Emperor from the elderly tyrant Tiberius. Tiberius, who had spent brooding years of self-imposed exile on the island of Capri, had become feared and despised because of the cruel executions of his critics in the Roman army.

But it seemed as if the embittered old emperor might have done some sort of penance by appointing Gaius Caesar as his successor. The young man was a great-grandson of Augustus and son of the soldier Germanicus, one of the unsullied military heroes of the Roman Empire.

As a baby, Gaius had often been taken by his father on Roman army campaigns and the legionaires who doted on the child adopted him as a lucky mascot. They dressed him in a tiny uniform complete with hand-crafted boots, called caligae. And they gave him the fond nickname 'Caligula' – little boots. In four brief years that nickname was to strike terror into the hearts of the citizens of Rome and even the old soldiers who helped to rear him.

Caligula had a wild streak of youthful extravagance and an appetite for sexual adventuring. But if his elders thought he would grow out of such excesses as he adopted the mature responsibilities of Emperor, they were mistaken. His youthful excesses masked a depraved insanity which only surfaced when he began to revel in the full power of his new office.

The first six months of Caligula's reign were a spectacular 'honeymoon' period for the citizens of Rome. He quickly won their affection by giving away most of the treasury of Tiberius in generous tax rebates and cash bonuses for the soldiers of the garrison in Rome. And he paid small fortunes to the soldiers he trusted most – the broad-shouldered German mercenaries who made up his personal bodyguard.

With reckless disregard for the worried senators who warned him he would bankrupt himself and the office of Emperor, he began to lavish unheard-of expense on the blood-letting rituals of the circuses in the Roman amphitheatres.

From all parts of the Empire, a sinister menagerie of lions, panthers, elephants and bears were captured in the forests and deserts to be brought to Rome and bloodily butchered in staged 'hunts' in the arenas, to the delight of the spectators.

Prize money for gladiators and charioteers was doubled and trebled to encourage them to fight each other to the death at the circuses. The shows were breathtaking extravaganzas, wildly acclaimed by their audiences – and they made Caligula an Emperor to be admired and applauded.

The popularity of the circuses also helped his subjects turn a blind eye to the fact that Caligula had made his three sisters leave their husbands and move into his palace in Rome to share his bed. And it helped to stifle any misgivings about reports that the fun-loving young Emperor spent many nights wandering the city with his guards, indulging in orgies with the prostitutes before burning their brothels to the ground.

In AD 38, with his reign only a year old, Caligula was still a popular Emperor when he fell ill with a fever. The circuses suddenly stopped.

Sympathetic Romans gathered in their thousands day and night outside his palace. All traffic of chariots and handcarts, and the noise of music and trade in the street were banned within half a mile of the palace, while the citizens prayed for Caligula's recovery.

For a month he hovered between life and death. Then the fever broke. The Emperor awoke weakened but growing stronger every day. But he had gone stark, raving mad.

Calling his friends and family around him, he confided: 'I wasn't really ill, I was just being reborn as a God!'

And with just enough money left at his disposal, Caligula celebrated with a programme of circuses which surpassed all his previous spectaculars. He was determined that everyone should enjoy themselves as much as he did. Trade and commerce almost ground to a halt as Caligula declared day after day a public holiday so that none of the citizens might have an excuse for not attending the circuses.

The constant bloody carnival soon took its toll. For the Romans, it was too much of a good thing. And for Caligula's purse, it was an expense he could no longer support. With most of his money gone in spendthrift celebration, even the Emperor felt the pinch of the expense of fresh meat to feed the lions being prepared for their daily battle with gladiators – who were themselves deserting the circus because of the falling prize money.

And when one mediocre circus featured mangy, underfed lions and paunchy, middle-aged gladiators lured from retirement, it was unacceptable to the crowds, who demanded more and more excitement each time. They rose in the 30,000 seat amphitheatre and actually booed the Emperor.

The mad Caligula reacted swiftly. The ringleaders who had led the jeering were seized by his guards and dragged away to the cellars under the arena. There their tongues were cut out and, choking on their own blood, they were forced into the arena to do battle with the wild animals.

The Roman crowd, used to seeing trained professional 'huntsmen' kill the lions, were stunned into silence by the sight of their fellow citizens being made to

> The victims who suffered most from the sexual depravity of
> the Emperor Caligula were members of his own family. It
> is likely that his own grandmother, who was besotted by
> him as a boy, introduced him to sex. As a 13-year-old, he
> began to have an incestuous affair with his sister Drusilla,
> who was one year older than him. When he became
> emperor he forced his two other sisters, Agrippinilla and
> Lesbia, to divorce their husbands and to share his bed with
> him. But it was Drusilla who paid the ultimate price. When
> she became pregnant, the emperor believed that she was
> going to give birth to his child and that the baby of their
> incestuous union would be endowed with God-like powers.
> Drusilla died in one night of bloody butchery, when
> Caligula disembowelled her to pluck the unborn baby from
> her womb. The emperor announced that his beloved sister
> had died of a crippling disease and her body was hastily
> bound in a tight shroud and buried before any mourner
> could see the bestial wounds and dismemberment he had
> inflicted on her.

face the beasts. But Caligula enjoyed the scene immensely, whooping and clapping until the last of the insolent hecklers had been killed and dragged back to the cages by the emaciated lions.

As he left the arena with a mad glint in his eye, he told the Captain of the Guard wistfully: 'I only wish all of Rome had just one neck so I could cut off all their heads with one blow.'

Caligula had cowed even the bloodthirsty Romans into shocked submission. Still he needed more money to stage even more circuses and to keep paying his army for their shaken loyalty. And mad though he was, he knew that nothing would bring the wrath of his disenchanted subjects down on him quicker than a hefty increase in their taxes.

At least he had solved the problem of the food bill for the lions. From then on, the common criminals of Rome's jails were transported to the amphitheatres at night and fed to the lions. He began to ease his other financial problems with a series of trumped-up treason charges against some of the capital's wealthiest citizens. Their vast estates and fortunes were seized as fines and punishment, and the paid informers who gave perjured evidence against them were rewarded with a few gold coins.

With all of Rome turning against him, the Emperor seemed to see some sense at last and turned to the time-honoured way of raising cash – plundering the captive peoples of France and Spain.

He reserved the last of his Imperial revenues for one bizarre display in the Bay of Naples, where he moored 4,000 boats in a floating causeway – to give the lie to a prediction by a soothsayer who had told him as a boy that he had as much chance of becoming Emperor as crossing the bay and keeping his feet dry.

Caligula galloped across a wooden road of ships laid with turf, flanked with artificial gardens and mock taverns, to loot the city of Puteoli. Caligula then returned to Rome happy that he had proved the soothsayer wrong.

That night a storm wrecked almost half the ships still riding at anchor, and Caligula swore he would take his revenge on Neptune, the God of the Sea. The loss of the ships hasn't dampened his spirits enough to prevent him throwing a party for his favourite horse Incitatus, 'the swift', and presenting the animal with more classical paintings to join the collection already hanging on the walls of its marble bedroom. And Incitatus was 'promoted' from Senator to Consul of the Roman Empire.

Broke and desperate to recoup the cost of his Bay of Naples escapade, Caligula threw all caution to the wind. His guards rounded up ordinary citizens in the street and forced them to contribute every coin in their purses to the Emperor's treasury. Holding back a single coin could mean instant death.

When his loyal guards explained that they had even managed to rob the city's prostitutes of their meagre earnings, Caligula hit on his most obscene idea for raising even more revenue. At a family meeting in his palace, he raged at his sisters Agrippinilla and Lesbia: 'Everyone else in Rome has to work to support me, but I never see any money from you. Now it's your turn to work.'

By imperial decree, Caligula announced that his palace was to be opened as a brothel, with his sisters as prostitutes. Eminent senators were ordered to turn up at the enforced sex orgies and pay an entrance fee of 1,000 gold pieces. To the shame of the most noble men of the Senate, they were then summoned to return

---

Rome's enemies were equally capable of cunning cruelty. Mithridates was king of Pontus, a state on the Black Sea, now part of Turkey, for 59 years from 124 BC. In a surprise attack, he seized Syria and part of Asia Minor, taking thousands of Romans captive. Then he secretly instructed his generals to arrange a day of massacre. When the date arrived, 100,000 Roman men, woman and children were dragged out on the streets from their homes and slaughtered without mercy.

---

to another series of orgies and to bring their wives and daughters as prostitutes to join Caligula's sisters.

When Rome had been bled almost dry, Caligula decided to look further afield and, to the relief of his countrymen, set out to plunder his way through the captured provinces of France and Germany. He sent word ahead to the military garrison commanders and provincial governors in France that he wanted all the richest men in their areas to be assembled in Lyons to meet him. Nervously the Roman administrators complied, fearing that Caligula might rob and kill the

---

The young Emperor Nero never looked like being a threat to his fellow Romans when he succeeded to the supreme title at the age of 17 on the death of his stepfather Claudius. A foppish, bloated young poet who also fancied himself to be a talented musician and gifted architect, he showed no inclination to follow his predecessors as a warrior and great general. In the 13 years of his reign, he liked to pick on imagined enemies he could easily crush.

In 64 AD, when Rome was devastated by a fire which burned for a week. It was rumoured that Nero had started the blaze himself to rebuild the city and practise his amateurish architectural skill. But, far from accepting any blame, Nero found the perfect scapegoat for the blaze. The Christian religion was claiming a growing number of converts in Rome and Nero delighted in dreaming up cruel and bizarre new tortures for them. Instead of 'noble' gladiatorial contests in the circuses, he fed Christians to the lions. The wide roads leading to the arenas were lined with crucified Christians, coated in tar and set alight to form avenues of glowing torches to lead the audiences to the spectacle.

The citizens of Rome revelled in such delights. It helped them overlook the fact that Nero had murdered his own mother and his wife. But they drew the line when they discovered that he had castrated a slave and 'married' him to live as man and wife. When he heard he had been declared a public enemy and ordered to be flogged to death, the whimpering emperor clumsily committed suicide by slitting his own throat. His conceited dying words: 'This is a terrible loss to the world of art.'

French noblemen and provoke another Gallic uprising. But the tortured mind of the Emperor had produced an outrageous compromise. The rich merchants were being offered the bargain of a lifetime, a chance to buy some of the 'treasures' of Caligula's palace at knock-down prices.

So began the weirdest 'auction' any of them had ever witnessed. Caligula himself did the bidding on behalf of his captive buyers, bidding merchant against merchant until he was satisfied he had taken every piece of gold from them. When his sales assistants, the Imperial Guard, passed out the merchandise to the baffled bidders, the French merchants found they had unwittingly paid thousands of pieces of gold for packages of cloth which contained only old sandals and mouldy pieces of cheese.

With another small fortune in running expenses, Caligula set off for the Rhine, vowing to exterminate his German enemies. In one small skirmish, his legions captured about 1,000 prisoners. Caligula picked out only 300 men from the dishevelled ranks and ordered the remainder to be lined up against a cliff, with a bald man at each end. Satisfied he had enough prisoners for a swaggering triumphal entry to Rome, he ordered his Legions: 'Kill every man from bald head to bald head.'

Then he set off for his last great 'battle'. Camping outside the port of Boulogne, he ordered his dispirited and nervous army to line up on the beaches. Roman archers formed ranks at the water's edge. Huge catapults and slings were dragged on to the sand dunes to support the infantrymen; massed troops of cavalry waited on the flanks. All eyes were set on the horizon, watching disbelievingly for the appearance of some distant enemy.

Then Caligula rode with imperial majesty into the shallow water. With blood-curdling oaths, he unsheathed his sword and swore revenge on the sea god Neptune who had wrecked his ships in the Bay of Naples. The soldiers watched in silence as Caligula slashed at the foam with his sword. Then he ordered the catapults to be fired into the sea. The infantry charged, trampling the waves. The archers shot their arrows at the breakers. The shallow waters were pierced with spears and the cavalry rode in and out of the surf, stabbing the seawater with their swords.

'Now for the plunder', shouted an overjoyed Caligula. And each man had to begin looting the sea – gathering piles of sea shells in their helmets.

It was too much. The mighty Roman army had been reduced to clowning for their insane Emperor.

As Caligula began the long march home, the long-overdue conspiracy to rid the empire of the bestial lunatic quickly gathered strength. When Caligula entered Rome, bringing the straggling German prisoners and a handful of Britons he had captured from a trading boat in Bologne, together with tons of sea shells, the Senate was seething and the Army close to revolt.

For the next month they plotted. They let the mad Emperor rant and rave and award himself great honours for his 'victories'. Caligula drew up plans for all the statues of the Gods in Rome to be beheaded and replaced with an image of his own head. He danced through his palace in silken women's clothes and carried on blatant love affairs with young men he selected to be his bed partners.

But his days were numbered.

There was no mass uprising to overthrow him, just the sudden anger of one old soldier who had reached the end of his tether.

To Cassius Chaerea, colonel of the Imperial Guard, was given the most menial task of tax collecting. As an honourable soldier, he was sworn to give total obedience to his Emperor, no matter what the provocation. But when Cassius was ordered to torture a young girl falsely accused of treachery, he broke down and wept at the girl's pain and innocent anguish. Word of the veteran soldier's tears reached Caligula and the Emperor began to taunt him with shouts of 'cry-baby'.

To make sure all of the Guard knew of his insults, he teased Cassius mercilessly each day when he issued the new password for the Guard. Cassius was given the password personally by Caligula and had to repeat it in turn to each of his junior officers. The passwords had always been stern military slogans like 'victory' and 'no surrender'. Cassius had to repeat a new series given to him by the mocking Emperor, slogans like 'perfume and powder' and 'kiss me soldier'.

Cassius's sense of honour finally outweighed loyalty to a madman. In January AD 41, he waited in the covered walkway which separated Caligula's palace from his private theatre and sent in word to the Emperor who was watching rehearsals for a new play a troupe of young Greek dancing boys had arrived to perform for him. The perverted Emperor couldn't wait to meet the youngsters. He abandoned the audience and, as he hurried along the passageway, the old soldier Cassius stepped forward.

'I need the password for today, Emperor,' he told Caligula.

'Oh, yes,' said the leering Emperor. 'Let me see now. I think the password for today should be "old man's petticoat".'

It was to be his last insult. Cassius drew his sword and smashed Caligula to the ground.

With ten thrusts of the sword, from the skull to the groin, he ended the rule of the Divine Emperor Caligula. Seconds later he strode into the theatre and told the audience: 'The show is over, the Emperor is dead.'

There was a stunned silence. Then a roar of applause louder and more joyous than any heard during four years of depraved circuses and orgies of the wicked reign of Emperor Caligula.

Vlad the Impaler

If Dracula ever walked the earth as a creature of flesh and blood rather than a figure of fiction, then the person who deserved that terrible title was Vlad Tepes. But the legend of Count Dracula is a fairy-tale compared with the catalogue of terror, torture and sheer blood lust that marked the violent life of Tepes – otherwise known as Vlad the Impaler.

Vlad Tepes ruled over Walachia, now part of Romania, between 1456 and 1476. His father had been given the title 'Dracul' (meaning Dragon) because that creature was the emblem on his shield. His son, Vlad the Fifth, gave the title a new meaning by his habit of drinking the blood of his victims, of whom there was no shortage of supply. And his ingenuity in devising ever more horrible forms of death for his enemies was awesome.

On one occasion, he sat down to dinner surrounded by a large number of slowly dying victims. When one of his guests, sickened by the stench and the screams, made the mistake of complaining, Vlad had him impaled 'so that he could be above the smell'.

Twelve years of his reign were spent imprisoned in Hungary where, denied the pleasure of human victims, he pursued his solitary hours in the torture of animals.

Yet Vlad the Fifth was a hero in his own country, a brilliant general who ferociously set about putting an end to decades of internal strife and who then turned his attentions towards the Turks whose territorial ambitions were a perpetual threat to his borders. When the Turks sued for peace, Vlad summoned their envoys before him and had their hats and coats nailed to their bodies, using short nails to prolong their agonies.

Hungarian company director Sylvestre Matushka was tried in 1932 for causing the deaths of 22 people for his sexual gratification. He gained pleasure from witnessing catastrophe on a grand scale and sated his lust in a most extraordinary way. In August 1931 he set off an explosion that derailed an express train near Berlin, injuring 16 people. A month later he repeated the crime, blowing apart a Budapest-Vienna express and killing 22. He was apprehended while attempting a third explosion and jailed for life.

Impaling his victims on stakes was Vlad's favoured method of execution. He once triumphantly impaled 20,000 of his enemies. On another occasion, he partook of a hearty breakfast in a field of impaled peasants. He generally insisted that the stakes be made not too sharp – so that his victims would suffer more.

But there were other ways of avenging himself on those who offended him. A group of protesting peasants were invited to a feast at one of his homes, which was then locked and set on fire. He put down one rebellion by making it known that the bodies of plotters would be fed to the crabs, and the crabs then force-fed to their families – a threat he gleefully carried out. He also forced wives to eat the roasted bodies of their husbands and made parents cannibalize their children.

Vlad's excesses were not simply due to a cruel nature. He was a sadist who gained a perverted pleasure from his deeds and whose habit of drinking his victims' blood made him the model for the Dracula myth.

Vlad the Impaler's terrible rule came to an end in 1476 when he was killed in battle against the Turks – although it is believed that the blow that felled him came from one of his own lieutenants.

Gilles de Rais

While Vlad the Fifth was gaining infamy for his barbarity, a noble contemporary of his was gaining glory at the other end of Europe. Gilles de Rais (or de Retz) was a Marshal of France, one of the richest and bravest noblemen in the land, cultured, sophisticated and pious. His main claim to fame was that he fought alongside Joan of Arc. But his claim to infamy is in many ways more horrific than even Vlad's . . . for de Rais secretly tortured and killed hundreds of children to satisfy his craving for the shedding of blood.

Born in 1404, de Rais married into an equally noble family at the age of 16. He owned five vast estates, had a private chapel that required the attendance of 30 canons and was so esteemed in the eyes of the court that he was appointed to the post of Marshal so that he could personally crown King Charles VII of France. Of proud and muscular bearing, he was a brilliant warrior, being instrumental in securing Charles's victories over the English. He rode alongside Joan of Arc and was followed by a personal retinue of 200 knights.

Yet for all those glittering prizes, de Rais maintained a sick and savage secret. He was guilty of what a contemporary described as 'that which the most monstrously depraved imagination could never have conceived.'

He is said to have sadistically tortured and murdered between 140 and 800 children. Obsessed with the letting of blood, he would order his servants to stab his young victims in their jugular vein so that the blood would spurt over him. He was alleged to have sat on one dying boy while drinking his blood.

Ten years after Joan of Arc's trial for heresy, de Rais was charged with the same offence after he attacked a priest. Haughtily refuting that accusation, he was then charged with murder. In the words of his ecclesiastical accusers, he was a 'heretic, sorcerer, sodomite, invocator of evil spirits, diviner, killer of innocents, apostate from the faith, idolator.'

There was good reason for the Church to have fabricated the case against de Rais. He was a secular challenge to their power over the king and his court, and if found guilty the Church stood to seize his lands. No effort was spared in preparing the most damning case: de Rais's servants were tortured until adequate evidence was given against their master.

De Rais himself was probably not tortured. Yet he made a full and ready confession – not only to the murder of 140 children, of which he was charged, but to the murder of 'at least 800.'

Two rational reasons were given for this slaughter. The first was the influence on him of a book, an illustrated copy of *Lives of the Caesars* by Suetonius, which included graphic descriptions of the mad Emperor Caligula's sadistic excesses. The second was the approach of an Italian alchemist, Francisco Prelati, who promised the secret of turning iron into gold by black magic rites and sacrifices. But the real reason for the mass killings de Rais perpetrated could only have been what we now know as paedophilia and sadism – both carried out on a scale probably unequalled before or since.

Predictably, de Rais was found guilty and in a show of public contrition and humility begged forgiveness from the parents of the children he admitted slaughtering. Like Joan of Arc before him, he was sentenced to death by fire. But as an act of 'mercy' for not recanting his confession, he was first garrotted to death before being thrown on the flames on 26 October, 1440.

A mass murderer who was never caught, and whose reign of terror ended as suddenly and mysteriously as it had begun, stalked the streets of Cleveland, Ohio, between 1935 and 1938. Known as 'The Mad Butcher of Kingsbury Run,' he killed more than 12 men and women, chopping up the bodies into small pieces and leaving them in neat piles in alleys and on wasteland. Sometimes the victims, usually vagrants, would have parts of other corpses mixed in to the grisly pie. Few of the victims' heads were ever found – and the identity of the killer remains a mystery.

The Beane Family: the Ghouls of Galloway

Human monsters who practise vampirism or cannibalism are a vile but fortunately rare breed. Yet there is one case where such beings have not only worked as a team but as an entire clan. They were the notorious Beane family of Galloway, Scotland, made up of Sawney Beane and his wife, their eight sons, six daughters, 18 grandsons and 14 granddaughters.

Sawney (known as 'Sandy') Beane was the vagabond son of a road-mender and ditch-digger who lived near Edinburgh in the late fourteenth century. Driven out of town because of his n'er-do-well ways, Sawney fled with his young mistress to the rugged west coast of Scotland, where he settled in a cave and began to raise a family on the proceeds of sheep stealing and robbing travellers.

Their home provided a safe haven for their nefarious activities since its precise location was not known outside the family and because its entrance was blocked by the tide most of the time. But by 1435, at which time the Beane clan had increased by incestuous union to 48 members, the authorities were forced to act.

An entire tract of Galloway was prey to the ravages of the Beanes. And it was not just money, animals or property that travellers risked losing . . . it was their lives and bodies. For the evil clan had turned to cannibalism as the easiest and most satisfying way of both disposing of their victims and feeding their family.

James I of Scotland issued orders that the scourge of Galloway be ended and personally took charge of the force he assembled to clean up the coast. On the first foray of this policing operation, Beane's Gang was caught in the act. They were surprised while attacking a man and his wife and fled, leaving the woman's disembowelled body on the roadside.

With the help of dogs, the king's men tracked the Beanes to their lair. Inside the cave they found a charnel-house far exceeding in horror their worst nightmares. There were bundles of stolen clothes, saddles, food and valuables. There were animal carcasses. But in addition there were human corpses, both male and female, some dried, some smoked, some pickled and some salted. They hung, dismembered or still whole, from the damp roof of the cave.

All 48 Beanes were captured and taken to Leith where, after a show trial, the men had their hands, feet and private parts severed. As they bled to death, the women were burned alive – savage justice for the murder of dozens, and possibly hundreds, of innocent victims who ended up as dinner for Sandy Beane's bestial family.

Kürten and Haarman: the German 'Vampire' Killers

The label 'vampire' conjures up visions of dark, misty forests and bleak castles. But one of the most famous vampires in history was no part of this ancient mythology. The scenes of his appalling crimes were in twentieth-century urban Germany. His name was Peter Kürten and because of his vile deeds he became known as 'the Vampire of Düsseldorf'.

Kürten was a brutal sadist who first practised his perversions as a child of nine while working for the local dog-catcher near his home-town of Cologne-Mulheim. The youngster loved to torture the animals he rounded up, eventually progressing from dogs to pigs, sheep and goats. He was drawn hypnotically to the sight of blood and loved nothing better than to chop the head off a goose or swan and gorge himself on the blood that spurted out. Gradually Kürten switched from animals to human victims.

As a boy, he drowned two playmates swimming in the Rhine but there deaths were clean, easy, almost mundane. As an adult, he sought excitement through theft, fraud, arson and the beating of prostitutes. But the thrills he experienced were not enough and he coolly planned the ultimate crime, premeditated murder.

Strangely for such a calculating fiend, his first attempt failed. He attacked a girl in a wooded park, leaving her for dead. The victim, however, recovered and crawled away, too ashamed ever to report the incident.

His next attempt was tragically successful. The victim was an eight-year-old girl whom he strangled and raped before cutting her throat. The murder took place in 1913 but it was 17 years before the full story was known . . . related by Kürten himself at his trial.

Without emotion, he told the court: 'I had been stealing, especially from bars and inns where the owners lived on the floors above. In a room above an inn at Cologne-Mulheim I discovered a child asleep. I seized her head and strangled her for about a minute and a half. She woke up and struggled but lost consciousness.

'I had a small, sharp penknife with me and I held the child's head and cut her throat. I heard the blood spurt and drip on the floor. The whole thing lasted about three minutes, then I locked the door and went home to Düsseldorf.'

The following day, Kürten returned to the scene of the crime, sitting at a cafe opposite the bar where the girl had been murdered. 'People were talking about it all around me,' he said. 'It did me good.'

There was a tragic sequel to this murder, of which Kürten must have been fully aware. The butchered girl's uncle became prime suspect in the case. He was arrested and tried for murder. After a shameful trial, the poor man was acquitted but the stigma of the accusation haunted him until his premature death two or three years later.

Meanwhile, Peter Kürten, who had been called up for service in 1914, deserted within days and spent most of World War One in jail. Even when freed, he turned again to crime and was imprisoned for fraud. Finally released in 1921, he seemed to make a concerted effort to attain respectability. He got married, albeit to an ex-prostitute, gave up crime and took a job in a factory. He dressed smartly, spoke courteously and was well liked by his neighbours.

In 1925 the monster reverted to form. He employed prostitutes and beat them within an inch of their lives. Then he began attacking complete strangers in the street, mesmerized by the sight of their blood.

Kürten's savagery became uncontrollable in 1929. He accosted two sisters, aged 14 and five, as they walked home from a fair, strangled both and cut their throats. Within 24 hours, he pounced on a housemaid and stabbed her repeatedly in an uncontrollable frenzy until the blade of his knife broke off in her back. The girl's screams alerted passers-by who arrived in time to save her life but not to catch her attacker.

The city of Düsseldorf was by now in a state of panic. Police had a file of more than 50 attacks they believed had been committed by the man referred to as 'The Vampire'. But there was no suspect, no evidence, no link between the horrified victims and the quiet, self-controlled murderer.

Then, in 1930, the police were led literally to Kürten's door. A young country girl, newly arrived at Düsseldorf's main railway station, was being pestered by a stranger who promised to direct her to a cheap hotel. Just as the man's advances became frighteningly persistent, a second man arrived on the scene and intervened. As the first offender skulked away the 'rescuer' introduced himself – as Peter Kürten.

The girl was invited to recover from her ordeal with a meal at Kürten's home, after which he walked with her into the city's Grafenburg Woods and viciously assaulted her. Just as she was about to pass out, Kürten did what he had never done before . . . he allowed his victim to go free. He asked her if she could remember where he lived and, after naively accepting her assurance that she could not, he escorted her to a public thoroughfare and walked calmly away.

Incredibly, perhaps through a sense of shame, the girl did not go to the police,

At the same period that Fritz Haarmann was butchering innocents in Hanover, another German, the landlord of a rooming house in Munsterberg, Silesia, was also killing vagrants. Cannibalistic Karl Denke disposed of more than a dozen men and women, pickling their bodies for later consumption. Denke, seemingly a deeply religious man who played the organ at his local church, hanged himself in prison awaiting trial.

and the Vampire of Düsseldorf might even then have escaped capture except for an extraordinary coincidence. The young girl wrote of the incident to a friend but incorrectly addressed the letter. A postal official who opened it to seek the sender's address could not contain his curiosity and read the account of the attack. He immediately called in the police.

Detectives found the girl and made her retrace her steps to Kürten's home. There, they spotted Kürten but he had seen them first and fled through the streets. Under threat of capture, the killer turned to his unsuspecting wife. He met her in a restaurant where she worked and over double helpings of lunch, he confessed to her, in a matter-of-fact way, his many crimes. His disgusted wife arranged a further secret meeting but instead went to the police, who lay in wait for Kürten at the rendezvous.

In court, 47-year-old Kürten was as cool as ever. He horrified judge and jury by the calm, clinical manner in which he related in sickening detail the long catalogue of his crimes. He told how he had strangled, stabbed or clubbed to death his innocent victims and had then drunk the blood from one person's slashed throat, from another's wounded forehead and from another's half-severed hand.

His own defence counsel called him 'the king of sexual delinquents; uniting nearly all perversions in one person; killing men, women, children and animals — killing anything he found.' His lawyer was making a plea for a ruling of insanity, but to no avail.

Kürten was sentenced to die by guillotine and on the morning of his death, 1 July, 1932, he ate a hearty meal twice over, then told a prison doctor of his last hope . . . to experience what he described as 'the pleasure to end all pleasure'. It was, said Kürten, 'that after my head has been chopped off I will still be able to hear, at least for a moment, the sound of my own blood gushing from the stump of my neck'.

It is incredible that two 'vampire' killers could turn up in the same country in the same period. Yet while 'the Düsseldorf Vampire', Peter Kürten, was beginning to gain infamy for his deeds, another brutal monster was coming to the end of his reign of terror. He was Fritz Haarmann, 'the Hanover Vampire'.

At the end of World War One, Haarmann, then aged 39, emerged from a five-year jail sentence for theft and returned to his home town of Hanover to try to scrape together a living in the chaos of post-war Germany. The business he chose was as a purveyor of meats, pies and second-hand clothes in a poor area of the city. He prospered because of the cheap and simple source of his raw materials . . . murdered young men and boys.

Haarmann spent his evenings and nights prowling Hanover's railway stations and back alleys to seek out the human flotsam sleeping rough there. He would offer those who were jobless or homeless the chance of free food, lodging and companionship. In return, they would be sexually abused and often murdered. Their bodies would be butchered, their clothes sold and their flesh put into Haarmann's tasty pies.

The method of murder gave rise to Haarmann's sobriquet as 'Vampire of Hanover' – he would kill his victims by biting through their throats.

Incredibly, police and voluntary workers, who must certainly have suspected Haarmann, not only turned a blind eye to his nefarious activities but actively encouraged him. He became a police informer, passing on details of suspicious newcomers to town, of planned crimes and of hidden loot. So close was his relationship with the police that when in 1918 the parents of one 17-year-old boy reported their son missing after being seen in Haarmann's company, the ensuing search of the killer's room was no more than cursory. The murderer was later to boast at his trial: 'When the police examined my room, the head of the boy was lying in newspaper behind the oven.'

The following year Fritz Haarmann met the accomplice who was to speed up the 'production line' at his cooked meats plant. His name was Hans Gans; He was just 20 but was already a heartless, vicious thug whose job it was to pick out the victims ready for the executioner. Together, they began disposing of boys and young men at a prodigious rate.

Hanover had by now gained an unenviable reputation as the city where people could vanish from the streets without trace while the police were apparently powerless to act. In fact, the police could have acted and saved many lives, but they found Haarmann's information so helpful that they effectively gave him immunity. They even failed to respond to complaints about the one-way traffic of boys into Haarmann's rooms, the buckets of blood carried out and the bloodied clothes and suspect meat (labelled as pork) which he was selling.

Eventually, the discovery of two human skulls, one of a youngster, on the bank of the River Leine forced police to act. They searched the riverside and discovered more human remains. Boys playing nearby found a sack packed with human organs. And the dredging of the river bed raised more than 500 human bones. Haarmann's blood-spattered apartments and workshops were raided.

In December 1924 Haarmann and Gans went on trial. 'How many victims did you kill?' asked the prosecutor. Haarmann replied: 'It might be 30, it might be 40, I can't remember the exact number.' Asked how he had killed his victims, Haarmann replied dispassionately: 'I bit them through their throats'.

While Hans Gans received a life sentence (of which he subsequently served only 12 years) the Vampire of Hanover was predictably sentenced to death, having been found sane and entirely responsible for his bloody deeds. Before being beheaded, he declared: 'I will go to my execution as if it were a wedding.'

Herman Mudgett and the Chicago 'Torture Castle'

If there were a league table of mass killers, the name of Herman Webster Mudgett would be high on the list. He is reckoned to have murdered at least 200 victims – mainly young ladies – for the sheer pleasure of cutting up their bodies.

Mudgett researched his dreadful pastime at America's Ann Arbor medical school. An expert in acid burns, he boosted his student allowance by body snatching. He would steal corpses, render them unrecognizable, then claim on life insurance policies he had previously taken out under fictitious names. He got away with several of these frauds before a nightwatchman caught him removing a female corpse and the errant student fled.

Mudgett next turned up in Chicago where, under the alias 'Dr H. H. Holmes', he ran a respectable pharmacy without a hint of scandal. So successful was he that in 1890 he bought a vacant lot and set about building a grand house.

But this was no ordinary home. It contained a maze of secret passages, trap doors, chutes, dungeons and shafts. Suspicion was averted during the construction of what later became known as the 'Torture Castle' by the expedient of hiring a different builder for each small section of the house.

The house was finished in time for the great Chicago Exposition of 1893 when the city filled with visitors, many of whom were to be Mudgett's prey. He lured girls and young ladies to his 'castle' where he attempted to seduce them before drugging them. They were then popped into one of the empty shafts that ran through the building. The hapless girls would come round only to find themselves trapped behind a glass panel in an airtight death chamber into which would be pumped lethal gas.

The bodies would be sent down a chute to the basement which contained vast vats of acid and lime and, in the centre of the room, a dissecting table. Here Mudgett would cut up the corpses, removing particular organs which took his fancy and disposing of the rest in the vats.

Mudgett later admitted to having murdered 200 girls during the Chicago Exposition alone, and the orgy of bloodletting might have continued for much longer but for the phoney doctor's greed. He had murdered two visiting Texan sisters and, rather than quietly dispose of their remains, he set fire to the house in an attempt to gain the insurance money and make good his escape from Chicago.

The insurance company refused to pay and the police began an investigation into the blaze. Strangely, the police work was not pursued vigorously enough to produce any evidence of Mudgett's bloody activities – but the killer did not know this, and he fled.

This time he went south to Texas, where he traced relatives of the sisters he had so clumsily murdered. Having ingratiated himself with them, he tried to swindle them out of a $60,000 fortune. They were suspicious so Mudgett again took to the road, this time on a stolen horse. Police caught up with him in Missouri, where, using the name H. M. Howard, he was charged with a further fraud attempt. With the help of a crooked lawyer, he was granted bail – and promptly absconded.

Mudgett next turned up in Philadelphia where an associate in crime had been operating insurance frauds at the mass killer's behest. In an apparent accident one day in 1894, this co-conspirator blew himself up. In fact, he had been murdered by Mudgett who ran off to Toronto with his victim's wife and their three children. Their young bodies were later found in the basements of two rented houses.

It was not any of his many murders that finally brought Mudgett to justice but the jumping of bail in Missouri and the theft of a horse, a capital offence in Texas at that time. Detectives traced Mudgett through his aged mother who was happy to give them the whereabouts of the son of whom she was so proud.

The mass killer was arrested with his mistress in Boston and was charged with horse stealing and fraud. It was only at this stage that police searched the burned-out Chicago Torture Castle. They pieced together the remains of 200 corpses. Mudgett confessed to the murders of all of them. He was hanged on 7 May, 1896.

The Marquis de Sade

When police raided the house of 'Moors Murderers' Ian Brady and Myra Hindley in 1965, they found, along with the remains of one of their victims, the collected works of the Marquis de Sade. De Sade and Adolf Hitler's *Mein Kampf* were read as 'Bibles' in the killers' household. Although Hitler's philosophy is political and de Sade's sexual, both are in their own way equally dangerous. Both are able to snare the weak-minded. Both can turn mild men and women into monsters.

De Sade's distorted view of life, morality and sexual fulfilment is flaunted in books like *Justine, Juliette, Philosophy In The Bedroom* and *120 Days Of Sodom*. Stories of sexual deviation are told with relish. The extent of the perversions are limited only by de Sade's imagination – and that is considerable.

The man who gave his name to sadism was born Donatien Alphonse François De Sade on 2 June, 1740 in pre-Revolutionary Paris, which was a hotbed of vice and corruption. Related to the royal house of 'Condé, his father was a court diplomat and his mother a lady-in-waiting to the Princesse de Condé. Educated by his uncle, the Abbé de Sade of Ebreuil, he grew up good-looking, wealthy and spoilt. By the age of 18 he had experimented in every form of sexual adventure he could devise. But it was not enough. His over-fertile imagination began to invent new and terrible perversions to fuel his fantasies. The principal tenet of his philosophy was that the finest form of sexual pleasure is achieved through cruelty and pain.

De Sade served in the army during the Seven Years' War, leaving in 1763 and marrying the daughter of a judge. But within a month he was having an affair with an actress known as La Beauvoisin and was inviting prostitutes into the marital home at Arceuil. There he put his sadistic theories into practice with numerous victims, many of them strangely willing to subject themselves to his cruel whims. But some complained about their sexual abuse and de Sade was ordered to be detained in jail at Vincennes.

Within weeks he was freed and, despite having fathered two sons and a daughter by his long-suffering wife, he returned to his old ways. This time, his activities created a national scandal. In 1768 he hired a Paris prostitute called Rose Keller whom he locked up and tortured to such a degree that she complained to the authorities. De Sade was sent to jail in Lyons.

Possibly because of his family connections, he again secured an early release and in 1772 moved to Marseilles where in the busy port his pockmarked valet,

Latour, found for him a ready supply of prostitutes. But, as ever, his sensual experimentation was his undoing. De Sade fed the girls sweetmeats laced with various supposed aphrodisiacs. The girls were sick, believed they had been poisoned and complained to the police. The marquis and Latour fled.

At Aix, master and servant were sentenced to death in their absence and were executed 'in effigy'. The fugitives were finally captured and thrown into the fortress of Miolans. But de Sade still seemed to have the ability to get out of prison as easily he had got himself in. He escaped and hid away with his wife at their château. By now she too was debauched, both were in debt and further trouble with the authorities was inevitable. His wife became an enthusiastic partner in his perversions and when a new scandal broke involving young boys, both husband and wife fled.

The Marquise de Sade sought refuge in a convent while her husband bolted to Italy with his latest mistress – his wife's own sister, the Canoness de Launay. A year later, in 1777, they foolishly risked returning to France and de Sade was arrested in Paris. Thrown into the dungeons at Vincennes and then into the notorious Bastille, he suffered at the hands of harsh warders and fellow prisoners. The cruelty he had always been ready to mete out to others was now his lot.

His enforced isolation did, however, allow him to develop his blasphemous philosophy through his writing. In de Sade's eyes, there was no god but nature – and nature was not only the creator of beauty but also of destruction, through earthquake, flood, fire and tempest. Man's destiny, he believed, ran parallel with nature, and man's destructive impulses had to be obeyed in the same way as his more gentle ones were. So a truly 'complete' man should fulfil himself by becoming a monster.

De Sade propounded such lofty thinking as a camouflage for his real designs which are clear to see in books like his elegantly titled *120 Days Of Sodom* which was written in the Bastille on a single roll of paper about 12 metres (39 ft) long.

> Ex-monk Joseph Vacher was committed to an asylum in 1893 and was released, supposedly cured, a year later at the age of 25. A series of mutilation murders followed across a wide area of south-east France. Vacher, who was leading the life of a tramp, killed and disembowelled eleven victims, five of them young boys. The 'French Ripper' was arrested in 1897 for an assault on a woman and was jailed for three months. In prison, he wrote to the authorities admitting all his crimes and asking to be sent back to the asylum. Judges accepted his confessions but not his plea to be treated as insane; he was executed in 1898.

The Marquis de Sade (based on contemporary descriptions)

He would probably have spent the rest of his days in prison but for a strange quirk of fate. In the chaos of the French Revolution – the Bastille itself was stormed on 14 July, 1789 – De Sade was freed.

Despite his aristocratic background, he became 'Citizen Sade', head of one of Paris's ruling revolutionary committees. As such, he managed to save his father-in-law from the guillotine – but only just escaped it himself. Strange as it may seem, 'Citizen Sade' began to deplore the unbridled brutality of France's new rulers and was accused of being a 'moderate'. He was sentenced to be guillotined but was overlooked in the prison line-up on his day of execution. The following day, Robespierre, hard-line leader of the revolutionary Convention, was overthrown and de Sade was safe once more.

In desperate poverty, he set up home with a young, widowed actress, Marie-Constance Quesnet, and wrote, among other books, *Justine* and *Juliette*. But it was these works that finally ended his freedom for ever. In 1801, on the basis of his writings, he was judged insane and locked up in Charenton asylum. Napoleon Bonaparte himself ordered that he never be released.

Visited by his actress mistress, he continued writing books and plays, which were performed by the asylum inmates. On 2 December, 1814 he died. His son visited Charenton, collected 13 years of his work and burned the lot.

A will was discovered. Written nine years previously, it instructed that his body was to be buried in the midst of a particular thicket on his old estate and the grave sown with acorns so that over the years it would be obliterated. He wrote: 'The traces of my grave must disappear from the face of the earth as I flatter myself that my memory will be effaced from the minds of men'. His wishes were ignored and de Sade the atheist was given a Christian burial, a stone cross being erected above his grave. Shortly afterwards the grave was broken into and the body stolen. The skull later came into the possession of a leading phrenologist who read de Sade's bumps and declared that he was a man of 'tender character and love of children'.

The contribution de Sade left to the world of literature is slight – but his contribution to criminality is considerable. The sickening philosophies he propounded have taken seed in the minds of the bad and the mad, the weak and the willing, murderers and mutilators from the beginning of the nineteenth century to the present day. Because he could so well express the fantasies of his own evil mind, others who followed him have been encouraged to act out their own. Indirectly, he may have been responsible for more murders than any other individual in peacetime history. The name of the Marquis de Sade is synonymous with evil.

THE WORLD'S
GREATEST
CROOKS &
CONMEN

Contents

Acknowledgements

For contributions, criticism and constructive advice, the author would like to thank the following: Roger Boar, Robin Corry, Terry Hasler, David Williams, Marian Davidson, Rob Robbins, David Nicholson, Sonia Roberts, Geoff Barker, Jeremy Beadle, Clive Doig, Ann Mayhew and Stella Duggan.

Introduction

THE DEVIL, they say, has all the best tunes. He also has some of the best stories.

Like it or not, the rascals, scoundrels and rogues of this world are generally more interesting characters than the good guys. In fact, as well as fiction, their names and their escapades are often better remembered than those of the heroes.

To prove it, we have gathered together in this volume a remarkable array of men and women whose deeds, although never laudable, nevertheless make compelling reading.

They're not all malicious, hardened criminals, of course, some of the characters in this book are even rather lovable.

You may not approve of them. . . . But you can't help admiring them!

Nigel Blundell

Chapter
One

Thieves and Villains

'Crimes, like virtues, are their own rewards'
George Farquhar

How the great escaper became a runaway success

A handsome, weatherbeaten man of 52 strode out to greet waiting crowds in Bridgetown, Barbados. His reception was tumultuous. In the carnival atmosphere of cheering and singing, he announced exultantly 'Champagne for everyone – the drinks are on me!'

Yet the hero of the moment was no popular republican, no victorious sportsman. He was a crook – and not a very good one at that. His name: Ronald Biggs.

In 1963, eighteen years earlier, a gang of thieves held up a mail train at a remote spot in the English countryside and got away with £2½ million in used banknotes. The daring robbery was labelled the crime of the century.

Best-known of the so-called Great Train Robbers was Ronnie Biggs. Not because he was one of the gang leaders – his part in the raid was relatively minor – but because of his amazing ability, after later escaping from jail, to keep one step ahead of the law.

Every night used banknotes were sent from Scotland by rail to London to be destroyed. The money travelled in a special coach which formed part of the regular night mail train from Glasgow to Euston. The amount varied but always rose dramatically after a Bank Holiday. On August 3, the gang believed, it might be as much as £4 million.

The gang were a colourful bunch. Principal among them were: Bruce Reynolds, aged 30, fond of the 'good life', who considered himself a cut above London's East End criminal fraternity; Gordon Goody, a 32-year-old tough loner with a sharp taste in clothes and girls; Ronald 'Buster' Edwards, aged 30, club-owner, and devoted family man; Charlie Wilson, 32, a resourceful criminal friend of Reynolds; Jimmy White, a quiet 42-year-old ex-paratrooper; Bob Welch, 32 a South London club owner; Tommy Wisbey, a 32-year-old bookmaker; and Jim Hussey, aged 30, who ran a Soho restaurant.

The gang also brought in three specialists: 'wheels' man Roy James, 23, a silversmith and racing driver; Roger Cordrey, a 38-year-old florist who was an expert at 'adjusting' railway signalling equipment; plus a retired train driver.

At the last minute, they also recruited a small-time thief and decorator, with a pretty wife, engaging smile and a yearning for the luxury life he could never afford. His name was Ronald Biggs.

Bridego Bridge in Buckinghamshire was the lonely spot where the gang decided to rob the train. Their base was isolated Leatherslade Farm, 26 miles away.

At around midnight of August 2, these motley 'soldiers' of fortune, dressed in an assortment of commando gear, set out from the farm for Bridego Bridge with two Land-Rovers and a lorry.

Cordrey switched on two warning lights – one several hundred yards up the track, another closer to the bridge. The first would cause the train to slow, the second would bring it to a halt. The gang also cut the lines to trackside emergency telephones and to nearby farms and cottages.

Aboard the train at precisely 3 am, driver Jack Mills looked out for the usual green trackside light. But tonight it was amber. He put on the brakes and throttled back the mighty diesel. The overhead signal gantry came into sight. It glowed red. Mills stopped the train and asked his fireman, David Whitby, to use the emergency telephone beside the gantry to find out what was going on.

Whitby vanished into the darkness. Mills heard him ask someone: 'What's up, mate?' Then nothing. In fact, Whitby had run into Buster Edwards. Bundled down the embankment, he was pinioned to the ground.

Back in the cab of the train, driver Mills was being attacked from both sides. He was overpowered from behind and hit twice across the head.

The engine and two front coaches, including the one carrying the money, were separated from the train and were moved the short distance to the bridge by the ex-driver. The gang then smashed the doors and windows of the High Value Packages Coach with an axe and crowbars. Five Post Office guards were made to lie on the floor while the gang unloaded 120 mailbags along a human chain which led down the embankment and into the back of the lorry.

Then, sweating but jubilant, they drove back in their convoy to Leatherslade Farm. All had gone according to plan, but for the blow on the head received by driver Mills. It proved to be a big 'but' – for that moment of violence weighed heavily against the robbers at their trial.

But, for the time being, the future looked rosy. The gang spent the rest of the night counting out the money, setting aside sums for major bribes and backhanders, and sharing out the rest. In all, there was £2½ million.

Having concocted their alibis and arranged to salt away their shares until the

---

Bold front

A beautiful girl toured the big stores in Denver, Colorado, and made dozens of purchases – but only from male assistants. The girl paid for the goods with a credit card which she offered, still warm, from her bikini top. The girl got away with at least $1,000 of goods before anyone bothered to check whether her credit card was genuine.

hue and cry was over, they went their separate ways, brimming with confidence. It was short-lived . . .

Damning evidence had been left behind – fingerprints, clothing and vehicles. Although the robbers had arranged for an associate to stay at the farm and clean it from top to bottom, the job was never done. The contract was bungled.

Detectives had no difficulty in identifying the men from fingerprints and palm prints. A Monopoly board was a mine of information to forensic scientists. Soon the faces of the robbers were on 'wanted' posters all over Britain.

Within a year, most were in jail. The sentences meted out for 'a crime against society' shook the thieves – and created public sympathy. Goody, Welch, James, Wisbey and Hussey all got 30 years, although they were eventually released after serving 12. Wilson and Biggs also got a 30-year term. Cordrey was given 14 years and freed after seven. But some of the robbers were to give the police enormous trouble in the years to come.

White evaded arrest for three years before being captured in 1965, and was jailed for 18 years, of which he served nine.

Reynolds and Edwards hid out in London for almost a year, then fled to Mexico City. They spent money at a frightening rate and both eventually returned to Britain.

In 1966 Edwards surrendered. He was given a 15-year sentence and served nine. Reynolds was arrested in 1968 and received 25 years. He was released in 1978.

In prison the train robbers were kept under the closest security because two of them had made sensational escapes . . .

In 1965 Wilson escaped from Winson Green Prison, Birmingham, and joined Reynolds and Edwards in Mexico City. But he too tired of the place and moved to a smart home near Montreal, where he was caught in 1968. He returned to continue his 30-year sentence and was freed 10 years later.

The second escape was even more sensational – and launched a criminal legend. In July 1965 Ronald Biggs was 'sprung' from London's Wandsworth Prison by a daring group of associates. He scaled the wall and landed on the roof of a waiting furniture van.

After undergoing plastic surgery in France to restyle his nose and cheek-bones, Biggs collected some of his share of the loot and flew to Australia. He set up home in a Melbourne suburb, took a job as a carpenter and was joined by his wife Charmian and their three sons. There they lived under assumed names for several years, with only one event to mar their happiness – the death in a car crash of their eldest son.

Eventually Biggs received a tip-off that Scotland Yard detectives were on to him and that he was in imminent danger of arrest. This time he fled to Brazil. Life without his family was difficult. He settled near Rio de Janeiro and

Ronald Biggs relaxing on a beach near his home in Rio de Janeiro

sought solace in drugs, alcohol and women.

Early in 1974 a reporter of a London newspaper tracked him down and set about writing his story. But the paper's executives tipped of Scotland Yard about their projected scoop. On February 1, 1974, Chief Superintendent Jack Slipper and another police officer arrived in Rio to arrest Biggs. To their dismay they learned that Brazil had no extradition agreement with Britain. The Rio police refused to hand him over.

Then Biggs's young Brazilian girl-friend, Raimunda, announced that she was pregnant. It was news which left the lucky father-to-be overjoyed – simply because the father of any Brazilian child could not be deported.

So Biggs went free again. And Slipper, after his much-publicized swoop, flew home alone.

It was not till 1981 that the great escaper found himself back in prison, not thanks to Scotland Yard, but to a gang of kidnappers.

Masterminding the kidnap plot was a 36-year-old ex-British Army sergeant named John Miller. He and his four-man team arrived in Rio in April and befriended the unsuspecting Biggs, long separated from Raimunda but living with six-year-old son Mike. One night, outside a Copacabana bar, the gang overpowered him, gagged him and stuffed him inside a sack, which they bundled into a waiting van.

Biggs was smuggled out of the country through the northern port of Belem, put aboard a chartered yacht and taken outside Brazilian territorial waters.

The kidnappers and their hostage sailed north to the Caribbean where, in an extraordinary auction, the hapless Biggs was held to ransom.

Ringleader Miller based himself at a Barbados hotel and told the assembled representatives of the press that he would 'sell' Biggs to the highest bidder.

But now the operation went wrong. The yacht on which Biggs was held broke down and, as it drifted into Barbados waters it was seized by coastguards. The kidnappers quietly dispersed and Biggs was thrown into prison to await extradition to Britain.

As Biggs languished in a cockroach-infested cell in Bridgetown, Barbados, hope must almost have gone. Extradition was surely only a formality. But it proved otherwise.

Biggs's closest friends in Rio were Cockney John Pickston and his Brazilian wife Lia. They hired top lawyer Ezra Alleyne to fight the extradition. After three weeks of legal wrangling, the island's Chief Justice, Sir William Douglas, ruled that the extradition treaty between Barbados and Britain was not valid.

Biggs walked free – with £30,000 for the costs of his case.

The crowds outside the court swept him through the streets in an impromptu display of Caribbean dancing. The delighted Biggs shouted: 'Isn't it bloody marvellous? I just don't believe it. Champagne for everyone.

Even more emotional was Biggs's return to Brazil. At Rio airport the tough train robber was reduced to tears as he was reunited with son Mike.

They clung to one another as Biggs said: 'I didn't know if I would ever see you again.' He gave the boy a table tennis game he had spent the last of his money on. And little Mike gave his father an Easter egg and twenty pictures he had painted – all inscribed 'Welcome home Daddy.'

Then the tired ex-train robber was handed a brand-new Brazilian passport, an amazing gesture by the adopted country where he had become a national hero. He waved the passport above his head and vowed: 'This marks a new chapter in my life. I am now able officially to work for a living. I'm going to get a job . . . anything honest!'

The underground 'mole' behind the world's biggest bank robbery

The 1976 raid on the Nice branch of the Société-Générale was the biggest bank robbery ever. Afterwards, owners of rifled strongboxes put in claims totalling £6 million, but French police believe the haul could have been nearer £50 million.

Most of the raiders, who tunnelled from a sewer into the bank's vaults, were never caught. The mastermind, Albert Spaggiari, was arrested but escaped from a courtroom and was believed to have headed for South America. To the French, he became something of a cult hero. He even wrote a book about the robbery, which was made into a film.

Spaggiari evidently set his heart on big-time crime in his teens. At 16 he applied in writing to join a group of Sicilian bandits, but received no reply. Two years later he joined the army and served as a paratrooper in Indo-China, where he had three citations for bravery in action. But after staging a robbery at a nightclub he was court-martialled, jailed and dishonourably discharged.

He then joined the OAS and went to Algeria. The OAS hated France's President, General de Gaulle, and Spaggiari claimed to have organized an assassination attempt – along the lines of the one featured in Frederick Forsyth's thriller, *Day of The Jackal*. When de Gaulle visited Nice, Spaggiari had him in the sights of a rifle from the upper window of his mother's shop. The reason he did not fire was that his OAS chief failed to give the order.

A year later Spaggiari was arrested with four accomplices for printing and distributing right-wing pamphlets. Police searching their print shop and homes discovered an illegal cache of arms and ammunition. Because of his previous record, Spaggiari got four years' imprisonment, while his friends were put on probation.

After his release, he became a photographer, opening a shop and specializing in smart weddings and pictures of the rich and famous who pass through Nice.

His work brought him in contact with the town's top people, and he cultivated a friendship with the mayor, Jacques Médecin. Later Médecin became France's Minister of Tourism and took Spaggiari with him on a tour of Japan as his official photographer.

Spaggiari used the profits from his photographic business to invest in a chicken farm in the hills. He lived there with his wife Baudi, his collection of German imperial army spiked helmets and an armoury of guns, ammunition and explosives. It was at the farm that he and his accomplices plotted the biggest bank raid ever.

Spaggiari, lean and handsome and always smoking a big Dom Miguel cigar, was a popular and respected character in Nice.

The city was considered by many to be the crime capital of southern France, having inherited the dubious honour from Marseilles. Violence and gang warfare were a part of everyday life. At stake were the rich pickings from drugs, vice and robberies.

Much of the illicit profit ended up in safe-deposit boxes in bank vaults. Other boxes in the vaults of the Société-Générale would have held assets undeclared for tax reasons. Many victims of Spaggiari's raid claimed much less than they had lost – for fear of attracting the attention of the tax inspectors or the police.

Some of the boxes broken open by the thieves held humble secrets. One was filled with coffee, sugar and biscuits, presumably hoarded in case of the outbreak of World War Three. Others held chocolates, toffees, cigarettes and flasks of alcohol, belonging to secret smokers, drinkers and dieters who could not resist the occasional lapse.

Spaggiari is thought to have got hold of a map of the town's sewer system with the help of a highly placed town hall official. He rented a safe-deposit box at the Société-Générale to note the layout and security system.

To check for electronic sensors, he left a wound-up alarm clock in his box, to see if its ringing set off detectors. It did not. There was no alarm system in the vaults because they were considered impregnable. The walls were 5 ft thick.

Spaggiari decided to tunnel from the nearest sewer to the vaults, then break through the masonry walls with electric drills. After 18 months' planning, the gang entered the sewer system via a small underground river.

They reached the vaults of the Société-Générale by digging a tunnel 24 ft long and 4 ft high. It took them two months, working by night and laboriously carrying their equipment in and out every evening and morning. They carried the soil away in plastic sacks, to dump in the hills above Nice. The tunnel, supported at the correct intervals by jacks, was constructed so professionally that when police discovered it they first checked on ex-miners.

The gang broke through to the vaults on the evening of Friday, July 20, 1976. They brought in an air pump to set up a ventilation system. Then they opened safe-deposit boxes with jemmies, taking notes, gold and jewellery, and scattering share certificates and private documents over the floor.

The gang could have worked undisturbed until the early hours of Monday morning but for one piece of bad luck – rain.

Their getaway sewer was a main storm drain. A heavy downpour threatened to flood it and on Sunday the gang made a hurried escape in rubber dinghies after rifling 317 of the 4,000 deposit boxes in the vaults.

Before leaving, they welded shut the door leading to the bank to give themselves a few more hours before the robbery was discovered. A bank employee who tried the door on Monday morning assumed it was stuck and it was not until lunchtime that a professional was called in to cut through it.

In their haste, Spaggiari and his gang left behind thousands of pounds' worth of equipment. Police found heavy-duty blow torches, 27 gas cylinders, 11 crowbars, pit-props, sledgehammers, jemmies, bolt-cutters, lamps, hacksaws, rope, pliers, hammers, spanners, drills, cooking stoves, eating utensils, empty wine bottles and the remains of meals. On one wall was scrawled the message: 'Without anger, without violence, without hatred'. Above it was the peace symbol.

While bank employees were still trying to free their welded-up vault door, the raiders were counting and sharing their loot, a task which took them from Monday morning until Wednesday evening.

Spaggiari was eventually traced through a shop from which he had bought equipment for the raid – and by the Dom Miguel cigar butts found in the vaults.

On March 10, 1977, Spaggiari was being questioned by an examining magistrate about the disposal of the loot, which he steadfastly claimed to have handed over to an underground OAS-style group. The prisoner complained to the magistrate that the room was stuffy and moved towards a window, apparently for some fresh air. He threw the tall casement open and jumped.

Spaggiari fell 20 ft, landed with an expert paratrooper's roll on a parked car, and sprang on to the pillion of a waiting motorbike. As he sped away, he turned and made a rude gesture to the police. After a 15-minute journey to the airport, he caught the early evening flight to Zurich.

After his escape, sightings were reported in Spain and South America. But it was felt in France that some police were only half-hearted in their efforts to catch the thief whom many regarded as a folk hero.

17

He escaped to prove his innocence

Alfie Hinds was the Houdini who ran the police ragged in the 1950s when he escaped three times from prison. He broke out each time to protest his innocence of a robbery conviction which landed him 12 years in jail.

Alfie's running battle with the police and the whole legal system began in 1953 when he was convicted of taking part in robbing London's big department store, Maples, of £30,000 in wages.

Alfie, who was born in 1917, had a criminal past. He had been to approved school and Borstal, and during the Second World War had deserted from the army.

But after his marriage in 1947 to Peg Stoodley, a docker's daughter, Alfie went straight. He opened a business dealing in war surplus goods and second-hand cars, and handling demolition work. Peg and Alfie had a son, born in 1948, and a daughter born in 1951.

Throughout his trial at the Old Bailey Alfie protested his innocence. The police claimed he had led a gang which blew open the safe and escaped with the wage money. Alfie said he was at home with Peg when the store was robbed.

But the jury didn't believe him and the judge, Lord Goddard, sentenced Alfie to 12 years preventive detention.

Alfie, describing the trial as a 'farce', was determined to fight back. The campaign to prove his innocence was to involve him in 31 court appearances between the time of the Maples robbery in 1953 and the final hearing in 1965.

His first appeal for a fresh hearing was rejected by the courts. So Alfie decided he must get out to draw the public's attention to his case.

In 1956 he was cooped up in Nottingham Prison, studying law with a driving determination to use every twist and turn of the legal system in his fight for freedom.

His plan was to escape to Eire where he believed he could convince an Irish jury of his innocence.

There were two escape plans then being hatched at Nottingham – one a mass break-out and another involving just one man – a smash and grab driver who was serving eight years.

Alfie said: 'I did not join the mass attempt. My problem was that if I broke prison I was committing a crime. The golden thread which ran through all my years of imprisonment was that I must not commit one crime in order to prove

Alfie Hinds on his way to prison accompanied by a huge police guard

that I was innocent of another.'

He discovered that if he escaped at the same time and by the same route as another prisoner, but provided he had not been involved in any planning, all he could be accused of was 'escape from lawful custody', which was not a criminal offence.

Alfie knew of the one-man escape plan but never let on. When his fellow prisoner made his break, Alfie simply tagged along.

Reunited with Peg, he moved to the Clapham area of London. He bombarded the newspapers with letters explaining the reason for his escape. He even promised to give himself up if he could get an inquiry.

Despite the publicity, no new hearing was promised. So Alfie took the ferry to Ireland. Then he contacted Peg, getting her to send over some money to buy a cottage a few miles south of Dublin.

But in August 1956 it all went wrong. Alfie was arrested as he went to pick up a consignment of tools from a Dublin shipping company.

Back in Pentonville, Alfie spent two years in fruitless legal wrangles trying to prove that he had been unlawfully brought back from Eire and that the Maples case should be reopened. But even as he made a succession of court appearances, a second escape plan was forming in his mind.

Alfie decided to make his getaway during one of his many visits to the Law Courts in London. Each time he arrived, his escorts removed his handcuffs, took him for tea in the staff canteen in the basement and then upstairs to the lavatory before his hearing started.

Alfie arranged with an old friend, due for release from Pentonville Prison, to make a key for the lavatory and leave it taped to the underside of one of the canteen tables.

On the day he planned to escape, Alfie was escorted as usual to the Law Courts. Down in the canteen, his trembling fingers groped beneath the table – and closed round a packet. It was unexpectedly big for a key but he managed to slip it into his pocket without arousing the suspicion of the prison officers.

Warily he undid the package in his pocket. Inside, to his surprise, was a padlock. What was it for?

Tea finished, Alfie and his guards made their way up the stairs to the court and the lavatory. One glance at the door showed Alfie that the plans had changed. 'There', in his own words, 'were two of the biggest and brightest nickel-plated screw-eyes I had ever seen, one on the door itself and the other in the right-hand jam.'

'I assumed my prison friend had been unable to fit the lock and that this was his solution.'

Rushing ahead of his escorts, the padlock gripped firmly in his right hand, Alfie opened the door to the lavatory with his left hand. As they entered, he slammed it shut.

Within a second, the padlock was in place and Alfie was away again, down the stairs and out into the street. There, waiting to take him to London Airport was his brother Bert and a friend, Tony Maffia.

At the airport they found they had missed the Dublin flight. So they drove to Bristol. There, as a result of a circulated description, Bert was mistakenly arrested as the escaper. Alfie, sitting quietly in the airport lounge, was picked up as a suspected accomplice. But at the police station a prison officer arrived and identified the right man. Back went Alfie to Pentonville.

· In June 1958 Alfie made his final escape – this time from Chelmsford Prison in Essex. As with his first break-out, he waited until just one man was on his way 'over the wall' – and followed him.

This time his fellow escaper was Londoner Georgie Walkington, serving seven years, who planned to escape from the prison yard with the aid of some keys.

Once outside, both men made a dash for a waiting car and were away before police had time to set up road blocks. They stayed together in a caravan in Kent before going their own ways.

Georgie was caught at a London dog track but Alfie reached Ireland by boat from Liverpool. Using assumed names, he set himself up as a car dealer in Dublin.

Things went well – until Alfie was caught smuggling cars across the border between Northern Ireland and Eire. His fingerprints were sent away for identification and the startled Customs men only then discovered that their smuggler was none other than the king of the escapers.

He was sent to prison for six months in Belfast for smuggling before being returned to Britain in November 1960 to finish his 12-year sentence.

Within a month Alfie was making legal history. An appeal to the House of Lords was finally under consideration. In December he made several visits to the House Appeals Committee – the first time that a prisoner had been permitted to argue in person before the noble peers.

Hoodwinked

A raider put a pillowcase over his head and held up a store in Riverside, California. But after blundering around and knocking into display counters, the bandit got the message that it is always best to cut eye-holes in the mask! He raised a corner of the pillowcase to find his way out of the store, was instantly recognized by a customer, and was later arrested by police.

But again his hopes were dashed. His application for leave to appeal to the Lords was thrown out.

A few days later Alfie was on his way to the top security prison, Parkhurst, on the Isle of Wight.

Then, in 1962, he got his lucky break. Ex-Chief Superintendent Herbert Sparks, who had investigated the Maples robbery, had written a series of articles for a Sunday newspaper. One of them told how he had caught Alfie Hinds. It implied, of course, that Hinds was guilty. In January 1963 Alfie issued a writ for libel against the detective. Just over a year later the case was heard. Alfie spent six days in the witness box.

In his summing up the judge, Mr Justice Edmund Davies, asked the jury: 'Has Hinds spoken with the voice of truth about the Maples robbery, or is he a plausible liar who appears to have attracted to himself in some quarters wholly unmerited sympathy and support?'

After five hours of deliberation the jury found for Alfie and awarded him £1,300 damages.

The following day Alfie heard that the Home Secretary, Henry Brooke, had ordered his immediate release.

Despite his lawyer's advice, Alfie refused to stop battling to completely clear his name. He still insisted on a retrial and in November 1965 his appeal opened at the Court of Criminal Appeal. But it was to be the old disappointments all over again. His appeal was dismissed by the court and later by the House of Lords.

Alfie had won his case with the libel jury but had been unable to get the original conviction against him removed.

He went to live in semi-retirement with Peg in St Helier on the island of Jersey, becoming a do-it-yourself property developer, buying up old properties and renovating them himself.

His keen and agile brain, which had become sharpened through endless hours of battling in the courts, earned him a place in the Channel Islands Mensa Society – an organization for people of super-intelligence.

Warm thanks

A 27-year-old pregnant Swedish girl named Else Haffner won the sympathy of magistrates when she appeared before them on a shoplifting charge. They put her on probation – but their character judgement was soon shown to be faulty. As Else left the court at Malmo, Sweden, she was arrested again . . . and charged with walking out in a fur coat belonging to one of the magistrates.

Ice-cool crooks

I ce-cool nerve seems to be the principal qualification for a life of crime. It was certainly needed in the case of The Great Frozen Asset Robbery.

In 1980, staff at pubs and clubs in Camden, North London, were baffled by the pools of water which appeared under their cigarette machines. They discovered that an ingenious crook had got away with thousands of cigarettes by making ice 'coins' and putting them in the slots. Then he would vanish with his loot while the evidence literally melted and evaporated.

The coolest courage, plus a dash of sheer daring, helped a thief who had been caught red-handed by a woman as he fled from her house carrying a shotgun and the family silver in a plastic bag.

With police patrol cars and a Royal Air Force helicopter on his tail, the fugitive raced away on foot, abandoning his getaway car. Then, on a sudden inspiration, he stopped to seek sanctuary – at a police college.

The brazen bandit knocked on the door of the college at Bramshill, Hampshire, and asked if he could use the phone. He called a cab – and disappeared.

Even more daring were the thieves who stripped the lead from the roof of a police station in Coventry. The building, which the police authority was trying to sell at the time, had to have £5,000 spent on it to make the roof waterproof again.

'If you can lift it, take it' seems to be the motto of the criminal crowd. A banner advertising a crime prevention week in Reading, Berkshire, was stolen. And another thief took the trouble of removing a cardboard cut-out of a Canadian Mountie from a police exhibition at Aylesbury, Buckinghamshire.

A couple who broke into a chemist's shop in Ilkeston, Derbyshire, made a bed from disposable nappies, downed a bottle of energy-giving drink and made love before leaving with goods worth £144.

A gang broke through an elaborate security system to raid the home in Turin, Italy, of a wealthy businessman who earned his fortune making burglar alarms.

After a bigger haul were the three men who boarded an El Salvador Airlines DC-6 jet at Miami airport in 1979. They filed a flight plan for Haiti and took off, stealing the plane. The theft was discovered when the real crew arrived.

One crook who made a clean break was the 23-year-old convict who literally swept out of a Paris jail. He was given a broom and carried on brushing, unnoticed, through the gates and away.

But for sheer cheek, there is no case to beat that of the British bridegroom who invited his boss to the wedding. The bridegroom, a 34-year-old chauffeur, for once did not have to take the wheel, as he and the guests – boss included – were whisked by limousines to the church in Grimsby.

Two of the bridegroom's best friends, however, were not invited to the wedding. They had a prior engagement that very day. For while the bridegroom stood at the altar saying 'I do', his two friends were hard at work – snatching a safe, containing between £15,000 and £20,000, from the boss's home.

The chauffeur, however, did not long enjoy wedded bliss. The conspiracy was uncovered and he was jailed for three years.

The criminal clergy

A dog collar is no deterrent when it comes to fleecing the innocent. The Rev Harry Clapham didn't mind where the cash came from. Even his own flock stumped up to line his pockets, and when he was caught he went to prison for three years.

But the Rev William Dodd, active almost two centuries earlier, who strayed just once and forged the signature of a lord on a bond, paid dearly for his crime – he was executed.

Harry Clapham was the vicar of St Thomas's Church in Lambeth, South London, in the 1930s when he stumbled on the perfect way to rip off the unsuspecting public.

While visiting a patient in hospital, he noticed piles of postal orders and cheques on a desk in an official's office – the result of an appeal for subscriptions to the hospital.

It was like a vision to someone struggling to keep a wife and two children on a vicar's salary of £400 a year, particularly to someone who was as addicted to money as the Rev Clapham.

When he got back to South London he laid his plans to cash in on the public's good nature. Nobody, he thought, would ever suspect a minister of the cloth of pocketing the proceeds of an appeal. And he was right.

He first set about buying a list of people who were well known for their generosity and who usually contributed to charity appeals.

Then he wrote begging letters explaining how desperately his church needed cash for restoration work and to help the poor of the parish. The response amazed even Harry Clapham. Cheques and postal orders poured in as a result of his heart-rending appeals.

His main helper was Constance Owens who worked as his secretary and book-keeper. She was a former schoolteacher who dressed as a nurse and called herself Sister Connie.

Clapham drafted in a small army of volunteers to work in the vestry sending out begging letters as fast as they could stick down the envelopes. It was later estimated that they were issuing up to 200,000 letters a year.

Clapham then played his trump card. He arranged for his brother Willie to move south from their home town of Bradford, Yorkshire, and take over a small sub-post office. Clapham now had a place where he could cash the mounting pile of postal orders and cheques without the risk of someone asking awkward questions.

As the money continued to pour in, so he began to live the life of his dreams. Decked out in expensive hand-made suits, he holidayed in such places as the West Indies and the Holy Land and drove around in expensive foreign cars.

By the late 1930s the Charity Commissioners began to get suspicious of the Rev Clapham. Scotland Yard was called in and, although they found plenty of activity at the church, there was no evidence that the vicar was involved in a massive fraud.

But then Clapham made a fatal mistake. He applied to a charity for assistance. He told them he was a poor clergyman trying to put his son through Cambridge. To qualify for a grant, his income would have had to be less than £400 a year.

This time he was arrested and charged with attempting to obtain money under false pretences.

In June 1942 he was found guilty at the Old Bailey of 21 charges and sent to Parkhurst Prison on the Isle of Wight to serve a three-year sentence.

He was defrocked while in prison but was released early because of ill health. Waiting for him was Sister Connie, his secretary and helper at St Thomas's.

They lived together in a small cottage in the country until he died in 1948. He left her £9,000, but the rest of his ill-gained fortune, estimated at £200,000 – worth about £2 million today – was never recovered.

Barely worth it

Drinkers got a shock when they flocked to a pub in Norfolk, England, which was advertising topless bar staff. The staff were all men.

The Rev William Dodd was a well-known and well-respected public figure in the 18th century. But that didn't save him from the gallows. . . .

Dodd worked hard for many charities and everyone agreed that he was a kind, Christian gentleman. He even had the confidence of the King to whom he was chaplain.

But just before Christmas 1776 Dodd found himself in debt. He didn't owe a lot but his creditors were pressing for payment. So he forged the signature of Lord Chesterfield who lived close by, on a bond for £4,200.

Shortly after the bond was cashed, an investigator who worked for the firm that loaned the money found a discrepancy in the signature. The document was shown to Lord Chesterfield and the game was up.

The firm demanded their money back immediately but Dodd was unable to recover it all and was sent for trial.

Lord Chesterfield refused to help the cleric or even put in a good word for him, despite the fact Dodd had been his teacher and had treated him almost like a son.

Dodd was convicted at the Old Bailey in February 1777 and sentenced to death. Despite a huge public outcry, petitions for mercy and a deputation from the Lord Mayor of London and the Common Council to the King, he was hung at Tyburn.

The politician who faked his own death

Sixty-five-year-old Mrs Helen Fleming was happy to help the pale Englishman who approached her on Miami Beach on a grey, blustery day in November 1973.

Mrs Fleming who ran the Fontainebleau Hotel beach office, had already talked to him some ten days before. He had then told her that he was in Florida on business and that on a previous trip all his possessions had been stolen from the beach. That was why he now asked Mrs Fleming to be good enough to look after his clothes while he went for a swim. The old lady was glad to oblige such a polite, well-spoken gentleman.

The Englishman also impressed on Mrs Fleming his name. He mentioned it several times, and she had no trouble in recalling it later. The name was . . . John Stonehouse.

Stonehouse, 48-year-old Member of Parliament, strolled down the beach to the choppy sea – and vanished. He left behind him a wife, two children, a mistress, a constituency, several ailing companies and debts of about £800,000.

Next morning, James Charlton, a director of one of Stonehouse's companies, who had travelled to Miami with him, reported to the police that his partner had not been seen all night. A search was organized but no body could be found. It was assumed by everyone that he had drowned.

But John Stonehouse had not drowned. His 'death' was simply the final step in an amazingly devious plot.

At the time of his supposed death, Stonehouse was in fact strolling along Miami Beach to a derelict building near the Fontainebleau. There he retrieved a hidden suitcase containing clothes, money, travellers' cheques, credit cards and a passport – all in the name of Joseph Markham. He took a cab to Miami International Airport, boarded a plane to San Francisco and booked into a hotel there under his assumed name.

Over the next week he made his leisurely way by air to Australia. From room 1706 of the Sheraton Hotel, Honolulu, he made two phone calls to his beautiful mistress, Sheila Buckley at a London hotel. He went night-clubbing in Honolulu, sight-seeing in Singapore, and on November 27 flew into Melbourne.

There, in the heat of a southern summer, 'Joseph Markham' lazily acquired a suntan, planned a reunion with his young mistress, and congratulated himself on the success of the most brilliantly executed and foolproof deception of the decade . . . or so he thought.

John Thomson Stonehouse had always been an arrogant man. His conceit made him few friends as he carved a career in politics and business. He wanted to be a millionaire but he ended up in debt. He aimed to be Prime Minister but he ended up in jail.

Stonehouse first entered the House of Commons as a Labour MP in 1957, and subsequently held various ministerial posts, including Postmaster General. But when Labour lost power in 1970 he was offered only a minor post in the shadow cabinet. He turned it down and decided to use his political contacts to enter the business world and 'make a million'.

Financial independence, he told his beautiful wife Barbara, would allow him to return full-time to politics and make an attempt at the Labour leadership. But again his ambitions outstripped his ability.

Stonehouse formed 20 companies in five years, including a merchant bank. One by one they ran into trouble. His little empire only lasted as long as it did because of the way he manipulated funds between one company and another. Whenever the accountants were due to inspect the books of one company, cash would be pumped into it from another so that trading figures looked good.

It was a survival system that could not last. Finally, Stonehouse owed more than £1 million. Banks and credit card companies were demanding £375,000 and he had signed personal guarantees, that he had no chance of honouring, to the tune of £729,000.

By 1974 Stonehouse knew that a Department of Trade investigation was imminent. It would expose him as a liar and a cheat, signal the collapse of his companies, and lead to personal ruin, disgrace – and possibly prosecution for fraud. So he turned to the only ally he could fully trust – his mistress.

Mrs Buckley, 20 years younger than her lover, first worked for Stonehouse as his secretary when he was Minister of State for Technology. With her long black hair, full lips and flashing eyes, the 22-year-old beauty was a popular figure in the Commons. But she had eyes only for her boss. Separated from her husband, in 1973 she moved into a nearby apartment and became Stonehouse's mistress. Her pet name for him was 'Dum Dum'.

After her divorce in 1973, on the grounds of her husband's adultery, Sheila Buckley and her 'Dum Dum' set in motion a plan to salvage as much as possible from what remained of Stonehouse's companies. His eventual aim was to tuck away a nest-egg of more than £100,000 in banks in Switzerland and Australia and use the money to establish himself and his mistress in a new life together with fresh identities in New Zealand.

But first John Stonehouse had to 'die'. . . .

The initial step was to find someone else, someone who was *really* dead, so that he could assume that man's identity. As MP for Walsall, Staffordshire, Stonehouse tricked a local hospital into giving him details of men of his age who had died in the wards. He told them he had money to distribute to widows and that he was carrying out a survey. They gave him two names.

He used the same cover story when he called on Mrs Jean Markham and told her how sorry he was that her 41-year-old husband Joseph had died some weeks earlier of a heart attack.

He extracted from Mrs Markham all the information he needed for his plot to steal her dead husband's identity – particularly the fact that since Mr

---

Thieves in a flap

Cat burglars couldn't believe their eyes when they found a giant 2½ ft dog flap in the back door of a house they were about to rob in Berkshire, southern England. They crawled through, subdued a 4-ft Great Dane called Jasper and fled with £5,000 of jewellery.

Markham had never travelled abroad he had not needed a passport.

Then Stonehouse repeated his act with Mrs Elsie Mildoon, whose husband Donald had also died in the same hospital.

Everything was now ready. Stonehouse obtained copies of the two men's death certificates. Then he applied for a passport in Markham's name. He had himself photographed in open-necked shirt with hair brushed straight back, large spectacles, and a wide grin to distort his features.

He signed copies of the photograph, certifying it to be a true likeness of Joseph Markham, in the name of Neil McBride MP. Stonehouse knew that McBride was fatally ill with cancer. He died two months later.

On August 2, 1974, the Passport Office issued British Passport Number 785965 in the name of Joseph Arthur Markham. Stonehouse had his new identity.

In order to establish Markham as a real person, he got him a private address in a cheap London hotel and a business accommodation address as J. A. Markham, export-import consultant. He opened a bank account as Markham, deposited sums of money in it, then transferred the money to another Markham account with the Bank of New South Wales in London. He flew to Switzerland and put large sums in special Markham accounts there; and he obtained an American Express credit card in the dead man's name.

By November 1973 Stonehouse had no fewer than 27 different accounts in his own name in 17 banks, as well as nine accounts in the names of Markham or Mildoon. The ground plans had been well laid for his disappearance. But there was still one more major test to make.

On November 6 Stonehouse flew to Miami, supposedly to try to raise a big investment to save his ailing merchant bank. On the beach he chatted with Mrs Fleming. He travelled out under the name of Markham, even buying his plane ticket with a Markham credit card. No one was suspicious. The dummy run was a success.

Ten days later he was back in Miami on his final business trip this time travelling on his own passport – and it was then that he performed his vanishing trick on Miami Beach. A day later the Miami Beach Police Department contacted London with the message: *John Stonehouse presumed dead*.

And 'dead' John Stonehouse might have stayed – but for the most astonishing stroke of bad luck.

The day after his arrival in Australia, Stonehouse called at the Bank of New South Wales in Collins Street, Melbourne. There he checked that Aust. $24,000 had been transferred from London in the name of Markham. He withdrew $21,500 in cash and walked down the road to the Bank of New Zealand, where he introduced himself as Donald Mildoon. He said he was planning to emigrate to New Zealand and wished to deposit $21,500 in cash.

John Stonehouse surrounded by crowds as he leaves Brixton prison

The teller to whom he handed the money was 22-year-old Bryan King. Later, returning from lunch, Mr King spotted Mr Mildoon emerging from the Bank of New South Wales. Mildoon strolled down the street to the Bank of New Zealand. There he deposited another $2,200 in cash.

The young man was suspicious. He told his boss, who telephoned the Bank of New South Wales. 'No,' he was told, 'We have no customer by the name of Mildoon. But we do have a newly arrived British immigrant named Markham who has been drawing out large sums of money in cash.'

The bank notified Victoria State Police and from that moment Stonehouse, alias Markham, alias Mildoon, was watched. The police did not have to wait long for his next move. For the following day Stonehouse boarded a plane at Melbourne Airport and flew to Copenhagen for a secret meeting with Sheila Buckley.

On December 10 he was back in Melbourne. While he was paying a call on his bank, Stonehouse's apartment was visited by Detective Sergeant John Coffey of the Melbourne Fraud Squad. He found nothing incriminating – but a book of matches caught his eye. They came from a hotel which Coffey had once photographed while serving as a steward on a cruise liner almost 20 years earlier. The hotel was the Fontainebleau, Miami Beach.

Coffey had Stonehouse closely tailed 24 hours a day. His actions were entirely unsuspicious. The only regular event in his life was his daily walk to buy *The Times*: but he could never wait until he was home to begin reading it. He always searched through it intently as he stood on a street corner.

Coffey bought copies of the newspaper, trying to discover what the Englishman was looking for. All that he found were reports about the disappearance of another Briton, Lord Lucan, wanted for the murder of his family's nanny.

Coffey naturally assumed that Mr Markham and Lord Lucan were one and the same man. But three days later he read about inquiries into the affairs of another missing Englishman, John Stonehouse MP, who had vanished from the Fontainebleau Hotel, Miami Beach. Coffey remembered the book of matches.

Victoria police called Scotland Yard and asked them urgently to airmail photographs of both Lucan and Stonehouse. The Yard also supplied the information that Stonehouse had a long scar on his right leg.

Early in the morning of Christmas Eve, Coffey and other detectives, armed with revolvers, arrested 'Mr Markham'. At first Stonehouse refused to answer questions. But when his right trouser leg was raised to reveal a scar described by Scotland Yard, he admitted his real identity.

In the fugitive's pocket was a letter addressed to Donald Mildoon. It read: 'Dear Dums, do miss you. So lonely. Shall wait forever for you.' It was from Sheila Buckley – one of many she wrote to Stonehouse while he was on the run.

THE WORLD'S GREATEST CROOKS AND CONMEN

Nothing to declare

A customs officer was suspicious about a lorry that had just driven off an English Channel ferry at Dover, Kent. He sauntered up to it, knocked on the side and shouted: 'Are you all right in there?' Back came the reply from 22 illegal Asian immigrants: 'Yes!'

On the day of his arrest in Melbourne, Stonehouse telephoned his wife Barbara. Unknown to either of them, the call was recorded. Stonehouse apologized to her, describing what had happened as a 'brainstorm' and explaining that by adopting another identity he hoped to set up a new life.

He concluded with an amazing request. He asked his deserted wife to fly out to Melbourne and to bring his mistress as well. 'Bring Sheila,' he said, 'and we'll link up. If the Australian authorities will allow it, I will remain here and start a new life. . . .'

Stonehouse then spoke to his 14-year-old son, Matthew, telling him that he would understand it all one day and urging him to be brave.

He ended the call with a final plea to his wife to fly to his side with Sheila Buckley in tow: 'Please tell her . . . and try to persuade her. I know she'll need enormous support. The poor girl's been going through hell like you have. I feel for you both.'

Incredibly, wife and mistress flew out separately to join Stonehouse who was by now out on bail. But after an emotional scene, with Stonehouse threatening to commit suicide, Barbara returned home. Sheila Buckley stayed on in Australia with her lover – a sort of phoney honeymoon for them both – until in April 1975 an extradition order was signed. Three months later the couple were flown back to Britain. Finally, in April 1976 their trial began at the Old Bailey.

It cost the British taxpayer an estimated £750,000 to bring John Stonehouse to justice. There was a six-week preliminary court hearing, six barristers involved in the 68-day trial, and a subsequent civil enquiry cost £100,000.

For almost two years an eight-man Scotland Yard fraud team had been tied up sifting through mountains of documents. They had visited America, Australia, Switzerland, Holland, Hawaii and Liechtenstein. Witnesses were brought from Australia and Hong Kong; altogether more than 100 people gave evidence in court.

On August 6, 1976, guilty verdicts to 14 charges involving theft, forgery and fraud rang out in the Old Bailey's historic Number One Court.

Jailing Stonehouse for seven years, the judge, Mr Justice Eveleigh, said: 'You are no ill-fated idealist. In your evidence, you falsely accused people of cant, hypocrisy and humbug – when your defence was all these things.'

Sheila Buckley collapsed in tears as she was given a two-year suspended sentence for helping her lover spin his web of fraud. Throughout his years in prison, she stood by him. He suffered two heart attacks and for several days seemed close to death in a prison hospital. Sheila Buckley visited him regularly.

Stonehouse served only three years of the seven-year sentence. And when he left jail, sick, bankrupt and broken, Sheila and he moved in to a small £13-a-week love-nest in an unfashionable area of London.

In February 1981 the couple married at a secret ceremony in the small Hampshire town of Bishop's Waltham. Perhaps at that ceremony the new Mrs Stonehouse recollected the words she spoke to reporters after her lover's arrest in Australia in 1974 . . . 'If I had the same decisions to make all over again tomorrow, I feel certain that those decisions would remain the same.'

Bandit forgot to remove the cork from his gun!

Irishman Eddie McAlea planned the hold-up of a watchmaker's shop with clockwork precision. He bought a cheap imitation .38 revolver, two reels of caps and a pair of women's tights for a mask.

Outside watchmaker Philip Barrett's shop, Eddie tightened his grip on the revolver and slipped the tights over his head. Then he sprung into action. He burst into the shop shouting 'This is a stick up. Get down!'

But no one moved. For Eddie, 37, had forgotten to take the cork out of the barrel.

When he realized his career as a big-time crook was up, the bungling bandit went out with a bang. As he fled into the street, he ripped off his mask – and Mr Barrett recognized him. For only the day before, Eddie had sold him his own watch.

Eddie was later caught and was hauled up before Liverpool Crown Court, where he was jailed for 30 months after admitting assault with intent to rob and possessing an imitation firearm. The court heard that Eddie, who asked for a psychiatric report on himself, had been released from prison only six days earlier.

Watchmaker Mr Barrett said: 'At first I thought the robbery was the real thing. But when I spotted the cork stuck in the barrel, I knew the fellow must be daft. It's the kind of story Irish jokes are made of.'

Bungling bandits

Plenty of crooks are caught because of their incredible clangers. A gunman who robbed a Paris grocer lost his hat as he ran away. Inside was his name and address, and police were waiting for him when he got home to count his loot.

An Italian bank robber tripped over a doormat when he burst into a Milan bank. As he fell, his mask dropped and his revolver went off. He clambered up, ran towards the cashier but lost his footing again on the slippery floor, grabbing the counter for support and dropping his gun.

As customers and staff began laughing, the robber fled in embarrassment – straight into the arms of a policeman who was writing him a ticket. He had left his car illegally parked.

A bungling bandit in Denver, Colorado, crashed his getaway car into a lamp post but escaped on foot. Back home, however, he was fumbling for his door key when he shot himself in the leg. Police caught up with him clutching his leg with one hand and his loot with the other.

There was trouble in store for a West German shoplifter who shinnéd down a drainpipe to escape police. He leapt from an 8 ft wall and found himself in the exercise yard of Dusseldorf jail. Warders found six stolen watches in his pocket, and before long he was doing time.

Two British burglars put police in the picture when one of them found a camera in the house they were raiding. For a joke, he took a photograph of his accomplice. But they dropped the camera as they made a quick getaway, and Tyneside detectives returned it to the owner, a 75-year-old woman. Three months later she had the film developed; among the snaps was a picture of a

---

Repentant robber

A bandit walked into a bank in Davenport, Tasmania, put a bag on the counter and ordered the girl teller: 'Fill it up – I've got a gun.'

She put all her loose cash in the bag and when the raider demanded more she got bundles of notes from other tellers. Eventually the robber told her: 'That's enough for me' – and walked out with about £5,000.

Minutes later he reappeared, put the loot back on the counter and told the astonished bank teller: 'Sorry, I didn't really mean to rob you.' Then he waited for the police to arrive.

---

burglar carrying the loot. Police picked up both men within a few hours.

A mugger in Majorca made the mistake of trying to snatch the handbags of two German great-grannies. The women, both 77, tied him up, locked him in the boot of his car and drove him to a police station in Palma. He was taken to hospital suffering from shock.

When a Missouri crook stole a car with a radio-telephone, his number was soon up. Police listened to his calls, and swooped when he arranged a business meeting in Kansas City.

A not-too-bright British bungling burglar had no trouble breaking into an apartment in Chester. It was getting out again that had him foxed. Not even an axe would budge the front door after it jammed shut. The red-faced raider opened a bottle of Scotch as he waited for the owner to turn up and turn him in.

Safebreakers in England's West Midlands were baffled when their oxyacetylene torch failed to cut through a door. It was not hot enough because they had forgotten to turn up the oxygen. After several hours they finally melted a hole large enough to put a hand through. It was not until they had been captured and brought to court that they learned that the door had not even been locked.

Another would-be bandit armed himself with a toy revolver for a raid on a Yorkshire village store that was planned to the last detail. He had his motorcycle parked for a fast getaway and wore his full-face crash helmet as a mask. But he forgot one thing – round the helmet, in inch-high letters, was painted his name! Police had little trouble tracing him.

Chapter Two

Frauds and Swindlers

'Successful crimes alone are justified'
John Dryden

Evita: the glamour and the greed

Eva Peron was the champion of the poor. They adored her. They lavished their humble devotion upon her with an almost religious fervour. They called her Santa Evita – 'Little Saint Eva'.

In the years following World War Two she was a heroine to Argentina's descamisados – the 'shirtless ones' – whose idolatry made her, for a while, the most powerful woman in the world.

As wife of Argentinian military leader Juan Peron, Eva moved regally among the masses, distributing gifts to the poor. Without warning, she and her retinue would dramatically appear in a peasant village and hand out sweets to the children and food packages to their parents.

The grateful recipients of her largesse wore rags. Eva boasted furs, finery and glittering jewellery. To outside observers, the contrast seemed incongruous. Yet that, Eva always insisted, was how her people wanted it. She was the only glamour in their impoverished existence, she argued, and they needed her.

But that glamour was not just for show. It was many years before the full truth was known, but beautiful Evita and her handsome husband – those two champions of Argentina's poor and oppressed – had spent all their years in power busily lining thier own pockets.

Eva Duarte was the illegitimate child of a poor provincial woman. She was born in 1919 – though she always claimed, with ruthless feminism, that it was 1922. By the time she was 15, she had moved to Buenos Aires with her first lover and was trying to get jobs as an actress.

She was 24 when she met Colonel Juan Peron, who was twice her age. She was then a small-time radio starlet earning £4 a week as a disc-jockey and heroine of the station's soap operas. Peron and the other leaders of Argentina's right-wing military junta arrived at the radio station to appeal for funds for the victims of an earthquake. Colonel Peron, still straight-backed and athletic, was captivated by her deep, seductive voice.

From that moment on, it was Eva who regularly appealed for funds for Peron's Social Services Ministry. In doing so, she built his political charisma. She became his spokeswoman.

'He doesn't care a button for the glittering uniforms and the frock coats,' she purred. 'His only friends are you, the descamisados.'

When the too-powerful Peron was ousted by the junta in 1945, it was Eva who single-handedly regimented the support of the young officers and the

Eva Peron in 1947

workers to reinstate him.

Two years later she married him. And the following year, with Eva at his side, Juan Peron was swept into the presidential palace on the shoulders of the descamisados and with the backing of the powerful unions.

As wife of the president, Eva Peron's ambitions and her past became even more starkly conflicting. She dripped with diamonds, wrapped herself in mink.

When she was snubbed by the genteel, aristocratic ladies who ran the nation's charities, Eva sacked them all and launched the Eva Peron Social Aid Fund. She ordered dresses from France and directed second-hand clothes to the farms and shanty towns. Children were showered with toys. The people were mesmerized. They worshipped her.

Juan Peron's power was based on the trade unions, Eva's on the descamisados. Their regime seemed unassailable. But when Eva sickened with incurable cancer Juan Peron faced the loss of his popular 'voice'.

Eva grew thin and shrunken. At those few political functions she attended, she had to be physically supported by her husband. She complained: 'I am too little for so much pain.'

On July 26, 1952, at 8.25 pm, Eva Peron died. She was 33. Almost on her last breath, her body was rushed away to be embalmed by an eminent pathologist who had been standing by for weeks. He operated on her emaciated body, replacing her blood with alcohol and then with glycerine, which kept the organs intact and made the skin almost translucent.

The nation went into an orgy of mourning. Two million people filed past her coffin. Seven were killed in the crush. There were plans to build memorials to her throughout Argentina. Most of them got no further than the drawing board. For in 1955 a period of roaring inflation led to Peron's overthrow.

The deposed president fled to Spain, where he remained in exile for 20 years. Meanwhile, his successor, General Lonardi, made every effort utterly to discredit the Perons.

He opened the Perons' homes to the public. On display were 15 custom-built sports cars, 250 motor scooters, the safes where Peron kept his $10 million in 'ready cash'. Much, much more had been salted away abroad.

Also revealed were Juan Peron's secret Buenos Aires love nests – apartments lined with furs and mirrors where 50-year-old Peron had satisfied his predilection for teen-aged girls.

The new military rulers also put on display Eva's vast wardrobe of clothes and jewels. But strangely, in her case, the effect was only to gild her glittering reputation. Eva had never hidden her beautiful clothes and gems from her worshipping descamisados. It seemed not to matter to them that almost all of her wealth had been milked from the charities she had so ostentatiously championed.

Never give a sucker an even break!

Phineas is an unusual name. Biblically, it means 'he with a brazen mouth'. In the case of Phineas T. Barnum, the greatest showman the world has even seen, it was extremely apt.

Big-mouthed Barnum would tell the most outrageous lies to lure his American audiences. They were persuaded to pay to view his 'cherry-coloured cat' – only to find themselves staring incredulously at an ordinary black alley cat which, according to the sign, was 'the colour of *black* cherries'! They would queue to see 'the horse with its tail where its head should be'. Spectators would be led into a tent where a perfectly ordinary horse would be tethered in a stall – back to front, with its tail in the feeding trough!

Phineas Taylor Barnum, born July 5, 1810, lured millions of sensation seekers to his museums and circus tents by creating and exhibiting well-publicized fakes and phonies such as these.

There was his 'Feejee Mermaid' which he claimed had been fished from the Pacific in 1817. Thousands paid their 10 cents to see this marvellous freak that in reality was the result of a taxidermist's art and Barnum's imagination. The upper part of the mermaid was a monkey and the lower part a fish.

In 1841 Barnum opened the American Museum in New York. It housed a permanent exhibition of art, curiosities and natural history, and Barnum boasted: 'I mean people to talk about my museum, to exclaim over its wonders, to have men and women all over the country say that there is no place in the United States where so much can be seen for 25 cents as in Barnum's American Museum.'

Most of the exhibits really were remarkable . . . and quite genuine. There was a fantastic working model of the Niagara Falls and the first Punch and Judy show ever seen on that side of the Atlantic. There was also a live hippopotamus and a flea circus. But such was Barnum's distaste for plain speaking that he billed the hippo as 'the Great Behemoth of the Scriptures' and the fleas were advertised as 'insects that can draw carriages and carts'. Of course, the carriages and carts were suitably insect-sized.

Another of Barnum's attractions was an African elephant which had been a big draw in the London and Paris zoos. It was called Jumbo and it has given its name since to everything from jumboburgers to jumbo jets. It died in 1885 after being struck by a train during a tour of Canada.

At the other end of the size scale was mighty midget 'General' Tom Thumb.

Barnum's half-brother Philo mentioned to the showman that the five-year-old phenomenon was being exhibited at Bridgeport, Connecticut. Barnum dropped everything, raced to see the tiny fellow and signed him up on the spot to work for him at $3 a week.

Tom Thumb, born January 4, 1838, had weighed more than 9 pounds at birth and had developed normally until the age of six months. Since then he had not grown another inch. At the age of five he still stood just 2 ft 1 in tall.

Anyone else might have thought this extraordinary enough in itself. But not Barnum. He billed the lad as 'General Tom Thumb' a dwarf of 11 years of age, just arrived from England'. He trained the midget to be 'autocratic, impudent and regal' and made him learn by heart appalling, stilted, pun-filled speeches which he recited to enrapt audiences. Barnum dressed him at different times as Napoleon, a Roman gladiator and Cupid. Tom Thumb became Barnum's roving ambassador (and publicity agent) and during a British tour was even introduced to Queen Victoria.

Phineas T. Barnum is credited with coining the phrases 'There's a sucker born every minute' and 'Never give a sucker an even break'. It has also been suggested that the following famous words, generally attributed to Abraham Lincoln, were in fact spoken by Barnum: 'You can fool all the people some of the time and some of the people all of the time, but you cannot fool all the people all the time'.

Barnum learned these elementary rules of showmanship at an early age. In his home town of Bethel, Connecticut, he worked in a barter store, where goods were paid for not in cash but in kind. So much suspect merchandise was offered to the store that the rule of the house was to make sure of a good bargain by automatically offering faulty goods to the customer in return. 'Everything in that store,' said Barnum, 'was different from what it represented.' Burnt peas were sold as coffee beans and cotton offered in place of wool.

Barnum learnt a few useful lessons in Bethel. But he earned little money. So in 1843 he took his family to New York and established a sideshow. His very first exhibit secured his fortune. Posters plastered all over Manhattan announced:

'The greatest curiosity in the world, and the most interesting, particularly to Americans, is now exhibiting at the Saloon fronting on Broadway; Joice Heth, nurse to General George Washington, the father of our country, who has arrived at the astonishing age of 161 years, as authentic documents will prove, and in full possession of her mental faculties. She is cheerful and healthy though she weighs but 49 pounds. She relates many anecdotes of her young master . . .'

Barnum had not invented Joice Heth. She really existed. She was a hideously ugly old negress whom Barnum had come across in a sideshow in Philadelphia. She was blind and partly paralyzed, but Barnum borrowed money to buy her from her exhibitor and put her on show in New York. Joice would answer

Phineas Taylor Barnum, the great American showman

questions from the audience about her supposed career as Washington's nurse; any errors in her replies – and there were many – were excused on the grounds of her failing faculties.

So astute was her new owner that he even wrote anonymous letters to the newspapers calling into question the veracity of the old lady's claims. His reasoning, echoed by many a publicity man since, was that it is better to have people talking about you than not. Bad publicity is still publicity.

Joice Heth died in 1836. And Barnum, of course, found a way of making mileage of the event. He engaged a leading surgeon to perform an autopsy on the raddled old hag – in front of an invited audience. Unfortunately for Barnum, the surgeon's verdict was that Joice Heth was no more than 80 years old. Barnum was labelled a charlatan but he protested that he had been duped just like everyone else. It kept his name in the news!

Barnum's career in conmanship continued for a further half-century, with only one major setback. In 1865 fire destroyed his fabulous American Museum. A fireman single-handedly carried the 400-pound Fat Lady to safety but the 7 ft 11 in World's Tallest Woman had to be rescued by crane along with her friend the Human Skeleton. Wild animals escaped through the streets of New York and an orang-utan caused havoc in a nearby block of offices. It was big news, Barnum made sure of that.

The damage was put at $500,000 and Barnum was insured for only a tiny fraction of it. Yet by the time of his death in 1890, he had recouped his fortunes. He left $5 million – proving that 'there's a sucker born every minute'.

The bank robber aged nine

A nine-year-old freckle-faced youngster munched a chocolate bar in a New York court in March 1981, as a judge heard evidence that he was America's youngest bank robber.

The boy was said to have walked into a bank, pulled out a toy cap-pistol, held up a clerk, and walked out with just over $100.

If he hadn't been so small, the security cameras might have detected him in time. As it was, he skipped out a good few steps ahead of the guards. With the FBI and the police on his trail the boy spent all but $20 of his loot on hamburgers, chips, three picture shows and a wrist watch which played a tune. Then he turned himself in.

His lawyer said that the boy was brought up on a constant diet of TV crime shows. The day after watching *FBI* and *Policewoman* he got out his toy gun and went to the bank.

Cheats who bet on a racing 'certainty'

Doping horses and bribing jockeys was part and parcel of the American racing scene when gangsters fancied a flutter. Bookmakers refused to accept bets from the most notorious race-fixers, but in 1921 they fell for a coup orchestrated by one of Chicago's crime kings – and it was all above board.

Arnold Rothstein was at New York's Belmont Track when he had the brainwave that was to land him one of the biggest legitimate killings in racing history. Surveying the crowds clustered round the bookies, he realized the men taking the bets would be too busy to think clearly as the big race action hotted up. He turned to trainer Max Hirsch, and said: 'What have we got running?'

The only horse with a real possibility of winning was a five-year-old called Sidereal, but Hirsch, planning to scratch him for a bigger race the following week, had left him behind in the stables.

'Get him here,' snapped Rothstein. 'I'll get the money organized.'

The gangster took no chances that his men would be recognized. He borrowed 40 runners from acquaintances who owed him favours. They spread the bets through all the on-course bookmakers in small amounts.

Slowly the horse's odds dropped from 25–1 to 15–1. Then, five minutes before the off, a second wave of bets was laid. The odds crashed to 3–1, then 8–5, as bookmakers at last realized they had been caught.

There was nobody with whom they could lay off their bets, since all faced a heavy payout – nobody, that is, except Rothstein.

He agreed to accept bets worth $125,000 at 8–5, which guaranteed him against loss. If Sidereal won, he collected $850,000. In the unlikely event of it losing, he still made $40,000.

Sidereal romped home in the six-furlong sprint. Rothstein celebrated by going on to a poker game – and winning another $50,000.

The 1844 Derby at Epsom was the scene of an audacious coup on the other side of the Atlantic. Twenty-nine horses went into the frame that year for the premier classic of the English flat-racing season. Favourites were The Ugly Buck, recent winner of the 2,000 Guineas, and Colonel Jonathan Peel's entries, Orlando and Ionian.

A fancied dark horse, however, was Mr A. Wood's Running Rein. It had won an important race for two-year-olds at Newmarket eight months earlier, when owned by Mr A. L. Goodman. And though there had been an objection then from Lord Rutland, who claimed the horse was at least a year older than stated, it was overruled through lack of evidence.

A few days before the Epsom race, stewards received a letter from a group of racegoers led by Lord George Bentinck, second son of the Duke of Portland. It said there were strong doubts about whether Mr Wood's colt was really Running Rein, and urged the stewards to demand proof of identity and age. By a curious coincidence, a similar complaint was lodged by Lord Maidstone against another horse in the field, Leander.

The stewards insisted that, as far as they were concerned, everything was in order. But the two owners were warned to expect an objection if their horses were first past the post. Neither withdrew their mounts, and both lined up at the start on the big day. A sudden rush of bets on Running Rein had cut the colt's odds to 10–1.

Leander made the early running, but after a half of a mile he was overtaken – and kicked – by Running Rein, who held on to beat Orlando by three-quarters of a length.

Orlando's owner, Colonel Peel, immediately slapped in his objection, claiming, on evidence supplied by Lord George Bentinck, that Running Rein was really a horse called Maccabaeus, and that, contrary to the limit on entries to three-year-olds, the horse was four years of age.

Jockey Club stewards upheld the protest, and awarded the race and stakes to Orlando. But Mr Wood refused to let the matter rest there. He decided to contest the decision by taking Colonel Peel to court at Westminster. On July 1, before Baron Alderson and a special jury, he claimed the horse's pedigree was a true one. He lost his plea because he could no longer produce the horse. The court was told it had vanished.

The true villain of the piece was not Mr Wood but former owner Abraham Levi Goodman.

Lord George Bentinck's detective work had revealed that Goodman had been owner of both Running Rein and Maccabaeus, and had sold the latter to Wood as Running Rein – on condition he ran him in the Derby. Since Maccabaeus was a far superior runner, and looked almost identical, he hoped to cash in at long odds. In the event Goodman had backed the horse to win £100,000 and then fled abroad when the row blew up.

Crime fits penalty

A burly centre-forward, sent off for violent conduct during a soccer match, said, 'If I'm to be sent off for that I may as well commit it.' He then hit the referee in the face. A London court fined him £20.

But incredibly, a second fraud attempt had been carried out in the race. Leander, who had to be destroyed after Running Rein's kick, was also a 'ringer'.

Ironically, if Leander had finished second, the Running Rein coup might have succeeded. Leander's owners would hardly have objected – since, at five, their horse was *two* years above the race's age limit!

Greyhound racing has also had its share of scandals as crooks and con-men have attempted to bash the bookies. Most have failed. But at London's White City on December 8, 1945, a gang pulled off the most spectacular swindle in the history of the sport. They got clean away with more than £100,000.

It was the 9.30 race, the last on the card, and second favourite Fly Bessie led at the first bend, closely followed by Jimmy's Chicken. Then, to the amazement of the 16,000 crowd, the dog began to swerve drunkenly and lose ground. One by one, the others also started stumbling . . . all except the rank outsider, a white hound called Bald Truth.

He streaked home 15 lengths ahead of the second dog, with favourite Victory Speech trailing in fourth.

No one was more amazed than Bald Truth's owner, Colonel B.C. 'Jock' Hartley, wartime director of the Army Sports Board. The dog had only been brought in as a late substitute to increase the field to five, and his £2 bet on it was ruled more by his heart than his head.

He sat speechless as fans shouted and growled, and track officials delayed making the official announcements. Surely it would be declared 'no race'.

But there was nothing the officials could do. No. 4 went up in lights; Bald Truth was the winner. Bets would be paid.

The affair, however, was far from over. Chief Inspector Robert Fabian of Scotland Yard was called in to investigate the coup, which followed a series of minor frauds at tracks around the country.

Slowly the pieces of the puzzle were fitted into place. The swindlers had used a dope called cholocretone. It was untraceable in pre-race examinations, but had an alcoholic effect as the dogs heated up during a race.

Investigators decided that the culprit had crept into a disused kennel, used to store straw and timber. Then, when all eyes were on the track during the penultimate race, he had crawled out, fed drugged pieces of fish to all the dogs except Bald Truth – the only white dog in the field – and returned to his kennel until the coast was clear.

Meanwhile the rest of the gang were placing bets with bookies all over the country and on the course, bringing the price down from 33–1 to 11–2 by the start.

Despite a £1,000 reward offered by the Greyhound Racing Association, the swindlers were never caught.

Derby Day at Epsom in 1844

Years later a crooked businessman, politician and philanthropist, Horatio Bottomley, attempted the most ingenious racing coup of all time. But, sadly for him, it was no more than an attempt.

Bottomley, a wheeler-dealer trader born in London's tough East End, bought his way into parliament through much-publicized charity work. He financed Australian gold-mines and made £3 million by juggling funds between his many companies, despite being served with 67 writs of bankruptcy.

He was also a racehorse owner and an inveterate gambler. And he knew that the only way to be certain of winning a race was to own every horse running.

That, Bottomley decided, was exactly what he would do!

The schemer scoured Europe for a country where racing rules were lax and where there was a racecourse to suit his devious purposes. He eventually chose Blankenberg, a Belgian seaside resort, where the course meandered through sand dunes, often obscuring the field from the spectators.

There were to be six horses in the race, and all were owned by Bottomley. The politician hired dozens of associates to place bets on his behalf – bets on the precise order in which the six horses would romp home.

The six jockeys were, of course, also in the pay of Bottomley who instructed them to sort themselves out into the required order as they raced off.

On the day of the race, disaster befell. A thick mist blew in from the sea and the jockeys could not even see one another. Their leader's startled cries to his fellow jockeys were muffled by the mist – and the six of them galloped to the finishing line in entirely the wrong order.

The betting 'coup' of the century ended as a fiasco. Bottomley lost a fortune, the first in a line of major setbacks that ended with a seven-year jail sentence for fraud in 1921.

Tout hits censor trouble

John Trevelyan, a man with a special interest in films, was accosted by a tout as he left his office in London's Soho.

Tout: 'How much would you like to see a blue movie?'

Trevelyan: How much will you pay me to see it?'

Tout: 'But you don't understand. You have to pay me to see it'.

Trevelyan: 'No, you don't understand. You have to pay me. It's my job.'

Tout: What do you do, then?'

Trevelyan: 'I'm head of the British Board of Film Censors.'

The unbelievable Horatio Bottomley

As we have seen from the unsuccessful racecourse fraud described in the previous chapter, Horatio Bottomley had the gift of the gab. He could charm people into parting with their money – and often talk his way out of trouble afterwards.

Bottomley was born in London's East End in 1860 but he rose to become a Member of Parliament and a conman with few rivals.

From an early age he knew what he wanted – money, fame, women and a successful political career. After first working as a solicitor's clerk and then a shorthand writer at the Law Courts in London, he turned his attentions to making money – big money – by fraud.

Together with friends, he launched a publishing company. Through another friend he bought some properties, including a printing works in Devon, for more than £200,000. Then he sold them to the publishing company for £325,000.

The trouble was that most of the properties were worthless. Bottomley knew it but the directors of the publishing company had been taken in by him.

Charged with fraud and sent for trial, Bottomley defended himself with such skill that he won. He so impressed the trial judge that he suggested that Bottomley should consider becoming a lawyer!

Bottomley's next move was into the Australian gold boom. By 1897 he had made a small fortune from promoting gold mines. Despite his success, his firms failed regularly and he was constantly being served with writs for bankruptcy.

Yet the public continued to pour their money into his ventures.

His method was simple. He would start a company, declare high dividends and as a result the price of the shares would rocket. Then he and his conspirators would sell the shares at the inflated price.

When the company started to sink, as it invariably did, up would pop Bottomley with a new company, offering to take over the old firm, backed, of course, by more funds from the unsuspecting shareholders.

Bottomley was instrumental in founding the *Financial Times* newspaper and the jingoistic magazine *John Bull*; he was elected to Parliament to represent the London constituency of Hackney South.

Although married, he kept a succession of young mistresses in love nests throughout the country.

At his home in Upper Dicker, near Eastbourne, Sussex, he lived the life of the local squire. But in 1912 he suffered a major setback when forced to resign from

Horatio Bottomley in 1927

Parliament because of a bankruptcy case.

Undeterred, he carried on as usual with his business enterprises and when hostilities broke out in 1914 used his demagogic powers in *John Bull* to support the war effort. He also made stirring recruiting speeches up and down the country – for which he charged a fee!

In 1918, with the war over, he was re-elected to Parliament for his old constituency. One year later he launched his biggest swindle and sealed his own fate . . .

Victory Bonds had been issued by the Government with a face value of £5, although investors could buy them at a discount price of £4 15 shillings. For ordinary working people this was still a lot of money; so Bottomley launched his Victory Bond Club. People were able to invest as little or as much as they wanted and the club would buy the bonds for them.

Bottomley was hailed as the friend of the little man – an image he loved to cultivate. What the investors didn't know was that their hero had siphoned off about £150,000 of the estimated half-million pounds that had flowed into the club in six short months.

The beginning of the end came when Bottomley started and then dropped a criminal libel case against one of his former partners, Reuben Bigland, who had accused him of a swindle.

By this time, the Chancery Court was investigating his empire and in 1922 he was prosecuted at the Old Bailey for fraudulent conversion of the funds of the Victory Bond Club.

This time Bottomley's glib tongue didn't sway the jury. After hearing evidence that he had used the money from the club to pay off £10,000 worth of debts, spent £15,000 on his burning passion for horse-racing and another £15,000 to buy and exhibit a German submarine, they took just 30 minutes to find him guilty. He was sentenced to seven years penal servitude but was released on licence in 1926. He tried to restore his old lifestyle, but in vain.

Horatio Bottomley, ex-millionaire, died in poverty in 1933.

Tea break

A woman who was picking blackberries from a cluster of brambles growing along the wall of London's Wormwood Scrubs prison noticed a rope and a wooden ladder drop down the side of the wall. Three men followed. 'I didn't raise the alarm,' said the woman. 'They told me they were nipping out for a cup of tea and planned to go back later.'

Going cheap – some of the world's best-loved landmarks

In 1925, within the space of a few weeks, a plausible Scottish rogue named Arthur Furguson sold off three of London's best-known landmarks to gullible American tourists. Buckingham Palace went for £2,000, Big Ben fetched £1,000 and Nelson's Column was sold for £6,000.

That anyone could fall for such obvious confidence tricks seems beyond belief. Yet Furguson was a past master at the art of gentle persuasion, thanks to his training as an actor. He appeared in repertory company melodramas throughout Scotland and northern England, once acting the role of an American conned by a trickster. Perhaps it was this part which inspired him to move south to London to try his hand in earnest at the con game.

The ex-actor would take up his position near a London monument, studying it with an air of rapt concentration. Soon a tourist would make an inquiry about the history of the monument and Furguson would engage him in conversation.

Once, while pacing around Trafalgar Square, he was approached by an American tourist from Iowa. Yes, said Furguson, the tower in the centre of the square was Nelson's Column, erected in honour of the great admiral. But sadly, he said, it would not be there for long. It was to be sold and dismantled along with several other landmarks to help repay Britain's vast war loan from the United States. And it was he, Furguson, who as a ministry official had been given the task of arranging the sale.

Yes indeed, Furguson informed the gentleman from Iowa, he was reluctantly authorized to accept a bid for the column even at this late stage. Furthermore, since the tourist was so obviously a lover of great art, he could arrange for him to jump the queue.

A cheque for £6,000 promptly changed hands and the American was left with a receipt and the address of a demolition company. It was only when the demolition company refused to consider carrying out the job of knocking down one of London's most historic sights that the American at last began to suspect that he had been taken for a ride.

Furguson used much the same ploy to dispose of the Big Ben clock tower and the King's royal residence of Buckingham Palace. Then, encouraged by his success in extracting cash from trusting Americans, he emigrated late in 1925 to enjoy this fount of easy money.

Within a few weeks he was back in action. In Washington DC, he met a Texas cattleman admiring the White House. Pretending to be a government agent, Furguson spun a slender yarn about how the administration was looking for ways of cutting costs. Now, if the Texan would care to lease the White House at a knockdown rent of $100,000 a year . . .? Furguson was in business again.

Moving on to New York, the wily Scotsman explained to an Australian visitor that, because of a proposed scheme for widening New York Harbour, the Statue of Liberty would have to be dismantled and sold. A great loss to the US, but would it not look grand in Sydney Harbour . . .? The Australian immediately began to raise the $100,000 that the con-man asked for the statue. But his bankers advised him to make a few further inquiries, and the police were tipped off.

This time Furguson had really slipped up. He had allowed the Australian visitor to take a souvenir snapshot of himself with the Statue of Liberty in the background. Police were immediately able to identify him as a man they had been watching.

Furguson was arrested, and a court sentenced him to five years in jail. When he came out, the master-hoaxer retired from the ancient monuments business and, until his death in 1938, lived in California – languishing in luxury on his ill-gotten gains.

The Balfour snowball

Jabez Balfour started with nothing and ended with nothing. But in between he made millions – by getting the public to invest cash in fraudulent companies.

Balfour became one of the most respected men of the late Victorian era. He was a Justice of the Peace, Mayor of the London suburb of Croydon and Member of Parliament for Burnley, Lancashire. He was on the point of landing a top Government job when his empire crashed and he was forced to flee the country.

Balfour is said to have originated the snowballing technique (whereby one company finances another) when, in 1868, he set up the Liberator Building Society. Over the next few years there followed a succession of companies such as the Lands Allotment Company, George Newman and Co. and the Real

Jabez Spencer Balfour

Estates Co. In 1882 he founded the London and General Bank with the main aim of processing the mass of dubious cheques that flowed from one into another of his companies.

While his companies bought and sold land and properties to one another – always of course with huge profits for Balfour and his cronies – the subscriptions poured in from the unsuspecting public.

The small investors believed in Balfour. Every year, regular as clockwork, they got eight per cent interest on their savings. Each time Balfour floated a new company it would be oversubscribed as the public flocked to invest.

Balfour was a success and they wanted to be part of it. What they didn't know was that their dividends were being paid out of new subscriptions and were not derived from any real company profits.

As the years passed, the snowball gathered speed and Balfour's business transactions became more and more complicated, his money-spinning schemes even bolder. He not only captivated his devoted investors but also dominated his business colleagues and employees, some of whom were genuinely honest men, others out-and-out villains.

Unlike some of his fellow con-men, there had never been a breath of scandal about Balfour. He had had a strict non-conformist upbringing and he carried this image of trust and respectability into his business and political life.

Large snowballs may take time to melt – but melt they do.

Suddenly in 1892, one of his companies collapsed, owing £8 million. It came out of the blue, quite stunning the financial world, so accustomed to Balfour's successes. Investors, and indeed the entire nation, were shocked at the news.

The only person not caught by surprise was Jabez Balfour. He was well prepared. While Britain was counting the cost of his 20 years of scheming and stealing, he was heading for South America, where he disappeared for three years.

Then, unhappily for him, he was recognized by a visitor to the little Chilean town of Salta. The man reported his discovery to the British Consul who eventually, after a long struggle, managed to extradite Balfour back to Britain to stand trial at the Old Bailey.

Some of the top legal brains of the time were lined up against Balfour. Masses of papers and legal documents were piled high on the court benches as they fought to show how he had swindled his way to millions.

It didn't take long for the jury to decide that he was guilty. He was sent to prison for 14 years with the words of the judge, Mr Justice Bruce, ringing in his ears: 'You will never be able to shut out the cry of the widows and orphans you have ruined.'

Balfour served his time and was planning to start up in business again when he died of a heart attack.

Bank busters extraordinary

Innumerable con-men have tried and failed to get the better of the mighty Bank of England. But it took four American financial wizards just six weeks to swindle 'The Old Lady of Threadneedle Street' out of £100,000 at the height of the Victorian era.

Their method was simple and it made George Macdonnel, Edwin Noyes, George Bidwell and his brother, Austin, rich men. But not for long.

They took advantage of a banking procedure that differed from the American system. The Bank of England had a well-established business in buying bills of exchange at discount rates.

The owner of a bill could take it to the Bank and exchange it for cash before it was officially due to be bought back by the finance house that issued it to raise capital. The Bank kept the bills until the end of the financial quarter when they were due to be repaid in full by the finance houses.

Macdonnel discovered that the Bank did not check whether bills were genuine before buying, as was done at home in America. He knew that a forgery would not be discovered until the end of a financial quarter, allowing the conspirators plenty of time to get away.

He sent word to his friends, the Bidwells, who joined him in London to launch the scheme in November 1872. Austin Bidwell opened an account under a false name at the Bank of England's branch in London's smart West End. Austin Bidwell must have been a very persuasive character, or the branch officials very gullible, for the Bank did not even check his identity, references or address. They seemed more than happy to have £2,000 on deposit from the smooth-talking American 'businessman'.

The conspirators' next move was to pay £8,000 in foreign currency into Bidwell's account. Any doubts entertained by the branch manager, Colonel Peregrine Francis, were surely allayed by the knowledge that his American customer was credit-worthy. Bidwell announced that he was planning to open a

---

What a gas!
Ronald Carr's gas-meter fiddle was a double disaster. He altered the meter the wrong way, so he ended up paying more instead of less. And in court at Rochdale, Lancashire, he was fined £75 for trying to steal the gas.

---

factory in Birmingham and might need to be granted credit. Francis quickly agreed. In order to strengthen confidence in Bidwell, the conspirators set about trading with genuine bills of exchange.

By the New Year of 1873 the time was right for the conspirators to move in for the kill. Bidwell informed Francis that his Birmingham factory had started to thrive and that he expected to be involved in some large financial transactions over the next few weeks.

Meanwhile, the men had been making faithful copies of their genuine bills of exchange. At this point they brought in from America Edwin Noyes, the fourth conspirator. His task was to present the bills of exchange and to help the gang change gold sovereigns for paper money which could be transported more easily.

In the six weeks up to the end of February 1873, Noyes exchanged a total of 94 bills, totalling £102,000. The plot came to light when the gang thought they still had three weeks of safety before the end of the financial quarter. In his haste to forge exchange bills, Macdonnel had failed to put dates on two of them. Bank manager Francis returned the bills to the finance houses that had supposedly issued them, to find that he had been duped. Noyes was the only member of the gang still in Britain and he was arrested as he went to close his bank account. Austin Bidwell was arrested in Cuba, his brother George was caught in Edinburgh and Macdonnel was extradited from New York.

When the case came to trial at the Old Bailey in August 1873, the evidence against the four men was so overwhelming that the defence lawyers did not even bother to address the jury. All four men were sentenced to penal servitude for life. Austin Bidwell was released after 17 years, Macdonnel and Noyes after 18 years. But George Bidwell, a con-man to the last, convinced the prison doctor that he was near to death and was released on compassionate grounds after only six years in jail. As soon as he was released, he made a remarkable recovery from his mystery illness.

A bevy of bottoms

Dozens of seemingly unrelated people received special invitations to a surprise dinner at a top London hotel. Nobody knew anyone else at the dinner but, as they introduced each other, they discovered that the guest list was made up of Winterbottoms, Sidebottoms, Littlebottoms, Witherbottoms, Highbottoms, Lowbottoms and plain ordinary Bottoms. One of these many Bottoms had called all the other Bottoms together for a joke.

The bouncing Czech who sold the Eiffel Tower at a knock-down price!

The idea came to Victor Lustig in a flash. There he was lounging in his Paris hotel room in March 1925 idly perusing the newspapers when he came across an item that made his eyes widen. The Eiffel Tower, said the report, was in need of major renovation. It had even been suggested that the city's most famous landmark should be demolished and rebuilt. . . .

To an artist, inspiration can come in a flash – and Victor Lustig was nothing if not an artist. The only difference was that his art was outside the law – he was a genius at deception. And the news item in that Paris paper opened up the opportunity for the coolest confidence trick of the present century.

First, Lustig (or 'Count Lustig', as he styled himself) acquired some printed notepaper from the French Ministry of Posts, which was responsible for maintaining the monument, and invited five French businessmen to a secret meeting at the Crillon Hotel, Paris.

When they arrived, they were ushered into a private suite by Lustig's 'ministerial secretary', a fellow con-man named Robert Tourbillon. The five were then sworn to secrecy and told the terrible news: that the Eiffel Tower was in a dangerous condition and would have to be pulled down.

There was sure to be a public outcry over the demolition of such a well-loved national monument, so the French government had to ensure total security. This was why five highly respectable and trusted members of the business community had been specially chosen for their loyalty and discretion.

The five flattered fools fell for Lustig's ruse completely. They each agreed to submit tenders for the value of the 7,000 tons of scrap metal that would be produced by demolishing the tower. Then they went away to make their calculations.

Lustig, however, had already picked out his candidate, a scrap metal merchant named André Poisson, one of the provincial nouveaux riches anxious to make a name for himself in the Paris business world. When, within the week, all five bids were in, Lustig accepted Poisson's and invited him back to the hotel to give him the good news.

It was then that the con-man played his master-stroke. He asked Poisson for a bribe to help the deal go smoothly through official channels. The duped dealer agreed willingly, and gave the back-hander in cash. If he had ever had any suspicions, they were now allayed. After all, a demand for a bribe meant that Count Victor must be from the Ministry!

Poisson handed over a banker's draft. In return, he received an utterly worthless bill of sale.

Lustig and Tourbillon were out of the country within 24 hours. But they stayed abroad only long enough to realize that the outcry they had expected to follow their fraud had not materialized. Poisson was so ashamed at being taken for a ride that he never reported the hoax to the police.

The 'count' and his partner returned to Paris and repeated the trick. They sold the Eiffel Tower all over again to another gullible scrap merchant. This time the man did go to the police, and the con-men fled. They were never brought to justice, and they never revealed just how much money they had got away with.

To a man like Lustig, proud of his art, selling the Eiffel Tower not once but twice was the pinnacle of a long career in confidence trickery. Born in Czechoslovakia in 1890, he had worked his way through Europe, using 22 aliases and being arrested 45 times.

He emigrated to America – but found the pickings so rich among the wealthy passengers on his Atlantic liner that he returned to make the transatlantic trip over and over again!

During the roaring Twenties, when 'making a fast buck' seemed to be all that life was about, Lustig preyed on the avarice of the greedy and gullible.

His cardinal rule when setting up a 'prospect' was to listen. Lustig never sold hard; he always let his victim do the talking, while the con-man showed deep interest. He would seek out his victim's political views and religious preferences and concur wholeheartedly to make him feel he had found a kindred spirit. But at the end of the day, the most crucial common interest would always be money.

Rags-to-riches multi-millionaire Herbert Loller had amassed all the money he could ever need. But he still wanted more, however dubiously it was acquired. Lustig demonstrated to him a machine which duplicated banknotes, and sold it to him for $25,000. Of course, it never worked. But by the time Loller discovered the fact, Lustig had disappeared to the next town, with another name and a new identity.

In the bootlegging days, Lustig insinuated himself into the company of Al Capone. It took a very brave, or perhaps foolhardy, man to tangle with the Chicago gangster, but Lustig actually tried to swindle him out of $50,000. The con-man told him he had a system that would ensure he doubled his money on Wall Street within two months.

Lustig took the money but after a while even he got cold feet and returned the $50,000 intact to Capone. The gangster must have taken a liking to the genial

Victor Lustig

fraud, because he forgave him and even gave him a $5,000 'tip' for his troubles.

Lustig's associations with the Capone gang continued for several years and led the trickster into an area of crime in which he found himself out of his class. That crime was counterfeiting.

By 1934 a special team of federal agents had been assigned to capture Lustig and his old Capone associate William Watts and to stem the flow of forged $100 bills which the pair were producing at the rate of $100,000 a month.

After tapping their phones for several months, the agents thought they had enough evidence. The pair were arrested and, although Lustig offered to reveal the whereabouts of all the counterfeit engraving plates if he were freed, he was thrown into New York's dreaded Tombs prison.

He didn't remain there long. One morning wardens found his cell empty and a sheet missing. They discovered it dangling from a window. Lustig had gone to ground again.

The master fraud may well have learned his lesson by now. After his jailbreak he fled to Pittsburgh and took on identity number 23 – that of quiet, retiring Mr Robert Miller. But luck was against him. A tip-off led police to his apartment and, after arrest number 47, he was put back in jail to await trial.

The outcome was the worst Lustig could have expected. In December 1945 he was found guilty of distributing a staggering $134,000,000 in counterfeit bills and was sentenced to 20 years imprisonment – the first part of it to be served on the escape-proof island of Alcatraz.

'Count' Victor Lustig, king of the con-men, served only 11 years of his sentence. He died in Springfield Prison, Missouri, in March 1947.

But what of Lustig's partner, Robert Arthur Tourbillon, the man who acted out the role of his 'secretary' in the greatest confidence trick of the century, the sale of the Eiffel Tower? Tourbillon, or 'Dapper Dan Colins' as the police knew him, had almost as amazing a career as Lustig himself.

Born in 1885, Tourbillon's first job was as a lion-tamer in a French circus. His act was called the Circle of Death and it involved his riding a bicycle around a pride of lions. Circus life was too tame for him, however, and at an early age he turned to crime.

He was 23 when he emigrated to America and was 31 when he first went to jail – for, of all things, 'white slavery'. He emerged from prison four years later determined to stick to the one crime he was best at: fraud. Until then, he had been known among the criminal fraternity as The Rat (after his initials) but he now styled himself 'Dapper Dan Collins', bought himself the smartest clothes in New York and set sail for his homeland, France.

He lived for several years in Paris, mainly off the proceeds of rich, old ladies who fell for the Casanova charm of this suave 'American'. In 1925 he and Victor Lustig pulled off their Eiffel Tower fraud and afterwards both men went to ground.

Further bad luck brought Tourbillon to the end of the road. Two American detectives who were in Paris with an extradition warrant for another crook heard about the suspicious exploits of 'Dapper Dan', sought him out – and recognized 'the Rat'. They arrested him and returned him to New York aboard the liner *France*. It was an amazing voyage. Tourbillon was given the freedom of the ship and, on his money, the trip turned into one large party for passengers, crew, criminal and detectives.

Amazingly, when the liner reached New York and Tourbillon was arraigned before a court, the robbery charges that had been brought against him failed to stick and he was freed. But not for long. . . .

In 1929, Tourbillon was charged with defrauding a New Jersey farmer out of $30,000 savings and was jailed for two years. He served 16 months and left jail vowing to return to France. Whether he did so or not, no one knows – for after speaking to reporters outside the jail, Tourbillon was never heard of again.

The match king who struck it rich

I var Kreugar struck it rich and created one of the biggest financial empires ever seen. The wily Swede, who captured almost three-quarters of the world's supply of safety matches, built his empire on a gigantic fraud.

He, conned millions of pounds from investors and banks in Europe and America before the bubble burst in 1932 and Kreugar – the man the world knew as The Match King – shot himself through the heart in his Paris apartment.

Kreugar was already a rich man when he embarked on his mammoth fraud. Born in Kalmar, Sweden, in 1880, he went to America when he was 19. When he returned to Sweden in 1908, he had amassed a tidy sum from dealing in South African gold and diamond shares.

Once home, he went into partnership with a friend called Toll. Between them they set up a building company which went from strength to strength, using many new techniques Kreugar had picked up while in America.

By 1914 Kreugar and Toll were wealthy. Then, suddenly, Kreugar quit and took over his family's ailing match business. He had taken the first steps on the rocky road to fame, fortune and suicide.

Kreugar was ruthless. By 1917 he had created the Swedish Match Company, of which he was president, by taking over or crushing all his competitors.

From this position of strength, he began to build a succession of companies. Each one was tied to the next by such a complicated web that only Kreugar knew how it all strung together. He wrote his own company reports and declared the profits and dividends.

Such was the success of his companies that investors fought to put their money in. What they didn't know was that most of the high dividends they received on their investments came not from profits but from money people had already invested in other Kreugar companies.

Kreugar had such tight control of his empire that everyone believed his valuation of its profits. It was almost impossible for anyone to unravel the deliberately complex figures in his reports.

Kreugar wanted desperately to be known as the world's Number One wheeler-dealer. He was already leading a frantic life of fast cars and mistresses in many European capitals when he decided to build himself a massive headquarters in Stockholm.

It was a huge commercial palace full of marble columns and fountains. His own office was magnificent with rich carpets, mahogany panels, beautiful decorations and a bank of telephones on his desk to impress even the most important of clients.

By 1921 Kreugar had established such a reputation and had such vast reserves of money available to him through investors and bank loans that he could embark on his final plan – to control the world's match market.

He knew what he wanted and he didn't care how he got it. If a rival company wouldn't sell, Kreugar either cut off their supplies of raw materials or sent in the thugs on his payroll to persuade or blackmail them into submission.

By 1922 the match industries of Sweden, Norway, Denmark, Finland and Belgium were in his hands.

In countries where the match industries were state-owned he simply offered to make loans to the governments in return for the right to total control of the industry. To do this he needed money – many millions, all of which he raised in America by persuading bankers and private investors to sink their cash into yet another of his new companies.

Much of the money went straight into Swiss banks. Not because he wanted to steal it. He just wanted it under his control so that he could use it as and when he wanted.

Over the next two years he loaned more than £150 million to 20 countries, giving him control of 65 per cent of the world's match production.

But the Wall Street stock market crash of 1929 sealed the fate of the Match King. As credit began to dry up all over the world, so many of Kreugar's clients who had borrowed money began to miss their repayments.

At the same time Kreugar still had to find the money for the governments to whom he had promised loans. He had to retain the confidence of his investors and creditors or his financial edifice would collapse.

He even resorted to straight trickery to get new loans from banks, using a receipt from one bank to get credit from another.

The final reckoning came in 1931 when he tried to sell one of his companies to the giant American-owned ITT corporation. Their investigation of the company books showed £7 million was missing. They called off the deal.

When the news broke, everyone wanted their money out of the Kreuger companies.

The Match King tried desperately to keep up the price of his shares by buying them with millions of pounds of his own money. But it was to no avail. The following year, when he heard the Swedish Bank were investigating one of his phoney deals involving forged Italian bonds, he went to his Paris flat and shot himself.

It has been said that Kreugar never intended to keep the money he conned for his personal use. If that had been the case, he would simply have disappeared when things started to go wrong instead of spending his personal fortune trying to prop up his empire.

No, say many who knew him, he just wanted to be Number One.

Titles for sale

Maundy Gregory made a mint out of selling titles to people desperate for honours. But the man who rubbed shoulders with kings, prime ministers and earls ended his years in exile and died in a wartime German hospital.

The artful conman was born in 1877, the elder of two sons of a Hampshire clergyman. His first job was as a teacher but he gave that up and went on the stage as an actor. He had some moderate success for several years before deciding to go into the business side of the theatre.

So in 1907 he opened up an office in London's Charing Cross Road as an impresario. His career in theatre management was short-lived. After two years he backed a musical extravaganza which collapsed, leaving him broke.

But although his business was in ruins, Gregory had made many useful contacts in high places. The scene was set for the Honours salesman supreme to move into the big time.

Like most conmen, Gregory oozed charm and confidence. He was kind and considerate to anyone he thought could help him, sometimes showering them with gifts. He dressed the part, too, with a diamond watch chain strung across his well-tailored suits.

He built up his image as a man of influence by launching a magazine, *The Whitehall Gazette and St James Review* – which was stoutly anti-Communist – and starting his own club, The Ambassador, in Conduit Street, London. Then he set up a palatial office in Parliament Street, close to Downing Street, with a commissionaire at the front door dressed deliberately as a Government messenger.

No one knew exactly where he fitted into the Establishment, but his victims were too flushed with the possibility of a knighthood or a peerage to enquire too deeply.

His con-trick was made that much easier by the fact that shortly after the end of the First World War the Prime Minister, Lloyd George, was openly selling off honours in a bid to boost his political funds – and to make sure he had plenty of supporters in the House of Lords.

Gregory had two ways of relieving his victims of their cash.

His first was to discover through his many contacts who was already in line for a knighthood or a baronetcy. Then he would check discreetly to see who on the list wanted an honour enough to pay for it. His rates varied but he usually charged £10,000 for a knighthood, £35,000 for a baronetcy and about £50,000 for a peerage.

The victim would be sent a letter suggesting a meeting to discuss a matter of great confidence. Many paid up, completely unaware that they would have got the honour anyway.

Plaster cast

Police in Sydney, Australia, ordered a drink-driving clampdown in 1970. They were keeping a discreet watch on one downtown club when they saw a customer stagger out of the door and fall down the front steps.

He picked himself up, stumbled to the car park, spent a few minutes trying to unlock the car, got in, crashed the gears and took off.

A police car followed, stopped him and gave him a roadside breath test. The test was negative. They took him to the police station for another test. Also negative.

Meanwhile the car park outside the club emptied as members drove off in a hurry. Puzzled police escorted the 'drunk' back to the car, and asked what he did for a living.

'I'm a professional decoy,' he said.

Just one call

A robber in Reno, Nevada, agreed to let a garage owner he was holding up make just one phone call. The owner called the police, who arrested the young raider on the forecourt.

His second method was to look for a rich businessman who he knew would pay for an honour and then use his contacts in the Government to get the man's name on the Honours List.

Gregory had a field day until a change of Government spelled disaster. The Conservatives, under Stanley Baldwin, were determined to stamp out the trading in honours and passed a new Act of Parliament in 1925 which made it illegal.

Undeterred, Gregory carried on as usual, but the big guns of the Conservative Party were out to stop him. They even infiltrated one of their top officials into his organization to get a list of people to whom Gregory had promised honours.

Then, in 1933, Gregory made a big mistake. He offered Commander Edward Leake a knighthood for £10,000. Gregory was arrested and tried at Bow Street Court under the 1925 Act. The Commander told the court how he had received a letter from a complete stranger offering an introduction to Gregory, who over one of his usual expensive lunches made his proposal.

Gregory told him how it would cost money to open the right doors to get him a knighthood and how he had done it many times in the past. The Commander went straight to Scotland Yard.

Gregory at first pleaded not guilty but later changed his plea to guilty. He was sentenced to two months in jail.

No further evidence was offered – and many people in high places breathed easily again. A long-drawn-out trial could have meant the exposure of many prominent people who had already done business with Gregory.

After his release, Gregory survived another scandal, over the mysterious death of Edith Rosse, a woman he had been living with for some years, before he slipped out of the country to live in Paris. There he remained as Sir Arthur Gregory until he died aged 64 in a German hospital in 1941.

Chapter
Three

Artful Tricksters

'The fear of the criminal is the same as the fear of
the artist: both are terrified of exposure.
It is basic to their nature.'
Richard Linder

The great Howard Hughes rip-off

It was billed as the publishing coup of the decade. But it proved to be the literary hoax of the century. The project was the 'autobiography' of the richest eccentric in the world, the legendary multi-millionaire recluse Howard Hughes.

The man behind this ambitious venture was an author named Clifford Irving, a man who, despite never having met Hughes, planned to write the mystery man's life story and sell the book to a publisher as being Hughes's own words.

Hughes was a sick, semi-senile man, possibly drug-addicted, and a fanatical recluse. He would allow nobody near him apart from the tight circle of Mormon male nurses who tended his needs in a succession of hotel-suites around the world,

Clifford Irving was an altogether different character. Born in New York in 1930, he was an incurable adventurer. Educated at art college and Cornell University, he sailed the Atlantic and lived with California's beatniks and Kashmir's drop-outs. He ended his ramblings when he married a pretty, slim blonde named Edith and settled down to write on the Mediterranean island of Ibiza.

His New York publishers, McGraw-Hill, encouraged him in his work and he attained moderate success. It was to McGraw-Hill that Irving turned when he wanted to sell his 'publishing coup of the century'.

Irving's amazing lie was this. . . . He had sent a copy of one of his own books to Howard Hughes for his critical comments. Hughes had replied in the kindest terms. The two had hit it off so well that Irving had boldly suggested 'ghosting' a Howard Hughes autobiography. And, to Irving's surprise, the old recluse had agreed.

McGraw-Hill fell for the bait. They agreed that Hughes would receive a hefty payment for allowing a series of tape-recorded interviews with Irving. And, of course, the author himself was to get large advances on the project. The total sum: one-and-a-half million dollars!

None of this went to Hughes. Roughly half of it was paid out – and all went into Irving's pocket. Not that it stayed there for long. The spendthrift author splashed out on luxury trips around the world. Wherever he went, he claimed to be keeping secret appointments with Hughes or his associates.

McGraw-Hill constantly fired off telegrams to Irving enquiring about the progress of the book. The author would reply from one five-star hotel or another, stressing the extreme difficulties of his task and Hughes's paranoid insistence on secrecy. Craftily, he maintained the publishers' interest by mailing them sample sections of the manuscript and providing letters supposedly sent to him by Hughes.

The sample chapters contained tantalizing quotations supposedly transcribed from tape-recordings made by Irving with Hughes. Some conversations were said to have taken place over the phone, others in person. The contents of the texts were mainly lies – but lies cleverly intertwined with rumour and half-truth and embroidered with the gleanings of newspaper libraries.

Irving's art-school training came in useful at this stage. For the letters signed by Hughes were in reality written by Irving to himself. The forgeries were so perfect that they fully satisfied the more doubtful sceptics at McGraw-Hill. At one stage, when the publishers became worried about the delay in receiving substantial parts of the manuscripts, they secretly took the Hughes letters to New York's leading handwriting analysts – who confirmed without doubt that they were indeed written by the old man.

Not all of Irving's work was pure fiction, however. The author had a secret source of hitherto unpublished revelations about the recluse. The source was Hughes's former aide, Noah Dietrich, who had made copious notes about his long liaison with the billionaire. Dietrich had been planning to turn this material into a book of his own. But Irving secretly borrowed the aide's notes, copied them and proceeded to lift from them some of the more interesting tit-bits.

McGraw-Hill were well and truly hooked. Tempted by fantastic stories of Hughes's secret World War Two missions, of his friendship with novelist Ernest Hemingway and of his glamorous, globe-trotting life-style, they kept the money pouring in. It arrived by post in the form of cheques made out to Hughes. They were paid into a Swiss bank account but the money did not remain there for long. The account, in the name of H. R. Hughes, had been opened by Edith Irving, using a passport forged by her husband.

Irving must have known that his amazing confidence trick could not last for ever. But when the crash came, it was from the most unexpected direction. By an amazing coincidence, someone else had been plotting a similar scheme to Irving's. A rival publishing house had taken the bait and proudly announced that an authorized biography of Hughes was shortly to be printed.

For a while, panic reigned at McGraw-Hill. The scene of confusion was repeated at the Time-Life organization which had agreed to buy the serialization rights to the Irving book. But the man at the centre of the storm remained as cool as ever. Irving produced a new forged letter from Hughes denouncing the rival book as a fake – and demanding more money for his own.

Raising the price was a master-stroke. McGraw-Hill once again fell for Irving's tale. But for the first time they had to show their own hand and announce the existence of the Irving book.

That sealed the conman's fate. Hughes ordered his lawyers to hold a press conference at which reporters who had followed the astonishing saga of the billionaire recluse were allowed to question Hughes by telephone. The Irving 'autobiography' was denounced, yet the trickster continued his protestations of innocence.

The man who finally shattered Irving's story was Robert Dolan Peloquin, a super-sleuth who had won the title 'Sherlock Holmes of the jet age'. This handsome 6ft 1in American lawyer had spent 16 years in the service of the US Government, taking on the con-men of the Mafia and the sophisticated criminals of the computer world. He was one of Bobby Kennedy's closest aides when the assassinated politician was America's Attorney-General.

Peloquin later left Government service to become president of Intertel, a private international intelligence agency based in Washington DC, with branches throughout the world. Ex-Scotland Yard head of CID Sir Ranulph Bacon joined him on the staff of what has been called 'the world's most formidable private investigating firm'.

It was at Intertel that Peloquin took a call from Chester Davis, lawyer for legendary recluse Hughes, who was alarmed at impending publication of the 'autobiography', and wanted Peloquin to prove the book was a fraud.

This meant knocking holes in publisher McGraw-Hill's claim that Hughes had collaborated with Irving. They based their claim on cheques made out to and endorsed by H. R. Hughes, and deposited in a numbered Swiss bank account. McGraw-Hill said handwriting experts had verified the signatures on them as that of Howard Hughes. But they refused to let Intertel see the cheques for themselves.

The controversy over the book was headline news. And that helped Peloquin get the evidence he needed. An executive of McGraw-Hill went on America's early-morning Today TV programme, brandishing three cheques worth a total of $650,000 and cashed by H. R. Hughes. Peloquin immediately obtained a video tape of the show, froze the frames where the cheques appeared, and had enlargements made of the prints.

It was just possible to see the name of the Zurich bank which had endorsed the payments. Peloquin was on the first available plane.

In Zurich, he was told that H. R. Hughes was a woman. Her description gave him a hunch. He phoned his Washington HQ and asked for a photograph to be wired to him. Four hours later he was back in the bank. The woman in the picture had her hair in a different style, but officials were almost sure she was H. R. Hughes. The picture, of course, was of Irving's wife.

Clifford Irving with his wife Edith and their two sons

Within minutes, the information had been cabled to Chester Davis, who called in the US Attorney in Manhattan. Irving and his wife were arrested.

Irving denied all until the very end. But his lies were finally seen for what they were when internationally famous singer Nina, the beautiful blonde half of the Nina and Frederick folk duo, revealed that at a time when Irving had supposedly been closeted with Howard Hughes, the author had really been with her.

In 1972, Edith Irving, distraught over the stories of her husband's womanizing, was sent to jail for two years in Switzerland. After hearing her sentenced, Irving sobbed: 'I have put my wife in jeopardy. She has suffered terribly. I have heard her cry herself to sleep at night.'

Then he too went down. After cracking and confessing all, Irving was fined

---

Shock of recognition

Swashbuckling silent screen hero Douglas Fairbanks senior was a great hoaxer. He had a special chair electrically wired to give mild electric shocks to anybody who sat in it. But he came unstuck once when a female fan sat in the chair. He applied the current but she showed no reaction. When he asked if she was feeling all right she explained: 'I thought one always felt like this when meeting a wonderful movie star like you, Mr Fairbanks.'

$10,000 and sentenced to 30 months' jail in the US. He was also ordered to pay back some of the $500,000 he owed McGraw-Hill.

Edith Irving served only 14 months of her sentence and her husband 17 months. But they were never reunited. Edith won a divorce and remarried her husband's former tennis partner. Clifford himself moved down to Mexico with a young woman friend.

There he set about writing another book, legitimately this time. It was a detailed, dramatic account of how he pulled off his $1½ million superhoax. He needed it to sell well in order to pay off his huge debts. And, ironically, the book was given a huge and topical sales boost soon after with the death in 1975 of the one man whose fabulous wealth had made the hoax of the century possible – Howard Hughes.

Who'll buy a tall story?

The one or two-paragraph items at the foot of newspaper pages are known in the trade as 'fillers'. Over the years they have become something of an art-form to journalists versed in the crafts of cliché, brevity and deadpan humour. Often, to serve these overriding interests, strict truth has come off second best.

The most famous, most imaginative and certainly the most audacious of these filler writers was Louis T. Stone, from Winsted, Connecticut. His career from 1895 to his death in 1933 consisted of paid lying.

It all began when he was working as a young cub reporter and needed $150.

What he actually needed was a story he could sell to the big-city papers. And since there wasn't a story, he decided to invent one.

He filed an account of the Wild Man of Connecticut who roamed through the forests without ever being caught. The story attracted the attention of New York editors, but was quickly spotted as a hoax. Stone, however, had learned a lesson that was to serve him well for the next 38 years.

He realized there was a demand for tall tales and set out to feed the market with gems like these . . .

'I have seen with my own eyes a man in this town – name of Samuel – who had such trouble with the flies buzzing round his old bald head, he painted a spider up there and that sure did scare all them doggoned flies away.'

And this one: 'In the next smallholding to me is a farmer who had a wonderful chicken who laid a red, white and blue egg on July 4th'.

And this: 'We have a cow that is so modest she only allows women to milk her. And another cow down Winsted way produces burning, hot milk, having been grazed on a horseradish patch.'

And this: 'I have seen and heard a cat with a harelip that could whistle Yankee Doodle'.

This too: 'One of the chicken farmers near here always plucks his chickens humanely – with a vacuum cleaner'.

These were all actual stories written by Stone and published as true – but editors just couldn't get enough of them. Many knew they were hoaxes but the readers enjoyed them so much they continued to print them. Certainly the people of Winsted appreciated Stone's efforts. As visitors drove in to the town, billboards greeted them with this sign:

'Winsted, Connecticut, founded in 1779, has been put on the map by the ingenious and queer stories that emanate from this town and which are printed all over the country, thanks to L. T. Stone.'

Stone is also commemorated by a bridge named in his honour. It spans a stream called Sucker Brook.

Lovely leg-pull

An official document circulated in October 1969 by the Ministry of Education and Science stated that West German scientists led by Professor Kitzelbein, had proved that girls with longer and shapelier legs were more intelligent. The report was a hoax pulled by Michael Proctor, First Secretary at the British Embassy in Bonn. And 'Kitzelbein'? It means leg-tickler!

The master-faker who even took Goering for a ride

How many of the treasures of the world's museums and art galleries are genuine and how many fakes will probably never be known. The art forgers are just too clever for most experts.

According to ex-forger David Stein, 'I can open an art catalogue anywhere in the world and recognize my own work.' Master-faker Elmyr de Hory said of the experts: 'They know more about fine words than fine art.' And Hans van Meegeren described them as 'arrogant scum'.

Van Meegeren is recognized as the greatest art forger of all time. But his criminal career was revealed only through the most amazing sequence of events. . . .

After the fall of Nazi Germany in 1945, Hermann Goering's priceless collection of old masters was uncovered at his Berchtesgaden mansion. Most had been looted from churches, galleries and private collections during the German march through Europe. A few, however, had been honestly purchased, and one of these was a painting entitled *Woman Taken in Adultery*. It was signed by Jan Vermeer, the 17th-century Dutch master.

In those first days after the war's end, the hunt was on throughout newly liberated Europe for collaborators. And when it was discovered that Goering's agents had paid £160,000 for the painting from a dealer in Amsterdam, Dutch police thought they had found someone who had been too generous to the Nazis. That someone was van Meegeren.

At that time van Meegeren was a rich nightclub owner who had amassed a small fortune by selling previously undiscovered old masters to major art galleries. Apart from the painting purchased by Goering, he had sold six other works signed by Vermeer to Dutch galleries.

Van Meegeren was arrested and thrown into prison to await trial as a collaborator -- a charge which could carry the death sentence. He was interrogated daily for three weeks without changing his story. Then, when he was finally brought to court, he came up with the most astonishing defence.

He said that, far from collaborating with the Nazis, he had actually duped them. He had not sold Goering a Vermeer but a van Meegeren -- the old master's work was a fake he had painted himself. And he had sold dozens of others for vast sums around the world.

At first the judge did not believe him. But he gave van Meegeren a chance. Placed under guard in his Amsterdam studio, he was told to paint another

Hans van Meegeren

THE WORLD'S GREATEST CROOKS AND CONMEN

Vermeer that would fool the experts. He did so – it was titled *Jesus Among the Doctors* – and he was freed.

The master-forger's freedom was, however, short-lived. For as more and more van Meegerens came to light, he was brought to trial again, this time charged with deception. He was jailed for 12 months, but died of a heart attack six weeks later at the age of 57.

What made van Meegeren embark on his career of forgery? Surprisingly, in view of the huge sums his fakes fetched, the motive was not money. Van Meegeren was a relatively successful painter who had his first major exhibition at The Hague when he was 33. It was a sellout, yet the critics slated it.

Foremost among them was a pompous professor, Dr Abraham Bredius, who dismissed van Meegeren's work with contempt. Over the years, the struggling painter's pent-up anger and frustration over Bredius's attacks found an outlet. Van Meegeren began to paint copies of the works of the artist whom Dr Bredius admired most of all: Vermeer.

Throughout 1936 van Meegeren remained in self-imposed exile in a rented villa in France, working on his masterpiece, a perfectly executed 'Vermeer' which he titled *Christ and the Disciples at Emmaus*. He 'aged' the painting 300 years by a process he had painstakingly developed.

In 1937 he put the painting on the market through a Paris lawyer, claiming that it had been in the possession of a Dutch family living in France. The family, so the story went, had fallen on hard times and now needed to sell their heirloom.

Naturally enough, the lawyer first approached Dr Bredius who, as the world's leading authority on Vermeer, could vouch for the painting's authenticity. He had no hesitation in doing so.

But not only did Bredius give his stamp of approval to the painting, he also – to van Meegeren's great delight – claimed the work as his own discovery. Bredius urged that it be bought for £50,000 by Rotterdam's Boyman's Museum. Bredius would often go there to study it – and van Meegeren to gloat over it.

Busting out all over

Perhaps the most prolific forger of sculptures was Giovanni Bastianini who before his death in 1868 turned out terracotta busts by the dozen under contract to an art dealer. They were considered to be perfect examples of Renaissance sculpture, and the Florentine faker's works appeared in museums around the world. There are still two in London's Victoria and Albert Museum.

Disgust at the ignorance of art 'experts' and anger at the dishonesty of dealers prompted another artist, Elmyr de Hory, to go into the faking business.

De Hory, a stateless Hungarian, received the greatest accolade of all when another famous faker, Clifford Irving, the American author later jailed for his forged biography of Howard Hughes, wrote a book about the artist entitling it simply *Fake*.

It was reported that paintings by the stateless Hungarian artist were among millions of dollars' worth of fakes sold to a Texas millionaire. The ensuing scandal made de Hory famous, although he insisted that he had never tried to pass his own work off as that of someone else. He said he had never put a famous signature to one of his own paintings – even when that painting was in the precise style of a sought-after artist.

In 1974, at the age of 60, de Hory was taken from his home on the Spanish island of Ibiza and jailed on Majorca. There was no formal charge, and the artist was out again after four months.

Like so many with his talents, he never disguised his contempt for the international art pundits who 'know more about fine words than fine art'. He claimed he could paint a portrait in 45 minutes, draw a 'Modigliani' in 10 and then immediately knock off a 'Matisse'.

'The dealers, the experts and the critics resent my talent,' he said, 'because they don't want it shown how easily they can be fooled. I have tarnished the infallible image they rely upon for their fortunes.'

Almost as quick on the draw as de Hory, but displaying rather more daring, was another brilliant artist, David Stein, who for a brief but mind-boggling four-year reign was undisputed king of the art forgers.

He was a talented painter in his own right, but the high prices paid in the art world were too great a temptation to resist. Working in watercolours or oils, he recreated the styles of some of the world's best-known artists – living and dead.

The dead gave David Stein no trouble, but the living led to his downfall.

Pressed for time one day, he rushed off three watercolours he had promised a dealer. Working furiously in his New York apartment, the whole fateful operation took just seven hours. At six in the morning he was lying in bed dreaming up ideas for the paintings. At one o'clock the same day he was handing a satisfied art dealer the 'genuine' works of French artist Marc Chagall, each with its own certificate of authentication.

In those seven hours he had treated the paper he used with cold tea to give it the impression of ageing, executed the watercolours, forged the certificates of authentication and Chagall's signature, and had the pictures professionally framed.

The art dealer was delighted when Stein handed over his 'find'. He examined the three forged Chagalls and, without ever suspecting the truth, began

Michelangelo's 'Antique'

**There is nothing new about the forgery of art-works.
Michelangelo himself is reputed to have raised much-needed
funds as a struggling young man by selling to a Rome cardinal a
statue of Cupid which the artist had first stained and buried to
age it into an 'antique'.**

haggling with Stein over the price. Eventually a cheque for $10,000 changed hands.

The dealer was so proud of his new acquisitions that he determined to show them to someone who had newly arrived in New York – Marc Chagall himself. For, while Stein had busied himself with the forgeries, Chagall had been flying into the city to supervise the installation of two huge murals he had painted in the Metropolitan Opera House.

The dealer had already fixed an appointment to see Chagall and, at their meeting, expected that the great artist would be delighted to see three of his earlier works again. Chagall's reaction at first bewildered then horrified him. 'Diabolical!' said the Frenchman, 'They are not mine.'

Had 31-year-old Stein stuck to Cézannes, Renoirs or Manets, he would have got away with it. As it was, the police came to arrest him that evening. The daredevil forger said afterwards: 'As they arrived at my front door, I left through the back with a glass of Scotch in my hand!'

He made his way to California and it was there that his luck ran out. He was arrested and confessed all. 'If only I had stuck to dead men,' he moaned when he was later indicted on 97 counts of grand larceny and counterfeiting.

While in jail, Stein shared his knowledge of faking with the New York Police Department, helping them create a special art forgery squad. With remission, he served just 16 months and, on his release, he left his three American galleries and half-a-million dollars a year income to return to his native Europe.

This was when the half-French, half-British Stein made his second mistake. He had not realized that the French police also wanted to ask him a few questions. That error cost him another two-and-a-half years in jail.

In the early 1970s, a free man at last, Stein decided to forget the old masters and stick to painting Steins. His fame as a brilliant forger aided his success and he later set up businesses and homes in both London and Paris.

But Stein was still angry at those people he regarded as the real fakers of the art world, the band of ignorant people who claim to be experts.

'A lot of the art world is fake,' he said. 'About two or three hundred of my forgeries are still on the market listed as originals.'

Which is the Mona Lisa?

The rich American collector felt the stirrings of greed. Here he was being offered a work of art that experts agreed was priceless for a knock-down figure of $300,000. It did not matter to him that the men offering the Mona Lisa for sale had stolen it from the Louvre Museum in Paris.

To own such a masterpiece was all he wanted and, who knows, after the fuss had died down maybe his children or his great-grandchildren could one day profit by its sale?

What he never suspected was that the same secret offer had been made to five other Americans. Six Mona Lisas – and not one of them was the real thing!

But the genuine masterpiece *had* been stolen, on August 21, 1911, when three thieves dressed as workmen came out of their overnight basement hiding place and coolly took it off the wall.

The gang consisted of art forger Yves Chaudron, con-man Eduardo de Valfierno, and Italian burglar Vincenzo Perrugia. They knew it was unlikely that the people they tricked would realize that their copy was a fake. Even if they did, they could not go to the police and admit to being part of a shady deal. Their reputations were at stake.

Chaudron and Valfierno had operated a similar scheme in South America. The trick there was to offer to steal a particular painting for a crooked dealer who would then sell it to a client.

Pretending to be art experts, they would ask a gallery owner to allow them to examine the picture. When it was down from the wall, Valfierno would cunningly line the back of the canvas with a forgery of the original painted by Chaudron.

On another visit, with the crooked dealer in tow, the victim would be invited to place his mark on the back of the picture he wanted stolen. Unwittingly, he would be marking the back of the fake. He later received his 'stolen' picture and the gallery owners never knew their part in the con-trick.

If the victim did wonder why the picture still hung on the gallery wall, Chaudron and Valfierno would tell him that a copy of the original had taken its place while the theft was being investigated. Super-salesman Valfierno even produced phoney newspaper cuttings telling of the crime to convince buyers.

The two rogues made enough money to afford the trip to Paris and to live in style there. It was only a matter of time before the Mona Lisa inspired the con-trick of a lifetime.

Perrugia's help was enlisted because, besides being a small-time criminal, he had once worked in the Louvre and knew his way about. He had put the glass in the box that protected Leonardo da Vinci's masterpiece.

Although Chaudron and Valfierno made almost two million dollars from the sale of the forgeries to unsuspecting Americans, they never got the chance to sell the Mona Lisa itself. Perrugia stole it from them and fled to Italy where he clumsily tried to sell it himself.

The gang were uncovered and the Mona Lisa was returned to the Louvre where, under heavy guard, behind a thick glass panel, and surrounded by electronic alarms, it remains today.

The theft of the Mona Lisa was not the first time that the Louvre had been taken for a costly ride. Its worst blunder was revealed in 1903 when a Parisian painter claimed that he was the creator of one of its most treasured possessions – a beautifully intricate golden headdress called the Tiara of Saitaphernes.

The claim was untrue. The tiara was a fake, sure enough. But the man who had made it was not the Parisian painter. Its creator was a Russian goldsmith, Israel Rouchomowsky.

Rouchomowsky did not want the false claimant to take credit for his work, so he travelled to Paris to put the record straight. The administrators of the Louvre continued to deny that the tiara was a fake until the old Russian produced the original designs he had drawn for the headdress eight years earlier – and, to rub salt in the wounds, began working on a new tiara, as intricate in every detail as that in the Louvre.

The faker famous for his 'Sexton Blakes'

Brilliant faker Tom Keating rocked the art world he despised with his amazing imitations of the works of great masters. In 1979, at the age of 62, he went on trial at the Old Bailey for forgery. But all the charges were dropped when his health deteriorated.

Keating, a big bearded ex-naval stoker, called his fakes, in Cockney rhyming slang, 'Sexton Blakes'. At first he painted them to get even with the dealers who had, he reckoned, exploited him.

As a young man, he had lived in a damp prefab with his wife and two children, and was paid £5 a time to copy other artists. He angrily quit the job when he found his paintings on sale in galleries for £500.

'Those dealers are just East End blokes in West End suits,' he said. 'They

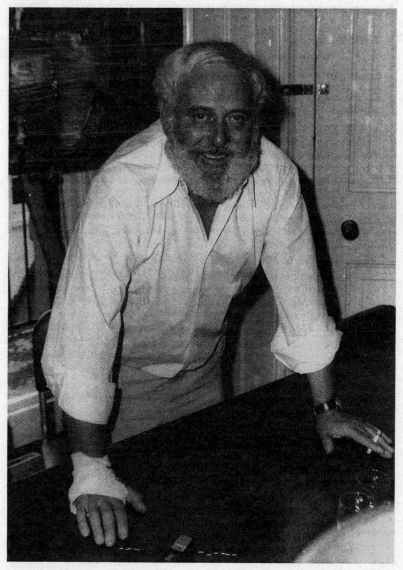

Artist, Tom Keating

Fake Madonna

America's Cleveland Museum of Art had to remove from display one of its most prized possessions, a wooden Madonna and Child, supposedly carved in Italy in the 13th century. In fact, it was carved around 1920 by an Italian art restorer, Alceo Dossena. His fake was only discovered when in 1927 the sculpture was X-rayed and modern nails were found to be embedded in the wood.

The museum put the Madonna and Child in its basement and looked around for other works to replace it. Three weeks later it bought a marble statue of Athena for $120,000. It, too, was a Dossena fake.

---

don't give a damn about the paintings. All they're after is the profit.'

In the 1950s his marriage broke up and he went to Scotland to restore murals. While he was there he began imitating the works of other painters and sending them to auction.

He returned to London in 1960 for his most important commission – restoring the pictures in Marlborough House which had been empty since the death of Queen Mary in 1953.

One day he met Queen Elizabeth while carrying out the restoration of a giant painting by Laguerre of the Duke of Marlborough.

In his book, *The Fake's Progress*, Keating recalls: 'The Queen came up the stairs and gazed at it in astonishment. She turned to me and mentioned that she had run up and down the stairs hundreds of times as a little girl but had not been aware these beautiful pictures were on the wall. "Well they are madam," I said. "And there's a lot more under the black varnish on the other walls."'

Then, according to Keating, the Queen watched him use a solvent to clean a section of the painting.

The work at Marlborough House was an isolated job for hard-up Keating. Most of his time would be spent turning out his 'Sexton Blakes' by the score, giving most of them away but selling others through auction rooms.

In 1963 he read a book on the 19th-century artist Samuel Palmer and became captivated by him. He scoured the art galleries looking for examples of Palmer's work to copy. At the Tate, said Keating, he touched one 'and a strange sensation went through me like an electric shock'.

Keating was a perfectionist. He was always careful about selecting the right paper or canvas. And he claimed that the spirit of Palmer would guide his hand.

'I'd sit in my little sketching room waiting for it to happen,' he explained. 'I have never drawn a sheep from life but then Palmer's sheep would begin to appear on the paper. Then Palmer's *Valley of Vision Watched Over by the Good Shepherd in the Shadow of Shoreham Church*. With Sam's permission I sometimes signed them with his own name, but they were his, not mine. It was his hand that guided the pen.'

It was also in 1963 that Keating met Jane Kelly, a pretty convent-educated schoolgirl busy studying for her exams. In Bohemian coffee bars, she and her friends would cluster round the painter, treating him almost as a guru.

Jane was 17, Keating 46. Yet, after the death of her boy-friend in a road accident, they fell in love – and the impressionable teenager became the painter's mistress. They moved to historic Wattisfield Hall in Suffolk, where Jane restored pictures and Keating embarked on a prodigious output of fakes.

When, at the Old Bailey in 1979, Keating was shown his most famous fake – a sepia, ink-wash of *Sepham Barn* sold for £9,400 as a genuine Palmer – he told the jury: 'I am ashamed of this piece of work.'

He had no recollection of painting it, he said. It had, however, been done using modern materials, the main figure of a shepherd was 'un-Palmerish' and the flock of sheep 'unsheep-like'. It was the sort of painting, he confessed, that he would normally have burnt or thrown away.

Looking at another work subsequently sold for £2,550, Keating appeared bemused and said: 'That must have taken me about half an hour. It's just a doodle. It has the ingredients of Palmer but not his technical ability of aesthetic appeal'.

The 'doodle' was of a barn at Shoreham, which had been sold at a country auction for £35. It was later sold by a London gallery to Bedford Museum for £2,550 after restoration work by the National Gallery.

Bemusing the Met

In 1918 the New York Metropolitan Museum of Art paid $40,000 for the 7-ft statue of an Etruscan warrior which had supposedly been buried since pre-Roman days. One arm of the warrior was missing, as was the thumb of his other hand.

In 1960 Alfredo Fioravanti confessed to the museum that he was one of six men who had created the statue between them 50 years earlier. He produced the warrior's missing thumb to prove it. The thumb fitted perfectly.

In 1975 the same museum had to withdraw from display a beautiful 'Greek' bronze horse when it was shown to be a fake. The horse had been one of the museum's most popular attractions.

After the sale of *Sepham Barn*, Keating and Jane went to live in Tenerife. There, Jane met a Canadian with whom she fell in love and whom she later married. The nine-year affair between Jane and Keating was over. They met again seven years later – when Jane gave evidence at the Old Bailey about Keating's famous fakes. The scandal, which ruined many reputations in the art world, broke after an expert had written in *The Times* suggesting *Sepham Barn* was not genuine.

By Keating's own rough count, no fewer than 2,500 of his fake pictures are hanging in galleries or on collectors' walls. No one will ever know which are fakes and which are old masters. Not even Tom Keating who, after his trial was stopped, continued turning out his paintings – at a price.

Because of his notoriety, Keating's works became highly prized. 'Suddenly everyone wants to own a Keating,' said one gallery owner. 'Prices have doubled in a month. His paintings are going round the world.'

Keating was offered a £250,000 contract from one London gallery and a £30,000 commission for a single portrait. He turned both down.

'I have enough work to make me rich beyond my wildest dreams,' he said. 'But I've met many millionaires and they have all been miserable. All I have ever wanted to do is to paint. I would give all the damn things away if I could afford to. Painting is God's gift, not mine, and it should be used to bring pleasure.'

At the height of his fame, a television film was made about the master-faker's life and work. Director Rex Bloomstein got to know him well. He said of Keating:

'He was a very emotional man. When painting, he would cry and shiver. He said he felt the artist come down and guide his hand. he was the most fascinating, complex person I have ever met.'

Crowning jest

In 1902 hundreds of upper-crust Americans received invitations to the Coronation of Edward VII and Queen Alexandra of England. Attached to each invitation was a set of instructions about the proper attire for the Coronation. Wealthy Americans were asked to turn up in costumes typifying the origins of their titles. Coal barons might wear miners' helmets, judges might carry six-shooters, and railway tycoons might sport guards' whistles. The invitations were, of course, a hoax. But they were cleverly adapted facsimiles of the genuine articles.

The pitfalls of literature

Two of the most famous forgers of all time were teenagers. Both lived in the 18th century, both forged literature, and their names were Thomas Chatterton and William Henry Ireland.

Chatterton became known as 'the Marvellous Boy'. Before he was 10 he had taught himself how to write in Gothic characters by copying from an old Bible. In 1765, when only 12, he started producing ancient poems which he claimed he had found in an old chest in the local church. He said they had been written by a priest named Thomas Rowley, possibly around Chaucer's time – 400 years earlier.

Not only did these odes convince scholars of their antiquity but they also received some fine critical acclaim. Spurred by his success, Thomas left his native Bristol for London. But the London experts were not fooled so easily and declared his works to be forgeries.

Although he had a minor success with his own poems and political satires, Thomas Chatterton's career was soon in ruins and at 17 he took his own life.

In his will, he left 'all the young ladies my letters and poems. I leave my mother and sister to the protection of my friends if I have any.'

Chatterton was later recognized to have been a budding genius. He became an inspiration to later poets such as Wordsworth, Shelley and Coleridge. He was immortalized in a painting by Henry Wallis and is the only forger to have had an entire opera written about him – Leoncavallo's *Chatterton*.

The other teenage forger of that time was William Henry Ireland who, although not so talented, also made the stage – with a Shakespearian production which he wrote himself.

William had started early by handing over spurious Shakespearian manuscripts and artefacts to his father, a London bookseller and Shakespeare enthusiast. William claimed that while working as a solicitor's clerk, a mysterious gentleman had entrusted all the documents into his safe-keeping. These he showed his father, who showed them to friends – and the news of the Shakespeare discoveries spread like wildfire.

What began as a jape rapidly turned into an industry. The young Ireland produced a land deed and other private papers of William Shakespeare. Then he got bolder and produced original transcripts of parts of *King Lear* and extracts from *Hamlet*. These were so convincing that even the diarist and biographer James Boswell paid homage. He said: 'I now kiss the invaluable relics of our bard to thank God that I have lived to see them.'

With this sort of success under his belt, Ireland really went to town. At the age

Thomas Chatterton

of 17, he 'discovered' a brand new Shakespearean play which no one had seen before. He called it *Vortigern*.

The play was produced at the Drury Lane Theatre on April 2, 1796. The actor-manager John Kemble, who was to play the lead, had his doubts about the authenticity of the piece and suggested that it would have been more appropriate to open the play a day earlier on April Fool's Day. But although the play did open on April 2, Kemble got the last laugh. In Act Five there was a speech which contained a line that brought the house down. . . .

'And when this solemn mockery is ended. . . .'

The audience hooted the rest of the play off the stage. The first performance of *Vortigern* was also its last and the game was up for Ireland. The rest of his forgeries were detected and the teenager confessed to everything – although his old father could never bring himself to believe that his treasured possessions were all fakes.

The bullet that found its mark 20 years late

Henry Ziegland thought he was a dead man. Standing before him was an angry young man, gun in hand, telling him that he was about to kill him. The gunman was the brother of Ziegland's ex-girlfriend, who had just committed suicide after being jilted. The brother was out for revenge.

The gunman pulled the trigger. The bullet grazed Ziegland's face and buried itself in a tree. Ziegland fell to the ground and stayed still, as the brother, thinking he had accomplished his mission, turned the gun on himself and blew his brains out.

The murder that never was occurred in Honey Grove, Texas, in 1893. Over the next 20 years, Ziegland put the incident from his mind. One day in 1913 he decided to fell the tree on his land under which the shooting had occurred. It was a tough job, so he used dynamite.

He drilled a hole in the tree trunk, filled it with explosive and set the fuse. The explosion blasted fragments in all directions – and sent the old bullet through Henry Ziegland's head, killing him instantly.

Chapter Four

Brigands and Outlaws

'The Devil, depend upon it, can sometimes do a very
gentlemanly thing'
Robert Louis Stevenson

The most wanted men in the West

What was the truth about the Wild West? Our ideas tend to have been formed by characters like Tom Mix, Gene Autry, the Lone Ranger and Roy Rogers. Screen idols through the years have portrayed the cowboy as a slick, good-looking, gun-totin', lariat-twirling goodie in a white hat, or scheming, scowling baddie in a black hat.

Hollywood took the names of men like Billy the Kid, Jesse James and Butch Cassidy and turned them into heroes. But few of the folk who lived and died in the 19th-century West would have agreed. . . .

Baptist minister's son Jesse Woodson James strolled into the Clay County Savings Bank in Liberty, Missouri, on February 13, 1866, and took the liberty of relieving cashier Mr Greenup Bird of $60,000.

It was the start of a bloodthirsty war that the James boys and their daring cousins, the Youngers, waged throughout Kansas and Missouri. They got away with gunning-down train guards and bank tellers because nobody knew what the villains looked like – since none of them ever had his photograph taken.

Jesse would openly stroll around Nashville and Kansas City, calling himself Mr Howard, and on one occasion even bought a drink for a Pinkerton Agency detective searching for him.

Detective Bligh confided to 'Mr Howard' that his last wish would be to confront Jesse James. Later James sent him a note: 'Go ahead and die. You've seen Jesse James.'

Jesse loved playing to the crowd. On one occasion during a Missouri train hold-up, he personally presented the guard with his latest press cuttings.

The day Jesse and his boys slipped up was when they tried to rob the First National Bank in Northfield, Minnesota. The townsfolk had been tipped off that the gang were on their way, and as they arrived in town they were met with a hail of bullets, grapeshot and even bricks. Two of the gang were blown to pieces, three Younger brothers were captured, but Jesse got away.

The man who finally put paid to Jesse James was a gunslinger named Bob Ford, who joined the gang after secretly agreeing with the authorities to assassinate James for a free pardon and part of the reward money.

On April 3, 1882, Jesse, then aged 35, got up to straighten his favourite 'Home, Sweet Home' picture on the wall of his bunkhouse abode. Ford blew off the back of his head, and his brains scattered across the floor.

The owner of the house where Jesse died, at St Joseph, Missouri, chopped up

The only authentic portrait of Billy the Kid

the floor and sold the blood-stained wood-shavings for five dollars a time.

The James gang's greatest partners in crime were the Younger family. Cole Younger, then 28, first teamed up with Jesse's gang in Logan County, Kentucky, in 1868, to rob the local bank.

Cole had already met Jesse as one of Quantrill's Raiders at the massacre of Lawrence, Kansas, where, in one of the most unparalleled acts of savagery in the West, 150 men and boys were shot by William Quantrill's Confederate guerillas.

Cole had a passionate love affair with Myra Belle Shirley, the 18-year-old daughter of a Dallas horse-breeder. After two disastrous marriages, she went on to achieve notoriety as Belle Starr.

The other Younger brothers – Bob, 18, Jim, 26, and John, 28 – later joined Cole in the James gang. John died from a Pinkerton bullet and the surviving three were captured and jailed for life after the Northfield, Missouri shoot-out.

Butch Cassidy and the Sundance Kid were turned into posthumous superstars thanks to one successful film. In real life, neither were heroes – although a cut above some of the other crooks of the age.

Butch Cassidy was born Robert Leroy Parker in 1867 in Beaver, Utah, but later changed his name as a token of respect to his idol Mike Cassidy who taught him the arts of rustling and horse stealing.

In his youth, Butch was involved in everything from petty larceny to train and bank hold-ups. But it wasn't until he was released from Rawlings Penitentiary, Wyoming, that he decided to get his own gang together. They soon became known as the Wild Bunch.

Legend has it that Butch, eulogized by contemporary posters as a cheery, affable character, never shot directly at a man. When pursued by a posse he would always fire at the horses.

Trains were the speciality of Butch and his Wild Bunch. One day they scooped $30,000 from a Union Pacific express by detaching the last car and blowing it and the safe inside to smithereens. They followed this success with three more train raids until Pinkerton agents got on the gang's trail.

The Pinkertons and the railroad's own crime fighters forced the gang to seek refuge in South America. Around 1909 (some say in Bolivia, others in Uruguay), Butch and his chief cohort in crime, Harry 'Sundance' Longbaugh, either committed suicide or were shot dead in a battle with troops.

Harry Longbaugh had got his nickname when, as a boy, he served 18 months in jail at Sundance, Cook County, Wyoming, for horse stealing. Thereafter, he called himself the Sundance Kid.

The Kid had no raindrops falling on his head – only 'wanted' posters. In late 1901, Sundance and his lady love, Etta Place, sailed for Buenos Aires after being run out of the US by the Pinkertons.

The Wild Bunch. Butch Cassidy is seated on the right and the Sundance Kid on the left.

He continued robbing banks and trains, managing to keep one step ahead of the law by hiding out among local Indians, until his death alongside Butch Cassidy.

The most famous gunfighter of the West was a soft-spoken, agreeable young man named William Bonney, better known as Billy the Kid. Believed to have been born in New York, he moved west with his family and became a cowboy in Lincoln County, New Mexico. There he worked for an English ranch owner John Tunstall, who befriended him.

In March 1878, two killers riding with the posse of corrupt Sheriff Brady of Pecos blasted Tunstall to death. When Bonney, then aged 19, heard of his benefactor's death, he grabbed a pair of Colt 44s and went looking for the two killers.

Billy found them and shot them dead. Then, with a price on his head, he teamed up with a gang whose members put paid to Sheriff Brady.

By now, Bonney's fame was spreading. People began talking about a gunslinger named Billy the Kid.

THE WORLD'S GREATEST CROOKS AND CONMEN

State Governor Wallace tried to con Billy into giving himself up. Wallace hired the Kid's one-time friend, Pat Garrett, who persuaded Billy to testify at an inquiry into gang warfare in Lincoln County in exchange for a light sentence.

The Kid walked smack into the trap – but shot his way to freedom. Unknown to Billy, Garrett was made Sheriff of Lincoln County in recognition of his treachery.

Still trading on their old friendship, Garrett guessed that eventually the Kid would head towards the hideout of a mutual friend, Pete Maxwell.

Garrett got there first, urging Maxwell to persuade Billy to surrender. But as they were talking, Billy walked in – straight into two slugs from Garrett's Colt.

Billy the Kid, 21, sprawled dead with 19 notches on his gun. But he could never add up. He had actually killed 21 people in less than two years to avenge his friend and earn himself a place in American legend.

The Wild West is packed with stories of vicious outlaws. But one robber who stood apart was Black Bart. He was always courteous, never hurt anybody and stole only from the treasure box and mailbags, never from the passengers.

Bart's first hold-up was on a blazing hot day in 1875 when he stopped a Wells Fargo stagecoach near Sonora, California. As the horses struggled up a hill, a strange armed man jumped out from the bushes. He wore a flour sack on his head, with holes cut out for the eyes, and a long, white coat.

He ordered the driver to throw down the box and mailbags, and he shouted to his hidden accomplices to shoot if anyone offered resistance. The driver saw six guns poking out from the bushes. They were all trained on the stagecoach.

What followed that day has passed into Western folklore. For when a petrified woman passenger threw her purse at Bart's feet, he calmly picked it up. With a gracious bow, he returned the purse and said he was interested only in the treasure box and mailbags. Not passengers' money or valuables. The strange robber took his loot and told the driver to continue his journey.

For several years, Black Bart robbed in his cavalier manner. His reputation and courteous ways became the talk of California. And he never earned more than £250 from each of his stagecoach robberies, since most gold and valuables were by then transported by train

The man given the task of nailing Black Bart was Jim Hume, Wells Fargo's chief detective.

He soon realized that Bart was cunning and resourceful. When he visited the scene of that first robbery, Bart's 'gang' were still there   six sticks poking through the bushes.

Hume learned little about Bart. He left no clues, his trail just petered out and he seemed to walk everywhere rather than ride.

Bart became bolder and even left Hume his name and a poem at the scene of

Charles E. Bolton, alias Black Bart

one of his crimes. Then Black Bart began to slip up.

After a series of hold-ups, Hume visited houses in the area and learned that a grey-haired, hitch-hiking stranger with a grey beard, white moustache and two missing front teeth had stopped to have dinner. A picture of the hooded raider was at last emerging.

A laundry mark on a handkerchief finally led to Black Bart's capture in 1882. The thief managed to escape unharmed when he was interrupted by a young gunman as he was about to rob a coach. But he blundered by leaving his sleeping-roll and his handkerchief.

Jim Hume had no trouble tracing the laundry mark to a San Francisco laundry – and that led him to a Mr Bolton. He was an elderly man, softly spoken, with grey hair, grey beard, white moustache and two missing front teeth.

Mr Bolton explained his long absences from home by saying that he had to make frequent visits to his mine. But there was no mine, and Jim Hume knew he had his man when Black Bart's clothes were found at Bolton's home.

Black Bart was arrested and, courteous to the end, returned much of the money taken on his raids. For their part, Wells Fargo made charges only on one hold-up and forgot about the others.

By now, the gentlemanly thief had become a popular hero. The judge must have had a soft spot for him, too. He was jailed for six years. It could have been worse.

Black Bart Bolton may have been one of the last stagecoach robbers – but he is remembered first and foremost as the outlaw who wouldn't hurt a fly.

Worst of the 'goodies'!

If the baddies of the Wild West were bad, the goodies were often worse! The men whose job it was to dispense law and order were frequently as lawless as their criminal quarry.

In the West, theatrical farces were put on in saloons and dance halls. But perhaps the most farcical scenarios were those staged by the local judges: and the most unorthodox of all these dispensers of justice was Judge Roy Bean.

A former Civil War guerilla, Judge Roy was a gambler, saloon-keeper and one-time smuggler who got the judge's job in Vinegaroon, Texas, at the age of

Judge Roy Bean

56 because he had picked up a smattering of law while running a construction camp saloon. Mindful of his background, he would regularly stop trials to serve liquor to counsel, jury and defendants, and play a couple of hands of poker before resuming.

He made his own laws and meted out his own fines, most of which he pocketed. He once doubled as a coroner after a worker had fallen 300 ft to his death. Bean did not think the coroner's five-dollar fee was enough, so he searched the body and found $40 and a revolver.

Said Judge Roy: 'I find this corpse guilty of carrying a concealed weapon – and I fine it $40.'

It is doubtful whether a twerp like Wyatt Earp ever became Marshal of Dodge City or even Tombstone. Chroniclers of the West said he brought peace and prosperity to the two frontier towns. But the myth was hatched by writer Stuart Lake, who sold a story to the *Saturday Evening Post*, praising 'lawman' Earp.

Earp, born in 1848, was only briefly a lawman. He took the job of Marshal of Lamar, Missouri, but soon decided that hunting buffalo in Kansas was more fun.

He became a card-sharp and worked a double-act in Wichita – as a gambler by night and a policeman by day. After being thrown out of town, he became assistant Marshal of Dodge City, a member of the local church, an alcoholic and womanizer. His two great boozing buddies were Ford County Sheriff Bat Masterson and James Henry 'Doc' Holliday.

The people of Dodge became fed up with Earp's activities and fired him. In 1879, Wyatt, his brothers and Doc Holliday arrived in Tombstone, Arizona, and set out to make their fortunes by fair means or foul.

Wyatt worked for Wells Fargo before being offered the job of keeping the peace in one of the town's gambling dens. His cronies were installed as croupiers, his brother Virgil became acting Marshal (after the murder of the unfortunate incumbent) and the Earp fortunes prospered.

In 1881 the Tombstone stage was held up. Rumour had it that Earp, Holliday and Masterson had masterminded the robbery with the help of the Clanton Gang. Nevertheless, it was the Earp brothers and Masterson who led the unsuccessful posse in its search for the raiders!

When, later that year, he had his shoot-out with the Clantons at the famous OK Corral, Earp made sure that nobody was left alive to put the finger on him.

Earp soon left Tombstone and, after running saloons in Alaska and Nevada, died in Los Angeles in 1929 at the age of 80. Stuart Lake's biography immortalizing the 'noble lawman' was published after his death – and was denounced by relatives as 'a pack of lies'.

But Wyatt Earp was a paragon of virtue compared with his friend John 'Doc'

Wyatt Earp

Holliday. Holliday was an alcoholic, an inveterate gambler, was tubercular and a walking skeleton with a dangerous temper. He would kill at the slightest provocation.

He originally came west from Baltimore, with qualifications as a dentist, because the climate was better for his health. He did other people's health no good at all. Holliday had gunned down 14 men even before the famous OK Corral shoot-out. Doc died in 1887, a victim of raging consumption. He was just 39.

In their quest for a character who really symbolized law and order in the cow towns, Wild West chroniclers hit upon one James Butler Hickok.

Long-haired, cold-eyed, Wild Bill Hickok was a Union scout in the Civil War who became a professional gambler and once shot dead a dealer who had been producing aces from the bottom of the deck.

Stories about his gunfighting prowess – most of which he had dreamed up himself – won him the job of Marshal of Abilene, Kansas. But he was sacked after shooting wildly at a party of roistering drunks and killing one of his own deputies instead.

Hickok went on a wild spree of boozing, gambling and whoring. In 1876, he was shot in the back during a poker game. He too was 39 when he died.

In his heyday, Wild Bill Hickok had teamed up with Buffalo Bill in his famous travelling stage show. The two men had a lot in common. Both were liars and both liked the bottle.

Buffalo Bill (real name William Frederick Cody, born Iowa, 1846) was a Pony Express rider, buffalo shooter, Indian fighter, cowpuncher, intrepid scout and incredible boaster.

He was encouraged in this latter practice by the wildly exaggerated claims of author Ned Buntline who churned out 121 dime novels supposedly based on the life of Buffalo Bill.

One boozy afternoon in North Platte, Nebraska, overhearing that no festivities had been planned for the forthcoming July 4 celebrations, Cody spontaneously organized a local talent contest, advertising for cowboys to display their skills.

He expected a hundred. Over a thousand cowboys turned up. That was the start of the famous Buffalo Bill Wild West Show which toured the West for 30 years and was even seen on Broadway and across Europe. Queen Victoria was in the audience when it toured Britain.

Like all good hard-living, hard-drinking entrepreneurs, Buffalo Bill Cody died in 1917 – broke.

The ugliest gals in the West

Beauty, grace, fresh-faced femininity . . . the famous gals of the old West had none of these. Despite their portrayal on cinema screens as glamorous, gun-totin' ladies, these women were often worse than their violent menfolk. And from the photographs that have been passed down to us, we know that the one thing they lacked was good looks. In fact, most of them were downright ugly!

Calamity Jane in 1880

Belle Starr and Indian Blue Duck

They had names like Calamity Jane, Belle Starr, Dutch Annie, Blonde Marie, Madame Moustache, China Mary and Big Nose Kate.

Often they would just as soon shoot you as take you to bed. And for 30 roistering years in the mid-1800s they drank, fought, shot and loved their way into Western legend.

Calamity Jane (born Martha Jane Caaery) got her nickname because so many of her lovers wound up on Boot Hill. She was a drunkard, chewed tobacco, swore like a cavalry trooper and packed an equally hefty punch.

She became a mule-skinner, an army scout, served under General Custer and fell in love with Wild Bill Hickok, near whose grave she was buried in 1903. Calamity was also the biggest liar in the West.

Belle Starr was a notorious outlaw who loved and bore a child to Cole Younger and who rode with Jesse James. Born Myra Belle Shirley, she married an Oklahoma Indian named Sam Starr and was sent to jail with him for horse-stealing.

She also had affairs with bandit Jim Reed (shot dead), a man named John Middleton (shot dead by Sam Starr), Indian desperado Blue Duck (also shot by Starr) and another Indian, Jim July, who survived her. Sam Starr himself was shot dead in a gunfight. And Belle was shot in the back while out riding in 1889. She was 41.

Poker Alice was really Alice Ivers, daughter of an English schoolteacher, who married a card-sharp mining engineer. She won her nickname by spending more time at the gaming tables than at home.

She smoked large cigars, wore outlandish, expensive clothes and, after the death of her husband, opened a brothel. She was as fast with a gun as she was with the cards, and in her long career she shot dead at least two men.

She died virtually penniless in 1930 at the age of 79.

Dutch Annie, Blonde Marie, Madame Moustache and China Mary were all brothel queens, vying with each other for the favours of the hard-drinking, hard-loving frontiersman. They had their counterparts in every cattle-town from the Dakotas to New Mexico.

Big Nose Kate, born Kate Fisher, was a dance-hall girl who attached herself to the Earp gang and became girl-friend to 'Doc' Holliday somewhere between Dodge City and Tombstone.

Holliday must have been shortsighted as well as an alcoholic for Kate was the ugliest of the lot. But she did establish Tombstone's first dance-hall in a specially built marquee.

Pauline Cushman was one of the sexiest, wildest, man-destroying predators in the West. A one-time actress turned bar-fly, she would goad men into gunfights and then sleep with the winner. In San Francisco music-halls, men would go wild as she came on stage, firing six-guns into the ceiling.

Dick Turpin, 'king of the road'

'**S**tand and deliver!' Travellers on the muddy, rutted, bumpy roads of Britain trembled at that cry for almost 200 years. But these travellers, although in peril of losing their purses, were seldom in fear of their lives. For many of the highwaymen who haunted the main routes through England between the early 1600s, until 1815, when a permanent police force was introduced, were gallant men. Rather than common thieves, they were often toasted as gentlemen who happened to have fallen on hard times.

Over the years an aura of glamour surrounded those dashing, charming perfectly behaved brigands of the night. They were heroes of literature and even of song – as in the most popular opera of the 18th century, *The Beggar's Opera*. But no highwayman was made more famous than the young man known as the 'King of the Road' – Dick Turpin.

Turpin was born in 1705 at the Bell Inn in the village of Hempstead, Essex. The inn, since renamed the Rose and Crown, was owned by his father, an ex-butcher. At 16, Dick was apprenticed to a London butcher, but the move to the big city gave him extravagant tastes and at night he became a footpad to eke out his modest income.

Completing his apprenticeship, young Turpin returned to Essex, married and set up in business as a butcher on his own account. He wasn't successful, however, and again he turned to crime. In 1729 he was caught selling stolen carcasses and he went on the run. He became a housebreaker, a cattle thief, a smuggler, a deer poacher in Epping Forest – and eventually a highwayman.

In 1736 one of the best-known criminal partnerships of all time was forged. Turpin was 'working' the Cambridge road out of London when he saw an immaculately dressed horseman approaching. 'Stand and deliver,' demanded Turpin. But the inexperienced highwayman received in reply only a laugh of derision from his intended victim, who was none other than the most famous brigand of the day, Robert King, known as the 'Gentleman Highwayman'.

Their partnership ended a year later in a shoot-out with London police. Turpin had earlier held up a horse dealer and stolen his prize racehorse. It was a reckless act as the horse would certainly be recognized. Sure enough, Turpin was spotted riding through the city. In an ambush, King was shot by the police, King's brother was accidentally shot by Turpin, and the highwayman fled.

He fled north, to Cambridge, Lincoln and finally Yorkshire, all the time making a living by sheep stealing. In Yorkshire, under the name of John Palmer, he would hunt with the local hounds, dine with the local gentry, and

Dick Turpin

dally with the local ladies, in between 'business trips'.

After one particularly wild night of revelry near York, Turpin began firing off his pistols in the street and ended up in jail while magistrates investigated his recent misdemeanours. Desperate that his real identity should not be discovered, he wrote to his brother back home at the Bell Inn, Hempstead.

> Dear Brother,
> I am sorry to acquaint you that I am now under confinement in York Castle for horse stealing. If I could procure an evidence from London to give me a character, that would go a great way towards my being acquitted. I had not been long in this country before my being apprehended, so that it would pass off the readier. For Heaven's sake, dear brother, do not neglect me. You will know what I mean when I say
>
> > I am yours
> > John Palmer.

Unfortunately for Turpin, the postmaster at Hempstead was Dick's old schoolmaster, James Smith, the man who had taught the young Turpin to read and write. Incredibly, he recognized his ex-pupil's handwriting and reported the matter. Smith was sent to York to identify Turpin and received £200 reward.

Dick admitted all, was tried and inevitably sentenced to be hanged. While awaiting execution he sat chained in leg-irons in York Prison cheerfully welcoming a steady flow of admiring visitors.

On the morning of April 7, 1739, Turpin was led through crowds of onlookers to the gallows on what is now York racecourse. 'All the way', according to a witness, 'he bowed repeatedly and with the most astonishing indifference and intrepidity.'

Standing undaunted, head held high, Dick Turpin hurled himself from the platform to ensure a brave but speedy end to his daredevil days.

But what of the most famous story of all about the dashing highwayman? According to tradition, books, films and television, Turpin once rode his horse Black Bess non-stop 200 miles from London to York to avoid capture. It is a romantic tale . . . but pure fiction.

Winning ways

In 1928, Liberian President Charles King put himself up for re-election. He was returned with an officially stated majority of 600,000 votes. King's opponent in the poll, Thomas Faulkner, later claimed that the election has been rigged. When asked to substantiate his allegations, Faulkner pointed out that it was difficult to win a 600,000 majority when the total eligible electorate was less than 15,000.

The most heroic legend in the history of crime

He was a criminal, a violent outlaw and highway robber who, with a band of common thieves, plundered the traffic of the king's highway. Yet he is the most enduring hero of his age. His name: Robin Hood.

It is a name that, against all the odds, has survived 600 years. Detail about him has always been scant. His nefarious activities, if true, were in any case minor. And he was not immortalized in any great literature. The illiterate peasantry of the Middle Ages passed on his name, his fame and his supposed deeds by word of mouth from one generation to another – in ballads and fireside stories. As a result, an obscure criminal, with no place in history, acquired international fame. He is the subject of films and television series which owe more to scriptwriters' imagination than to historical research.

How much of the Robin Hood legend is true? Historians over the centuries have debated the issue, challenging his adventures, and disagreeing on the vital question as to whether there even was an outlaw called Robin Hood in Sherwood Forest in the late 13th or early 14th century.

Some believe that the stories of the sprite-like hero may be connected with a mythological pagan woodland spirit. Robin was a name often given to fairies, and green is the supposed colour of the wood spirits – Robin Hood is always depicted as wearing green. There is also a theory that the outlaw was the incarnation of one of the characters depicted in ancient May Day ceremonies. 'Maid Marian' may also have appeared in the celebrations, as Queen of the May.

However, records do show that in the 13th and 14th centuries there lived in Wakefield, Yorkshire a real Robin Hood who may have been the legendary outlaw. This Robin, christened Robert Hood, was born in about 1290. His father, Adam Hood, was a forester in the service of John, Earl Warenne, lord of the manor of Wakefield. The surname in old court documents is variously spelt Hod, Hode and Hood.

On January 25, 1316, Robin Hood's 'handmaid' is recorded as having been brought before a court for taking dry wood and 'vert' from the 'old oak'. Vert is the old English term for trees which provide shelter and food for deer. She was fined twopence. Other court records for the year 1316 show that Robin Hood and his wife Matilda paid two shillings 'for leave to take one piece of land of the lord's waste' to build a five-roomed house.

In 1322, Robin's landlord – at this time, Thomas, Earl of Lancaster – called his tenants to arms in rebellion against King Edward II. A tenant had no choice but to obey his lord implicitly, and Robin Hood followed the earl into battle as an archer. The revolt was crushed. Lancaster was tried for treason and beheaded. His estates were forfeited to the king and his followers were outlawed.

Robin Hood fled into Barnsdale Forest, which at that time covered about 30 square miles of Yorkshire and was linked to Nottinghamshire's Sherwood Forest, with an area of 25 square miles. The forests were traversed by the Roman-built Great North Road, with its rich pickings for robbers. And so the legend of Robin Hood was born.

One of Robin's supposed escapades along this highway concerns the haughty Bishop of Hereford, who was travelling to York when he came across the outlaw leader and some of his companions roasting venison. Taking them for peasants, and infuriated by the flagrant breach of forest laws, the bishop demanded an explanation. The outlaws calmly told him that they were about to dine. The bishop ordered his attendants to seize them.

The outlaws begged for mercy but the bishop swore that he would show them none. So Robin blew on his horn, and the unhappy bishop found himself surrounded by archers in Lincoln green. They took him prisoner, with all his company, and demanded a ransom, amusing themselves by making him dance a jig around a large oak tree. The tree is no longer there but the ground on which it stood is known as Bishop's Tree Root.

Several other oak trees in Barnsdale and Sherwood are associated with Robin Hood and his band. Centre Tree, half way between Thoresby and Welbeck, is said to be the marker from which Robin Hood's network of secret routes stretched through the forest. But the most famous tree is Major Oak, at Birkland. It is reputedly a thousand years old and has a girth of about 29 feet. Alfred, Lord Tennyson visited this oak in the 19th century and in his poem 'The Foresters', has Little John referring to it as '. . . that oak where twelve men can stand inside nor touch each other'.

Among the stories passed down the centuries about Robin Hood's prowess is that of a visit he made with his closest friend, Little John, to Whitby Abbey. The abbot asked them to demonstrate their skill with the bow by shooting from the monastery roof. Both did so, and the arrows fell either side of a lane at Whitby Lathes – more than a mile away. The abbot had two stone pillars erected on the spots where the arrows fell. The pillars survived until the end of the 18th century. The fields on either side were also named after the event: Robin Hood's Close and Little John's Close.

Little John, who was Robin's second-in-command, got his nickname because of his height. He was said to have died at Hathersage, in Derbyshire, and his grave there was reopened in 1784. In it were found the bones of an exceptionally tall man.

J. Gilbert.

ROBIN HOOD & GUY, OF GISBORNE.

Best of both worlds

Police in Venezuela issued a warrant for the arrest of a known criminal. Unfortunately for them, the man's house was built slap across the Venezuela-Colombia border. When they called to arrest him, he ran into his bedroom, locked the door and phoned his lawyer. The bedroom was in Colombian territory and the offence with which he was to be charged was not punishable in that country. The Venezuelan police gave up.

Robin and his men certainly got around. Robin Hood's Bay, away on the Yorkshire coast, was named after him. It was here that the outlaws were reputed to own several boats, which they kept for fishing and for possible escape from the authorities.

On one of his journeys, Robin Hood visited St Mary's Church, Nottingham, where a monk in the congregation recognized him and alerted the sheriff. Robin drew his sword and slew 12 soldiers before being captured. But before he could be brought to trial, Little John led a band of the outlaws into Nottingham and rescued him. They also sought out the monk and murdered him.

But it was Robin Hood's supposed championing of the underdog that made him into a folk hero. His robbing of the rich and gifts to the poor, and his flouting of unpopular authority, became an inspiration to the oppressed peasantry of old England.

On one famous occasion Robin Hood was supposed to have met King Edward II. The story goes that the king, hearing that the herds of royal deer in Sherwood were diminishing because of the appetites of Robin Hood and his band, determined to get rid of the outlaws. So he and his knights disguised themselves as monks and rode into the forest.

They were met by Robin Hood and some of his band, who demanded money. The king gave them £40, saying that was all he had. Robin took £20 for his men and gave the rest back to the king. Edward then produced the royal seal and told the outlaw leader that the king wished to see him in Nottingham. Robin summoned all his men to kneel before the seal and swear their love for the king. They then invited the 'monks' to eat with them – and fed them on the king's venison. Later Edward revealed his identity and pardoned all the outlaws – on condition that they would come to his court and serve him.

The story is told in *A Lytell Geste of Robyn Hood*, published in 1459. It may not be complete fiction – the king was certainly in Nottingham in November 1323 and the story of his action fits what is known of his character.

A few months later, in 1324, the name of Robin Hood appears in the household accounts of Edward II. There is a record of wages paid to him until

November of the same year. After that date, he vanishes into folklore again. Perhaps after enjoying the free life of an outlaw, he was unable to settle in service, even for his king.

Robin Hood's adventures in the forests continued until about 1346 when he is reputed to have died at Kirklees Priory. The prioress there, said to be his cousin Elizabeth de Stainton, is reputed to have hastened his death, when he begged her to help relieve his pain during an illness, by bleeding him until he was too weak to recover.

On his death-bed, so the story concludes, Robin Hood managed to blow his famous hunting horn, which summoned his faithful companion Little John to his side. Robin then shot an arrow from the window of his room and asked to be buried wherever it might fall.

Richard Grafton, who wrote a story about the outlaw band in 1569, said that a tomb was set up at that point by the prioress. But the reason is not flattering to the Robin Hood of popular legend. Grafton wrote:

'The prioresse of the same place caused him to be buried by the highway side, where he had used to rob and spoyle those that passed that way. And upon his grave the sayde prioresse did lay a very fayre stone wherein his name was graven. And the cause why she buried him there was that for the common strangers and travailers, knowyng and seeyng him there buryed, might more safely and without feare take their journeys that way, which they durst not do in the life of the sayd outlawes. And at either end of the sayde tombe was erected a crosse of stone, which is to be seen there at present.'

The stone is no longer there. But the spot claimed to be the grave of Robin Hood can still be seen to this day.

Skulduggery on the high seas

Between 1550 and 1750, thousands of British sailors turned to piracy in the West Indies, the Mediterranean and along the coast of Africa. Some merchants who dabbled in piracy were well rewarded for their services to their country – for most of the victims, mainly French, Portuguese and Spanish, were Britain's enemies.

Francis Drake was knighted for his voyages of discovery, even though Queen Elizabeth I knew he had engaged in piracy, an offence punishable by death; but her 'daring little pirate' had made his queen rich and was an honoured subject.

For other sailors, piracy was a chance to escape a harsh, unrewarding home life and resort to a career of cunning and violence.

John Avery went to sea as the mate of a trading vessel and soon proved his daring by leading a mutiny in 1694. He and his adventurous crew plundered merchant ships. But he established his reputation as the con-man of the high seas by his skill in deceiving victims to part with their valuables without even resorting to violence.

Off the coast of Guinea he took down the skull and crossbones flag, the 'Jolly Roger' trademark of piracy, and hoisted the English flag in its place. The natives, knowing they could trust the English, rowed out and came aboard Avery's ship to trade their valuable gold. It soon became obvious that they had fallen into a clever trap and Avery sent them packing – making sure they left the gold behind.

Avery even tricked fellow pirates into handing over their booty without drawing his cutlass. The pirate captains, based in Madagascar off the African coast, were continually bickering about the way treasure was shared out. Using his great powers of persuasion, Avery convinced the captains that they should entrust their booty to him for safe keeping. Avery kept it so safe that they never saw it – or him – again! But Avery failed to hang on to his ill-gotten gains. A group of scheming merchants tricked him out of his loot and the pirate captain died in poverty in his native county of Devon.

Avery's cheek was surpassed by that of Captain Charles Vane, one of the most impudent pirates of all. In 1718, Britain, under pressure from European countries, sent warships to the Bahamas to put an end to the operations of pirates.

But Vane knew the ships were on their way. When the heavily armed fleet sailed into the pirate bay they were greeted by Vane's vessel sailing straight towards them, flying flags of welcome. The smartly dressed captain and his crew politely saluted the incoming ships and sailed cheekily past them out into the ocean. The salute was returned by the British ships and officers who docked to find they had been duped by the pirate ringleader.

It was a love affair between one of Vane's former seamates, John 'Calico Jack' Rackham, and Anne Bonny that led to one of the most notorious eras in pirate history.

Anne, an adventurous and spirited girl, dressed as a sailor to join Rackham's wild crew so as to be near her beloved Jack. Anne knew she would be in danger if the men found her out, because a woman on board a pirate ship was supposed to be a sign of bad luck. Anne fooled the crew long enough to prove she was as tough as any man on board, and the pirates accepted her. Her trickery had paid off. She revelled in adventure and was always one of the first to leap aboard any Spanish or Portuguese ships under attack.

Sir Francis Drake

When Captain Rackham captured a pirate ship in 1720, Anne found a worthy companion on board – Mary Read, a tough girl who had fled the slums of London for a thrilling and adventurous life.

Both girls got a chance to show their bravery when their ship was attacked by an armed vessel sent from Jamaica to arrest Rackham's pirates. As the faint-hearted men cowered below the decks, Anne and Mary stayed above to fight. When the ship was eventually captured and the crew brought to trial, Anne and Mary both escaped the gallows.

They kept up their trickery to the very end and fooled the judge into letting them go. He believed their story that they were both expecting babies and should be spared!

Romantic reign of the swashbuckling heroes

For 100 years, until the mid-18th century, the entire southern coastline of England was ruled by romantic, swashbuckling bands of smugglers. From the Essex marshes to the rocky cliffs of Land's End they were heroes – 'our brave lads' – to most of the population.

The profits from smuggling were immediate and enormous. From the time of the Norman Conquest, English fleeces were exchanged for fine French wines without more than lip service being paid to the laws that imposed import duties on all foreign luxuries. But not until the 18th century did 'free trade' develop to the point that it involved just about every owner of a lugger that could navigate the Channel on a dark night.

For many a farmer's boy or country inn-keeper's son, a gloomy night and the noises that came through it held few terrors. In fact, by the time he was 16 he might have been starting an apprenticeship that could eventually lead to riches and power.

There were many steps to climb in the 'organization'. He might start by merely holding the horses at one of the interchange points, where London buyers took over smuggled goods for delivery to inland customers. He would almost certainly graduate to the status of tubman, hauling heavy bales and kegs up the beaches to hiding places in caves or lonely churchyards.

He might go on to become a batman – a cudgel-wielding 'heavy' who watched the backs of the tubmen and was ready to spring into action at the first sign of trouble from the Revenue men. Or if the boy's father owned a fishing boat he might begin by actually helping to ferry contraband across the

Channel, learning the route between two coves with no help from the stars.

A lad who knew how to read and write would always be in demand, for the smugglers needed scrupulously kept accounts. In this violent world it could mean sudden death to short-change buyers or sellers. But practically every country craft could be adapted: coopers were needed to fashion cunning barrels with a false skin to hold tea or spirits, and boatbuilders to construct craft with false bottoms and sides or secret compartments where barrels could be hidden.

As the trade developed into a full-scale industry, big money was needed, and in the first half of the 18th century crime syndicates virtually took over the south coast. And, like syndicates in every age, they did not stop at one crime but added extortion, bribery, highway robbery and murder.

It became increasingly obvious to the government that it was losing vast sums of money in duty, and a corps of preventive officers was built up, who, despite the inefficiency and cupidity of senior Customs officials (many of whom were themselves customers of the smuggling rings) and the bribes offered by the smugglers, displayed integrity and courage and faced every sort of danger to make arrests. Many undoubtedly died in lonely coves or alleyways.

In the year 1733, Revenue men seized 54,000 pounds of tea and 123,000 gallons of brandy – the tip of the iceberg, for they rarely captured more than 10 per cent of an illegal cargo. Tea bought at 3½p a pound in Holland sold in England at anything from 17p to 25p; French brandy bought for £1 a keg fetched £4 in the UK.

This was how Thomas Johnson, who made a fortune out of smuggling and lost £11,000 at the gaming tables, managed to return to his old trade and make a second fortune. And it was in this way that Arthur Gray, who with his brother William masterminded the notorious Hawkhurst Gang, was able to retire (though still planning and financing local operations) to a £10,000 mansion.

At the height of its power, the Hawkhurst Gang, holding sway in Kent and Sussex, was capable of assembling an armed band of 300 men to recover a cargo of tea impounded by the Customs. In October 1747, the men marched from mid-Kent to Dorset, stormed the Poole Customs house and marched back with their booty.

On the outward journey they were cheered through the villages, but as news spread of the sadism with which they had murdered two harmless old men suspected of being informers, the ordinary people started to turn against them. It was the beginning of the end for the gang which, though powerful, relied heavily on the goodwill of the countryside.

Once the gang's influence was broken, and its leaders hanged or transported, its place was taken by the ruthless Ruxley gang, working out of a Hastings cove known as Bo-Peep – (the name, today, of a railway junction). It took 200

A popular print of smugglers from the 1840s

dragoons to subdue the Ruxleys, and even then they might have won the day had they not also been involved in territorial struggles with a gang from Folkestone.

In Devon and Cornwall, contraband regularly travelled the routes followed today by the Plymouth, Roscoff and St Malo ferries. Typical of famous Cornish smugglers was John Corlyon, of Coverack, who, when his boatbuilding business failed, set up as a smuggler and made a handsome living.

There was a strict law against signalling from the shore to a smuggling vessel, but John got round it very simply. If the coast was clear, his wife hung a red shirt from her washing line. If no red shirt appeared, the Revenue men were around. How could they prosecute someone for *not* giving a signal?

Another notable Cornish smuggler was Henry Cuttance, who was captured by a press-gang and taken to sea. He escaped by throwing his hat over the side with a cry of 'man overboard!' As the crew sought the drowning man, Henry slipped over the other side of the vessel and swam the $2\frac{1}{2}$ miles to safety. . . .

Most smugglers encouraged the tall tales that were told about their exploits – and if they had a supernatural twist which kept the credulous away, so much the better. Even today there's a tale of the 'demon drummer of Hurstmonceux Churchyard'; it's a fairly safe bet that the original drummer was a smuggler, detailed to deter the local inhabitants.

Many smuggling yarns became entangled with more ancient folklore. Certainly this was the case with Cruel Coppinger, who so terrorized the people of Welcombe Mouth, on the north Devon and Cornish border, that his name was used to quieten children and became inextricably linked with Viking raiders.

Even today, people of the Romney Marshes, Kent, retell stories about the sinister parson-cum-smuggler named Dr Syn, convinced that they are recounting local history. In fact, the character made his debut in novels written in the 1920s.

Smugglers loved such names, none more so than the Cornish Carters, a father and eight sons who styled themselves the Kings of Prussia because they moored their boats in Prussia Cove.

Jack Rattenbury, who began his smuggling career at the age of nine, working on his uncle's boat, liked to be described as the Rob Roy of the West. Flogged so severely with a rope's end for losing the rudder that he never spoke to his uncle again, Jack, who published his autobiography *Memoirs of a Smuggler* in 1937, was probably the last of the old-style swashbuckling smugglers.

By the early 1800s, times were getting hard for real-life smugglers. By then they had to evade not only an increasingly efficient Customs service but also Navy press-gangs, who recognized them as ideal recruits for their boat-handling and gunnery skills. And desperate men, prepared to accept the gallows or transportation as one of the risks of their profession, often reformed rather than face the harsh discipline of life aboard a warship of Nelson's day.

Chapter
Five

Signs of the Times

'For man's greatest crime is to have been born'
Pedro Calderon de la Barca

Computer crooks

The most sophisticated swindlers of modern times are the skilled thieves who are cashing in on the world's fastest-growing crime wave: computer frauds.

Computers, of course, are triumphs of human invention. But these technological marvels can also be extremely stupid – because they never, never ask questions. And even when a computer fraud is uncovered, the company is often too embarrassed to report it to the police.

Probably only about ten per cent of such crimes ever result in police investigation, representing the mere tip of an iceberg whose likely size is illustrated by the fact that in Britain alone more than 50 Scotland Yard detectives are working full-time on £100 million worth of computer frauds.

Two young British computer experts gave up their jobs to form a company advising firms on the dangers of computer-assisted crime. They claimed: 'A computer fraud can be perpetrated in a fraction of a second – the time it takes to blink.' They came across the chief of one computer centre who netted £25,000, from one company, then moved on to take £75,000 from another.

But not every computer cheat is so ambitious. One programmer working for a cigarette company rigged the computer so that it credited him with free savings coupons which he then exchanged for gifts.

Such a fiddle would be no more than child's play to American computer crooks, who currently operate a £100,000 million-a-year growth industry.

One ingenious American bank employee with access to a computer programme devised a system whereby he added 10 cents to every customer service charge of less than $10 and $1 on those above $10. He credited the difference to an account he had opened for himself under the unlikely name of Zzwicke.

The fraud should have gone totally undetected. But the bank, as a promotional stunt, decided to make gifts to the first and last names on their alphabetical list of clients. Last, of course, was Mr Zzwicke!

A variation on the same stunt was played at another bank where an employee ordered the computer to 'lose' 10 cents from every client's account and add it to the last account on the tapes. He then opened an account under a fictitious name beginning with 'Z'.

The fake Mr Z got away with a windfall month after month – until a genuine Mr Z became a client of the bank. His name appeared even further down the alphabet, so when he noticed the inexplicable increase in his monthly account he rang the bank to ask why!

Other fiddles attempted by staff with technical know-how include the case of the man who instructed the computer to ignore all cheques drawn on his own account, and the Washington tax clerk who programmed an Internal Revenue Service computer to list all unclaimed refunds, then sent them to his relatives!

One slippery customer cashed in on a bank computer to the tune of $100,000. He opened an account at a Washington DC branch, thus obtaining a supply of deposit slips. He knew that the computer recognized not the signature on the slips but the individualized magnetic ink symbols printed on them.

So one day he surreptitiously substituted slips from his own paying-in book for those left out on the counters for the convenience of customers who had forgotten their own deposit books. All money paid in on these forms, no matter what names and numbers were entered, went straight into the fiddler's account. After three days he withdrew his balance and vanished.

One of the first Americans to exploit the vulnerability of computers – and company bosses who use them without understanding their intricacies – was accountant Eldon Royce, who stole more than a million dollars between 1963 and 1969.

Angry that his employers – a fruit and vegetables wholesale organization – had failed to keep their promise of profit-sharing, Royce decided to take profits of his own kind.

His firm bought hundreds of different types of produce from hundreds of growers, and sold them to scores of dealers. Thousands of lorry, storage, packing and service transactions were involved. And with prices fluctuating throughout the day, only a computer could keep track.

Royce planned his rake-off carefully. He added fractions of a cent to the price of items bought by his company, and took fractions of a cent off the cost of items it sold. The computer then spread the differences across the various accounts, so that the books balanced. Every so often, Royce drained off his secret surplus by writing a cheque to one of the 17 bogus companies he had set up.

Eventually Royce fell victim to his own cleverness. Exhausted by the constant need for vigilance and meticulous accounting, he realized, when his firm's profits suddenly shot up, he could not put a stop to the rake-offs without

---

The boomerang brick

A young, would-be burglar stopped outside a jeweller's shop in the English seaside resort of Brighton one wintry night in 1981. From beneath his coat he produced a brick. He took aim and threw it at the window. The brick hit the reinforced glass, rebounded and knocked the raider unconscious.

Stanley Rifkin speaks to reporters upon his release from jail on bail

arousing suspicions. He confessed and was jailed for 10 years.

But the master of computer frauds was the man who became a multi-millionaire in minutes.

Stanley Rifkin had once worked as a computer programmer at a Los Angeles bank. Since the staff still knew him, he had no trouble in gaining access to the bank's wire room, where he memorized the day's codes. He then plugged in to the computer terminal and transferred $10 million to his own account!

Rifkin was caught only after a woman accomplice confided in a man she believed was a crooked bank employee. Unfortunately, he turned out to be an FBI agent.

Even FBI agents were surprised when they caught the person who had tuned into a computer to erase 10 million items from its memory bank. The culprit was just 13 years of age!

Using a phone in his New York school, the boy had called up a computer-communications network's ex-directory number. He then kept the direct line to the computer constantly engaged while he tried various codes to gain access to the system. Eventually, by trial and error, he managed it.

The 13-year-old later explained that his ruse began as a game when classmates suggested that they try to order the computer from the local Coca-Cola distributor to deliver free Coke to all their homes!

The clerk who 'invested' his bank's £32 million

Marc Colombo was a little man with big ideas. As a lowly foreign-exchange dealer working for a British bank in Switzerland, he saw fortunes changing hands daily. Fluctuations in the values of the world's leading currencies opened up enticing opportunities for men shrewd and brave enough to buy when the price was right and sell at a profit.

Colombo, a handsome 28-year-old, was one of only 16 employees at the Lugano branch of Lloyds Bank International. Lugano was the smallest of the organization's 170 branches – yet after Marco Colombo had finished with it, its name was better known than any other in the world!

The Middle East war of 1973 led to an oil embargo by Arab states. This sent foreign exchange rates crazy and made Colombo believe that the dollar's value would tumble while the Swiss franc remained strong. So he struck what is

Marc Colombo, foreign exchange dealer and Egidio Moembelli, branch manager

known as a forward deal with other international money dealers.

In November 1973, he agreed that – at current rates – his bank would buy US $34 million with Swiss francs the following January. He thought that the dollar's value would have fallen by that time and he would be able to use cheap dollars to buy back his francs. But instead the dollar went from strength to strength.

He now realized he had cost Lloyds about £1 million. He wasn't too worried. After all, his bank had just declared half-yearly profits of £78 million.

One person who had to be kept in the dark, however, was the bank manager, Egidio Mombelli. Having worked for Mombelli for a year, Colombo knew that, if he kept up a show of confidence, his boss would not suspect a thing. But he had to recoup his losses.

Without Lloyd's knowledge, Colombo continued to speculate. After pinning his faith on the dollar falling, which it did not, he changed his tactics, believing it would go on rising. Instead it eventually fell.

Lloyds had a £700,000 daily limit on debts or holdings. Colombo went way above this. The only records he kept were in his diary. The bank and the Swiss

banking authorities had no clue as to what was going on.

And neither did his colleagues or the unfortunate Mombelli. To them, Colombo was a hard-working, trustworthy employee.

But everything changed in August, 1974. It was then that a Lloyds Bank man in London was told by a top French banker that their Lugano branch had 'reached its limit with us'. Lloyds' offices in Queen Victoria Street were on the alert. Phone calls showed that a German bank had also been doing huge currency deals with Lugano.

A plane from London took Lloyds chiefs to Lugano the next day. They interviewed Colombo, Mombelli and the man in charge of all three of Lloyds' Swiss branches, Karl Senft. A mass of documents and the three Swiss employees accompanied the bankers back to London.

It took a full weekend to sort out the mess. At the end, Lloyds men were shocked to find that there was £235 million still tied up in the dangerous 'forward' deals. Colombo had believed in putting all his golden eggs in one basket. A sum greater than the combined capital and reserves of all three Lloyds banks in Switzerland was staked. The bank records had shown a mere £36,000.

Lloyds had to call in the Bank of England to unscramble things. The Governor himself agreed to allow them to transfer vast quantities of money to Lugano so that the deals set up by Colombo would be honoured.

The bank's international money market director, Robert Gras, also had his work cut out. He had to buy in the dollars Colombo had agreed to sell, without people realizing. It was a tricky operation which could be made vastly more expensive if international money men knew Lloyds were over a barrel.

It took three weeks of quietly feverish activity to settle the debts and, at the end, the world was told that Lloyds in Switzerland had lost a horrific £32 million. Never before – in Switzerland or in Britain – had such a loss been known. Lloyds' London shares immediately lost £20 million when chairman Sir Eric Faulkner broke the news.

By that time, Colombo and Mombelli and their families had gone into hiding away from the eager questioning of the Press.

A year later both appeared in Lugano's court on charges of criminal mismanagement, falsification of documents and violations of the Swiss banking code. Colombo denied that he had accepted illegal commissions or had any criminal intent, but he did admit breaking the dealing limits and conducting unauthorized transactions. He also slammed Lloyds Lugano branch for its lax systems of checking and criticized the 'frustrating' spending limits that had been placed on him. Colombo seemed unmoved when the prosecution described him as the 'mouse that made Lloyds tremble' and accused him of throwing money about like a man at a casino.

'Being a foreign-exchange dealer is always a hazardous operation,' he told them. 'It is a gambler's profession.'

He was unrepentant about the extent of his speculation. 'There was the pride of the foreign-exchange dealer who will not admit failure,' he told the court. 'I was at all times convinced that I could recoup my losses, but it only takes something a little unforeseen to upset the market. I was a prisoner of events.'

Even if Colombo had ended up with a profit he would still have faced the sack for breaking banking rules. But he claimed he would have netted £11 million for Lloyds if they had allowed his currency deals to stand.

Mombelli, 41, admitted that he had never understood what was happening and said he had signed papers without realizing what they were.

'It's a foreign-exchange Mafia,' Mombelli said after the trial. 'For every dealer you need at least four administrators to check what he is doing. They do things no ordinary banker understands.'

The two men walked from the court, much to Lloyds' amazement. Colombo received an 18-month suspended sentence and Mombelli one of six months, with a £300 fine each. The judge accepted that the two had not been out to line their own pockets.

Would you credit it!

Everybody has one birth certificate. But in America in the late 1970s, too many people had more than one – and officials estimated that it was costing the country a staggering £20 billion a year.

The cashless society had gone credit-card crazy. And as criminals had fewer chances to grab huge hauls of money, a new breed of con-man sprang up, ready to cash in on false credentials.

It was all based on the birth certificate. For a small fee, and the answers to a few questions, anyone could obtain a copy of his or her certificate – or anybody else's. Every year more than 10 million certificates were requested, and 80 per cent of these were despatched by post. Checks on applications were minimal.

Armed with the precious birth certificate, criminals could create a total 'paper person'. They could claim social security cards or driving licences, open bank accounts, collect welfare benefits, obtain credit cards.

In greatest demand were certificates of people who had died in infancy. There was then no danger of meeting the person whose identity had been usurped. And once a safe new identity had been established, all things were possible. . . .

In Chicago the authorities arrested a welfare scrounger – and discovered that as well as milking the Illinois coffers of £80,000, she had used 250 aliases in 16 different states to obtain social security benefits.

She had posed as an unemployed mother or as a widow. She used the names of eight different dead 'husbands' and at least 31 addresses. She had claimed for 24 children. When she came to court, even her own lawyer was not sure he knew her right name.

In California, well-dressed con-men called at the homes of people advertising expensive cars for sale in local newspapers. Introducing themselves with false identity cards, they agreed a price, produced a banker's draft, and drove off – taking care to leave after the banks had shut for the day.

Next morning, when the car seller discovered that the cheque was worthless, the gang had already disposed of the car. Using fraudulently obtained documents, they had sold it to a legitimate dealer – and disappeared.

In Los Angeles, the murder-suicide of lovers Patty Bledsoe and Robert Hinkley in 1974 revealed a more sinister confidence trick. The couple had credit cards, driving licences and social security cards in at least four names other than their own. They had used them as proof of identity in cashing counterfeit pay cheques from the Western Gillette Trucking Company. In one weekend, they collected £9,000.

By the time the banks were refusing to honour the worthless cheques, the couple were involved in the second stage of their plot – using the money to buy cocaine in Colombia, then re-entering America on forged passports to sell it on the streets.

Apart from criminals, illegal immigrants were believed to be using the birth certificate trick to establish legitimate bona fides. And in 1976 there were estimated to be eight million of them in the U.S., an annual tax burden of nearly £7,000 million.

A series of 'paper people' scandals forced the Government to act. An 80-strong Federal Advisory Committee on False Identification was set up to investigate. And after a year's deliberations, it recommended matching birth and death records, and criminal penalties for fraudulent use of birth certificates. Stricter standards were also introduced to vet applicants for driving licences and welfare benefits.

The day the bubble burst

I t was the greatest financial catastrophe in Britain's history: the day when the so-called South Sea Bubble burst. The Bubble was a massive fraud perpetrated by the South Sea Company, which was formed in 1710 and which collapsed spectacularly exactly 10 years later.

The aims of the company had been honest but its aspirations grandiose. The South Sea Company quite simply invited the public to invest in it on such a scale that the profits would be sufficient to pay off the entire national debt.

Britain's growing middle class rushed to put their money into the venture. So successful was it that hundreds of other get-rich-quick companies sprang up in its wake. An infectious gambling fever swept the country.

One of the new investment companies floated shares for building pirate-proof ships, another went in for planting mulberry trees and breeding silkworms, and a third started importing jackasses to improve the quality of British mules.

There was even a company formed for insuring girls against losing their virginity!

Yet some of the businesses were quite soundly based. One revolutionary venture was 'for paying pensions to widows' and another 'for insuring people against thefts and robberies'.

The boom lasted until 1720, by which time the South Sea Company had amassed enormous debts through inexpert trade deals. But the momentum behind the company was too great to allow it to admit defeat – and bankruptcy.

Sentence a walkover

Two students convicted of siphoning about three gallons of petrol ·
from a parked car got four miles to the gallon. The court at
Monroe, North Carolina, sentenced them to walk 12 miles.

So a new share issue was put on the market to pay for the company's past
mistakes. They were all snapped up.

Then the rumours began. The panic to sell was unprecedented. Nothing like
it was again seen until the Wall Street crash 200 years later. As the shares fell
and panic swept the land, the law stepped in, barring all companies trading
without a licence. The result was commercial chaos. Hundreds of firms went
bankrupt and hundreds of investors committed suicide.

It was at this point that the Prime Minister, Sir Robert Walpole, intervened.
He realized that the South Sea Company must be rescued. He ordered the Bank
of England to take over £9 million of the South Sea stock and the wealthy East
India Company to be responsible for a similar amount.

He also ordered an examination of the South Sea's books. The result: £2
million was confiscated from the estates of dishonest directors and distributed
among the badly battered shareholders.

Also well satisfied were those in the know who got out before the Bubble
burst. Among them was Spencer Compton, Speaker of the House of Commons,
who reputedly made a £80,000 profit.

Cops who stung them in style

In the hit movie, *The Sting*, Robert Redford and Paul Newman played a
couple of con-men who cheated a gang boss out of a fortune in a gambling
den. It was all fun and fiction – but it did hold a lesson for America's hard-
pressed police forces. It showed them how to play the crooks and con-men at
their own game.

In 1976, shortly after the film's release, federal agents tried out a sting
operation in California, setting up a string of seven fake warehouses for
receiving stolen goods. The Sting Squad, posing as crooks, brought up every
crime haul offered, from jewellery to guns and stolen cars. Contraband and

stolen property worth millions of dollars was recovered and more than 200 arrests were made in the Los Angeles area.

Most of the crooks were rounded up by inviting them to parties in celebration of their profitable crimes. Among the men booked was a professional killer who offered the con-men cops his services to get rid of underworld rivals.

Since then, Sting Squads have pulled off more than 50 successful similar operations, recovering over $250 million in stolen goods and putting more than 200 crime bosses behind bars.

But the greatest sting of all was pulled in Flint, Michigan, where the local Mr Big was a 'fence' – a receiver of stolen goods – known to his many underworld associates as Lucky. About $1 million of hot property had passed through his hands up to the time of the announcement of his untimely death.

Sixty crooks turned up for the funeral service. But no sooner had they taken their seats than the doors burst open and every man in the room was arrested – by the Sting Squad!

The whole fencing operation had been masterminded by undercover federal agents. Mr Big was really Walter Ryerson, a 40-year-old Treasury Department investigator. He grew a beard, let his hair grow, wore expensive suits and spent months infiltrating the local crime ring. And he was in on the kill with the rest of the squad at the funeral service held in his honour.

A further 300 crooks were rounded up. Ryerson had video-taped and recorded all his business transactions. As one crook said: 'You just don't know who you can trust these days.'

Million-dollar bank roll

Most folk would, without hesitation, hand in any lost valuables found in the street. But the public's honesty was sorely tested the day that someone mislaid a million dollars in the centre of an American city in 1981.

The money belonged to a Philadelphia bank and was being taken by a security firm to its headquarters less than three miles away. The money was stacked on a metal trolley in the back of a security van.

Half-way along the route, it would seem that a series of bumps 'tricked' the automatic mechanism on the locks into opening the van doors. The trolley, with its million-dollar load, rolled out of the van and trundled down the street.

The guards sitting up front in the security van did not know anything was amiss and drove into the distance. Witnesses said that the trolley ran along the street until it bumped into a pavement. A passing car drew to a halt, two men stepped out, gleefully loaded the two canvas bags of cash and drove off.

Police later interrogated the guards, suspecting a plot. But a detective said: 'These guys are as pure as snow. We are satisfied there was no conspiracy. It was just an incredible accident.'

All the missing money was in old banknotes and the security firm held out little hope of tracing it. They said they 'still hoped these people will turn out to be honest passers-by and will return the money' – and they offered a $50,000 reward to the two fortune finders.

There were no takers. . . .

Lousy luck that landed a couple in jail

Every con-trick or deception needs a certain amount of help from lady luck. But in 1938, even the man behind the crime could not believe his good fortune when an incredible string of coincidences conspired to place the wrong man in jail – and put him within an ace of getting away with £18,000.

Just before Christmas, banknotes worth the equivalent of £9,000 disappeared over a weekend from the safe of a small business in the Hungarian capital of Budapest. Police questioned the owner and his £100-a-month book-keeper cashier, the only men who knew the combination. The cashier had been the last to leave the office on the Friday before the crime, and his fingerprints were the only ones on the safe.

The case took a dramatic turn three weeks later. Detectives learned that on the Monday following the robbery, a woman had opened an £8,500 bank

---

Raiders on the run!

Thieves were on the run after raiding a pharmacy in the southern English village of Alresford, Hampshire . . . their £100 haul of tablets included 600 laxatives. Police, who warned that the tablets would produce a 'violent reaction', said: 'We've no idea how long these men will remain loose.'

Living for licks
A 14-year-old London boy, accused with his brother of stealing £50, told police that he spent £25 of the money in two weeks – on ice-cream.

---

account using the name Anna Nagy. It was a common name in Hungary – but police knew it was also the maiden name of the cashier's wife, who was eight months pregnant.

Inquiries revealed that the couple had spent the equivalent of £700 on a Christmas shopping spree. Their purchases included a radiogram, a baby carriage, and furniture for a nursery. Circumstantial evidence seemed to implicate the cashier. He was arrested and thrown into jail while police prepared the prosecution.

In those days, bank depositors in Hungary were not required to give an address. So the only hope of identifying Anna Nagy rested with the teller who took her money, and her signature on the deposit slip. Here again, a twist of fate stacked the odds against the cashier. The bank teller had died of a heart attack before police could interview him. And though there was no similarity between the autograph of the woman who deposited the money and the cashier's wife, police argued convincingly that she would want to disguise her handwriting, and be under strong emotional pressure, thus accounting for the shaky, uncertain writing.

When the case came to court, the prosecution said every Anna Nagy on the register of voters had been checked. And despite extensive publicity in the newspapers, no unregistered woman of that name had come forward. The evidence was considered conclusive. The cashier was convicted and jailed.

There the matter might have rested, had it not been for the handwriting expert called in by the Budapest criminal court to compare the two signatures.

The graphologist, Hanna Sulner, remained convinced that the woman who had opened the bank account was much older than the cashier's wife, possibly with a physical infirmity that made writing difficult. She went to see the cashier in his cell. He was bewildered and defeated, protesting his innocence with resigned despair. Their Christmas spree was with money saved over their four years of marriage, he explained. He had opened the safe on the Friday, but only to take out wages.

Next Hanna visited the wife in hospital. She had given birth to her baby, but was suffering from a nervous breakdown after the ordeal of the court case. Hanna was convinced she had not deposited the cash, but the distressed woman only sobbed: 'They'll never believe you.'

The couple's lawyer was equally gloomy. Why, despite nationwide publicity, had nobody come forward to claim the cash?

Then, at last, there came a stroke of luck. Hanna was discussing the case with a doctor friend over lunch, and reacted angrily to suggestions that she was letting her sympathy run away with her judgement.

'It's a question of science,' she snapped. 'That deposit slip was signed by someone much older than the cashier's wife, somebody with a handicap that made writing difficult.'

'You mean she could have been ill?' asked the doctor.

'Yes.'

'Have the hospitals been checked?'

It was so devastatingly simple that Hanna cursed herself for not thinking of it before.

The first hospital she tried had an Anna Nagy, who had already been questioned before being admitted to give birth to twins. The second knew of no Anna Nagy. But the third. . . .

Here was the answer to the mystery. A middle-aged woman from a village near the Rumanian border had been admitted just before Christmas for a serious eye operation. She had travelled to Budapest bringing her savings, and had put them in the bank for safe-keeping. Now she was convalescing, half-blind and unable to read newspapers.

Hanna asked her to sign her name on a slip of paper. The signature was identical to that on the bank form. The cashier was completely exonerated on appeal, and released to build a new life with his wife and child.

His place in prison was taken by the real culprit. He had crept into the deserted office over the weekend and raided the safe, wearing gloves. He knew the business would be reimbursed by the insurance company, which would double his takings from the crime. For he was the owner of the firm.

Grave justice

A gravestone in a churchyard in Sheldon, Vermont, bears this epitaph to an unknown burglar shot while robbing a store on October 13, 1905: 'Here lies a burglar – this stone was bought with money found on him.'

Chapter
Six

The Spoils of War

'War is much too serious a thing to be left
to military men'
Briand

The love cheats who listened in at Madame Kitty's

Madame Kitty's pleasure palace was the talk of Berlin's high society. All a newcomer had to do was turn up at her door and use the codeword: 'I come from Rothenburg'.

She would produce a lavish photograph album of her 20 most ravishing beauties, complete with personal details . . . and the client would take his pick. After a 10-minute wait, savouring the delights to come over a generous drink, he would be confronted by the girl who whisked him off to her boudoir and pandered to his every whim.

So enticing were Madame Kitty's ladies that visiting dignitaries, army generals and embassy staff could not resist sampling the pleasures behind the elegant third-floor doors of the fashionable house.

But sex was seldom what it seemed at 11 Giesebrechtstrasse. And the most satisfied smiles were usually on the faces of men who never availed themselves of the establishment's facilities.

The house that attracted the elite of Germany's diplomatic corps and armed forces had, in fact, been set up by a hard-headed Nazi intelligence chief who was banking on customers abandoning their common sense amid their sensual delights.

He was not disappointed. For months, indiscreet pillow talk gave eavesdropping Gestapo officers the evidence they needed to keep Hitler one step ahead ir controlling his own people, and manipulating leaders of other countries.

But the great deception eventually came unstuck . . . because another conman got in on the act.

Operation Kitty had been sparked off in 1939 by Gruppenführer Reinhard Heydrich, later notorious as the Butcher of Prague, but then the feared, ruthless, ambitious head of the Nazi SS network.

For some time he had been worried by careless security leaks in high places. With war fast approaching, it was essential to identify and eliminate loose tongues. The quickest way of doing that was to put suspects through the passion test, tempting them to blabber with wine and beautiful women.

Obersturmführer Walter Schellenberg, cunning chief of the SD – the Nazi central security organization – was ordered to infiltrate an exclusive brothel and enlist girls willing to pass on information they overheard.

But Schellenberg was not a man to do things by halves. The order gave him the idea for an ingenious surveillance blanket check. Instead of using a brothel, he would take it over completely. A team of hand-picked, specially-trained beauties would file reports immediately after sex-and-secrets sessions with celebrities.

And just in case anything slipped their minds, every room would be bugged, so that other agents in a basement control room could record every word, sigh and exclamation of bliss.

Only one bordello fitted the bill perfectly . . . and fate had made taking it over a simple matter.

Kitty Schmidt was then 57. For years her pension had been known as the most luxurious house of ill repute in the city, frequented by the most distinguished and influential figures in German society. Her charges were high, but that was the price clients paid for complete discretion.

Hitler's rise to power had disturbed Kitty. Rough and ready Brownshirts were replacing the gentle Jewish bankers and businessmen on whom she had built her reputation, and the police were no longer so obliging about letting her operate without harassment.

Cautious Kitty began transferring takings to London via Jewish refugees she helped smuggle abroad. By 1939 she had amassed several thousand pounds in British banks – and on June 28 she left Berlin to start spending them. She got as far as the German-Dutch border. SD shadows had tailed her from the capital, and brought her back to Gestapo HQ in Prinz Albrechtstrasse.

Schellenberg was waiting with a bulky dossier and a list of crimes: helping Jews to escape, illegally exchanging German marks, illegally transferring money abroad, attempting to leave Germany without permission, using a forged passport. The charges spelled death or an open-ended term in a concentration camp.

But the Nazi was prepared to be reasonable. 'If you can do something for me,' he said, 'I may be able to do something for you.'

Kitty, with no room to bargain, agreed to his astounding suggestions. She would hand her brothel over to the SD, ask for no explanation, do what she was told, and sign an official secrets document which meant death if she divulged one word of what was going on.

Workmen moved into 11 Giesebrechtstrasse to give it a sinister refurbishment. The interior was gutted and rewired, with microphones in every bedroom, lounge and corridor. A multi-core cable ran along the guttering, down a drainpipe, and into the bricked-off cellar.

Here five monitoring desks, each with two record turntables, were installed. Conversations from ten rooms could be recorded simultaneously on wax discs.

Meanwhile, SD Untersturmführer Karl Schwarz was finding girls to coax the unwary into filling the records with indiscreet words. Berlin's vice squad carried out an unprecedented number of raids on brothels, nightclubs and street corners. Hundreds of girls were grilled, then rejected as 'emotionally unreliable'.

Psychiatrists, doctors, language consultants and university professors all helped Schwarz whittle his short-list of 90 girls down to 20 in seven days of non-stop tests and interrogation.

The breathtaking beauties they selected were taken to a sealed-off wing of the officers' academy at Sonthofen. For seven weeks they went through a gruelling course of foreign languages, unarmed combat, marksmanship, foreign and home politics, economics, use of codes and ciphers.

They had to memorize charts of military uniforms and decorations. German radio interviewers demonstrated how to solicit secrets in seemingly innocent conversation.

By March 1940 all was ready for the launch of Operation Kitty. Schwarz briefed the madame in her newly redecorated parlour. 'Carry on as before', she was told. 'Welcome all your old customers. Keep on your existing girls.'

'But every so often, we will send along someone special. On no account introduce him to one of your regular staff, but show him this album of 20 girls. When he makes his choice, phone for her. She will arrive in 10 minutes. You will not discuss the client with her, and she will leave immediately he has gone.'

When Kitty asked how she would recognize the special visitors, she was told: 'They will use the codeword "I come from Rothenburg."'

Twelve days later, a young SS officer on leave was used to test the system. Schwarz and his colleagues tuned in as the unsuspecting man prattled about his home, his relatives and his devotion to the Führer.

But the girl had learned her lessons well. When she flattered his fighting spirit, he began bragging of his unit's imminent transfer, adding: 'If you ask me, the Führer's got his eye on Sweden.'

Schwarz was delighted with the success of the eavesdropping, even if he did have to arrange a court martial. And there were many more to follow as the supply of Rothenburg romeos was stepped up.

Soon the 20 girls were making love round the clock as special guests outnumbered genuine customers. The Gestapo had to send in extra food and drink as the celebrities exhausted Kitty's ration supplies.

During 1940 nearly 10,000 people climbed to the third floor. And in one month, 3,000 love sessions went on record.

Count Galeazzo Ciano, Italy's Foreign Minister, amazed listening agents one night with a tirade about Hitler's shortcomings as statesman, soldier and lover. When Schwarz forwarded a transcript to the Führer, relations between the two countries were never the same again.

In September, Schellenberg himself took over the earphones when Nazi foreign minister Joachim von Ribbentrop arrived at Kitty's salon with his

Gruppenführer Reinhard Heydrich, later known as the Butcher of Prague

Spanish opposite number, Don Ramon Serrano Suner. He overheard a bizarre Spanish plan to occupy Gibraltar, and was able to warn SS chief Heinrich Himmler in time to squash it.

Another visitor was Major-General Sepp Dietrich, commander of Hitler's personal bodyguard. He dropped no secrets, but caused problems of a different sort – he demanded all 20 girls for a party. Schwarz rounded up as many as he could – and Dietrich amazed the listeners with his stamina.

Only once did the codeword fail . . . when a soldier turned up who really was from the town of Rothenburg.

And the only time the recording and listening equipment was turned off was during Reinhard Heydrich's increasingly frequent 'tours of inspection'.

By this time, though, the Germans were not the only people listening in at Madame Kitty's.

Towards the end of 1940, Lljubo Kolchev, a junior press secretary at the Rumanian Embassy stumbled over some wires as he wandered down Giesebrechtstrasse.

Untersturmführer Schwarz, supervising the rerouting of cables from the No. 11 cellar to a new recording post at SD HQ in Meineckestrasse, automatically reached out to prevent the man falling. Schwarz had no way of knowing that the casual pedestrian was really Roger Wilson, a British spy.

Wilson had heard the 'Rothenberg' stories going round the embassy. Now, as he saw SD men in civilian clothes pretending to be workmen, and the multi-core cable in the drainpipe, he knew those stories were fact.

London ordered him to keep tabs on the salon without rousing suspicion, and Wilson became a regular visitor, keeping his eyes and ears open. Later a communications expert was sent in to fix wire taps to three of the wires in the cable.

From December 1940 until 1943, when Operation Kitty was closed down, Britain and the Allies shared some of its most intimate secrets.

But the salon's heyday had passed. Bombing raids reduced the flood of celebrities to a trickle, and Heydrich was increasingly using the love-and-listen

---

Case for the defence

A man who pleaded not guilty to purse-snatching in Tulsa, Oklahoma, decided to present his own defence. He began by asking the woman victim: 'Did you get a good look at my face when I grabbed your bag?' Not surprisingly, he was found guilty and jailed.

network to settle old scores with rivals in the Nazi hierarchy. Discipline was becoming ever more lax, with the 20 sex spies often staying on at the brothel for strictly forbidden drinks parties.

In July 1942 a bomb finally landed on Kitty's empire, scattering her elegant furniture and rich drapes all over Giesebrechtstrasse. Schwarz threw a ring of soldiers round the street, removed any incriminating evidence of the bugging, then set Kitty up again in the undamaged ground floor of the building.

Within a year, it was all over. The SD handed the house back to Kitty, and most of the beautiful agents decided to stay with her. Kitty had to sign another pledge to reveal nothing of what had gone on. It was a promise she kept until her death in 1954, aged 71.

Walter Schellenberg, the man who dreamed up the great deception, was arrested by the Allies in 1945. But they never got their hands on the 25,000 discs recorded during the operation. They vanished from the files at Gestapo headquarters as the Russians entered the smoking rubble of what had been Hitler's capital.

Do they still exist? No-one can be sure. But they were glimpsed once, in 1963, by author Peter Norden in a top-secret storeroom at the headquarters of the East German state security service in East Berlin.

The captain of Köpenick

Uniforms fascinated 57-year-old Wilhelm Voigt. After all, he had been familiar with them, in one form or another, for quite some time. Indeed, for no less than 27 years he had worn prison uniform himself, serving sentences for various petty crimes. Recently released from jail, he now looked in awe and envy at the smart captain's uniform hanging in the window of a second-hand shop in Potsdam near Berlin.

The price tag on it was equal to a whole week's wages from Voigt's job as a cobbler. But he didn't hesitate for long. He walked into the shop, tried the uniform for size and bought it on the spot.

It was 1906 and life held very little hope for the ex-jailbird. What the poor cobbler yearned for was respect from others, pride in himself and a little nest-egg for his old age. With his newly acquired uniform, he saw the chance of getting the lot.

Voigt first made a careful study of the local militia – how they marched, how they saluted, how they issued and obeyed commands. Then he decided on a dress rehearsal for his grand plan. A brewers' exhibition in Berlin gave him the opportunity.

The exhibition was well under way, the hall crowded, when 'Captain' Wilhelm Voigt stalked through the door. At every stand, there were nods from the tradesmen and shy but admiring sideways glances from the ladies. This flattered the ex-convict immensely, but what really delighted him was the reaction whenever he passed a soldier. The man would immediately leap to attention and salute stiffly. Voigt's dummy run had worked perfectly.

The gleeful cobbler then put the final touches to his master-plan. It was a scheme that took full advantage of the Prussian awe of authority and at the same time paid back the Kaiser's pompous government officials and bureaucrats who had refused to return his passport and identity card following his last stint in jail.

Voigt polished up his buttons and donned his uniform once more. Then he marched off to a big Berlin barracks and waited for his chance. It was not long before a corporal and five grenadiers marched towards the barracks gate.

'Corporal, where are you taking those men?' barked Voigt.

'Back to the barracks, sir,' said the corporal.

'Turn them round and follow me,' Voigt snapped. 'I have an urgent mission for them on direct orders of the Kaiser himself.'

The phoney captain led his little army back up the road. On the way, he ordered four more soldiers to fall in and follow him. With 10 men behind him, Wilhelm was now a force to be reckoned with. So commandeering a bus was easy – in the Kaiser's name, of course.

Their destination was Köpenick, an outlying district of Berlin. Once there, Voigt lined his troops up for inspection, then marched them off to the town hall.

'You're under arrest,' he snarled, bursting into the parlour of Dr Langerhans, the burgomaster.

'Where is your warrant?' asked the startled official.

'I am acting under orders,' replied Voigt. 'And my warrant is the men I command.'

The burgomaster, himself a reserve officer, knew that orders were orders. But he was still concerned that the 'captain' looked rather old for his role, and that his cap badge was upside down! Again he demanded his authority.

This time Voigt's rage knew no bounds. He said he had been sent by Berlin to check on missing municipal funds, that Dr Langerhans was suspected of fraud and that he was being placed under guard immediately. He then summoned the Inspector of Police and told him to get his men onto the streets in case of public disorder.

Despatching some of his men to collect the mayor's wife, Voigt turned his attention to the borough treasurer's office. 'You are under arrest,' he told the official. 'I am ordered to confiscate all your funds.' Fortunately the treasurer did not suspect that anything was wrong.

Meekly, the treasurer unlocked his safe and handed over 4,000 marks, worth about £650. Wilhelm handed over a bogus receipt, signed 'Von Aloesam, Captain, Guards Regiment.'

Ordering his men to hold the prisoners outside, Voigt eagerly ransacked the office, looking for a passport and identity card. But this time he was clearly out of luck.

Unsuccessful in his search for a new identity, Voigt decided to play the captain for a little longer. He ordered the Inspector of Police to commandeer a number of carriages from wealthy townsfolk and had the entire town council bundled inside and sent off to Berlin under armed guard. There they were delivered to General Moltke who, realizing the absurdity of the situation, roared with laughter and sent them packing.

The general also took the precaution of sending an armed party back to Köpenick to arrest the 'captain' before he did any more damage. But they arrived too late. Voigt had fled.

He had scuttled back to the railway station retrieving a bundle of civilian clothes he had previously deposited in the left luggage office. A quick change, and the captain was Wilhelm Voigt again – speeding back to Berlin on the first train.

Next day, the newspapers were full of the exploits of the mystery man who had taken authority down a peg or two. Voigt was delighted, even when a 25,000-mark reward was put on his head. But as the days went by and still no culprit had been arrested, he began to feel cheated of the recognition he had earned. So he planted a photograph to help lead police to him. And, after ten days, they came to arrest him at breakfast time.

The trial was a sensation. The poor little cobbler who had pricked the pomposity of both army and government was a national hero. And there were great rumblings of discontent when the judge handed out a heavy four-year sentence.

But Voigt didn't serve the full term. The Kaiser, who was said to have muttered 'lovable scoundrel' when told of his exploits, gave way to public sympathy and pardoned him after 20 months.

At last Wilhelm Voigt left jail a famous figure, his ambitions fulfilled. All except one – money. The 4,000 marks had been recovered almost intact and Voigt was again penniless. He was forced to perform a vaudeville act in the United States . . . until an invitation from a rich Berlin dowager changed his life. Captivated by the sheer audacity of his deeds, the old lady granted him a life pension which enabled him to retire in comfort to Luxembourg. He died there in 1922 at the age of 72.

Satan in satin

When his Great Army of the Potomac was crushed at Bull Run, Abraham Lincoln knew there had been treason in his government – and that behind the treachery was a beautiful but deadly woman. He called on General George B. McClellan to take command of the shattered Union Army. And together they turned to Allan Pinkerton, founder of Pinkerton's Detective Agency and internationally known manhunter. Now he was to become a hunter of women. Specifically, his prey would be Mrs Rose O'Neal Greenhow – 'Rebel Rose' – whose Washington spy ring was like a noose around the Union throat.

Rich, brilliant and seductive, the 44-year-old widow lived in an elegant mansion that had become the favourite gathering place of Washington's elite. She made no secret of her Southern sympathies or her flaming love affairs. She claimed to have been James Buchanan's mistress and the power behind his presidency. She also boasted that her current affair with Senator Harold Wilson had led to the trapping of Union forces at Manassas and the Bull Run catastrophe. There would later be documentary proof of her claim when Rebel archives were taken after the fall of the Confederate capital of Richmond, Virginia.

As chairman of the Senate's Military Affairs Committee, Wilson knew Lincoln's secret war plans. He had confided those secrets to Rose Greenhow, who routed them to another of her lovers in the Confederate high command, using as courier a female operative who crossed Union lines disguised as a farm-girl.

The contest between Rose and Pinkerton became a classic duel of wits. Rose made the first move, inviting him to a lavish house party where she tried every blandishment on the no-nonsense Scot. But when Pinkerton failed to take the bait, she became his deadliest enemy.

In the weeks that followed, Pinkerton and his men kept a constant watch on her home. Rose knew of the surveillance and openly laughed at it. Her own female operatives, all stunningly beautiful, continued to pass in and out of the house, and the great of Washington still vied for her favours.

The treacherous Wilson was a constant caller, and General McClellan angrily told Pinkerton that military secrets were reaching the enemy daily. Without further delay, Pinkerton arrested Mrs Greenhow in her home. Under the lady's furious eyes, he ordered a search of the premises and turned up damning evidence.

There was the cipher by which she had communicated with the enemy.

Rose O'Neal Greenhow with her daughter in the courtyard of the Old Capitol Prison   147

There were Senator Wilson's passionate love letters. There was a list of Rose's couriers and fellow conspirators, most of them wealthy and powerful. Worse, there were copies of official information on the movement of troops, the sizes and quantities of ordnance, and blueprints of the forts defending the city.

The grim-faced Pinkerton wanted Rose and her co-conspirators hanged, but Lincoln and McClellan vetoed the idea. Some of the traitors were so highly placed that the already shaky administration could have toppled.

For five months Lincoln wrestled with the problem, while Pinkerton kept Rose under house arrest in her home. But on January 18, 1862, she was transferred to Washington's Old Capitol Prison.

No spy in history has enjoyed kinder prison treatment. With the Greenhow fortune still at her disposal, she was given a suite of rooms on the second floor where guards brought her catered meals and champagne from her own cellars.

In Rose's case, prison discipline was suspended entirely. Her powerful friends came and went at will, and the guards retired politely when Senator Wilson was a guest. Another frequent caller·was Gustavus V. Fox, Assistant Secretary of the Navy, who was reckless enough to divulge the government's naval plans.

To everyone's surprise, Rose had taken up knitting, and balls of coloured wool were delivered to her through the Provost Marshal's office. She turned out an endless supply of socks, sweaters and tapestries and presented them as gifts to some of her callers.

Suspicious, Pinkerton intercepted one of the female visitors and took a close look at her tapestry. It held a cunningly concealed message for the Confederates – a coded outline of the information Rose had gleaned from Fox.

Even Lincoln agreed now that a woman who could spy from behind bars was too dangerous a prisoner to keep.

In June 1862, Pinkerton escorted her to Fortress Monroe, where she signed a pledge 'not to return north of the Potomac' until the war was over. 'But then I shall return,' she assured him. 'And after we have burned your White House to the ground, I think we shall hang Old Abe in my yard to frighten away the crows.'

In fact, she was never to return.

Jefferson Davis, President of the Confederate States, sent her from his capital of Richmond to London in order to recruit money and sympathy for the Rebel cause. There she published a book of memoirs reviling Allan Pinkerton and detailing her affairs with Lincoln's traitorous friends. Suppressed in the United States, her book was an overnight sensation in England.

But on Rose's return voyage, the blockade runner carrying her was grounded on a shoal off the coast of Wilmington, North Carolina.

Too impatient to wait for rescue craft, Rose set out for shore in a small boat. The boat capsized in heavy seas, and her body was never found.

Double Deutsch

The Oxford University dons who turned up for a lecture by the eminent psychologist Dr Emil Busch were puzzled but impressed. The man they had come to see after answering an advertisement in an Oxford newspaper had a flowing beard, a strong German accent and a strange way of haranguing his audience so that most of what he said was unintelligible. They later learned that 'Dr Busch' was one of their undergraduates, and his entire speech had been gibberish.

She left many questions behind her.

Never exposed during his lifetime, Harold Wilson went on to become a Vice-President of the United States. Gustavus V. Fox escaped without a rebuke. And though he knew their identities well, Lincoln took no action against any of the traitors who had worked so intimately with Rebel Rose.

It may have been a fatal mistake. Historians agree that these same conspirators could have been in league with John Wilkes Booth, the demented actor who brought Lincoln's life to a violent end.

The general who died twice

What is the most difficult thing in the world to fake? Is it is signature? A banknote, perhaps? Or an old master?

The answer must surely be: Your own death! Yet that is exactly what an extraordinary military gentleman by the name of Michel Ney is believed to have achieved in the winter of 1815.

Marshal Michel Ney was one of Napoleon Bonaparte's most able generals. But after his army was defeated at Waterloo, Napoleon was exiled at St Helena – and Ney, less lucky than his leader, was sentenced to death by firing squad.

Shortly after nine o'clock on the morning of December 7, Ney was led by a contingent of the troops he had once commanded into the Luxembourg Gardens in Paris. He was placed against a wall where he addressed his men in the most emotional terms.

A British Diplomat witnessed the execution. He said that Ney shouted to the firing squad: 'Comrades, when I place my hand upon my breast, fire at my

Marshal Michel Ney

heart.' The soldiers levelled their rifles, Ney put his hand to his chest, a volley rang out, and Ney fell, his coat stained with blood.

According to the observer, the body was then whisked away, with suspicious haste. It lay in a hospital overnight and was buried in the cemetery of Pierre la Chaise early the following day. Madame Ney did not attend the funeral. Only one distant relative was there to see the famous general laid to rest.

Three years later in Florence, South Carolina, a middle-aged French teacher using the name Peter Stuart Ney claimed that he and Marshal Ney were one and the same person. He said he had been saved from execution by a plot hatched by his old soldiers – with the aid of his former enemy, the British Duke of Wellington, who had been horrified by the ignoble fate proposed for a fellow general.

The teacher explained that the Paris firing squad had aimed above his head. He said that he had held in his hand a container of blood, which he had released when he struck his chest. He had then been smuggled by ship to America.

Nobody believed Peter Ney – until a doctor examined him and agreed that marks on his body conformed to Marshal Ney's battle scars. The teacher also claimed that during the passage to America he had been recognized by a fellow passenger – a soldier who had once been in his command. The man was later traced and confirmed the story. The French teacher also boasted a remarkably intimate knowledge of Marshal Ney and his family and of military tactics.

Then renowned New York handwriting expert David Carvalho examined letters written by the teacher and by the general. He had no hesitation in stating that they were written by the same person.

Six years after his Paris 'execution', one of Ney's pupils brought him a newspaper reporting the death of Napoleon on St Helena. The teacher fainted before his class and was carried home. Later that day he tried to cut his throat, but the knife broke in the wound.

Peter Ney – or Marshal Michel Ney – died peacefully in South Carolina in 1846. The last, weakly-spoken words of this frail old man were: 'I really am Marshal Ney'.

Chapter Seven

Imposters and Usurpers

'A face shaped by lotus petals, a voice as cool as
sandalwood, a heart like a pair of scissors, and
excessive humility; these are the signs of a rogue'
Sanskrit proverb

The Tichborne claimant

The largest and most ludicrous impostor of all time was an Australian cattle slaughterer from Wagga-Wagga named Arthur Orton – a corpulent con-man who became known through an amazing string of legal battles in the 1870s as 'The Tichborne Claimant'.

In March 1854 Sir Roger Charles Doughty Tichborne, a young British soldier and heir to a fortune, set off round the world to try to forget a disastrous love affair. He had fallen in love with his cousin, Katherine Doughty, but being Catholics, they could never wed.

Heartbroken, Tichborne resigned his commission in the Sixth Dragoon Guards and set sail in the small Liverpool sailing ship, the *Bella*, for South America. There his family hoped he would get over his romance.

After visiting Rio de Janeiro, the *Bella* headed north for New York – and was never seen again. Only the ship's log-book was found, floating 400 miles out to sea.

Roger's mother, Lady Tichborne, refused to accept the loss. She advertised in newspapers around the world for any information that could help locate her son. Shortly afterwards her husband died. In her grief she was more than ever convinced that Roger must still be alive. Then in 1866 came startling news – a letter from her son, supposedly dead for 12 years. She was overjoyed.

Unfortunately the Dowager Lady Tichborne was being hoodwinked by an altogether impossible claimant, cattle slaughterer Arthur Orton. Even at first glance he was an unlikely candidate. Sir Roger Tichborne had been a slight, sallow-faced man weighing barely nine stone. Arthur Orton was a ruddy-faced roly-poly 24-stone giant.

If Orton's appearance was dramatically different to young Tichborne's, so was his background. Orton was the youngest of 12 children of a poverty-stricken family living in the East End of London. He had gone to sea, deserted his ship in South America, returned briefly to England and, in 1852, emigrated to Australia.

Thirteen years later, deep in money troubles, he saw one of the Dowager Lady Tichborne's advertisements and, in a last desperate move to stave off bankruptcy, announced that he had estates in Britain.

After writing to the excited Lady Tichborne, hinting at a shipwreck, Orton raised several thousand pounds on the strength of his inheritance and sailed to Europe with his wife and baby daughter to meet the woman he hoped would become his mother. This dramatic meeting took place in Paris where the Dowager was then living. Orton insisted that the curtains be kept drawn – so this first encounter between son and mother took place in semi-darkness.

The impostor spoke to the old lady about his childhood. He mentioned meetings with his grandfather – who had died before Roger was born. He spoke of his old school, Winchester – whereas Roger had been educated at Stonyhurst. He alluded to his early Army service in the ranks – Roger had been a commissioned officer.

There were other discrepancies. Roger had a tattoo on his left arm. Orton had none. And Roger spoke fluent French. When his former French-language tutor questioned Orton, he found that the Wapping ex-seaman could not understand a word.

Yet the grief-stricken old lady who had lived so long in hope didn't care. She was convinced that Orton was her son. She explained away his errors of fact by saying: 'He confuses everything as in a dream.'

Orton could scarcely credit his luck. It didn't matter that no other members of the family believed him; he was sitting on a goldmine as long as the old lady lived. She immediately made him an allowance of £1,000 a year.

Orton now began to overstep the mark. Upon Sir Roger Tichborne's death, his younger brother Alfred had inherited the family estates. But he too had died young and Alfred's baby son, Henry, had taken the title. Orton now claimed his inheritance from Henry.

The case took over five years to prepare. Orton used the time to research the family history and even employed as servants two former members of Sir Roger's old regiment so that he could pick their brains about their former officer. Consequently no fewer than 30 of Roger's fellow-officers signed an affidavit that Orton and their dead comrade were one and the same person.

But just before the case opened, Orton lost his trump card. The Dowager Lady Tichborne died. So did her solicitor, who, strangely, had been one of Orton's most enthusiastic supporters. Undeterred, he proceeded.

The trial of the Tichborne Claimant opened on May 11, 1871. It continued for 103 days, during which time Orton produced over 100 witnesses prepared to state under oath that he was none other than Sir Roger Charles Doughty Tichborne. The family could muster only 17 witnesses to refute the claim.

Yet throughout the lengthy trial there were so many inconsistencies in Orton's story that although the old lady might have been fooled, a court of law was not deceived. The case collapsed and Orton was immediately arrested and charged with perjury. A new trial opened which lasted 188 days, ending on March 1, 1874, with Orton being sentenced to 14 years imprisonment.

The longest-ever British trial had spanned 1,025 days. Orton served 10 years and then had the nerve to return for another attempt on the Tichborne fortune. When this failed, he ended up exhibiting himself around the music halls. He died in a cheap lodging house on All Fools' Day, 1898.

Secret lives of military men

O ne of the most plausible impostors of all time was Dr James Barry. Noted for his dashing good looks, he joined the British army as a surgeon in 1816. He rose through the ranks to become the most skilled of physicians and later attained the exalted rank of Inspector General.

He showed conspicuous gallantry in campaigns around the world, even surviving a nasty wound in his thigh. He was greatly admired by his fellow officers. But the astonishing fact about our brave hero was that Dr James Barry was a woman.

No one knows who she really was. But it is recorded that in 1808, at the age of 13, she was accepted as a medical student at Edinburgh University in the name of James Barry. Fellow students said that she was somewhat nervous when walking out in rough neighbourhoods, that she refused to box and that she had the odd habit of keeping her arms folded over her chest.

But she wasn't a coward. In the army she became a noted duellist, and on one occasion after being insulted she gave a good account of herself with bare fists.

A fellow officer, however, did detect a certain 'effeminacy in his manner', and also praised 'his' conversation as being greatly superior to that usually heard at the mess table.

Only after Barry died was the dark secret discovered. To everyone's utter astonishment their Inspector General was revealed to be a woman. Even her own physician and her servant of 30 years were unaware of her true sex. But that wasn't the only shock. Further examination showed that Barry had been a mother.

The authorities were left with the perplexing question: why did this woman spend 53 years of her life as a man?

She is commemorated today in the Royal Army Medical College in Chelsea with a room called the Barry Room. It is the only part of the college where

---

Sex tale with no difference

Embarrassed police at Southend, Essex, could not be sure whether a long-haired suspect was male or female despite his (or her) assurances that he (or she) was a man.

They settled the problem by calling a police surgeon to find out whether he (or she) should be searched by a policeman or a policewoman. 'He' turned out to be a 'she'.

visiting ladies are permitted to remain unaccompanied.

An earlier case of a distinguished personage who chose to live in the guise of another sex was that of Chevalier D'Eon – a Frenchman who lived in the mid-18th century.

Being very feminine in looks, he took to swordsmanship to prove his masculinity. He became the greatest swordsman of his day and a highly successful French spy. Sent by Louis XV to spy on the Russian Court, the Chevalier dressed up as a woman, became lady-in-waiting to the Czarina and gathered much valuable information.

D'Eon's impersonations did not end with his spying days. He later came to London to the Court of St James as the French Ambassador. But because Louis XV had intimated that D'Eon was actually a woman, he turned up dressed as one, remaining in that guise for the rest of his life. Even so, many courtiers would lay bets as to whether the diplomat was really a man or woman.

Duelling and fencing at that time were learned and practised by most men in society. Despite his dress, the Chevalier became a fencing master of great renown and taught the aristocracy the fine art of duelling.

But this extraordinary man came to an even more extraordinary end. During a lesson he suffered a mortal wound when he fell on his opponent's sword – after tripping over his own skirts!

Thérèse and her priceless brick

Thérèse Humbert was the daughter of a French peasant, and she made a fortune out of a most audacious confidence trick. She drew inspiration from her father, who had lived his life in Toulouse on borrowed money raised against a vast inheritance – 'proof' of which he kept in an old sealed chest. When he died, his creditors called to claim the contents. They opened the chest and found a solitary house brick.

Like father like daughter, Thérèse fashioned a master-plan. She moved to Paris where she found a job as a washerwoman in the household of a government official. Here she deceived the boss's son into believing she was coming into money and he married her.

In due course, Thérèse had what appeared to be a fantastic windfall – a legacy of $20 million. She explained that it had been left her by Robert Henry

Taken for a ride

There was something the learner drivers did not know about their instructor – he had no licence himself. And the instructor used a stolen car for his lessons.

He was found out after driving a stolen car past a red traffic light and crashing into two other vehicles at Middlesborough, Yorkshire.

He was taken to court, where it was discovered that he ran a driving school and even branched out into coach-hire business – despite the fact that he had been banned from driving for 15 years.

Crawford, an American from Chicago. She had met him on a train two years previously and nursed him when he later suffered a heart attack.

The amazing story soon got around and when the young ex-washerwoman arrived at the bank, she received a warm welcome. She explained to the manager that Mr Crawford had actually left half of his fortune to be split between his two nephews in America and Thérèse's younger sister Marie. Out of the latter, Thérèse was to get an annual annuity but the full amount would not be realized until Marie reached the age of 21.

In addition, Thérèse explained, under the terms of the will and by agreement with the Crawford nephews, all the documents and deeds relating to the settlement were to be kept locked in her safe.

Thérèse told the manager: 'I am not allowed to open it until Marie comes of age, under penalty of forfeiting all claim upon the Crawford millions.' Then, predictably, she asked for a loan. It was readily granted.

The conniving trickster used the same ploy on several other banks. One Lille banker alone advanced her, over the years, seven million francs. And nobody ever questioned the contents of her safe – a massive contraption she kept hidden and locked in her splendid mansion bought with borrowed money.

Thérèse's position was now practically unchallenged . . . until the Lille banker, M. Delatte, happened to visit America. While there he tried to contact the Crawford family in Boston, where they were supposed to be living. Nobody in Boston or Chicago had ever heard of them or the deceased millionaire, Robert Henry Crawford.

The investigation proved disastrous not for Thérèse but for Delatte. His body was found floating in the East River in New York. The murderer was never caught.

With Marie's 21st birthday looming up, Thérèse now concocted a plan to make more crooked money, financing her brothers in a life insurance scheme that offered tempting returns. Instead of investing the incoming money, she spent it or paid off her more pressing creditors. Now she was 'La Grande Thérèse' and bankers and financiers pleaded with her to allow them to invest money in her schemes.

Then one high-ranking banker, Jules Bizat, decided to investigate. What he discovered shocked him – particularly as his own family had given the Humberts a small fortune – and he alerted the Prime Minister, Pierre Marie Waldeck-Rousseau.

The Premier decided against exposure but investors had to be warned. A series of scathing articles appeared in the influential newspaper *Le Matin*. Yet Thérèse's own lawyer believed so fervently in the truth of the Crawford inheritance that he threatened to sue the newspaper for libel and offered to open the safe to prove her virtue.

Thérèse, understandably, was horrified at this suggestion and covered up by protesting that such a procedure would dash all hopes of her getting her money. But the lawyer insisted that the safe should be opened to clear her name. Thérèse was trapped in the web of her own lies.

Two days before the safe was due to be opened, a mysterious fire broke out in Madame Humbert's apartment, totally gutting everything inside the room – except the safe. It was fireproof.

Some of France's leading financiers gathered around the safe on May 10, 1902. Thérèse was not present when the door was swung back to reveal . . . a brick!

Thérèse was later caught and sentenced to five years in prison. The safe, complete with brick, went on show in a Paris shop window, where it became one of the great tourist attractions of the year.

The 'count' from the backstreets of Sicily

For seven years, Count Cagliostro dazzled the high society of Europe's most fashionable cities. Royal courts marvelled as his magic elixirs performed apparent miracle cures. Scientists gasped at the gold and gems he could seemingly create from ordinary metal. Religious leaders believed him when he spoke of conversations with Moses and Solomon.

London, Paris and Strasbourg were bewitched by his glittering life-style.

THE WORLD'S GREATEST CROOKS AND CONMEN

Tales of his achievements spread like wildfire. A Baltic state offered him its throne. Ministers at the Tsar's Moscow court lined up relatives for him to heal.

Then, in France, he was thrown into the Bastille for a crime of which he was innocent. And shocked princes and priests learned that the count they had fêted was not what he seemed.

He was, in fact, a humble Sicilian named Giuseppe Balsamo. Born in a poverty-stricken back street of Palermo, in 1743, he had been living on his wits since stealing enough money from the church poor box and his uncle's savings to flee the island. He roamed the Mediterranean, staying for a while in Egypt, before settling to a lucrative life of crime in Rome, peddling home-made beauty creams and aphrodisiacs, copying paintings, forging banknotes and wills.

Here he met and married Lorenza Feliciani, a beautiful 15-year-old slum girl. Lorenza became the bait to lure rich victims into Balsamo's clutches. She was to help him reach the heights of fame and fortune – and send him tumbling to disgrace.

It was 1777 when the couple arrived in London. Rome had become too hot for them after a series of spectacular confidence tricks, and they had wandered for 10 years through southern Europe and North Africa, perfecting the art of deception. Now they were ready for the big time.

Overnight, Giuseppe and Lorenza Balsamo became Count Alessandrio di Cagliostro and Countess Serafina. He claimed he had stolen her from an Oriental harem. They lived up to their titles with the richest clothes and jewellery, elegant coaches and hordes of servants in sumptuous livery. When people asked where their money came from, admirers whispered that the Count had the power to turn base metals into gold.

The truth was more prosaic. The couple had arrived with £3,000, the proceeds of their Mediterranean adventures.

But shortly after arriving in London, Balsamo had joined a London lodge of Freemasons. Such Orders were spreading quickly throughout the Continent, with the richest, noblest men clamouring to join. Balsamo progressed quickly, being elected Grand Master of his lodge. And that opened many doors to him in Europe when he began travelling.

In Paris, he invented what he called an 'Egyptian Rite' order of Freemasonry, appointing himself head as Grand Cophta. This entitled him to collect heavy initiation fees and membership dues. And whereas Freemasonry was for men only, he opened a female lodge, with Lorenza in charge as the new Queen of Sheba.

Gullible Parisians flocked to join, lured by the promise of learning some of the Grand Cophta's secrets. The Queen of Sheba confided to duchesses that though she looked 30 – which she was – she was really 60. Her husband's magic five-drop potion kept her looking young.

Guiseppe and Lorenza Balsamo at their meeting with Comte de St. Germain

Listeners promised to keep her 'secret' – and became even more desperate to pay any price that the cure-all count demanded for his elixirs. His suave charm, irresistible bedside manner and touches of luxury – wrapping pills in gold leaf – all helped him get away with extortionate charges for herbal remedies any doctor could have prescribed.

As the Grand Cophta's fame spread, more and more countries demanded to see this man of magic powers for themselves. The nobles of the independent Baltic state of Courland were so impressed that they proposed crowning the count king. He wisely declined.

In Moscow one of the Tsar's ministers urged Cagliostro to cure his insane brother. The count deigned to inspect the patient, who was brought before him, securely bound. Acting on the count's instructions, the Russians untied the madman, and he charged his would-be benefactor, threatening to kill him. The count knocked him aside, then had him thrown into an icy river. Amazingly, when pulled out, the man was sane and apologetic.

But it was after he moved to Strasbourg in 1780 that Count Cagliostro achieved his greatest fame. By this time, he was claiming to have been born before Noah's flood, to have studied under Socrates, to have talked with Moses, Solomon and Roman emperors, to have drunk wine at a wedding feast in Cana, Galilee. And he was dating his letters 550 B.C.

He was also still confidently dispensing potions which cured patients whom ordinary doctors had given up as lost causes. The French government set up a commission of eminent medical men and scientists to investigate several unorthodox healers, and they pronounced many of Cagliostro's cures genuine, while admitting they could find no scientific explanation.

Soon his achievements came to the attention of the arrogant archbishop of the city, Prince-Cardinal Louis de Rohan. A servant was sent to summon Cagliostro – but returned alone with a message.

'If the prince is ill, let him come to me and I will cure him,' the count had said. 'If he is not ill, he has no need of me and I have no need of him.'

Such impudence was unheard of. But once de Rohan overcame his initial rage, he was intrigued enough to invent a minor ailment to justify visiting the man everyone was talking about. And so began the patronage that was to establish the count as one of Europe's most powerful men – and drag him down to despair.

When Cagliostro cured the Prince-Cardinal's brother, Prince de Soubise, of scarlatina – something the greatest doctors of Paris had failed to do – adulation knew no bounds. The count's effigy began appearing on snuff boxes, shoe buckles, rings and medallions.

Then de Rohan overstepped himself. Anxious to ingratiate himself with Queen Marie Antoinette, with whom he had fallen out of favour, he hatched a bizarre plot to obtain a diamond necklace she wanted. When King Louis XVI learned he had been forging letters in the queen's name and disguising a woman as the queen, he had the Prince-Cardinal arrested – and his protégés, the Cagliostros, were also thrown into the Bastille.

A public trial completely cleared them of involvement in the conspiracy, and nine months later they were escorted home in triumph by thousands of delighted supporters. But the damage had been done. Under intense interrogation. Lorenza had revealed too much about the tricks of Balsamo's trade. Slowly the truth about his money, his elixirs, his life-style began to emerge.

The furious Louis kicked the couple out of France, with dire warnings not to return. Again they wandered Europe, growing increasingly poor and shunned. Finally, Lorenza, tiring of her husband now that the glamour, riches and excitement had gone, persuaded him to return with her to Rome.

It was a crazy blunder – any Roman Catholic joining the Freemasons was subject to excommunication as a heretic. Yet Balsamo compounded his career by creating a new Egyptian Rite Masonic Lodge to try to revive his fortunes.

The papal police quickly seized him, and on April 7, 1791 he was found guilty of heresy and sentenced to die. Lorenza had denounced him, hoping to save herself. She was locked away in a convent for the rest of her life.

The Pope's mercy saved Balsamo for a while. The death sentence was commuted to life imprisonment in the dungeons of Italy's strongest fortress, San Leo. And there, on August 26, 1795, Count Alessandro di Cagliostro, the man who had proclaimed himself immortal, died, aged 52.

Is there a real doctor in the house?

The strange case of the queen and the bogus baron made the Dutch people look uneasily at their Head of State. For it was the second time that Queen Juliana of the Netherlands had been duped by a fraud 'psychiatrist'.

Her 'confessor' was really a Dutch labourer, Henry de Vries, 35. He shared a flat with the royal dressmaker, who introduced him to the queen as Baron David James Rothschild. The 69-year-old monarch took an instant liking to him and appointed him her psychiatrist.

Guards at the Soestdijk Palace, in The Hague, were so used to his frequent visits that they did not bother to check his papers. He was eventually exposed in 1978 when he applied for a police permit to hold a World Wildlife party in the grounds of the palace.

When the scandal broke, de Vries fled to France. Queen Juliana and her husband, Prince Bernhard, went on a long sea cruise in the late Aristotle Onassis's luxury yacht, *Christina*.

There were increasing fears at home that Juliana's powers of judgment were not all they should be. For she had been duped in the 1960s by another bogus 'psychiatrist', Greet Hoffman, whose powerful sway over her had caused a public outcry.

The former Dutch queen is just one of many victims of the age-old art of medical trickery – perhaps the greatest exponent of all being the resourceful impostor Ferdinand Demara.

Demara posed as a naval surgeon and saved many lives with his deft, self-taught surgery. He signed on the Royal Canadian Navy destroyer *Cayuga* during the Korean War when there was a desperate shortage of medical men.

The authorities accepted Demara's credentials, dispensing with the usual red tape, including fingerprint examination. His papers stated he was Dr Josephy Cyr, of New Brunswick. In fact, 30-year-old Demara had stolen them from Dr Cyr at a time when he was posing as a professor.

Once aboard the *Cayuga* as a surgeon-lieutenant, Demara's skills were called into immediate use: the captain needed a tooth extracted.

The bogus doctor sat up all night reading medical text books. Next morning he successfully removed the commander's tooth.

Sterner challenges soon followed. Nineteen badly wounded Korean civilians battled through the sea in a junk to beg for help from the *Cayuga*.

'I had to keep one basic principle in mind,' Demara recalled. 'The less cutting you do, the less patching up you have to do afterwards.'

The civilians responded well to the Canadian 'doctor's' skills. He had similar success with a South Korean soldier who was brought to him with a bullet near his heart.

Demara carried out cardiac surgery aboard ship as if he had been performing similar operations all his professional life. He later saved another soldier who had been smashed in the chest by a dum-dum bullet.

His downfall came when the Navy insisted on publicizing his heroic work. The real Dr Cyr read the story and an inquiry began. Investigations showed that, apart from posing as a doctor and a professor, Demara had also hoaxed his way across America disguised variously as a Trappist monk, a psychologist, a deputy sheriff, a prison warder and an instructor of theology.

He used forged references to get the jobs. Yet, once accepted, he invariably made a success of them. Indeed, had he not been so good a surgeon, he might still be conning his way through life – instead of reforming and settling down as a religious counsellor at a Californian hospital.

Young Barry Vinocur was praised for saving the life of an infant when he diagnosed a rare blood disease at the prestigious medical faculty of the University of California, San Francisco. He was so well regarded that he was deputed to lead a land and air emergency team for sick new-born babies.

Yet Vinocur was no doctor – he was a 33-year-old college drop-out with no formal medical training, who fast-talked his way into a job as a medical technician at a hospital in Cleveland, Ohio. Then he faked his physician's licence by using the medical records of his own cousin.

It was in Cleveland that Vinocur decided to create his false identity, after watching a real doctor vainly attempting to insert a catheter in the vein of a patient who was screaming in agony.

'I put on gloves and picked up the needle,' he said. 'I broke out in a cold sweat – and then put the needle in. It was then that I realized that I could do all these things myself.'

Vinocur's sham was uncovered in 1980, when a court put him on probation and ordered him to perform 100 hours of community service. The former 'doctor' was left with only one relic of his amazing days in the hospital wards: a textbook on intensive-care medicine which he had co-written with three real doctors.

Vinocur never made much money out of his good-natured duplicities. But Frank Abagnale – alias Dr Frank Williams – claimed to have been a millionaire twice over.

'I stole every nickel and blew most of it on gourmet food and luxurious living,' he said. 'But I never felt I was a criminal. I was simply a poseur and swindler of astonishing ability.'

His greatest coup came by chance after he had moved to Georgia in 1964, posing as Dr Frank Williams, a children's specialist. A neighbour was chief resident doctor at a nearby children's hospital, and invited 'Dr Williams' to look around.

Soon he was on the hospital staff – after reading every book he could find on children's diseases. If a term cropped up that he did not understand, Abagnale would surreptitiously consult a medical dictionary. But as a rule, when other doctors gave their diagnosis, he was only called on to nod agreement.

Eventually Abagnale realized his improbable role was putting young lives at risk and he resigned, having drawn a hefty salary for 11 months.

Next Frank Abagnale, alias Frank Williams, became 'Robert Conrad'. He put aside his medical text books and began studying borrowed law books, finally forging a degree for himself from Harvard Law School. He practised law for nine months before a colleague became suspicious.

Robert Conrad then became 'Frank Adams PhD, sociology teacher.' With fake documents he was hired by a Utah college as a teacher for three months.

Nobody was any the wiser. Said Abagnale: 'I just read a chapter ahead of the students and selected passages to emphasize.'

Then came a con-trick on a major American airline. Posing as a pilot, he got them to issue him with a uniform to replace his own 'stolen' one. With forged licence and identification as 'Captain Frank Williams' he flew as a standby co-pilot, with the crew on the flight deck.

But the con-man came down to earth with a bump in 1971. He was jailed for 12 years after admitting hundreds of charges. He was paroled four years later.

While in prison, Abagnale wrote a book on his life, aptly titled *Catch Me If You Can*, and came out a minor celebrity. He even appeared on the Johnny Carson TV show.

With his specialized knowledge, he started up businesses in Houston and Denver with an annual turnover of about $3 million. His speciality . . . crime prevention.

The 'professor' with an academic act

Thousands of former American college students owe their qualifications to the professor who never was. They were guided to examination success by a man who hoaxed his way into a series of top university posts – and proved he was suited for the job he had no right to hold.

Marvin Hewitt, born the son of a Philadelphia policeman in 1922, was a loner as a child. He discovered advanced mathematics at the age of 10, and was soon so well versed in the subject that neither his family nor his playmates could understand a word of what he was talking about.

He yearned to continue his studies at university, but could not qualify because routine schoolwork bored him. He left secondary school early, at 17, and for six years worked unhappily in factories and freight yards.

Then a newspaper advertisement caught his eye. A military academy needed a senior preparatory school teacher. Hewitt applied, claiming he was a Temple University graduate, and landed the post.

For the first time in his life he felt at home – admired and respected by pupils and fellow teachers alike. When the spring term finished, he decided to further his own education – as an aerodynamicist at an aircraft factory. He picked out a name from a universities' *Who's Who* list and landed a job on the strength of the borrowed qualifications. With his knowledge of advanced mathematics, even the most complex tasks were simple.

That summer, growing in confidence, he chose a fresh name for another post in education. Julius Ashkin was about Hewitt's age, had had a promising career at Columbia University and was about to start work as a teacher at the University of Rochester.

Hewitt usurped his name and qualifications, and applied to Philadelphia College of Pharmacy and Science for a job as physics teacher. He got it, at $1,750 a year. Students watched with admiration as their new master did complicated calculus in his head. And at the end of the year his classes did as well as any others in departmental examinations.

The only dark cloud on Hewitt's horizon was his salary. He felt Ashkin was entitled to better things. So he began writing to other colleges, enhancing his prospects by introducing the Christie Engineering Company in his list of references. This was a simple matter of getting letterheads printed, and hiring a secretarial service to handle mail.

Soon the Minnesota Bemidji State Teachers College sent Christie an inquiry about physicist Ashkin. They received a glowing testimonial – and Hewitt landed a job at $4,000 a year.

On the strength of his new-found means, Hewitt married. His wife Estelle was unperturbed by his bizarre explanation that because he had qualified under an assumed name he had to continue using it. She was even prepared to have all her 'Mrs Hewitt' mail delivered to a post-office box, and to put off her parents when they wanted to visit the couple.

Despite such precautions, Hewitt was running into problems. The president at Bemidji had also attended Columbia University, and was ever-ready to discuss mutual friends and acquaintances with 'Ashkin', a fellow campus old boy.

It was time to move on, and Hewitt decided to return to higher education, where he could mix with minds he considered more his equal.

Out came the Christie notepaper again, and back came an interview offer from the physics department at St Louis University. Hewitt was too scared to go, and wrote excusing himself, saying he could not get away on the suggested date. To his surprise, he was offered the post anyway, at $4,500 a year.

Now Hewitt was in his element. He was teaching graduate courses in nuclear physics, statistical mechanics and tensor analysis. He was proud of lecturing at Ph.D. level. Students liked him and fellow staff respected him, even if some did comment on inexplicable gaps in his knowledge of basic physics.

THE WORLD'S GREATEST CROOKS AND CONMEN

But again the close links between colleges and academics put his future in peril. A professor who travelled occasionally to Argonne National Laboratory, Chicago, for research, returned one day to tell Hewitt that he had run into an old friend who had worked with Ashkin at Columbia – and remembered him well.

Hewitt was now living on his nerves every time his colleague went to Chicago. But amazingly, the conversations at Argonne, faithfully reported on the professor's return, did not give the imposter away.

In the spring of 1948, Hewitt got another shock. An article appeared in the journal *Physical Review* – written by the real Julius Ashkin. Hewitt dashed to see his professor, and explained that he had written the paper, but signed it from Rochester University because that was where he had done the work on which it was based. Although his explanation was accepted, Hewitt wisely decided that there was a limit to how long his luck could last at St Louis.

He applied to the University of Utah at Salt Lake City, and received the red carpet treatment when he arrived for his interview. Glowing references from St Louis and Columbia backed up the good impression he made. Nobody realized that they were references for two different men. And nobody checked with Rochester University.

A dean at Columbia had even given Hewitt a quite unexpected 'insurance' bonus. He told Utah there had been two Ashkins on his books.

The Utah authorities were so delighted to get their man, they appointed him to a $5,800-a-year position as full professor. Hewitt had now overtaken the man whose qualifications he had borrowed. The real Ashkin was still an assistant professor at Rochester. It was the moment he had dreamed of. But his joy was not to last for long.

A month after he began work as head of department, a letter arrived addressed to 'Dr Julius Ashkin (?)'. It demanded that the masquerade be ended, but added:

'Let me assume that you are versed in theoretical physics and that you are a fundamentally decent man. I should then be willing to help you to relieve yourself of what must have become an almost unbearable burden. It is on these assumptions that I have decided not to take any immediate steps to notify university officials.'

The letter was from the real Julius Ashkin. And though he kept his word, one of his colleagues at Rochester was less merciful and tipped off the authorities. Hewitt was hauled before the Utah president and had to admit the truth. Generously, the authorities offered him the choice of staying on as a research fellow, to qualify for the degrees he needed to hold his position legitimately, or of transferring to another college to qualify.

But Hewitt was too shaken by events to take up either offer. He slunk back disgraced to his mother's home in Philadelphia, and for 18 months laid low, supported by his family and in-laws.

Then, in the spring of 1950, he launched a new bid for bogus academic fame. He wrote to a teachers' placement agency, announcing that George Hewitt, D.Sc., John Hopkins, was available for a posting. Qualifications included work as research director for the giant RCA communications company.

Hewitt had invented an RCA vice-president, and given him an address in Camden, New Jersey where letters could be sent – and answered by Hewitt.

The dead-letter ploy worked again. Hewitt took up an appointment teaching electrical engineering at Arkansas University's college of engineering, and flung himself into the work. Apart from lessons, he gave a local engineering society a lecture on 'The Orthogonality Property in Microwave Transmission.' He also presented a paper on 'The Theory of the Electron' at the Arkansas Academy of Science, and worked on two research programmes.

Then an RCA chief came to the university seeking engineering recruits. 'We have your former research director here,' he was told.

'Oh yes, who's that?'

'George Hewitt.'

'Who?'

It was back to Philadelphia for Hewitt. But by now he had twin baby sons to support as well as a wife. So he became Clifford Berry, Ph.D., Iowa State College, and took a post at New York State Maritime College.

Bored by teaching undergraduates, he tried to gatecrash technical industry. But this proved a tougher nut to crack than colleges. So he became Kenneth Yates, Ph.D., Ohio State University. And in January 1953 he began work teaching at the University of New Hampshire.

Again he was unmasked. One of his students in theoretical physics and relativity became suspicious of lapses in his tutor's knowledge. Checking a copy of the *American Men of Science* catalogue, he found the real Yates was working near Chicago for an oil company.

Confronted by the facts, Hewitt again owned up and quietly resigned. 'I always do all I can to straighten things out,' he said. But this time, any hopes he had of reappearing quickly in a new area were dashed. The news leaked to a newspaper, and quickly his career as a bogus boffin was splashed over every front page in the country.

Hewitt had always caused more trouble to himself than to anyone else. He said wistfully: 'If they'd only let me be a professor, I'd never want anything else or lie. I lied only to get those jobs. I was a good teacher, I've never really hurt anyone.'

The Princess from Javasu

One mild April evening in 1817 near the village of Almondsbury in Gloucestershire, a mysterious beautiful girl appeared. She was aged about 20, was penniless, lost and bewildered and spoke a tongue that no-one had ever heard before.

It was obvious she was in need of food and shelter, and a kindly magistrate, Mr. Worral, took pity on her and invited her into his house. There he and his wife tried to illicit some information from her about where she'd come from and who she was. But all the girl would say was 'Caraboo!' Over and over again: 'Caraboo! Caraboo!' Mr and Mrs Worral asked in sign language if that was her name. She nodded.

At least that was established. But not much else was forthcoming. She seemed to get excited by an oriental picture, would only eat food if she prepared it herself in a special way, and she insisted on sleeping on the floor.

As luck would have it, after a few weeks a Portuguese appeared on the scene – Signor Manuel Eynesso, who had spent some time in the Far East. He was called round to meet Caraboo and after a short time alone with her, announced he could understand every word she spoke.

This truly amazed everyone, including Caraboo – since she didn't understand what she said herself.

According to the Portuguese 'interpreter', Miss Caraboo was a princess in her country, an island near Sumatra called Javasu. After a war in which the Boogos, or cannibals, killed her mother, she was kidnapped by Malay pirates who sold her into slavery. She was bought by a ship's captain whose vessel visited a southern African port and then continued on to Europe to an unknown destination. Princess Caraboo escaped her master while the ship sheltered from a storm and she swam ashore. She wandered round the countryside for many weeks before finding refuge in the village.

Signor Eynesso's sensational disclosures amazed the whole country. More experts came from all over the examine the mysterious princess. And she certainly didn't let them down. She performed wild dervish-like dances, twirling around holding one leg in the air. She confused the greatest linguists with her strange tongue. And she drew up characters of the 'Javasu' language.

Yet all this was an elaborate fraud and imposture . . . by a cobbler's daughter from Devon called Mary Baker. She had dreamed up the act to get into a wealthy household and escape from her impoverished and boring environment.

The Portuguese, Eynesso, had been an added bonus and when they were alone Mary had somehow persuaded him to join in the deception.

Princess Caraboo

But Mary's fame as Princess Caraboo soon led to her downfall. A Bristol woman named Mrs Neale read an account of Caraboo. The description of the princess was identical to a girl who, Mrs Neale claimed, lodged with her for several weeks. A meeting between Mrs Neale and Caraboo was arranged.

Mrs Neale immediately recognised Mary and exposed her. The girl confessed. But with her background of family poverty, desertion by her parents and near starvation, everybody took pity on poor Mary. She was given the passage money to go off to America to make a new life.

America didn't work out either for this exotic adventuress. Seven years later she was back in Bristol trying to exhibit herself as Princess Caraboo for a shilling a peep. But she wasn't successful, and she ended her days selling leaches to people who wished to avoid physician's bills by bleeding themselves.

The saved exotic

Another imposter supposedly from far-off shores was a remarkable man who called himself George Psalmanazar. In 1703 he arrived in London claiming to be from Formosa, a country about which little was known at the time. He also claimed to have been converted to Christianity and sponsored by the Bishop of London as an important convert. He was immediately lionized by London society, including Dr Johnson, as 'a saved exotic'.

Doted on by the famous, he was given chambers and asked to translate the Bible into his native tongue. He couldn't, of course, although he burned candles at his window all night to convince people he was working on the project. But he did invent a Formosan language, lectured on the country and offered to teach the language to future missionaries. And in 1704 he wrote an Historical and Geographical Description of Formosa.

As was the 'custom' in Formosa, he only ate raw meat and he astonished Londoners with tales of the annual sacrifice of 18,000 infants to the pagan Formosan gods. He claimed the average life expectancy was 100 years, guaranteed by a regular diet of snakes' blood for breakfast.

This was an age when average life expectancy was a meagre 40 years and people's diet basically consisted of meat and potatoes. Obviously, a life-span of 100 years would have been unheard of.

He also strongly advocated a daily dip. Again, this astounded people. Londoners bathed very seldom and preferred to use scent to disguise bodily smells. However, it is debatable whether he practised what he preached.

Then a strange thing happened to George. Impressed by the kindness and generosity of Londoners, he really was converted to Christianity. He repented, confessed everything, was forgiven – and lived out the rest of his days like a saint. But the two things he never revealed were where he actually came from and who he really was.

Chapter
Eight

Pranksters and Hoaxers

'Life is a joke that's just begun'
Sir W.S. Gilbert

The Piltdown 'missing link'

In 1912 two men made monkeys out of the world's scientific establishment. One of them was a quiet, studious English country lawyer and respected amateur geologist named Charles Dawson. But it is the name of the other that has gone down in history – Piltdown Man.

Piltdown Man was the title given to a prehistoric humanoid skull which Dawson claimed to have discovered in a gravel pit near Piltdown Common, Sussex. He had been tipped off about bones in the pit by a workman. Dawson had spent many days searching the pit. First he turned up a few tiny fossilized bone fragments. Then he found flint tools, fossilized teeth – and finally parts of a skull.

The lawyer packaged up his treasures and sent them to an acquaintance, one of the world's leading authorities on the history of man, palaeontologist Dr Arthur Smith Woodward of the British Museum.

Woodward was so excited that, at the first opportunity, he sped down to Sussex to join Dawson at the gravel pit. His enthusiasm knew no bounds, for here at last was the discovery that scientists had anxiously awaited for half a century – the proof of Charles Darwin's controversial Theory of Evolution.

When Darwin published his *Origin of Species* in 1859, he was denounced as a crank and even a heretic. Even the more level-headed critics demanded to be shown some proof of his theory. Where, they asked, was the Missing Link? Why had no one ever discovered any fossilized remains of the creatures that Darwin claimed linked man with the ape? Here thought Woodward, was that proof.

He and Dawson carefully sifted through the gravel pit debris in the area where the first bones had been unearthed. More finds were made and other experts called in. They agreed – Piltdown Man was indeed the Missing Link.

They pointed to the thick bone structure of the skull fragments, to the tiny brain area, to the ape-like jaw – and, above all, to the teeth which were ground down, not in the manner of an ape, but as human teeth are worn away.

Woodward painstakingly pieced together the finds until they formed the greater part of a complete skull – and announced that what they had unearthed was a creature, half-man half-ape, which had lived 500,000 years ago. Although the skull was that of a woman, the find was officially named *Eoanthropus dawsoni* – Dawson's Early Man.

The announcement threw scholars worldwide into dizzy delight. Piltdown was scheduled to be named a National Monument. Dawson became a hero. Woodward wrote a book about this discoverer of 'the earliest Englishman'. The British Museum displayed the skull with a pride bordering on rapture.

Even the local public house changed its name to The Piltdown Man.

Mr Charles Dawson and Dr A Smith Woodward

Trippers travelled by the coachload to view the site of this earth-shattering find.

Dawson continued his excavations in the Piltdown area and, over the next few years, pieced together parts of a second skull. The finds only ended when he died in 1916, at the age of 52. Others continued the search but no further evidence was ever found.

The drying-up of the discoveries after Dawson's death was realized later to have been no coincidence. For Piltdown Man was a fake.

The skull was indeed that of a human, but the jaw and teeth were those of an orang-utan. The teeth had been filed down to look like human teeth, then the skull had been skilfully stained and aged before being broken up and buried in the gravel pit.

Right from the start, a few sceptics had raised doubts about the authenticity of Piltdown Man. But the cynics were not allowed access to the relics to make more thorough tests. All requests to have the samples scraped and probed were turned down. It was not until 1949 that one of Woodward's successors at the British Museum, a young geologist, Dr Kenneth Oakley, was allowed to take samples of the skull fragments and subject them to chemical tests. His verdict: the skull was not 500,000 years old but 'only' 50,000 years old.

Oakley, too, was wrong. In 1953, using newly developed techniques of age assessment, more extensive tests were made by a committee of paleontologists.

They finally and officially declared Piltdown Man a fake.

Who had perpetrated such an elaborate and outrageous confidence trick at the expense of the scientific world?

Although nobody was ever able to prove it, Hoax Suspect Number One has always been Charles Dawson. He had never sought money on the strength of his 'discovery'. But he was ambitious for academic distinction. And once a visitor had once walked into his laboratory uninvited to find Dawson busy over a bubbling crucible – staining bones.

The other prime suspect was Australian-born Sir Grafton Elliot Smith, one of the leading experts then employed by the British Museum. He had the temperament for such a massive practical joke. His possible motive: to liven up the deathly atmosphere pervading the famous mausoleum.

Whoever the culprit was, he took his secret with him to the grave – and left behind some very red scholarly faces.

The gigantic hoax

George Hull pulled off a giant of a fraud – literally. The cigar-maker from Binghampton, New York, decided to line his pockets with a scheme that was big in every way.

In 1868 Hull read about a race of giants that were supposed to have inhabited the earth. Anyone who discovered the remains would be on to a fortune, he thought. People would pay dearly to see such a giant.

So Hull set about 'making' his own giant. He bought a massive block of gypsum from a quarry in Iowa and sent it secretly to Chicago to be carved into a 10-ft-high naked giant.

Thanks Pal

Report in a Sussex newspaper:
'Mr Michael Vanner, of Bexhill Road, St Leonards, a defendant in a recent case at Hastings Magistrates' Court, wishes to state that Mr Melvin Peck, whom he pleaded not guilty to assaulting, was not a passer-by, as stated, but is a friend of his.'

When it was complete the stone was treated with chemicals to make it look as though it had been buried beneath the earth for millions of years. Then, unknown to his cousin William Newell, he buried the stone giant on Newell's farm in New York State.

Hull bided his time. With a bit of gentle persuasion he got Newell to start drilling for water on the farm. Wells were sunk all over the farm and in October 1869 the 'giant' was discovered.

Newell was overjoyed. He bought a tent, erected it over the find and charged the public 50 cents to see the marvel. The news that some genuine fossilized bones had been found close by added to the attraction.

It was now time for Hull to make his move. He returned to his cousin's farm and persuaded him to increase the admission price to one dollar. He even got Newell to read a lecture on the giant which he had specially written.

The crowds flocked by coach and train to see what Newell termed the Eighth Wonder of The World. Experts were also taken in until one, Oliver Wendell Holmes. bored a hole in the skull and found it was solid.

But the public were not put off. They still turned up in their thousands to see the giant.

The end came when a private investigator traced the connection between Hull and Newell and got on the trail of the block of gypsum. The game was up. Hull confessed to his con and renamed the giant Old Hoaxey. It still exists today, resting in the New York State Farmer's Museum.

It has been estimated that Hull and Newell picked up about £55,000 from their giant swindle.

'Princes' who fooled the navy

While the officers and men of the *Dreadnought* prepared for their VIP visitors, an elegant man in top hat and morning coat was introducing himself to the stationmaster at London's Paddington Station. He announced himself as Herbert Cholmondely of the Foreign Office and he demanded a special train to be laid on immediately to convey a party of Abyssinian princes to Weymouth.

Cholmondely was none other than William Horace de Vere Cole. It was he who had sent a telegram and it was he who had recruited five of his friends to perpetrate one of the most imaginative and elaborate hoaxes of all time.

The four princes who boarded the special train at Paddington on February 7 were really Cole's accomplices in this amazing confidence trick. All had been heavily made up, bearded and robed by theatrical make-up expert Willy Clarkson. It was his best day's work.

Clarkson watched proudly as the Abyssinian potentates were ushered into a specially prepared carriage. Beneath the elaborate disguises were famous novelist Virginia Woolf, sportsman Anthony Buxton, artist Duncan Grant and judge's son Guy Ridley. Accompanying them as an 'interpreter' was Virginia Woolf's brother Adrian. And bringing up the rear the 'man from the FO', Cole himself.

The group's reception at Weymouth was better than the hoaxers had ever dreamed of. A red carpet stretched from the train down the platform and through the station concourse. Waiting beyond was a guard of honour which they graciously inspected.

The party was taken by launch to the *Dreadnought* which had been bedecked with bunting for the royal visit. They were ceremoniously piped aboard.

The princes were invited to inspect the mighty ship. As they wandered around they handed out visiting cards printed in Swahili and spoke Latin in a strange accent. 'Bunga-bunga,' they exclaimed whenever they were shown some awesome aspect of the warship.

They overacted their roles to a ludicrous degree. They asked for prayer mats at sunset and they even tried to bestow Abyssinian honours on some of the senior officers.

On three occasions they almost gave the game away. The royal guests were offered a princely repast aboard the *Dreadnought*; they declined and Cole had to explain that their religious customs precluded them from eating or drinking at sea. The real reason for their refusal, however, was a warning by make-up man Clarkson that if they tried to eat anything, their false lips would fall off!

Later the hoaxers' hearts sank as they were introduced to an officer who was related to Virginia Woolf and who had met Cole on several occasions. The officer looked both of them square in the face yet failed to recognize either.

The third moment of panic occurred when Anthony Buxton sneezed and one half of his moustache flew off but he stuck it back again before anyone noticed.

The visit ended with Press photographs and an uproarious journey back to London during which the tricksters laughed themselves hoarse. The Royal Navy hierarchy were left congratulating themselves as being paragons of protocol – while Cole congratulated his phoney princes on the hoax of the decade.

The entire operation had cost Cole £4,000. But he counted it money well spent in his one-man campaign to bring the posturing and the pompous down a peg or two.

Oh come, all ye trustful!

Theodore Hook was a poet and wit who lived nearly 200 years ago in Regency London. Hook's hoaxes began gently enough – they were more in the nature of fun and japes – but his most ambitious one involved hundreds of London celebrities, including royalty.

Once at the Drury Lane Theatre he hid under the stage during the performance of a tragedy. When the leading actor began his crucial soliloquy, Hook accompanied him with a tune on a penny whistle. The stage was also the scene for another of Hook's pranks. He walked on in the middle of a performance and delivered a joke letter to the leading man telling him he had inherited a fortune. The actor apologized to the audience, jubilantly announced his good luck – and walked off stage, bringing the performance to a close.

Hook didn't become too popular with theatregoers. But he has to be remembered for one of the greatest hoaxes in history. It took place on November 10, 1810, as the result of this wager he made with a friend:

'I wager I can make an ordinary house in an ordinary street – how about this one, for example, No 54 Berners Street – the most famous address in the whole of London.'

His friend, obviously thinking he was on to a good thing, eagerly accepted the bet.

Over the next few days Hook began writing letters to hundreds of people. Then on November 10, Theodore Hook and his friend rented a room in the house opposite No. 54, a shabby, nondescript little dwelling occupied by a widow named Mrs Tottenham.

At precisely 9.0 am the first of many callers arrived. It was the coalman, with several sacks of coal that had never been ordered. Then came the fishmonger, the florist, the butcher and the cabinetmaker.

Hook had written to all these merchants and many more asking them to come to No. 54 Berners Street at the appointed hour on November 10. There were chimney sweeps, undertakers, doctors and dentists, cabs, carriages and carts.

Under various absolutely credible pretexts, Hook had invited not just tradesmen and merchants, fashionable medics and professionals to the house, but also really important personages. With hundreds of people pouring into Berners Street, Hook happily watched the resulting confusion. But his greatest triumphs were yet to come.

The Governor of the Bank of England arrived – to keep an appointment with a criminal who was to reveal inside information on a major counterfeiting

Theodore Edward Hook

fraud. The Archbishop of Canterbury turned up – to collect a large bequest for the Church of England. Then came the Lord Mayor – to collect a special philanthropic donation on behalf of the City of London. The Lord Chief Justice, too, came and went. And the Lord Chancellor.

The day was crowned with the arrival of a detachment of guards, the chief of police and none other than the Duke of York, who was son of the King of England and Commander-in-Chief of the British Army.

Hook had, without doubt, won his wager. London was brought to a standstill, as traders, merchants, diplomats and the hoi-polloi struggled to make their way to and from Berners Street. But at that time, of course, only two people knew who was behind the scheme. The secret cost Hook's friend £1,000. Hook discreetly left the country.

'Poor old prospectors' struck pure gold!'

On a summer day in 1872, two grizzled prospectors, Philip Arnold and John Slack, ambled into the Bank of California in San Francisco. They had with them a drawstring sack, which they cautiously handed to the teller.

'How about keeping this for us,' Slack drawled, 'while me'n him go and get drunk?'

The teller agreed, but as soon as the prospectors had left the bank he peeked at the contents of the pouch. Then he rushed into the office of his boss, the financial czar William Ralston, a man whose greed matched his girth. Expecting to see a few pinches of gold dust, Ralston opened the sack. A cataract of living fire spilled across his desk – a fortune in uncut diamonds.

At the end of a feverish three-day search, Ralston found the missing prospectors in a saloon. But even after he'd sobered them up they proved tough customers.

Grudgingly they admitted to having found a diamond field 'bigger than Kimberley'. But they said they hadn't acquired title to the land and refused to tell him where it was located. Much as they would appreciate Ralston's financial backing, anyone who inspected their find must agree to make the entire journey blindfold.

Ralston agreed, sending his mining engineer David Colton. The man returned in three weeks, wild with excitement. It was all true, Colton said, displaying his own find – a fistful of diamonds.

Ralston paid the two miners $50,000, put another $300,000 aside for their use, and promised them an additional $350,000 when their project started producing. Others who contributed money included Baron Anthony de Rothschild, the editor Horace Greeley, General George B. McClellan, and Charles Lewis Tiffany, founder of the world's greatest jewellery business.

To pull in still more smart money, Ralston sent another inspection party to the field. Again, they were led by Arnold and Slack. The visitors travelled by rail to Rawlings, Wyoming, where the prospectors blindfolded them and took them on a long trek through wild rangeland.

When the blindfolds were lifted, the view stunned them. Ant hills in the valley shimmered with diamond dust. More than that, there were rubies scattered across the terrain like plums in a pudding.

When the party returned home with their astonishing report, Ralston's avarice knew no bounds. His first step was to dump the two old-timers.

The game, he told them, was far too rich for their blood. Bullying them with threats of strange legal manoeuvres, he persuaded his grizzled victims to accept $700,000 for their share. Apparently hoodwinked by a great robber baron, they took the money and ran.

By now the diamond lode was a worldwide sensation, but eminent geologist E. W. Emmonds doubted the whole story – he had seen no signs of diamonds anywhere in Wyoming.

Doubling back on his trail, he located the great discovery. He was immediately alerted by the fact that the site lay only a few miles from the rail-line. The blindfolded members of Ralston's party had simply been led round in circles. Then he found that the 'ant hills' were man-made and there was something very strange about all the diamonds. The first one he picked up showed the marks of a lapidary tool. Emmons wired the bad news to San Francisco. The field had been 'salted'.

It hit the money marts with bombshell force, and by nightfall Ralston's diamond syndicate had become a joke.

It was revealed that the prospectors had visited Europe before setting up the con-trick, covering their tracks by sailing from and returning through Halifax, Nova Scotia. In Europe they had spent $35,000 – their life savings – on the gems they scattered across Wyoming soil.

Public sympathy was with the hoaxers, and they were never prosecuted. Slack later drifted away to parts unknown, Arnold to Kentucky, where he founded his own bank. But it did little better than that of William Ralston, whose great institution collapsed in 1875.

The dismantling of Manhattan Island

The 19th century was not a golden age for America. Two wars and several economic depressions left little to laugh about. Yet, possibly because of these traumas, it seems to have been a boom time for hoaxers.

No hoax can have been more ridiculous than the project dreamed up by two tricksters in 1824 to slice off Manhattan Island and put it back again the other way round! Yet, incredibly, many people believed them.

It was claimed that Mayor Stephen Allen was seriously worried about the Battery, the island's southern end, where many new buildings had been erected. It was starting to sag dangerously under the weight, and could sink at any moment with great loss of life and property.

The plan was to amputate the Island at the Kingsbridge or northern end. It would then be floated down past Ellis Island, turned round and moored in a safer position.

Cautious at first, hundreds of workmen and contractors were later completely sold on the idea. They swarmed into the parnters' plush office to get in on the historic project.

In the next eight weeks, the pair collected an array of mammoth saws 100 ft long with 3-ft teeth. Even paying some salaries in advance, they hired 300 labourers to do the sawing.

They also found two dozen oars 250 ft long and signed up another 2,000 men to row the island across the bay. Gigantic anchors were leased to hold the island firm in case of a storm.

Second-hand surgery

Francis Murphy amputated a toe and undertook complicated hip surgery on an elderly woman during 17 successful operations at Redhill General Hospital, southern England. And it was not until after he was sacked – for a row with a senior consultant – that the hospital discovered he was a phoney who had learned his techniques from his medical student wife. Murphy, who had conned other hospitals in England, Canada and Ireland, was jailed for two years.

Edgar Allan Poe

On the big day, dozens of greedy contractors, hundreds of workmen and thousands of sightseers turned up to launch the project. Also there was Mayor Allen, who was simply trying to find out what on earth was going on. The only people not around were the two promoters of the project. They were never seen again.

Another great hoax of the age was perpetrated by a newspaper that tried to make its own news. Desperate to increase its readership, the *New York Sun* ran stories of an amazing telescope with a huge lens that magnified objects 42,000 times. According to the reports, the telescope showed that there was life on the Moon, including a strange ball-like creature that rolled at great speeds. During these sensational reports, the paper's circulation rose from 2,500 to 19,000.

Another great newspaper hoax was author Edgar Allan Poe's account of a transatlantic crossing by balloon. Millions of readers eagerly awaited for Poe's reports – which the famed horror-story writer made up from start to finish.

Then there was the 'Terrible Turk' – not a person but supposedly a chess-playing robot that drew huge audiences. This bizarre-looking contraption took on all-comers and made strange machine sounds as it played. It took years – and lots of money for its owner, Johann Maelzel – before someone found that the real chess genius was a dwarf hidden inside the 'Terrible Turk'.

Who do you think you're kidding?

Hoaxers come in all shapes and sizes – and a multitude of disguises. Some perpetrate their cunning uses for money, others – like the honest hoaxers in this final chapter – carry out their con-tricks just for the joy of making a lot of suckers look silly!

But only one man has ever been able to hit the hoaxers' highspot – a fake entry in the American edition of *Who's Who*. That man was Professor Rutherford Aris, a noted chemical engineer who was already listed in the book. But when the *Who's Who* compilers wrote asking him to fill in any further biographical details, they incorrectly addressed the letter to 'Aris Rutherford'.

Professor Aris wrote back with details of a completely new fictional character whose birthplace was a Scotch whisky distillery, whose job was as a whisky consultant, and whose hobby was drinking the stuff. *Who's Who* printed the lot.

One of America's most persistent pranksters was humourist Edgard Nye.

Alan Abel, international hoaxer

Once, when travelling by train with poet James Whitcomb Riley, he spotted a ticket inspector approaching. Nye, who had been looking after the tickets, said to his friend: 'I've lost one of them. Quick, get under the seat'.

The poet complained but obeyed. However, when the inspector arrived at their seats, Nye handed to him, not one, but both tickets. 'Who is the other ticket for?' asked the inspector. 'For my friend,' said Nye, pointing under the seat with one hand, while tapping his temple knowingly with the other.

More recently, another American joker, comedian Alan Abel, played a trick on the entire nation. He formed the Society Against Indecency of Naked Animals to persuade owners to dress their dogs, cows and other animals in special underwear to preserve the creatures' modesty. It was meant to be a joke but the Press and public took the whole idea seriously.

At the height of the Vietnam War, President Lyndon Johnson asked if he could visit an air-base to cheer up some of the boys who were about to be drafted to south-east Asia. The visit was duly arranged. But by the time the President turned up, the troops who were on their way to war had tried to drown their sorrows to such an extent that they were deemed unfit to be paraded before him.

Then one of the Army's public relations men had a brainwave. Instead of using the outgoing troops, another batch of young men were introduced to Johnson. They were a laughing, joking, hand-shaking squad whose morale was at an all-time high – because they had just come *back* from Vietnam.

President Johnson was most impressed: so much so that he extended his visit to be able to wave the soldiers goodbye. Which meant the Army having to put their homecoming troops straight back into a plane and flying them round in circles until Johnson had left the base.

One hoax which is known to be pure fiction is the novel of Penelope Ashe. Miss Ashe appeared to have one of the sure-fire American best-sellers of the 1970s with her book, *Naked Came the Stranger*, a story of sex in suburbia. In just three days, 20,000 copies were sold, paperback rights were bought and 18 film companies made inquiries. It even got a write-up in the prestigious *New York Times Book Review*.

But at the end of the week, publishers and agents began to worry because all their attempts to track down Penelope Ashe were hitting dead-ends. That's when New York newspaper columnist Mike McGrady announced: 'The book is a hoax.'

McGrady had invented Miss Ashe so that he could produce his idea of a really abysmal novel. He recruited 24 co-authors, and they polished off the whole book, a chapter each, in just three weeks. None of them had expected the novel to be quite as successful as it turned out.

Another literary hoaxer was Cyril Henry Hoskins. Clever make-up helped him pull off a remarkable con-trick.

THE WORLD'S GREATEST CROOKS AND CONMEN

Hoskins wrote a string of money-spinning books about his life in a non-existent Tibetan monastery. He called himself Lama Lobsang Rampa, and claimed that a hole had been drilled in his shaven head to accommodate a spiritual 'third eye'.

Thousands of people thought there was magic in the air one morning when astronomer Patrick Moore told radio listeners tuned to the British Broadcasting Corporation that at exactly 9.47 am the planet Pluto would pass behind Jupiter, producing an increased gravitational pull from the heavens.

Moore said that when that happened people would feel lighter, and he invited them to jump into the air to experience a floating sensation. That was how thousands of people across Britain came to be leaping into the air at 9.47 am on April 1, 1976 – April Fools' Day. Hundreds of listeners actually rang the BBC afterwards to say that the experiment had worked!

Famous BBC broadcaster Richard Dimbleby fooled the nation nine years earlier – on April 1, 1957 – when he showed a television documentary about the spaghetti harvest in Italy. Viewers saw the spaghetti wafting in the wind as it 'grew' from the branches of trees. Because he was such a distinguished broadcaster, thousands believed him.

One radio station had a hoax played on it when it invited a VIP visitor, His Serene Highness Prince Shubtill of Sharjah, to be interviewed about oil exploration in the Persian Gulf. The interview was recorded for a news bulletin on Liverpool's Radio City, and the prince left after being fêted by the management.

But his Serene Highness was prankster Neville Duncan, a bank computer expert . . . and his impersonation was discovered 20 minutes too late when interviewer Peter Gould, a crossword fanatic, realized that Prince Shubtill's name was not Arabian after all, but an anagram for Anglo-Saxon bull****.

There was panic in 1977 when an unknown electronics wizard broke into a peak-hour national newscast on British television and announced that beings from outer space had landed in Southern England. TV station and newspaper switchboards were jammed, but the hoaxer was never discovered.

But creatures from outer space are small fry compared to the giant monster of Loch Ness. Sightings of the famous 'Nessie' have been reported for more than 1,000 years, but in 1972, experts believed they had at last captured the 'beastie'.

What they did not know was that, some weeks earlier, the crew of a British cargo vessel taking live elephant seals from the Falkland Islands to a zoo in England had found one of the seals dead. They threw the body overboard and it was picked up in the nets of a fishing boat. For a prank, the fishermen dumped the body in Loch Ness.

It was found there by zoologists organizing a large-scale search for the monster. The experts packed the half-ton, 15-ft giant in ice, loaded it into a van

Richard Dimbleby

and headed south for England to announce their news to the world.

However, locals alerted the police to the monster-snatchers' activities and the order was flashed to all cars: 'Nessie must not leave Scotland – she belongs to us'. Roadblocks were set up and the van was eventually stopped on the Forth Road Bridge. The phoney Nessie was impounded by police. Its true identity was revealed only after a blaze of publicity.

Money, purely and simply, was the aim of the Trodmore Hoaxers, a gang who invented a complete Cornish town, which they called Trodmore. But the only piece of fictitious real estate in which they were interested was the racecourse.

Just before a Bank Holiday, one of the gang, calling himself 'Mr Martin of St Ives' delivered to the editor of *The Sportsman* a racecard for Trodmore. It duly appeared in the paper. None of the horses ever ran, but the 'winner' was later announced. It was a horse called Reaper, and the gang had placed dozens of bets on it with bookmakers throughout London. They got their money and were never caught.

Another sporting hoax – for fun, this time, not money – was perpetrated on the organizers of the 1976 British Open golf tournament. One of the contestants who was accepted for the tournament was Mr Maurice G. Flitcroft, a Barrow-in-Furness shipyard worker who had never even tried to play a full 18 holes of golf in his life. But, as his professional partners stamped and fumed, the cheeky Mr Flitcroft managed to blunder round the course – in 121 shots!

Hot pants

A 30-year-old Lebanese businessman flew to Copenhagen airport to pick up four sample pairs of jeans for his brother's clothing company. But when he opened the package he got a shock – it contained £120,000 in different currencies. The money belonged to a London company.

The Lebanese stared into the parcel, then made up his mind. He picked up the bag, returned to the airport and bought a ticket to Athens via Frankfurt. Then he disappeared, leaving his wife and three children back in Copenhagen.

Said the deserted wife: I can't blame him. He did the right thing.'

THE WORLD'S GREATEST
SERIAL KILLERS

ACKNOWLEDGEMENTS

Corbis UK Ltd/Bettmann 19, 23, 36, 118
Hulton Getty Picture Collection 40, 62, 63
Rex Features 47, 75, 78, 83, 93, 126, 129, 152, 168, 169, 179, 180

Contents

Introduction

According to the FBI Handbook, a serial killer is someone who has murdered more than four people. This must have been done over a period of time, however – going down the local McDonald's and taking everybody out in one go does not count, because although the body count may be high, the perpetrator would be a spree killer, not a serial killer. In order to qualify as serial killer, the killings therefore have to take place one after another, like an old-fashioned newspaper serial (which is how the term came to be coined).

Indeed, the serial killer is a modern, mass-media phenomenon: although there were multiple murderers throughout history, such felons only became known as serial killers when the police discovered the bodies of their victims consecutively, the resultant press reports chilling the blood of the reading public and giving the impression that no one was safe.

Serial killers' motivations are often sexual. Some like to mutilate the bodies of their victims and sometimes resort to cannibalism. They seem to like to see how far they can travel beyond the usual bounds of morality. They frequently exhaust the possibilities and seem relieved when they are caught, quickly admitting their many crimes. In other cases they become so high on the thrill of living in a moral vacuum, in which every whim can be instantly acted out, that they become careless or unlucky.

Thankfully, most of the world's greatest serial killers described in this book have been caught. But beware: some of them are still out there.

1 ❖ Jack the Ripper

Jack the Ripper was the first serial killer to come to public attention. Although he killed only five women for certain – a pitifully low body count compared to those who came after him – he must count as one of the world's greatest serial killers because today, over a century since his savage murder spree ended, his name still chills the blood. In the East End of London, where he went about his gruesome business, tours of his murder sites are conducted. Experts still speculate about his identity. Each new serial killer that hits the headlines is compared to him. This is fame – or notoriety - indeed.

Jack the Ripper qualifies as the first true serial killer because his ten-week campaign of murder was a media event. Indeed, he courted the press, writing to the newspapers and giving them his sobriquet. He even sent them body parts of his victims that had been excised during his bizarre mutilation of their corpses. The Ripper's murderous activities gripped the public's imagination like no single individual's crimes before them and London was paralysed by fear. Again thanks to the mass media, Jack the Ripper was soon as famous in New York, San Francisco, Paris, Sydney and Berlin as he was in London. In Arles, the painter Vincent Van Gogh had been avidly following the accounts of his deeds in the French newspapers before he sliced off part of his ear (some biographers have concluded that he was influenced by the Ripper's method of dissection).

Whitechapel was the Ripper's stamping ground. In 1888, when the killings started, there were 62 brothels in the London district, along with 233 boarding houses that catered for prostitutes and their clients. On top of that there was also an army of older, pox-ridden, middle-aged alcoholics who offered their sexual favours in alleys and doorways for the price of a slug of gin.

On the night of 3 April 1888 the 45-year-old Emma Elizabeth Smith solicited a well-dressed gentleman. Later that night she collapsed in the arms of a police constable, saying that she had been attacked by four men. A foreign object had been shoved up her vagina and she died a few hours later. What connected her death to the Ripper's subsequent murders was the fact that her ear had been cut off. Then, on the night of 7 August 1888, Martha Tabram was stabbed to death. There were 39 wounds on her corpse, mainly around her breasts and vagina – the areas of the body that the Ripper liked to mutilate when he had the time. Both Martha Tabram and Emma Elizabeth Smith had been attacked from behind. The police assumed that (like the Ripper's later victims) the women had turned their backs on their client and had hoisted up their skirts for rear-entry sex when they were attacked. It is not known for certain that these two women were killed by Jack the Ripper, but their killer was never caught and their murders shared many similarities with the Ripper's slayings.

The first woman definitely to have been killed by Jack the Ripper was the 42-year-old Polly Nichols, whose body was found in Buck's Row, Whitechapel, at 3.15am on 31 August 1888. Although she had fought her attacker she had not cried out, for her murder had taken place under the window of a sleeping woman who had not been woken by the struggle. She also appeared to have turned her back on her attacker, who slashed her throat twice, so savagely that he almost decapitated her. There were deep wounds around her sexual organs, too, although no body parts had been removed. The doctors who examined the corpse speculated that the attacker had some medical knowledge and was possibly a doctor himself.

The police concluded that Polly had turned away from her killer during the assignation (a common practice among London street prostitutes of the time). She had therefore had her back to her killer when he pulled his knife, which was why she had not cried out. He had then put the knife to her throat and had pushed her forward on to it, which explained the depth of the wound. It also meant that the blood from the arteries and veins in her neck would have spurted forward, away from the killer, enabling him to escape from the scene unsullied.

With the murder of Polly Nichols the police realised that they had a maniac on their hands who seemed to be motivated by a hatred of prostitutes. Detectives were accordingly sent into the East End to search for men who mistreated prostitutes. The name 'Leather Apron' came up several times during the investigation and a shoemaker called Pizer was arrested. Although he used a leather apron and sharp knives in his trade, his family swore that he had been at home on the three occasions on which women had been attacked in this manner.

On 8 September 1888, in various pubs in Whitechapel, the 47-year-old Annie Chapman bragged that the killer would meet his match if he ever came near her. She was wrong, however. She was subsequently seen talking to a 'gentleman' in the street; having apparently struck a bargain they went off arm in arm. Half an hour later she was found lying dead in an alleyway. Her head was connected to her body by only a strand of flesh. Her intestines had been thrown over her right shoulder and the flesh from her lower abdomen over her left. Her kidneys and ovaries had been removed.

The killer had left a blood-soaked envelope bearing the crest of the Sussex Regiment. It had been reported that Martha Tabram had been seen in the company of a soldier shortly before her death and the newspapers now speculated that her wounds could have been caused by a bayonet or army knife.

Three weeks after the death of Annie Chapman the Central News Agency received a letter that gloated about both the murder and the tantalising clues that had been left. The author expressed his regret that the letter had not been written in the victim's blood, which had gone 'thick like glue', and promised to send the ear of his next victim. The letter was signed 'Jack the Ripper'. At last the murderer had a name. On 30 September 1888 the Central News Agency received another letter from the Ripper, apologising for not having enclosed an ear, as promised. But he nevertheless had exciting news for the papers, he wrote: he was going to commit a 'double' – two murders in one night.

At 1am on the night on which the letter had been received the 45-year-old 'Long Liz' Stride, a Swedish prostitute whose real name was Elizabeth Gustaafsdotter, was found lying in a pool of blood; her throat had been slashed. The delivery man who discovered her body heard her attacker escaping over the cobblestones. At around the same time the 43-year-old prostitute Catherine Eddowes was being thrown out of Bishopsgate Police Station, where she had been held for being drunk and disorderly. As she walked towards Houndsditch she met Jack the Ripper, who cut her throat, slashed her face and cut her ear, though not severing it completely. He also opened up her stomach, pulled out her intestines and threw them over her shoulder. Her left kidney was found to be missing altogether.

The murder of two women in one night – so soon after a letter from the Ripper promising just that – sent London into a panic. Queen Victoria demanded action, but the police had no idea where to begin. (The public did not even have that great fictional detective Sherlock Holmes to turn to, for he did not make his debut in *Strand* magazine for another three years.)

In a blaze of publicity, East End resident George Lusk set up the Whitechapel Vigilance Committee with which to patrol the streets. For his pains, two weeks later Mr Lusk received a small package through the post. It was from Jack the Ripper and contained half of Catherine Eddowes' kidney; the other half, an accompanying note explained, had been fried and eaten. On hearing this Queen Victoria concluded that the Ripper must be a foreigner: no Englishman would behave in such a beastly way, she asserted. A Cabinet meeting was called to discuss the matter and the government consequently ordered checks on all of the ships that were tied up in London docks. This action proved merely to be a huge waste of police manpower and in the meantime the Ripper continued on his grisly business.

On the night of 9 November 1888 Mary Kelly was seen soliciting a 'well-dressed gentleman' on the streets. Mary was unlike the Ripper's previous victims, being attractive and young – just 24. She was not a full-time prostitute, only going on to the streets occasionally, when she needed to pay the rent. She was furthermore killed indoors and was also the only one of the Ripper's victims to cry out. Despite her screams, the Ripper was not disturbed and spent more than an hour going about his dreadful task.

Mary Kelly's clothes were found folded neatly on a chair, from which it was assumed that she had brought her 'gentleman' back to her room and had taken off her clothes in readiness for sex. The theory was that it was then that he had pulled a knife. Unlike the Ripper's other victims, Mary had been facing her killer and had cried out on seeing the knife. Some time between 3.30 and 4am a woman who had been sleeping in the room above had heard Mary scream 'Oh, murder' before going back to sleep.

The Ripper slashed Mary's throat, almost decapitating her. As she was facing him, some of her blood must have splashed onto his clothes, which were found burnt in the stove. Then the Ripper set about his dissection work. He cut off both of her breasts and put them on the table, placing her severed nose and flesh from her thighs and legs alongside. Her forehead and legs were stripped of flesh and her abdomen was slashed open. Her liver and intestines were removed and her hand shoved into the gaping hole in her belly. (Mary was three months pregnant when she died.) There was blood around the window from which the Ripper was thought to have escaped. He would have been naked, except for a long cloak and boots.

The next day the rent man called and discovered Mary's mutilated corpse. He called the police, who were horrified and, once again, baffled.

Mary Kelly was last woman whom we know to have been a victim of the Ripper. Other murders followed that may either have been his handiwork or the work of a copycat killer. In June 1889, for example, the headless corpse of Elizabeth Jackson, a prostitute who worked in the Chelsea area, was found floating in the Thames. The following month the body of Alice McKenzie, a prostitute working in Whitechapel, was found; her throat had been cut from ear to ear and her sexual organs cut out. Frances Cole, a streetwalker known as 'Carroty Nell' because of her flaming-red hair, was also found dead in Whitechapel with her throat cut and slashes around her abdomen. Her assailant may have been planning a more thorough mutilation, but had been disturbed by a policeman, who reported having seen a man stooping over the body who had run away before the constable could get a good look at him.

The newspapers had already produced an image of the Ripper that had seized the public's imagination. It was based on a description given by the friend of Mary Kelly who had seen her with a client on the night of her death. She said that he was 5 feet 6 inches (1.65 metres) tall, about 35 and well dressed, and that he had had a gold watch chain dangling from his waistcoat pocket.

Mary had been heard in conversation with the man. 'Will you be alright for what I have told you?' he had asked. 'All right, my dear', she had replied, taking him by the arm. 'Come along, you will be comfortable.' A few hours later a roast-chestnut vendor had seen a man matching the same description, wearing a long cloak and silk hat, with a thin moustache that turned up at the ends. Ominously, he was carrying a black bag, which could have contained surgical instruments. 'Have you heard that there has been another murder?' the man had asked. 'I have', the chestnut vendor had replied. 'I know more of it than you do', the man had said as he walked away.

The Ripper was never caught, and over the past century an enormous number of theories have been put forward regarding who he was. The police alone came up with 176 suspects, of whom perhaps the most likely was a Russian physician, Dr Alexander Pedachenko, who had worked under an assumed name at a Camberwell clinic that catered to prostitutes, including four of the victims. He had died in an asylum in St Petersburg after killing a woman in the Russian town. A document naming him as the Ripper was said to have been found in the basement of Rasputin's home in St Petersburg after the monk's murder in 1916; sceptics, however, have pointed out the house did not have a basement.

Another popular suspect was a Dr Stanley, a Harley Street physician who had contracted syphilis from a prostitute called Kelly in Whitechapel. It was said that he had gone about killing prostitutes out of vengeance until he hit upon the right one. Stanley subsequently fled to Buenos Aires, in Argentina, where he died in 1929 after supposedly confessing all to a student.

At the time of the murders Jewish immigrants to the East End were blamed for having perpetrated them. It was said that they represented ritual Jewish slaughters and had been performed by a *shochet*, a butcher who kills animals according to Talmudic law. The *shochet* theory was given some credence by a strange message that was found scrawled on a wall in Whitechapel after the murder of Catherine Eddowes, which said 'The juwes are not the men that will be blamed for nothing'. It was also noted that 'juwes' was a Masonic spelling of 'Jews', which gave rise to the theory that the murders had been part of a Masonic rite. The police commissioner, Sir Charles Warren, himself a leading Mason, had the graffiti removed in order to prevent the inflammation of anti-Jewish sentiments. He resigned from the police force after the murder of Mary Kelly, admitting his utter failure to solve the case.

A Polish Jew named V Kosminski, who lived in Whitechapel and had furthermore threatened to slice up prostitutes, was a suspect, but later became insane and died in an asylum. Another Polish immigrant, Severin Klosowich – alias George Chapman – was also under suspicion. A barber and surgeon in Whitechapel, he kept sharp knives for bloodletting and the removal of warts and moles. He also poisoned three of his mistresses and went to gallows in 1903. A further suspect was Thomas Cutbush, who was arrested after the murder of Frances Cole for stabbing women in the buttocks; he died in an mental institution, too.

A newspaper reporter named Roslyn D'Onston wrote to the police in 1888 accusing Dr Morgan Davies, a surgeon at the London Hospital in Whitechapel, of being Jack the Ripper. Yet D'Onston was himself a suspect; a failed doctor and a drug addict, he was said by some to have killed the women in order to give his career a fillip. It was claimed that the stories that he published in the newspapers contained details about the murders that were never released by the police. D'Onston subsequently became a Satanist; his fellow devil-worshipper, Aleister Crowley, claimed that he had ritually murdered killed the women in an attempt to become invisible.

The insomniac G Wentworth Bell Smith, who lived at 27 Sun Street, off

Finsbury Square, became a suspect because he railed against prostitutes, saying that they should all be drowned. For his part, Frederick Bailey Deeming confessed to the Ripper's murders. Deeming had murdered his wife and children in England and had then fled to Australia, where he had killed a second wife; he had been about to murder a third when he was arrested in Melbourne. It is thought that his confession was an attempt to postpone, if not evade, his trip to gallows. Another popular suspect was the 'Lambeth Poisoner', Dr Thomas Neil Cream, who poisoned a number of prostitutes during the 1890s. Before he was hanged he told his executioner 'I am Jack the . . .', just as the trap opened.

The police's prime suspect was Montague John Druitt, an Oxford graduate and scion of a once wealthy family. After failing as a barrister, Druitt became a school teacher. Unable to keep his homosexual urges under control, he was dismissed for molesting a boy. He then moved to Whitechapel, where he was seen walking the streets. In December 1888 his body was fished out of the Thames; there were stones in his pockets and he appeared to have drowned himself.

Somewhat surprisingly, the secretary of William Booth (the latter the founder of the Salvation Army), also found himself on the list of suspects – apparently he had said 'Carroty Nell will be the next to go' a few days before the slaying of Frances Cole. Another man, the alcoholic railway worker Thomas Salder, was arrested after the murder of Alice McKenzie; he also knew Frances Cole, but was released due to lack of evidence.

Although Sherlock Holmes was not around to solve the case, his creator, Sir Arthur Conan Doyle, was, and used all of his considerable powers of reasoning to deduce that the Ripper was a woman. According to his theory, 'Jill the Ripper' was a midwife who had gone mad after having been sent to prison for performing illegal abortions.

The spiritualist William Lees staged a seance for Queen Victoria in an attempt to discover who the Ripper was, but the results frightened him so much that he fled to the Continent. The Ripper, he believed, was none other than the queen's physician, Sir William Gull. The theory that was later developed was that Prince Eddy, the Duke of Clarence – Victoria's grandson and heir to the throne – had secretly married a shop girl called Crook, who had borne him a child which was placed in the care of one Mary Kelly. Gull and some of his Masonic cronies, it was said, went about killing prostitutes until they got to Kelly and retrieved the child. Gull's papers were examined by Dr Thomas Stowell and were discovered to name Prince Eddy, who died of syphilis before he could ascend the throne, as Jack the Ripper. Another suspect was James Kenneth Stephen, the prince's tutor and possibly also his lover; the pair frequented homosexual clubs in Whitechapel together.

The painter Frank Miles, an intimate of Oscar Wilde, was named as the Ripper, too, but the truth is that the identity of Jack the Ripper will probably never be known.

2 ❖ The Boston Strangler

The man who came to personify the modern serial killer was the Boston Strangler, who terrorised the USA's Boston area for two years. No one was ever charged with the Boston Strangler killings, but a man did confess to them: his name was Albert DeSalvo.

DeSalvo was the son of a vicious drunk. When he was 11 he watched his father knock out his mother's teeth before bending back her fingers until they snapped – this was just another ordinary day in the DeSalvo household. When they were children, DeSalvo's father sold him and his two sisters to a farmer in Maine for just $9. DeSalvo escaped, and after he had found his way home his father taught him how to shoplift by taking him to a shop and showing him what to steal. His father would also bring prostitutes back to the family apartment and make the children watch while he had sex with the women.

Perhaps unsurprisingly, the young DeSalvo soon developed a lively interest in sex. He made numerous conquests among the neighbourhood girls, as well as earning a healthy living from the local gay community, members of which would pay him for his services. DeSalvo continued his sexual adventuring in the army until he met Irmgaard, the daughter of a respectable, Catholic family, in Frankfurt-am-Main, Germany. After marrying Irmgaard, DeSalvo returned to the USA with his wife, where he was dishonourably discharged from the army for sexually molesting a nine-year-old girl; he only escaped criminal charges because the girl's mother wanted to protect her daughter from publicity.

DeSalvo next became a professional thief, making his living by breaking and entering. At home he appeared to be the perfect family man, although his prodigious sexual appetite was more than his wife could cope with: his demands for sex five or six times a day annoyed, and finally repelled, Irmgaard. DeSalvo then began to hang around the campus area of Boston on the lookout for apartments shared by young, female students. He would knock on the door with a clipboard and introduce himself as the representative of a modelling agency before asking whether he could take the measurements of the women who lived there. He was a charming man and sometimes succeeded in seducing them (occasionally they would seduce him). On other occasions he would just take their measurements – either when they were clothed or, as he preferred, naked – and promise that a female representative would call later. He never assaulted any of the women, who sometimes complained that no one had made the promised, follow-up visit. The police called him 'Measuring Man'.

At around that time DeSalvo was arrested for housebreaking and was consequently jailed for two years. Prison soured him, and when he was released he began breaking into houses throughout New England, tying up women and raping them. Known as the 'Green Man' because he wore a green shirt and trousers, the police throughout Connecticut and Massachusetts guessed that his assaults numbered in the hundreds. DeSalvo himself later claimed more than a thousand, bragging that he had tied up and raped six women in one morning.

In 1962 DeSalvo began to concentrate his activities on Boston, also adding murder to his repertoire. His first victim was the 55-year-old Anna Slesters, whose body, which had been left in an obscene pose, was found in her apartment. DeSalvo had strangled her and had then tied the cord that he had used to kill her in a bow around her neck. This became his trademark. Two weeks later he murdered the 55-year-old Mary Mullen, whom DeSalvo subsequently said had reminded him of his grandmother. Then he raped and strangled an 85-year-old nurse, Helen Blake. For her part, Nina Nichols fought back, scratching some flesh from his arms before he strangled her. On 19 August the 75-year-old Ida Irga was raped and strangled and on the following day DeSalvo murdered the 67-year-old Jane Sullivan.

The Boston police force soon realised that a maniac was at work and began questioning all known sexual deviants. DeSalvo, however, had a police record for housebreaking alone – the details of his sexual deviancy appeared only in his army file.

DeSalvo took a long autumn break from his murderous activities, but by the time of his wedding anniversary – 5 December 1962 – his brain was so overheated by violent sexual images that he felt that it was going to explode. Seeing an attractive girl go into an apartment block, he followed her and knocked on the door of her apartment, pretending to be a maintenance man who had been sent by the landlord to check the pipes. She did not let him in, so he tried the same ploy at the next apartment, whose door was opened by a tall, attractive, 25-year-old African-American woman called Sophie Clark. This time DeSalvo reverted to his 'Measuring Man' routine and remarked upon her curvaceous figure. When she turned her back he pounced on her, and after he had subdued her he stripped, raped and finally strangled her. As with his other victims, before leaving he propped up her naked body, spread her legs and tied the cord that he had used to strangle her in a bow under her chin.

Three days later DeSalvo made a return call on one of the women, a 23-year-old secretary, whom he had previously visited as the 'Measuring Man'. After Patricia Bissette had invited him in for a coffee she turned her back, whereupon he grabbed her around the throat, raped her and then strangled her with her own stockings. DeSalvo's next victim, however, fought back so violently – biting, scratching and screaming – that the Boston Strangler fled and she escaped with her life, but she was so distraught that the description that she gave of her attacker was practically worthless.

The failed murder seems to have marked something of a turning point in DeSalvo's career of crime, because from then on his attacks became even more violent. On 9 March 1963, for example, he entered the apartment of the 69-year-old Mary Brown on the pretext of fixing the stove. He had brought a piece of lead pipe with him, which he used to beat in her head. When she was dead he raped her and then stabbed her breasts with a fork, which he left sticking from her flesh. Although he maintained his *modus operandi* by strangling her, this time the victim was already dead when he did so.

Two months later DeSalvo took a day off work and drove to Cambridge, Massachusetts. Spotting a pretty girl, a 23-year-old student named Beverley Samans, on University Road, he followed her back to her apartment. Once inside, he tied her to her bedposts, stripped, blindfolded, gagged and then repeatedly raped her before strangling her with her own stockings. But this was no longer enough for him and before he left the apartment he pulled a penknife from his pocket and started to stab her naked body. Once he had started he could not stop, and when her body

The Boston Strangler - Albert DeSalvo. Photographed 25th February, 1967.

was discovered it was found to bear 22 savage wounds. After his frenzy had subsided DeSalvo calmly wiped his fingerprints from the knife, dropped it into the sink and went home.

On 8 September 1963 the Boston Strangler struck again. This time it was a straightforward case of rape and strangulation, the 58-year-old Evelyn Corbin being strangled with her own nylons, which he left tied in his signature bow, but around her ankle, in a departure from his usual style.

By this time the people of Boston and the surrounding area were in a state of panic. The Strangler seemed to come and go at will. The police had no useful description of the killer and no clues – they seemed powerless. In desperation they brought in a Dutch psychic, Peter Hurkos, who had had some success in other cases, but he failed to identify the Boston Strangler.

While the USA – and particularly John F Kennedy's home state of Massachusetts – was in mourning following the assassination of the president, the Boston Strangler struck again, raping and strangling Joan Gaff, a 23-year-old dress designer, in her own apartment before tying her black leotard in a bow around her neck. DeSalvo later said that he did not know why he had killed her; 'I wasn't even excited', he commented. After he had left her apartment, he revealed, he had gone home, played with his children and watched the report of Joan's murder on television. Then, he said, he had sat down and had his dinner, without thinking of her again.

On 4 January 1964 the Boston Strangler killed for the last time. His victim was the 19-year-old Mary Sullivan. He gained access to her apartment, tied her up at knife point and raped her before strangling her with his bare hands. Her body was left sitting up in bed, with her head lolling against her right shoulder. Her eyes were closed and a viscous liquid dripped from her mouth down her right breast. Her breasts and sexual organs were exposed and a broom handle protruded from her vagina. More semen stains were found on her blanket and a New Year's greeting card that the killer had found in the apartment was placed between her toes.

Later that year a woman reported having been sexually assaulted by a man who had used the Measuring Man routine, but otherwise the Boston Strangler's activities stopped. This was because DeSalvo had again been arrested for housebreaking. In jail his behaviour became increasingly disturbed and he was transferred to a mental hospital in Bridgewater, where he was diagnosed as being schizophrenic.

Although DeSalvo was in custody, the police still had no idea that they were holding the Boston Strangler. But in the Bridgewater hospital another inmate – who had killed a petrol-station attendant and was himself a suspect in the Boston Strangler case – listened to DeSalvo's deranged ramblings and began to put two and two together. He then persuaded his lawyer to speak to DeSalvo. In his taped interviews with the lawyer DeSalvo discussed facts about the murders that the police had not revealed. He spoke of the positions in which he had left the bodies, the ligature that he had used to strangle each victim, as well as the other wounds that he had inflicted. He also admitted to two murders that had not yet been attributed to the Boston Strangler.

Despite his admissions DeSalvo was a mental patient who was plainly unfit to stand trial and whose confession was legally worthless. He was therefore not prosecuted for the rapes and murders to which he had admitted. There was no doubt, however, that he was indeed the Boston Strangler, even if he could only be charged with robbery and other sexual offences unconnected to the Strangler's activities. He was sentenced to life imprisonment and transferred to Walpole State Prison. On 26 November 1973 the 36-year-old DeSalvo was found dead in his cell, stabbed through the heart.

3 ❖ The Campus Killer

Like Albert DeSalvo, Ted Bundy also had the power to charm women, many of whom paid for their susceptibility with their lives. For three years during the 1970s Bundy preyed on young female students on college campuses across the USA, killing at least 19 young women and maybe as many as 40.

Bundy was well educated, ran his own business, had been a noted high-school athlete and worked for both the Republican Party and the Washington State Crime Commission. He even became a counsellor at a Seattle rape-crisis centre after having been screened for 'balance and maturity'. He had one significant problem, however: his sexual impulses were so strong that he could not control them. He later said that after his first attacks he had had to wrestle with his conscience, but had subsequently begun to desensitise himself to his crimes. He claimed not to have caused his victims unnecessary suffering, but said that he had had to kill them after he had raped them in order to prevent them from identifying him. He admitted deliberately terrorising his victim – or rather victims –in only one case: when he kidnapped two girls at the same time, intending to rape each in front of the other before killing them both.

From an early age Bundy had been a compulsive masturbator, and after glimpsing a girl undressing through a window he had become a Peeping Tom. He later became obsessed by sadistic pornography. His long-time girlfriend, Meg Anders, described how he liked to tie her up with her own stockings before having anal sex with her, but said that she had put a stop to this sex game when he almost strangled her. For years they maintained a normal sexual relationship while Bundy indulged his perverse cravings elsewhere. And what he craved was total control over an anonymous victim, whom he often strangled during sex. Indeed, his attitude to sex was ambivalent: although his victims were always attractive young women, he liked to defile their bodies by stuffing twigs and dirt into their vaginas or sodomising them with aerosol cans or other foreign objects. When they were discovered, some of the bodies of his victims, although partly decomposed, were found to be wearing newly applied make-up and to have freshly washed hair – he had kept them for the purposes of necrophilia.

Bundy began his murderous career in his home town of Seattle. His first victim was Sharon Clarke, into whose apartment he broke while she was asleep before hitting her around the head with a metal rod. Although she survived – albeit with a shattered skull – she could not identify her attacker; nor was there any indication of the motivation for the attack.

Soon afterwards, young women began disappearing from the nearby campus of the University of Washington. Six went missing within seven months. The clue to what may have happened to them came from the Lake Sammanish resort in Washington State, when a number of women reported having been approached by a young man calling himself Ted. He had had his arm in a sling and had asked them to help him to lift his sailing boat off the roof of his car. Once in the car park, however, they had found that there was no boat, whereupon Ted had then said that they would have to go to his house to get it. Although most of the women had declined his invitation to accompany him, it seemed that Janice Ott had agreed to go. And a few hours later Denise Naslund went missing from the same area; she had been seen with a good-looking, dark-haired young man. The remains of Janice Ott, Denise Naslund and another unidentified young woman were later found on waste ground. Their bodies had been dismembered and eaten by animals. Witnesses at the University of Washington subsequently said that they had seen a man wearing a sling, and more bodies were also found on wasteland.

The police had two suspects: Gary Taylor and Warren Forrest. Taylor, a former convict, had been arrested by the Seattle police for abducting women under false pretexts. For his part, Forrest, a park attendant, had picked up a young woman who had agreed to pose for him. He had taken her to a secluded part of the park, where he had stripped her naked and tied her up. He had then taped up her mouth and had fired darts at her breasts before raping and strangling her and leaving her for dead. His victim had survived, however, and had identified her attacker. The problem for the police was that although both men were in custody the attacks continued.

By now Bundy's girlfriend was growing suspicious of him and called the police anonymously to give them his name. But her tip-off was just one among the thousands of leads that the police had to follow up and it was overlooked.

Serial Killer Ted Bundy, who was killed by electric chair at 7am on 24th January, 1989. Before his death, he managed to escape from secure institutions on two occasions.

Nevertheless, things were becoming a bit too hot for Bundy in his home state, so on 30 August 1974 he quit his job in Seattle and moved to Salt Lake City, where he enrolled at the University of Utah's law school. On 2 October he abducted Nancy Wilcox after she had left an all-night party. On 18 October he raped and strangled the 18-year-old Melissa Smith, the daughter of the local police chief; her body was found near Salt Lake City. He abducted the 17-year-old Laura Aimee from a Hallowe'en party in Orem; her naked body was discovered at the bottom of a canyon. He tried to pick up a pretty young French teacher outside her high school, but she refused to go with him. The 17-year-old Debbie Kent did, however, disappearing on 8 November from a school playground in which the key to a pair of handcuffs was later found.

A week later he approached the 18-year-old Carol DaRonch in Salt Lake City. Bundy pretended to be a police detective and asked her for the licence number of her car, explaining that someone had been trying to break into it. He then invited her to accompany him to the police station in order to identify the suspect and she obligingly got into his car. Once they were in a quiet street he handcuffed her and put a gun to her head when she began to scream. Despite being handcuffed, Carol managed to get out of the car, whereupon Bundy chased after her with a crowbar, which he swung at her head. Carol was just able to deflect it when at that moment a car drove down the street. Seizing her chance, she threw herself in front of it, forcing it to stop; after she had jumped in the car drove away.

Carol gave a good description of her attacker to the Utah police, but shortly thereafter Bundy moved to Colorado. In January 1975 Dr Raymond Gadowsky reported that his fiancée, Carolyn Campbell, was missing from her hotel room in Snowmass Village, a ski resort. A month later her naked body was found in the snow; she had been raped and her skull smashed in. Julie Cunningham disappeared from nearby Vail, and the remains of Susan Rancourt and Brenda Bell were found on Taylor Mountain. The body of Melanie Cooley was discovered just ten miles (16 kilometres) from her home. Unlike the other victims she was still clothed (although her jeans had been undone), but the police were nevertheless convinced that the motive for her murder was a sexual one. The Colorado attacks continued: Nancy Baird vanished from a petrol station, while Shelley Robertson's naked body was found down a mine shaft.

One day a highway patrolman was cruising through Granger, Utah, which had recently been plagued by a series of burglaries. He noticed Bundy's VW driving slowly, without its lights on, and indicated that he should pull over. Instead of complying, however, Bundy sped off, causing the patrolman to give chase. On catching up with him the patrolman asked him what he had in the car, to which Bundy replied 'Just some junk'. The junk turned out to be a ski mask, handcuffs, some nylon stockings and a crowbar. Bundy was detained for having committed a traffic offence and was later released. On the following day he was arrested at his apartment in Salt Lake City and charged with possessing tools with which to commit burglary, but he was again released on bail.

The police had impounded Bundy's car, however, in which they discovered maps and brochures of resorts in Colorado, some of which coincided with the places from which the girls had disappeared. Forensic experts found a hair in the VW that matched that of Melissa Smith. A witness recognised Bundy from Snowmass Village. Furthermore, Carol DaRonch picked him out of a line-up.

Bundy was charged with kidnapping and was subsequently tried, found guilty and sentenced to a period in jail of from one to fifteen years. Then he was extradited to Colorado to stand trial for the murder of Carolyn Campbell. In court Bundy came across as an intelligent and person-able young man – the sort who could have had any girl whom he wanted – and it seemed unlikely to many that he could have been responsible for the terrible sex attacks.

In Aspen, Colorado, Bundy was given permission to conduct his own defence, even being allowed to use the law library. It was there that he managed to give his guard the slip, jump from a window and escape. He was recaptured eight days later. Bundy continued to protest his innocence and was able to spin out the pre-trial hearings by using skilful, legal, stalling tactics. In the meantime he had lost weight. One day, while stand-ing on a stack of legal books in his cell, he managed to cut a hole under the light fitting with a hacksaw blade. He then squeezed through the 1-foot-square (30-centimetre-square) hole, stole a police car and got clean away.

Bundy made a murderous tour of the USA before settling in Tallahas-see, Florida, a few blocks from the sorority houses of Florida State Univer-sity. On the evening of 15 January 1977 Nita Neary saw a man lurking in front of her own sorority house. She was about to phone the police when a fellow student, Karen Chandler, staggered from her room, blood streaming from her head, screaming that she had just been attacked by a madman. Her room-mate, Kathy Kleiner, had also been attacked and her jaw broken. The 21-year-old Margaret Bowman had been sexually assaulted and stran-gled with her own tights. The 20-year-old Lisa Levy had also been sexually assaulted: Bundy had bitten off one of her nipples and had sunk his teeth into her buttocks before beating her around the head. She died on the way to hospital. Cheryl Thomas had been viciously attacked in another build-ing, too, but survived. The police could elicit only a sketchy description of the attacker from his victims.

On 8 February, in Lake City, Florida, Bundy abducted the 12-year-old Kimberley Leach, sexually assaulted and strangled her, mutilated her sexual organs and dumped her body in a pig shed.

Bundy was now short of money, so he stole some credit cards, along with a car, and did a moonlight flit from his apartment, on which he owed rent. But the stolen car was a giveaway and he was stopped by a highway patrolman, whereupon Bundy attacked him and tried to escape. The patrolman caught up with him, however, and clubbed him unconscious. At the police station Bundy admitted that he was wanted in Colorado. For their part the Florida police had begun to link him to the Tallahassee attack. When they tried to take an impression of his teeth he went berserk and it took six men to hold his jaw open. The impression was subsequently found to match the teeth marks on the buttocks of the murdered student, Lisa Levy, as well as those on the body of Kimberley Leach.

Bundy was charged with the murder of the child. At his trial he again conducted his own defence, cannily using points of law with which to prolong the court case and charming the jury with his personality. The evidence against him was too strong, however, and Bundy was found guilty of murder and sentenced to death. All the while protesting his innocence, he managed to postpone his execution for another ten years. Eventually, when all the legal avenues had been exhausted, he broke down and confessed to nearly 40 murders. 'I deserve to die', he said.

At 7am on 24 January 1989 Bundy went to the electric chair. He is said to have died with a smile on his face. On death row Bundy had made a detailed confession, thereby aiding a number of academics who were studying serial killers. He had also received sacks full of mail from young women whose letters dwelt on various cruel and painful ways in which to make love – it seems that even on death row he had not lost his charm.

4 ❖ Ten Rillington Place

John Reginald Christie got his kicks by murdering women and sexually abusing their corpses. He went about his grisly business in his shabby house in Notting Hill Gate, London, whose address – 10 Rillington Place – has since become infamous.

Christie was born on 8 April 1898 in Halifax, Yorkshire. His father, Ernest, a designer for Crossley Carpets, was a pillar of local society, being a leader of the Primrose League (an organisation intended to promote morality among the working classes) and a founder member of the Halifax Conservative Party. He was also a stern disciplinarian and his son was terrified of him. 'We almost had to ask if we could speak to him', he later wrote. Christie also had other problems within his family: one of seven children, he was completely dominated by his older sisters.

Christie did well at school and sang in the choir. He was first a boy scout and then an assistant scout master. But there were other, deeper, tides flowing within Christie. When he was eight, for example, his grandfather died and Christie reported having felt a trembling sensation of both fascination and pleasure on seeing the body.

After leaving school Christie started work at the Gem Cinema in Halifax. One day he was part of a gang of boys and girls who went down to the Monkey Run, as the local lovers' lane was known. They paired off and Christie found himself with a girl who was much more sexually experienced than he was. Intimidated, he could not rise to the occasion and when word of it got around his friends started taunting him, calling him 'Reggie-no-dick' and 'Can't-do-it-Reggie'.

At the age of 17 Christie was caught stealing at work and sacked, whereupon his father kicked him out of the house; he had to sleep on the family's allotment and his mother took him food. He then drifted from job to job until he was called up to serve as a soldier during World War I. He was gassed in France before being sent home and discharged from the army with a disability pension.

On 20 May 1920 Christie married the long-suffering Ethel Waddington. He got a job as a postman, but was caught stealing money from letters. In 1921 he was jailed for nine months. Two years later he was bound over for posing as a former officer. Following a violent incident he was put on probation, and when he was sent down for another nine months for theft Ethel left him. In 1929 he was sentenced to six months' hard labour for assaulting a prostitute. A Roman Catholic priest befriended him, but Christie stole his car, which earned him another spell in prison.

On his release Christie wrote to Ethel asking her to come back to him and she foolishly did so. They moved to London, and on a visit to Ethel's family in Leeds Christie boasted of his 'big house in London' and his servants. In fact, he and Ethel lived in a shabby little flat in North Kensington, with no servants. He never earned over £8 a week, which was the going rate for a junior clerk.

On the outbreak of World War II in 1939 Christie became a special constable in the War Reserve Police. No checks were carried out to see if he had a criminal record, but in any case he seemed to be a reformed character. He was never much liked, however, because of his petty-mindedness – indeed, Christie and another special constable were known as the 'rat and the weasel'.

Although he was balding, Christie still regarded himself as a charmer. Deep down, however, he feared and hated women. 'Women who give you the come-on wouldn't look nearly so saucy if they were helpless and dead', he thought. He took pride in hiding his violent intentions from the women whom he took back to 10 Rillington Place, and by the time that they arrived there it was too late for them to save themselves.

His first victim was an Austrian refugee, the 17-year-old Ruth Fuerst. Ruth worked in a munitions factory, but because the pay was poor she supplemented her income with the proceeds of a little prostitution. Christie had met her while he was trying to trace a man who was wanted for theft; she had asked him to lend her ten shillings and Christie had invited her home. On one hot, August afternoon in 1943, while Ethel was in Sheffield, she called again at 10 Rillington Place. At first Christie refused to engage in sexual intercourse, but Ruth encouraged him. Once the sex was over he strangled her. Christie said that he had felt a great sense of peace after he had killed Ruth. He had been fascinated by the beauty of her corpse and had wanted to keep it, but his wife had returned home unexpectedly that night and he had had to bury Ruth's body in the garden. He compared his début in murder to an artist's first painting. 'It was thrilling because I had embarked on the career I had chosen for myself, the career of murder. But it was only the beginning', he later said.

Christie left the police force at the end of 1943 and went to work at the Ultra Radio Works in west London, where he met an attractive, 31-year-old woman, Muriel Eady. Muriel suffered from catarrh and Christie claimed that he had a remedy for it. On one afternoon in October 1944 she therefore went to see him at 10 Rillington Place and he showed her what he claimed was his patent inhaler. In fact, it was nothing more than a jar containing perfumed water that had two holes in its lid with rubber tubes leading from them. Christie then persuaded Muriel to inhale his remedy through one of them; unbeknownst to her the other tube was connected to the gas pipe. The perfume in the jar concealed the smell of gas and when Muriel lapsed into unconsciousness Christie had sex with her and then strangled her. He was thrilled by the notion that his second murder was much cleverer than the first.

In 1948 Timothy Evans, a lorry driver, and his wife, Beryl, moved into the top-floor flat at 10 Rillington Place. Born in Merthyr Vale on 20 November 1924, Evans was educationally challenged and also had a speech impediment (when he was a child he could not even pronounce his own name). His schooling had been held back further by a foot injury which caused him to spend long spells in hospital. Evans' father had walked out on his mother before Timothy was born (his mother subsequently procured a certificate saying that he was presumed dead). She later remarried and the family moved to Notting Hill Gate, where Timothy married a local girl, Beryl Thorley, in 1947.

Evans was 24 when he saw the 'To Let' sign outside 10 Rillington Place. He and the pregnant Beryl were still living with his mother and stepfather and because the young couple desperately needed a place of their own they took the cramped attic flat. Charles Kitchener, a railway worker with failing eyesight, lived on the floor below. He kept himself to himself and was often in hospital. The ground floor was occupied by John and Ethel Christie. Shortly after the Evanses moved in Beryl gave birth to a baby daughter, whom they named Geraldine. The Evanses and Christies were soon getting on well and Ethel, who was fond of the baby, looked after Geraldine when Beryl was working part-time.

In the summer of 1949 Beryl became pregnant again. There was little money coming in and the Evanses were behind on their hire-purchase payments. Beryl, who was still only 19, wanted an abortion, but Timothy, a Roman Catholic, forbade it. The adamant Beryl then discovered that there was a back-street abortionist on the Edgware Road who would do the job for £1. When Christie heard of her plan he told Beryl that he could help her out by performing the abortion himself. She in turn told Timothy of Christie's offer, who said that he had not realised that Christie knew anything about medical procedures. In order to reassure him Christie showed him the St John's Ambulance Brigade's first-aid manual; Evans, who was illiterate, knew no better.

On 8 November 1949 Evans came home to find Christie waiting for him with bad news: the operation had not been a success, Christie explained, and Beryl had died. Christie begged Evans not to go to the police, saying that he would be charged with manslaughter because Beryl had died during an illegal abortion. Evans' first concern was who would look after Geraldine and therefore suggested his mother, but Christie said that he would find someone else to care for the baby. When Evans returned from work on 10 November Christie said that he had delivered the child to a couple in East Acton, and that evening Evans assisted Christie in disposing of Beryl's body down the outside drain.

Christie helped Evans to sell off his furniture and Evans then returned to Wales with £40 in his pocket. He was plagued by guilt, however, believing that as a Catholic he should have stopped Beryl from having the abortion; if he had done so, he reasoned, she would still have been alive. So he walked into Merthyr Vale's police station and confessed. Evans thought that he could take the blame for Beryl's death without implicating Christie, whom he considered to be his friend. He therefore told the police that he had obtained a bottle that contained something that would make his wife miscarry from a man whom he had met in a transport café. He had not intended to give it to his wife, he said, but explained that she must have found it while he was out at work. When he returned he had found her dead and had opened a drain outside the front door into which he had dropped her body.

The Merthyr Vale police contacted their counterparts at Notting Hill Gate, who sent police officers to 10 Rillington Place. It took three of them to lift the manhole cover over the drain, only to find that it was empty. Back in Merthyr Vale the police then challenged Evans' statement: he could not possibly have lifted the manhole cover himself, they said. Unable to continue the pretence, Evans made a second statement, this time telling the truth: Christie, he said, had performed an illegal abortion on his wife, who had consequently died; together he and Christie had disposed of the body.

The police had searched 10 Rillington Place, but not very thoroughly – they did not even notice Muriel Eady's thighbone, which was propped up against the garden fence. Christie made a statement saying that he had overheard the Evanses quarrelling; Beryl had complained that her husband had grabbed her by the throat, he elaborated. The police believed Christie – after all, the man had been policeman.

The house was searched again and this time Beryl's corpse was found. It had been wrapped in a green tablecloth and hidden behind a stack of wood in a downstairs washroom. Beside it was the body of the 14-month-old Geraldine. Both had been strangled. An autopsy revealed that there was bruising in Beryl's vagina and that her right eye and upper lip were swollen. In the police view this evidence confirmed their belief that Beryl's murder had been a simple 'domestic'.

Evans' trial took place at the Old Bailey in the January of 1950. Standing in the witness box, Christie apologised to the judge for speaking softly, explaining that this was the result of having been gassed during World War I. The court was also told of his service as a special constable. His long record of petty crime was not mentioned and the impression was given that he was a solid citizen whose word was not to be doubted. When he was asked if he had performed an illegal abortion on Beryl Evans he denied it, saying that he had been lying ill in bed on the day of Beryl's death.

Evans cut a much shabbier figure. He was out of his depth in the court-room and gave his evidence poorly. His allegation that his wife had died during an illegal abortion performed by Christie held no water with the court as the evidence proved that she had been strangled. Furthermore, he could not explain the death of the baby. The jury deliberated for just 40 minutes before returning a verdict of guilty. The sentence imposed by the judge was death by hanging.

Evans maintained to the end that Christie had killed both his wife and daughter. There was some public disquiet about the verdict and a petition bearing nearly 2,000 signatures was presented to the home secretary appealing against the verdict. It did no good and Evans was hanged on 9 March 1950.

Christie later said that on 14 December 1952 he had been woken when his wife, Ethel, went into convulsions. She seemed to have overdosed on phenobarbital and Christie decided that it was too late to get help. It would be kindest to put her out of her misery, he reasoned, so he put a stocking around her neck and strangled her. Unsure of what to do with it, he then left his wife's body in the bed for two days before pulling up the floor-boards in the front room and burying her under them. The couple had been married for 32 years.

Over the next four months Christie sold his furniture to fund a sex-and-murder spree. The 25-year-old prostitute Rita Nelson had just discov-ered that she was pregnant when, on 12 January 1953, she visited 10 Rillington Place, where Christie strangled her, subsequently shoving her body into an alcove in the kitchen. The 26-year-old Kathleen Maloney was lured into his flat to pose nude while he photographed her. Instead she was gassed and sexually abused, her body then also being placed in the alcove.

Christie had more trouble with his final victim, Hectorina MacLennan. He had met her in the café in which he picked up prostitutes and had offered her somewhere to stay. She had turned up at 10 Rillington Place with her boyfriend, however. After they had been there for three nights Christie at last found her alone on 6 March 1953. He gave her a drink and offered her a whiff of his inhaler, which she did not enjoy. Following a struggle Christie strangled her and had sex with her corpse. He then bun-dled her body into the alcove, joining those of Rita Nelson and Kathleen Maloney, propping her up into a sitting position, with her bra hooked to Maloney's leg.

After that Christie built a false wall in front of the alcove and papered over it. He sublet the flat to a couple called Reilly, took his dog to the vet to be put to sleep and moved out. The landlord subsequently evicted the Reillys and gave Beresford Brown, who was living in the flat that had previously been occupied by the Evanses, permission to use the kitchen in the ground-floor flat provided that he cleared it out. After Brown had removed the clothes, rubbish and filth that Christie had left behind him, he started to redecorate the kitchen. He had wanted to put up some brackets on the rear wall, but when he tapped it he found that it was hollow. Pulling away some of the wallpaper, he saw a papered-over, wooden door. On opening it he discerned a partially clothed woman's body sitting on a pile of rubbish. Brown promptly called the police.

The police soon discovered that there was more than one body at 10 Rillington Place. A thorough search of the alcove revealed a second, wrapped in a blanket, and then a third, whose ankles had been tied together with plastic flex. All three had been strangled. Next, the corpse of Ethel Christie was found under the floorboards in the front room.

The police quickly realised that John Reginald Christie was the man for whom they should be searching and issued his description to the press. His picture appeared in every national newspaper and appeals for information regarding his whereabouts were made over the loudspeaker systems at football matches. Soon the whole country was looking for a slight, balding, middle-aged multiple murder. There were numerous reported sightings of Christie, but few were genuine.

Meanwhile, in the tiny garden of 10 Rillington Place, the police had unearthed the skeletons of two more women, which, they estimated, had lain buried for about ten years. Both women had been strangled and the skull of one was missing.

On the day that he left 10 Rillington Place Christie had moved into a hotel in King's Cross Road. He had soon moved on, however, tramping back and forth across London homeless and alone. At around 11pm on the night of 19 March 1953, at the height of the biggest manhunt that the country had ever known, Norman Rae, the chief crime reporter of the Sunday newspaper the *News of the World*, received a phone call. 'Do you recognise my voice?' the caller asked. Rae did: he had met Christie during the trial of Timothy Evans. 'I can't stand any more', said Christie. 'They're hunting me like a dog.' In return for a meal, some cigarettes and a warm place in which to sit, Christie promised that he would give the *News of the World* an exclusive. They arranged to meet at 1.30am, outside Wood Green's town hall, and as Rae parked outside it two policemen walked by. It was pure chance, but Christie ran off, thinking that he had been double-crossed.

Two days later PC Thomas Ledger stopped a man near Putney Bridge, who, in response to the constable's questioning, said that he was John Waddington, of 35 Westbourne Grove. The young policeman then asked him to turn out his pockets, one of which proved to contain a newspaper cutting from 1950 concerning Timothy Evans' murder trial. The hunt for Christie was over.

Christie made a detailed confession, providing a separate – and self-serving – explanation for each killing. The prostitutes had forced themselves upon him, he said, and things had got out of hand. His wife had had to be put out of her misery. The murders of Muriel Eady and Beryl Evans had been mercy killings, too.

At his trial Christie pleaded insanity, but could not disguise the fact that he had carefully planned the killings (which he described with a chilling lack of contrition as 'those regrettable happenings'). He had even constructed a special apparatus with which to gas four of his victims. Christie was found guilty and sentenced to death. There was no appeal and he was hanged at Pentonville Prison at 9am on 15 July 1953.

There remained a legal problem, however, in that Timothy Evans had been convicted of the murder of his wife, Beryl, and their daughter, Geraldine – murders to which Christie had subsequently confessed. A formal inquiry was therefore set up, which concluded that two murderers had been operating at 10 Rillington Place; Christie had told the truth at Evans' trial, it reasoned, but had lied at his own. It was not until 1966 that Evans received a royal pardon, after which his body was exhumed from the grounds of Pentonville Prison and was reburied in consecrated ground.

5 ❖ Jerry Brudos

On 10 May 1969 a fisherman angling from a bridge across the Long Tom river in Oregon, in the USA, saw what he took to be a large package floating in the water. On looking closer, however, he realised that it was the bloated body of a young woman, which had been weighed down by a car's gearbox. The body was identified as being that of the 22-year-old

Linda Salee, who had vanished two weeks earlier. The corpse had been in the water for too long to determine whether Linda had been raped, but it was noted that curious burn marks surrounded puncture wounds a few inches below her armpits.

Police frogmen searching the area then found another body, which had been anchored in the water by means of a cylinder head. It belonged to the 19-year-old Karen Sprinkler, who had disappeared on 27 March; it was estimated that her corpse had been in the water for six weeks. The dead woman was fully clothed and was wearing a black bra that was plainly too big for her. Her breasts were missing and the bra had been padded out with screwed-up paper. Both Karen and Linda had been strangled.

The skeleton of the 16-year-old Stephanie Vilcko was later washed up in a creek along the same river. She had disappeared from her home in Portland, Oregon, the year before. The Oregon state police also had two other missing girls on their books: the 19-year-old encyclopaedia seller Linda Slawson, who had gone missing during a sales trip in the Portland area; and the 23-year-old Jan Whitney, whose broken-down car had been discovered on a highway near Lebanon, Oregon.

Linda Salee and Karen Sprinkler's bodies had both been tied up with electrical flex and the police therefore thought that the murderer might be an electrician. But the corpses had been weighed down with car parts, too, so it was equally possible that he might be a mechanic. As Oregon was full of electricians and car mechanics, these speculations did not take them further forward.

Karen Sprinkler had been a student who lived on the Corvallis campus of Oregon State University. Several of the other girls there now reported that they had received phone calls from a man who claimed to be a psychic, as well as a veteran of the Vietnam War. He had used a variety of names and had always ended the conversations by asking the girls for a date; when they had refused he seemed offended. However, one of the more daring girls had indeed met him for a date. He had been fat and freckled, she said, and she had thought that there was something odd about him. During their conversation he had told her that she should be sad. When she asked why he replied 'Think of those two girls whose bodies were found in the river'. When she declined his invitation to go for a drive with him he said that she was right to be circumspect, asking 'How do you know I wouldn't take you to the river and strangle you?'

A week later the man phoned the girl again, whereupon she called the police, who seized him when he arrived at the college to pick her up. His name was Jerry Brudos and he was a 30-year-old electrician who lived in Salem, which lies between Corvallis and Portland. The police did not have any evidence on which to hold Brudos, so they had to release him, but while investigating his background they soon discovered that he had a history of violence towards women and had spent time in a state mental hospital because of his sexual deviancy.

Brudos' deviant behaviour had begun when he was five and had taken home a pair of women's patent-leather shoes that he had found in a rubbish dump. He was trying them on when his mother discovered him. She was furious and told him to throw the shoes away, but he nevertheless kept them and wore them secretly. When his mother learned of this she burnt them and beat him. At school he became obsessed with women's high-heeled shoes and even stole a pair of his teacher's. When he was caught and made to confess he was asked why he had done it, but he responded that he did not know and ran from the room.

At 16 he lured his neighbour's daughter to his bedroom. While Brudos was out of the room a masked man burst in brandishing a knife and forced the girl to strip, after which he took pictures of her nude. When the masked man left Brudos reappeared. The masked man had locked him in the barn, he said. At 17 he had taken another girl for a drive when he stopped on a deserted road, dragged her from the car and forced her to undress. She was saved by a passer-by who had heard her screams. This time the police were called and Brudos lamely protested to them that this girl had been attacked by a weirdo. When the police searched his bedroom, however, they found a box of women's shoes and underwear. Brudos was sent to Oregon State Mental Hospital for treatment and was discharged after nine months.

His condition did not improve and he began attacking young women and stealing their shoes. Members of his family were afraid that he was well on his way to becoming a rapist, but then, to their great relief, he fell in love with a 17-year-old girl called Darcie and married her. They had their first child eight months later. Married life seemed to calm Brudos. His wife even indulged his obsession with photographing her in the nude, but later became concerned about the increasingly disturbing poses that he wanted her to adopt. Then, when his wife was in hospital having their second child, Brudos saw a young woman in the street who was wearing attractive shoes. He followed her home and choked her until she was unconscious before raping her.

As well as being an electrician, Brudos was also a mechanic who ran a one-man car-repair business from the garage of his home. He had furthermore been working in Lebanon, Oregon, close to the place where Jan Whitney's car had been discovered. The police found lengths of rope in Brudos' home, too, one of which was tied in the same kind of knot that the killer had used when trussing up the corpses.

Although the police were convinced that they had identified the right man they still did not have enough evidence with which to make an arrest. Then they discovered that they had a potential eyewitness to Brudos' criminal activities: a 15-year-old schoolgirl had been attacked by a fat, freckled man with a gun in Portland just two days before Linda Salee had disappeared. She had screamed, but the man had grabbed her around the neck, whereupon she had bitten his thumb and he had beaten her unconscious. When a car had fortuitously approached he had run off.

The girl identified Brudos from his mug shot and the police were on their way to arrest him when they saw his station wagon driving towards Portland. When it was stopped by highway patrolmen Brudos' wife was found to be driving; Brudos himself was hiding under a blanket in the back

Jerome Brudos
with his wife.

of the car. When he was made to change into prison overalls at the police station it was revealed that he was wearing women's underwear.

Brudos withstood questioning for five days. After that he began to talk about his interest in women's shoes and admitted tailing a pretty girl before breaking in to her home in order to steal her shoes. Next he shared his obsession with women's underwear; his favourite fetish, he said, was a large, long-waisted, black bra that he had stolen from a washing line. It was the type of bra that had been found on the body of Karen Sprinkler.

Then Brudos confessed everything, including the murder of the two missing women whose bodies had not been found. In January 1968, he revealed, Linda Slawson had come to his house selling encyclopaedias and wearing high-heeled shoes that he had found irresistible. Brudos had told her that his wife had visitors and asked her if she would mind discussing the encyclopaedias in his workshop. Having agreed, she was sitting on a stool running through her sales patter when he knocked her unconscious with a lump of wood. Then he strangled her. His mother and children were upstairs in the house at the time, so he gave them money and told them to go to a local hamburger joint. When they had gone he rushed back to the workshop and undressed the corpse, discovering to his delight that Linda was wearing attractive underwear. Making use of a box full of women's underwear that he had stolen from clothes lines he began to dress and undress the corpse as if it were a doll. That night he also chopped off Linda's foot, which he kept in the freezer and used to try on women's shoes. He dumped the rest of her body in the river, using a cylinder head with which to weigh it down.

Ten months later he was driving home from his job in Lebanon when he noticed that a car had broken down on the motorway. Brudos stopped and explained to the driver, Jan Whitney, that although he was a car mechanic they would have to drive to Salem to get his tool box. On arriving at his house together, he then ran inside alone, ostensibly to get his tools. Instead, however, he went in to check that his wife was not at home. Having ascertained that Darcie was not in he slipped silently into the back seat of the car, threw a leather strap around Jan's neck and strangled her. He then sodomised her corpse before beginning his game of dressing and undressing the body. This time he took photographs, breaking off from time to time in order to violate the body. Brudos then decided to prolong his pleasure by leaving Jan's body hanging from a hook in the locked garage. In that way he could come and play with it whenever he felt the need. He later cut off one of her breasts to make into a paperweight.

Two days after the murder his perverted secret was almost discovered when a car crashed through his garage wall. Although a policeman looked into the garage he did not spot Jan's body hanging there, shrouded as it was by dust and gloom. That night Brudos weighed down the corpse with scrap iron and dumped it in the river.

Four months later, while Brudos was driving past a department store, he spotted a young woman wearing a miniskirt and high-heeled shoes. He parked the car and chased after her, but she vanished into the crowd. On his way back to his car he saw Karen Sprinkler in the car park, pulled a gun and forced her to get into his station wagon. Brudos' family was away, so he knew that he was in no danger of being disturbed. Karen begged for her life, saying that she would do anything he wanted if he did not kill her. He asked if she was a virgin, to which she replied that she was and also told him that she was having her period. It made no difference, for he made her lie on the garage floor and raped her. Next he forced her to pose in high-heeled shoes and sexy underwear while he took pictures of her. After that he tied her hands behind her back, put a rope around her neck and threw the end of it over a beam, pulling it slowly until she suffocated. 'She kicked a little and died', Brudos said. He then violated Karen's corpse, cut off her breasts and dumped her body in the river.

Linda Salee was buying her boyfriend's birthday present when Brudos flashed a fake police badge at her and told her that he was arresting her for shoplifting. He then drove her to his garage. When they arrived Brudos' wife came out the house on to the porch, so Brudos ordered Linda to stand still in the darkness. At that moment a single scream could have saved her life, but instead Linda meekly did as she was told. After Darcie had gone back inside Brudos took Linda into the garage and tied her up before going to have his dinner. When he returned he found that she had freed herself. Although there was a telephone in the garage she had not called the police – 'She was just waiting for me, I guess', Brudos told his interrogators with a smile. Linda then tried to fight back, but the petite 22-year-old was easily subdued by Brudos, who put a leather strap around her neck. 'Why are you doing this to me?' she gasped. Pulling the rope tight, he raped her as she died. Brudos then strung up her corpse and jabbed two syringes into her sides, through which he ran an electric current intended to make her dance, but only succeeding in burning her flesh. On the following day he raped her corpse again. He considered cutting off her breasts, but did not like her pink nipples, preferring brown ones; he nevertheless made a mould of her breasts before throwing her body into the river.

On searching Brudos' garage the police found his lingerie collection, along with photographs of his victims either posing in the underwear or hanging from the ceiling. Brudos had incriminated himself in one shot by capturing on film his own reflection in the mirror. A female breast, hardened with epoxy, was also found on the mantelpiece in the living room.

After pleading guilty to four counts of murder, Brudos was sentenced to life imprisonment. Utilising his gift for all things electrical, he set up a computer system in jail, being permitted to order shoe and underwear catalogues from the outside world in return.

The police could not believe that Darcie Brudos was unaware of her husband's murderous activities. She was charged with abetting the murder of Karen Sprinkler, but was subsequently found not guilty.

A year after Brudos was sent to jail the body of Jan Whitney surfaced. It was so badly decomposed that it could only be identified by means of dental records. Linda Slawson's body was never found.

6 ❖ Brides in the bath

The notorious 'Brides in the Bath' killer, George Joseph Smith, discovered that murdering women could prove a lucrative occupation, provided that he had enough sex appeal in order to get them to the altar first. Although far from good-looking and poorly educated, the petty criminal from east London found that he had what it took to become a lady-killer. His formula was simple: he married his victims and then dispatched them when they were naked and at their most vulnerable.

By the age of 25 Smith had spent most of his adult life in jail for petty thieving. In an effort to go straight he opened a baker's shop in Leicester, under the alias George Oliver Love. It was there that he met a friend of one of his shop assistants, the 18-year-old Caroline Thornhill. Within weeks he had wooed and wed her. Then his shop failed, and with it his plan to pursue a legitimate career. With his young wife acting as his accomplice, he embarked upon a new life of crime. Caroline would take a job as a housemaid with a wealthy family and steal their valuables; Smith would sell

'Brides in the Bath' murderer George Joseph Smith, posing with a female companion.

them and the pair would then move on. They got away with it for nearly two years, but when Caroline tried to pawn some silverware the pawn-broker smelt a rat. She was arrested and Smith did a runner. After being sent to prison for a year Caroline resolved to rid herself of her cowardly husband.

While Caroline was in jail Smith made his way to London. Unable to afford the rooms that he rented, he resolved his plight by means of the simple expedient of marrying his landlady – bigamously. On her release Caroline also went to London, where she by chance bumped into Smith on Oxford Street. She called a policeman, who arrested him; he was subsequently sentenced to two years' hard labour.

By the time that he got out of jail Caroline had emigrated to Canada. Smith moved back in with his second 'wife', but things did not work out between them, so he set out on a career as a swindler and serial bigamist. In 1908, with £90 that he had conned out of an unsuspecting spinster, he opened an antiques shop in Bristol. He took on a housekeeper, the 28-old Edith Pegler. Within a month she had become wife number three.

Leaving Edith in charge of the business, his antique-dealing cover gave him the perfect excuse for travelling the country in search of new victims to marry. The wooing-and-winning process sometimes took months rather than weeks. In order to explain his unduly long absence to her, he once claimed to have been abroad and told the unsuspecting Edith that he had sold a Chinese figure for £1,000.

Edith occasionally accompanied her husband on his travels and was with him in Southampton when he spotted Sarah Freeman, whereupon Edith was promptly sent home while Smith went about his business. Sarah initially resisted his advances, however, and it took him four months to get her up the aisle. After being married by special licence they set off for London – Sarah had just £90 in cash. Then, in their lodgings in Clapham, Smith spotted his new wife's bank book and lost no time in suggesting that she take out all of her money and hand it over to him. Soon he was £300 the richer. For a treat, he later took her to the National Gallery, where he sat her down on a bench and said that he was going to the lavatory. When he had not returned after about an hour, Sarah asked an attendant to go into the gents and look for him, but he was not there. When she eventually returned to their lodgings she found that her jewellery, clothes and other belongings had gone, along with Smith.

Florence Wilson, a widow from Worthing, married Smith in 1908. Her dowry was twenty gold sovereigns and two large, white, £5 notes. After Smith had pocketed the money he suggested that they visit the Anglo-French Exhibition at London's White City. He left her sitting on a bench while he went to buy a newspaper, but did not come back.

Bessie Mundy, a handsome woman in her mid-thirties, fell for a similar trick. She had married Smith believing him to be called Henry Williams. After a few weeks she had returned home to find her husband, as well as her life savings, gone. He had left a note accusing her of having given him venereal disease. Eighteen months later she saw him on the promenade at Weston-super-Mare. 'Henry?' she enquired tentatively. 'My dearest Bessie', he exclaimed, 'I have been searching the country for you. It was all a terrible mistake.' He then sat her down on a bench and explained that when he thought that he had contracted venereal disease he had decided to do the honourable thing: leave home rather than risk passing it on to her. The £150 that he had 'borrowed' from her had been used to pay back a loan. By the time that he had discovered that he did not have VD after all he had lost track of her and had since been combing the country trying to find her. He was only in Weston-super-Mare, he said, because he had heard that she was there. Soon they were locked in a tearful embrace. Back at her lodgings, Bessie announced to her landlady that she had been reunited with her husband. The landlady was suspicious and wired Bessie's aunt, but by the time that she arrived the lovebirds had flown.

To seal their new-found happiness, the reconciled couple went to a solicitor and had wills drawn up, each naming the other as the sole beneficiary. Bessie had £2,500; Smith was, as always, penniless. They then moved to Herne Bay, in Kent, where he set himself up as an art and antiques dealer. Because the house that they were renting did not have a bath Smith ordered a £2 tub from the local ironmonger; since it did not come with taps or fittings Bessie was sent to the ironmonger to bargain two shillings and six pence off the price. Despite the reduction, Smith omitted to pay for it when the bath was delivered on the next day.

On the day after that Smith took Bessie to their doctor, saying that his wife had had a black-out during a fit. Bessie seemed well enough, but the doctor nevertheless prescribed bromide of potassium, a sedative. Two days later the doctor was woken in the early hours by Smith beating on his door – Bessie had had a second fit, Smith said. Although she was hot and clammy when the doctor examined her, it was a humid July night and she showed no other signs of having had a fit. Even so, he provided another bottle of bromide of potassium.

Bessie seemed to be in good health on the following day, but on the morning after that the doctor received a note from Smith asking him to come at once because Bessie was dead. Once at Smith's house the doctor found Bessie's naked body floating face upwards in the bath; her right hand was clutching a bar of soap and her mouth and nose were under the water. Smith said that he had left the house to buy herrings for breakfast and that he had found her dead upon his return.

The inquest returned a verdict of accidental death. Smith sobbed decorously throughout and then buried his wife in a pauper's grave. The bath was returned to the ironmonger (Smith had still not paid for it). After the reading of Bessie's will and receiving his legacy Smith sold up and moved on.

In the following year Smith married the 25-year-old Alice Burnham, the buxom daughter of a rich fruit farmer, in Southend; this time he used his real name. Money soon found its way out of her account into his and he used it to insure her life for £500. She also made a will in his favour. They then set off for a belated honeymoon in Blackpool. The first boarding house that they inspected had a piano, but no bath. They took a room – with a bath – at a second boarding house for ten shillings.

Within days Alice became ill. She complained of headaches and a doctor prescribed some tablets. Soon afterwards the landlady was having dinner when she noticed a damp patch on the ceiling, which seemed to be growing bigger. Smith then came in saying that he had just bought some eggs for their breakfast the next morning and disappeared upstairs. Moments later he cried out, asking for a doctor to be called. When the doctor arrived he found Smith in the bathroom. His wife was in the bath, naked and dead. The inquest returned a verdict of accidental death. Like Bessie, Alice was buried in a pauper's grave, Smith inheriting her estate of £600.

A few weeks after the outbreak of World War I Alice Reavil was listening to a band in Bournemouth when she was picked up by Smith. This time he was masquerading as Charles Oliver James, a gentleman with a private income from land in Canada. They were married within less than a week.

On the pretext of opening an antiques shop Smith persuaded Alice to hand over the £76 that was in her post-office savings account. She also gave him the £14 that she had made from selling her furniture. (They were moving to new accommodation, he had said, and the rest of her belongings had been loaded onto a barrow and taken away.) Then Alice's husband took his new bride for a walk in a nearby park. After sitting her down on a bench he went off to find a lavatory, never to return. All that she had left was a few shillings and the clothes that she stood up in, but at least she had escaped Smith's clutches with her life.

In December 1914 Smith married Margaret Lofty, a clergyman's daughter, in Bath. He called her Peggy and she thought that his name was John Lloyd. After the marriage service they took a train to London and rented rooms in Bismarck Road, Highgate. On the following evening, after the landlady had boiled up water for Mrs Lloyd's bath, she heard a splashing sound, a sigh and then the front door slamming. A few minutes later Mr Lloyd entered with a bag of tomatoes, which, he said, were for his wife's dinner. Announcing his intention to ask her whether she was ready for them, he went upstairs and found Peggy lying dead in the bath.

After haggling with the undertaker, Smith had Margaret Lofty interred in a common grave for £1 off the standard burial price. He then returned to Bristol to spend Christmas with Edith, bringing her a present of Margaret Lofty's dresses, from her bridal trousseau.

Smith had made a fatal mistake in the murder of Margaret Lofty, however. Until then his killings had taken place in seaside resorts, where details of the inquests only appeared in the local papers. But Margaret had drowned in a bath in London and the mass-circulation Sunday newspaper the *News of the World* picked up on the story. Its headline, 'Bride's tragic fate on the day of her wedding', attracted the attention of Alice Burnham's father, who alerted Scotland Yard to the similarities between the deaths of Margaret Lofty and his daughter.

Although the inquest into Margaret Lofty's death in Highgate had returned a verdict of accidental death, the police began to keep an eye on 'Mr Lloyd'. A month later police detectives arrested him at a lawyer's office in Shepherd's Bush as he was trying to speed up the probate procedure on Margaret's will. He was charged with making a false declaration on his marriage certificate, whereupon 'Mr Lloyd' admitted that his name was really George Joseph Smith.

While Smith was being held in Bow Street police station, officers from Scotland Yard set off to follow his trail, their investigations taking them to 40 seaside resorts. After interviewing over 150 witnesses the police compiled 13 points of similarity between the untimely deaths of Bessie Mundy, Alice Burnham and Margaret Lofty.

The dead women were then exhumed and the Home Office pathologist Dr Bernard Spilsbury quickly established that they had died neither as the result of an accident nor of suicide, but had been murdered by Smith. Each of the women had been quite relaxed when Smith had entered the bathroom, he believed. Smith had then knelt by the bath, putting one arm under the victim's knees and then pulling them upwards. Next he had put his other hand on top of her head and had pushed it under the water. The whole thing would have happened so fast, Spilsbury thought, that the woman would have died of shock rather than of drowning.

On 23 March 1915 Smith was formally charged with the murders of the three women. Even though Britain was fighting the Great War at the time there was still intense public interest in the 'Brides in the bath' case. Caroline Thornhill – Smith's first and only legitimate wife – risked attack by German U-boats to make the two-week trip from Saskatchewan to attend the committal hearings. As Smith was committed for trial at the Old Bailey Caroline burst into tears, along with half-a-dozen other women in the courtroom.

Throughout his trial Edith Pegler stood by Smith (who protested his innocence), as did a flock of female fans, who queued around the block for seats in the courtroom. In a private room a nurse in bathing dress played the victim in a staged demonstration of Spilsbury's theory. The jury watched as Inspector Neil of Scotland Yard grasped her feet and pulled them upwards, simultaneously forcing her head under the water. Although the nurse was submerged for only a matter of seconds she had to be revived by means of artificial respiration.

Smith was found guilty of murder and sentenced to death. He wrote to Edith Pegler from Pentonville Prison, calling her 'his one true love'. The last words on his lips when he went to the gallows on 13 August 1915 were 'I am innocent'.

The day after Smith was executed his only legal wife, Caroline Thornhill, married a Canadian soldier. Soon afterwards Bismarck Road was renamed Waterloo Road as a result of anti-German sentiment. The bath in which Margaret Lofty had died was bought by Madame Tussaud's for display in its chamber of horrors. One of the other baths used by Smith to murder his 'brides' is kept in Scotland Yard's Black Museum.

7 ❖ Bluebeard

The legendary Bluebeard – Gilles de Rais – was a distinguished French soldier who saw battle against the English at the side of Joan of Arc. After she was captured and burnt at the stake (a punishment in which some say de Rais took great pleasure) he returned to his estate, where he kidnapped, tortured and killed perhaps as many as 140 children. His servant, Poitou, lured de Rais' victims to his castle, where his master sodomised them while simultaneously strangling them or cutting off their heads; he also enjoyed disembowelling them and then masturbating over their entrails. Some 50 dismembered bodies were found in a disused tower in the castle when he was arrested, although he later confessed under torture that he and his followers had murdered over 800 children.

France produced a second Bluebeard in the person of the notorious lady-killer Henri Desiré Landru, who, the French police estimated, killed nearly 300 women. Despite his small stature, bald head and pointed beard his strong powers of attraction enabled him to seduce almost any woman that he pleased.

As a young conscript Landru had impregnated his attractive young cousin, Mademoiselle Remy, and had been forced to marry her. On leaving the army he decided to become a con man, but was not a very successful one, being arrested four times between 1900 and 1908. Landru had fathered three illegitimate children and maintained a love nest for his assignations, but that had strictly been a matter of pleasure and he now decided that he would use his seductive skills to make a living. In 1914, using a number of aliases, he therefore placed advertisements in the lonely hearts' columns of various newspapers, saying that he was a wealthy bachelor who was seeking the companionship of a respectable woman. His plan was simple: when women answered his advertisements he would seduce them, marry them, take their money and then murder them.

His first victim, Madame Izoré, vanished shortly after replying to his advertisement, along with 15,000 francs. A 39-year-old widow, Madame Cuchet, was the next to respond to one of his advertisements. When she announced that she was going to marry Landru some suspicious members of her family went to visit him; on arriving, however, they found that he was out. They seized the opportunity to search the villa that he was renting in Vernouillet and found a huge bundle of love letters, but when they alerted Madame Cuchet to their discovery she did not believe them. Soon afterwards she, as well as her 16-year-old son, disappeared.

In 1915 a widow named Madame Laborde-Line, who was originally from Buenos Aires in Argentina, left Paris saying that she was going to live with a wonderful man whom she had met in Vernouillet. After her subsequent disappearance Landru cashed in her securities and sold her furniture, piece by piece, from a garage in Neuilly. Madame Guillin, along with 22,000 francs, was the next to vanish; her furniture also ended up in a garage sale in Neuilly. When Landru forged Madame Guillin's signature in an attempt to withdraw 12,000 francs from her account he was questioned at the bank. Claiming that he was Madame Guillin's brother-in-law, he explained that she had suffered a stroke and was no longer able to handle her own financial affairs.

Moving on to the village of Gambais, he enticed another widow to his villa with the promise of marriage. She, too, disappeared, and the residents of Gambais began to notice that black smoke belched from the chimney of Landru's villa at odd hours.

Landru then placed another advertisement in the lonely hearts' columns, which said that he was a 'widower with two children, aged forty-three, with a comfortable income' who wanted to meet a 'widow, with a view to matrimony'. The 45-year-old Madame Collomb, who worked as a typist and had saved 10,000 francs, answered it and Landru quickly proposed to her. Although her mother disliked Landru and warned her against marrying him the lovesick Madame Collomb took no notice and joined her fiancé at his villa in Gambais, never to be seen again.

On 11 March 1917 the 19-year-old Andrée Babelay told her mother that she was going to be rescued from her life of poverty: she had met a rich man on the Paris underground-railway system, the Métro, and they would soon be on their way to his villa in Gambais to get married, she said. Madame Babelay never saw her daughter again. (Andrée was the only one of Landru's known victims who yielded him no financial profit, although she briefly satisfied his almost incessant need for sex.)

His next conquest was Madame Buisson, a 47-year-old widow who was worth around 10,000 francs. She disappeared after informing her relatives that she was getting married. Landru later appeared at her apartment bearing a note that had ostensibly been signed by Madame Buisson authorising him to take her furniture. It went straight to his garage sale in Neuilly.

Gille De Rais. Also known as Bluebeard, he fought with Joan of Arc.

A matrimonial agency introduced Madame Jaume to Landru. She was last seen on 25 November 1917, leaving her apartment with him. A few days later Landru withdrew 1,400 francs from her account.

The 36-year-old Madame Pascal had very little money, but Landru kept her in an apartment in Paris and saw her on and off for a year. Then he grew tired of her sexual charms and took her to Gambais.

Although Madame Marchadier did not have much money either, she did have a large house on the rue St Jacques. After escorting her and her two dogs on a trip to Gambais Landru sold her house and all of her belongings.

Although Landru tried to avoid the relatives of his victims, nearly two years after the disappearance of Madame Buisson her sister, Madame Lacoste, recognised Landru as he was walking with an attractive young woman down the rue de Rivoli in Paris. She followed the pair into a china shop, where he ordered a delivery of crockery using the name Lucien Guillet and giving an address in the rue de Rochechouart. Madame Lacoste went to the police, who visited 'Guillet's' apartment on the rue de Rochechouart, where they found Landru lying naked in bed with Fernande Segret, a 27-year-old clerk. The lovers were planning a trip to Gambais.

The police discovered a notebook in Landru's pocket in which were written the names of some of his victims. On searching the villa at Gambais they found the personal effects of a large number of unknown women. They also discovered Landru's voluminous correspondence. His letters were sorted into seven groups, headed 'No reply'; 'Without money'; 'Without furniture'; 'To be answered *poste restante*'; 'To be answered to initials *poste restante*'; 'Possible fortune'; and 'In reserve for further investigation'. In all, Landru had written to 283 women, of whom almost none could be located. The police then dug up the garden, exhuming the corpses of three dogs, but no human remains. However, in the villa's stove they found ashes and tiny fragments of bone.

At his trial the prosecution said that Landru had drugged and then strangled his victims, after which he had chopped up the corpses into tiny pieces and burnt them. But Landru taunted them with the challenge 'If I am a murderer produce your bodies'. For its part the defence maintained that Landru was no mass murderer, but rather a white-slaver who had abducted and sold his victims to brothels in South America. The prosecution, however, pointed out that most of the missing women were in their fifties and that Landru had kept their false teeth, hair and breasts.

Landru remained cool throughout the proceedings. When the presiding judge asked him if he was a liar Landru replied 'I am not a lawyer'. The women of Paris flocked to see Bluebeard in court and Landru played to the gallery. When he left the court after the death sentence had been pronounced he turned and enquired of his female devotees 'I wonder if there is any lady present who would care to take my seat?' On the day of his execution a priest asked Landru if he wanted to make his confession; in response Landru pointed to the guards who were about to escort him to the guillotine and said 'Sorry, but I do not want to keep those gentlemen waiting'.

Landru maintained his innocence to the end. Yet he had drawn a picture for his defence attorney while awaiting execution, and when the daughter of the lawyer in question had the picture cleaned in 1963 a full confession was found on the back in Landru's handwriting.

8 ❖ Carl Panzram

During the early years of the twentieth century the German-American Carl Panzram went on a life-long campaign of murder and mayhem. He claimed to have killed 21 people, to have committed thousands of burglaries, robberies and arson attacks and to have sodomised more than 1,000 men.

Born in 1891 to a family of immigrant Prussian farmers in Warren, Minnesota, Panzram became a criminal as a young boy. His father had deserted his family soon after Panzram's birth and his mother could not control him. When he was just eight years old he was brought before a juvenile court for being drunk and disorderly. Then, after burgling the house of a well-to-do neighbour, he was sent to reform school, where the discipline was rigid, if not sadistic. Panzram burned the place down.

Released in 1906, he began his war against the world in earnest, starting in the west, where he committed a string of robberies and assaults. While travelling the country he was raped by four hoboes, which instilled a new mode of revenge in him: 'Whenever I met a hobo who wasn't too rusty looking,' he later wrote in his autobiography, 'I would make him raise his hands and drop his pants. I wasn't very particular either. I rode them old and young, tall and short, white and black'. Having ended up in Montana State Reformatory, he quickly escaped from jail, robbing and burning down several churches over the next couple of months. Then he joined the army, only to be court-martialled on 20 April 1907 for insubordination and pilfering US-government property. Three years spent at Fort Leavenworth, where he crushed rocks under the blistering Kansas sun, honed his meanness to the sharpness of a razor's edge.

After his release in 1910 Panzram headed for Mexico, where he joined up with the rebel leader Pascaul Orozco, who fought alongside Pancho Villa and Emiliano Zapata during the Mexican Revolution. He later returned to the USA, leaving a trail of murder, robbery, assault and rape in his wake as he moved north through California and the Pacific Northwest region.

Arrested in Chinook, Montana, for burglary, he was sentenced to a year in prison, but escaped after eight months. A year later Panzram was arrested again, this time while using the alias Jeff Rhoades; he was given a two-year jail sentence. Paroled in 1914, he immediately resumed his life of crime. In Astoria, Oregon, he was once more arrested for burglary and was offered a minimal sentence if he revealed the whereabouts of the goods that he had stolen. Although he kept his side of the bargain he was sentenced to seven years' imprisonment. Outraged at this injustice, Panzram escaped from his cell and wrecked the jail. After the guards had beaten him up he was sent to Salem's correctional facility, the toughest prison in the state. Almost as soon as he arrived there he flung the contents of a chamber pot into a guard's face, for which he was beaten unconscious and chained to the floor of a darkened cell for 30 days. This punishment did not break his spirit, however, and he spent his time in the hole screaming words of defiance.

The facility's warden was shot dead during an escape attempt, and although the new warden was even tougher Panzram still managed to burn down the prison's workshop, as well as a flax mill. He also went berserk with an axe and incited a prison revolt, for which he was given another seven years in jail. By now, however, the atmosphere in the prison was so tense that the guards would not venture into the yard, so the warden was dismissed. The next warden was an idealist who believed that Panzram might respond to kindness. When Panzram was next caught trying to escape the warden told him that he was the 'meanest and most cowardly degenerate' that the prison authorities had ever seen. Panzram agreed with this description, but to his astonishment instead of punishing him the warden let him leave the jail on condition that he returned that evening. Although Panzram walked through the prison gates with no intention of going back he did, in fact, return that evening. The liberal regime was maintained and Panzram continued to respond to it, that is until he got drunk with a pretty nurse one night and absconded, only to be recaptured after a gunfight. He was returned to a punishment cell, where he was fed a diet of bread and water, also being beaten and sprayed with a fire hose. Finally, the ever resourceful Panzram constructed his own tools and hacked his way out of the prison in May 1918.

He headed east, stealing $1,200 from a hotel in Maryland and then boarding a merchant ship bound for South America. He jumped ship in Peru, where he worked in a copper mine. In Chile, he became a foreman for an oil company, later, for no apparent reason, setting fire to an oil rig. Back in the USA he stole $7,000 from a jewellery shop and $40,000 in jewels and liberty bonds from the New Haven home of the former US president, William Howard Taft. With the money he bought a yacht, and after hiring sailors to help him to refit it he raped and shot them before dropping their bodies in the sea. He killed ten in all.

Panzram served a six-month jail sentence in Bridgeport for petty theft before being arrested again for inciting a riot during a labour dispute. Jumping bail, he headed for western Africa, where he continued his murder spree. On one occasion he was approached by a 12-year-old boy who was begging for money. 'He was looking for something. He found it, too', wrote Panzram later. 'First I committed sodomy on him and then I killed him.' He smashed in the boy's head with a rock: 'His brains were coming out of his ears when I left him and he will never be deader', Panzram enthused. Panzram once decided to go crocodile-hunting and hired six black porters to guide him through the backwaters, later shooting them in their backs and feeding them to the crocodiles.

Back in the USA Panzram raped and killed three more boys. In June 1923, while he was working as night watchman for the New Haven Yacht Club, he stole a boat, killing a man who clambered aboard and tossing the body into New York's Kingston Bay. He was eventually caught attempting to rob an office in Larchmont, New York, and was sentenced to five years in Sing Sing. The guards there were unable to handle him, however, and he was sent to Clinton Prison in Dannemora, which was considered to be the end of the line for hard cases such as he. There he received savage beatings and also smashed his leg after falling from a high gallery. He spent his days plotting his revenge against the whole human race, amongst other things planning to blow up a railway tunnel when there was a train in it; to poison an entire city by putting arsenic in its water supply; and to start a war between Britain and the USA by blowing up a British battleship in US waters.

When he tried to escape from Clinton Prison he was tortured by having his hands tied behind his back and then being suspended by a rope from a beam. He could endure this for 12 hours on end, all the while screaming and cursing his mother for having brought him into the world. Despite his horrendous treatment at the hands of the guards, one of them, Henry Lesser, sympathised with Panzram and persuaded him to write his autobiography. Panzram did so, making no excuses for himself in it, saying that he had broken every law of God and humanity and furthermore commenting that if there had been more laws in existence he would have broken those, too.

Released yet again in 1928, Panzram hit the Washington-Baltimore area like a one-man crime wave, committing eleven robberies and one murder. He was soon arrested. At his trial he addressed the jury, saying 'While you were trying me here, I was trying all of you. I have found you guilty. Some of you I have already executed. If I live, I'll execute some more of you. I hate the whole human race'. The judge sentenced him to 25 years in jail. 'Visit me', Panzram retorted.

At Fort Leavenworth Panzram told his guards 'I'll kill the first man that bothers me'. True to his word, he murdered the mild-mannered, civilian prison-laundry supervisor Robert G Warnke with an iron bar. After a hasty trial Panzram was sentenced to death by hanging. Meanwhile, Lesser had been hawking Panzram's autobiography around the literary establishment, which included the legendary newspaperman H L Menken. People were impressed by it, but when Panzram heard that they were thinking of starting a movement to work for his reprieved he protested, saying 'I would not reform if the front gate was opened right now and I was given a million dollars when I stepped out. I have no desire to do good or become good'.

The Society for the Abolition of Capital Punishment also stepped in to try to save his neck, but he told it to forget it. Hanging would be a 'real pleasure and a big relief' for him, he said. 'The only thanks you or your kind will ever get from me for your efforts is that I wish you all had one neck and I had my hands on it. I believe that the only way to reform people is to kill them. My motto is: "Rob 'em all, rape 'em all and kill 'em all."' He even turned on Lesser in the end, writing in his last letter 'What gets me is how in the heck any man of your intelligence and ability, knowing as much about me as you do, can still be friendly towards a thing like me when I even despise and detest my own self'.

The end could not come soon enough for Carl Panzram. He was standing on the gallows on 11 September 1930 when the hangman, a son of Indiana, asked him if he had any last words. Panzram replied 'Yes, hurry it up, you Hoosier bastard. I could hang a dozen men while you're fooling around'.

9 ❖ Harvey Glatman

The *Los Angeles Times* journalist Robert Dull had separated from his pretty, young, blonde wife, Judy, because he objected to her modelling in the nude for other men, but the bust-up had not been acrimonious. She had invited him to her flat on 1 August 1957 to talk about a divorce, but when he arrived she was not at home. Her flatmate, Lynn Lykles, said that she had left several hours earlier with a photographer called Johnny Glynn. Over the next two hours two other photographers called, saying that the 19-year-old Judy had failed to turn up for a session. No one answered the phone number that Glynn had left, so Dull called Judy's family and friends. After ascertaining that none of them had seen her he called the police.

Lynn gave the Los Angeles Police Department (LAPD) a description of Glynn: he was short, with jug-handle-like ears, she said, and looked rather scruffy and dishevelled. He had visited the flat two days earlier, when another of her flatmates, Betty, had showed him Judy's portfolio, which had captivated him. He had phoned that morning, she continued, saying that he had a rush assignment and asking Judy to act as his model. Judy had been reluctant to do so, however, as she had a busy schedule ahead of her; Betty's description of him had made her rather suspicious, too. But when Glynn had said that his studio was being used for another assignment and that they would therefore have to shoot the pictures in her flat she had agreed. When he had turned up at the flat he had brought no photographic gear with him because, he explained, a friend had lent him his studio. He had agreed to the fee that Judy asked and the two of them had then left. That was the last time that anyone saw Judy alive.

Descriptions of both Judy and the mysterious photographer were circulated, but there was little else that the LAPD could do. However, Judy's disappearance did make the newspapers and for weeks Police Sergeant David Ostroff was kept busy following up potential leads. Ostroff also studied the file on a beautiful young actress named Jean Spangler, who had vanished eight years earlier.

Five months after Judy's disappearance a rancher and his dog discovered a skull lying in the desert near the Interstate 60 motorway, over 100 miles (161 kilometres) east of Los Angeles. When the police arrived they unearthed a half-buried skeleton clad in women's underwear and the remains of a brown dress like the one that Judy was wearing when she was last seen. Tufts of hair attached to the skull showed that the dead woman had been a blonde; furthermore, the skeleton measured 5 feet 4 inches (1.6 metres), the same height as Judy.

Eight months after Judy Dull went missing another woman in the Los Angeles area disappeared. A divorcée and mother of two, the 24-year-old Shirley Ann Bridgeford had gone on a blind date with a short, dishevelled man with prominent ears called George Williams. Police Sergeant Ostroff soon came to believe that Johnny Glynn and George Williams were the same man. Three months later Ruth Rita Mercado, a 24-year-old stripper and nude model who used the stage name Angela, also vanished. Although Ostroff added her file to his dossier he was still no nearer to catching the culprit. Then, however, the police got lucky.

On the evening of Monday, 27 October 1958, Officer Thomas F Mulligan, of the California Highway Patrol, turned into a dark street in the dusty town of Tustin, 35 miles (56 kilometres) south of Los Angeles. The light thrown by his motorcycle headlamp revealed a couple struggling, so he stopped and called out to them. Seeing that the woman was holding a gun and that her clothes were in a state of considerable disarray, Officer Mulligan pulled out his own pistol and ordered them to stop, whereupon they put up their hands. The woman, who identified herself as Lorraine Vigil, claimed that the man had tried to rape and kill her. The man did not deny her allegations.

Lorraine was a secretary who was determined to break into modelling, she later explained. A friend, who ran a modelling agency, had called her that evening and had asked her if she wanted to undertake a photographic assignment. Although her friend knew the photographer, who was called Frank Johnson, she had warned Lorraine to be a little wary of him. Lorraine had accepted the job and the photographer had later picked her up from her flat on Wiltshire Boulevard. Heading downtown, he had driven past the modelling studio on Sunset Strip that the agency had said would be the venue for the session. When Lorraine had mentioned this he had said that he was taking her to his studio in Anaheim, but then he had driven through Anaheim as well.

He had stopped on the dark road in Tustin and had pulled out a gun. Having ordered her to keep quiet, he had then produced a length of rope. Seeing this, Lorraine had said that she did not want to be tied up and would do anything that he wanted. At that moment a car had driven by and Lorraine had made a lunge for the door handle, whereupon the gun had gone off, the bullet grazing her thigh. In the resultant split second of confusion she had thrown herself at her assailant, causing the car door to fly open. They had fallen out of the car on to the road, and Lorraine had bitten her attacker as hard as she could. He had then dropped the gun, which she grabbed. She was in the process of trying to shoot the fake photographer who had attacked her when Officer Mulligan arrived.

At Santa Ana police station the photographer who called himself Frank Johnson revealed that he was, in fact, Harvey Murray Glatman, aged 30. It was furthermore discovered that Glatman lived no more than a few streets from Ruth Rita Mercado's San Pico Boulevard flat. When they visited the address that he had given the police found a run-down, white-shingle bungalow. Inside, the walls were covered with nude pin-ups, some of which featured bound and gagged young women. Among Glatman's meagre possessions were found a number of lengths of rope.

Glatman agreed to take a lie-detector test; when the name Angela – Ruth Rita Mercado's professional name – was mentioned the stylus leapt, and within minutes Glatman had confessed to killing Ruth. Then he said 'I killed a couple of other girls, too'. It turned out that he had quite a story to relate.

Harvey Glatman was born in Denver, Colorado, in 1928. He was a mummy's boy who did not get on well with other children. When he was 12 his parents noticed red welts encircling his neck and after persistent questioning forced him to admit that tightening a rope around his neck gave him sexual satisfaction. The family doctor told his worried parents that he would grow out of it. At school Glatman was unattractive to girls and would instead gain their attention by grabbing their purses. This was not a very effective method of courtship, however, and at 17 he therefore took more direct action by pointing a toy gun at a girl and ordering her to undress. After she had screamed and run away Glatman was arrested, fleeing to New York on being released on bail.

In New York Glatman turned his perverted urges into a way of life, robbing women at gunpoint and later graduating to burglary, for which he spent five years in Sing Sing. He seemed to respond to psychiatric help in prison and became a model prisoner. On his release he went back to Colorado and began working as a television repairman – a job that allowed him to enter other people's homes quite legitimately (he would sometimes sneak into their bedrooms). His mother then lent him the money with which to set up a television-repair business in Los Angeles.

Glatman confessed everything to the police. Judy Dull, he said, had been the girl of his dreams. After he had picked her up he had driven her to his makeshift studio, where he had asked her to take off her dress and put on a pleated skirt and cardigan instead. He had then produced a length of rope and had tied her up. The shots that he was taking, he had explained to her, were for the cover of a true-life crime magazine, which was why she had had to be bound and gagged.

He had taken some pictures of her, but the sight of the helpless Judy had been too much for him; bound as she was, she could not resist as he had slowly undressed her. After that he had put a gun to her head and had told that he would kill her if she cried out for help; she had nodded, whereupon he had untied her gag. Glatman had next made her pose on the sofa for more explicit bondage photographs and had then raped her twice. When he had finished he told her that he would take her to a remote spot in the desert, where he would release her.

He had let Judy put on her brown dress and had then driven her into the Nevada Desert. After spreading a blanket on the ground in a lonely spot he had again made her pose for erotic photographs, some with a noose around her neck. When Glatman had grown tired of taking pictures he had tied the loose end of the noose around her ankles and had pulled it until she was dead. Glatman had apologised to Judy's corpse before burying it in a shallow grave and had kept her shoes as a keepsake. Although he had originally intended to get a thrill from photographing and raping a beautiful woman – naked, bound and gagged – Glatman found that the killing had given him the greatest satisfaction of all and was determined to do it again.

Glatman had then registered in the name of George William with a dating agency and the agency had fixed him up with a date with Shirley Ann Bridgeford. When he had picked up Shirley he could see by her reaction that she found him a disappointment, but she had nevertheless gone with him.

Glatman had driven her south, out of Los Angeles towards San Diego. He had stopped in the Anza Desert and had tried to put his arm around her, to which she had responded that she did not feel that this was appropriate behaviour on a first date. He had then suggested that they went for a meal and she had seemed relieved. He had driven with one hand on the steering wheel while trying to fondle her with the other. She had again tried to fend him off and he had soon grown angry. He had stopped the car and had pulled out his automatic pistol, ordering her to get into the back of the car and undress. She had refused, so he had torn off her clothes and then raped her.

That had not been the end of Shirley's hideous blind date, however. Next he had driven her into the desert, where, after unpacking his photographic gear, he had made her pose on the same blanket on which he had killed Judy Dull. After having forced her to lie on her front he had tied a rope around her neck and garrotted her. He had taken her red knickers as a memento and had left her body where it lay, covered with brushwood because the ground was too hard to dig a grave in.

Five months later Glatman had spotted an advertisement in the newspaper offering the services of a nude model called Angela. He had called her before visiting her on the evening of 23 July 1958. She had taken one look at him, however, and had refused to let him in, but because he had liked her appearance he had pulled out his gun and had forced his way into her flat.

He had ordered Angela to undress at gunpoint and had then tied her up and raped her. After that he had announced that they were going for a little picnic, whereupon he had driven her to a deserted spot about 30 miles (48 kilometres) from where he had murdered Shirley Ann Bridgeford. Much as he had enjoyed killing Shirley and Judy, he had later thought that those murders had been over too quickly and had decided that in this instance he would take his time. The two of them had accordingly spent the day together, eating, sleeping and drinking. Glatman had also occasionally forced Angela (or Ruth Rita Mercado, as she was known when she was not at work) to pose for him. He had furthermore repeatedly raped her. Ruth had been very compliant, he said, clearly having decided that her only chance of surviving was to try to please him. After 24 hours spent toying with his victim, however, Glatman had garrotted her in the same manner in which he had dispatched his previous two victims.

After making his detailed confession Glatman helped the police to find the remains of Ruth Rita Mercado and Shirley Ann Bridgeford. Although his lawyers suggested that he plead guilty but insane, Glatman pleaded guilty without caveat, thus opting for a quick execution rather than a life spent in a mental institution. He died in the gas chamber on 18 September 1959.

10 ❖ The Vampire of Düsseldorf

Peter Kürten terrorised the German city of Düsseldorf during the year of 1929. He was sexually aroused by blood and flames, as well as by the notoriety that his monstrous crimes bestowed upon him.

Kürten's childhood was a catalogue of abuse. His father was a violent drunk who physically and sexually abused his wife and 13 children. At the age of nine Kürten drowned two of his playmates in the river Rhine, a dogcatcher who shared the Kürtens' house furthermore encouraging Peter to torture animals. Peter was also sexually precocious and began indulging his enormous sexual appetite with farm animals, soon discovering that stabbing the animal during the act increased his satisfaction. (He later took up with a prostitute.)

Convicted for theft, he was sent to jail, where his sexual longings became sublimated into gruesome fantasies. On his release he strangled a young woman in a wood while they were having sex. Subsequently finding himself back in prison, Kürten deliberately flouted prison rules in order to be put into solitary confinement, where he worked on developing his erotic fantasies. After being released again he next added arson to his repertoire of crime. He was then called up, but later deserted from the army, an action which landed him in prison once again. He was in the process of breaking into a house in 1913 when he discovered a 13-year-old girl asleep in bed; on raping and strangling her it was then that he discovered murder as a pleasure in its own right. Soon afterwards he attacked two strangers in the street with an axe, achieving orgasm at the sight of their blood.

Kürten spent World War I in jail for burglary. When he was released he wooed his future wife with a mixture of sweet talk and threats of appalling violence. His intended was stoical: a former prostitute, she had spent four years in jail for shooting a man who had failed to fulfil his promise to marry her and she put up with Kürten's strange ways as a form of atonement. He was physically gentle with his wife, although he admitted that he could only have sex with her by fantasising about being violent to someone else. During the early years of their marriage they lived in the small town of Altenburg. Kürten worked hard and was a political activist, but from time to time he sought out women for brutal sexual encounters. They later moved back to Düsseldorf, where Kürten again took up arson. 'I got pleasure from the glow of the fire, the cries for help', he later said. 'It gave me so much pleasure that I got sexual satisfaction.' He also attacked four or five women, strangling them to the point of unconsciousness.

On 3 February 1929 his assaults assumed a new ferocity when he attacked a woman in the street, stabbing her 24 times with a pair of scissors. A week later he stabbed a workman to death, subsequently also raping and strangling an eight-year-old girl before mutilating her body with a knife. He half-strangled four women during his attacks and also murdered two children. He killed and buried the 20-year-old Maria Hann, later returning to her grave and digging up her corpse because he wanted to frighten people by nailing her body to a tree in a perverted form of mock crucifixion. He murdered two women with a hammer, severely injuring two others. Then he killed a five-year-old girl, buried her and sent a map of the grave site to the newspapers; Kürten joined the crowd that rushed to the scene, discovering a fresh source of sexual pleasure in the fear and outrage of the people around him. Kürten continued his attacks, assaulting ten more women. After having been battered or half-strangled, those who escaped gave a description of their attacker to the police.

By this time the police had interviewed more than 9,000 people and had investigated 2,000 clues in connection with Kürten's crimes. His name had even come up during the investigation, but the woman who had accused him of being her attacker was eventually fined for wasting police time. When a woman whom Kürten had raped bumped into him on the stairs outside his flat, however, Kürten knew that his time was up. He accordingly confessed everything to his wife and urged her to go to the police to collect the reward for identifying him. She did not believe his story at first, and it was only when he started relating every detail of his assaults with evident relish that she was convinced.

Kürten had planned one more act of mass murder, but was prevented from carrying it out when his wife went straight to the police and arranged for him to give himself up. In custody, Kürten made a full confession, admitting many crimes that the police had not yet heard about. He often did not even know his victim's name. 'I went out with my scissors', ran one typical confession. 'At the station a girl spoke to me; I took her to have a glass of beer and we then walked towards the Grafenberg woods. I seized her by the throat and I held on for a bit . . . I threw her down the river and went away.'

After having been found guilty in court Kürten was studied by Professor Karl Berg, who described him as the 'king of the sexual perverts'. 'I have no remorse', Kürten told Berg. 'As to whether recollection of my deeds makes me feel ashamed, I will tell you. Thinking back to the details is not at all unpleasant. I rather enjoy it.'

Kürten received a huge amount of mail while he was being held in prison. Around half of the letters that were sent to him spelt out the cruel and unusual punishments that the writers would have liked to have inflicted upon him. The other half consisted of fan mail, including a large number of love letters from women.

The death penalty was very unpopular in Germany at that time and there was therefore widespread protest when Kürten was sentenced to death. Kürten himself was unconcerned about the sentence, however – indeed, when he heard that he would be able to experience the ultimate pleasure of hearing the blood gush from his neck for the split second during which his head was being severed he relished the prospect. And on 2 July 1930, after a final meal of Wiener schnitzel, fried potatoes and white wine, Peter Kürten went eagerly to the guillotine.

11 ❖ The Moors murderers

Ian Brady and Myra Hindley still rank as perhaps the world's most infamous killers. Their bizarre and deviant sexual relationship drove them to torture and murder defenceless children for pleasure in a case of serial killing that appalled the world. The idea that Hindley may one day be released from prison elicits howls of protest from the public. Nobody – least of all himself – however, has ever contemplated freeing Brady.

When Hindley met Brady he was already deeply warped: a 21-year-old stock clerk at Millwards (a chemical company in Manchester), his mind was full of sadistic fantasies. He had a collection of Nazi memorabilia and listened to recordings of Nazi rallies, while in his lunch hour he read Adolf Hitler's autobiography *Mein Kampf* ('My Struggle') and studied German grammar. He believed in the Nazi cause and regretted that he had not been part of its terrible excesses.

For her part, Hindley was known as a loner. Her first boyfriend had died when she was 15; she had not been able sleep for days afterwards and had turned to the Roman Catholic Church for consolation. At school it was noted that she was tough, aggressive and rather masculine, and that she enjoyed contact sports and judo, none of which suited her to the genteel life of 1950s' Britain. At the age of 19 she became a typist at Millwards, where she met Brady. He impressed her immediately: she considered most of the men whom she knew to be immature, but Brady dressed well and rode a motorbike. 'Ian wore a black shirt today and looked smashing . . . I love him', she confided to her diary.

For nearly a year Brady took no notice of her, however: 'The pig. He didn't even look at me today', she wrote more than once. Finally, in December 1961, he asked her out. 'Eureka!' her diary says. 'Today we have our first date. We are going to the cinema.' (The film that they saw was *Judgement at Nuremberg*, which was about the trial of Germany's leading Nazis following World War II.) Hindley rapidly surrendered her virginity to Brady, later writing 'I hope Ian and I love each other all our lives and get married and are happy ever after'. Yet their relationship would not be as innocent as her hopeful worlds suggest, for Hindley soon became Brady's

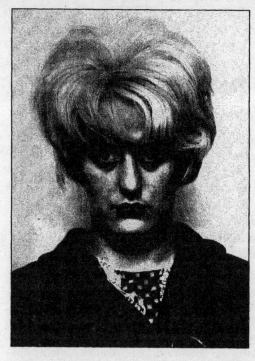

Moors Murderer Myra Hindley. This picture was taken during her trial.

sex slave. He introduced her to sexual perversion and urged her to read his books on Nazi atrocities. They also took pornographic photographs of each other and kept them in a scrapbook; some showed weals across Hindley's buttocks that had been left by a whip.

Hindley subsequently gave up babysitting and going to church. Within six months she and Brady were living together at her grandmother's house; because her grandmother was a frail woman who spent most of her time in bed they had the run of the place. Brady persuaded Hindley to bleach her brown hair a Teutonic blonde and dressed her in leather skirts and high-heeled boots. He often called her Myra Hess – or 'Hessie' – after a sadistic, Nazi, concentration-camp guard.

Life with Brady made Hindley hard and cruel. She did anything that Brady asked of her and did not balk at procuring children for him to abuse, torture and kill. Their first victim was the 16-year-old Pauline Reade, who disappeared on 12 July 1963 on her way to a dance. They persuaded Pauline to go for a walk on the nearby Saddleworth Moor, where they killed and buried her. Four months later Hindley hired a car and abducted the 12-year-old John Kilbride; when she returned the car it was covered

Ian Brady, who along with Myra Hindley, killed and buried children on Saddleworth Moor.

with mud from the moors. Brady and Hindley laughed when they read about the massive police hunt that was being undertaken to find the missing boy.

In May 1964 Hindley bought a car of her own, a white Mini van. During the following month the 12-year-old Keith Bennett went missing; like their other victims, Hindley and Brady had buried him on Saddleworth Moor. At Brady's behest Hindley then joined a local gun club and bought pistols for them both, which they practised firing on the moors. While they were there they visited the graves of their victims, photographing each other kneeling on them.

On 26 December 1964 they abducted the ten-year-old Lesley Ann Downey. This time they were determined to derive the utmost perverted pleasure from their defenceless victim. They accordingly forced her to pose nude for pornographic photographs and then tortured her, recording her screams, before strangling her and burying her with the others on Saddleworth Moor.

Brady now wanted to extend his sphere of evil influence, aiming to recruit Myra's 16-year-old brother-in-law, David Smith, to their perverted circle. Brady showed Smith his guns and talked to him about robbing a bank. He also lent him books about the Marquis de Sade (from whose name the word 'sadism' is derived) and persuaded him to write down quotations dictated by Brady. 'Murder is a hobby and a supreme pleasure' or 'People are like maggots, small, blind, worthless fish-bait', Smith obediently wrote in an exercise book under Brady's guidance.

Brady believed that he could lure anyone into his world of brutality and murder and bragged to Smith about the murders that he had committed. They were drinking at the time and Smith thought that Brady was joking, so Brady decided to prove his capacity for murder and simultaneously ensnare Smith by making him party to a killing.

On 6 October 1965 Brady and Hindley picked up Edward Evans, a 17-year-old homosexual, in a Manchester pub. They then called Smith and asked him to come to their house at midnight. When he arrived he heard a cry coming from the sitting room. 'Help him, Dave', said Hindley, and Smith rushed into the room to find a youth in a chair with Brady sitting astride him. Brady held an axe in his hands which he brought down on to the boy's head, hitting him at least 14 times. 'It's the messiest', Brady said with some satisfaction. 'Usually it takes only one blow.' Brady then handed the axe to the dumbstruck Smith. (This was an attempt to incriminate Smith by putting his fingerprints on the murder weapon.)

Although Smith was terrified by what he had seen he helped to clean up the blood while Brady and Hindley wrapped the boy's body in a plastic sheet; the couple made jokes about the murder as they carried the corpse downstairs. After that Hindley made a pot of tea and they all sat down. 'You should have seen the look on his face', said Hindley, who was flushed with excitement; she then started reminiscing about the murders that she and Brady had previously committed. Although Smith could not believe what was happening he realised that he would be their next victim if he showed any signs of disgust or outrage. After a decent interval he made his excuses and left; when he got back to his flat he was violently ill.

Smith told his wife what had happened, who urged him to go to the police. At dawn, armed with a knife and screwdriver, the couple went out to a phone box and reported the murder. A police car picked them up and took them to the police station, where Smith told his lurid tale to incredulous policemen. When the police visited Hindley's house at 8.40am to check out Smith's story, however, they found Edward Evans' body in the back bedroom.

Brady admitted killing Evans during an argument and then tried to implicate Smith in the murder. Hindley merely said 'My story is the same at Ian's ... Whatever he did, I did'. The only emotion that she showed was when she was told that her dog had died: 'You fucking murderers', she screamed at the police.

The police found a detailed plan that Brady had drawn up for the removal from the house of all clues to Evans' murder. Curiously, one of the items listed was Hindley's prayer book; when the police examined it they discovered that a left-luggage ticket from Manchester Station had been stuck down its spine. On following up the lead at the left-luggage office the police found two suitcases containing books on sexual perversion, as well as coshes and photographs of a naked and gagged Lesley Ann Downey. The tape that had recorded her screams – which was later played to the stunned courtroom at Chester Assizes – was also discovered. Other photographs showed Hindley posing beside graves on Saddleworth Moor, and it was these that subsequently helped the police to locate the bodies of Lesley Ann Downey and John Kilbride.

At Brady and Hindley's trial the truly horrific nature of the murders was revealed. The pathologist disclosed that Edward Evans' fly had been undone and that dog hairs had been found around his anus; John Kilbride's body was discovered with his trousers and underpants around his knees. Hindley, it seemed, had been turned on by watching Brady perform homosexual acts on his victims. Later Brady let it slip that both he and Hindley had been naked when they had photographed Lesley Ann Downey in the nude, but otherwise the pair refused to talk about their crimes.

They were sentenced to life imprisonment. Brady did not bother to appeal against the sentence; Hindley did, but her appeal was rejected. They were refused permission to see each other in jail, although they were allowed to exchange letters.

Brady showed no contrition in prison and refused to allow his spirit to be broken, regarding himself as a martyr to his own perverted cause. He gradually became insane. Hindley, however, broke down and petitioned to be released. When her appeal was refused a warder (who was Hindley's lesbian lover) organised an abortive escape attempt, for which Hindley was sentenced to an additional year in jail.

She took an Open University degree and gave additional information about the whereabouts of her victims' graves to the police in a bid for mercy. Brady, however, countered her every move by revealing more of her involvement in the crimes, considering any attempt on her part to go free as an act of disloyalty to him. 'The weight of our crimes justifies permanent imprisonment', Brady told the Parole Board in 1982. 'I will not wish to be free in 1985 or even 2005.'

Hindley still hoped for parole, but public opinion was resolutely against it: after all, the families of their victims were still suffering.

12 ✦ Henry Lee Lucas

Henry Lee Lucas holds the record for being the USA's most prolific serial killer. He confessed to over 360 murders, of which 157 were investigated by the authorities and proved to have been committed by him – as for the rest, they took his word for it.

Lucas' mother, a half Native American Chippawa, was drunk for most of the time on the corn liquor that she bought with the proceeds of prostitution. Known to be 'as mean as a rattlesnake', she sent the seven children from her first marriage to a foster home. Lucas' natural father worked on the railways and lost both of his legs in an accident; Lucas himself was brought up by one of his mother's lovers, Andrew Lucas. His mother beat her children constantly and after one beating he was unconscious for three days and suffered brain damage; another such incident resulted in a glass eye. Lucas was also made to grow his hair long and to wear a dress.

Lucas was introduced to sex at the age of ten by the educationally challenged Bernard Dowdy, another of his mother's lovers. Dowdy would slit the throat of a calf and have sex with the carcass, encouraging the boy to do the same. Lucas enjoyed the experience and from childhood onwards associated sex with death. Throughout his childhood he continued to have sex with animals, sometimes skinning them alive for his sexual pleasure. At 14 he turned his perverted attention to women, beating a 17-year-old girl unconscious at a bus stop and raping her; when she came to and started to scream he choked the life out of her.

Convicted of burglary, he was sent to a reformatory when he was 15. Two years of hard labour on a prison farm did nothing to reform him, however, and on his release he resumed housebreaking, again being caught and sent back to jail. He escaped from prison, whereupon he met and fell in love with a young woman called Stella. They stayed together for four years and she agreed to marry him. Then his mother turned up demanding that her son take care of her and after a violent row Lucas killed her. This time he was sentenced to 40 years' imprisonment.

By 1970 the authorities considered Lucas to be a reformed character and released him. He killed a woman within hours of getting out of jail. In 1971 he was arrested for attempting to rape two teenage girls at gunpoint; the only excuse that he gave at his trial was that he craved women all the time. Released again in 1975, he then married Betty Crawford, but the marriage broke up when Betty discovered that he was having sex with her nine-year-old daughter, as well as trying to force himself on her seven-year-old child. Lucas then moved in with his sister, only to be thrown out when he started to have sex with her daughter, too.

In 1978 he met another sex-murder freak in a soup kitchen in Jacksonville, Florida. Ottis Toole was a sadist with homosexual tendencies who often dressed as a woman and picked up men in bars – he had even started to take a course of female hormones in furtherance of his ambition to have a sex change. Toole was also a pyromaniac who had an orgasm at the sight of a burning building.

Lucas and Toole became lovers and together embarked upon a series of violent robberies which frequently involved murder – often for the sheer pleasure of it. In Toole's confession he admitted that at around that time they had seen a teenage couple walking along a road because their car had run out of petrol. Toole had shot the boy while Lucas had forced the girl into the back of the car. After he had finished with her he had shot her six times and they had then dumped her body by the side of the road. (This was one of the cases that the police would later confirm.) Another incident had occurred outside Oklahoma City, when they had picked up a young woman called Tina Williams whose car had broken down. Lucas had shot her twice and had then had sex with her corpse.

Later in 1978 Lucas and Toole were in Maryland when a man asked them if they would help him to transport stolen cars. This was much too tame a sport for such hardened criminals, they explained, so he enquired whether they would be interested in becoming professional killers instead. They answered that they would, to which the man replied that the one condition was that they joined a Satanic cult.

Lucas and Toole subsequently claimed to have been inducted into the

Hand of Death sect in Florida by a man named Don Meteric. As part of the initiation ceremony Lucas had had to kill a man. He had lured his victim to a beach and had given him a bottle of whisky; when the man had thrown back his head to take a swig of it Lucas had cut his throat. As part of the cult's activities Lucas and Toole kidnapped young prostitutes, who were forced to perform in pornographic videos which often turned out to be 'snuff movies' in which the prostitutes were killed. The pair also abducted children, taking them across the border into Mexico where they were sold or used as sacrifices in Satanic ceremonies.

At around that time Toole introduced Lucas to his 11-year-old niece, Becky Powell, who was slightly educationally challenged. Becky was then living in Toole's mother's house in Florida, where they were also staying. Toole – who had been seduced by his older sister, Druscilla, before he became a homosexual – enjoyed watching the men whom he picked up make love to Becky or her older sister, Sarah. After Druscilla committed suicide, however, Becky and her brother, Frank, were put into care. Lucas then 'rescued' them and by January 1982 they were all on the run together, living off the money that they stole from small grocery shops. Becky called Lucas 'Daddy', but one night, when he was tickling her innocently at bedtime, they began to kiss; Lucas then undressed her before stripping off himself. Becky may have been only 12 at the time, he said, but she looked 18.

During his time with Becky Lucas continued his murderous rampage in conjunction with Toole. Lucas later outlined a typical two weeks in Georgia. In that short space of time they had kidnapped and murdered a 16-year-old girl before raping her dead body, as well as abducting, raping and mutilating a blonde woman. Another woman had been taken from a car park and stabbed to death in front of her children. During the course of one robbery the shop's owner had been shot; another man had died in a second robbery; in a third the owner of the shop had been stabbed; and in a fourth a woman had been tied up before being stabbed to death. Toole had also tried to force his sexual attentions upon a young man, whom he had shot after being spurned. Becky and Frank had often taken part in the robberies, also witnessing several of the murders.

Lucas and Toole eventually parted company, Toole taking Frank back to Florida while Lucas and Becky were given work with a couple named Smart who ran an antique shop in California. After five months the Smarts sent Lucas and Becky to Texas to look after Mrs Smart's 80-year-old mother, Kate Rich. A few weeks later Mrs Smart's sister visited her mother, only to find the house filthy. Lucas, it transpired, had been taking Mrs Rich's money in order to buy beer and cigarettes. On finding him drunk, in bed with Becky, the pair was fired.

They were trying to hitch a lift out of town when they were picked up by the Reverend Reuben Moore, who ran a religious community nearby called the House of Prayer. Lucas and the 15-year-old Becky quickly became converts and joined the community, living in a converted chicken barn. Becky then seems to have had a genuine change of heart and to have become homesick. She wanted to go back to Florida, she told Lucas, who reluctantly consented, whereupon the two set off to hitchhike to her home state. They settled down with their blankets in a field at nightfall. It was a warm, June night. A row then broke out about Becky's decision to return home and she struck Lucas in the face. He retaliated by knifing her through the heart, after which he had sex with her corpse, cut up her body and scattered the dismembered pieces in the woods. Becky was, Lucas later claimed, the only woman whom he had ever loved.

Lucas returned to the House of Prayer, where he, too, then seems to have had some sort of change of heart. One Sunday he dropped in at Mrs Rich's house to give her a lift to church. During the journey she asked him where Becky was, whereupon Lucas pulled out a knife and stabbed her; she died instantaneously. He then drove to a piece of waste ground, where he undressed and raped her corpse before stuffing it into a drainage pipe that ran underneath the road. He subsequently returned, placing her body in a dustbin bag and then burning it in the stove at the House of Prayer.

Sheriff Bill F 'Hound Dog' Conway, of Montague County, Texas, had begun to have his suspicions about Lucas when he reappeared without Becky. Now it seemed that he was linked to the disappearance of another woman, Mrs Rich, and Lucas was accordingly hauled into the sheriff's office for questioning. Lucas was both a chain smoker and a caffeine addict, so Conway deprived him of cigarettes and coffee, but still Lucas refused to break, saying that he knew nothing about the disappearance of Kate Rich and that Becky had run off with a lorry driver who had promised to take her back to Florida. Conway finally had to release him.

Soon afterwards Lucas told Reverend Moore that he was going to look for Becky. While heading for Missouri he saw a young woman standing beside her car at a petrol station; holding a knife against her ribs he forced her into her car. They then drove south, towards Texas. When she dozed off

Lucas pulled off the road, intending to rape her. She awoke suddenly to find a knife at her neck, whereupon Lucas stabbed her in the throat, pushed her out of the car on to the ground and cut her clothes off her body. After he had raped her corpse he dragged it into a copse and took the money from her handbag. He abandoned her car in Fredericksburg, Texas, and then returned to the House of Prayer.

While he had been away Reverend Moore had told Sheriff Conway that Lucas had given Becky a gun for safekeeping. Because Lucas was a convicted felon who had therefore forfeited his right to bear arms under US law this was enough to justify his arrest. After taking him into custody Conway again deprived him of coffee and cigarettes and this time Lucas began to crack; he was later found hanging in his cell with his wrists slashed.

After having been patched up in the prison hospital Lucas was put in a special observation cell in the women's wing. On the next night he cracked completely, starting to yell in the early hours of the morning. When his jailer arrived Lucas claimed that the light in his cell was talking to him. The prison officer, Joe Don Weaver, who knew that Lucas had already smashed the bulb in his cell, told him to get some sleep. Later on during the night Lucas called the jailer again and confessed that he had done some pretty bad things. Weaver advised him to get down on his knees and pray, but instead Lucas asked for a pencil and paper.

Lucas spent the next half an hour writing a note to Sheriff Conway, which read 'I have tried to get help for so long and no one will believe me. I have killed for the past ten years and no one will believe me. I cannot go on doing this. I have killed the only girl I ever loved'. Lucas then pushed his confession through the peephole in the door of his cell. After reading it Weaver called Sheriff Conway, who plied Lucas with coffee and cigarettes upon his arrival and asked about the murders. Lucas said that he had seen a light in his cell that had told him to confess his sins and then told the sheriff that he had killed Kate Rich. Sheriff Conway and Phil Ryan, a Texas Ranger, later asked Lucas what had happened to Becky Powell. Tears flowed from his one good eye as Lucas told of how he had stabbed, raped and dismembered her. The story left the two hardened law officers feeling sick and wretched. 'Is that all?' asked Ryan wearily, half hoping that it was. 'Not by a long way', replied Lucas. 'I reckon I killed more than a hundred.'

On the next day the Montague County police began to investigate Lucas' story. Near the drainage pipe in which Lucas had temporarily hidden Mrs Rich's body they discovered some of her underclothes, as well as her broken glasses. At the House of Prayer they found burnt fragments of human flesh, along with charred bones. Lucas himself took them to the field in which he had killed Becky. There they found her suitcase, which was full of women's clothing and make-up. Her skull and other parts of her body were discovered in an advanced stage of decomposition in nearby woodland.

Lucas began to confess to other murders, too – often in breathtaking detail. These were also investigated and confirmed. A week after he had begun to confess Lucas appeared in court, where he was charged with the murders of Kate Rich and Becky Powell. When he was asked whether he understood the seriousness of the charges against him Lucas replied he did, then admitting to about a hundred other murders. The shocked judge could scarcely credit this behaviour and asked Lucas whether he had ever had a psychiatric examination. Lucas replied that he had, but commented 'They didn't want to do anything about it . . . I know it ain't normal for a person to go out and kill girls just to have sex'.

Lucas' sensational testimony made the headlines in every newspaper in the country. Police departments in each US state and county began to check their records, while Lucas' confession was also run through the computer at the newly formed National Center for the Analysis of Violent Crime.

Toole, it was discovered, was already in prison: he had been sentenced to 15 years' imprisonment for arson and was currently incarcerated in Springfield, where he had been regaling a cell mate with the gruesome tale of how he had raped, murdered, beheaded, barbecued and eaten a child named Adam Walsh. The police were now forced to take his lurid stories seriously. Indeed, both Toole and Lucas now began to admit their crimes freely. They confessed to a series of robberies of convenience stores, for example, saying that at one they had tied up a young girl who had had wriggled free, so Lucas had shot her in the head and Toole had had sex with her dead body.

Lucas was next taken on a 1,000-mile- (1,609-kilometre-) long tour of his murder sites. In Duval County, Florida, he confessed to eight unsolved murders. The victims had been women ranging in age from 17 to 80; some had been beaten, some strangled, some stabbed and others shot (Lucas claimed that the Hand of Death had said that he should vary his coup de grâce.) Near Austin, Texas, Lucas pointed to a building and asked whether it had once been a liquor store; on being told that it had Lucas confessed to having murdered its former owners during a robbery in 1979. Lucas then led the police to a field in the same county in which he had murdered and mutilated a girl called Sandra Dubbs – he even pointed out where her car had been found.

It transpired that Lucas and Toole had cruised the Interstate 35 motorway murdering tramps, hitchhikers, men who were also robbed of their money and old women who had been abducted from their homes. Over a period of five years they had killed more than 20 people up and down that highway alone. One of their victims was a young woman whose corpse was later found naked, except for a pair of orange socks, near Austin. She had been hitchhiking along Interstate 35 when Lucas had picked her up; according to Lucas she had refused to have sex with him, so he had strangled her and taken what he wanted. Although she was never identified it was for her murder that Lucas was sentenced to death.

Despite his subsequent withdrawal of his confession to the murder of Becky Powell and his plea of not guilty, Lucas was found guilty of the crime and sentenced to life imprisonment, in addition receiving four further life sentences, two sentences of 75 years each and one of 67 years, all for murder.

During his confession Lucas had told the police that Toole had poured petrol over a 65-year-old man before setting him alight; the pair had then hidden so that they could watch the fire engines arrive. The police identified the man as being George Sonenberg, who had died four days later. Until then they had assumed that the fire was an accident, but Toole freely admitted to the killing and furthermore claimed to have started hundreds of other fires. It was for this particularly horrific murder, however, that Toole was also sentenced to death.

Both Lucas and Toole enjoyed their brief period of notoriety and relished revealing the ghoulish details of their shocking crimes. Further information about the Hand of Death was not forthcoming, however.

13 ❖ Dennis Nilsen

Dennis Nilsen was Britain's most prolific serial killer. Sadly, of all of his 15 victims only one – a Canadian tourist – was missed; the rest were homosexual drifters who were looking for money, love or just a place to stay for the night.

Nilsen was born in Fraserburgh, a small town on the bleak, north-eastern coast of Scotland, on 23 November 1945. His father was a Norwegian soldier who had escaped to Scotland following the German invasion of his country in 1940 and had married Betty Whyte, a local girl, in 1942. The marriage did not work out, however, and Betty continued to live with her parents before the couple divorced a few years later.

Dennis grew up living with his mother, elder brother and younger sister, but the strongest influence on his young life was that of his stern and pious grandparents. Their faith was so strict that they banned alcohol from the house and regarded the radio and cinema as instruments of the devil. Nilsen's grandmother would furthermore not cook on Sunday – the Lord's day – and their dinner therefore had to be prepared on Saturday.

The young Nilsen was sullen and intensely withdrawn. The only person who could penetrate his private world was his grandfather, Andrew Whyte, Nilsen's hero. A fisherman, he would regale the little boy with tales of the sea and of those of his ancestors who had been lost beneath its churning waves. When Whyte died of a heart attack at sea in 1951 he was brought home and laid out on the dining-room table. Dennis, aged six, was invited to view his grandfather's body and thus got his first sight of a corpse. From that moment on the images of death and love were fused in his mind.

He left school at 15 and joined the army. After basic training he was transferred to the catering corps, where he was taught how to sharpen knives and to dissect a carcass. During his time in the army Nilsen had only one close friend, whom he persuaded to pose for photographs sprawled on the ground, as if he had been killed in battle. On one night in Aden the drunk Nilsen fell asleep in the back of a taxi. He woke to find himself naked and locked in the boot of the car. When the taxi driver appeared Nilsen played dead, but as the Arab manhandled him out of the boot Nilsen grabbed a jack and beat him around the head with it. Nilsen never knew whether he had killed the man, but after that he began having nightmares about being raped, tortured and mutilated.

After spending 11 years in the army Nilsen left to join the police force. Part of his training included a visit to a mortuary; the partially dissected corpses that he saw there fascinated him. Although he did well in the police force his private life was gradually disintegrating. Death became an obsession with him, and he liked to masturbate while pretending to be a corpse, lying naked in front of a mirror with blue paint smeared on his lips and his skin whitened with talcum powder. His incipient homosexuality also began to bother him. After 11 months in the police force he caught two men committing an act of gross indecency in a parked car; because he could not bring himself to arrest them he decided to resign.

He then went to work interviewing unemployed applicants for benefit at the Jobcentre in London's Charing Cross Road, becoming the branch secretary of the civil-service union and developing increasingly radical political views. His work was nevertheless good enough to earn him promotion to the position of executive officer at the Jobcentre in Kentish Town, north London.

Despite his professional progress Nilsen was lonely and yearned for a lasting relationship. He had been aware of his attraction towards other men since his teens, but had somehow managed to repress it while in the army and police force. In 1975 he met a young man called David Gallichen outside a pub, with whom he later moved into a flat at 195 Melrose Avenue, in the Cricklewood district of London, along with a cat and a dog called Bleep. Gallichen, or 'Twinkle', as Nilsen called him, stayed at home and decorated the flat while Nilsen went to work. They made home movies together and spent a lot of time drinking and talking. The relationship did not last, however, and when Gallichen moved out Nilsen was again plunged into a life of loneliness.

On New Year's Eve in 1978 Nilsen met a teenage Irish boy in a pub and invited him back to Melrose Avenue. They had been too drunk to have sex and when Nilsen woke in the morning the boy was lying fast asleep beside him. He was afraid that when the boy woke up he would leave, and Nilsen wanted him to stay.

Their clothes were thrown together in a heap on the floor. Nilsen lent over and grabbed his tie, wrapping it around the boy's neck and pulling it

Dennis Nilsen, who was infatuated with the corpes of his victims.

tight. The boy immediately awoke and began to struggle. They rolled on to the floor while Nilsen kept on pulling the tie. Although the boy's body went limp about a minute later, he was still breathing. After going into the kitchen and filling a bucket with water Nilsen took the bucket to the bedroom and held the boy's head under water until he drowned. Now he had to stay with Nilsen. He carried the dead boy into the bathroom and gave him a bath. He then dried the corpse lovingly, before dressing it in clean socks and underpants. For a while he lay in bed holding the dead boy; after that he put him on the floor and went to sleep.

On the following day he decided to hide the body under the floorboards, but *rigor mortis* had stiffened its joints, making it hard to handle. He therefore left the body as it was while he went to work. After the corpse had loosened up Nilsen undressed it and washed it again, this time masturbating beside it. He found that he could not stop playing with, and admiring, the boy's body. All the time that Nilsen was playing with the corpse he expected to be arrested at any moment, but no one came: it seemed that the dead boy had not been missed by anyone. After a week of living happily with the corpse Nilsen hid it under the floorboards; seven months later he cut it up and burnt it in the garden.

Nilsen's first experience of murder had frightened him. He was determined that it would not happen again and decided to give up drinking. But because he was lonely and liked to go to pubs to meet people he soon slipped off the wagon. Nearly a year later, on 3 December 1979, Nilsen met Kenneth Ockenden, a Canadian tourist, in a pub in Soho. Nilsen took the afternoon off work to join Ockenden on a sightseeing tour of London, after which Ockenden agreed to go back to Nilsen's flat for something to eat. After a visit to the off-licence they sat in front of the television eating ham, eggs and chips and drinking beer, whisky and rum. As the evening wore on disturbing feelings began to grow inside Nilsen. He liked Ockenden, but realised that he would soon be leaving to go back to Canada. A feeling of desolation swept over him – it was the same feeling that he had had when he killed the Irish boy.

Late that night they were both very drunk. Ockenden was listening to music through earphones when Nilsen wrapped the flex of the earphones around Ockenden's neck and dragged him struggling across the floor. When he was dead Nilsen took off the earphones and put them over his own ears. He then poured himself another drink and listened to records. He stripped the corpse in the early hours of the morning and carried it over his shoulder into the bathroom. When the body was clean and dry he placed it on the bed and went to sleep next to it.

Later that morning he put the body into a cupboard and went to work. In the evening he took out the corpse and dressed it in clean socks, underpants and a vest. He then took some photographs of it before arranging it next to him on the bed. For the next two weeks Nilsen would watch television in the evening while Ockenden's body was propped up in an armchair next to him. Last thing at night he would undress it, wrap it in some curtains and place it under the floorboards.

Because Ockenden had gone missing from a hotel his disappearance made the news for a few days. Nilsen was again convinced that he was about to be arrested at any moment – after all, people in the pub, on the bus and in the off-licence had seen them together. But when there was still no knock on the door Nilsen felt that he could pursue his macabre hobby unfettered. He began deliberately to seek out his victims, going to pubs where lonely, young homosexuals hung out, where he would buy them drinks, offer advice and invite them back to his flat for something to eat. Many accepted.

One of those who did was Martin Duffey, who, following a disturbed childhood, had run away from home and had ended up sleeping in railway stations in London. He went home with Nilsen and crawled into bed after drinking two cans of beer. When he was asleep Nilsen strangled him and then dragged his unconscious body into the kitchen, filling up the sink and holding his head under water for four minutes. After that Nilsen went through his now standard procedure of stripping and bathing the corpse before taking it to bed. He talked to it, complimenting it on its physique, kissing it and masturbating over it. Nilsen kept the corpse in a cupboard for a few days; when it started to swell he put it under the floorboards.

The 27-year-old Billy Sutherland, on the other hand, died because he was a nuisance: Nilsen hadn't fancied him, but after meeting him on a pub crawl Sutherland had followed him home. Nilsen later said that he vaguely remembered strangling him – there was certainly a dead body in the flat on the following the morning.

Nilsen did not even know the names of some of his victims. Indeed, he was not that interested in them – only in their bodies, their dead bodies. To him, their seduction and murder were sad, mechanical processes, but once they were dead they really turned him on: just touching a corpse would give him an erection.

Nilsen would go out to work as if all was perfectly normal, but when he got home in the evening he would retrieve his latest corpse from its hiding place and play with it. To him it was a thrill to own such a beautiful body and he would engage the corpse in a passionate embrace and talk to it. When he was finished he would stuff it under the floorboards again.

Some of his murders were terrifyingly casual. Nilsen came across one of his victims, the 24-year-old Malcolm Barlow, for example, after he had collapsed on the pavement on Melrose Avenue. Barlow was an epileptic and said that the pills that he was taking made his legs give way, so Nilsen carried him home and called an ambulance. When he was released from hospital the next day Barlow returned to Nilsen's flat. Nilsen prepared a meal and Barlow began drinking, even though Nilsen warned him not to mix alcohol with the new pills that he had been prescribed. When Barlow indeed collapsed Nilsen could not be bothered to call the ambulance again and therefore strangled him, after that carrying on drinking until it was bedtime. By now the space under the floorboards was full of corpses, so the following morning Nilsen stuffed Barlow's body into the cupboard under the sink.

As the place was full up Nilsen decided that it was time to move. There were six corpses under the floorboards; several others had been dissected and stored in suitcases. He decided that he had better dispose of the bodies first and after a stiff drink pulled up the floorboards and began cutting up the corpses. He hid the internal organs in the garden, where birds and rats dealt with them. The other body parts were wrapped in a carpet and thrown onto a bonfire; a tyre was placed on top to disguise the smell.

Nilsen then moved to an attic flat at 23 Cranley Gardens, in the London district of Muswell Hill, in a deliberate attempt to put a halt to his murderous career – he could not kill people, he reasoned, if he had no floorboards under which to hide their corpses and no garden in which to burn them. Indeed, although he had several casual encounters at his new flat, when he picked up men at night he let them go in the morning, unmolested. He was elated because he believed that he had finally broken the cycle of killing.

When, however, John Howlett – or 'Guardsman John', as Nilsen called him – came back to Cranley Gardens Nilsen could not help himself and strangled Howlett with a strap before drowning him. A few days later he strangled Graham Allen while he was eating an omelette. The death of his

Dennis Nilsen, being transported by maximum security.

final victim, Stephen Sinclair, a drifter and a drug addict, upset Nilsen. When they met Nilsen felt sorry for him and bought him a hamburger. Having gone back with Nilsen to Cranley Gardens, Sinclair slumped in a chair in a stupor and it was then that Nilsen decided to relieve him of the pain of his miserable existence. He first got a piece of string from the kitchen, but finding that it was not long enough he instead used his one remaining tie to choke the life out of his unconscious victim.

Killing at Cranley Gardens presented Nilsen with a problem: how to get rid of the bodies of his victims. With no floorboards or garden he was forced to dispose of the corpses by dissecting them, boiling the flesh from the bones, dicing up the remains and flushing them down the toilet. Unfortunately, the drains in Muswell Hill were not built to handle bodies and those at 23 Cranley Gardens had been blocked for five days when, on 8 February 1983, the drain-clearance company Dyno-rod sent Michael Cattran to investigate.

Cattran quickly determined that the problem was not inside the house, but on the outside. Locating the manhole that led to the sewers at the side of the house, he removed its cover and climbed in. At the bottom of the access shaft he saw a glutinous, grey sludge, which smelled awful. As he was examining it more sludge came out of the pipe that led from the house. He called his manager and told him that he thought that the substance that he had found had originally been human flesh.

On the following morning Cattran and his boss returned to the manhole, only to find that the sludge had vanished. No amount of rainfall could have flushed it away, which meant that someone must have gone down there and removed it. Cattran put his hand inside the pipe that connected the sewer to the house and pulled out some meat and four small bones. One of the tenants living in the house told them that they had heard footsteps on the stairs during the night and that they suspected that the man who lived in the attic flat had been down to the manhole. They then called the police.

Detective Chief Inspector Peter Jay took the flesh and bones that Cattran had recovered to Charing Cross Hospital, where a pathologist confirmed that the flesh was indeed human. The tenant of the attic flat was still at work when Jay visited Cranley Gardens, but when Nilsen returned at 5.40pm Jay met him at the front door and introduced himself, saying that he had come about the drains. Nilsen remarked that it was odd that the police should be interested in drains, prompting Jay to explain that the drains contained human remains. 'Good grief! How awful', exclaimed Nilsen. Jay told him to stop messing about and asked 'Where's the rest of the body?' After a short pause Nilsen replied 'In two plastic bags in the wardrobe next door. I'll show you'. He then pointed out the wardrobe to Jay, the smell that emanated from it confirming what he was saying. 'I'll tell you everything', Nilsen said. 'I want to get it off my chest, not here, but at the police station.'

The police could scarcely believe their ears when Nilsen admitted killing 15 or 16 men. In the wardrobe in Nilsen's flat, however, they found two large, black, dustbin bags, one of which held a shopping bag containing the left side of a man's chest, including the arm; a second shopping bag contained the right side of a chest and an arm. A third held a torso which had no arms, legs or head, while a fourth was full of human offal. The unbearable stench indicated that the bags had been closed for some time. In the second dustbin bag were two heads – one whose flesh had been boiled away, the other largely intact – and a torso, whose arms were still attached to it although the hands were missing. One of the heads belonged to Stephen Sinclair (Nilsen had severed it four days earlier and had started to simmer it in a pot on the kitchen stove). The police found Sinclair's pelvis and legs under a drawer in the bathroom. There was another torso in a tea chest in Nilsen's bedroom, along with a skull and more bones. The police also examined the garden at 195 Melrose Avenue, where they identified human ash and enough fragments of bone to determine that at least eight people, and probably more, had been cremated there.

Nilsen was eventually charged with six counts of murder and three of attempted murder. His solicitor had one simple question for Nilsen: 'Why?' 'I'm hoping you will tell me that', Nilsen replied.

Nilsen had intended to plead guilty, in order to spare the jury and the victims' families the details of his horrendous crimes, but his solicitor instead persuaded him to claim diminished responsibility. He was sentenced to life imprisonment, with the recommendation that he serve at least 25 years.

14 ❖ Jeffrey Dahmer

Like Dennis Nilsen, the Milwaukee mass murderer Jeffrey Dahmer kept the corpses of his victims lying around his home. He went one step further than Nilsen, however: in an effort to possess them more completely he began eating their flesh, reasoning that they would thus become a part of him and therefore stay with him forever.

Dahmer began his murderous career at the age of 18, at a time when his parents were going through an acrimonious divorce. Dahmer's father had already left home, his mother was away on holiday and Dahmer was alone in the house, feeling very neglected. He therefore went out to look for company and picked up a hitchhiker, a 19-year-old youth named Stephen Hicks who had spent the day at a rock concert. They got on well and Dahmer took Hicks back to his parents' house, where they had a few beers and talked about their lives. When Hicks said that he had to go Dahmer begged him to stay, but Hicks was insistent, so Dahmer made him stay by picking up a heavy dumbbell, clubbing him around the head with it and then strangling him.

Dahmer dragged Hicks' body into the crawl space under the house and dismembered it with a hunting knife (he had had plenty of practice because his childhood hobby had been dissecting animals). Even though he had wrapped Hicks' body parts in plastic bags the stench of rotting flesh soon permeated the house, so that night Dahmer buried them in a nearby wood. Becoming afraid that local children would find the grave, he then dug up them up again, stripped off the flesh and pulverised the bones with a sledgehammer before scattering the remains around his garden and the neighbouring property. It would be ten years before Dahmer would kill again.

After that Dahmer moved to Milwaukee to live with his grandmother. A loner, he hung out in gay bars. If another customer chatted him up he would slip drugs into their drink and they would often fall into a coma. Dahmer made no attempt to rape them – he was simply experimenting – but when the owner of the Club Bar ended up in hospital Dahmer was barred from it. In 1986 Dahmer was sentenced to a year's probation for exposing himself and masturbating publicly in front of two twelve-year-old boys. He claimed that he had been urinating and promised the judge that it wouldn't happen again.

Six days after the end of his probation period he picked up the 24-year-old Stephen Tuomi in a gay club and went to the Ambassador Hotel with him to have sex. When Dahmer awoke he found Tuomi lying dead; there was blood surrounding his mouth and bruising around his neck. Dahmer had been drunk the night before and realised that he must have strangled Tuomi; now he was alone with a corpse in a hotel room and at any moment a porter would be checking to see whether the room had been vacated. In a controlled state of panic he rushed out and bought a large suitcase, into which he stuffed Tuomi's body before taking it back by taxi to his grandmother's house, the taxi driver even helping him to drag the heavy case inside. Dahmer then cut up the corpse and put the pieces into plastic bags, which he left outside for the refuse collectors. (He performed this task so well that he left no traces at all: when police investigating the disappearance of Tuomi called at the house there was no sign of the body. Dahmer had got away with his second murder.)

Companionship, sex and death were now inextricably linked in Dahmer's mind. Four months later he picked up a young, male prostitute and went back with him to his grandmother's house to have sex in the basement. Dahmer then gave the boy a drink laced with a powerful sedative and when the young man was unconscious he strangled him. He then dismembered the corpse, stripped off the flesh, crushed the bones to powder and scattered the remains. Two months later Dahmer met an impoverished, 22-year-old homosexual and offered him money to perform in a video. Having agreed, the man had oral sex with Dahmer in his grandmother's basement. When it was over Dahmer offered him a drink, drugged and strangled him and finally disposed of the corpse.

Dahmer's grandmother began to complain about the terrible smell that persisted even after the rubbish had been collected; she also found a patch of blood in the garage. By way of explanation Dahmer said that he had been skinning animals there, an excuse that she accepted, although she made it clear that she wanted him to move out. Dahmer consequently found himself a small flat in a run-down, predominantly black, area. On his first night there he lured Keison Sinthasomphone, a 13-year-old Laotian boy, to the flat and drugged him. The boy managed to escape, however, and Dahmer was arrested. Charged with sexual assault and enticing a minor for immoral purposes, he spent a week in jail before being released on bail.

Dahmer could not control his compulsion to kill and while out on bail picked up Anthony Sears, a handsome, 26-year-old bisexual. Fearing that the police were watching his flat, he took Sears to his grandmother's basement instead. After they had had sex Dahmer drugged Sears and dismembered his body, disposing of his corpse in the rubbish, but keeping his skull as a souvenir.

In court the district attorney pushed for a sentence of five years' imprisonment for Dahmer's assault on Sinthasomphone. For his part, Dahmer's attorney argued that the attack was a one-off offence, continuing that his client was a homosexual and a heavy drinker who needed psychiatric help, not punishment. Dahmer was sentenced to five years on probation, as well as a year on a correctional programme. It did not help, however, for Dahmer was now set in his murderous ways.

After picking up a young stranger in a club he offered him money to pose for nude photographs. Back in Dahmer's flat the youth accepted a drink, which Dahmer had drugged. When he lapsed into unconsciousness Dahmer strangled and stripped him before performing oral sex on the corpse. He then dismembered the body, again keeping the skull, which he

Cannibalistic serial killer Jeffrey Dahmer during his trial.

painted grey. He picked up another notorious homosexual, known as the 'Sheikh', and did the same to him, except that this time he engaged in oral sex before drugging and strangling him.

His next victim, a 15-year-old boy who had accepted Dahmer's offer of $200 for posing in the nude, was luckier. Although the boy undressed Dahmer had neglected to drug him before attacking him with a rubber mallet; Dahmer then tried to strangle him, but the boy fought back. Eventually Dahmer calmed down, and after the boy had promised not to inform the police he let him go, calling him a taxi. When he went to hospital for treatment the next day, however, the boy broke his promise and told the police what had happened. But because he begged them not to let his foster parents find out that he was a homosexual they dropped the matter.

The next time that Dahmer picked up a victim, a few weeks later, he craved more than his usual formula of sex, murder and dismemberment, having decided to keep the skeleton and to bleach it with acid. Although he dissolved most of his victim's flesh in acid he left the biceps intact and stored them in the fridge. When his neighbours began to complain about the smell of putrefying flesh that was coming from Dahmer's flat he apologised, saying that his fridge was broken and that he was waiting to have it fixed.

Dahmer's next victim, the 23-year-old David Thomas, was not gay. Although he had a girlfriend and a three-year-old daughter he nevertheless accepted Dahmer's offer to come back to his flat for money. After drugging him Dahmer realised that he did not fancy his latest pick-up, but killed him anyway, fearing that Thomas might otherwise cause trouble when he woke up. This time he took more pleasure in the dismemberment process, photographing it step by step.

The 19-year-old Curtis Straughter, an aspiring model, was engaged in oral sex with Dahmer when the sleeping potion took effect. Dahmer strangled him and again photographed his dismemberment; his skull was also kept as a trophy. The 19-year-old Errol Lindsey's murder proceeded along exactly the same lines, Dahmer offering him money to pose for nude photographs before drugging, strangling and dismembering him. The grisly process was once again recorded photographically and his skull was added to Dahmer's collection. The 31-year old deaf-mute Tony Hughes also accepted $50 to pose in the nude and was duly murdered, but by this time Dahmer had become so blasé about the whole procedure that he kept Hughes' body in his bedroom for several days before cutting it up.

Dahmer's next victim was Keison Sinthasomphone's older brother, the

14-year-old Konerak. As in Keison's case, things went badly wrong for Dahmer, who, after drugging, stripping and raping the boy, went out to buy some beer instead of strangling him. On his way back to the flat Dahmer saw a naked and bleeding Konerak talking to two girls on the street. When Dahmer tried to grab him the girls hung on to Konerak; one of them had called the police and two patrol cars soon arrived.

The police wanted to know what the trouble was about and Dahmer claimed that he and Konerak had had a lover's tiff. He managed to convince them that the 14-year-old Konerak was really 19, and after taking them to his flat showed them Polaroids of Konerak in his underwear which seemed to back up his story that they were lovers. The police, however, did not realise that the photographs had been taken earlier that day, while Konerak was drugged. Throughout all of this Konerak sat passively on the sofa thinking that his ordeal was over. In fact, it had only just begun: the police accepted Dahmer's story and left, whereupon Dahmer immediately strangled and then dismembered the boy. (The three policemen in question were later dismissed.)

On one occasion Dahmer was returning home after attending Gay Pride Day in Chicago when he picked up another would-be model, Matt Turner. Turner was also strangled and dismembered at Dahmer's flat. On meeting Dahmer in a gay club the 23-year-old Jeremiah Weinberger asked his former roommate whether he should go with him, to which the roommate replied 'Sure, he looks okay'. Dahmer seems to have liked Weinberger, for they spent the whole of the next day together having sex. Then, when Weinberger looked at the clock and said that it was time that he went, Dahmer asked him to stay for just one more drink. His head ended up next to Turner's in the freezer.

When Dahmer lost his job he knew that one thing alone would make him feel better. He accordingly picked up a 24-year-old man called Oliver Lacy and took him back to his flat, where he strangled him and sodomised his corpse. Four days later the 25-year-old Joseph Bradeholt – who was married, with two children – accepted Dahmer's offer of money for nude photographs and willingly engaged in oral sex with him. His dismembered torso was left to soak in a dustbin filled with acid.

By the time that Dahmer had killed 17 men – all in much the same way – he was becoming so casual about murder that it was perhaps inevitable that he would be caught. On 22 June 1991 Dahmer met Tracy Edwards, a young man who had just arrived from Mississippi. He was with a number of friends, so Dahmer invited them all to his flat for a party. He and Tracy would go ahead in a taxi to buy some beer, he said, instructing the others to follow later. Edwards went along with this plan, but did not realise that Dahmer was giving his friends the wrong address.

When he got there Edwards found that he did not like Dahmer's flat: it smelled funny and there was also a fish tank in which Dahmer kept some Siamese fighting fish. As Dahmer told lurid tales about the fish fighting each other to the death Edwards glanced nervously at the clock as he sipped his cold beer. After he had finished the beer Dahmer gave Edwards a drugged drink of rum and coke. When Edwards became drowsy Dahmer put his arms around him and whispered that they would go to bed. Within an instant Edwards was wide awake and telling Dahmer that it was all a mistake and that he had to be going. Before he knew it, however, his hands had been handcuffed and Dahmer was poking a butcher's knife at his chest while ordering him to undress. Realising the seriousness of the situation, Edwards knew that he had to humour the man, to make him relax, and slowly unbuttoned his shirt.

Dahmer then suggested that they go into the bedroom, and escorted Edwards there at knife point. The room was decorated with Polaroid photographs of naked young men; there were also pictures of dismembered bodies and chunks of meat. The smell in the room was sickening; the putrid aroma seemed to be coming from a plastic dustbin under the window. Edwards thought that he could guess the rest.

Dahmer wanted to watch a video with his captive friend, so they sat on the bed and watched *The Exorcist*. The gruesome film made Dahmer relax, while Edwards was frantically thinking of ways in which to escape. If Edwards did not comply with his requests, Dahmer then threatened, he would rip out his heart and eat it. Next he told Edwards to strip so that he could photograph him in the nude. As Dahmer reached for the camera Edwards seized his opportunity and punched Dahmer in the side of the head. When Dahmer crumpled up Edwards kicked him in the stomach and ran for the door. Dahmer managed to catch up with him and offered to unlock the handcuffs, but Edwards ignored him, wrenching open the door and running for his life.

Halfway down 25th Street Edwards spotted a police car and ran over to it, yelling for help. Once inside the car he explained to the policemen that a maniac had tried to kill him and directed them to Dahmer's flat. The door was answered by a well-groomed man who seemed calm and composed; the police began to have doubts about the story that Edwards had told them – that is, until they noticed the strange smell.

A contrite-looking Dahmer admitted that he had threatened Edwards, explaining that he had just lost his job and had been drinking. But when the police asked for the key to the handcuffs he refused to hand it over and became violent, whereupon the policemen pushed him into the flat and forced him to lie face down on the floor while they read him his rights. Then they began to look around the flat, one of them opening the fridge door. 'Oh my God,' he exclaimed, 'there's a goddamn head in here.' Dahmer began to scream like an animal and the police rushed outside to get some shackles with which to restrain him. After that they began their search of the flat in earnest.

They ascertained that the fridge contained meat – including a human heart –in plastic bags. There were three human heads in the freezer. A filing cabinet contained grotesque photographs, three human skulls and a collection of bones. Two more skulls were found in a pot on the stove. Another pot contained male genitals and severed hands, while the remains of three male torsos were found in the dustbin in the bedroom.

At the police station Dahmer seemed almost relieved that his murderous spree was over. He made a detailed confession and admitted that he had now reached the stage at which he was cooking and eating his victims' bodies.

Dahmer's cannibalism and necrophilia were the cornerstones of his plea of insanity, but the district attorney pointed out to the jury that if Dahmer were found to be insane and sent to a mental hospital his case would be reviewed in two years' time, further explaining that if he was then found to be sane he could be released. The jury found Jeffrey Dahmer guilty of 15 murders, for which he received 15 life sentences.

15 ✦ The Candy Man

The Texan town of Houston's Candy Man, the killer Dean Corll, did not realise that he was homosexual until he was drafted into the army at the age of 25. After being discharged 11 months later he went back to work in his mother's sweet factory. Although he was late in recognising the true nature of his sexuality he quickly learnt how to exploit his personal situation and began giving sweets to local boys, also being in a position to hire any boys that he fancied. Furthermore, his mother covered up for him; when one boy complained about Corll's sexual advances she sacked him. For their part, the other teenagers on the workforce made sure that they were never left alone with Corll.

At around that time Corll met a 12-year-old boy called David Brooks, who had a deeply insecure background. Brooks liked Corll, considering him to be good and generous (Corll paid him $5 a time for oral sex.) By the time that Brooks was 15 he was using Corll's flat as his second home. Corll lived in the run-down Heights area of Houston, in which children were always short of money and often high on drugs, making things easy for a predatory homosexual like Corll. Even after the sweet factory closed down Corll continued to be known as the kind man who gave sweets to children; the boys also knew that he gave away money in return for oral sex.

Corll seems to have committed his first murder during this period, for it is thought that he picked up and took home Jeffrey Konen, a 21-year-old student at the University of Texas who disappeared while hitchhiking. Konen's body was discovered three years later on High Island Beach (which later became one of Corll's favourite body-dumping grounds). It was so badly decomposed that forensic experts were unable to determine the cause of death. It was certainly murder, however, because the body was found bound hand and foot.

In 1970 Brooks visited Corll's flat, where he found two dead, naked boys strapped to a board. Corll, who was also naked, explained that he had killed the boys during sex and offered Brooks a car if he kept quiet. From then on Brooks, who was soon seen driving around in a green Corvette, acted as Corll's accomplice, helping to lure boys to Corll's flat, where Corll would rape and kill them while Brooks looked on. Brooks found the whole business highly lucrative, for Corll seemed to have an insatiable desire for young boys and penetrated them anally before strangling them. 'He killed them because he wanted to have sex and they didn't want to', Brooks later explained.

Corll developed a taste for double murders. In December 1970, for example, he picked up the 14-year-old James Glass and the 15-year-old Danny Yates when they were on their way back from church. Glass already knew and liked Corll and had visited his flat before. On this occasion, however, he and his friend ended up being tied to the board before being raped and strangled. Six weeks later the same fate befell the 17-year-old Donald Waldrop and his 13-year-old brother, Jerry.

Then, on 29 May 1971, the 13-year-old David Hilligiest and his friend, the 16-year-old George Winkie, vanished while on their way to the swimming pool. They had been seen together getting into Corll's white van. Although their disappearance was reported the police showed no interest in following up these cases and – like the others who had disappeared before them – listed the two missing boys as runaways. This was not good enough for David Hilligiest's parents, however, who had posters printed offering a $1,000 reward for information about their son's whereabouts. One of the boys who distributed the posters was Wayne Henley, a lifelong friend of David Hilligiest.

Later that summer the Hilligiests' younger son, the 11-year-old Greg, revealed that he had once played an exciting game called poker with David, Wayne Henley and David Brooks, who had once worked at the neighbourhood's sweet factory. David Hilligiest had gone missing once before, his parents then recalled. On that occasion they had found his bike outside the sweet factory and had discovered David inside with the manager, Dean Corll, a nice man who had given him sweets. They still did not put two and two together, however.

It later transpired that sometime before David Hilligiest went missing David Brooks had taken Wayne Henley to meet Corll, guessing that he could be potential victim. Corll, however, had quickly realised that Henley was a popular boy, and also that he would do anything for money. He soon began paying Henley $200 a time to deliver his friends to him. Henley would sit in the car while Corll cruised the district offering young boys a lift. With one teenager in the car already they felt that it was safe to get in, but would then be driven to Corll's flat to be raped and killed.

Henley soon took over from Brooks as Corll's major source of supply. He subsequently admitted to being present at the murders of at least nine boys and furthermore confessed to killing one himself. Henley had shot the boy in the head, he said, but his victim had not died immediately. When he had looked up at Henley and had said 'Wayne, why did you shoot me?', Henley had pointed the gun at him and had shot him again. Henley had also played an active role in the murder of the 18-year-old Scott Mark, who, unlike the younger boys, was no pushover. Mark had grabbed a knife and had tried to stab Corll, but Corll had disarmed him. Henley had then seized Corll's pistol and had aimed it at Mark while Corll strangled him.

Between them Henley and Brooks regularly supplied Corll with victims aged between nine and twenty. Corll continued to rape and kill the boys singly, as well as in pairs; he sometimes also castrated his victims. The local people were becoming increasingly concerned about their missing children, but still the police did nothing. Indeed, Corll's killing spree only came to an end when Henley made a near-fatal mistake and brought Corll a girl instead of a boy.

Henley had comforted the 14-year-old Rhonda Williams after her boyfriend, the 18-year-old Frank Aguirre, had gone missing (he was another of Corll's victims). She soon considered herself to be Henley's girlfriend and the two decided to run away together. This suited Corll, who was becoming tired of murder and was planning to go straight.

Corll now had a regular boyfriend, Guy, whom he had picked up in a public lavatory before taking him back to his flat, where they had become lovers. When Guy had expressed interest in a locked room in the flat Corll had vowed that he would never take Guy into it and nothing more was said. Corll also had a girlfriend called Betty Hawkins, whom he had been dating on and off for five years; she had two children, who called Corll 'Daddy'. Corll promised Betty that he would finish with Guy and they then planned to move to Colorado together.

Henley and Rhonda had planned to run away together on 17 August 1973, but Rhonda could not wait and left home nine days early, on 8 August, to join Henley. Henley had invited a friend named Tim Kerley to a paint-sniffing party that was being held at Corll's flat on that night and had no choice but to take Rhonda along. When they arrived Corll was furious: 'You weren't supposed to bring a girl', he yelled.

Corll eventually calmed down and they soon began to get high by sniffing acrylic paint that had been sprayed into a paper bag. Within an hour they had all passed out. When Henley awoke he found that he had been handcuffed and bound; the other two youngsters had been tied up as well, and Kerley was naked. Corll was now furious again: 'I'm going to kill you,' he told Henley, 'but first I'm going to have my fun'. He then dragged Henley into the kitchen, holding a .22 pistol against his stomach. This was the moment that Henley had long feared would happen: he had always believed that Corll would kill him one day, in order to get his hands on Henley's 14-year-old brother, Ronnie.

Having procured victims for Corll for two years Henley understood him well and knew how to sweet-talk him. He therefore said that he would be willing to participate in the rape and murder of the other two: Henley would rape Rhonda while Corll had Kerley. Corll agreed to this suggestion and released Henley. They then carried their bound victims into the bedroom, where Corll turned up the radio in order to drown the sound of any screams. Next he gave Henley a knife and ordered him to cut away Rhonda's clothing. After that Corll set about raping Kerley, but when Kerley began to struggle Rhonda grew distressed. 'Why don't you let me take her out of here?' Henley asked Corll. 'She doesn't want to see that.' But Corll ignored him, so Henley grabbed Corll's pistol and told him that they were going. 'Go on Wayne, kill me, why don't you?' taunted Corll, whereupon Henley pulled the trigger and hit Corll in the head with a bullet, causing him to stagger forward a few paces. When Henley fired again Corll fell through the bedroom door and Henley then emptied the clip full of bullets into his back.

After he had untied the other two they called the police. When they arrived Henley admitted to killing Corll and the others vouched for him – after all, he had done it to save them, they believed. A chance remark of Henley's alerted the police to the true story, however: he had told Kerley that if he hadn't been his friend he would have got $1,500 for him. The police then found a 17-inch- (43-centimetre-) long dildo in Corll's flat, along with other tools of the sadist's trade. Inside his white Ford van they also discovered rings, hooks and lengths of rope.

When questioned about all of this Henley confessed that he had taken money from Corll in return for procuring boys for him, furthermore admitting that he and Corll had also killed boys. There were a lot of them buried in a boat shed that Corll had hired three years earlier, Henley volunteered, later helpfully taking the police to it. Inside they found some possessions belonging to the missing boys, as well as bags of lime. They then started digging up the floor and soon the naked bodies of 17 boys were revealed. They had been bound and gagged; their genitals had sometimes been buried separately; and there were also body parts that did not belong to any of the 17 victims. Henley then told the police that more bodies were buried around Lake Sam Rayburn, as well as to the south, at High Island Beach. Twenty-three bodies were found in all; although Henley said that two more bodies were buried on the beach they were never located.

Brooks was surrendered to the police by his father. When Henley saw him he told him that he had confessed and warned him that if he, Brooks, did not do the same he would recant and blame everything on him. Brooks then admitted everything, too.

Twenty-seven bodies had been discovered by the time that the police abandoned the search, but both the extra body parts and the frequency of killing indicated that there were probably at least six or seven more. Forty-two boys were missing from the district in all, although some of them may have been genuine runaways.

The trials of Wayne Henley and David Brooks took place in San Antonio, Texas, in June 1974. Their insanity pleas were rejected and Henley was found guilty of nine murders – not including that of Dean Corll – and sentenced to 594 years' imprisonment. Brooks was found guilty of just one count of murder and was given a life sentence.

16 ❖ Wayne Gacy

Like Dean Corll, John Wayne Gacy, Jr also discovered that he was a homosexual relatively late in life. He was 22, and a married man, when, in 1968, he lured a youth into the back room of the fast-food franchise that he was operating. After handcuffing him he tried to bribe him to perform oral sex; when the youth refused Gacy tried to sodomise him, but his victim escaped. The young man reported Gacy to the police, who arrested him. After having been sentenced to ten years' imprisonment he became a model prisoner, who, because he had no history of serious crime, was released after 18 months. He then moved to Chicago, where he set up a construction firm.

Within a year of his release Gacy picked up another youth and tried to force him to have sex. Although he was again arrested the case against him was dropped when the young man did not turn up in court. Gacy then pulled a gun on another youth, who had approached him asking for work, and threatened to shoot him if he did not consent to sex. The youth called his bluff, even though Gacy had said that he had killed people before (this was true), and managed to leave unmolested. In fact, Gacy had already taken a number of teenage boys back to his home, where he had held them captive and sexually abused them over a number of days. When he had tired of them he had murdered them.

US mugshot of
John Wayne
Gacy.

In 1977 Gacy was accused of having sexually abused a youth at gunpoint. Although Gacy admitted having engaged in brutal sex with the boy he claimed that the youth had been a willing participant who was now trying to blackmail him. The police accepted his story and Gacy was released with a caution.

By this time Gacy was both a successful contractor and a leading light in the local Democratic Party who furthermore provided entertainment at children's parties by dressing up as a clown. He also hung out at notorious gay bars and in 1978 met the 27-year-old Jeffrey Rignall at one of these hangouts. Having invited the young man to share a joint with him in his car, once inside the Oldsmobile Gacy held a chloroform-soaked rag soaked over Rignall's face.

Rignall awoke to find himself naked in Gacy's basement, strapped to a device that resembled a pillory. Gacy, who was also naked, then showed Rignall a number of whips, along with more sinister sexual devices, and explained how he intended to use them. Gacy furthermore told Rignall that he was a policeman and that he would shoot him if he raised any objections. Gacy's subsequent abuse and torture of Rignall went on for hours. At times it was so painful that Rignall begged to die, but Gacy would then chloroform him again and wait until he had come round before starting again. Eventually Rignall promised that he would leave town without telling anyone what had happened to him.

Having blacked out again, Rignall later woke up to find himself fully dressed and lying in Chicago's Lincoln Park. Although there was money in his pocket his driver's licence was missing. He checked into a hospital, where it was discovered that he was not only bleeding from the anus, but also that his face and liver had been damaged by chloroform. Although sympathetic, the police had nothing to go on: Rignall could not give them the name, address or licence-plate number of his abuser.

Rignall remained determined to exact his retribution on his attacker. Renting a car, he followed the route along which he thought Gacy had driven him, which he vaguely remembered having registered through a haze of chloroform. On identifying the motorway exit that Gacy had taken he waited patiently there until he eventually saw Gacy's black Oldsmobile sweep by. Having noted down its licence-plate number he then followed the car, which Gacy parked in the driveway of 8213 West Summerdale Avenue. Rignall subsequently checked the land-registry records and discovered that the house in question belonged to John Wayne Gacy, Jr. He then took everything that he had uncovered to the police.

When they followed up Rignall's leads the Chicago Police Department ascertained that Gacy's suburban home was outside their jurisdiction, which therefore meant that they could not press felony charges against Gacy. For his part, Gacy agreed to give Rignall $3,000 towards his medical bills and the matter was then dropped.

Later that year Mrs Elizabeth Piest made a report to the local police saying that her 15-year-old son, Robert, had gone missing. He had been looking for a summer job and had said that he was going to visit a contractor who lived nearby. The neighbourhood pharmacist had then ventured that the contractor concerned must be Gacy, who had recently given him an estimate for the refurbishment of his shop.

The police phoned Gacy, who denied all knowledge of the missing boy. (In fact, Robert Piest was lying dead on Gacy's bed as they spoke.) On checking their records the police then discovered Gacy's earlier conviction for sodomy and went to see him. However, when Gacy refused to accompany them to the police station to discuss the matter they realised that they had no charge on which to hold him. After his house was put under 24-hour surveillance Gacy nevertheless managed to place Piest's body in a trunk and smuggle it into his car. He then jumped behind the wheel and raced off at top speed, leaving the police standing. Having lost his tail Gacy drove to the nearby Des Plaines river and dropped Piest's body into it. The police then obtained a search warrant, but the only potential clue that they found in Gacy's house was a receipt from a chemist that had been made out to Robert Piest. It wasn't much, but it was enough to justify continuing their surveillance of Gacy.

Gacy, however, was becoming cocky and one morning invited two of the policemen who had been stationed outside his house to join him inside for breakfast. As they sat down to eat the policemen noticed a peculiar smell, which they investigated. It turned out that Gacy had inadvertently switched off the pump that drained the basement and that the water that had flowed under the house as a result had disturbed the soil in which Gacy had buried 29 of his victims, which, armed with another warrant, the police subsequently disinterred. Another four bodies – including that of Robert Piest – were found in the Des Plaines river. The youngest of his victims had been nine, while the oldest had been fully grown men.

John Wayne Gacy, Jr was convicted of mass murder in 1980. Despite his known homosexuality, when he was on death row Gacy received fan mail from women who said that they admired him because he was a deviant and that they loved the excitement of a wild fight. Gacy died by lethal injection in 1994.

17 ❖ The Butcher of Hanover

The Butcher of Hanover – who was also known as the Werewolf of Hanover and the Vampire of Hanover – killed at least 27, and possibly as many as 50, young boys. He killed them by biting out their throats, after that selling their flesh to unwitting consumers on the black market that flourished in Germany following the end of World War I. When one woman grew suspicious about the origins of the joint of meat that she had bought she was told by the police that she should be grateful for finding such a fine piece of pork in these difficult times.

The Butcher of Hanover was a degenerate homosexual named Fritz Haarmann. Haarmann had had a difficult upbringing: his mother, whom he adored, had become an invalid soon after he was born, while his father was a mean and moody locomotive stoker, nicknamed 'Sulky Olle', who had tried to have his son committed to a mental institution on the grounds that he was feeble-minded.

Like many other serial killers, Haarmann started out as a petty criminal. As a youth, he wandered around Germany supporting himself by means of petty theft, swindling and picking pockets. For pleasure, however, he took to child-molesting. Other crooks regarded him as a simpleton who tried hard to please, and he developed a reputation among policemen for laughing when he was arrested.

Haarmann sat out World War I in jail. Following the crushing defeat of Germany, when the war ended he was released into a country that had been broken by the ravages of four years' war: families had been destroyed, the cities were full of homeless refugees and the country was in a state of near famine. To a man like Haarmann, this desperate situation presented a business opportunity that was not to be missed.

Posing as a policeman, Haarmann preyed upon the rootless young drifters who congregated around Hanover's main railway station. He would be there every night, offering cigarettes and chocolate to the new arrivals and then luring them back to his grim lodgings on the Kellerstrasse with the promise of a mattress for the night. Here Haarmann seduced or raped his victims before killing them.

Unaware of the fate of the boys who ended up in his care, the welfare workers at the station began to regard Haarmann as one of their team. The police were aware of his history of petty crime, but Haarmann was proving himself to be a useful informer. No one questioned the source of the second-hand clothes that he sold and his keenly priced joints of meat were sought after.

In September 1918 the parents of a 17-year-old youth reported that their son had gone missing and that he had been seen in the company of Haarmann. The police reluctantly questioned their useful informant, only to eliminate him from their inquiries. Six years later, at his trial, Haarmann boasted 'When the police examined my room the head of the boy was lying wrapped in newspaper behind the oven'.

This close shave with exposure merely served to convince Haarmann that he was unstoppable, and in September 1919 he teamed up with another homosexual degenerate, Hans Grans. Together they transferred their expanding operation to a flat on Neuestrasse. Although he was 20 years Haarmann's junior, Grans was nevertheless the dominant partner in the relationship, treating Haarmann little better than he would a servant and making sure that he took all the risks. It was Grans who picked out the pair's victims, once even instructing Haarmann to murder a boy 'because I like the clothes he's wearing'. (It has been calculated that during this period they were disposing of two victims every week through the black-market trade in meat.)

They executed their grisly business undetected for six years, a period that may well have lasted longer, for many of their victims were homeless and no one reported them missing. Furthermore, because of the economic chaos that existed in Germany at the time, the authorities were obliged to turn a blind eye to the black market. Haarmann and Grans became amazingly lax, however, carting around buckets of blood in front of their neighbours, for example, or chopping up bodies within earshot of other people before dumping the remains in the river Leine.

On 17 May 1924 some children found a human skull on the banks of the Leine. It would be the first of many, but at the time the police issued a statement saying that it had been put there by medical students as a sick joke; the statement did little to quell public fears. A pile of human remains was then discovered by a group of children playing in a meadow, and more than 500 human bones were subsequently found in the river. The newspapers now began writing about the 'Werewolf of Hanover' and one writer went so far as to claim that 600 people had disappeared in the city in the course of that year.

On 22 June 1924 Haarmann was arrested for trying to molest a boy in the street, whereupon the police searched his flat. Although its walls were spattered with blood and it was full of his victims' belongings, Haarmann protested that he was a butcher who also traded in second-hand clothes. The parents of children who had gone missing were invited to the flat to examine the clothes that had been found there, but no one recognised anything until one mother noticed that the son of Haarmann's landlady was wearing a coat that used to belong to her boy. It was only then Haarmann broke down and confessed everything.

Haarmann and Grans were jointly charged with the murders of 27 boys aged between 12 and 18. During their 14-week-long trial one newspaper wrote

Nearly two hundred witnesses had to appear in the box, mostly parents of the unfortunate youths. There were scenes of painful intensity as a poor father or mother would recognise some fragment or other of the clothing or belongings of their murdered son. Here it was a handkerchief, there a pair of braces, and again a greasy coat, soiled almost beyond recognition, that was shown to the relatives and to Haarmann. And with the quivering nostrils of a hound snuffling his prey, as if he were scenting rather than seeing the things displayed, did he admit at once that he knew them.

When the picture of one young boy was held up by the prosecution Haarmann revealed the depth of his callousness by turning to the boy's father and saying 'I should never have looked twice at a boy as ugly as your son'.

In court, Haarmann admitted to killing 30, or possibly even 40, youths – 'I really can't remember the exact number', he said. When the counsel for the prosecution asked how he had killed his victims Haarmann replied 'I bit them through their throats'. It was then that the newspapers began calling him the 'Vampire of Hanover'.

When he was found guilty, on 19 December 1924, Haarmann screamed at the judge and jury

Do you think I enjoy killing people? I was ill for eight days after the first time. Condemn me to death. I ask only for justice. I am not mad. It is true I often get into a state when I do not know what I am doing, but that is not madness. Make it short, make it soon. Deliver me from this life, which is a torment. I will not petition for mercy, nor will I appeal. I want to pass just one more merry evening in my cell, with coffee, cheese and cigars, after which I will curse my father and go to my execution as if it were a wedding.

Haarmann got his wish and was beheaded on the following day. His accomplice, Grans, however, served only 12 years in jail.

18 ❖ The Yorkshire Ripper

Peter Sutcliffe, the Yorkshire Ripper, picked up where his namesake, Jack, left off, like him (or her) specialising in killing prostitutes. By the time that he was caught 20 women had been savagely attacked, 13 brutally murdered and a whole community was living virtually under siege. During a reign of terror that spanned nearly six years he managed to elude the biggest police squad that has ever been assembled in Britain to date with the aim of capturing one man.

It started on 30 October 1975, when a Leeds milkman on his rounds saw a shapeless bundle lying on a bleak recreation ground. He went over to investigate and found a woman sprawled on the ground, her hair matted with blood and her body exposed. Her jacket and blouse had been torn open, her bra was rucked up and her trousers had been pulled down, below her knees. There were 14 stab wounds in her chest and stomach. The milkman did not see the massive wound on the back of her head that had actually caused her death. Having been attacked from behind, two vicious blows had been delivered with a heavy hammer, smashing her skull; the stab wounds had been inflicted after she was dead.

The body belonged to a twenty-eight-year-old mother of three, Wilma McCann, who had regularly hitchhiked home after spending nights on the town. She had died just 100 yards (91 metres) from her home, a council house in Scott Hall Avenue. Post-mortem blood tests showed that she had consumed 12 to 14 measures of spirits on the night of her death. Although her clothes had been interfered with, her knickers were still in place and she had not been raped. There therefore seemed to have been no overt sexual motive for her murder. Her purse, however, was missing, so in the absence of any other discernible motive the police regarded her murder as a callous by-product of robbery.

This opinion was reassessed, however, when a second killing occurred in Chapeltown (the red-light district of Leeds) three months later. Not all of the women who worked in the area were professional prostitutes: some women sold sex in order to earn some extra cash; others, such as the 42-year-old Emily Jackson, were enthusiastic amateurs who sold their bodies primarily for fun. Emily lived with her husband and three children in the respectable Leeds suburb of Churwell. On 20 January 1976 she and her husband went to the Gaiety pub on Roundhay Road, a popular venue with both Chapeltown irregulars like Emily and their prospective clients. After leaving her husband in the main lounge she went searching for business. An hour later she was seen in the car park getting into a Land Rover. At closing time her husband finished his drink and took a taxi home alone; his wife, he assumed, had found a client for the night.

Emily Jackson's body was found the next morning huddled under a coat on open ground. Like Wilma McCann, although her breasts had been exposed she was still wearing her knickers. She, too, had been killed by two massive blows to the head that had been inflicted by a heavy hammer. Her neck, breasts and stomach had been stabbed over 50 times, her back had been gouged with a Phillips screwdriver and the impression of the heavily ribbed sole of a size 7 Wellington boot was stamped on her right thigh (this was the only real clue). The post mortem indicated that Emily had had sex before the attack, although not necessarily with her murderer. Once again, there seemed to be no clear motive for the killing.

Over a year later, on 5 February 1977, the 28-year-old part-time prostitute Irene Richardson left her tawdry rooming house in Chapeltown half an hour before midnight in order to go dancing. On the following morning a jogger running through Soldier's Field, a public playing field a short car ride from Chapeltown, saw a body lying slumped on the ground. It turned out to be that of Irene Richardson. Because she was lying face down the three massive blows that had shattered her skull were obvious. Her skirt and tights had been torn off, her coat had been draped over her buttocks and her calf-length boots had been removed from her feet and lay neatly across her thighs. Her neck and torso were studded with knife wounds. The post mortem indicated that she had not had sex before her death and that she had died only 30 minutes after leaving her lodgings.

Following the murder of Irene Richardson the police were able to link the three cases: they were plainly the work of a serial killer. Parallels with the Jack the Ripper quickly sprang into the public imagination, and the murderer of Wilma McCann, Emily Jackson and Irene Richardson soon became known as the 'Yorkshire Ripper'.

It was obvious that the Yorkshire Ripper was preying on prostitutes in Leeds, so the working women of Chapeltown moved in droves to Manchester, London and Glasgow, while those who could not afford to travel so far from home began plying their trade in nearby Bradford. The York-shire Ripper's next victim, Patricia 'Tina' Atkinson, however, was a Brad-ford girl who lived in Oak Lane, just around the corner from the city's thriving red-light district. On the evening of 23 April 1977 Tina went to her local pub, The Carlisle, for a drink with friends and reeled out shortly before closing time. When nobody saw her the next day it was assumed that she was at home, sleeping off the effects of the previous night.

The following evening some friends visited her flat and found the door unlocked. Inside, they discovered her covered with blankets lying dead on her bed. It seemed that she had been attacked as she had entered the flat. Four hammer blows had smashed in the back of her head and she had then been flung on to the bed, after which her clothes had been pulled off. She had been stabbed in the stomach seven times and the left side of her body had been slashed to ribbons. There was also a size 7 Wellington-boot print on the sheet.

The footprint belonged to Peter Sutcliffe, who believed that he was on a moral crusade to rid the streets of prostitutes. The eldest of John and Kathleen Sutcliffe's six children, he was born in Bingley, a dour-looking town 6 miles (10 kilometres) north of Bradford. A timid child and later an inscrutable young man, he had always been regarded as something of an outsider. Being small and weedy he had been bullied at school and clung to his mother's skirts. Although his younger brothers had inherited their father's appetite for life, the opposite sex and the consumption of large quantities of beer, Peter liked none of these things. Despite taking no inter-est in girls, as an adolescent he spent hours preening himself in front of the bathroom mirror and later took up body-building.

After leaving school at 15 he took a job as a grave-digger at a cemetery in Bingley and regularly joked about having 'thousands of people below me where I work now'. During his three years as a grave-digger he devel-oped a macabre sense of humour. He once pretended to be a corpse, for example, lying down on a slab, throwing a shroud over himself and making moaning noises when his workmates appeared. For their part they called him 'Jesus', because of his biblical-looking beard. At his trial Sutcliffe claimed that he had heard the voice of God while working at the cemetery. He said that he had been digging a grave when he had heard a voice ema-nating from a cross-shaped headstone telling him to go out on to the streets and to kill prostitutes.

Despite the youthful Sutcliffe's good looks girls were not attracted to him. His first proper girlfriend was Sonia, a 16-year-old schoolgirl whom he had met in his local pub who suffered from the same type of introversion as Sutcliffe. On Sundays they would sit lost in conversation in the front room of her house. She would speak to other members of the Sutcliffe family only when it was absolutely unavoidable.

As a devout Catholic Sutcliffe was devastated when he learned that his mother was having an affair with a neighbour, a local policeman. His father arranged for all of his children – including Sutcliffe, who was accompanied by his bride-to-be, Sonia – to be present at a Bingley hotel to witness a humiliating confrontation with his wife. Having arrived at the bar believing that she was meeting her boyfriend, only to be greeted by her husband and children, Kathleen was then forced to show the family the new nightdress that she had bought for the tryst. This incident was particularly painful for Sutcliffe, who had earlier discovered that Sonia also had a secret boyfriend. Later in the same year, 1969, Sutcliffe carried out his first-known attack, following a row over a £10 note hitting a Bradford prostitute over the head with sock containing a stone. Psychiatrists later said that the discovery of his mother's affair had triggered his psychosis.

After a courtship lasting eight years Sutcliffe and Sonia were married. After spending the first three years of their married life living with Sonia's parents they then moved to a large, detached house in Heaton (a middle-class suburb of Bradford), which they kept immaculate.

On the evening of Saturday, 25 June 1977 Sutcliffe gave his wife a lift to the Sherrington nursing home where she worked at nights. With his neighbours, Ronnie and Peter Barker, he then went on a pub crawl around Bradford, ending up at the Dog in the Pound. At closing time they went to get some fish and chips. It was well past midnight when Sutcliffe dropped the Barker brothers at their front door, but instead of parking his white Ford Corsair outside his house Sutcliffe drove off down the main road, towards Leeds. At around 2am, illuminated by the street lights of Chapeltown Road, he saw a young woman wearing a gingham skirt. As she passed the Hayfield pub and turned left, down Reginald Terrace, Sutcliffe parked his car, got out and began to follow her down the quiet side street.

The next morning a girl's body was found lying next to a wall by a group of children on their way to a nearby adventure playground. She had been struck on the back of the head, dragged for 20 yards (18 metres) and then hit twice more. She had also been stabbed once in the back and repeatedly through the chest – the trademarks of the Yorkshire Ripper were unmistakable. But the victim had not been a prostitute: Jayne McDonald was only 16 and had just left school to work in the shoe department of a local supermarket. On the night of her death she had been out with friends in Leeds and was on her way back to her parents' home (which was just a few hundred yards from where her body was found) when she was attacked.

The murder of a teenage girl gave the investigation new impetus. By the September of 1977 the police had interviewed almost 700 local residents and had taken 3,500 statements, many of them from prostitutes who worked in the area.

Two weeks after the killing of Jayne McDonald the Yorkshire Ripper savagely attacked Maureen Long on some waste ground near her home in Bradford. By some miracle she survived, but her description of her assailant was too vague to be of help to the inquiry.

The investigation's staff was subsequently increased to 304 full-time officers, who had soon interviewed 175,000 people, taken 12,500 statements and checked out 10,000 vehicles. Their main problem was that they had no idea of the type of man for whom they were looking. It is furthermore doubtful whether anyone would have suspected the long-distance lorry driver Peter Sutcliffe. The 31-year-old was a polite and mild-mannered neighbour, a hard-working and trusted employee, a good son and a loyal husband. He was the sort of man who did jobs around the house or tinkered with his car at weekends. Nothing about him suggested that he was a mass murderer, and those who knew him would even have been surprised if they had seen him picking up prostitutes, although that was what he regularly did.

On Saturday, 1 October 1977 Jean Jordan climbed into Sutcliffe's new, red Ford Corsair near her home in Moss Side, Manchester. She took £5 in advance and then directed him to some open land 2 miles (3 kilometres) away that was used by prostitutes when entertaining their clients. They were a few yards from the car when Sutcliffe smashed a hammer on to Jean's skull, hitting her again and again – 11 times in all. He then dragged her body into some bushes, but before he could proceed further another car arrived and he made a quick getaway.

As he drove back to Bradford Sutcliffe realised that he had left a vital clue on his victim's body: the £5 note that he had given Jean was brand new; it had come directly from his wage packet and could therefore link him to the dead woman. He waited nervously for eight long days. During that time, however, nothing appeared in the press about Jean's body having been found, so he risked returning to Moss Side to try to recover the £5 note. Despite a frantic search he could not find Jean's handbag, and in his frustration he started to mutilate her body with a broken pane of glass. He even tried to saw off her head in an attempt to remove his hammer-blow signature, but the glass was not sharp enough to sever her spine. In the end he gave up, kicked the body several times and then drove home.

On the following day an allotment-owner discovered Jean's naked body. The damage to her head had rendered her unrecognisable and there was no evidence among her scattered clothing with which to identify her. (She was eventually identified from a fingerprint on a lemonade bottle that she had handled before leaving home for the last time.) The police did, however, find the £5 note and immediately set about tracing it. Over the next three months they interviewed five-thousand men, one of whom was Sutcliffe, but when the detectives saw Sutcliffe's well-appointed house they discounted him from their inquiries.

Sutcliffe's next victim was the 18-year-old Helen Rytka, who shared a miserable room next to a flyover in Huddersfield with her twin sister, Rita. Both were prostitutes who worked as a pair in the red-light district around Great Northern Street. Because the Yorkshire Ripper's murders had scared them they had devised a system which they hoped would keep them safe. Basing themselves outside a public lavatory, when one sister was picked up separately the other wrote down the number of the client's car; after giving their clients precisely 20 minutes they then returned to the lavatory. Ultimately, however, this system went terribly wrong.

On the snowy night of Tuesday, 31 January 1978 Helen returned to their usual rendezvous five minutes early. At 9.25pm a bearded man in a red Ford Corsair offered her the chance of making a quick £5, which she accepted, thinking that she could perform her services quickly and be back at the rendezvous before Rita returned.

Helen took her client to the nearby Garrard's timber yard. Because two men were already there Sutcliffe could not kill her straightaway and instead had sex with her in the back of the car. By the time that they had finished the men had gone, so as Helen got out of the back seat to return to the front of the car Sutcliffe swung at her with his hammer, but missed, hitting the door of the car. His second blow, however, struck her on the head and he then hit her five more times until the walls of the foreman's shed, which was just a few feet away, were spattered with blood. After that Sutcliffe dragged Helen's body into a woodpile and hid it. Her bra and black, polo-neck pullover had been pushed above her breasts; although she was still wearing her socks the rest of her clothes were scattered over a wide area. Her black-lace knickers were found pinned to the shed door by a lorry driver the next day.

Rita, who had waited for her sister at the lavatory, was desperately worried when she did not appear, but her fear of the police prevented her from reporting Helen's disappearance for three days. It was a police Alsatian that found the hidden body; Helen had been horribly mutilated and there were three gaping wounds in her chest, where she had been repeatedly stabbed.

The Yorkshire Ripper's latest victim had disappeared from a busy street, and the police later traced over a hundred passers-by, eliminating all but three cars and one stocky, fair-haired man from their inquiries. Although they appealed on the radio to any wife, mother or girlfriend who suspected that they were living with the Ripper to come forward no one did.

A few weeks later a passer-by spotted an arm sticking out from under an overturned sofa on wasteland in Bradford's red-light district. After initially thinking that it belonged to a tailor's dummy the putrid aroma that emanated from it sent him rushing to a telephone. The body was that of the 22-year-old Yvonne Pearson, a high-class prostitute who serviced the rich-businessmen trade in most of Britain's cities. She had been murdered two months earlier, ten days before Helen Rytka, and the killing bore all of the hallmarks of the Yorkshire Ripper. A hammer blow to the head had smashed her skull. Her bra and pullover had been pulled up, exposing her breasts, and her chest had been repeatedly jumped on. Her black, flared trousers had been tugged down and some of the sofa's horsehair stuffing had been rammed into her mouth.

Friends reported that Yvonne had spoken of her fear of the Yorkshire Ripper only days before she had disappeared. On the night of her death she had left her two daughters with a neighbour and was seen climbing into a car driven by a bearded man with black, piercing eyes shortly after 9.30pm. Sutcliffe had killed her with a hammer on wasteland in nearby Arthington Street and had then dragged her body to the abandoned sofa, jumping on her corpse until her ribs cracked. Although he had hidden her body the police deduced that the killer had become concerned when it had not been found because he had later returned in order to make it more visible, tucking a copy of the *Daily Mirror*, dated four weeks after her death, under her arm.

Two months after Yvonne Pearson's body was found the Yorkshire Ripper attacked the 41-year-old Vera Millward. A Spanish-born mother of seven children, Vera had come to England following World War II as a domestic worker. She lived with a Jamaican man and had resorted to prostitution in Manchester's Moss Side in order to earn money to help to support her family. On the night of Tuesday, 16 May 1978 she left home for the Manchester Royal Infirmary to get painkillers to ease her chronic stomach pains. She died in a well-lit part of the hospital grounds, Sutcliffe hitting her three times on the head with a hammer and then slashing her across the stomach. Her corpse was discovered by a gardener the next morning, lying on a rubbish pile in the corner of the car park.

Three months later the police again visited Sutcliffe, this time because his car-registration number had cropped up during checks carried out in Leeds and Bradford. They subsequently returned to question him about the tyres on his car. (They were looking for treads that matched the tyre tracks found at the scene of Irene Richardson's murder 21 months earlier.) As always, Sutcliffe was helpful and unruffled, giving them absolutely no reason to suspect him. Indeed, they didn't even think it worth asking Sutcliffe what his blood group was – the Yorkshire Ripper's was rare – or for his shoe size, which was unusually small for a man.

Suddenly the Yorkshire Ripper's killing spree stopped: for 11 months there were no more murders. The police speculated that he had committed suicide, taking his identity to the grave with him. It was all eerily similar to the disappearance of Jack the Ripper 90 years earlier.

Sutcliffe was not dead, however, nor could he suppress his desire to murder for much longer. On the night of Wednesday, 4 April 1979 he drove to Halifax, getting out of his car at around midnight and accosting the 19-year-old Josephine Whitaker as she walked across Savile Park playing fields. They spoke briefly, and as they moved away from the street lights he smashed in the back of the head with a hammer and dragged her body into the shadows. Her body was found the next morning.

In common with Jayne McDonald, Josephine Whitaker was not a prostitute. She lived at home with her family and worked as a clerk at the headquarters of the Halifax building society. After her murder no woman felt safe on the streets of Yorkshire after dark.

Two weeks before Josephine Whitaker died a letter arrived at Bradford's police station; it was postmarked Sunderland and dated 23 March 1979. The letter said that the next victim would not be killed in Bradford's Chapeltown district because it was 'too bloody hot there' as a result of the efforts of the 'curserred coppers'. This odd misspelling so closely aped Jack the Ripper's notes that it should have rung warning bells, but the police believed it to be genuine. Handwriting experts confirmed that it had been written by the same person who had sent two previous letters purporting to come from the Yorkshire Ripper. This one furthermore mentioned that Vera Millward had stayed in hospital, information that the police (wrongly) believed could only have been gleaned from Vera herself. On this basis they concluded that the writer of the three letters was indeed the Yorkshire Ripper.

Traces of engineering oil had been found on one of the letters and similar traces were now discovered on Josephine Whitaker's body. Next the police called a press conference asking members of the public to come forward with any information that they might have about anybody who could have been in Sunderland on the days on which the letters were posted. Although the response was overwhelming it ultimately produced merely more useless information that had to be checked, analysed and filed.

Then, on the morning of 18 June 1979, two months after Josephine Whitaker's death, a buff-coloured envelope, addressed in the same handwriting as the previous letters that the Yorkshire Ripper had allegedly sent, arrived at the police station. The envelope contained an audio cassette on to which had been recorded a 257-word message delivered in a broad Geordie accent. A huge publicity campaign was mounted and the public was invited to dial up and listen to the 'Geordie Ripper tape' in the hope that someone might recognise the voice. Within a few days more than 50,000 people had called in. Language experts had confirmed that the accent was genuinely Wearside and had pinned it down to Castletown, a small, tightly knit suburb of Sunderland. Eleven detectives were consequently installed in a Sunderland hotel and a hundred officers combed the town. Although only 4,000 people lived in Castletown the police could still not find their man – a cruel hoaxer who had a cast-iron alibi. The identity of the Geordie Ripper remains a mystery to this day.

In July 1979 Detective Constable Laptew again visited Sutcliffe, whose car had by now been spotted in the red-light district of Bradford on 36 separate occasions. Laptew became increasingly suspicious of Sutcliffe, but because the police force's attention was focused on the Geordie Ripper tape at that time his report was not followed up and Sutcliffe therefore remained free to return to Bradford to dispatch his eleventh victim.

On Saturday, 1 September 1979 Sutcliffe was cruising the streets around Little Horton, a residential area of Bradford, when, at about 1am, he saw Barbara Leach, a student, moving away from a group of friends outside the Manville Arms. He attacked her when she was just 200 yards (183 metres) from the pub, dragging her into a back yard before stabbing her eight times. He then stuffed her body into a dustbin and slung an old carpet over it; it was discovered the following afternoon.

Two high-ranking officers from Scotland Yard were sent to Yorkshire, but made no progress. Although a police task force from Manchester reviewed the £5-note inquiry and narrowed the field down to 270 suspects it, too, could get no further.

Like everyone else in Yorkshire Sutcliffe spoke to his family and friends about the Ripper. He made a point of picking up Sonia from work in order to protect her and was later reported to have told a workmate 'Whoever is doing all these murders has a lot to answer for'. On one occasion his colleagues at the depot even made a bet that Sutcliffe himself was the Yorkshire Ripper, at which he laughed, but said nothing.

The Yorkshire Ripper now took another break from killing, which lasted for nearly a year. Then, on Thursday, 18 August 1980, he struck for the twelfth time. His victim was Marguerite Walls, a 47-year-old civil servant who had been working late at the Department of Education and Science in Leeds that evening, leaving at 10pm to walk home. Her body was discovered two days later, under a mound of grass clippings in the garden of a magistrate's house. She had been bludgeoned and strangled, but because her body had not been mutilated the police did not at first realise that she was another of the Ripper's victims.

Three months later, after he had just finished eating a chicken dinner, Sutcliffe saw Jacqueline Hill, a language student at the University of Leeds, getting off the bus outside a Kentucky Fried Chicken fast-food restaurant. His fingers were still greasy from his supper when he viciously struck her down before dragging her body to some waste ground behind the shops and attacking it savagely. Death had befallen Jacqueline so suddenly that one of her eyes had remained open, and Sutcliffe now stabbed it repeatedly with a rusty Phillips screwdriver that he had sharpened into a fine point.

The Home Office appointed a special squad with which to try solve the case, but only six weeks after Jacqueline Hill's murder it reached the same conclusion as had the West Yorkshire police force – it had no idea of how to crack the case. What it needed was a bit of luck.

On 2 January 1981 Sergeant Robert Ring and Police Constable Robert Hydes started their evening shift by cruising along Melbourne Avenue, in Sheffield's red-light district. On seeing Olivia Reivers climbing into a Rover V8 3500 they decided to investigate. The driver – a bearded man – identified himself as Peter Williams. After saying that he did not want any trouble he scrambled out of the car and asked if he could relieve himself. When the policemen agreed he went over to the bushes that lined the street and dropped a ball-peen hammer and sharp knife from a special pocket in his car coat while pretending to urinate. The policemen did not notice him doing this while Olivia Reivers was remonstrating loudly with them, complaining that they were ruining her livelihood.

By the time that the man strolled back to his car, however, the police had discovered that the car's number plates were false. He was accordingly taken to the police station, where he admitted that his name was really Peter William Sutcliffe. During his interview Sutcliffe said that his main concern was that the police would tell his wife that he had been picked up with a prostitute. Otherwise he was calm and forthcoming and readily confessed that he had stolen the number plates from a scrapyard in Dewsbury. He was even allowed to go to the lavatory alone, where he hid a second knife in the cistern.

There was no concrete reason to suspect Sutcliffe of being the Yorkshire Ripper, but the police working on the case had so little to go on that when any man was caught with a prostitute his details had to be forwarded to the West Yorkshire police before he could be released. Sutcliffe was thus locked up for the night before being taken, unprotesting, to a Dewsbury police station the next morning. In Dewsbury Sutcliffe proved himself to be a chatty and eager interviewee. Indeed, he was so full of himself that he made two fatal mistakes: in passing, he mentioned that he had been interviewed by the Yorkshire Ripper Squad about the £5 note and that he had also visited Bradford's red-light district.

The Dewsbury police next called the Yorkshire Ripper Squad in Leeds, where Detective Sergeant Des O'Boyle discovered that Sutcliffe's name had come up several times during the course of the investigation. Having driven to Dewsbury, when O'Boyle called his boss, Detective Inspector John Boyle, in Leeds that evening, he told him that Sutcliffe's blood group was B – the rare blood group that the police knew the Ripper shared. Sutcliffe was accordingly locked into his cell for a second night.

Meanwhile, Sergeant Ring had heard one of his colleagues casually mentioning that the man whom he had arrested was being interviewed by detectives from the Yorkshire Ripper Squad. After rushing back to Melbourne Avenue he found the ball-peen hammer and knife that Sutcliffe had hidden in the bushes. Sonia Sutcliffe was furthermore questioned and their house was searched. Early in the afternoon of the next day O'Boyle told Sutcliffe that they had found a hammer and knife in Sheffield, whereupon Sutcliffe, who had been talkative up to this point, fell silent. 'I think you're in trouble, serious trouble', said O'Boyle. Sutcliffe finally spoke: 'I think you are leading up to the Yorkshire Ripper', he said. O'Boyle nodded. 'Well,' said Sutcliffe, 'that's me.'

Sutcliffe's confession took almost 17 hours to complete. He said that he had begun killing after a Bradford prostitute had cheated him out of £10 in 1969. (He mentioned nothing about hearing a voice from God at that stage.)

Sixteen weeks later Sutcliffe stood trial at the Old Bailey. The Crown Prosecution Service's barrister, the defence counsel and the attorney general, Sir Michael Havers, had all agreed that Sutcliffe was mentally ill, and that he was suffering from paranoid schizophrenia. The presiding judge would have none of this, however, and told both counsels that the jury would listen to the evidence and then decide whether Sutcliffe was a murderer or a madman.

Sutcliffe pleaded guilty to manslaughter. During his testimony he remained calm and self-assured, even managing a laugh when he recalled that when he was questioned about the size 7 Wellington boot-print stamped on Emily Jackson's thigh and Tina Atkinson's sheet the policeman who had been interviewing him had not noticed that he was wearing the boots in question. He also claimed that he had been acting on instructions from God to 'clean the streets' of prostitutes.

The jury found Sutcliffe guilty of 13 murders and he was sentenced to life imprisonment, with the recommendation that he should serve at least 30 years.

19 ❖ Jack the Stripper

The file on Jack the Ripper has never been closed. Neither has the file on Jack the Stripper – even though Scotland Yard is sure that it knows who killed six women in 1964 and early 1965 and left their naked bodies lying along the bank of the river Thames.

The police found the first body under a pontoon at Hammersmith on 2 February 1964. The victim had been strangled and the remnants of her underwear had been shoved down her throat; she was small, at 5 foot 2 inches (1.60 metres) tall, and was naked, apart from her stockings.

The body was identified as being that of Hannah Tailford, who was 30 years old and lived with her boyfriend in the West Norwood district of London. She had a three-year-old daughter and an eighteen-month-old son and was pregnant again. She was employed as a waitress and a cleaner and supplemented her meagre wages by working as a prostitute on the streets of Bayswater (her record showed four convictions for soliciting). She had disappeared from her flat ten days before her body was found, although a couple had seen her on Charing Cross Road only two days before that. She had appeared depressed and suicidal and they had tried to cheer her up, they said.

Forensic experts concluded that she had been dead for just 24 hours when her corpse was found and believed that she may have been drowned in a bath or pond before she was dumped in the river. Tide tables showed that she must have been dropped in the Thames at Duke's Meadow, in Chiswick, a popular spot with prostitutes and their clients. The police discovered that Hannah had been a star turn at sex parties and that she had often attended kinky orgies in Mayfair and Kensington. A foreign diplomat known for his perverted tastes had been one of her clients, but he had been out of the country at the time of her disappearance.

This gave the police little to go on. Although they believed that Hannah had been attacked and sexually assaulted (her knickers having been shoved into her mouth to stop her from screaming as she was killed) they could not even prove that she had been murdered. The inquest into her death recorded an open verdict.

On 8 April 1964 the naked body of the 26-year-old Irene Lockwood was found among the tangled weeds and branches on the river bank at Duke's Meadow. Irene was a pretty, young redhead who, like Hannah, had also worked on the streets of Bayswater and Notting Hill and had attended kinky parties, too (she had furthermore performed in blue movies). Both girls had solicited cab drives late at night and both had been pregnant when they died.

It was impossible to determine how either Hannah or Linda had died, although marks on the back of Irene's head indicated that she could have been attacked from behind. Like Hannah, the police believed that Linda had been killed elsewhere and then brought to Duke's Meadow. The police also suspected that both girls had been mixed up in a blackmail racket. They had found an address book and photographic equipment in Hannah's flat, while Irene's flatmate, Vicki Pender (who had been found battered to death a year earlier), had once been beaten up after trying to blackmail a client who had been photographed with her without his knowledge. The most striking similarity between the two killings, however, was that the victims were found naked; there was no sign of their clothes, which were never discovered.

On 24 April 1964 another naked female corpse was found, this time in an alleyway off Swyncombe Avenue in nearby Brentford, Middlesex. The victim, the 22-year-old Helen Barthelemy, had been strangled, probably from behind. Strangely enough, three of her front teeth had been extracted after her death. It was also established that she had been stripped of her clothes post mortem; fresh tyre marks in the alley furthermore indicated that she had been killed elsewhere and then dumped there.

Helen was also a prostitute. Educated in a convent, she had later become a stripper in Blackpool. She had served a prison sentence in Liverpool for luring a man into a trap, after which he had been robbed. She had then come to London, where she had gone on the game. She was known to cater for any sort of perversion, but would often entertain local black men for free because they were more sympathetic to her than her kinky clientele. One Jamaican man admitted having been with her on the night of her disappearance, but because he had a strong alibi he was quickly ruled out as a suspect.

The newspapers soon picked up on the story of the three similar killings, and because the victims' nudity was the most sensational aspect the tabloids dubbed their murderer 'Jack the Stripper'.

On reviewing its records Scotland Yard identified another case that matched Jack the Stripper's *modus operandi*. On 8 November 1963, three months before Hannah's murder, the body of the 22-year-old Gwynneth Rees had been found buried in a shallow grave in an ash tip near Chiswick Bridge. She was naked, except for one stocking, and had been sexually assaulted. The body had lain there since May or June of 1963 and it was thought that she may have been sunbathing when she was attacked. The police concluded that she had been another victim of Jack the Stripper.

Kenneth Archibald, a 24-year-old caretaker, then walked into Notting Hill's police station and confessed to the murder of Irene Lockwood. (He was already a suspect because his cart had been discovered in Irene's flat.) He said that he had met her in a pub on the night of the murder, after which they had quarrelled over money on some open land near Barnes Bridge. He had lost his temper, he said, and after placing his hands around her throat to stop her from screaming he had accidentally strangled her. When she was dead he had taken off her clothing and had rolled her into the river. Then he had taken her clothes home and had burned them.

Archibald said that he knew nothing about the murders of Hannah Tailford, Helen Barthelemy or Gwynneth Rees, however. Although he was charged with the murder of Irene Lockwood, when he appeared in the Old Bailey he retracted his confession, and as there was no other evidence against him the jury acquitted him.

The forensic scientists paid special attention to Helen Barthelemy's body, which had not been buried, like that of Gwynneth Rees, and had not come into contact with water. It was, however, filthy, as if it had been stored somewhere dirty before being dumped. A minute examination of the corpse's skin showed that it was covered from head to toe in tiny flecks of paint and it was therefore concluded that Helen's naked body had been kept near a spray-painting shop.

It was clear that the man who had killed Helen Barthelemy and the others sought the company of prostitutes in the Bayswater area. The police next organised an amnesty for women working on the streets in that area and appealed to any who had ever worried about odd or eccentric clients – especially those who had made them strip naked – to come forward. The women's response was overwhelming. Policewomen posing as prostitutes were also sent out on to the streets.

On 14 July 1964 another body was found. At around 5.30am a man who was driving to work down Acton Lane had to brake hard in order to miss a van that was speeding out of a cul-de-sac. He subsequently called the police and at the end of the cul-de-sac, outside a garage, they found the naked body of Mary Flemming.

The murdered girl had again been a prostitute who had worked in the Bayswater area. As with Helen Barthelemy, her clothes had been removed after her death and there were tiny flecks of paint all over her body. It furthermore appeared that before being dumped her body had been kept for approximately three days after her killing. Mary had been warned of the dangers of continuing to work the streets which Jack the Stripper was prowling and had taken to carrying a knife in her handbag. It had done her no good, however, for she had been attacked from behind, like the Stripper's other victims. No trace of her handbag, knife or clothes were ever found.

By this time Scotland Yard had interviewed 8,000 people and taken 4,000 statements, but it was still no nearer to finding the culprit. Plainclothes policemen now blanketed the area in which the murdered girls had worked, but despite their presence the body of the 21-year-old Margaret McGowan was found lying on some rough ground in Kensington on 25 November 1964. Margaret had been a prostitute and an associate of the society pimp Dr Stephen Ward (who stood trial during the Profumo scandal). Her naked body had lain on the open ground for at least a week when it was found, but before that the forensic scientists believed that it had been stored somewhere else. She had been strangled and her skin was also covered in tiny flecks of paint. The hallmarks of Jack the Stripper were unmistakable..

On the evening on which she had gone missing Margaret and a friend had been in the Warwick Castle, a pub on the Portobello Road, where they had talked about the murders. Margaret had then met a client and she and her friend had gone their separate ways. Her friend gave a good enough description of Margaret's client for the police to issue an Identikit picture of the man, but no one answering the description was ever identified. The police also noticed that Margaret's jewellery was missing, but a check on all the local pawn shops drew a blank.

Although Christmas and New Year passed uneventfully, on 16 February 1965 the naked body of the 28-year-old Bridie O'Hara was found lying in the bracken behind a depot in Acton. In common with the Stripper's previous victims she was short – 5 feet 2 inches (1.60 metres) tall – and worked as a prostitute. Along with her engagement and wedding rings her clothes were nowhere to be found (and never were). The corpse was furthermore covered with minute flecks of paint. This time, however, there was a new clue: one of her hands was mummified, which meant that it had been kept near a source of heat, which had dried out the flesh.

Scotland Yard now threw all of its resources into the case and ordered every business premises within an area of 24 square miles (62 square kilometres) to be searched for samples of paint that matched the flecks on the victims' bodies. The police also worked out that all of the Stripper's victims had been picked up between 11pm and 1am, their bodies being disposed of between 5 and 6am. They concluded that the murderer was therefore a night worker, probably a night watchman who guarded premises near a spray-painting shop. In addition, they speculated that he was a man of about 40 who had a highly charged libido and curious sexual tastes.

The police now dismissed a theory that had been put forward earlier, which held that the culprit was on a crusade against prostitution. They instead believed that because he could not satisfy his bizarre sexual requirements at home he turned to the prostitutes who would do anything for money. The detectives felt sure that the man went into a frenzy during orgasm, which resulted in the women's deaths. He could not help himself, they guessed, and had thus learned to accept that murder was the price that he had to pay for his sexual satisfaction.

This was not much to go on, but the police nevertheless held regular press conferences at which they stated that a list of suspects had been drawn up which they were working their way through. The killer would soon be behind bars, they promised. In fact, although the police had no such list and were not nearly as confident as they pretended, they felt that this strategy was the best way in which to keep putting pressure on the culprit.

The murders coincided with a ten-week cycle, and the police were determined to prevent the next one. They therefore threw a cordon around a 20-square-mile (52-square-kilometre) area of central London and recorded every vehicle that entered or left it at night. Anyone who was found to have moved in or out of the zone on more than three occasions was traced, the police then visiting their home under the pretext of investigating a traffic accident (in order to avoid embarrassing those who had been where they were not supposed to have been). The suspect was then interviewed out of his family's earshot.

Weeks of searching at last paid off when a perfect match was made between the paint flecks on the victims' bodies and paint found under a covered transformer at the rear of a spray-painting shop in the Heron Factory Estate in Acton. (The transformer itself also generated enough heat to mummify any flesh that was left near it.) Every car entering or leaving the estate was then logged and all 7,000 people living in the vicinity were interviewed. At specially convened press conferences the police announced that the number of their suspects was being whittled down to three, then two, and finally one. Once again, these statements were not true, but it is likely that the strategy behind the press conferences worked.

In March 1965 a quiet, family man who lived in south London killed himself, leaving a suicide note that said that he could not 'stand the strain any longer'. At the time the police took little notice of the man's death. By June 1965, however, they had concluded that Jack the Stripper had not struck again – the ten-week cycle had been broken – and because they wanted to know why he had stopped killing they began investigating the suicides that had occurred since the murder of Bridie O'Hara in January 1965. They discovered that this particular suicide victim had worked at a security firm at night. Despite an intensive search of his house and extensive interviews with members of his family no evidence linking him directly to the murders was ever found. Nevertheless, the killings seemed to have stopped and from the circumstantial evidence alone the police were convinced that the man had been Jack the Stripper.

By July 1965 the murder inquiry had been scaled down, to be wound up in the following year. In 1970 Scotland Yard announced that the south London suicide had been Jack the Stripper. It never named him, however, and, indeed, the file on the Jack-the-Stripper case remains officially open.

20 ❖ The Co-ed Killer

One young man's irrepressible sexual appetite – he killed young women and mutilated their bodies for his sexual pleasure – terrorised a small town in the US state of Michigan for more than two years. After he was caught he showed no remorse and was convicted of only one murder, and then only by the flimsiest forensic evidence.

At about 9pm on a warm Sunday in June 1967 Mary Pleszar, an attractive, brunette student, was walking down a street in the small, university town of Ypsilanti when a car pulled over beside her and a young man leaned out to speak to her. An onlooker assumed that he was offering her a lift which she appeared to refuse, whereupon the car drove off. After turning at the next corner, moments later it sped past the girl again and drove into a private driveway. By this time Mary had reached her block of flats and was safe – or so she thought.

On the following day Mary's flatmate phoned her parents to say that Mary had not come home. Concerned, they called the police, who proved unhelpful: Mary was 19 and students often stayed out all night at parties or with boyfriends, they said, to which her parents protested that their daughter was not that sort of girl. On the day after that the police issued a missing-person's report on Mary. Although a witness who responded to it said that he had seen the young man who had offered Mary a lift he was unable to give a detailed description of the youth or of the car that he was driving.

Four weeks later two boys came across a fly-covered mass of rotting meat – which they took to be a deer's carcass – near a secluded lover's lane 2 miles (3 kilometres) north of Ypsilanti. A pathologist subsequently identified it as being human flesh, and more specifically the corpse of a young woman who had been stabbed in the chest more than 30 times. An extensive search of the area failed to uncover the victim's clothes, but the searchers did find one sandal close to the corpse, which Mary's parents identified as belonging to their daughter. Fresh tyre tracks were also found beside the body.

At the funeral home where Mary's body was lying prior to burial the young man was seen again. Having asked the receptionist if he could take a photograph of the body as a memento for his parents the receptionist had replied that that was impossible; it was only when he was going out of the door that she noticed that he was not carrying a camera.

Almost exactly a year later Joan Schell, a 20-year-old art student, left her flat (which was just three streets away from where Mary had once lived) to spend the night with a girlfriend in nearby Ann Arbor. Her flatmate accompanied her to the bus stop, where they waited for three-quarters of an hour. Then a red car pulled up and a young man, who was wearing an East Michigan University sweatshirt, asked if they wanted a lift. Joan was suspicious at first, but because were two other men in the back of the car she thought that she would be safe enough. As she climbed

John Norman Collins arriving for his trial, 1969.

into the car she told her flatmate that she would phone her when she arrived in Ann Arbor. She never called.

Five days later Joan's body was discovered rotting in a storm drain. Her blue mini-skirt and white slip had been pulled up, round her neck, and she had been raped and then stabbed to death. Although she had been dead for almost a week the pathologist noted that her body had been in the storm drain for less than a day.

Extensive inquiries revealed that Joan had been seen walking with a young man on the evening on which she went missing. The witnesses could not be certain, but thought that the youth was John Norman Collins, a fine football and baseball player, an honours student and a devout Catholic – in short, a regular, all-American boy. He had a troubled background, however: his father had abandoned his family soon after his son was born and his mother's second marriage had lasted for only a year; her third husband, who adopted John and his older brother and sister, was an alcoholic who beat his wife. Unbeknown to the police, Collins was suspected of stealing $40 from his fraternity house, as well as of other petty thefts. Although he lived directly opposite Joan, when the police interviewed him he claimed that he did not know her.

Ten months later a thirteen-year-old schoolboy saw a suspicious-looking shopping bag in a cemetery. After telling his mother about it she accompanied him to the spot where he had found it, there discovering a girl's body hidden under a yellow raincoat; her skirt had been pulled up and her tights rolled down. The corpse was that of the 23-year-old Jane Mixer, a law student who had been reported missing a few hours earlier. The man whom the press was now calling the 'Co-ed Killer' had struck again.

Four days after that the body of the sixteen-year-old Marilyn Skelton was found lying in a patch of undergrowth. She had been brutally beaten and a tree branch had been jammed into her vagina. The urges that were driving this sexually obsessed serial killer were plainly becoming more urgent, and the police feared that he would soon kill again. Sure enough, three weeks later the corpse of the thirteen-year-old Dawn Basom was discovered lying amongst some weeds. The youngest victim yet, she was wearing only a white blouse and a bra, which had been pushed up around her neck; the rest of her clothes had been strewn over a wide area. She had been strangled with a length of electric flex and her breasts had been repeatedly slashed.

On 9 June 1969 three teenage boys found the body of a girl in her twenties near a disused farmhouse. She had been shot in the head and repeatedly stabbed; her clothes were scattered around her. Pathologists established that she had been dead for less than a day. Although the use of a gun was new, the police were convinced that this killing was the work of the Co-ed Killer. The town was now in a state of panic; a $42,000 reward was offered for information leading to the killer's capture and the police were heavily criticised for not apprehending him. In their defence they argued that they had little to go on.

On 23 July 1969 the 18-year-old Karen Sue Beineman, another student, went missing. She had last been seen in a wig shop buying a $20 hairpiece. There were two foolish things that she had done in her life, she told the shop assistant – one was buying a wig and the other was accepting a lift on a motorbike from the stranger who was waiting for her outside. The assistant agreed that the latter was stupid and took a look out of the window at the young man on the motorbike. She had to admit, however, that he looked decent enough.

Four days later a doctor walking near his suburban home stumbled across Karen Sue's naked body, which was lying in a gully. She had been raped and her knickers had been stuffed into her vagina; somewhat strangely, there were hair clippings inside them. The police had already begun to suspect that the murderer returned to the spot where he had dumped each corpse on several occasions, even moving it if he had the chance. Before the news of her death was made public the police therefore replaced Karen Sue's mutilated body with a tailor's dummy and staked out the area. It rained heavily that night, which diminished the visibility, but shortly after midnight an officer nevertheless spotted a man running out of the gully. Although the policeman tried to summon help his radio had been soaked by the rain and failed to work. The man got clean away.

It was then that a young campus policeman put two and two together. The description of the young man on the motorbike that had been circulated reminded him of a member of his fraternity house who had dropped out of college after having been suspected of stealing. The young man's name was John Norman Collins, and he had already been interviewed by the police. The policeman then showed a photograph of Collins to both the shop assistant from the wig shop and the owner of the shop next door; both identified it as being a picture of the man on the motorbike. After that the policeman went to interview Collins himself, expecting a confession from him; none was forthcoming, however, and Collins even refused to take a lie-detector test. On the following night Collins was seen by his flatmate emerging from his room and carrying a box that was covered with a blanket. The flatmate caught a glimpse of its contents: a handbag, as well as some women's clothing and shoes.

Police Corporal David Leik had been on holiday with his family and had therefore missed the latest developments in the Co-ed-killer case. After they had returned home his wife had taken some washing to the laundry room in the basement and had noticed that the floor was covered in black spray paint. Only one person had been in the house while they were away: Leik's nephew, John Norman Collins, who had been letting himself in to feed their dog. But why would he paint the basement floor? After receiving an urgent phone call telling him to report to work Leik went to the police station where he was told, to his surprise and disbelief, that Collins was a prime suspect in the Co-ed-killer case.

That evening Leik scraped some of the black paint from the basement floor with a knife; underneath the paint were brown stains, which Leik thought could be blood. Within two hours lab technicians had identified the brown stains as being varnish that Leik had spilled when he had painted some window shutters. A more extensive examination of the basement floor, however, revealed what later proved to be nine tiny bloodstains. Even more significantly, forensic experts discovered some hair clippings lying on the floor next to the washing machine which were subsequently proved to match the clippings that had been found in the knickers that had been stuffed into Karen Sue Beineman's vagina.

Collins was arrested that afternoon. Although he was shaken – and even tearful – he refused to make a confession. A search of his room revealed nothing, his box of gruesome mementos already having been disposed of.

The police knew that Collins ran four motorbikes and funded his activities by means of petty theft. On closer examination, however, it was found that his background was even more disturbed than had first been thought. His sister had become pregnant at the age of 18 and had married the child's father. Although the marriage did not last, when Collins discovered her dating another man he lost control of his temper, beating the man unconscious and hitting his sister repeatedly while screaming that she was a tramp. He furthermore seemed unable to express his sexual feelings in any normal way, and when his girlfriend moved close to him while dancing he chastised her for inciting lustful feelings in him. Later, when his defence attorney was trying to ascertain how well Collins would stand up to cross-examination, he called Collins' mother (who had a new boyfriend, but had not remarried) a 'kept woman', whereupon Collins' usually calm demeanour dissolved into uncontrollable rage.

The police case against Collins was still flimsy, so they began to try to track down Andrew Manuel, Collins' former room-mate, who had committed a number of burglaries with him. Using false names, he and Collins had also once hired a caravan, which they had not returned after their trip – it had been left in Manuel's uncle's back yard in Salinas, California. At around that time the 17-year-old Roxie Ann Philips had vanished from Salinas after telling a friend that she had a date with a man called John, from Michigan, who was staying with a friend in a caravan. Two weeks after her disappearance her body was discovered in a ravine; she had been strangled and her corpse also bore all of the other trademarks of the Co-ed Killer.

Manuel was found in Phoenix, Arizona, and was charged with burglary and stealing the caravan. He knew nothing about the murders, he said, although he did admit to leaving Ypsilanti after he had heard that the police suspected Collins of being the Co-ed Killer. Manuel was sentenced to five years' probation.

Collins went to trial charged only with the murder of Karen Sue Beineman. The prosecution's case centred on the identification of Collins by the wig-shop sales assistant and the hair clippings that were found in Karen Sue's knickers. For his part, the defence counsel questioned the wig-shop assistant's eyesight and contended that the comparison of 61 hairs from the knickers and 59 from the basement floor was insufficient evidence with which to convict a man of murder.

After long deliberation the jury returned a unanimous verdict of guilty and Collins was sentenced to a recommended period of imprisonment of from 20 years to life.

21 ✦ Women are doing it for themselves

Aileen Wuornos never made any secret of the fact that she hated men. When she hung out, drinking and popping pills, in the Last Resort, a Hell's Angels' bar in Port Orange, Florida, she would curse all men and boast that she would get even with this rotten, masculine world. For their part, the Hell's Angels put up with her, regarding her as just another outcast – like them – and calling her 'Spiderwoman', on account of the black-leather outfits that she wore.

Wuornos certainly came from a tough background. Her first recollections were of her mother screaming while her alcoholic father administered another brutal beating; when she was five he abandoned his family. Her mother died when she was 14, and by the time that she was 19 she was all alone in the world, her father having died in prison after having been convicted for sex offences and her only brother having died of cancer. Wuornos then took to prostitution and armed robbery. Although she occasionally worked as a barmaid or cleaner, with her love of alcohol and drugs she could never hold down a job for long. More often than not she spent her time hitchhiking around the highways of Florida, sleeping on the beach or at the roadside.

The Last Resort was more of a home to her than anywhere else. She sometimes slept on the porch or in the so-called 'Japanese hanging gardens', from whose trees the Hell's Angels would hang the Japanese motorcycles that they despised. She was known to one and all as a foul-mouthed, ill-tempered drunk.

When Wuornos was 27 she fell in love with the 22-year-old Tyria Moore. It was a deeply romantic affair and Wuornos believed that Tyria would put an end to her loneliness, never abandoning her as all the men in her life had. She petted and pampered Tyria, stealing in order to lavish her with luxuries.

In September 1990 Wuornos stole a car for Tyria, but when the two women took it for a spin down a dirt road the car went out of control and they subsequently abandoned it. The pair had been spotted, however, and had been reported to the police. Their descriptions were entered into the Marion County police computer, which then linked the two women to six murders that had occurred in the area. The victims had all been men whose bodies had been dumped miles from their cars. Each had been shot exactly nine times and a condom wrapper was found on the back seat of each of their cars.

Shortly after the incident with the stolen car Tyria left Wuornos and fled. In January 1991 the police traced her to Pennsylvania, where they arrested her for car theft. Tyria then broke down and blamed everything on Wuornos, who, she said, had enticed Tyria into a life of crime, also murdering and robbing in order to buy expensive gifts for her.

Wuornos was sleeping on the porch of the Last Resort when she was apprehended. At first she thought that she was being arrested for a five-year-old firearms' charge, but when the police dropped the names of the murder victims into the conversation she freely admitted having killed them.

She explained that she had usually been hitchhiking when her victim stopped his car to offer her a lift, although she had sometimes pretended that her car had broken down and that she needed help. Either way, once she had got into the car she had offered to have sex with the man and had then asked him to drive to a deserted spot. After having had sex she had then exacted her vengeance on all mankind, killing her victim and robbing him of his money, as well as his jewellery.

Even the hardened Hell's Angels were shocked that they had been harbouring a man-slayer in their midst. 'It's scary, man', said Cannonball, the barman at the Last Resort. 'Every one of those guys could have been one of them [Hell's Angels], and we would never have known where it was coming from . . . Mind you, I sorta think she would not have gone for a biker . . . we were her only folks . . . She was a lost soul, like most of us.'

22 ❖ The Night Stalker

On the night of 28 June 1984 the mutilated body of the seventy-nine-year-old Jennie Vincow was found lying spread-eagled on the bed of her one-bedroom flat in the Eagle Rock district of Los Angeles. She had been raped and her throat had been slashed so savagely that she had almost been decapitated; there was blood on the walls of the bedroom and bathroom and her flat had been ransacked. In violent LA, however, it was regarded as just another murder.

Nine months later the killer struck again. Maria Hernandez had just parked her car in her garage in the Rosemeade suburb of Los Angeles and was walking towards her flat when she heard footsteps behind her. On turning around she was confronted by a man holding a gun. Although he aimed the gun at her and pulled the trigger, the bullet miraculously ricocheted off her car keys and dealt her only a glancing blow. Even so, the impact was enough to knock her to the ground, whereupon the gunman stepped over her, giving her a vicious kicking as he did so, and made his way into her flat. Maria then heard a gunshot from inside the flat and staggered to her feet, only to come face to face with the gunman as he ran from the building. 'Please don't shoot me again', she begged, and after freezing momentarily the gunman took to his heels. Inside the flat Maria found her boyfriend, the 34-year-old, Hawaiian-born traffic-manager Dayle Okazaki, lying dead on the kitchen floor. He had been shot through the head.

There was only one clue to the murder: Maria told the police that the gunman was wearing a baseball cap which had the AC/DC logo embroidered on the front of it. AC/DC, an Australian heavy-metal rock band, had recently released an album called *Highway to Hell*, on which a track called 'Night Prowler' appeared. 'Night Prowler' was the *nom d'assassin* , or assassin's name, that Richard Ramirez, the killer responsible for the deaths of Jennie Vincow and Dayle Okazaki, preferred, and he therefore became annoyed when the newspapers insisted on calling him the 'Night Stalker'. Despite having killed Okazaki, his lust for blood was still not satisfied that night, and less than an hour later, when he was on his way home, Ramirez pulled the 30-year-old Tsai Lian Yu, a Taiwanese law student, from her car and shot her repeatedly. She died before the ambulance arrived.

Ten days later Ramirez entered the home of Vincent and Maxine Zazzara, which was half a mile from the San Gabriel motorway. Maxine was a successful lawyer, while Vincent had just fulfilled his lifetime's ambition to open his own pizzeria. Both of them were shot at point-blank range, and Maxine's naked body was mutilated after her death, Ramirez stabbing her repeatedly (the wounds making a pattern resembling a large, ragged 'T') and also gouging out her eyes. The bodies were found by their son, Peter, when he called in at the house on the following day.

On 14 May 1985 Ramirez broke into the home of William and Lillie Doi, shooting the 66-year-old William in the head as he lay sleeping. His wife, the 63-year-old Lillie, who was lying in bed next to William, was beaten repeatedly around the head until she told the intruder where their valuables were hidden. After that Ramirez handcuffed her and ransacked the house before returning to rape her.

A fortnight later Carol Kyle was awoken in her Burbank flat by a torch shining into her eyes, a man then pointing a gun at her and dragging her out of bed. Carol's terrified 12-year-old son was handcuffed and locked into a cupboard in the next room before his mother was raped. Despite her ordeal Carol was compassionate towards Ramirez, saying 'You must have had a very unhappy life to have done this to me'. Ramirez, however, shrugged off her compassion, replying 'I don't know why I'm letting you live. I've killed people before.' He then ransacked the flat looking for valuables. Satisfied with the jewellery that he had found, he finally went away, sparing both Carol and her son's lives.

At around the same time two elderly women, the 83-year-old Mabel Bell and her 80-year-old sister, Florence Long, an invalid, were attacked in their home in the LA suburb of Monrovia. On 1 June 1985 Carlos Venezuela, a gardener who did chores for the sisters, found Florence lying on her bed in a coma; there was a huge wound over her ear and a blood-stained hammer had been left on the dressing table. The barely conscious Mabel was found lying in a pool of her own blood on her bedroom floor. Both women had been beaten with the hammer, as well as having been cut and tortured – there were even signs that Ramirez had tried to rape the older sister, Mabel. The police concluded that the sisters had been attacked two days earlier.

As on previous occasions the culprit had ransacked the house; this time, however, some clues to the attacker's identity were discovered. Along with the hammer, a half-eaten banana was found on the dining table. He had also left what was soon to become his trademark: an inverted pentagram (the encircled, five-pointed star that is used in witchcraft). One was scrawled in lipstick on Mabel's thigh, while another was drawn on Florence's bedroom wall. Tragically, Mabel died six weeks after the attack, but Florence eventually regained consciousness and survived.

Now the Night Stalker's onslaught began in earnest. On the night of 27 June 1985 Ramirez slashed the throat of the 32-year-old Patty Elaine Higgins in her home in Arcadia. The same fate befell Mary Louise Cannon five days afterwards. Three days later, again in Arcadia, Ramirez savagely beat the 16-year-old Whitney Bennett with a crowbar; she survived. On 7 July Ramirez once again turned his attention to Monterey Park (where he had attacked Tsai Lian Yu and the Dois), the 61-year-old Joyce Lucille Nelson being found beaten to death in her home, while the 63 year-old Sophie Dickmann had been raped and robbed in her flat.

On 20 July Ramirez murdered the 66-year-old Maxson Kneiding and his 64-year-old wife, Lela, in their Glendale home before going on to kill

The 'Night Stalker'
Richard Ramirez.

the 32-year-old Chainarong Khovananth at his house in Sun Valley. After shooting Chainarong as he lay asleep in his bed Ramirez raped and beat up his 29-year-old wife, Somkid. He furthermore forced Somkid to perform oral sex on him and stole $30,000 in cash and jewellery, before raping her eight-year-old son also making her swear in Satan's name that she would not cry out.

Although the police had long ago concluded that they had a serial killer on their hands, their primary problem was that he followed no set *modus operandi*. He killed people with guns, hammers and knives; he raped both children and women – young and old – orally, anally and vaginally; sometimes he mutilated the bodies of his victims after death, but sometimes he didn't.

Some patterns in the Night Stalker's attacks were nevertheless emerging. The killer stalked quiet suburbs away from the city's main centres of crime, where home-owners were less security-conscious, for instance. He also tended to pick houses that were painted in beige or pastel yellow and that were usually close to a motorway. He made his entry through an open window or an unlocked door. Although burglary was clearly one of his motives, he also seemed to enjoy rape and sheer brutality. Pentagrams and other satanic symbols were furthermore commonly left by the killer.

On the night of 5 August 1985 Virginia Petersen, a postal worker, was woken by the sound of an intruder. Sitting up in bed, she cried out 'Who are you? What do you want?', whereupon the burglar laughed and shot her in the face. The bullet entered her cheek, just below her eye, and exited through the back of her head (miraculously, she survived). Her husband, Christopher, who was lying beside her, was woken by the shot and leapt to his wife's defence, which earned him a bullet in the temple. Christopher, who worked as a lorry driver, was, however, a tough guy whom it would have taken more than one small-calibre bullet to subdue. Diving out of bed, he chased his attacker. The intruder, who was not prepared for this, panicked and ran.

Like his wife, Christopher Petersen survived the ordeal, although he suffered from partial memory loss thereafter and had to live with a bullet lodged in his brain. For the first time, however, the Night Stalker had been put to flight, although this did not end his violent rampage. Three days later he shot a 35-year-old Asian man and beat up and raped his 28-year-old wife. In common with Somkid Khovananth she was forced to swear by Satan that she would not cry out, but this time he did not molest the couple's two young children, apart from tying up their three-year-old son, Amez.

By this time the public state of panic had reached fever pitch in Los Angeles. In the affluent suburbs locksmiths and burglar-alarm outfits were doing a roaring trade, while gun shops quickly sold out of their stock and local residents set up neighbourhood-watch committees. It was now that Ramirez took a holiday and travelled north to San Francisco, where, on the night of 17 August 1985, he shot both the 66-year-old Asian accountant Peter Pan and his 64-year-old wife, Barbara, through the heads in their home in the suburb of Lake Merced. Before leaving the scene of the crime Ramirez drew an inverted pentagram in lipstick on the bedroom wall, underneath it writing 'Jack the Knife'. At first the police thought that the Pans' murders were copycat killings, until they discovered that the bullets that had killed the couple matched the small-calibre rounds that had been used in the Los Angeles murders.

A week later Ramirez travelled to the small town of Mission Viego, south of Los Angeles, where he shot William Carns, a 29-year-old computer engineer, three times in the head before raping his fiancée, Inez Erickson (also 29), twice and ordering her to say 'I love Satan'. 'You know who I am, don't you?' Ramirez taunted. 'I'm the one they're writing about in the newspapers and on TV.' (William Carns survived the shooting, but suffered permanent brain damage. The couple never married.)

Inez had managed to observe Ramirez's rusty, old, orange Toyota leaving the house. James Romero III, a sharp-eyed youth, had also noticed the orange Toyota as it cruised the area and had noted down its licence-plate number. The car would prove to be the vital clue that put an end to the reign of the Night Stalker. After the police had circulated a description of it it was found in a car park in LA's Rampart suburb two days later.

Forensic scientists used a radical new technique when examining the car: they put a dab of Superglue on a saucer and sealed the doors and windows before placing the saucer in the car, the theory being that the fumes from the Superglue would react with the moisture contained in any fingerprints in the car and would then turn them white. The interior of the car was also scanned using a laser beam, which would be able to pick up any fingerprints on the car, including those that the culprit had tried to wipe off. The scan yielded one fingerprint, which a computer matched to a fingerprint belonging the twenty-five-year-old Ramirez, who had been arrested on three previous occasions in El Paso for marijuana possession.

Richard Ramirez, arriving at the court for his trial.

Soon afterwards Ramirez's photograph was on the front page of every newspaper in California.

Ramirez was quite unaware of these developments when he stepped off a Greyhound bus at Los Angeles' main bus station. He had been in Phoenix, Arizona, where he had obtained some cocaine, and was now on a high: he had killed 13 people so far and felt good about it – surely, he reasoned, he must be Satan's favourite son.

On going into a shop to buy a Pepsi he saw his face splashed across the Spanish language paper *La Opinion* that was lying on the counter by the till. He was also recognised by the cashier, as well as by other customers in the shop, causing him to make a run for it. Out on the street someone cried 'It's the Night Stalker' and Ramirez soon heard the wail of police sirens behind him. He knocked on a door, and when Bonnie Navarro opened it he shouted 'Help me' in Spanish. She slammed the door in his face, however. Ramirez tried to pull a woman from her car in the next street, but some bystanders rushed to her rescue. He then jumped over a fence into the garden where Luis Munoz was cooking a barbecue and was hit with Munoz's tongs. In the next garden he was prevented from stealing a red, 1966 Mustang by the 56-year-old Faustin Pinon, who had been working on the car's transmission and now grabbed him in a headlock. Ramirez broke free, but José Burgoin, a 55-year-old construction worker who had heard Pinon's shouts from across the street, picked up a steel rod and hit Ramirez with it. Although Ramirez stumbled away Burgoin soon caught up with him and clubbed him to the ground.

Deputy Sheriff Andres Ramirez pulled up in his patrol car in the nick of time, as far as Ramirez was concerned. 'Save me!' yelled the Night Stalker, commenting as his namesake handcuffed him 'Thank God you came. I am the one you want. Save me before they kill me'. Only the arrival of further police patrol cars stopped the angry mob from taking the law into their own hands, and even outside the police station a crowd soon gathered calling for him to be lynched.

Ramirez showed no contrition for his crimes, explaining to the police

I love to kill people. I love watching them die. I would shoot them in the head and they would wiggle and squirm all over the place, and then just stop. Or I would cut them with a knife and watch their faces turn real white. I love all that blood. I told one lady one time to give me all her money. She said no. So I cut her and pulled her eyes out.

In court he made satanic signs and even appeared with the inverted pentagram scratched into his palm. He told the judge 'You maggots make me sick. Hypocrites one and all. You don't understand me. You are not expected to. You are not capable of it. I am beyond your experience. I am beyond good and evil'.

Ramirez was found guilty of 63 crimes, including 13 murders. He was sentenced to 12 death penalties and over 100 years' imprisonment. When he was on death row many women wrote to him, sending provocative pictures, pledging undying love and even proposing marriage. When Ramirez accepted the proposal of Christine Lee, a divorcée, over that of the nude model Kelly Marquez it made headlines. Christine, a mother of two, bombarded Ramirez with pin-up-style pictures of herself and visited him over 150 times. She was undaunted by the fact that her husband-to-be was a serial killer: 'We really love each other and that's all that matters', she said. 'From the moment I saw him in prison I knew he was special. I couldn't believe he was the evil monster people were calling him. He's always been sweet and kind to me.'

23 ❖ Leonard Lake and Charles Ng

When a young Chinese man took a vice from a shop without paying for it the sales assistant ran to find a policeman. The officer followed the man to his car, who dumped the vice in the boot before running off when he spotted the policeman. Although the police officer gave chase the youth was too fast for him, and when he returned to the car he found a bald, bearded man standing next to it. The man explained that it had all been a mistake: he had now paid for the vice, he explained, and showed the officer the receipt. The policeman was suspicious, however, and examined the car, finding a holdall in the boot containing a .22 pistol, as well as a silencer. (Although it is legal to carry a handgun in the USA adding a silencer is against the law and usually indicates that the gun is likely to be used for some illegal purpose.)

The bearded man's Californian driving licence said that he was called Robin Scott Stapley. He hardly knew the youth who had run away, he told the policeman, but had been about to hire him for a job. Despite his explanation the officer took him to the police station for questioning. Once there the man asked for – and received – paper, a pencil and a glass of water. He then scribbled a note to his wife on the paper, which read 'Cricket, I love you. Please forgive me. I forgive you. Please tell Mama, Fern and Patty I'm sorry'. After that he swallowed a cyanide capsule, washing it down with the water. Within seconds he was dead.

The police subsequently discovered that the dead man was not Robin Scott Stapley, who had gone missing five months earlier. A few weeks after his disappearance, however, his camper van, which was being driven by a young Chinese man, had collided with a lorry. Although the young man had begged the lorry driver not to report the accident the latter was driving a company vehicle and therefore had no option but to do so.

It later transpired that the car that the bearded man had driven was registered to a Paul Cosner. When questioned, Cosner's girlfriend said that he had told her that he was selling it to a weird-looking man who had said that he would pay cash for it. Cosner had never returned after he had driven off to deliver the car.

When forensic scientists examined the car they found two bullet holes in the front seat and two spent rounds lodged in the upholstery; there were also bloodstains – human bloodstains – in the car. In the glove compartment they discovered some papers belonging to a Charles Gunnar, of Wilseyville, Calavers County, which was 150 miles (241 kilometres) north of San Francisco.

A call to Wilseyville's sheriff revealed that the Calavers County police already had their eye on Gunnar, as well as his young friend, a Chinese man named Charles Ng. They were suspected of handling stolen goods – videos, television sets, furniture and other household items – and had been selling furniture belonging to Brenda O'Connor and Lonnie Bond. Gunnar had explained to the police that the couple had moved to Los Angeles with their baby and had given Gunnar the furniture in settlement of a debt. There had furthermore been another mysterious disappearance in the area: a young couple had vanished from a camp site at the nearby Schaad Lake, leaving behind their tent, as well as a coffee pot sitting on the stove.

Following a computer check the dead man's fingerprints revealed that his real name was Leonard Lake. Lake had been charged with grand larceny and burglary in Mendocino County and had then jumped bail. It also seemed that he was linked with a number of other disappearances, including that of his younger brother, Donald, who had gone missing two years before, after setting off to visit Lake at a survivalist camp in Humboldt County. Charles Gunnar, the man whose identity Lake was using, had disappeared earlier that year after having acted as best man at Lake's wedding.

The trail inexorably led to the small ranch on Blue Mountain Road where Gunnar – that is, Lake – and Ng lived, and a team of policemen from San Francisco consequently visited it. Set within three acres of wooded grounds, the ranch was an ordinary-looking, two-bedroomed bungalow. Inside, however, it was far from ordinary, for the master bedroom was fitted out like a medieval torture chamber: there were hooks in the ceiling and walls, as well as boxes full of chains and shackles that could be used to immobilise someone who was lying on the bed. There was also a wardrobe full of flimsy nightgowns and sexy underwear, along with expensive video gear. The serial numbers confirmed that the video equipment belonged to Harvey and Deborah Dubbs; following the disappearance of the couple and their 16-month-old baby it had last been seen being carried from their flat by a Chinese removal man.

Lake had been a dedicated survivalist who had built a nuclear-fallout shelter in the garden. Inside the shelter the police found a storeroom containing food, water, candles and guns. Set into the floor was a sinister-looking trapdoor which led to another chamber. This subterranean room was also hung with hooks and chains, and the walls were covered with photographs of frightened-looking girls posing in their underwear. It was clear that all of the pictures had been taken in that very room. Next to this chamber was a tiny cell with a one-way mirror in its wall, which meant that anyone being held inside the room could be subjected to twenty-four-hour surveillance.

The bomb-shelter basement also contained filing cabinets, in which the police found more pictures, as well as a huge collection of video tapes. The first video cassette that they viewed was marked 'Kathy/Brenda'. It began by showing a terrified girl, who was handcuffed to a chair, being menaced by Charles Ng. Then Lake entered the frame and removed the girl's handcuffs, instead shackling her feet, after that ordering the girl to strip. She undressed reluctantly – she could clearly hardly bring herself to remove her knickers, but was forced to do so. 'You'll wash for us,' announced Lake, 'clean for us, fuck for us.' Later she was shown naked, being strapped to the bed and being told by Lake that her boyfriend was dead.

'Brenda' – who was later identified as Brenda O'Connor – also appeared in the video. Shown handcuffed to a chair, she entered into a chilling dialogue with Lake while Ng slowly cut her clothes off her. First she asked where the baby was, to which Lake replied that it had been placed with a family in Fresno. 'Why do you guys do this?' she then asked. 'We don't like you. Do you want me to put it in writing?' was the response. 'Don't cut my bra off', she pleaded, to which Lake replied 'Nothing is yours now'. 'Give my baby back to me. I'll do anything you want' Brenda begged, only to be told 'You're going to do anything we want anyway'.

Other videos showed women being shackled, raped, tortured and murdered. They featured all of the missing women of whom the police already knew and others that they recognised from missing-person's reports, along with over 25 more whom they never identified. It was plain that Leonard Lake and Charles Ng had been making 'snuff' movies for two years, for each of the tapes, which were clearly marked 'M Ladies' ('Murdered Ladies'), ended with the death of its reluctant female star.

The police also discovered a bloodstained chainsaw which had been used to cut up the bodies of Lake and Ng's victims; the body parts had then been incinerated and the bones scattered across the hillside at the back of the house. Other bodies were found intact, while in a narrow trench that ran across the garden the police discovered a number of corpses that were too decomposed to identify. Among the latter were the bodies of a man, woman and child, which could have belonged to Bond, O'Connor and their baby, the Dubbs family or, indeed, to any other man, woman and child who had had the misfortune to fall into Lake's gruesome trap. Two weeks of digging produced a total of nine entire bodies and 40 lbs (18 kilogrammes) of human bones. Identifying the corpses themselves was well-nigh impossible, but driver's licences and other papers confirmed that Robert Stapley, Paul Cosner and the couple from the camping site were all among the victims.

The police found Lake's diary in the files in the basement which indicated that his grisly career of murder had begun long before he moved into the ranch on Blue Mountain Road. Born in San Francisco in 1946, Leonard Lake had been rejected by both parents, being brought up with military discipline by his grandparents. Leonard's brother, Donald, was a sadist who tortured animals and tried to rape his sisters. Leonard protected his sisters, but at a price: they had to perform certain sexual favours for him. He also took nude pictures of his sisters and cousins, later also making pornographic films featuring his wife, 'Cricket' Balazs.

Although he was not the front-line hero that he subsequently claimed to have been, the Vietnam War changed him. Despite disguising his feelings by teaching, becoming a volunteer fire-fighter and doing charity work, he became deeply pessimistic. This pessimism eventually led him to survivalism, as well as to a life financed by petty theft and burglary.

Then Lake's marriage broke up, although his wife still acted as a fence for the credit cards and other items that he stole. After that the idea slowly began to grow in his mind that women were the cause of all his problems. He eventually found the release that he sought by killing his troublesome brother, Donald, whereupon he embarked upon a murder spree. (The police discovered a crude map of California that he had marked with crosses labelled 'buried treasure'. The crosses were believed to represent the graves of his early victims, but the map was too inaccurate for the police to investigate this theory.)

While staying in the isolated village of Miranda, in northern California, Lake came up with the idea for 'Operation Miranda': he planned to stockpile weapons, food, water and kidnapped women in preparation for the nuclear holocaust that he believed was nigh. 'The perfect woman is totally controlled,' he wrote, 'a woman who does exactly what she is told to and nothing else. There is no sexual problem with a submissive woman. There are no frustrations – only pleasure and contentment.' He then put Operation Miranda into practice with the help of Charles Ng.

Ng, the son of a wealthy Hong Kong family, was born in 1961. He was educated at a private school in North Yorkshire before being expelled for theft, therefore completing his studies in San Francisco. At the age of 18 he was involved in a hit-and-run accident and joined the US Marines in order to escape going to jail. Having been posted to Hawaii, his lifelong kleptomania then reasserted itself and he was arrested for the theft of ammunition and weapons worth over $11,000. After escaping from jail in Hawaii Ng returned to San Francisco where he met Lake, whom he looked up to. Together they embarked upon a full-time life of crime, later being arrested in Mendocino County for burglary. Ng was imprisoned (also serving time for his earlier theft in Hawaii) and spent some of his sentence at Fort Leavenworth. When he was paroled he joined Lake at the ranch and helped him to transform his paranoid fantasies into brutal reality.

Lake's journal describes how his sex slaves were obtained. Having invited unwitting couples and families to the ranch for dinner the men and children would be murdered straightaway. The women would then be stripped, shackled, sexually abused, humiliated and forced to perform menial chores around the house. Kept in a Spartan cell, they would also be used as the unwilling subjects of sexually sadistic videos. When a woman showed any sign of rebellion against her submissive role – or when her tormentor grew tired of her – Lake and Ng would kill her and film her death.

Psychological studies of Lake showed that he was in the final phase of the serial-murder syndrome when he was arrested: sated with blood, he felt that he had reached the end of a cul de-sac from which there was no way back. Having caused untold misery to others he was now bringing misery upon himself – the only way out was suicide.

Ng escaped to Canada, where he shot a security guard after having been caught shoplifting. He served a four-and-a-half-year sentence for armed robbery before being extradited to California to face charges of mass murder.

24 ❖ Son of Sam

At 1am on 29 July 1976 the 19-year-old Jody Valente and her friend, the 18-year-old Donna Lauria, were sitting in Jody's car outside Donna's home in the Bronx area of New York. It was a hot summer night and they were discussing their boyfriends. Finally Donna said goodnight and opened the car door to get out. As the door opened a young man who was standing a few feet away reached into the brown-paper bag that he was holding, pulled out a gun and dropped into crouching position. 'What does this guy want?' asked the alarmed Donna. The words had just left her mouth when a bullet struck her in the side of the neck, a second bullet smashing the window in the door and a third shattering her elbow as she raised her hands to protect her face. Fatally wounded, she tumbled out of the car on to the pavement, whereupon her killer shot Jody in the thigh, causing her to fall forward on to the car's horn. As the horn blared the killer made off.

Donna's father, Mike Lauria, who was about to take the dog for a walk, was halfway down the stairs of the family house when he heard the shots. Running outside, he found Jody conscious, though hysterical, and Donna lying collapsed on the ground. In the ambulance he entreated his daughter not to die, but it was too late: when Donna reached the hospital she was pronounced DOA – dead on arrival. Although Jody was treated for hysteria she nevertheless managed to give the police a good description of their assailant: he was a young, white male, about 30 years old, clean shaven, with dark, curly hair. He was not a rejected boyfriend (as the police at first speculated), Jody said – in fact, she had never seen him before. The only other clue to his identity was a yellow car that had been parked near Jody's, but it had gone by the time that the police arrived, and in any case New York is full of yellow cars.

(The car in question actually belonged to David Berkowitz. In the days leading up to the murder he had been looking for a job, but had spent the nights, he later said, 'Looking for a victim, waiting for a signal'. Demonic voices inside his head had told him to kill, he explained. 'I never thought I could kill her', he said of Donna Lauria. 'I just fired the gun, you know, at the car, at the windshield. I never knew she was shot.')

The northern Bronx, where the Laurias lived, is a predominantly Italian area, and the police therefore immediately suspected Mafia involvement in Donna's murder. However, the Mafia are usually scrupulous when it comes to contract killings: women and children are out of bounds. Besides, ballistics tests showed that the murder weapon was a Charter Arms, five-round, .44 Bulldog revolver, which had a powerful recoil and was grossly inaccurate at distances of more than a few yards – hardly a hit man's weapon.

On the other side of the East river from the Bronx lies the Queens area, a comfortable, middle-class district. Twelve weeks after the murder of Donna Lauria the eighteen-year-old Rosemary Keenan, a student at Queens College, went to a bar in the Flushing area of Queens where she met the twenty-year-old record salesman Carl Denaro, who was enjoying his last days of freedom before joining the United States Air Force. After having left the bar together in her red Volkswagen, Rosemary and Carl had parked and were talking when a man crept up on them. He may have thought that Carl, who was sitting in the passenger seat, was a woman on account of his long, brown hair. He pulled out the .44 Bulldog handgun that was tucked into his belt and fired through the passenger window five times. His shooting was wildly inaccurate, however, and only one bullet found its mark: as Carl threw himself forward to protect himself from the flying glass the bullet clipped the back of his head, knocking away part of his skull, but not damaging his brain. Although Carl was lucky, in that he recovered completely after a two-month stay in hospital, the metal plate that the surgeons had had to insert into his head ended his air-force career before it had even begun.

On the evening of 27 November 1976 two schoolgirls – the 16-year-old Donna DeMasi and her 18-year-old friend, Joanne Lomino – were sitting talking on the front porch of Joanne's home on 262nd Street in Queens. At the end of their conversation Joanne stood up and reached into her handbag for her front-door keys. It was then that the two girls noticed a man walking down the other side of the road. He was acting rather suspiciously: when he saw them he suddenly changed direction. After crossing the street at the corner he came over to them as if he was about to ask for directions, but instead he pulled a gun from his waistband and began firing at them. The two girls ran towards the front door, Joanne frantically searching for her keys. The first bullet hit her in the back; the second lodged in Donna's neck. They stumbled into the bushes as the gunman fired his remaining three shots, all of which missed. He then ran off down 262nd Street and was spotted by a neighbour still holding his gun.

The two wounded girls were rushed to Long Island Jewish Hospital, where Donna was found not to be badly injured (she made a full recovery after three weeks). But Joanne was not so lucky: the bullet had smashed her spinal cord, paralysing her from the waist down, and she would spend the rest of her life in a wheelchair. The neighbour who had spotted the gunman making his escape gave the police a description of him. One key feature that he mentioned was the young man's dark, curly hair, which was strange because the girls themselves said that he had had long, fair hair. Despite the discrepancy, the description nevertheless linked the shootings of Donna DeMasi and Joanne Lomino to the man who had killed Donna Lauria and wounded Jody Valente.

On 29 January 1977 the 30-year-old John Diel and his 26-year old girl-friend, Christine Freund, went to see the film *Rocky* in Queens. Afterwards they had dinner at the Wine Gallery, in Austin Street, where they discussed their forthcoming engagement. Soon after midnight the couple walked along several streets to where their Pontiac Firebird was parked. It was cold outside, and once inside the car their breath fogged up the windows. Although they were eager to get home they stopped for a moment to kiss, John then turning the key in the ignition. Before he could pull away, how-ever, he heard the blast of gunfire, whereupon the passenger window shat-tered and Christine slumped forward, bleeding. She died a few hours later in St John's Hospital of bullet wounds to her right temple and neck. She had never even seen her killer, but he had seen her – and so had the demon within him: Berkowitz later claimed that he had heard a voice command-ing him to 'Get her, get her and kill her'. After firing three shots and real-ising that he had hit her he felt calm again. 'The voices stopped', he said. 'I satisfied the demon's lust.'

After the murder of Christine Freund Berkowitz surrendered himself completely to his impulse to kill. After all, he reasoned, he was being rewarded by all of the publicity that he was generating: 'I had finally con-vinced myself that I was good to do it, and that the public wanted me to kill', Berkowitz later explained.

However, the New York Police Department (NYPD) was on his trail. Its ballistics lab had ascertained that the bullet that had killed Christine Freund had come from a .44 Bulldog handgun, which tied it to the murder of Donna Lauria and the shootings of Jody Valente, Carl Denaro, Donna DeMasi and Joanne Lomino. Yet apart from the mention of his dark, curly hair by Jody Valente and the neighbour in the DeMasi-Lomino case the descriptions of the gunman varied so widely that no one in the NYPD had concluded that the shootings were the work of a single individual.

Six weeks later, on 8 March 1977, Virginia Voskerichian, a 19-year-old Armenian student, left Columbia University in Manhattan and set off for her home in Forest Hills, Queens. At around 7.30pm she was nearing her home on Exeter Street when a young man approached her on the pavement. She politely stepped aside, whereupon he pulled out a gun, shoved it into her face and fired. Although Virginia raised her books in a vain attempt to protect herself, the bullet tore through them, entering her body through her upper lip, smashing several teeth and lodging in her brain. She collapsed in the bushes at the side of the street and died instantly. A witness saw a young man running away and later estimated that he was aged about 18 and was 5 feet 8 inches (1.75 metres) tall. No dark, curly hair was noted, however, because the murderer was wearing a Balaclava.

The killer was almost caught that very day. Minutes after Virginia's murder the police put out a 'Code .44' alert and two police officers were assigned to the southern end of the Bronx with orders to stop any car that contained a lone white man. Berkowitz had driven up to the checkpoint with his loaded .44 Bulldog lying in full view on the passenger seat of his Ford Galaxie and was third in line when the police called off the search. He could not believe his luck as he watched the officers walk away.

It was quickly proved that the bullet that had killed Virginia Voskerichian was of a .44 calibre and that the riflings on it matched the marks on the bullet that had killed Christine Freund six weeks before and just a few miles away. Two days later it was established that the same gun was responsible for the shooting of seven people.

On the afternoon of 10 March 1977 a press conference was held at One Police Plaza, the 13-storey, red-stone building that is New York's equivalent of London's New Scotland Yard. As Police Commissioner Mike Codd stood with some trepidation before New York's hard-bitten crime reporters and started to read his carefully prepared statement he had an inkling that he was about to unleash a wave of hysteria that would engulf the city. He began by saying that the murder of Donna Lauria nine months before was linked to the killing of Virginia Voskerichian a mere two days earlier. In both cases, he stated, the killer had used a .44 Bulldog revolver and the same gun had also been used in three other incidents. Worse still, in terms of securing his arrest, the killer apparently chose his victims completely at random. As the reporters pushed for further information Codd revealed that the police were looking for a Caucasian male, about 6 feet (1.83 metres) tall, of medium build, 25 to 30 years old, with dark hair. The .44 killer made the headlines the next day.

The policeman in charge of the investigation was Deputy Inspector Timothy J Dowd. Working under Dowd was Chief of Detectives John Keenan, who had a special reason for wanting to capture the .44 killer: his daughter was the young woman who had been in the car with Carl Denaro when he was shot in the head. 'I know he was aiming for her', Keenan subsequently said. 'So let's just say I put a little more than I had to into this case.'

The police realised that their chances of catching a lone, seemingly motiveless, murderer on the streets of New York were remote, so they asked for the help of every New Yorker. As a result tip-offs jammed the police switchboards and Dowd and his detectives had to follow up 250 to 300 leads a day. Berkowitz took pity on the police, however, and wrote them a letter, although dropping it into a letter box and letting the postal service deliver it was too mundane an option for him.

On the night of 16 April 1977 another young couple went to a cinema in New York. After the 18-year-old Valentina Suriani and her boyfriend, the 20-year-old Alexander Esau, had seen the film they went on to a party. At around 3am they were sitting in a borrowed Mercury Montego that was parked outside Valentina's block of flats in the northern Bronx, only three streets away from where Donna Lauria had been killed. Valentina was sitting on Alexander's lap, her legs stretched across the passenger seat, enjoying a prolonged series of goodnight kisses when a hail of bullets suddenly shattered the passenger window. Two hit Valentina's head, killing her instantly. Another two struck Alexander on the top of the head as he dived across the seat towards the passenger door; he died two hours later.

When the police arrived they found a white envelope lying in the middle of the road next to the car. It was addressed to Captain Joe Borelli, Dowd's second-in-command. The letter was written in capitals, was full of spelling mistakes and appeared to be the work of a madman. The writer claimed that he had been ordered to kill by his father, who was a vampire. His father's name, the writer said, was Sam (hence the killer's subsequent macabre sobriquet 'Son of Sam'). In the letter he professed to love the people of Queens, but nevertheless stated his intention of killing more of them – particularly the women (he spelt the word as if it rhymed with 'demon'). The writer signed off with a farewell message:

I SAY GOODBYE AND GOODNIGHT. POLICE: LET ME HAUNT YOU WITH THESE WORDS; I'LL BE BACK! I'LL BE BACK! TO BE INTERPRETED AS – BANG BANG, BANG, BANG, BANG, BANG – UGH!! YOURS IN MURDER, MR MONSTER.

By the time that the letter reached the police labs eight policemen had handled it and only tiny traces of the writer's fingerprints remained. He furthermore appeared to have held the letter by the tips of his fingers and there was therefore not enough of a print on the paper with which to identify the sender. Although the police consequently kept the existence of the letter a secret they showed a copy of it to the celebrated New York columnist Jimmy Breslin, who dropped hints about it in his column in the New York Daily News.

On 1 June 1977 Breslin himself received a letter from the .44 killer. It had been posted two days earlier, in Englewood, New Jersey, just across the George Washington Bridge from Manhattan. The New York Daily News, which was then the biggest-selling newspaper in the USA, held back publication of the full letter for six days as speculation about it, and therefore also the newspaper's circulation, mounted. On 3 June the New York Daily News ran the front-page headline: 'THE .44 CALIBER KILLER – NEW NOTE: CAN'T STOP KILLING'. On the next day the headline read: '.44 KILLER: I AM NOT ASLEEP'. In the Sunday edition it said: 'BRESLIN TO .44 KILLER: GIVE UP! IT'S THE ONLY WAY OUT'. This edition had sold out within an hour of going on sale, so the presses kept rolling and by the end of the day the paper had sold 1,116,000 copies – a record that was beaten only on the day on which Berkowitz was arrested.

The paper's editors assumed that public interest in the story had peaked on Sunday and therefore reproduced the letter in full in the Monday edition. Like the first letter that had been received by Borelli it was written entirely in capital letters and showed the same uncertain grasp of basic spelling. The letter was something of an anti-climax to the newspaper's readers as it was as rambling and incoherent as the letter that the .44 killer had sent to the police.

The writer signed off with the words:

NOT KNOWING WHAT THE FUTURE HOLDS I SHALL SAY FAREWELL AND I WILL SEE YOU AT THE NEXT JOB, OR SHOULD I SAY YOU WILL SEE MY HANDIWORK AT THE NEXT JOB? REMEMBER MS LAURIA.

THANK YOU. IN THEIR BLOOD AND FROM THE GUTTER, 'SAM'S
CREATION' .44.

Then there was a long postscript:

HERE ARE SOME NAMES TO HELP YOU ALONG. FORWARD THEM TO
THE INSPECTOR FOR USE BY THE NCIC: 'THE DUKE OF DEATH'. 'THE
WICKED KING WICKER', 'THE TWENTY TWO DISCIPLES OF HELL',
JOHN 'WHEATIES' – RAPIST AND SUFFOCATER OF YOUNG GIRLS.
    PS: J B PLEASE INFORM ALL THE DETECTIVES WORKING THE
SLAYINGS TO REMAIN.

At the police's request this last page was withheld from publication
because the police said that they did not want the existence of the NCIC –
the National Crime Information Center – to become public knowledge. Yet
the .44 killer certainly knew about it. Perhaps the real reason for their
request lay in the satanic undertones of the list of pseudonyms that the
killer gave: the 'Wicked King Wicker' presumably refers to 'Wicca' (witchcraft), while the 'Twenty Two Disciples of Hell' certainly sounds like a
satanic organisation. The name 'Wheaties' was enclosed within inverted
commas as if it were the nickname of the John who was supposedly the
'rapist and suffocater of young girls'. When they ran some checks, however, the police could find no trace of him. In fact, none of the names given
were much help either to the Omega team that was working on the case or
the NCIC. Nor were they any use to Breslin, who now began calling the .44
killer the 'Son of Sam'.

The 17-year-old Judy Placido went to the same Bronx school as
Valentina Suriani, whose funeral she had attended. On 25 June 1977, three
weeks after the publication of the letter that the .44 killer had written to
Breslin, Judy celebrated her high-school graduation at Elephas, a discotheque in Queens. There she met a handsome young man called Salvatore Lupo, who worked at a petrol station; they hit it off immediately and
soon went outside for some privacy. While sitting in a car Salvatore slipped
his arm around Judy's shoulders as they discussed the Son of Sam killings.
It was at that precise moment that their lurid speculations turned into murderous reality. A .44 bullet smashed through the passenger window, passing through Salvatore's wrist and into Judy's neck; a second bullet hit her
in the head, but miraculously failed to penetrate her skull, while a third
entered her right shoulder. The terrified Salvatore threw open the car door
and ran into the discotheque to get help, but it was too late: the shooting

was over and the attacker had fled. Although she had been hit three times Judy was quite unaware of having been shot and was shocked to see that her face was covered with blood when she glanced into the rear-view mirror. She, too, then jumped out of the car and headed for the discotheque, but only managed to cover a few yards before collapsing. Salvatore nursed a shattered wrist and cuts from the flying glass; in hospital it was ascertained that Judy had been fortunate to escape without serious injury.

The city was now in a state of panic and takings at discotheques and restaurants – particularly in Queens – plummeted. Newspapers' circulation soared: not only did they contain the gory details of the latest shooting, but they also speculated about the next killing. In the Son of Sam's letter to Breslin he had written 'TELL ME JIM, WHAT WILL YOU HAVE FOR JULY TWENTY-NINTH?' It was noted that 29 July was the date on which he had carried out his first murder. Was he planning to celebrate the killing of Donna Lauria with another?

New York's mayor, Abraham Beame, who was running for re-election, could not afford to wait to find out and quickly announced that even more officers were being seconded to the investigation. Overnight it became the largest single operation in the history of the New York Police Department: 200 men, recruited from every borough of the city, were seconded to the case and the investigation cost more than $90,000 a day to run. Volunteers, like Donna Lauria's father, Mike, furthermore manned special Son of Sam patrols, as well as a hot line, which was receiving at 5,000 calls a day by then. For their part, a team of psychiatrists tried to compile a profile of the killer, but the best that they could come up with was that he was 'neurotic, schizophrenic and paranoid'. This description was duly released by the police, but did not help anyone to identify the gunman.

Fortunately 29 July passed without incident and two days later, with a sense of relief, two sisters from Brooklyn, the fifteen-year-old Ricki Moskowitz and the twenty-year-old Stacy, decided to go out. While in a Brooklyn restaurant they were approached by a handsome young man who introduced himself as Bobby Violante. The next day Bobby and Stacy went to see the film *New York, New York*. Afterwards they went out to dinner before heading off for a quiet place where they could be alone. They drove to a secluded spot on Shore Parkway, near Coney Island, southern Brooklyn, which was used as an urban type of lovers' lane. They felt safe enough there: so far there had been no Son-of-Sam killings in Brooklyn; the nearest shooting had taken place 22 miles (35 kilometres) away, in Queens. What they did not know, however, was that a week beforehand a man claiming to be the Son of Sam had phoned the Coney Island police station to say that he would strike in that area next. Extra patrol cars had therefore been assigned to Brooklyn and Coney Island and Shore Parkway was patrolled regularly.

Bobby and Stacy pulled up under a street lamp, the only available parking spot on Shore Parkway. There was a full moon that night and because it was not dark enough for what they had in mind the pair went for a stroll in a nearby park. They walked over a bridge and spent a few minutes playing on the swings. Near the public lavatories they noticed a jeans-wearing man – whom they described as a 'hippie type' – leaning against a wall, but he was no longer there when they returned to the car. They were kissing in the front seat when Stacy suggested that they move on. Bobby, however, insisted on one more kiss. This was a mistake, for while they were embracing Bobby was hit in the face by two bullets, which blinded him and caused his eardrums to explode. Although he could neither see nor hear he felt Stacy jerk violently in his arms before falling forward. Fearing that she was dead, Bobby threw himself against the car's horn, fumbled at the door, called for help and then collapsed on to the pavement.

Tommy Zaino, who was sitting in the car in front, had seen the shooting in his rear-view mirror. He had watched as a man approached the car from behind before pulling out a gun; from a crouching position he had then fired four shots through the open passenger window. When Tommy's girlfriend, Debbie Crescendo, had heard the shooting she had asked 'What's that?' Tommy believed that he knew: 'Get down', he said. 'I think it's the Son of Sam.' Tommy had seen the gunman run towards the park and had then looked at his watch: it was exactly 2.35am. (A patrol car was just five streets away at the time.)

Stacy Moskowitz was still conscious when the ambulance arrived. Although one bullet had grazed her scalp the other had lodged in the back of her brain and she died 38 hours later. Bobby Violante survived, but his sight could not be restored.

Tommy Zaino gave a good description of the killer: he was stocky, with stringy, fair hair. This matched the description given by Donna DeMasi and Joanne Lomino, but did not fit the man with the dark, curly hair who had been described by Jody Valente and the neighbour in the DeMasi-Lomino case. The police therefore wondered whether he had been wearing a wig.

There were other witnesses, too. A beautician and her boyfriend had been sitting by the entrance to the park when they had heard the shots. They had then seen a man wearing a denim jacket and what they took to be a nylon wig jump into a light-coloured car and drive off, as if he had just robbed a bank. A young girl who had been riding a bicycle identified the car as being a yellow Volkswagen, while a nurse who had looked out of her window when she had heard the shooting also said that she had seen a yellow VW. It had almost collided with another car at an intersection and the second driver had been so incensed that he had chased the VW, only to lose it a few streets later. The VW's driver, the other motorist said, had had stringy, brown hair.

An even more vital witness took a little longer to come forward, however. She was Cacilia Davis, a 49-year-old widow who had been out with a male friend on the night in question. They had returned to her flat, which was two streets from the park, at around 2am and had then sat in her friend's car and talked for a few minutes, keeping an eye open for other cars as they did so because they had been forced to double-park. Cacilia had noticed a police car a little way ahead, along with two patrolmen, who were writing out parking tickets. Some way behind them was a yellow Ford Galaxie that had been parked by a fire hydrant; a few minutes beforehand a patrolman had issued it with a parking ticket. Next Cacilia had seen a young man with dark hair walk up to the Galaxie and irritably pull the parking ticket from the windscreen. After that she had invited her friend in for coffee, but he had declined, saying that it was late – it was 2.20am by then. At that moment the police car had pulled away, as had the Galaxie shortly thereafter, but because he could not get past her friend's car the Galaxie's driver had impatiently honked his horn. Cacilia had hurriedly got out of the car and her friend had driven off, whereupon the Galaxie had followed and quickly passed him before speeding off after the police car.

Minutes later Cacilia had taken her dog for a walk in the park and had noticed Tommy Zaino and Bobby Violante's cars, as well as a VW van. On her way home she had seen a man with dark hair and a blue-denim jacket striding across the road from the cars. As he glared at her she had observed that he was walking with his right arm held stiffly, as if something was concealed up his sleeve. He also looked rather like the driver of the Ford Galaxie whom she had seen earlier, she thought.

Cacilia did not come forward with this information immediately, however, for she realised that she was in danger if the man whom she had seen was indeed the Son of Sam: he could easily identify her and knew where she lived. It was not until two days after the shootings that she told a couple of close friends what she had seen. Thinking that she might be able to provide a vital clue as to the killer's identity they urged her to call the police, eventually doing so on her behalf. Although Detective Joseph Strano visited her and took her statement it caused hardly a ripple of interest among his colleagues, who considered Tommy Zaino to be the best witness to the shooting. Tommy had seen a man with fair, not dark, hair; moreover, the driver of the Ford Galaxie had left the scene of the crime before the shooting began.

By this time, however, Cacilia – who felt that she had risked her life to come forward – was no longer going to be ignored and threatened to go anonymously to the newspapers with her story. In order to humour her Strano interviewed her again, this time bringing a police artist to make a sketch of the man whom she had seen. He also took her on an expedition to the shops to see if she could pick out a similar denim jacket to the one which the man had been wearing. Yet nothing further was done to investigate her story.

The primary problem with Cacilia's evidence was that the local police said that they had not issued any parking tickets in the area on the night on which the shootings had taken place. The police cars that had been patrolling the area had been seconded from other boroughs, however, and it was thus ten days before four further parking tickets materialised. Three of the four cars that had been penalised were quickly eliminated. The fourth, a yellow Ford Galaxie with the number plates 561-XLB, was found to belong to a David Berkowitz, of 35 Pine Street, Yonkers – a suburban area just north of the Bronx. When Detective James Justus called the Yonkers police headquarters to investigate further, a switchboard operator named Wheat Carr answered. On explaining that he was working on the Son-of-Sam case and that he was running a check on David Berkowitz the woman shouted 'Oh, no'.

It turned out that not only did Wheat Carr know David Berkowitz, but that she had suspected that he was the Son of Sam for some time. It had begun the previous year, when her father, Sam Carr, had started to receive anonymous letters complaining about his dog. In October 1976 a petrol bomb had been thrown through the window of the Carrs' house at 316 Warburton Avenue, Yonkers. A neighbour had also been receiving anonymous letters and abusive phone calls, and on Christmas Eve a number of shots had been fired through their window; their Alsatian had also been killed. Then, on 27 April 1977, someone had entered the Carrs' back yard and had shot their black Labrador, Harvey.

On 10 June 1977 Sam Carr had received a phone call from Jack Cassaras, who lived in New Rochelle, on Long Island Sound, who wanted to know why Sam had sent him a get-well card. The card had mentioned that Jack had fallen off a roof, but Jack had claimed that he had not – and, indeed, had never – been on one. Sam, who could offer no explanation for the mystery, had invited Jack over to his house to discuss the matter. On Jack's arrival, about 20 minutes later, Sam had examined the card, which had a picture of an Alsatian on it. He had then told Jack about the bizarre things that had been happening.

Jack had driven home feeling even more puzzled, but his son had then told him that he thought that he had the answer to the enigma. In the previous year the Cassarases had rented a room above their garage to a certain David Berkowitz, who had complained about their Alsatian before suddenly leaving a few weeks later without asking for the $200 deposit on his room. Jack's son suspected that Berkowitz might have something to do with the card. When Mrs Cassaras had looked him up in the telephone directory she found that he had moved to 35 Pine Street, Yonkers. She had then called Sam Carr to ask him whether Pine Street was near his house; it was just around the corner from him, Sam had replied. Convinced that Berkowitz was responsible for the harassment that his family had suffered, Sam had therefore gone to the police, but they had explained that they could take the matter no further without more concrete evidence.

Craig Glassman – a police officer who lived in the flat beneath Berkowitz – had also been receiving abusive letters, and when rubbish was piled against his front door and set alight on 6 August 1977 (a week after the Moskowitz murder) he reported it. He also showed detectives two anonymous letters that he had received, which accused Glassman of being a spy who had been planted in the building by Sam Carr. Glassman and the Carrs were members of a black-magic sect that was to get him, the author alleged. The detective who examined the letters recognised the handwriting to be that of a man whom he was investigating – David Berkowitz.

Berkowitz was not the only suspect in the Son-of-Sam case, however – indeed, New York has a rich supply of potential serial killers. Besides, Berkowitz did not fit the description given by Tommy Zaino, nor did he drive a yellow VW. It was not until 10 August 1977 that detectives John Longo and Ed Zigo went to Yonkers to check out Berkowitz. On their arrival Zigo spotted Berkowitz's Ford Galaxie parked outside the block of flats in Pine Street. On closer investigation they saw that there was a bag on the back seat from which a rifle butt protruded. Although possession of a rifle does not require a licence in New York, Zigo nevertheless forced open the car. Inside he found another, more formidable, weapon: a Commando Mark III semi-automatic. He also discovered a letter in the glove compartment addressed to Deputy Inspector Timothy Dowd – the head of the Son-of-Sam investigation – which said that the next shooting would be in Long Island. Detective Zigo phoned the police station and told Sergeant James Shea 'I think we've got him'.

Police who had been rapidly ordered to Pine Street from all over the city staked out the car until Berkowitz – a stocky man, with a round, cherubic face and dark hair – turned up six hours later. When he got into the driver's seat he found himself looking down the barrel of a police revolver. 'Freeze!' yelled Detective William Gardella. 'Police!' Berkowitz simply smiled. Detective John Falotico then opened the passenger door, held his .38 to Berkowitz's head and told him to get out. When Berkowitz placed his hands on the roof of the car Falotico asked 'Who are you?' 'I am Sam', replied Berkowitz.

At One Police Plaza Berkowitz confessed to the shootings, as well as to sending the anonymous letters, furthermore admitting that his crime spree had begun on Christmas Eve in 1975. At about 7pm on that day he had driven to Co-op City in the Bronx, where his adoptive father lived. On seeing a young, Hispanic woman leaving a shop he had followed her before pulling out a knife and stabbing her in the back. Not realising what had happened, she had turned, screamed and grabbed his wrist, whereupon he had run away. On his way home, however, he had stalked the 15-year-old Michelle Forman and had stabbed her in the back and head. When she fell screaming to the pavement Berkowitz had again fled. Michelle had somehow managed to stagger to the block of flats where she lived and her parents had then rushed her to hospital, where it was discovered that she had a collapsed lung. Her other injuries were superficial, however, and she only spent a week in hospital. Berkowitz's first victim had not even reported the attack and was never identified. These early attacks had convinced Berkowitz that he needed a gun, and a friend called Billy Dan Parka had accordingly bought him a .44 Bulldog revolver in Houston, Texas, for $130.

Under interrogation, Berkowitz explained that he had been ordered to commit the murders by Sam Carr, via Carr's demonic dog, Harvey. Other demonic voices had accompanied him when he was stalking his victims, he claimed. Berkowitz was so forthcoming that his confession took only half an hour to complete.

Further inquiries revealed that Richard David Berkowitz had been an illegitimate child who had been given up for adoption as a baby. His natural mother, Betty Broder, was Jewish. At the age of 19 she had married the Italian-American Tony Falco, who had left her for another woman six years later. Betty had begun an affair with Joseph Kleinman, a married real-estate agent, in 1947 and had become pregnant by him, but when she told him that she was going to have a child he replied that she had better get rid of it if she wanted to continue seeing him. Their child was born on 1 June 1953 and was immediately adopted by a Jewish couple, Pearl and Nathan Berkowitz, who were unable to have children of their own. They called their new son David. When Pearl succumbed to cancer in 1967 the 14-year-old David was deeply upset by this new loss.

Two years later Nathan decided to move to Co-op City, in the Bronx. It had been a middle-class suburb, but gangs of youths soon began terrorising the neighbourhood. David's school marks plunged and he seemed to lose his sense of direction. A shy boy, he found himself becoming the victim of bullying, although others regarded him as being spoilt and something of a bully himself. He was big for his age, strong and an excellent baseball player, but preferred to play with children who were younger than himself. His biggest problem, however, was with girls (one friend recalled Berkowitz asking him if he wanted to join the 'girl-haters' club'). He only dated one girl in Co-op City: Iris Gerhardt. Although Iris liked his warm and obliging nature the relationship was never consummated, and while Berkowitz remained chaste it seemed to him that almost everyone else was having sex: 'After a while, at Co-op City there wasn't one girl who was a virgin', he said resentfully. In prison, Berkowitz later wrote 'I must slay women for revenge purposes to get back at them for all the suffering they caused me'.

When his friends started smoking marijuana Berkowitz was too inhibited to join in. Things became worse in 1971, when his father remarried, whereupon Berkowitz, who resented his stepmother and stepsister, joined the army (his spell in uniform did not last long, however). By the time that he returned home in 1974 Berkowitz had rejected Judaism and had become a Baptist. Nathan Berkowitz furthermore remembered watching his son standing in front of a mirror while beating his head with his fists. Things became so uncomfortable in the Berkowitz household that David moved out, renting a drab, one-room flat at 2151 Barnes Avenue in the Bronx. By this time Nathan was convinced that his son needed psychiatric help, but because he and his new family were moving to Florida nothing was done. With his adoptive father gone another door to sanity closed on Berkowitz.

Having known since the age of seven that he was adopted, because he was feeling isolated he now tried to trace his natural family. It took a year. Through the Bureau of Records he discovered that his real name was Richard Falco and that he had been born in Brooklyn. With the help of an old telephone directory he managed to locate his mother and an elder sister. A few days after dropping a card into his mother's letterbox she called him and they had an emotional reunion. He also met his 37-year-old sister and became a regular visitor to the house in which she lived with her husband and children. Berkowitz had found his family and was happy at last – or so it seemed.

During the first half of 1976 his visits to his mother and sister became increasingly rare. He complained of headaches. In February he rented the room above the Cassarases' garage in New Rochelle, but two months later suddenly moved to Pine Street, Yonkers. In July he killed Donna Lauria, marking the start of his year-long killing spree.

Now, however, the police had Berkowitz under lock and key. Judged sane enough to stand trial, Berkowitz pleaded guilty to all of the charges against him and was sentenced to 365 years in prison. Sergeant Joseph Coffey, who had conducted Berkowitz's initial interrogation, commented 'I feel sorry for him. The man is a fucking vegetable'.

Not everyone was satisfied with Berkowitz's conviction; the young, Yonkers-born investigative journalist Maury Terry was one who noted a number of inconsistencies in Berkowitz's story. For example, Berkowitz claimed that he had acted alone, but because descriptions of the killer varied wildly he could have had an accomplice. Terry also noted that some of the Son-of-Sam killings had been performed with ruthless efficiency, while others had been inept and bungled. He eventually concluded that Berkowitz had committed only three of the killings – those of Donna Lauria, Valentina Suriani and Alexander Esau.

Terry believed that Berkowitz was a member of a satanic organisation – the Twenty Two Disciples of Hell mentioned in the letter sent to Jimmy

Breslin from the Son of Sam – and that further members of the cult were actually responsible for the other murders (the killer in the Balaclava, Terry speculated, was a woman). However, when he managed to track down some of the cult's members – including Sam Carr's sons, John 'Wheaties' and Michael – in order to investigate his theory further he learned that they had all died mysteriously.

In February 1979 Berkowitz issued a statement from Attica Correctional Facility, where he was being held, saying that he was indeed involved with a satanic group. Then, on 10 July 1979, he was slashed with a razor by another inmate. The cut ran from the left-hand side of his throat to the back of his neck; it needed 56 stitches and nearly killed him. Berkowitz claimed that the attack was a warning from the cult that he should keep his mouth shut.

25 ❖ The Zodiac Killer

A brutal assassin who styled himself the 'Zodiac Killer' stalked the Bay area around San Francisco for over ten years. Like Jack the Ripper, he taunted the police with letters and clues. Also in common with the Ripper, he, too, was never caught and may even have moved on, to kill again.

His reign of terror began on a chilly, moonlit night at Christmas in 1968. A teenage couple had drawn up in their car in an open space next to a pump house on the Lake Herman road in the Vallejo hills overlooking San Francisco. This was the local lovers' lane and David Faraday and Bettilou Jensen were indifferent to the cold. Indeed, they were so wrapped up in each other that they did not notice another car pulling up about 10 feet (3 metres) away. Their amorous reverie was then rudely interrupted by gunfire, however. One bullet smashed through the back window, showering them with glass, while another thudded into the car's bodywork. Bettilou threw open the passenger door and leapt out. David, who was trying to follow her, had his hand on the door handle when the gunman leant in through the driver's window and shot him in the head, causing his body to slump across the front seat. Bettilou's attempt at flight was futile; as she ran screaming into the night the gunman ran after her; she had covered just 30 feet (9 metres) when he fired five shots at her. After she had collapsed

Artists impression of the 'Zodiac Killer'.

and died the gunman walked calmly back to his car and drove away.

A few minutes later another car drove down the quiet road. Its driver, a woman, saw Bettilou's body sprawled on the ground, but did not stop, instead speeding on, towards the next town, Benica, to get help. On the way she saw the flashing blue light of a police car approaching her and frantically switched her headlights on and off to try to attract the driver's attention. The car stopped and she told the patrolmen what she had seen. They then followed her back to the pump house, arriving there about three minutes later. Although Bettilou was dead David was still alive, but because he was unconscious he could not give them any information about what had happened. He died shortly after his arrival at the hospital to which they had rushed him.

There was little for the police to go on: the victims had not been sexually assaulted and nothing was missing (the money in David's wallet was still there). Detective Sergeant Les Lundblatt, of the Vallejo-county police force, investigated the possibility that they had been murdered by a jealous rival, but there were found to be no jilted lovers and no other amorous entanglements. The two teenagers were ordinary students whose lives were an open book. Six months later Bettilou Jensen and David Faraday's files had become just two of a huge number relating to unsolved murders in the state of California.

On 4 July 1969 their killer struck again. At around midnight at Blue Rock Park – another romantic spot, just 2 miles (3 kilometres) from where Bettilou and David were murdered – Mike Mageau was sitting in his car with his girlfriend, the 22-year-old waitress Darlene Ferrin. They were not entirely alone because other courting couples had also parked their cars there. Like Bettilou and David before them, Mike and Darlene were too engrossed in each other to notice when a white car pulled up beside them. It stayed there for only a few minutes before driving away, but then it returned and parked on the other side of the road. A powerful spotlight was suddenly shone on Mike's car, whereupon a figure approached them. Thinking that it was a policeman, Mike reached for his driver's licence. As he did so, however, he heard the sound of gunfire and saw Darlene slump in her seat; seconds later a bullet tore into Mike's neck. The gunman then walked unhurriedly back to the white car, paused to fire another four or five shots at them and then sped off, leaving the smell of cordite and burning rubber in his wake.

A few minutes later a man called the Vallejo-county police station and reported a murder on Columbus Parkway, telling the switchboard operator 'You will find the kids in a brown car. They are shot with a 9mm Luger. I also killed those kids last year. Goodbye'. When the police arrived Darlene was dead, and although Mike was still alive the bullet had passed through his tongue and he was unable to speak.

There was another lead for the police to follow up, however. Four months earlier Darlene's babysitter had noticed a white car parked outside Darlene's flat. Thinking that it looked suspicious, she asked Darlene about it. It was plain that the young waitress knew the driver: 'He's checking up on me again', she told the babysitter. 'He doesn't want anyone to know what I saw him do. I saw him murder someone.' The babysitter had had a good look at the man in the white car and told the police that he was middle-aged, with brown, wavy hair and a round face. When Mike could talk again he confirmed that the gunman had had brown hair and a round face. After that, however, the clues to the killer's identity petered out.

Then, on 1 August 1969 – almost two months after the shootings of Darlene and Mike, three local newspapers received handwritten letters. They all began: 'DEAR EDITOR, THIS IS THE MURDERER OF THE 2 TEENAGERS LAST CHRISTMAS AT LAKE HERMAN & THE GIRL ON THE 4TH OF JULY ...' (Like

David Berkowitz's letters, they were written in capital letters and contained basic errors in spelling and syntax.) The author gave details of the ammunition that he had used, leaving no one in any doubt that he was indeed the gunman. Each letter also contained a third of a sheet of paper covered with a strange code, which the writer demanded that the papers print on their front pages; if they did not, he warned, he would go on 'killing lone people in the night'. The letters were signed with another cipher – a circle with a cross inside it which looked ominously like a gun sight.

All three of the newspapers complied with the writer's demands and the coded message was also sent to Mare Island Naval Yard, where cryptographers tried to crack it. Although it appeared to be a simple substitution code the US Navy's experts could not break it. Dale Harden, a teacher at Alisal High School in Salinas, however, could. Having had the idea of looking for a group of ciphers that might spell the word 'kill', he managed to locate them and after ten hours' intense work he and his wife had decoded the whole of the message, which read: 'I like killing people because it is so much more fun than killing wild game in the forrest [sic] because man is the most dangerous of all to kill . . .' The killer then went on to boast that he had already murdered five people in the San Francisco Bay area and added that after he had been reborn in paradise his victims would become his slaves.

After the murderer's cryptic message was made public a tidal wave of information was offered by ordinary citizens: over 1,000 calls were received by the police, but none of them led anywhere. So the killer helpfully volunteered another clue, this time revealing a name, or rather a nickname, that he knew would attract the attention of the headline-writers. Writing again to the newspapers, he began his letters 'DEAR EDITOR, THIS IS ZODIAC SPEAKING . . .' He again gave details of the slaying of Darlene Ferrin that only the killer could have known. Yet although the killer's strategy increased his publicity profile the police were still no nearer to catching him.

On 27 September 1969 the 20-year-old Bryan Hartnell and the 22-year-old Cecelia Shepard – both students at the nearby Seventh-day Adventists' Pacific Union College – went for a picnic on the shores of Lake Berryessa, some 13 miles (21 kilometres) north of Vallejo. At around 4.30pm they had finished eating and were lying on a blanket, kissing, when they noticed a stocky man, with brown hair, walking towards them across the clearing.

Having disappeared momentarily into a copse, when he re-emerged he was wearing a mask and carrying a gun. As he came closer Bryan saw that the mask had a symbol on it: a white cross within a circle.

The man was not particularly threatening in his manner and his voice was soft. 'I want your money and your car keys', he said. Bryan explained that he only had 76 cents, but said that the masked man was welcome to that. The gunman then began to chat, telling them that he was an escaped convict and that he was going to have to tie them up with the clothesline that he had brought with him. Having forced Cecelia to tie up Bryan, he then trussed her up himself.

The gunman talked some more before calmly announcing 'I am going to have to stab you people', whereupon Bryan begged to be stabbed first, saying 'I couldn't bear to see her stabbed'. Having quietly agreed to this, the gunman sank to his knees and stabbed Bryan repeatedly in the back with a hunting knife. Although he was feeling dizzy and sick, Bryan was still conscious when the masked man turned his attention to Cecelia. Having initially appeared calm, after the first stab he went berserk, plunging the hunting knife into her body again and again while she frantically twisted and turned beneath him in a futile attempt to escape the blows. When she was finally lying still the man regained his composure. He got up, walked to their car, pulled a felt-tip pen from his pocket and then drew something on the door before strolling away.

A fisherman who had heard their screams ran towards them, to find both Bryan and Cecelia still alive. Napa Valley police officers were already on their way, having been alerted by an anonymous phone call in which a man's gruff voice had said 'I want to report a double murder', then going on to give the precise location at which the bodies could be found before leaving the phone hanging from its cord.

When the police arrived Cecelia was in a coma; she died two days later, in hospital, without having regained consciousness. Bryan recovered slowly and was able to give a full description of their attacker, but the police had already guessed who he was, for the sign that the killer had drawn on the door of their car was a circle with a cross within it. The police also located the phone booth from which the killer had reported the murder: it was less than six streets away from the headquarters of the Napa Valley Police Department. They furthermore managed to lift three good-quality fingerprints from it, although their owner's details were unfortunately not found among the police's records.

On 11 October 1969, just two weeks later, a fourteen-year-old girl was looking out of a window of her home in San Francisco when she witnessed a crime in progress. A taxi was parked on the corner of Washington and Cherry streets and she could see a stocky man, who was sitting in the front passenger seat, going through the pockets of the driver, who appeared to be dead. She called to her brothers to come and watch what was happening and together they observed the man getting out of the taxi, leaving the cab driver lying slumped across the seat, and wiping the door handle with a piece of cloth before walking off in a northerly direction. Although the children promptly called the police they did not give their evidence very clearly and the telephone operator who took the call (which was logged at 10pm) made a note that the suspect was an 'NMA' – Negro male adult – even though he was, in fact, white. Indeed, after the police had put out a general alert a patrolman actually stopped a stocky man near the scene of the crime and asked whether he had seen anything unusual; the man replied in the negative and because he was furthermore white the patrolman waved him on his way.

A stocky man was later seen running into the nearby Presidio – a military compound that contains housing and a park – whereupon the floodlights were switched on and the area was searched by patrolmen with dogs, but with no success. When they inspected the taxi the police found the driver, the 29-year-old Paul Stine, lying dead from a gunshot wound to the head. The motive for his killing, they thought, was robbery.

Three days later the San Francisco Chronicle received a letter from Zodiac. 'THIS IS THE ZODIAC SPEAKING', it said. 'I AM THE MURDERER OF THE TAXI DRIVER OVER BY WASHINGTON ST AND MAPLE ST [sic] LAST NIGHT, TO PROVE IT HERE IS A BLOOD STAINED PIECE OF HIS SHIRT.' (The piece of cloth enclosed with the letter was indeed found to match the shirt of the murdered taxi-driver. The bullet that had killed Stine was also identified as a .22 that had been fired from the same gun that had been used to kill Bettilou Jensen and David Faraday.) The letter went on to say: 'I AM THE SAME MAN WHO DID IN THE PEOPLE IN THE NORTH BAY AREA'. 'THE S. F. POLICE COULD HAVE CAUGHT ME LAST NIGHT', it taunted, before concluding: 'SCHOOL CHILDREN MAKE NICE TARGETS. I THINK I SHALL WIPE OUT A SCHOOL BUS SOME MORNING. JUST SHOOT OUT THE TIRES AND THEN PICK OFF ALL THE KIDDIES AS THEY COME BOUNCING OUT.' The letter was signed with the now familiar circle containing a cross.

The description of the man supplied by the children, as well as by the policeman who had stopped the stocky, white male as he was leaving the scene of the crime, matched those given by Darlene Ferrin's babysitter, Mike Mageau and Bryan Hartnell. A new composite image of the Zodiac Killer was now drawn up and issued to the public by San Francisco's chief of police, Thomas J Cahill. It depicted a white male, 35 to 45 years old, with short, brown hair, which possibly had a red tint; he was described as being around 5 feet 8 inches (1.75 metres) tall, heavily built and a wearer of glasses. This 'wanted' poster was plastered around San Francisco.

The Zodiac Killer's appetite for publicity seems to have been insatiable. At 2am on 22 October 1969, 11 days after the murder of Paul Stine, a man with a gruff voice called the police department in Oakland, just across the bay from San Francisco. After introducing himself as Zodiac he said 'I want to get in touch with F Lee Bailey. If you can't come up with Bailey I'll settle for Mel Belli. I want one or other of them to appear on the Channel 7 talk show. I'll make contact by telephone'.

The men for whom he had asked were the USA's two leading criminal lawyers, and although F Lee Bailey was not available at such short notice Melvin Belli agreed to appear on Jim Dunbar's talk show at 6.30 on the following morning. The show's ratings soared as people throughout the Bay area tuned in. At around 7.20am a man called in and told Belli that he was Zodiac, although he preferred to be called Sam. Then he said 'I'm sick. I have headaches'. The mystery caller was eventually traced to Napa State Hospital and proved to be a psychiatric patient.

The actual Zodiac continued his correspondence, however, writing to Inspector David Toschi, of San Francisco's homicide squad, and threatening to commit more murders. In another letter he claimed to have killed seven people – two more than the Zodiac Killer's official body count up till then. He later said that he had murdered 10, taunting the San Francisco Police Department (SFPD) with the score line 'ZODIAC 10, SFPD 0'. He furthermore gave cryptic clues as to his real name and shared his fantasy of blowing up school children with a bomb with the recipients of his letters.

The following Christmas Melvin Belli received a card saying 'DEAR MELVIN, THIS IS THE ZODIAC SPEAKING. I WISH YOU A HAPPY CHRISTMAS. THE ONE THING I ASK OF YOU IS THIS, PLEASE HELP ME . . . I AM AFRAID I WILL LOSE CONTROL AND TAKE MY NINTH AND POSSIBLY TENTH VICTIM'. Another piece of Paul Stine's bloodstained shirt was enclosed. Forensic handwriting experts feared that Zodiac's mental state was deteriorating.

On 24 July 1970 the Zodiac Killer wrote a letter that included the words: 'THE WOEMAN [sic] AND HER BABY THAT I GAVE A RATHER INTEREST- ING RIDE FOR A COUPLE OF HOWERS [sic] ONE EVENING A FEW MONTHS BACK THAT ENDED IN MY BURNING HER CAR WHERE I FOUND THEM'. The afore- mentioned woman was Kathleen Johns. On the evening of 17 March 1970 she was driving in the Vallejo area, with her baby in the car with her, when a white Chevrolet drew up alongside her. The driver indicated that there was something wrong with her rear wheel, so she pulled over and the other driver also stopped; according to Kathleen he was a 'clean-shaven and neatly dressed man'. He told her that her wheel had been wobbling and offered to tighten the wheel nuts for her, which she gratefully agreed to. When she drove off, however, the wheel that he had said that he had fixed came off altogether, whereupon the driver of the Chevrolet offered her a lift to a nearby service station. She again accepted his offer of help, but when they reached the service station he drove straight past it, reply- ing to her query as to why he had done so in a chillingly calm voice. 'You know I am going to kill you', he said.

Kathleen managed to keep her head, however, and when her abductor slowed down on the curve of a motorway ramp she jumped from the car while holding her baby in her arms, ran off and hid in an irrigation ditch. The driver then stopped the Chevrolet and started to search for her, using a torch that he had taken out of the boot of the car. Fortunately for Kath- leen, he was approaching the ditch in which she was cowering with her child when he was caught in the beam of a lorry's headlights. An hour later, having watched him drive off, Kathleen made her way to a police sta- tion to report what had happened to her. On seeing Zodiac's 'wanted' poster pinned to the wall of the police station she identified him as the man who had threatened to kill her. When the police drove her back to her car they found that it was now a burnt-out shell – it seemed that the Zodiac Killer had returned to set it alight.

Despite the new leads that Kathleen Johns had provided the police were still no nearer to catching the Zodiac Killer, although the Vallejo- county police believed that he was now the driver of a new, green Ford. The reason behind their suspicion was that the driver of such a car had once stopped and ostentatiously watched a highway patrolman who was parked on the other side of the motorway. After the patrolman had decided to ask him what he was doing and had driven through an underpass to reach him he had found the green Ford gone: it was now parked on the other side of the motorway, exactly where the squad car had been moments before. Zodiac subsequently played this cat-and-mouse game every day for two weeks.

Detective Sergeant Lundblatt was becoming increasingly convinced that the Zodiac Killer was a man named Andy Walker. Walker had known Darlene Ferrin and Darlene's sister had also identified him as the man who had waited outside Darlene's flat in the white car. He bore a marked resemblance, too, to the description of the man who was seen near Lake Berrylessa when Cecelia Shepard was stabbed to death. Walker was also known to suffer from bad headaches and to get on badly with the women with whom he worked. He had furthermore studied codes while in the army.

However, neither did his fingerprints match the one that had been left in Paul Stine's taxi nor did his handwriting equate to that on Zodiac's notes. The police then discovered that Walker was ambidextrous, which meant that his handwriting would change depending on which hand he used to write with. They also formulated the theory that the murder of Paul Stine had been so meticulously planned that the Zodiac Killer may have used the severed finger of an unknown victim with which to plant fingerprints in the taxi and thereby throw the police off his scent.

The police decided that they had to obtain Walker's palm prints in order to see if they matched those that had been found on the telephone that had been left dangling after the Paul Stine killing. An undercover policeman therefore asked Walker to help him to carry a goldfish bowl, but although Walker obliged the palm prints that he left were smudged. Walker soon realised that he was being targeted by the police, however, and approached a judge, who issued a court order which forced them to stop harassing Walker.

Letters from Zodiac threatening more murders were received; some were authenticated, but rendered few new clues. The only thing that the police could be sure of was that Zodiac was a fan of the comic operettas of Gilbert and Sullivan. He had taunted them with a parody of 'The Lord High Executioner', listing those people whom he intended to kill and using the refrain 'Titwillo, titwillo, titwillo', and there were furthermore no letters or killings during the entire run of San Francisco's Presentation Theater's The Mikado .

The police also deduced that Zodiac had a curious connection with water. Not only did all of the names of his crime scenes have some association with water, but in one of his letters he had claimed that the body count would have been higher if he had not been 'swamped by the rain we had a while back'. The police therefore reasoned that he lived in a low-lying area that was susceptible to flooding or that he perhaps had a basement in which he kept equipment for making his long-threatened bomb.

Next a K-Mart shop in Santa Rosa, California, was evacuated following a bomb threat made by a man who identified himself as the Zodiac Killer. Two months later Zodiac wrote another letter to the *San Francisco Chronicle* claiming to have killed 12 people and enclosing a map with an 'X' marking the peak of a mountain in Contra Costa Country, across the bay from San Francisco, from which an observer, he said, would be able to see the entire panorama of the area in which the murders had taken place. When detectives examined the location more closely, however, the spot marked was found to be within the compound of a naval relay station, to which only service personnel with security clearance were granted access.

The letters, which continued to come, now demanded that everyone in the San Francisco area wear lapel badges bearing the Zodiac Killer's symbol. When they did not comply he threatened Paul Avery, the *San Francisco Chronicle*'s crime writer who had been investigating the Zodiac story, whereupon journalists (including Avery), began wearing badges saying 'I am not Paul Avery'. Avery, who was a licensed private eye and a former war correspondent in Vietnam, also started carrying a .38 and practised shooting regularly at the police firing range.

An anonymous correspondent then tied the Zodiac slayings to the unsolved murder of Cheri Jo Bates, an 18-year-old college student who had been stabbed to death after leaving the college library in Riverside, California, on Hallowe'en in 1966. Although the police could not rule out a connection they could not prove a concrete link either. When Avery investigated it, however, he discovered that the police had received what they considered to be a crank letter about the murder five months after the killing. It was signed with the letter 'Z'. In a series of typewritten letters the author furthermore gave details of the murder that only the killer could have known. He also threatened more killings and wrote of a 'game' that he was playing. Handwritten letters were received, too, whose writing matched that of Zodiac's. Armed with this evidence, Avery managed to persuade the police to re-open the Bates case in the light of the Zodiac murders.

During 1971 there were a number of murders which could have been committed by Zodiac. Indeed, letters purporting to have come from him confessed to them, but he could easily have been claiming the credit for other people's handiwork.

At around 9pm on 7 April 1972 the 33-year-old Isobel Watson, who worked as a legal secretary in San Francisco, got off a bus in Tamalpais Valley. She had just begun walking home, up Pine Hill, when a white Chevrolet swerved across the road and nearly hit her. After the car had come to a halt the driver apologised and offered to give her a lift home; when Isobel declined he got out of the car, pulled out a knife and stabbed her in the back. Her screams alerted her neighbours, who came running out of their homes, whereupon the man jumped back into his car and sped off. After Isobel had recovered she gave a description of her attacker: he was a white man in his early forties, around 5 feet 9 inches (1.78 metres) tall, and had been wearing black-rimmed reading glasses. The police believed that there was a better than 50-50 chance that he was the Zodiac Killer.

As time went by, many of the detectives working on the Zodiac case were reassigned, and eventually only Inspector David Toschi was left. Agents from the Federal Bureau of Investigation (FBI) looked at the files, but even they could take the case no further. Zodiac's correspondence now ceased for nearly four years, but although psychologists believed that he was the type to commit suicide Toschi was not convinced that he was dead. He reasoned that Zodiac got his kicks from the publicity that his murders generated rather than from the killings themselves and that he would therefore have left a note or some other clue that he was Zodiac if he had killed himself. Then, on 25 April 1978, Toschi received confirmation that Zodiac was still alive when the *San Francisco Chronicle* received a letter from him. It mentioned Toschi by name and said that the writer wanted the people of San Francisco to know that he was back.

Robert Graysmith, the author of the book *Zodiac*, deduced that the eponymous murderer was a film buff. In one of his cryptograms, for example, he had mentioned the 'most dangerous game', which is the title of a film, in another calling himself the 'Red Phantom', which is also the name of a film. He furthermore frequently mentioned going to the cinema to see The *Exorcist* or *Badlands*, the latter a fictionalised account of the murderous spree of the Nebraskan killer Charles Starkweather.

The police used the information supplied by Graysmith, as well as the Zodiac Killer's obvious love of publicity, to try to trap him. When a film about the Zodiac killings was shown in San Francisco a suggestions box was installed in the lobby of the cinema, into which the audience was invited to drop notes containing any information or theories that they may have had regarding the murders. Inside the huge box was hidden a detective, who read every note by torchlight as it fell through the slot; he had been ordered to raise the alarm if any looked as though they could have come from the Zodiac Killer, but none did.

The Oakland police thought that they had captured the Zodiac Killer at one point. The suspect was a veteran of the Vietnam War who had seen the Zodiac film three times and had been apprehended while masturbating in the cinema's lavatory after a particularly violent scene. They were soon proved wrong, however, for his handwriting did not match Zodiac's. Amid a welter of recrimination Toschi was transferred from homicide following (baseless) accusations that he had forged the Zodiac letters for self-promotion. The police in the Bay area now began to believe that the Zodiac Killer was either dead or serving time for another crime in a prison outside the state. On the other hand, maybe he reckoned that his time was running out, having nearly been caught following the killing of Paul Stine.

Robert Graysmith was not convinced by these theories, however. He had managed to link the Zodiac killings with the unsolved murders of 14 young girls, usually students or hitchhikers, in the Santa Rosa area during the early 1970s. Although most of them had been found naked, with their clothes missing, they had generally not been sexually molested. Each had been killed in a different way, as if the murderer had been experimenting to ascertain which method was best. Graysmith now reckoned that Zodiac's body count could be as high as 40.

Graysmith believed that Zodiac's symbol - a cross within a circle – was not intended to represent a stylised gunsight, but rather the projectionist's guide that is shown on screen during the lead-in to a film. He traced a promising-sounding suspect through a cinema in San Francisco on whose ceiling the constellations were painted: the man, Graysmith was told, had filmed some murders and kept the gruesome footage in a booby-trapped can. Another suspect of Graysmith's was a former boyfriend of Darlene Ferrin, who had also been a resident of Riverside at the time when Cheri Jo Bates was murdered. He lived with his mother, whom he loathed, and dissected small mammals as a hobby. During the crucial 1975 to 1978 period, when the Zodiac Killer had been quiet, he had been in a psychiatric institution after having been charged with molesting children at the school where he was employed. Graysmith could not pin the Zodiac murders on either of his suspects, however. He published the story of his investigation in 1985.

In 1990 a series of murders was perpetrated in New York by someone who claimed to be Zodiac. Although descriptions of the New York killer did not match those given by the witnesses to the Zodiac murders in California, a man can change a lot over 20 years. Who can tell where he may strike next?

26 ❖ The Hillside Strangler

Between October 1977 and January 1979 the Los Angeles area was plagued by a series of killings. Although these were attributed to the 'Hillside Strangler they turned out to be the work not of one man, but of two murderous cousins.

It had started as a discussion over a beer, when Kenneth Bianchi had asked his cousin, Angelo Buono Jr, what it would be like to kill someone. This was no drunken banter and they consequently decided to find out exactly how it would feel.

The 25-year-old Bianchi had been raised by foster parents in Rochester, New York State. In 1977 he had moved to Los Angeles, where he stayed with his cousin, Buono, who was 17 years his senior. The intellectually sub-normal, yet streetwise, Buono used to bring prostitutes back to his house in Glendale, where he ran an upholstery business. Within months of Bianchi's arrival in California the aforementioned question of murder came up and they accordingly resolved to kill one of the prostitutes whose services Buono used. It would be the beginning of a murder spree that would claim the lives of 12 young women.

Their first victim was the 21-year-old Hollywood prostitute Elissa Kastin, whose naked body was found on a hillside on Chevy Chase Drive on 6 October 1977. The police believed that she had been murdered else-where and that her body had later been dumped there. Indeed, like those that were to follow her, she had been lured to Buono's home, where she had been savagely raped and killed.

By the end of November 1977 five more young women had fallen victim to the putative Hillside Strangler, and a pattern to the killings was beginning to emerge. The bodies of all of the women, who were mainly part-time prostitutes, had been discovered on hillsides around Los Angeles. Their wrists and ankles bore the marks of ropes and they had been stripped naked, raped and sometimes also sodomised. Their corpses had subsequently been carefully cleaned by the killers so that no clues to their own identities remained. From analysing samples of the sperm that had been left inside the women, however, the police knew that two men had been involved, but they kept this information from members of the press, who, presuming that the perpetrator was a single man, had come up with the nickname the 'Hillside Strangler'.

The murderers were clearly enjoying their notoriety, for all of the naked bodies – often arranged in lascivious poses – had been dumped by roadsides, where they were certain to be discovered. Because the corpses had also been left near police stations it was speculated that the killer was taunting the police. In fact, Bianchi had applied for a job with the Los Angeles Police Department (LAPD), and although he had been turned down police officers had taken him on patrol during the course of the investigation.

The killers chose their victims by cruising around Los Angeles in Buono's car. When they saw a likely target they would stop and get out. Flashing fake badges, they would claim to be undercover policemen and order the woman to get into what they said was an unmarked police car. The woman would then be driven to Buono's home, where she would be tied up, tortured and abused by both men before being strangled.

Their second victim was the 19-year-old Yolanda Washington, whose corpse was discovered lying beside the Forest Lawn cemetery on the night of 18 October 1977. Her spread-eagled, naked body had been meticulously cleansed and the only clues to her death that remained were the marks of the ropes that had restrained her during her final hours of torment. Two weeks later the 15-year-old Judith Miller was found dead on a hillside above a Glendale road. Her neck, wrists and ankles all bore rope marks and she had been violently raped before being strangled.

On the night of 20 November 1977 Bianchi and Buono murdered three girls, one of whom – Dolores Cepeda – was only 12 years old. Dolores' body was found lying alongside that of the 14-year-old Sonja Johnson in Elysian Park. On the same night the corpse of the 20-year-old Kristina Weckler was discovered on a hillside in Highland Park. Three days later the casually discarded body of the 28-year-old Jane King was found lying on an exit ramp of the Golden State motorway.

Things went quiet for a bit after that, until, on 17 February 1978, the naked body of Cindy Hudspeth was discovered in the boot of a car. Cindy had been registered with a modelling agency which kept a record of its clients' assignments, leading the LAPD to hope that a breakthrough was at last in sight. Although police officers interviewed a security guard named Ken Bianchi, nothing came of it. The killings, however, mysteriously ceased.

Buono's home was filthy and because Bianchi could no longer stand living there he left his cousin's house and moved to Bellingham, in Washington state, where he took a job as a security guard and again applied to join the local police force. For the rest of 1978 there were no more killings and the special murder squad that had been formed in Los Angeles to track down the Hillside Strangler was therefore disbanded.

However, in January 1979 the bodies of two young women were found in the back of a locked car in Bellingham. Diane Wilder and Karen Mandic had been hired by a young man from a security firm to 'house-watch' a luxury residence in Bellingham while the alarm system was being repaired, or so he had said. Their corpses were subsequently discovered near the house and on investigating further detectives learned that there had been nothing wrong with the alarm system. On checking with the Coastal Security Company (for which Bianchi worked) Bianchi's name came up and it was established that he was the security guard who had hired the women to look after the house. The police then found a note of the address of the house, as well as its front-door key, in Bianchi's lorry. A number of blood- and semen-stained articles of clothing were furthermore discovered in his house, along with Karen Mandic's telephone number. Meanwhile, forensic experts were examining both car and bodies in an attempt to link him to the killings.

Bianchi now claimed to be suffering from multiple-personality disorder and said that one of his personalities – Steve – was a sex killer. Six Washington-state psychiatrists duly certified him insane, which, according to the law in Washington, saved him from receiving the death penalty (hanging) for the two murders. Bianchi then plea-bargained a deal with the state prosecutors: if he was allowed to serve out his life sentence in California (where he thought the jails to be more comfortable) he would turn state's evidence again Buono in the Hillside-strangler case.

The Los Angeles prosecutors, however, considered Bianchi's evidence to be worthless – after all, he had been declared insane by six psychiatrists in Washington state. Thereafter the Hillside-strangler case became one of the longest and most expensive trials in US criminal history. Halfway through it Bianchi even tried to sabotage it by protesting that he was innocent.

More than 400 witnesses were heard before the two men were finally convicted, of whom one of the most important was the 27-year-old daughter of the actor Peter Lorre. Catherine Lorre identified Bianchi and Buono as the two men who had stopped her in Hollywood claiming to be police officers. Along with her identity card, she had showed them a photograph of herself with her famous father. This had saved her life, for the murderers had decided that killing the daughter of a celebrity would have caused the police to redouble their efforts to catch them.

The trial dragged on from 16 November 1981 to 14 November 1983, and at the end it Judge Ronald George told the pair 'I am sure, Mr Buono and Mr Bianchi, that you will only get your thrills by reliving over and over the tortures and murders of your victims, being incapable as I believe you to be, of ever feeling any remorse'. Bianchi – who was considered to have broken the terms of his plea bargain – was transferred to Washington state to serve his sentence of life imprisonment in Walla Walla Prison, while Buono, who was also sentenced to life, was sent to Folsom Prison in California.

27 ✦ The Wests

Number 25 Cromwell Street, Gloucester: an ordinary house in an ordinary terrace. The man of the house, Fred West, was cheerful and hard-working. His wife, Rosemary, was a busy, lively mother. They were generally liked by their neighbours. Although there was some gossip about the number of men who visited the house late at night, and some said that they disciplined their children too harshly, it was nothing that they felt that they should tell the police or social services about. The Wests, however, had some minor legal problems: during the 1970s the upper floors of the house had been divided into cheap bedsits and Fred, a builder by trade, had added a single-storey extension to the rear of the property without obtaining planning permission for it.

The story of what was actually going on behind the façade of this apparently ordinary house began to unravel during the summer of 1992. Police Constable Steve Burnside was patrolling his Gloucester beat when a group of young people came up to him and told him that children were being abused at a house in Cromwell Street, which was owned by a man named 'Quest'. Although the young informants were unsure of the facts, it was enough to warrant further police attention and as a result social services eventually took the five of Wests' children who were under sixteen into care. Fred and Rosemary were charged with a number of sexual offences, including rape and buggery, but the case against them was dropped when two prosecution witnesses refused to testify. Fred and Rosemary hugged each other in the dock and then returned to their old ways as if nothing had happened.

Detective Constable Hazel Savage, however, who had investigated the initial allegations, remained convinced something terrible was going in Cromwell Street. During quiet chats with the West children she had won their trust; they seemed particularly concerned about the disappearance of Fred and Rosemary's 16-year-old daughter, Heather, who had last been seen on 29 May 1987. Her parents had not even reported her as being missing, and when questioned had said that she had left home of her own accord, 'with a lesbian in a blue Mini'. But the children said that Fred would often joke about Heather being 'under the patio', and Savage believed that these 'jokes' were made a little too often to be simply the product of poor taste. On 23 February 1994 she therefore obtained a search warrant enabling her to gain access to the property at Cromwell Road and the following day the police started to dig up the garden.

A mechanical digger was brought in to remove the topsoil. Then, in the pouring rain, an 'archaeological-type dig' began, under the aegis of the Home Office pathologist Professor Bernard Knight. Supervised by Detective Superintendent John Bennett, a team of 30 officers, working in relays, began sifting shovelfuls of sodden earth through a sieve in the search for clues. At night the work continued under the glare of arc lights. On the second day a trowel hit something hard and the loose soil was scraped away to reveal a human skull. It was thought to be Heather's, and on 25 February 1994 Fred and Rosemary West were arrested. 'I didn't kill her', shouted Fred, as the couple was driven away in a police car.

Rosemary West - the serial killer poses at a birthday party.

After the police had interviewed her Rosemary was released without charge. By the time that her husband appeared in Gloucester magistrates' court a few days later to be formally charged with murder two more bodies had been found. Both were badly decomposed, having lain in the garden for 16 years.

One of the bodies was identified as being that of Shirley Ann Robinson, a lodger at 25 Cromwell Street who had last been seen in 1977. At the time of her death she had been 18 years old and heavily pregnant. According to Liz Brewer, another lodger, Fred West was the father of her child and Rosemary West had also been pregnant with another man's child at the time. 'The Wests had told Shirley they had an open marriage', said Liz. 'Fred didn't seem to mind his wife expecting by another man.' When Shirley had disappeared the Wests had informed Liz that Shirley could not cope with the growing tension between Fred and Rosemary and had gone to visit relatives in Germany. 'I was told she probably wasn't coming back', she said.

Over the next five days the bodies of two more women were unearthed in the cellar of the house. The situation was becoming so gruesome that the police officers involved in the excavation were given stress counselling; 40 more policemen were also seconded to the investigation. The police now

Fred West who, along with his wife Rosemary, buried many of their victims around the garden or in the house.

thought that there were five more bodies in the house and two further corpses buried in a field near Fred West's former home in Much Marcle. At 25 Cromwell Street the floorboards were lifted, fittings were ripped out and 200 tons of soil were excavated from the garden. In addition, the police opened up the chimney breast and broke up the bathroom floor using pneumatic drills. They furthermore discovered that the basement had been dug out to a depth of 5 feet (1.5 metres), which had undermined the foundations of the house.

Next a sixth body – again that of a young woman – was found buried under the cellar and it was then that the police brought in a ground-penetrating radar system. Developed during the Falklands Conflict to locate plastic landmines, it was the first time that this technology had been used in a murder investigation. The device cost £2,000 a day to rent. A seventh body was located under concrete in the cellar; the eighth was buried 4 feet (1.2 metres) beneath the bath on the ground floor (Fred's brother-in-law, Graham Letts, had helped him to lay the concrete floor there in 1987). The ninth, that of the 15-year-old Carol Ann Cooper, was discovered behind a false wall in the bathroom. Carol had last been seen on 10 November 1973; she had been in care at a children's home in Worcester at the time, but had been let out for the weekend to visit her grandmother.

The police also sealed off the nearby 25 Midland Road, the Wests' former home. Other bodies were thought to have been buried in a cornfield, known as Fingerpost Field, on the road between Much Marcle and Dymock. They decided that up to 30 properties at which Fred West had lived or worked would also have to be searched.

By 11 March 1994 Fred West had been charged with eight murders. Throughout the investigation he had been questioned by relays of detectives, who had found him to be co-operative 'some of the time'. From their interviews with him they had been able to piece together the bare bones of his life story.

Frederick Walter Stephen West was born on 29 September 1942 in Much Marcle. He lived with his parents and siblings at Moor Court Cottages and developed his powerful physique while working as a farm labourer. His mother's favourite son, Daisy was believed to have seduced him when he was 12. His father, Walter – also a farm labourer – enjoyed incestuous relationships, too, and regarded his daughters as sexual playthings; Fred would follow in his father's footsteps.

At the age of 19 Fred was arrested after having impregnated a 13-year-old girl. When questioned by the police he was unabashed and openly admitted to molesting young girls, asking 'Doesn't everyone do it?' Although West escaped a charge of statutory rape when his victim refused to give evidence in court, his mother threw him out of the house and he went to live nearby, with his Aunt Violet. He then started work as a lorry driver, soon afterwards meeting the woman who would become his first wife: a blonde, 18-year-old waitress named Catherine 'Rena' Costello.

Rena was already five months pregnant by another man when she married Fred on 17 November 1962. Fred gave the baby, Charmaine, his surname, and he and Rena then had a child of their own, Anne-Marie. They moved briefly to Lanarkshire and then to a caravan park in Bishop's Cleeve, near Cheltenham. The marriage was already in trouble because West wanted to play sadistic sex games, which Rena hatred. When she subsequently disappeared West told friends that she had taken up with an engineer and had returned to Lanarkshire. She was never seen again. Meanwhile, West had started seeing the 15-year-old Rosemary Letts.

Rosemary Pauline Letts was born on 29 November 1953 in Barnstaple. Her father, William Letts, was a steward in the Royal Navy who battered and bullied his wife and treated their seven children with appalling severity (he was later diagnosed as being schizophrenic). As the third-youngest of his children, Rosemary escaped the worst of his father's attentions, however. When the family moved to Bishop's Cleeve her mother walked out, taking Rosemary and her two younger brothers with her. Later in the same year Rosemary met the 27-year old Fred West at a bus stop and they soon began going steady. Fred had probably already committed one murder – maybe two – by this time, while the 15-year-old Rosemary was making a little pocket money from prostitution.

Rosemary's parents disapproved of the relationship and put Rosemary into care, but when Rosemary attained her independence at the age of 16 she moved in with West and his two daughters at the local caravan site. In 1970 they had a daughter of their own, Heather. Thereafter the Wests moved to a two-storey, pebble-dash house in Midland Road, Gloucester, along with Fred's daughter, Anne-Marie. Charmaine had been put into care in 1969, but was later returned to Fred, going missing shortly afterwards. The Wests apparently abused her viciously, on the grounds that she was 'not one of theirs', and at Rosemary's trial witnesses told of seeing Charmaine standing on a chair, her hands tied behind her back, while Rosemary beat her with a wooden spoon.

The police believed that Fred had killed Charmaine at around this time and that when Rena had come looking for her daughter he had killed her, too. Neither was reported missing and when Rosemary was asked where Charmaine was she replied 'She's gone off with her mother'. West certainly did not expect any problems to be caused by his first wife when he married Rosemary on 29 January 1972 at Gloucester Registry Office, for on the marriage certificate he entered his marital status as 'bachelor'. Three days later the Wests moved into 25 Cromwell Street. Here they would create their own fantasy world, a world in which Rosemary not only gave free reign to Fred's desire for sadistic sex, but actively indulged in it herself. The house in Cromwell Street was also home to a family of nine children, at least two of which were fathered by another man (West was furthermore said to have fathered as many as 24 children by different women). Because his wages were not enough to support such a large family the Wests supplemented their income by taking in lodgers and by Rosemary's prostitution under the working name of 'Mandy Mouse'.

Neighbours remembered Fred West as being a devoted father who loved taking his children to the seaside and worked hard for a number of local employers. Using his do-it-yourself skills he turned 25 Cromwell

Street into a temple to Formica. The downstairs front room was turned into a bedroom for Rosemary; set into the floor was a trap door which led down to the cellar, which West converted into two rooms in which four of the children slept. There was another bedroom, with a lace-canopied bed, on the first floor, as well as a sitting room containing a fully stocked bar, television and video (this storey was out of bounds to the children). On the top floor was one more bedroom, which was kept locked. It contained a four-poster bed that was fitted with spotlights and a concealed microphone; whips, chains, manacles and bondage gear were also to hand. It was here that they shot home-made, hard-core pornographic films starring the Wests and the punters who paid for Rosemary's services as a prostitute.

The couple lived for sex and were both constantly on the lookout for young women whom they could use as sexual playthings. Rosemary played a key role in this, Fred later explaining that it was a lot easier to pick up girls when he had Rosemary in the car with him because their victims felt more secure with a woman being present. After the young women had been lured to Cromwell Street their faces were bound with sticky, brown parcel tape and plastic breathing tubes were stuffed into their nostrils. Then their limbs were tightly bound and they were repeatedly raped and tortured. After they had died their bodies were mutilated – some say cannibalised – and their remains were then tossed unceremoniously into pits that had been dug in the cellar or back garden. (No one thought it odd that Fred did a lot of do-it-yourself work around the house – after all, he was a builder.)

By 8 April 1994 the police had identified every one of the nine bodies that had been found at 25 Cromwell Street. They were all those of young women aged between 15 and 21. Four had last been seen waiting for buses.

Lynda Gough, a seamstress who worked at the Co-op in Gloucester, had disappeared in April 1973 – just two weeks before her twentieth birthday – when she had left her parents' home to move into a flat in Gloucester. Her distraught parents had made enormous efforts to find her. The Swiss-born Thérèse Siegenthaler, a 21-year-old sociology student at Woolwich College in south London, had left her Lewisham home for the Holyhead ferry on 15 April 1974 to hitchhike to Ireland. She had boasted that because she was a judo expert she could take care of herself. The third body found in the garden was that of the 17-year-old Alison Chambers, who had been placed with a firm of solicitors in Gloucester under the Youth Training Scheme. Alison had run away from her home in south Wales and had written to her mother saying that she was staying with a 'big family'.

The police team then moved to Letterbox Field, on Stonehouse Farm at Kempley. After a trench 135 feet (41 metres) long had been dug and 160 tons of soil removed the remains of West's first wife, Rena, were found. She had gone missing at the age of 24 and her remains were identified on 14 April 1994, which would have been her fiftieth birthday. A quarter of a mile away, at Fingerpost Field, in Stonehouse Coppice, police found the remains of Anna McFall, a nanny who had been employed by Rena who had vanished during the early 1970s at the age of 22. The remains of Charmaine West, who had disappeared in 1971 at the age of eight, were found under the kitchen floor at 25 Midland Road.

Up until this time it had been assumed that Fred West alone was responsible for the murders. On 21 April 1994, however, Rosemary West was jointly charged with a 67-year-old man with raping an 11-year-old girl and assaulting a 7-year-old boy, causing actual bodily harm. Although man was released on bail Rosemary continued to be held. Two days later she was charged with having sexual intercourse with the same girl without her consent. After that she was charged with the murders of Lynda Gough, Carol Ann Cooper, Lucy Partington, Thérèse Siegenthaler, Shirley Hubbard, Juanita Mott, Shirley Robinson, Alison Chambers, and finally, on 26 May 1994, of her own daughter, Heather. Fred West had already been accused of all nine murders, as well as of the murders of two people whose remains had been found at Midland Road and Letterbox Field, but who had not yet been identified. His younger brother, John Charles Edward West, was accused of raping two underaged girls, along with Rosemary.

The most extraordinary thing about the West case was that they had got away with it for so long: for more than two decades the Wests' secret careers as sadistic sexual torturers and murderers of young women had flourished unchecked. West had killed his first victim – Anna McFall, from Sandhurst, Gloucestershire –before he had even met Rose. West had made Anna pregnant while she was working as a nanny for him and Rena in 1967 and had murdered her because she wanted him to leave Rena. The next two to die were Rena and little Charmaine. The police believed that West had killed his wife when she came looking for her daughter in 1971 and that Charmaine was strangled a few hours later.

Victim number four was the nineteen-year-old Lynda Gough. A local girl, she had become friendly with some of the Wests' lodgers at the Cromwell Street house and had moved in herself in March 1973. She had found herself becoming unwillingly involved in the Wests' twisted sex games and was dead within a matter of weeks. Her body had been buried under the bathroom floor; tape had been wound thickly around her head and her dismembered limbs had been piled on top of one another.

The fifth victim was the 15-year-old Carol Ann Cooper, who lived in a children's home in Worcester and was last seen boarding a bus on the way to her grandmother's on the night of 10 November 1973. Although West admitted killing her he said that Rosemary had not been involved. Number six was the twenty-one-year-old Lucy Partington. A devout religious student, she was studying medieval English at Exeter University when the Wests spotted her waiting at a bus stop in Cheltenham as they drove back from a Christmas visit to Rosemary's parents in Bishop's Cleeve on the night of 27 December 1973. At 25 Cromwell Street she endured a week-long ordeal of rape and torture. West did such a sloppy job dismembering her body that he cut his hand and had to go to hospital.

The next of the Wests' known victims was the Swiss-born Thérèse Siegenthaler. The 21-year-old had been hitchhiking to Ireland for a holiday when West had picked her up in his lorry near Chepstow. She was then taken to Cromwell Street, where she was imprisoned, tortured and raped. When the police unearthed her remains at Cromwell Street some of her body parts were found to be missing. Number eight was the fifteen-year-old Shirley Hubbard, a schoolgirl from Droitwich who had disappeared on 14 November 1974 while she was travelling by bus from Worcester to her parents' home. She, too, had been forced to wear one of West's 'mummy'-style masks before being repeatedly raped.

The 18-year-old Juanita Mott was picked up as she hitchhiked into Gloucester from her home in Newent on 11 April 1975. Lured to their home by the Wests, she was then trussed up with 17 feet (5 metres) of grey, plastic clothesline and her own stockings. After the Wests had finished with her Fred killed her with a blow from a hammer before decapitating her body and burying it in the cellar. Their tenth victim was Shirley Robinson. A bisexual, the eighteen-year-old had shared three-in-a-bed sex sessions with the Wests during early 1978 before becoming pregnant with West's child and falling in love with him (Rosemary had also been pregnant in 1978 with the child of a West Indian man). Rosemary had become jealous of Shirley and had put pressure on her husband to get rid of her. He had complied: Shirley's body was found next to that of her unborn child in the garden of 25 Cromwell Street.

A few months after Shirley had disappeared the Wests had latched on to the 16-year-old Alison Chambers, who was living in a children's home in Gloucester at the time and was exactly the kind of vulnerable girl that they liked. One of her friends was a lodger at 25 Cromwell Street and she visited the house regularly. The Wests had asked her to become their nanny and shortly after she had moved in they had involved her in their sadistic sex play. The police found her body underneath the Wests' lawn.

Their last-known victim was Heather West. Born in 1970, Heather was thought to have been the product of an incestuous relationship between Bill Letts and his daughter, Rosemary. Fred had made her life a living hell: when she had refused to let him molest her he had beaten her viciously. When she vanished, on 17 June 1987, the Wests told friends that she had run away from home.

The Wests were reunited in the dock of Gloucester's magistrates' court on 30 June 1994. West brushed his wife's neck with his hand and bent down to speak a few words to her, but Rosemary ignored him and refused even to glance at him. As they rose to leave the court after the brief hearing West tried to touch his wife again, only to receive the same response. They appeared together again for one last time in December 1994, when Rosemary West again pointedly ignored her husband.

On New Year's Day, 1995, Fred West was found hanged in his cell in Winson Green Prison. He had made a rope by plaiting strips of sheet together. Standing on a chair, he had then tied his home-made rope to a ventilator shaft, put the noose around his neck and kicked away the chair. (Things had not gone to plan, however, for the fall had not broken his neck and he was slowly strangled to death instead.) His suicide left Rosemary to face ten murder charges alone, along with two counts of rape and two of indecent assault. Her trial, which was presided over by Mr Justice Mantell, opened at Winchester Crown Court on Tuesday, 3 October 1995.

An early witness was Caroline Owens, who had been picked up by the Wests while she was hitchhiking in 1972. They had bound, beaten and raped her, she said, further alleging that Fred West had threatened that he would murder her. A witness described as 'Miss A' also said that she had been abused by the Wests at 25 Cromwell Street. And Anne-Marie, Fred's daughter, described how she had been raped by Fred and Rosemary at the age of eight; West had told her that she 'should be grateful' and that all fathers did this to their daughters. She had become pregnant by her father at the age of 15, but he had arranged an abortion.

In her defence Rosemary West claimed that she was innocent. She said that her husband had manipulated her into participating in the assault on Caroline Owens, but stated that she did not know 'Miss A'. She furthermore denied all knowledge of the murders, as well as of the alleged assault on her stepdaughter, Anne-Marie. The defence played four of Fred West's taped interviews with the police, in which he had admitted to committing the murders and had said that Rosemary had played no part in them. The prosecution then called Janet Leach as a rebuttal witness. She had sat in on the police interviews with West and testified that when she and West were alone together after the interviews he had given a different version of his story, explaining that he had lied to the police in order to protect Rosemary, who had committed some of the murders. West had also told her that there were at least 20 more bodies that had not been discovered by the police.

The jury found Rosemary West guilty of all ten counts of murder. In passing sentence Mr Justice Mantell said 'Rosemary Pauline West, on each of the ten counts of murder of which you have been unanimously convicted by the jury the sentence is one of life imprisonment. If attention is paid to what I think you will never be released. Take her down'. He also ordered that the outstanding rape charges against her should be left on file.

On 19 March 1996 Rosemary West lost her appeal against her conviction. Meanwhile, the police continued their investigations into the deaths of nine other girls who had visited Cromwell Street and were never seen again.

28 ✦ The Backpacker Killer

After meeting in Australia in 1992, two British backpackers, Caroline Clarke and Joanne Walters, teamed up together to hitchhike around the south of the country, leaving a hostel in Sydney in April and then heading south. In September a jogger found their remains in a shallow grave at a place called Executioner's Drop in the Belanglo Forest. In the October of the following year, 1993, two more corpses were discovered in the same area. They belonged to James Gibson and Deborah Everist, both of whom were 19 and from Melbourne, who had disappeared in 1989.

It was soon begun to be feared that a serial killer was at work and an intensive search of the region was therefore set in motion. On 1 November 1993 the body of the 23-year-old Simone Schmidl, from Germany, was unearthed nearby; she had last been seen in January 1991. On the following day the skeletons of the 21-year-old Gabor Neugebauer and his 20-year-old girlfriend, Anja Habschied – two more German backpackers, who had disappeared two years previously – were found. Both victims had died from multiple stab wounds and Anja had also been beheaded.

Over 300 police officers were then ordered to comb a vast area of remote woodland and scrub for clues and other graves. It was the biggest murder hunt in Australia's history. One clue was identified: cartridges from a .22 Ruger were found near the grave of the 22-year-old Caroline Clarke which matched some spent cartridges that had been discovered at an isolated farmhouse.

After searching their records the New South Wales police thought that they had identified the serial killer's eighth victim. In 1991 the body of a 29-year-old Australian mother, Diane Pennacchio, had been found in a wood; last seen leaving a bar near Canberra, she had been stabbed to death sometime thereafter. Although her body had been found more than 100 miles (161 kilometres) from the others, she had been buried in the same, distinctive way. All eight had been found lying face downwards, with their hands behind their backs, alongside a fallen tree trunk; a small wigwam of sticks and ferns had been constructed over each body.

By the beginning of 1994 the 'Backpacker Killer' was making the headlines world-wide. Then a 24-year-old British woman came forward and told the police that she had been hitchhiking in the Belanglo Forest in January 1990 when she had been picked up by a lorry driver. When he had started acting strangely she had leapt out of the vehicle and had run into the woods. As she fled the driver had fired a gun at her, but had missed. Another British backpacker, the 25-year-old Paul Onion, also told the police that he had been hitchhiking in the same area in 1990 when he had accepted a lift from a man who had later pulled a gun out of the glove compartment. As Paul was fleeing the man had shot at him, thankfully missing his intended victim. Paul was able to identify the driver's car, as well as picking out his photo from the New South Wales police's collection of mug shots.

Following a dawn raid on 22 May 1994 a 49-year-old lorry driver and gun fanatic named Ivan Milat was arrested. Parts of a rare, .22-calibre, Ruger rifle were found hidden in his bungalow and ballistics tests later linked it to cartridge cases that had been picked up at the scenes of two of the killings. It was also identified as the weapon that had been used to kill Caroline Clarke, Milat's fingerprints furthermore being found on the gun.

Ivan Robert Marko Milat was consequently charged with the deaths of seven backpackers. Although he pleaded not guilty the jury did not believe him and Milat was accordingly sentenced to life imprisonment.

29 ❖ The Gay Slayer

Colin Ireland, London's 'Gay Slayer', wanted to achieve notoriety as a serial killer. He revelled in the fact that the details of his hideous murders were reported week by week by a fascinated press and furthermore telephoned police detectives to taunt them: 'I've got the book', he would say (meaning the FBI Handbook). 'I know how many you have to do.' After he had murdered his fifth victim – which officially classed him as a serial killer – he phoned up and boasted 'I've done another one'.

There is no doubt that Ireland was deranged character. The illegitimate son of a newsagent's assistant in Dartford, Kent, he never knew his father. His mother remarried when he was 12 and he did not get on with his step-father, who beat the boy for the slightest reason. Always something of a loner, he then became 'difficult' and was sent to a school for maladjusted children. After having been expelled for arson he began a life of petty crime, which took him firstly to borstal and eventually to prison. At the same time he became obsessed with both uniforms and the newly fashionable cult of survivalism, moreover making it plain to his friends that he hated 'queers'.

In 1990, at the age of 35, the 6 feet (183 metre) tall Ireland, who now weighed 15 stones (95 kilogrammes), married the landlady of a pub in Newton Abbot. He dumped her on their honeymoon, however, before returning to the pub, plundering it and then making off in her car. By the end of 1992 he had two failed marriages behind him and was working at a night shelter for the homeless in Southend. Shortly before Christmas he had a violent row with a gay man at the shelter and upon being sacked set about taking his revenge on all homosexuals. He began frequenting the Coleherne, a pub in the Earl's Court district of London that was popular with homosexual men who were into sado-masochism (S & M). Ireland later told detectives: 'I had gone there with the idea that if someone approached me something would happen. It would be some sort of trigger – a stepping over the line in a way'.

On 8 March 1993 Peter Walker, a 45-year-old theatre director, stepped over that line when he accidentally spilled some water on Ireland's jacket and begged Ireland to punish him for it by beating him. They then took a taxi to Walker's flat in Battersea for a sado-masochistic sex session, Ireland having come equipped with a cord, knife and pair of gloves. Walker eagerly submitted to being tied to the bed. 'Once I had tied him up I knew my intentions were different from his', Ireland said later. 'I'm not sure if I really set out to kill him, but it went from there . . . In the end I killed him with a plastic bag. I put it over his head.' Two days later he called the Samaritans, as well as a newspaper, asking them to visit the flat to take care of Walker's dogs.

On 28 May 1993 Ireland returned to the Coleherne and fell into conversation with Christopher Dunn, a 37-year-old librarian. Like Peter Walker, Dunn was a masochist who was into bondage – perfect for Ireland's purposes. The two men went back to Dunn's flat in Wealdstone, where Ireland handcuffed the willing Dunn to his bed. Dunn's pleasure

**Colin Ireland -
London's 'Gay Slayer'.**

Colin Ireland who was described as having an aggressive character. He was deeply disturbed since childhood.

quickly turned to dismay, however, as he watched Ireland rifle through his wallet and pull out the money that it contained, along with his cash-point card. When Dunn refused to tell Ireland his PIN (personal identification number) Ireland burnt Dunn's testicles with a cigarette lighter until he complied, then strangling him with a length of cord.

Ireland's third victim was Perry Bradley III, a 35-year-old sales director from Sulphur Springs, Texas, whose father was a congressman. The bisexual Bradley was another *habitué* of the Coleherne, where, on 4 June 1993, he met Ireland, shortly thereafter taking him to his smart, Kensington flat. Although Bradley was not really into S & M Ireland eventually persuaded him to let Ireland tie him up, going through his wallet once Bradley was trussed up and helpless. 'At one point I was thinking of letting him go', Ireland said in his statement to the police. 'Then I thought it's easier to kill him. I walked round and pulled the noose.' Ireland was becoming increasingly afraid of being caught and now feared that he would look conspicuous walking the streets alone while it was dark. He therefore settled down to listen to the radio until morning, wiping away his fingerprints after dawn and then leaving the flat.

Andrew Collier, the 33-year-old warden of a block of sheltered-accommodation flats in east London, was another Coleherne regular. After having been picked up by Ireland on 7 June 1993 Collier took him to his flat in Dalston. While the two men were having a drink they heard an altercation on the street and went to the window to see what was happening, Ireland leaning out of the window and accidentally leaving a fingerprint on the outside of the window frame. Afterwards Collier consented to Ireland tying him up and once he was helpless Ireland strangled him with a noose. Ireland was then inspecting the contents of Collier's wallet when he found some medical papers: 'I was going through his documentation and I became aware he had AIDS', Ireland said. 'He didn't warn me . . . I went fucking crazy. I burnt certain areas of his body. He loved his cat, that was his life – so I did the cat with a noose, draped it over the body.' The cat was actually arranged so that its mouth was around Collier's penis, its tail having been stuffed into his mouth. Ireland later told the police 'I wanted him to have no dignity in death. It was a way of saying to the police "What do you think of that?" It was like a signature to let them know I'd been there. I was reaching a point where I was just accelerating. It was just speeding up, getting far worse.'

After Collier's killing Ireland phoned the police and asked them whether they were still investigating the murder of Peter Walker. He taunted them, saying 'I will do another. I have always dreamed of doing the perfect murder'. Then Ireland laughed about killing Collier's cat – following the call that he had made about Peter Walker's dogs the press had been speculating that the killer was an animal lover.

On 13 June 1993 Ireland killed for the fifth, and last, time. His victim was the 42-year-old, Maltese-born chef, Emanuel Spiteri. 'I'd seen him a couple of times at the Coleherne', said Ireland. 'He was obviously the leather type.' Having accompanied Spiteri to his flat in south London, Ireland then tied him up and tortured him in an attempt to make him reveal the PIN for his cash-point card. Spiteri, however, resisted, screaming 'You will just have to kill me'. 'He was a very brave man, but I couldn't allow him to stick around', explained Ireland, continuing 'I killed him with a noose.'

It was at this point that Ireland telephoned the police and bragged that he had now taken five lives, which, he claimed, made him a real serial killer and hence 'famous'. What Ireland did not know, however, was that when he and Spiteri had passed through Charing Cross station on their way to Spiteri's home in Hither Green they had been filmed by the station's security cameras. A description of the man whom the police wanted to question was first issued to the public and then the British Transport Police's video of Spiteri with his killer was shown on television.

On 20 July 1993 Ireland walked into a solicitor's office in Southend and revealed that he was the man who had been filmed with Spiteri, whereupon the solicitor advised him to go to the police. Having done so, Ireland told police officers at New Scotland Yard that although he had indeed gone to Spiteri's flat with him he had left shortly afterwards; a third man had also been present, he claimed. The police quickly demolished Ireland's story, however: one of his fingerprints was found to match that left on the frame of Collier's window and the police also recognised Ireland's voice from his anonymous phone calls. Realising that the game was up Ireland confessed to all five murders en route to the magistrates' court.

At the Old Bailey Ireland pleaded guilty to five counts of murder. On sentencing him to serve five life sentences Mr Justice Sachs said

By any standards you are an exceptionally frightening and dangerous man. In cold blood and with great deliberation you killed five of your fellow human beings in grotesque and cruel circumstances. The fear, brutality and indignity to which you subjected your victims are almost unspeakable. To take one human life is outrageous. To take five is carnage. You expressed your desire to be regarded as a serial killer – that must be matched by your detention for life. In my view it is absolutely clear you should never be released.

30 ❖ The Monster of Florence

In 1968 Antonio Io Bianci was making love to Barbara Locci in the front seat of his car when they were both shot dead, Barbara's husband being subsequently arrested and convicted of the murders. It would be six years before Signor Locci could prove his innocence and establish that the double murder was the first atrocity committed by a serial killer who preyed on courting couples in Tuscany who later became known as the 'Monster of Florence'.

While Signor Locci was languishing in jail another courting couple was killed in a car. The police established that they had been shot with the same .22-calibre Beretta pistol that had been used in the Bianchi and Locci murders; the female victim had furthermore been mutilated. During the course of the next year two more people were killed in a similar manner. Although a German couple was murdered, too, neither of them was mutilated (they were homosexuals and their killing was probably a mistake).

Upon Signor Locci's release the Monster of Florence appeared to suspend his activities. He struck again in 1981, however, stabbing his female victim some 300 times. Four months later, in October 1981, another woman was murdered and mutilated. The Monster of Florence continued to wage his campaign of murder over the next four years. The slayings followed a rigid pattern: all of the men were shot through the driver's window before the women were killed, their bodies then being dragged from the car and mutilated with a knife (their left breasts were generally hacked off). Ballistics tests revealed that all of the 67 bullets that were fired in a total of 16 murders came from the same gun, all also being marked with the letter 'H'. The Monster of Florence's final attack, in 1985, differed slightly from the rest, however. He slaughtered his last victims – a French couple – in their tent, cutting off a section of the woman's genitalia (which he later posted to the police) during his grisly mutilation of her body.

The Florence police handled the case badly. Numerous false accusations were made and one man who had been named as the killer committed suicide by cutting his throat. Another five were jailed for the killings, three of whom were released when the Monster struck again while they were behind bars; because there was no evidence against a fourth a judge released him, while the fifth man remained the subject of controversy.

During the course of the Monster of Florence's bloody reign of terror the police received scores of anonymous notes identifying Pietro Pacciani as the killer. Pacciani was a peasant farmer who had been convicted of murder in 1951 and jailed for 13 years for killing a rival in love. (Pacciani had followed his 16-year-old fiancée upon seeing her going into the woods with another man; when he could no longer stand the sight of them making love he had stabbed the man 19 times before raping the terrified girl next to the mutilated corpse.) The police speculated that if he was indeed the Monster of Florence the embittered Pacciani had sought to avenge himself on other couples. Key to their thinking was the theory that it had been the sight of his fiancée's exposed left breast during her seduction that had triggered Pacciani's initial attack and that this was also why the Monster usually amputated the left breasts of his female victims. Pacciani had again come to the police's attention in 1987, subsequently being convicted of molesting his two daughters and accordingly being jailed.

His name was fed into a computer, along with those of more than 100,000 people who had had the opportunity of carrying out the Monster of Florence's crimes. The computer identified just one suspect, however: Pacciani. Convinced that Pacciani was the perpetrator of the murders, the police searched his farm in minute detail for evidence, but nothing was found. They were on the point of giving up when a bullet was unearthed which was later found to match those that had been used in the murders.

Although a weapon was never recovered Pacciani was charged with murder. His trial dragged on for six months before the jury finally convicted him, whereupon he was jailed for life in 1994. Subsequently, however, a judicial review reassessed the flimsy evidence against him and after its ruling that his conviction was unsafe Pacciani was released from prison in 1996. As far as anyone knows the Monster of Florence is still at large.

31 ❖ The Rostov Ripper

Following the collapse of the Soviet Union during the early 1990s the rest of the world – as well as its own people – discovered that Russia, along with the other former Soviet republics, could produce serial killers that were more than a match for any found in the West.

The first such notable case was that of Nikolai Dzhumagaliev, the killer cannibal who was known as 'Metal Fang' because of his white-metal, false teeth. Dzhumagaliev operated in Kazakhstan during 1980, picking up tall, attractive women in the capital, Alma-Ata, before taking them for a walk along the river bank, where he raped them and then hacked them to death with an axe. On the night following each murder he would invite friends to dinner and serve them roast meat, his reign of terror coming to an end when two of his guests found a woman's head and entrails in his fridge. Charged with seven murders, Dzhumagaliev was found to be insane and was sent to a psychiatric hospital in Tashkent. He escaped in 1989, however, and after trying to pick up women in Moscow fled to Uzbekistan, where he was eventually captured. Yet terrible as his crimes undoubtedly were, Metal Fang's reputation as a serial killer would soon be eclipsed by that of the 'Rostov Ripper'.

At first sight Andrei Romanovich Chikatilo, a former schoolteacher, was a mild-mannered grandfather. He was also an apparently happily married man – if slightly henpecked – although some thought his habit of sleeping in the bathroom a little odd. Those who were closer to him, however, knew that he was haunted by the memory of a cousin who had been killed and his body subjected to cannibalism during the 1934 Ukrainian famine. Even so, no one who knew Chikatilo would have believed that he had tortured, murdered, raped, mutilated and eaten as many as 53 victims, many of them children, between 1978 and 1990. (There may have been more: because Chikatilo's victims were loners and strays some disappearances may have gone unreported.) During the course of the 12-year murder investigation 500,000 people were questioned; Chikatilo himself was arrested and interrogated twice, but was released on both occasions.

It was Chikatilo's sexual problems that sparked his murder spree. His wife, Fayina, later admitted that her husband had not been able to make love to her properly. He had therefore turned to prostitutes and had bought a shack to which he would take them for sex. This strategy ultimately proved unsuccessful, too, however, and his inability to perform sexually seems to have enraged him.

His first victim was a pretty nine-year-old named Lena Zakotno. In December 1978 he lured her to his shack, where he tried to rape her; having failed to do so, he then murdered her. It was then that he discovered that he was only able to have sex with someone when they were dead. Afterwards he disposed of Lena's body in a river. Chikatilo was suspected of being involved in Lena's death after neighbours reported seeing a light burning in the shack during the night on which Lena had vanished. He was interviewed nine times about the murder before suspicion fell on another man who lived nearby. The man confessed, was found guilty and executed.

Chikatilo then embarked upon a career of prolific murder – 11 bodies were found in 1984 alone. With the sixth sense of the natural predator he would pick out the weak and vulnerable, hanging around bus stops and railway stations looking for prostitutes and runaways. He would also stalk potential victims on buses and trains or target them in the street. His favourite targets were homeless drifters who were unlikely to be missed, or else solitary children on their way to school.

A lone child could be tempted by a packet of chewing gum, while a drifter would jump at the offer of a meal or a chance to watch a video. After all, Chikatilo looked for all the world like a kindly grandfather.

'As soon as I saw a lonely person I would have to drag them off to the woods', he later told the police. 'I paid no attention to age or sex. We would walk for a couple of miles or so through the woods and then I would be possessed by a terrible shaking sensation.' He then murdered his victims before raping and mutilating their corpses. Sometimes he disembowelled them and cut out or bit off their organs; fearing their deathly gaze, he would usually pluck out their eyes, and would furthermore bite off their nipples in a sexual frenzy.

The police found themselves out of their depth: 'We just couldn't imagine what sort of person we were dealing with', said Lieutenant Colonel Viktor Burakov, who led the murder hunt. 'This was the height of sadism, the like of which we had never seen.' At the height of the murders the police mounted a regular surveillance of the woods around Rostov. Although Chikatilo himself was stopped in an isolated, wooded area in 1979, he persuaded the police that he was an innocent hiker and after noting down his name and address they let him go.

Chikatilo's wife and friends were baffled when he gave up his teaching job of ten years in 1981 for the position of a lowly supply clerk in a loco-motive-repair shop in Rostov. His new job gave him the opportunity to travel, however, and he extended his murderous activities to St Petersburg, the Ukraine and Uzbekistan. The manhunt, which was led by detectives seconded from Moscow, now stretched to Siberia.

In 1983 he was arrested close to the scene of one of the murders, the police finding a length of rope and a knife in his briefcase. A sample of his blood was taken, but because it proved to belong to a different group to that of the semen samples that had been recovered from the victims' bodies Chikatilo was released. (At that time the Soviet police did not know that in extremely rare cases secretions from various parts of the body can have dif-ferent serological groupings; Chikatilo was one of those rare cases.)

During the summer of 1984 Chikatilo was forced to take a break from murder when he was arrested and jailed for three months for the theft of three rolls of linoleum. Over the month following his release Chikatilo relieved his pent-up frustration by slaughtering eight people.

Chikatilo's murderous campaign was only halted because the police had a stoke of luck. In November 1990 a policeman stopped Chikatilo in the street after spotting bloodstains on his face. When the body of his final victim, a young boy, was later discovered nearby witnesses reported having seen a middle-aged man hanging around the railway station while the boy bought a ticket. Having run a check on 25,000 possible suspects detectives put Chikatilo under heavy surveillance on reading the police report pertaining to his having been stopped while covered with blood. Six-hundred policemen were drafted in to cover the station and adjoining woods and some were watching on 20 November 1990 when Chikatilo approached a teenage boy at the railway station. He was immediately arrested.

Under interrogation Chikatilo readily confessed to murdering 11 boys and 42 women and girls during his reign of terror, although he claimed that 'there may be more'. Of his known victims the youngest was Igor Gudkov, a seven-year-old who had strayed from his home; the oldest was the 44-year-old prostitute Marta Ryabyenko. Upon realising that her husband was the Rostov Ripper Chikatilo's wife, as well as his two grown-children, went into hiding.

Chikatilo was 56 when he went on trial in Rostov on 14 April 1992. Throughout the proceedings he sat in chains within an iron cage that had been built around the dock. On the first day of the trial proceedings were delayed for half an hour while the hysterical crowd bayed for his blood, Chikatilo merely rolling his eyes and waving pornographic magazines to inflame the audience further as first-aiders administered sedatives to the families of his victims. The two-volume indictment listed thirty-five child victims and eighteen women. The facts of the case were not contested and the only matter upon which the court had to decide was whether or not Chikatilo was sane; experts from Moscow's Serbsky Institute, Russia's leading institute of psychiatry, testified that he was.

It took Judge Leonid Akabzhanov an hour and a half to read the verdict on 15 October 1992, during which he concluded that 52 of the 53 murders had been proven. He expressed fierce criticism of the police, however: 'If they had done their job in 1978 after the first killing 52 lives could have been saved', he said, continuing: 'Or if they had not released him after questioning in 1984 at least 20 people would not have died'. Of the accused he said: 'He ruthlessly and cold-bloodedly dismembered his victims, pulling them apart while they were still alive'. The judge then sentenced him to death, outraging Chikatilo: 'I fought in Afghanistan', he ranted. 'I was a partisan who defended the barricades; I fought for a free Russia.' The courtroom was in pandemonium when he was finally taken from the iron cage for the last time.

On 14 February 1994 Andrei Chikatilo, whom the press was now calling the 'world's most sadistic and perverted killer', was executed by means of a single bullet to the back of the head after President Boris Yeltsin had rejected his appeal for clemency.

32 ❖ The Terminator

The Ukrainian serial killer Anatoly Onoprienko was sentenced to death in 1999 after having been convicted of murdering fifty-two people, including ten children in villages across Ukraine, most of them during a three-month killing spree. The former sailor, who had become known as 'The Terminator', admitted the killings, saying that he had been driven by a higher force.

In its eagerness to join the European Union (EU) the Ukraine had in the meantime complied with EU requirements in suspending its death sentence, however, and in 1999 Onoprienko was therefore still being held in a tiny, 9- by 5-feet (2.7- by 1.5-metre) cell at the nineteenth-century prison in Zhitornir, 8 miles (13 kilometres) west of Kiev, while his fate was being decided. Because Onoprienko relished killing even the toughest guards on death row took no chances with him.

'The first time I killed I shot down a deer in the woods', he later reminisced. 'I was in my early twenties and I recall feeling very upset when I saw it dead. I couldn't explain why I had done it, and I felt sorry for it. I never had that feeling again.' Onoprienko's first human victims were a couple whom he had seen standing by their Lada car on a motorway. 'I just shot them', he said. 'It's not that it gave me pleasure, but I felt this urge. From then on it was almost like some game from outer space.'

After that he terrorised the Ukraine for months, slaughtering men, women and children alike, wiping out entire families in cold blood, battering children and raping one woman after having shot her in the face. 'To me killing people [was like] ripping up a duvet', he explained. 'Men, women, old people, children – they are all the same. I have never felt sorry for those I killed. No love, no hatred, just blind indifference. I don't see

Ukranian serial killer Anatoly Onoprienko who was sentenced to death in 1999 after killing 52 people.

them as individuals, but just as masses.' On one occasion he had killed a young girl who was praying, having just seen him kill both of her parents. 'Seconds before I smashed her head [in] I ordered her to show me where they kept their money', he said. 'She looked at me with an angry, defiant stare and said "No, I won't". That strength was incredible. But I still felt nothing.'

The Ukraine had been plunged into panic when Onoprienko's savagery reached its climax in early 1996, when he committed about forty murders in three months. The determined force that he used was almost unbelievable: he blew the doors off homes on the edges of villages, gunned down adults and beat children with metal cudgels, stealing money, jewellery, stereo equipment and other valuable items before burning down his victims' homes. 'To me it was like hunting. Hunting people down', he explained. 'I would be sitting, bored, with nothing to do. And then suddenly this idea would get into my head. I would do everything to get it out of my mind, but I couldn't. It was stronger than me. So I would get in the car or catch a train and go out to kill.'

Although he took pleasure in the 'professionalism' of his crimes, Onoprienko claimed that he had derived no pleasure from killing. 'Corpses are ugly', he confided. 'They stink and send out bad vibes. Once I killed five people and then sat in the car with their bodies for two hours not knowing what to do with them. The smell was unbearable.' Investigators feared that his final tally of victims was higher than 52 – with some justification, for there appeared to have been a long gap between murders when he roamed illegally around other European countries.

After weeks of tests and interviews a commission consisting of the Ukraine's top psychiatrists and psychologists concluded that Onoprienko was not mentally ill, rather that his main motivation for murder appeared to have been money: he killed to steal. The fact that he had grown up without parents and had been sent to an orphanage by his elder brother may have explained why he had slaughtered entire families, they speculated. Indeed, his most frenzied killing spree had occurred after he had moved in with a woman (who said that he had always been very loving) and her children. The couple had intended to marry, Onoprienko having proposed to his girlfriend with a ring that he had forcibly removed from the finger of one of his victims only a few hours earlier.

For his part, Onoprienko – who claimed that he was a good-natured person and a sensitive music-lover – maintained that he was possessed. 'I'm not a maniac', he said.

It's not that simple. I have been taken over by a higher force, something telepathic or cosmic, which drove me. For instance, I wanted to kill my brother's first wife, because I hated her. I really wanted to kill her, but I couldn't because I had not received the order. I waited for it all the time, but it did not come . . . I am like a rabbit in a laboratory, part of an experiment to prove that man is capable of murdering and learning to live with his crimes. To show that I can cope, that I can stand anything, [I] forget everything.

Onoprienko was finally caught after the Ukraine had staged its biggest manhunt, which involved 2,000 police officers and more than 3,000 troops. He was eventually arrested in April 1996 at his girlfriend's house, near the Polish border, as the result of an anonymous tip-off.

During his trial, which took place in his home town of Zhytomyr, Onoprienko stood locked within a metal cage in the courtroom. He described